KNOWLEDGE AND THE FUTURE OF MAN

AN INTERNATIONAL SYMPOSIUM

EDITED BY

WALTER J. ONG, S.J.

Saint Louis University

Initiating the Sesquicentennial
of Saint Louis University
1818–1968

A Clarion Book
Published by Simon and Schuster

A CLARION BOOK
PUBLISHED BY SIMON AND SCHUSTER
ROCKEFELLER CENTER, 630 FIFTH AVENUE
NEW YORK, NEW YORK 10020
ALL RIGHTS RESERVED
INCLUDING THE RIGHT OF REPRODUCTION
IN WHOLE OR IN PART IN ANY FORM
COPYRIGHT © 1968 BY HOLT, RINEHART & WINSTON, INC.
REPRINTED BY ARRANGEMENT WITH HOLT, RINEHART & WINSTON, INC.

FIRST PAPERBACK PRINTING 1968

MANUFACTURED IN THE UNITED STATES OF AMERICA
PRINTED BY MURRAY PRINTING CO., FORGE VILLAGE, MASS.
BOUND BY ELECTRONIC PERFECT BINDERS, INC., BROOKLYN, N.Y.

*Grateful acknowledgment is made to Présence Africaine, Paris,
France, for permission to reprint four lines of a poem by Claude
Laleau which first appeared in L. S. Senghor's* Anthologie de la
Nouvelle Poésie Nègre et Malgache (*Presses Universitaires de France,
Paris, 1948*) *and translated by Samuel Allen in* Africa Seen by Ameri-
can Negroes (*Présence Africaine, Paris, 1958*).

TO ALL THOSE
WHO FROM THE BEGINNING
HAVE CONTRIBUTED
TO MAN'S GROWTH
IN KNOWLEDGE
AND UNDERSTANDING

❧

CONTENTS

PREFACE

K
NOWLEDGE AND THE FUTURE OF MAN is a theme touching both the future itself and the present, which prepares for the future. The theme relates also in a special way to the past in the collection of studies offered here. The year 1968 marks the sesquicentennial of Saint Louis University, the oldest university in the United States west of the Mississippi River, which has chosen this theme, Knowledge and the Future of Man, to unify the symposia and other academic events celebrating its sesquicentennial. As a prelude to these events, through its Committee for the Sesquicentennial, the university has planned the present book for the general public under the conviction that this same theme is of great interest far beyond the university and the academic world as a whole.

The distinguished scholars contributing to this collection thus write not merely for Saint Louis University but for the world. The studies here are all original works, done especially for this sesquicentennial volume, where they are now printed for the first time. Each contributor addresses himself in his own way to the general subject of Knowledge and the Future of Man in terms of his own field of competence and special interests.

Saint Louis University was founded by Bishop Louis William Du Bourg as Saint Louis Academy "for young gentlemen" in 1818, when the City of St. Louis was a pioneer settlement of some three thousand people. In 1828 it was placed under the direction of the Society of Jesus (informally known as the Jesuit order), a Catholic religious order of men committed largely to educational work since shortly after its founding in 1540. The State of Missouri was admitted to the Union in 1821, and in 1832 the Missouri General Assembly granted the first university charter west of the Mississippi to the trustees, all members of the Society of Jesus.

Grown to an institution with thirteen different faculties or schools, seventy-seven departments, and nearly twelve thousand students, in 1967 Saint Louis University became the first American Catholic university to reconstitute its board of trustees with a majority of laymen and a lay chairman. The university proposes to grow further still as a great Catholic educational center to which the Society of Jesus continues its full commitment with the increased stress on lay responsibility and ecumenical sharing particularly favored since the Second Vatican Council. The fourth half-century of the university dawns at a propitious time, when the knowledge explosion to which the intellectual developments of the past have led offers all universities opportunities to discharge responsibilities in teaching and research and in civic, national, and global cooperation with even more devotion and success than in the past. The present volume salutes what lies ahead.

WALTER J. ONG, S.J.
For the Committee for the Sesquicentennial
Joseph J. Simeone, Faculty Chairman

St. Louis, Missouri
January, 1968

I

THE ENVIRONMENT OF LEARNING

1

KNOWLEDGE IN TIME

WALTER J. ONG, S.J.

Saint Louis University

M AN IS A VENTURE in knowledge. The story of knowledge and its uses, good and bad, is the story of man.

Man's knowledge is essentially incremental. It not only accumulates but also metabolizes and grows, feeding on other things and on itself. Its potential is unlimited, which means that when it is true as true can be, and certain beyond the shadow of a doubt, it is also incomplete.

This book is concerned with what happens as knowledge grows and what will happen as man puts his increasing knowledge to use in the future.

Knowledge did not always grow so fast as it does now. Its growth has accelerated from an extremely slow start. Insofar as quantitative statements about knowledge have meaning, we can be fairly certain that there was a time toward the beginning of man's history when knowledge took 10,000 years—perhaps even 100,000 years—to double, and that at a later period it doubled in 1000 years, and still later in 500 years. It has been estimated that today man's knowledge doubles every 15 years. We are used to this tempo of development of knowledge and find it hard to believe how slowly knowledge advanced before the development of writing. In some stone-age cultures, the same pattern for a hand axe or spear point persisted for thousands upon thousands of years. In such cultures massive social and psychological structures evidently almost immobilized knowledge.

But virtual immobilization was necessary. It insured against loss. Before the invention of writing (only some 5500 years ago, around 3500 B.C.) knowledge was not only in short supply but also devastatingly insecure. In cultures without records, it could easily leak away. Gargantuan efforts were needed simply to conserve knowledge by keeping it fixed either through recitative formulas for such knowledge or, for nonverbalized knowledge, through such cultural institutions as the tradition of unvarying spear-point design. Without writing, mere retention of the knowledge that had accumulated (no one knew quite how) proved so formidable a task that even apart from the risk of loss if set patterns were varied, the subsistence economies of early mankind could afford neither the time nor the energy for planned knowledge expansion. This state of affairs persisted to a greater or lesser degree for centuries after the invention of writing and even beyond the invention of print until the implications of print for storing and shaping knowledge were digested into the social consciousness and individual psychological structures.

Until print was thus interiorized, cultures remained largely what David Riesman has well labeled "tradition-directed." In such cultures, when expansion of knowledge actually did occur, it was likely to pass with little notice. Thus medieval European thinkers, for example, went far beyond Aristotle in the development of formal logic, moving toward modern symbolic logic (though without the symbols or variables of modern logic, so that the movement was all the more arduous). But they appear to have been aware hardly at all that they had made vast new discoveries. The essential intellectual need was still felt to be holding onto what was known. Eric Havelock's intriguing *Preface to Plato* and Frances A. Yates's seminal work on *The Art of Memory* have made it clear how early world views and thought structures inherited from antiquity and still widely operative as late as the seventeenth century were in great part determined by the need to hold knowledge in patterns that served ready recall. You knew the things that lent themselves to memory schemes.

Memorization and the iconographic imagination, which memorization encourages, constituted a style of life. The Ramist "method" or way of abstractly organizing knowledge and communication, which swept the most technologizing parts of Europe in the sixteenth and seventeenth centuries, was in great part a tantalizingly simple memory system, disguised as science and made plausible by diagrams that could be given ready currency by print. The method proved short-lived, for the new invention of printing, which Ramism exploited, was actually making mnemonic systems in the mind less necessary, as our various computing machines have finally made them obsolete. Knowledge storage was effected more and more outside the mind, first by writing, then by print, finally by our electronic circuitry. But those living through the changes induced by new knowledge storage and retrieval and communication developments are never entirely aware of what the changes are. Hence of necessity they lean on obsolescence and even find obsolescence exciting.

For the advancement of learning, storage of knowledge is essential, but insofar as knowledge is mere "information" or "structure" its storage and retrieval are not truly intellectual tasks. As artificial extramental information storage and retrieval systems (writing, print, and electronics) evolved, the mind was freed more and more to do its proper work of thinking, and the acceleration of knowledge got under way. To store and organize knowledge, oral cultures had to devote vast amounts of time to reciting it. Learning *was* in effect memorizing. Early chirographic cultures recorded knowledge and began to analyze it. Late chirographic cultures, such as that of medieval Europe, codified it. The typographical culture of the Renaissance indexed it; indexes were not unknown in manuscripts, but they remained relatively inefficient until print could produce hundreds of copies of a text with all the words in exactly the same place on the page, at which time indexing became a major selling point for learned works. Today we have computerized knowledge, which is to say that not merely have we set up outside the mind exponentially more effective information storage and retrieval systems but also, more basically, that we are actually breeding knowledge outside the mind. The computer is a special milieu in which knowledge can be cultivated outside its normal habitat.

Of course, the computer breeds knowledge only insofar as knowledge involves structures of "information"—that is, insofar as it can be quantified, directly or indirectly. This means that the computer can do almost anything with knowledge except think about it, which is to say it can do everything but decide with reference to an actual, existing situation whether something is true or false. An actual, existing situation is always one in which there are nonquantified and even nonconceptualized factors. It is, in other words, a noncomputerized situation. Computer verdicts concerning "truth" or "falsity" are vacuities. Either before or after they are arrived at, they have to be applied by someone who *really* knows. But the computer frees the mind to apply knowledge (to judge truth and falsity) in many situations more complex and sweeping than any the mind could compass without computerization.

Not only do new knowledge storage, retrieval, and communication systems (the "media") accelerate the growth of knowledge, but the growth of knowledge also of course accelerates the development of new media. Scripts grow out of the knowledge accumulated in oral culture, the alphabet out of greater knowledge accumulated in a pictographic script culture, alphabetic letterpress typography out of structures of knowledge favored by a chirographic or manuscript culture, and electronic circuitry out of the vast store of knowledge which typography made possible and put at the service of modern science.

When we look to the speed with which the media develop, we find that here, too, there is a spectacular acceleration. Only after being on earth some 500,000 years (to take a fairly good working figure) did man move from his original oral culture, in which written records were unknown and unthought of, to literacy. The first script appeared around 3500 B.C. In another two thousand years the alphabet put in its appearance, around 1500 B.C. By the mid-1400s of the Christian era alphabetic letterpress printing appeared in west central Europe. In another four hundred years the telegraph was devised. Within another sixty years, the wireless. Thirty-five years more brought television. A few decades later we had the whole panoply of spacecraft, Telstar, electronic computers in vast quantity, and countless related devices. Each advance exploited antecedently existing knowledge more efficiently than had the advances that went before, for new knowledge does not simply layer itself onto existing knowledge but interacts with it. It is not an additive but a multiplier.

The total pattern of acceleration in knowledge is thus a complex one. Of itself, knowledge grows and accelerates its own growth. This growth also produces new media, which further accelerate growth (and of course change the structure of knowledge and of the psyche, as will be seen later). The new media themselves, finally, appear in an accelerating sequence, more and more of them faster and faster as time moves on.

II

We have reached a period today when the accumulation of knowledge has made possible insights of new clarity and depth into the history of knowledge itself. Growth of knowledge soon produces growth in knowledge about knowledge, its constitution, and its history, for knowledge is of itself reflective. Given time, it will try to explain not only the world but itself more and more.

What has happened and is happening to knowledge can be considered under several more or less distinct headings: (1) growth in knowledge of the physical universe; (2) growth in knowledge of man and his life world, including his sense of history; (3) increased exteriorization of knowledge (connected with the development of "objective" science); (4) interiorization of knowledge; (5) thrust into the future and growth in responsibility; (6) the permanent limitations of growth. We can take these up in order.

KNOWLEDGE OF THE PHYSICAL UNIVERSE

When marveling about growth in knowledge, many persons focus immediately on our increase in knowledge of the physical universe during the past hundred years (since Darwin) or perhaps three hundred years (since Newton). Here results of increased knowledge are indeed striking. Discoveries in the physical sciences often lead to the production of "hardware" or other products that are highly visible and palpable and that enable man to dominate his physical environment spectacularly: steam engines, telegrams, radar, jet-propelled spacecraft, plastics, television. Knowledge is power. In the early 1600s Francis Bacon gave this old com-

monplace its best publicized utterance, and Thomas Hobbes
soon reiterated Bacon's cosmopolitan Latin in plain English.
But Bacon and Hobbes only stated the aphorism. We have
lived it, particularly regarding the physical sciences.

Even at his imaginative best, early man could not quite
foresee what we have lived through. Bacon had thought of
better organizing or "methodizing" the knowledge already on
hand and of exploiting nature by achieving a better grasp of
"forms." He hardly conceived of breaking through the kinds
of frontiers that Newton, Darwin, and Planck have put behind us.

The breakthroughs began with two seventeenth-century
developments: the application of mathematics to the physical
sciences and an intent and minute observation of nature unknown to earlier ages, which, contrary to the still popular
persuasion, had not consciously thrown out induction in favor
of deduction but had simply supposed that ordinary observation sufficed for inductive purposes and which thus had not
troubled with controlled experiment. Anyone could tell immediately that a heavy body "naturally" falls faster than a
light body because when stones and feathers were thrown out
a high window at the same time, the stones reached the
ground first. Despite Newton's laws of gravitation, they still
do.

Experimentation to prove they do not or should not had to
do less with ordinary experience than with pure science. But
physical science seldom stays pure, and the new sciences in
the seventeenth century and later made themselves felt in
practical ways very soon. Indeed, post-Newtonian science was
in alliance with practical craftsmanship from the very beginning. The closely controlled observations called for by the
new mathematization and experimentation themselves demanded finely constructed tools, such as telescopes and
microscopes and vacuum pumps. The new sciences used
knowledge-producing tools more than earlier science had ever

done, and it was a natural thing for the artisans who could make delicate machines for research purposes to make scientifically designed machines for practical purposes. A new breed of thinker arose, the "inventor." "Projectors" the eighteenth century still called them disdainfully, with little sympathy for the Thomas A. Edison syndrome.

We have long ago passed the stage where "inventors" seem intruders on the intellectual scene. The physical sciences have paid off in practical contrivances and processes so abundantly as to make us even discredit science that does not have immediate application. Systematized, formalized knowledge has penetrated the whole of life. In a technologized society not only automobiles and television sets but even soap and apples cannot be produced effectively without a store of systematized, formalized knowledge. Artisan's rule-of-thumb skills have largely yielded to science and are yielding more and more daily.

The result has been a new texture for life itself. Man is dealing constantly with complex, formalized structures rather than with "nature," whether it be in planting corn specifically designed for his region's rainfall and temperatures or crossing a neighborhood street intersection, which he must do by following traffic lights programmed to the city-wide diurnal flow of traffic. It is misleading to imply, as Jacques Ellul and others do, that these formal patterns are something alien to man, a self-subsistent intrusion on his life. They are in fact very human structures devised by human beings in order to make their lives bearable, to give them more security, privacy, and personal independence than early man ever knew. (Philippe Ariès has shown in *Centuries of Childhood* how lacking in security, privacy, and independence were living conditions for even the well to do through the eighteenth century and later. The crowding in our slums today was normal to earlier urban life; it has become intolerable because now for the first time it can be avoided and indeed is avoided by most city dwellers.)

It is not the inhuman effects of technological living—our being "dominated" by machines, whatever that may mean—but the human effects that pose our problem. The science that underlies technological living has given a new shape to the contents of the human mind. In earlier ages abstract, formalized thought was dominantly philosophical and religious. Knowledge of the physical universe, while it was not so thin as the popular impression today would have it, was still relatively jejune and unsatisfying. Today the physical sciences have become so rich and fecund that the mind can lose itself in them for a lifetime.

The mere bulk of learning in the physical sciences is overwhelming. Devising systems to abstract, store, and retrieve the results of each year's new research has become a major problem. Even with the best of such systems, it is occasionally less time consuming to repeat certain bits of research than it would be to comb the vast float of extant literature for needed information.

The overwhelming weight of detailed knowledge regarding the physical world carried within technological cultures calls for a special balance in man's consciousness as he learns to address himself and the world around him. Technological man has a personality structure different from that of nontechnological man. The stages of culture described by David Riesman as successive tradition-directed, inner-directed, and other-directed are relevant here. Technological man may be inner-directed or other-directed or on the border line between the two, but he cannot be tradition-directed as primitive peoples are. (This is by no means to say that technological man has no traditions; he does have them in great number, but he is also likely to reflect on them and analyze them.) To move a nontechnologized culture into the scientific, technological world demands far more than supplying those in such a culture with "information." It demands a restructuring of personality which inevitably forces the painful psychological, political, and ideological dislocations seen in the developing countries today. We can hope to understand and to deal with these dislocations better than we now do. But we can hardly hope to eliminate them totally.

Meanwhile, it is defeatist to suppose that man's attention to the physical world is some kind of degradation. There are dangers here, of course, dangers of total absorption, but of itself man's present managerial position over some of the natural world (some of it only, a tiny fraction, for there is no question of managing the galaxies) means that the material world is being more spiritualized by being more subjugated to the mind.

KNOWLEDGE OF MAN AND HIS LIFE WORLD

If advance in the physical sciences has been spectacular, it has, nevertheless, in fact not been conclusively greater than advance in knowledge elsewhere. A little attention to library acquisitions and bibliographies today as compared with 150 or even 10 years ago makes it patent that insofar as increments in various knowledges are comparable, the humanities and the social and behavioral sciences are growing seemingly as fast as the physical sciences. By far, most of the intellectual and literary and cultural history on library shelves today had not been written 150 years ago. A hundred and fifty years ago most of our linguistic knowledge concerning the thousands of languages man speaks or has spoken did not exist. Neither did most of sociology, anthropology, psychology, and countless other subjects dealing with the human life world as such.

Moreover, in these fields knowledge often grows geometrically because here, perhaps more than in the physical sciences, different and even remote areas of knowledge have a way of interacting with one another today to form new and productive configurations. Psychology and linguistics yield the composite field of psycholinguistics, itself closely allied to cultural anthropology. Analysis, especially historical analysis, of literary forms, of scientific discoveries, of styles in painting, and of political institutions daily throw more and more light on one another.

In addition, the humanities are automatically enlarged by growth of knowledge in the sciences. Every science, not only the social and behavioral sciences, has a history, which is a matter for humanistic study. And the humanities seize on technological interventions for their own specific purposes and thus extend themselves into new areas. Opposition between technology and the humanities is more imaginary than real. The printing press, a technological device, was developed largely under Renaissance humanist auspices, and the use of computers for textual study and other humanistic purposes is already becoming commonplace.

Advances in the humanities and social and behavioral sciences have combined with advances in the physical sciences to affect radically man's sense of his life world and sense of identity, if we take sense of identity to mean the sense of where one comes from and how one relates to those other than oneself, how one fits into what one knows of the universe.

Changes here have been too vast to enumerate, but some of their forces can be seen in the changes regarding man's sense of time. Until quite recent years man had no very effective idea of the real time scales applying to the universe of which he was a part. Today our frames of reference have been brought more into accord with actuality, the macroscale frames largely by the natural sciences and the (relatively) microscale frames by the humanities and social sciences. We know that it took the universe some five to ten billion years of active evolution to produce the conditions making life pos-

sible on our earth. We know that social structures and psychological structures have evolved irreversibly over periods of
tens of thousands and hundreds of thousands of years. Even
though it is not always explicitly attended to, the past is a
massive fact in the sense of identity of any well-educated
man today, that is to say, of any man thoroughly in touch
with his surroundings. We no longer think of ourselves as
beings who inhabit a cozy (but savage) universe that began
some 6000 years ago, as Western man often used to do, nor
do we think of time in terms of unreal cyclic patterns such
as the Hindu kalpa (4,320,000,000 years), an imaginative
projection having nothing to do with researchable fact and
indeed running counter to such fact. Today we know the
past as something with which we are in publicly and cir-
cumstantially verifiable contact, and as affecting the real
present in ways that are matter for scientific, cosmological,
and historical study.

The immensity of space has likewise lately become known
to us and affected our sense of identity, but it has done so
less directly, for space is mostly beyond us, in a real sense.
If and when man gets to the moon, he will be roughly only
1/400 of the distance to the sun and an infinitesimal fraction
of the distance to the nearest star outside the solar system.
Most of space is permanently remote from us. We feel little
kinship with Betelgeuse or with galaxies millions of light
years away. But time is in us: the material in our own bodies
is five to ten billion years old. Our modern sense of measured
time has revolutionized all knowledge dealing with man's
life world at least as drastically as Planckian and Einsteinian
discoveries have revolutionized modern physics. The appearance of studies such as Martin Heidegger's great work
entitled *Being and Time (Sein und Zeit)* signals the overwhelming sense of time in which modern man is plunged.
From antiquity man has speculated philosophically about the
nature of time, but only in recent generations have his phi-

losophy and his whole life world become immersed in it. This immersion in time is what commits modern man to change and propels him irresistibly into the future.

Knowledge concerning man and his life world, which includes his artistic and literary productions, also is power, quite as much as knowledge of physical science is. It is most obviously power in the social and behavioral sciences, which lend themselves readily to use, moral or immoral as the case may be, aiding in the solving of human problems or implementing manipulations of human beings as though they were things. Knowledge in the humanities is power, too, for the humanities give us greater insight into the nature of man, and this insight provides ground for greater control over man's behavior, again for good or evil. To understand a people's psychology in order to deal with them on a practical footing, it is advisable to study their literature and art. Such study can be undertaken more productively today than ever before because of the immense advances, effected over the past few generations, in comparative literary and art history and in criticism.

Humanistic knowledge grows in complex fashion because what is new mixes constantly with what is very old. The humanities draw directly on knowledge that is rooted in pre-history, and even the newest discoveries in the humanities are likely to have antique counterparts: psychological literary criticism may draw on Freud's description of the Oedipus complex, but Freud himself is rooted in Euripides, who in his drama put his finger directly on Freud's problem two thousand years earlier. Still, Euripides is not Freud. Freud knew more, even about Oedipus, and so does the competent present-day critic. Even when we fully avow how much our present knowledge of man derives from the ancients, we must still be aware that what we today know about man in terms of his whole life world immeasurably exceeds what earlier man could get at. We have the advantage both of the general accumulation of learning and also of the greater penetration of time and space which has made cross-cultural studies possible.

EXTERIORIZATION OF KNOWLEDGE

As knowledge has grown, it has become both more exteriorized and more interiorized. Early man's knowledge tended to merge the exterior and interior worlds. Even in a technologized culture, the child's consciousness must first be formed in an intersubjective world of personal relationships —mother, father, other human beings. Primitive man remained close to this world in his adult cosmology, too. The universe was anthropomorphic in a myriad of ways. Lonely for his own kind on an earth that was underpopulous, early man commonly filled the empty forests and air and waters with living beings—wood nymphs, gnomes, spirits of all sorts, nereids—not entirely unlike himself. Totemic systems blended the animal and human in ways that still enchant and puzzle anthropologists and philosophers down to Maurice Merleau-Ponty and Claude Lévi-Strauss. Even so sophisticated a cosmology as that of Aristotle and Ptolemy was basically animistic and anthropomorphic: the putative celestial spheres surrounding the earth and bearing the planets were taken to be living, intelligent beings. Only through their mediation did change take place in our dull sublunary world. We can see these early constructs of physical science as partly projections from man's own interior, minimally "objective." They connect in part with early man's proclivity for interiorizing, auditory syntheses (the music of the spheres) rather than objective, visual syntheses (the universe held together by measurements).

At the same time, early cultures often exteriorized man's own interior to a degree that would make us acutely uncomfortable. Tribal patterns of thought and activity overpowered the individual. Visitors from technologized cultures living with the people in nontechnologized society often find themselves unnerved by the almost total lack of privacy: life is lived as a kind of total exposure, with almost no opportunity for withdrawal into oneself. Of course, before writing was invented, individual study of a subject was impossible. Thought advanced either obscurely in the gradual evolution of social institutions and language or by being publicly talked out, which is to say it advanced communally. Oral cultures had no Aristotles or Scotuses or Newtons or Einsteins. To a degree, morality itself consisted in external arrangements: touching a dead body even inadvertently could render one ritually impure and vaguely guilty, even though it was not strictly a prohibited action.

Post-Copernican, post-Newtonian man has in great part (not entirely, as he often thinks) foresworn allegiance to these primitive views that half-humanized and thus half-interiorized the external world and at the same time half-exteriorized man's interior consciousness. The interior and exterior are thought of as separate—all too much so, particularly since Plato and Descartes. The external world is now conceived of more typically as a visual synthesis, a set of things defined by surface, a congeries organized not by sound and resonance but by a certain structured disposition in space, something essentially picturable. Although the world in which we live presents itself to all the senses, we habitually consider it as something that is, above all, seen, and perhaps touched (but here only to a degree: touch works for stones but not for clouds). Essentially, the world is "objects," things with surfaces abutting on one another. Our knowledge has progressed, in the physical sciences particularly, when we have thought of the world only this way, keeping ourselves and all interiority out of the focus of attention. Technology has to do with objective things, apprehended from outside, devoid of personal resonance. Eventually, our knowledge has become focused on exteriority so intently that we have tended more and more to regard man himself and perhaps even God as a thing. We are by now acutely aware of the corner we have been painting ourselves into. We talk incessantly of the dangers of depersonalization. We fear being reduced to a mere Social Security number, a computerizable quantity.

INTERIORIZATION OF KNOWLEDGE

But all the while that knowledge was in a sense being exteriorized and depersonalized, a counter movement has also been under way. Ours is not only an exteriorizing, depersonalizing age but also an interiorizing, personalizing one. No other age has been so explicitly conscious of the human person as ours is. Although early society was deeply personal in some ways, its organization communal and feudal, based on personal ties rather than on issues and analytically conceived programs, it was also in other ways terribly impersonal, and unavoidably so. Often it showed little respect for human life. Capital punishment for crimes such as stealing or even for what we would consider misdemeanors took a staggering toll every day in the most civilized countries of Europe as late as the sixteenth century and beyond, when crowds comparable to those attending professional baseball and football games today still regularly assembled to view hangings and the subsequent savage mutilation of the body of the victim (drawing and quartering) carried out, in accordance with the law, before the victim expired. Punitive mutilation was common: one met on the streets men and women whose ears or noses had been cut off or who had been branded for punishment. In this general context of unprogrammed and programmed violence, religious persecution, which strikes us today as so horrible when seen in isolation and which was indeed horrible enough, shows itself also as almost incidental —a manifestation in one particular life area of patterns of savagery accepted everywhere.

In such a world it is not surprising that philosophical thought, too, attended relatively little to the person as person. The good life of the Greek philosophers simply wrote off the slaves and lower classes as not worth consideration. The higher ranges of speculation in the Greek tradition were largely concerned with "forms" and grew much more directly out of the physics of the time than out of explicit attention to the humane. The term "metaphysics," that is, post-physics, which was used for the highest reaches of philosophical thought, suggests the general state of affairs. Deep interest in the human as human was of course discernible in philosophy from the start, but when abstract thought moved in on man's life world, somehow or other it atomized this world into a congeries of virtues and vices. The richness of human life was caught in something of its integrity by early art and literature, but even here, we are now beginning to understand, the economy of knowledge inherited from primitive oral culture tended to dissolve human complexities in abstract virtue-and-vice polarities. Oral modes of thought persisted long after the arrival of writing and even print, losing their dominance only when the romantic movement overwhelmed the ancient rhetorical and dialectical educational tradition.

Major intellectual developments focusing explicity on the person as person can be traced directly to early Christian theology in the first ecumenical councils through the Second Council of Constantinople (A.D. 553), as Denis de Rougemont has suggested in *Man's Western Quest*. Here the early Church thoroughly thrashed out problems concerning the person of Christ and the difference between Father, Son, and Holy Spirit precisely as persons, further elaborating the Scriptural insistence on the personal relations of each individual human being to God. Philosophy, however, picked up little of the theological concerns centered around the Trinity of Persons. Only in the nineteenth century (that is, during the industrial revolution) did philosophy become highly anthropologized, centering itself more explicitly on man as man. In our own day this anthropologizing has culminated in the personalist philosophy of Gabriel Marcel, Karl Jaspers, and others. Personalist philosophy (and complementary reverse personalism, such as Sartre's) are just as typical of twentieth-century civilization as technology is.

Interiorizing, personalizing trends in thought are too diffuse and too numerous to be listed here in detail, but something of what they come to can be seen in the history of of literature. Literature of course always personalizes its matter in the sense that it has somehow to do with man in his lived experiences, with human problems and hence with the interior, human consciousness. But its personalizing potential has been progressively intensified as the focus of plotting has moved over the ages from the more exterior world of fixed social institutions, exteriorized adventure, or episodic exploit, to the human interior directly realized through stream-of-consciousness or interior monologue and related techniques. Such a movement can be traced variously in Greek tragedy from Aeschylus through Euripides, in Elizabethan drama from its crude para-academic beginnings through Shakespeare, or again in the history of the novel, which in two centuries evolved from the relatively exteriorized machinations of Fielding's eighteenth-century *Tom Jones* to the baroque interiority of Joyce's twentieth-century *Finnegans Wake*. Indeed, the novel itself as a genre comes into being late because it depends on advanced interiorization of attention, if we accept Lionel Trilling's well-founded view that a novel is essentially a critique of a complex society which sees through the obvious, exterior, somewhat fraudulent surface of that society to some deeper (interiorly realizable) truth. As a personalized critique of society, though far less interiorized than Joyce, Fielding's work is more interiorized than is John Lyly's *Euphues* of nearly two centuries earlier.

Something similar to what has happened in literature has

also happened in art, as José Ortega y Gasset has explained in *The Dehumanization of Art and Other Essays:* the focus has moved from representations of the exterior world to more and more concern with representations of inner states of mind. Obvious parallels suggest themselves in music.

Perhaps the most pervasive interiorization of knowledge today is coming about in our understanding of history. In place of what used to be more or less standard history, consisting of accounts of military and political ventures, we are developing a sense of history as basically cultural and psychological. We know now that psychological structures change as cultures change: much of the current popular interest in the "media" feeds on a vague awareness of this fact, which has been the concern of scholars quite clearly since Freud's *Civilization and Its Discontents* and indeed from the time of Giovanni Battista Vico (1668–1744). External historical events are shaped by personality structures, which themselves are the result of external historical events and cultural patterns, all these interacting with a certain amount of incalculability insofar as free human decisions (always in very limited existential fields) are also in play.

To the best of modern historians the world is not simply a series of external happenings so much as it is a concatenation of interior states of consciousness: both exterior and interior need to be accounted for, but the principal focus is on the latter. Personalist philosophies of intersubjectivity have their effect here in showing how interpretation of exterior reality itself demands and builds on relations of persons to persons. The Jesuit paleontologist and cultural historian, Pierre Teilhard de Chardin, has gone further in interpreting personal, interior consciousness as the focus of the entire evolutionary process, cosmic, organic, and historical. In *The Phenomenon of Man*, in *The Future of Man*, and in others of his works, Teilhard attends to the way the physical universe evolves toward "inwardness" and consciousness and to the way consciousness itself evolves as man fills and organizes the earth.

Looking to historiography in these perspectives and with the eyes of the future, we might say that history is deposited as personality structure. You and I in our own particular consciousness are our own history, and collectively we are the history of mankind. History is the way we are. It is why we confront ourselves and other men and the world the way we do. To say this is not to imply any kind of fatalism or total determinism. Man is free, and history itself involves free choice. But man must make choices within situations that are actually presented to him and that he does not choose. History is a fabric woven by choice out of necessity. In such a fabric, choice regards the present and the future. The necessities, interior as well as exterior, in which choice asserts itself often derive from the past.

What we are beginning to learn about the effects of history in the organization of consciousness and personality structures has almost limitless implications for our understanding of knowledge itself and its development. For knowledge exists in dependence on given personality structures. A tradition-directed culture cannot produce highly original speculative thought because the personality structured to such a culture cannot function independently of accepted tribal patterns and, indeed, cannot even want to experience itself as "original." Tradition-directed cultures are, roughly, oral cultures or cultures in which script has not been sufficiently interiorized to change psychic organization. Eric Havelock has shown in his *Preface to Plato*, mentioned earlier, how Plato's highly speculative philosophy, and in particular his "ideas," were dependent on an attitude toward the world made possible only by writing, which prepares the psyche for the fixity and remoteness from the human life world that the "ideas" stand for.

Our growing awareness of the variant psychological struc-

tures produced by different cultures and in particular of the
need for knowledge to be detribalized in the sense of personally interiorized (as in David Riesman's "inner-directed"
character) in order to produce a technological thinker is
affecting our sense of global understanding. We are reaching
the point where we may no longer regard "elections" in which
a predictable winner piles up 99 percent of the vote as
frauds managed so naïvely as to be merely quaint. We can
begin to appreciate that such more or less enforced patterns
of publicly manifested conformity found in neotechnological
cultures are doubtless due in great part to old tribal or tradition-directed personality structures, which cannot be eradicated in a day. The divisions of opinion on which a democracy
thrives could paralyze a personality formed in a newly technologized or half-technologized milieu, in which the older
tribal organization of consciousness calling for nondeviance
is still operative.

We are also, or should be, long past the stage where we
label members of still earlier, pretechnological, oral cultures
"lazy" because their members do not take enthusiastically to
the ethic of "hard work" which technological cultures automatically structure into their successful members' psyches.
We know that persons in pretechnological cultures are
perfectly capable of doing things that are quite as difficult
and demanding as the tasks of an assembly-line worker or a
junior business executive but that their outlook on existence
is at root so communal that the idea of "making something of
yourself" will necessarily appear to them unrealistic and even
unmanly. Man, they feel, is supposed to live in a world of
human events, not in constant traffic with such things or
abstractions as technological life demands. To make a fetish
of work is to dehumanize oneself, to become a machine. The
problem facing developing nations, as an increasing number
of psychological studies shows, is not a problem of exhorting
lazy people to work hard, but more profoundly, that of re-

structuring personalities or of structuring young, forming personalities in the ways that technological life requires for its members if they are to survive as human beings. Our growing knowledge of knowledge is making us more adept at describing socially determined differences in personality structures. But we are as yet far from knowing how to change them.

THRUST INTO THE FUTURE AND GROWTH IN RESPONSIBILITY

The growth of knowledge is certainly one of the factors thrusting modern man into the future. Very primitive peoples tend to live from hand to mouth more than more developed civilizations do. Growth into a planned economy has come about gradually. Manufacture of clothing and weapons showed planning for the future, which the planting of crops further intensified. Later the large civil governments developed in antiquity relied on intensive planning, as in the elaborate irrigation work along the Nile in ancient Egypt. At first governmental planning had been largely to maintain the precarious status quo, but with colonization and empire it meant also plotting major changes for individuals and regions, though seldom avowed changes in style of life. Yet even in style of life, some programmed change was possible as early as among the ancient Romans, for example, because these peoples had enough knowledge of climate, natural resources, engineering (particularly for their roads), and writing (an absolute essential, as Harold Innis has made clear) to have some control over the future.

Today, however, programming the future has entered a new stage. Earlier time scales, related more or less to the duration of a few generations, have been superseded. We think habitually of the future of the human race on earth a hundred years from now, or five hundred years, or two thousand years. In the control of natural resources—the soil and

its products, food crops, forests, fisheries, water power—we
already effectively plan in ways that will determine conditions
of life in the next few centuries, and it is in part our ability
to do this which gives our life the future pitch it has. But
the principal reason for the thrust into the future which
makes our state of mind today different from that of earlier
man is our knowledge of cosmic and organic evolution. We
are aware that we live in an evolving universe, pitched into
the future. The world is structured in patterned change. Not
only can man change things; he can change the very pattern
of change as well.

Our awareness of patterns of development extends beyond
the exterior universe into knowledge itself. As time goes on,
we learn more and more about how knowledge comes into
being, about learning processes and processes of discovery,
about how knowledge can be not merely stored and communi-
cated but also brought into existence as well as increased.
We engineer knowledge itself in advance, as the Rockefeller
Foundation helped do a few decades ago when it found the
increment of knowledge in the life sciences inadequate and
hence made the decision to divert large funds into stepping
up the increment here, a decision that helped produce within
a few years our new understanding of DNA and the genetic
code of living organisms. The ability to program knowledge
gives man a kind of exponential control over nature. If knowledge is power, knowledge of how to generate knowledge is
power over power.

With his present sense of an evolving universe, his store of
knowledge, and his awareness of knowledge as power, man
today quite naturally feels his life role to be largely that of a
manager. Of course, not every man and woman even in a
highly technologized society thinks of himself or herself as an
active global planner, but everyone knows that this is now
the role of the human race taken as a whole. From national
planning commissions of all sorts down to science fiction and

comic strips, the mythology of global and, to a very limited extent, cosmic management permeates all levels of society and all economic levels.

We know that if we are responsible today more than ever before for the conditions we live in, we shall also be still more responsible in the future. In the past when civil disorders occurred or wars broke out, man could put it down to the inescapable state of human affairs, to vices bred into men. No one in his right mind would deny that today we have our share of real vices, but we are at the same time aware that breakdowns in society must be accounted for by a great many things other than vice—lack of education, of economic opportunity, the revolution of rising expectations, the unthinking use of the mass media of communication, and a great many other social developments over which we can exercise control even though we may not yet have learned how to do so very effectively.

The buildup of knowledge and the proliferation of means for storing and communicating knowledge that makes man's managerial role possible and imperative also, of course, creates severe strains in society. There is a great deal of illusion in loose talk about "turnover" in knowledge, which mistakes knowledge for a commodity and thus confuses it with agglomerates of "information," forgetting that true knowledge in human beings cannot "replace" earlier knowledge but must somehow be integral with earlier knowledge in order to be functional or even psychologically possible at all. Nevertheless, even when we write off the cheap equations such talk relies on, we must still note that the rapid increase in knowledge divides the generations. The mode of assimilating the store of human knowledge, and particularly the "image field" used in managing it, probably differs considerably between those who are twenty years old and those who are fifty. Such differences should not be minimized. But neither should they fill us with despair. They are not unbridgeable but simply take work to bridge. A good many persons in their fifties and beyond are doing the best work interpreting just such differences between the generations. It is paradoxical that only a relative oldster such as Marshall McLuhan can interpret the younger generation to themselves and that to many of his own generation his interpretation remains incomprehensible. It would be more paradoxical if all the younger persons understood and none of the oldsters did. Such is not the case. Some of both groups do. His interpretations and those of others like him in fact do bridge the chasm.

A more serious problem created by proliferation of knowledge and man's resulting managerial responsibility is that of withdrawal. Withdrawal symptoms show up more and more in technologically advanced societies. Often they are factitious and even meretricious: the beatnik or hippie is not really "dropping out" but looking desperately for an in-group that will satisfy his own demands. Often, seeming withdrawal is merely a way of securing attention without responsibility. Nevertheless, it creates real problems, and the withdrawal syndrome is certainly connected with the pressures of managerial expectations. The sociological studies show that hippies come typically not from the underprivileged but almost entirely from among the relatively well to do or the very wealthy, where the pressures of responsibility in one way or another make themselves felt. Withdrawal, real or simulated, will probably be a major problem with us for a long time.

The countervailing factor to withdrawal is the possibility of cooperation which modern technological society offers and indeed has to a great extent implemented. We fail all too often to be aware of the fantastic cooperative ventures that the human race has by this time achieved, despite the dissensions that still tear at the national and international fabrics. Man is a cooperating animal, and the earliest human traces on earth show the results of joint action. By the time of the Old Empire in Egypt, shortly after 3000 B.C., cooperative endeavor (not all of it voluntary, but any means) could raise the pyramids. The organization evident in such early works is overwhelmingly impressive, given the conditions of communication and transport under which it was achieved. But in intricacy of detail, it is negligible compared to the cooperation required today for airing a single television program, if one considers all of what is really involved in bringing together the persons and equipment as well as the actual operation of the latter: the skills going into the design and manufacture of television apparatus, the intricacies of program planning, the transportation systems needed for moving personnel to and from the studio (carefully engineered automobiles, subways, freeways patroled by helicopter, traffic-light engineering, and so on ad infinitum). And if the cooperative effort in producing a pyramid or even a medieval gothic cathedral is, for all its wonder, small compared to that needed for a single television broadcast, it is infinitesimal compared to that required to launch a rocket to the moon. Massive cooperation is the hallmark of technological society. Even the routine cooperative activity of a single metropolis in the course of one day surpasses all powers of conceptualization. No one can really disengage himself from the cooperative network of modern living, and in point of fact, few ever really want to.

III

Despite incidental problems it has created and heavy burdens it has imposed on man, the knowledge explosion as described thus far here appears unmistakably as a tremendous achievement and boon. Is this all there is to say about it? Hardly. For human life is tragic at its root, and for all the progress we have made, we have in another sense made no progress at all. The heady sense of growing control over the physical world around us, of growing knowledge concerning man himself, his physical and psychological makeup, and the way he fits historically into the cosmos and into his own social structures can in the long run foster an illusion. For with this kind of knowledge we have actually learned no more at all about what man has always really wanted to know.

The basic, ultimate questions concerning either the exterior universe or our interior consciousness still yawn before us. What is the universe *doing?* If the cosmos is a happening, *what* is going on? What is life all about? Where did my consciousness come from, this "I" that I and I alone can utter, which no one else can savor no matter how much I may wish to share it with him? How could this "I," this spark, without which for me the whole universe ceases to be, once not have been and now actually exist? What is the meaning of my life? What value have my actions? *Why* do I want *others* to judge *me*—approvingly of course, but objectively, on my own merits? What is to be the meaning of my death? The growth in knowledge which we have just reviewed does not lead us toward answers at this level.

It does, of course, bring to light a great deal of new material which can be related to such questions. It also eliminates some false assumptions bearing on such questions: matter is not more spiritual as one moves upward from the earth's surface, as Aristotle thought it was. Moreover, our growth in knowledge enables us to articulate psychological and other complexities which earlier man could not formulate very satisfactorily even when he was acutely aware of them. But enrichment and improved articulation of questions only tantalizes us here so long as it fails to move us further toward satisfying answers. Having discovered as much as we have about the intricacies of the universe, we feel more than ever the urgency of knowing what it is about as a whole. Knowing human history as we do, and thus knowing a great deal about how society has got to where it is, aware that in clearly discernible ways social evolution is patterned, it is natural that we want to know where history is heading. Our knowledge of particular details is now so massive that it can of course distract us from these larger questions for a long time. We have no evidence, however, that this knowledge distracts anyone from them for good. When you raise the questions, others know very well what you are talking about although they may not agree with what you say about them or even with how you formulate them.

Everyone thinks of these things, even though he may try to turn the thought off from time to time or almost for good or may become outraged if the questions are openly broached. It is fashionable, or was a few years ago, to say that life is absurd (a variant of the old statement that it is meaningless). Such a statement may be titillating and can certainly be titillatingly presented. But it accomplishes little. We have not the slightest indication that those who utter or receive it either with composed acquiescence or with starry-eyed excitement cease at all to wonder just the same as before. If they did, the cult of absurdity would not have the shock value it lives on, if it is still alive.

Moreover, not only does our growth in knowledge fail to enter into the basic questions of existence, it also fails to make existence more radically satisfactory for the individual than it would be otherwise. Corporately, knowledge has advanced, but somehow the advance does not touch the individual at the center of his being. How can it? Each of our lives is fresh and unique, a brand new venture into integrity. Knowledge, no matter how much of it is available or how much structure the past experience of man has given it, still has somehow to be built by the individual self into the pattern of a new and induplicable consciousness.

The task can be crushing. Disabilities that most grossly interfere with the individual's functioning as a human being can be ameliorated, and in this sense life can be made more satisfactory: we can realistically hope to eradicate malnutrition and to control more effectively fatal or seriously crippling diseases, or perhaps even inhuman patterns of urban overcrowding, unemployment, and education or lack of education—although we have not been brilliantly successful here. But when all this is done and man's physical needs are filled and his intellectual environment made more habitable, he is still liable to interior collapse. Environment is mostly people, real or imagined. Pressures less visible and tangible but more real than those that may afflict the individual's body can bear in on his mind.

Adequate diet and housing and access to all the sensual and intellectual pleasures that can be dreamed up will not eliminate suicide. And although psychiatry can be of some help, its practitioners certainly do not look forward to an imminent or even an ultimate state of universal well-being. Life is not that way. The psychiatrist can only help man to live with the difficulties that are part of all men's lot. Typically, he spends far more time getting a patient to acknowledge the permanent existence of difficulties than he does in abolishing them.

Our inability to handle our social problems better is due in part, although not entirely, to the problems of the individual. We will always have social problems because whatever else we can do and must do, we have no way of eliminating all individual collapse.

Finally, apart from its limited range and effectiveness, our growth in knowledge holds in its very self threat as well as promise. Most knowledge can be misused, and the power it gives can certainly be misused. There is a touch of death in what man learns. Not a few of the great inventions most useful for peaceful purposes—explosive powder, rocketry, and atom power among them—have been first developed and used to kill other men.

For all these reasons, man's growth in knowledge is both

challenging and tragic. Despite all his progress, man remains a permanent threat to himself, "a being darkly wise and rudely great."

He can and does thrive under such conditions because he is also a being who hopes. As in the past, so today hope concerning the human condition belongs to men not quite settled in the material world immediately around them, much though they may love it, men who sense material reality as something pointing, however darkly, outside itself, an essential intimation of otherness, a something suggesting something it is not. For the fact is that out of his contact with the world around him this question constantly arises in man's mind: Is there something more than this immediacy? And beyond this the further question: Why does this question itself arise, why does man ask whether there is not something more?

In the Hebreo-Christian tradition, this intimation of something more than immediate, sensible reality is subsumed in faith in a personal God, a God who is concerned, to whom men matter. Such faith connects with experience of things, but it relates most directly to man's experience of persons. Man's relationship to God belongs primarily in the realm of personal relationships. It is of a piece with the world in which man speaks to man, heart to heart, in which the mysterious words "I" and "you" are uttered, the world that eludes science but in which all science rests, since it is only a person, an "I," who knows, who can learn, and who can communicate what he learns to others. All science exists in the consciousness of always unique persons, whom science can never get at, for only I know what it feels like to be me, and only you know what it feels like to be you, and what has science to say when death attacks this relationship in which I know you and you know me? Out of what Martin Buber has well styled the primary word of relationship, of binding together, "I-thou," there arises faith as this is known in the Hebrew and Christian heritage.

This personal relationship is not an isolating relationship, since it comes into being in the human community, where the individual discovers his own being, and also in the related community of the faithful. The community of the faithful among the Hebrews constituted the Chosen People. Among Christians the community of the faithful, the Church, is called the People of God—an ancient concept today disseminated by the Second Vatican Council as perhaps never before. The communal grounding of the faith of the People of God further emphasized the personal character of this faith, for community is a relationship between persons, not things.

Like other personal relationships, this faith is of itself abiding. Through it men cling to a personal God in the face of the worst conceivable disasters, like Job, who resisted the attempts of his friends to rationalize the miseries of his life as nothing more than equitable punishments from God's hand. Job knew better. All explanation of evil proved only partial explanation. Finally Job declared his faith in divine providence in the face of what he knew he would always have to live with—his own inability completely to comprehend God's intent and what in fact the full pattern of existence comes to. Despite this inability to comprehend—or indeed because of it, insofar as it showed Job's creaturely status before God —Job believed in God and trusted God fully, leaving himself in God's hands with hope. Job comes to this conclusion not because of reason, or any new explanation he has received or devised, but neither because he feels God is acting against reason. He comes to the conclusion, "I disown what I have said and repent in dust and ashes" (Job 42:6), because God has raised him to a new experience, a new grasp of reality through an encounter with Himself. The solution is a matter not of a scientific or philosophical formula but of Job's own personal relationship to God. He hopes not in any principle of total understanding but simply in God.

Despite the great advance in knowledge and the great

promise further advance holds for the future, there will always be room for this kind of faith, for knowledge is clearly not moving at all in any direction that would engage the problems of existence that faith meets head-on. The Christian's faith partakes of Job's but moves even further into greater hope, for the Christian's faith tells him that God has brought man into personal partnership with himself through the Incarnation, by taking to Himself human nature, entering into this historical, material world in Jesus Christ. This same faith of course is not remote from the growth of knowledge but rejoices in this growth. First, this growth is a good in itself, and faith rejoices in natural good. Secondly, faith can indefinitely deepen its own understanding of itself, and since the man of faith is rooted in the natural, secular world, faith stands to gain by every advance in secular understanding.

One might argue of course, as some do, that Christian faith solves the problem of man's destiny all too well. It eliminates all tragedy, we are told, and with tragedy some of the greatest of man's literary and artistic creations. Does it not make suffering and disaster unreal, or try to, by presenting both as simply preludes to eternal happiness? Even the worst disaster is dissolved in ultimate bliss. The cross is eliminated by the Resurrection.

All students of faith and tragedy do not by any means acquiesce in such an interpretation. To many, including the present writer, such an interpretation badly misses the point of suffering as seen in Christian teaching. Tragedy is tragedy and has to be lived through, by the Christian as by others. Man's relationship to nature is in the last analysis tragic. For it ends always in death.

> Million-fuelèd, ' nature's bonfire burns on.
> But quench her bonniest, dearest to her, her clearest-selvèd
>   spark

Man, how fast his firedint, ' his mark on mind, is gone!
Both are in an unfathomable, all is in an enormous dark
Drowned.

The Jesuit poet Gerard Manley Hopkins has no illusions
about death's absoluteness here in "That Nature Is a Heracli-
tean Fire." Nature ultimately wipes out the individual:

> Manshape, that shone
> Sheer off, disseveral, a star, ' death blots black out; nor mark
> Is any of him at all so stark
> But vastness blurs and time ' beats level.

With Christ, too, suffering and death were real. His
death interrupted his ongoing work, the momentum of his
entire mission. He did not plan his death. It was something
he underwent, a *passio* or passion, not an action, something
that happened to him, not anything he contrived. In Hopkins'
words again, in his letter of July 3, 1886, to R. W. Dixon,
Christ's "career was cut short and, whereas he would have
wished to succeed by success . . . he was doomed to succeed
by failure; his plans were baffled, his hopes dashed, and his
work was done by being broken off undone. However much
he understood all this he found it an intolerable grief to
submit to it. He left the example: it is very strengthening,
but except in that sense it is not consoling." It was Christ's
personal acceptance, his reaction to tragedy, which cost
dearly but was founded on his personal love for his Father
that raised (did not eliminate) tragedy itself to a loftier
action of self-offering and through this brought redemption.

The Christian view of man's career on earth thus ends
in a mystery for contemplation, not in a neat diagram an-
nihilating either evil or the problem of man himself. It is
a view that proposes enlarged perspectives, not narrowed
exclusiveness, truly Catholic in the root sense of this term,
"through-the-whole," a view that on the one hand does not

carry the eye through all the mists but on the other hand is not at all a tentative view but a committed one. Faith makes demands. Christians are called on to die for their faith rather than deny it, and their typical heroes are those who have done so, the "witnesses" or martyrs.

Still, this commitment to something beyond does not in the least exonerate the Christian from the common obligation of all men to do something about the here and now and the future of man on earth. The Christian is committed to this world, or should be, for all the reasons that the complete secularist can urge—the alleviation of suffering, the improvement of living conditions, the promotion of world peace, the general improvement of mankind, and the advance of knowledge not only insofar as it is power but also simply because knowledge is eminently human and a good in itself. Besides these reasons, the Christian can also propose to himself a further and particularly Christian one for advancing the natural, secular world and man's role in it, a reason deriving from his faith: in Christian teaching, not only did God create this world, but he also became incarnate in it, both giving himself to it and taking it to himself in the human nature of Jesus Christ, sharing its miseries and its glory. The Incarnation enhances the worth of the natural and indeed transvaluates it by giving it even a divine significance through adoption. Thus the particular motivation of the Christian as a Christian in his commitment to the natural world is not simply a powerful, or even the most powerful, motivation among others on the same footing but rather a motivation of a transcendent sort, which sees the natural values of the universe in all their integrity caught up into something beyond themselves. Insofar as a Christian does not opt for a program of secular improvement, he is derelict in a particularly desperate way.

The history of benevolent and charitable social organizations among Christians shows a general awareness of commitment to this world even when lack of understanding of natural forces and of control over them has encouraged a psychology of withdrawal. But today we are more than ever intensely aware of Christian secular commitment. Our age has seen a tremendous growth in Christian theology of the secular world, and it has become more and more common-place that secularization has Hebrew and, even more, Christian roots, if we understand by secularization the tendency to give the secular world an intrinsic value of its own (although not necessarily an ultimate value), as contrasted with secularism, which can refer to the belief that the this-worldly is all there is. The historical fact is that modern secularization, like the science and technology that go with it, in all the 500,000-year history of mankind across the surface of the globe had really only one effective starting point in time and space: a culture of the sixteenth and seventeenth centuries which had lived through a massive experience of Christian teaching. The roots of knowledge run everywhere through all human cultures, but the beginnings of modern science are clearly identifiable.

Back of this culture lay the world of medieval Europe in which universities in the present-day sense of the word began and to which, in one way or another, all universities in the world today trace some of their roots. In his *Science and the Modern World* Alfred North Whitehead has made the point that the extraordinary patience needed to attack a problem scientifically demands faith in the intelligibility of the universe and that historically the great impetus to this act of faith has been the Hebreo-Christian teaching that God made everything, that he is actually concerned about everything in its least detail, and that he is all-wise, the clear implication being that, however hard the answer may be to find, there is always an answer to any question that is properly put and thus that infinite patience and labor in research and reflection are ultimately worthwhile no matter how difficult the matter in hand may be. For all their rationality, even the ancient Greeks had not been so strongly convinced of universal intelligibility. They were haunted by the suspicion that here and there the world was or might be terrifying chaos. This idea of universal intelligibility became widely compelling in twelfth-century and thirteenth-century Europe, when at Paris, Bologna, Salamanca, Oxford, Cambridge, and elsewhere the first universities were taking form and the scholastic thinkers there were developing the scrupulous attention to logical detail characteristic of the modern mind.

It is conventional to state that the first universities matured the distinction between faith and reason which gave the natural, secular world its own intellectual autonomy. But this distinction must not be taken to be more absolute than it actually was. Even with the distinction, reason and faith interacted. Reason was not simply established within a realm in which its own processes ruled but, if Whitehead is right, was also actually strengthened within its own realm by faith, which conveyed its own assurance that reason was worthwhile. Moreover, if reason was indebted to faith for this encouragement, faith itself was helpless without reason, for it needed reason to explicate its own interior organization.

The feeling for knowledge to which universities today are heirs thus traces to complex noetic structures in the past. In these structures the two intellectual worlds, that in which man comprehends and controls nature and that in which he faces his ultimate concerns, were allied at the very time that they were distinct. The alliance and the distinction between the two persist today. Secular knowledge and faith are still related in ways both uneasy and telling. In the midst of our present knowledge explosions, it will take effort to keep alive a fruitful relationship between the two intellectual worlds. But if knowledge is to be advanced—which is virtually the same as saying, if man is to survive—we have to maintain a firm, if inevitably precarious, hold on both.

2

THE FUTURE OF
UNIVERSITY EDUCATION AS AN IDEA

CHARLES MUSCATINE
University of California, Berkeley

I F THE effect of knowledge is to be read in our formal
institutions, the picture of our education in the future
will be close to that of our future itself. "Education of
many different kinds," said scientist Roger Revelle recently
to a congressional committee, "will become the central activity of the people of the United States." Management
professor Warren G. Bennis calls education "the most distinctive characteristic of our society." Sociologists have
named ours a "post-industrial" era, meaning an era in which
the manager moves over to make room for the scholar. "The
university's invisible product, knowledge," writes Clark Kerr,
"may be the most powerful single element in our culture."[1]
In this context, "university education" implies activities of
such scope and importance as to threaten the very identity
of the university. To anyone but the most uncritical booster,

---

[1] Roger Revelle, "Science and Social Change," presented to the
House Committee on Science and Astronautics, Jan. 26, 1966; Warren
G. Bennis, "The Coming Death of Bureaucracy," *Think*, 32, No. 6
(Nov.–Dec., 1966), 34; Daniel Bell, *The Reforming of General Edu-
cation* (New York: Columbia University Press, 1966), p. 86; Clark
Kerr, *The Uses of the University* (Cambridge, Mass.: Harvard Uni-
versity Press, 1964), p. vi.

in fact, the prospects for university education, while fascinating, are not uniformly hopeful.

It has already become conventional for university people to worry over their future in terms of resources. The population projections and the steady rise in our educational norms are impressive enough: by the year 2000 we may expect between 55 and 71 percent of our college-age youths, that is, between thirteen and sixteen million of them, to be enrolled as "undergraduates" in our "colleges," with another two million in "graduate schools" to boot.[2] I use the quotation marks expecting that the structure of the university will have changed a good deal in the interval. (The extreme alternative—that universities remain essentially the same but just get bigger and more numerous—is almost too awful to contemplate and stands outside our calculations.) Even if we assume—by analogy with what has happened with universal high school education—that in the future many more millions of healthy, active American youths will be able to be safely detained within the classrooms of more and bigger conventional "colleges," some will have found access to more modern institutions, consciously redesigned to meet problems that are obvious today.

In fact, as the demand for university education grows, downright repressive measures may be required to keep higher education from drastic change. For the very alteration of the scale of education will bring problems that even the doubling and redoubling of conventional resources will never answer. The bigger campus will tend to generate and have to fight impersonality, but it will also generate cosmopolitanism and sophistication. It will justify more complex equipment in laboratories and theaters and enjoy a greater variety of talents in faculty and students. More innovative still

[2] Alan M. Cartter and Robert Farrell, "Higher Education in the Last Third of the Century," *Educational Record*, 46 (spring, 1965), 119–28.

will be the students' wider social base and range of ideology. On a small campus the rare student with deviant attitudes is cowed or ostracized; on a big campus he joins a club or a movement. The "new generation of students," with its rich mixture of innovative social, political, and moral propensities, can be expected to flourish as college populations rise.

Along with the numbers of students, the mighty expansion of knowledge will transform university education. With an increase in the "graduate" orientation of students, "post-doctoral" studies, refresher courses, and "continuing education" for the sciences and learned professions, the "learning period" will lengthen and the student community will stretch indefinitely through the higher-age groups. The increase in the general maturity of "students" should force the abandonment of much of the disciplinary hardware designed in the nineteenth century for youthful Protestant seminarians and naïve frontier mechanics. There will, indeed, be no time to waste on the ordinary sticks and carrots, on routine quizzing and grading; but better understanding of how people learn will be applied directly, with as little nonsense as possible.

It seems inevitable that the near future will alter the roles of university student and teacher; in this case economy, learning theory, and the rate of obsolescence of knowledge may all three be pushing in the same direction. There will be less routine classroom lecture-and-recitation, because in the first place the faculty will have less time for it. The trend toward dividing the professor's teaching time with research and public service will continue as long as research and public service remain socially and professionally justifiable and as long as well-compensated scholars and scientists, in demand elsewhere, can resist the naked fiats of university administrators and reformers.

When the professor enters the classroom it will be on new terms, largely dictated by his own intellectual situation. In many fields a major force will be the threat of obsolescence, which will make it imperative for the professor to remain abreast of current research, to keep his teaching in close contact with examples of research, and in so doing to emphasize the learning of principles rather than facts. This will mean the abandonment of the "survey" approach in many introductory studies, in favor of the "problems" approach— to teach a method, a stance, a conceptual grasp of a discipline that will be useful long after all the current information is out of date. This approach, by and large, calls for discussion, experimentation, emulation, and the cultivation of personal discovery, rather than for formal indoctrination; it suggests an expanded role of the teacher as guide, explicator, counselor, and critic rather than as formal lecturer. Some of the time for this highly expensive kind of teaching activity will be bought by canceling many of the unnecessary informational courses that are now routinely offered, along with a good deal of the tedious numbers game of grading and credit keeping that goes with them. We are discovering that "contact hours" does not equal education.

But there will never be enough professors to go around, and the university will have to augment its teaching power from other sources. New technology may be of some help, especially with the irreducible busy work and with whatever rote learning and drill work survive in the curriculum. But the major new teaching assistance will come from the students themselves, in the form of discussion groups, seminars led by the more experienced, and a great deal of independent study. Current experiments in this direction are prompted by the hypothesis that the deepest kinds of learning require less constant presence of the teacher than we have hitherto imagined.

Another major new source of university teaching power will be the surrounding community of scientists, technicians, artists, and cultivated people of all sorts. Many can be brought in on a part-time basis to exchange their professional knowledge for the pleasure of teaching. Furthermore, if the university is forced to concentrate on teaching general principles, the up-to-the-minute professional details will have to be left to institutes and training centers close to industry, government, and the professions.

In all this we can already see a profound change in the structure of the university, or rather, a blurring of the notion of the university as a definable structure at all. Here even the "multiversity," with its multiplicity of loci and functions, begins to lose its outlines. As nearly everyone heads for a university education; as the learning period lengthens indefinitely; as the shifting student community expands to include new classes, new age levels, new ranges of ideology; as the procedures of teaching lose their current simplicity and the criteria of learning become more subjective and indefinite; as the conception of who *may* teach includes more and more of those who *can* teach; as professional teachers become more implicated in the worlds of business and government; as more and more "university" instruction goes on in extramural institutions and in field studies here and abroad—the university will tend to lose its character as a place with clear geographical and intellectual boundaries, a place where one spends a definite amount of time and acquires a certain amount of knowledge. It will become, rather, a point or center from which knowledge and teaching radiate into the surrounding environment, and the possible relations of individuals to it will have many gradations, altering with age and circumstances. Some of our current problems of determining just who is to be officially considered a "student" are early symptoms of this condition, as are the growing student taste for off-campus living and other signs of the disintegration of the traditional university community.

However unrealistic this picture may seem in specific detail, it is a plausible one in its outlines, given what we can expect of the future role of knowledge in our culture. If anything, the picture may be a sentimental one. If it predicts more change in a few decades than the university has managed in centuries, it may still be predicting the survival of too much university. In an environment that promises to be almost totally compact of knowledge, the edges of educational institutions will naturally tend to become invisible. Indeed, we might well ask whether there is any reason other than a sentimental one not to expect and not to accept the university's gradual assimilation into the knowledge-producing and knowledge-consuming environment, finally to become indistinguishable in a web of other activity centers of similar purpose.

Resistance to change in the university has indeed a large sentimental component, as well as a large component of insecurity. For some university people the promised uncertainties and ambiguities of the future are simply intolerable; their passionate clinging to the old ways is a clinging to the most comforting symbols of the university's identity. Others are less sentimental than skeptical: in changing so much, they feel, we will not be able to preserve for the university its proper role as conservator and propagator of values of the past. But it would repay these loyal defenders of the university to scrutinize proposed innovations carefully before opposing them. The kinds of changes I have described above are actually a very mixed bag. If most of them threaten to blur the university's physical and intellectual boundaries, at least some of them, if vigorously used, promise a countervailing rehabilitation of the university as a moral force. The fostering of individual responsibility for learning, studies in the field and by one's self, the cultivation of dialogue and debate over real problems—this kind of innovation makes for independence of spirit and for critical thinking. In the coming environment they may well prove to be more valuable symbols of the university idea than any number of cherished traditions. For this we have as witness yet another class of opponents of innovation who (usually beneath appeals to "quality" and to "discipline") actually fear that innovation may embarrass the university with too much moral force altogether.

There are, in short, profound political reasons for preserving the identity of the university, though paradoxically, we shall have to change that identity greatly in order to be able to preserve it at all. To meet the issue more crudely and immediately we need only turn from the problem of knowledge-as-environment to the related problem of knowledge-as-power. Here we have to face it: most educational development today is propelled by the new economic and political potentialities of knowledge, particularly of scientific knowledge. What are the chances that the university will not in one way or another lose its autonomy and identity in the general competition for economic and political power?

Whatever the answer may be, it is mixed with several difficult paradoxes. For millennia we have dreamt of the ideal of the philosopher-prince, or at least of the philosopher at the elbow of the prince. Now its fulfillment seems at hand; but as the scholar flies off to Washington, we wonder where scholarship leaves off and political ambition begins. I refrain from adding to the rich literature on "University Research and the Federal Government." The paradoxes and the dangers are obvious enough.[3] For the whole century of our land-grant universities we have accepted the idea of some sort of collaboration between scholarship and industry. This collaboration has latterly become exceedingly fruitful and close—so close, in fact, that we can now begin to discuss "The Corporation as a College." A recent General

[3] One of the best treatments I have seen is Gerard Piel, "Federal Funds and Science Education," *Bulletin of the Atomic Scientists*, 22, No. 5 (May, 1966), 10–15. On pp. 13–14 Piel cites testimony that in engineering even teaching follows closely the patterns set by defense-supported and space-supported research.

Motors advertisement boasts of an employee, who, "passing up scholarships at two universities, . . . decided instead on the General Motors Institute in Flint, and was graduated with an engineering degree." A Yale economics professor describing "the new corporate curriculum" suggests that it could range from elementary English composition to "courses more advanced than those available in the universities."[4]

As I have suggested above, the universities will need some help from government and industry; what is unpleasant is the prospect that they will receive all too much help, and that in the process "university education" will lose the only subject that has to be taught in a university and that will never appear in the "corporate curriculum," namely, Criticism. By Criticism I mean informed and unconstrained evaluation, the skill that in a democracy we hope every citizen will learn to exercise.

In naming Criticism—in its broadest sense—as the characterizing activity of the university, I am of course invoking an old *idea* of the university that seems lately to be losing ground. It is losing ground to the notion, profoundly typical of our times, that we don't need an idea of a university if we have a description of one. As the Foreword to Clark Kerr's *The Uses of the University* puts it: ". . . in the discussion that follows, analysis should not be confused with approval or description with defense." Nevertheless, the normative idea of the university has its proponents. It is what Gerard Piel has in mind when he says that the university has an obligation to the citizen that is prior to its obligation to the government: "For the university is the seat of the citizen's sovereignty; it is the institutional embodiment of the immunity that hedges his liberty."[5] It is this idea that informs the thinking of those who look to the university as the

---

[4] See *Commentary*, 42, No. 6 (Dec., 1966), p. 62, for the ad; and Neil Chamberlain in *The Atlantic*, 215, No. 6 (June, 1965), 102–4.
[5] On p. 11 of the article cited above.

last source of responsible guidance amid the breakup of the old authorities. It is held perforce by those who, not trusting naked intelligence, are looking for a place that will teach how knowledge can be developed with moral sensitivity.[6]

The university has never anywhere fully exemplified this idea, but we need the idea nonetheless. Whether we shall have even an imperfect but working model of it in the future remains to be seen. We have glanced darkly at forces of disintegration within and without the university and have observed some elements of curricular and organizational change that might make for integrity. What other defenses does our idea of the university have? What, for instance, can be expected of the great university disciplines: natural science, social science, and the humanities?

Too much has been written recently of weakness and venality among our scientific entrepreneurs; it would be fairer to give the scientists another generation in which to become accustomed to their new social status and to ask whether there are forces within the scientific discipline itself that will tend to generate and preserve the critical spirit. The answer, on paper, is yes. If the sciences deal with intrinsically unmoral data, they can deal with them in ways that would seem to have profound moral implications—with skepticism and creative insight, critical detachment, rationality, the demand for verification, the recognition of the tentativeness of knowledge. To the extent that we still have some good science teaching, its qualities will rub off on some students and must be counted among the forces that will preserve the university idea. Looking at science education as an enterprise, we see that the scientists have not gone much beyond this fortuitous rubbing-off. They have

[6] See, among others, Kenneth B. Clark, "Intelligence, the University, and Society," in *The American Scholar*, 36, No. 1 (winter, 1966–67), 23–32; John William Ward, "The Trouble with Higher Education," in *The Public Interest* (summer, 1966), pp. 76–88; J. H. Plumb in *The Saturday Review*, Nov. 26, 1966, pp. 29, 57.

been teaching physics and chemistry and genetics proper, that is, as science, and they have been teaching them better and better to prospective scientists. But with pitifully few exceptions criticism of science stops at the borders of the technical field. In this, science teachers have been widely short-changing the prospective nonscientists, whose appreciation of science depends on seeing it in the context of their culture, its history, and its values.

Perhaps we should not ask too much of the natural scientists in these boom times. Success and excitement are not the best conditions for philosophical self-examination. Besides, Criticism in the social and moral realms is not the natural scientist's professional forte. But can we say the same of the social scientist and the humanist? We may readily observe that detachment, impersonality, and rigorous scientific objectivity, when they are practiced as ends in themselves and to the exclusion of all else, can render a man and his work morally sterile. This may not affect the gross production of knowledge, but for the idea of the university it is crucial. The most serious betrayal of this idea today is the moral anesthetization of the social sciences and humanities which generally goes on in the name of "science," "research," and "objective scholarship."

About the full condition of the social sciences I cannot pretend to much authority. I know enough of the relative decline of political theory and economic history and of the vogue of "mathematical" economics and politics to make me worry. Most of all, I am concerned that so very few of the social scientists I know of are saying (or have ever said) anything so unsettling about society as to require protection by the academic freedom and tenure that society has generously vouchsafed them.

With the humanities I am in more familiar territory. Where else should Criticism flourish but in the humanities? Of criticism with a small *c* we have plenty—this is an "age of criticism"—but of studies informed with large moral vision we have little. The case of philosophy is typical. Metaphysics and idealism are nearly dead, trampled in the rise of "scientific philosophy," now largely concerned with the critical analysis of logic and language. One hears that this tool sharpening is just a phase, prelude perhaps to a grand new attempt to grasp this sorry scheme of things entire. We can only hope so.

The teaching of literature is in slightly better case, if only because literature's academic establishment is a formidable one, including many of our creative writers. Even so, the teaching of non-Western literature is generally neglected, and the established departments of the European literatures are widely suffering for lack of fresh talent. Let us concentrate on English, a prospering field marked by continually impressive feats of scholarship and criticism.

As Professor John Gerber has recently made clear in a witty and plausible historical sketch,[7] for the last century the trend in literary studies in America has ever been toward detachment. The revolt from factualism loudly heralded by the New Criticism thirty years ago did not turn teacher and student back to the emotional appeal and moral relevance of literature but rather substituted the detachment of critical analysis for that of Germanic scholarship. The New Criticism's corrective for studying matters extraneous (and often irrelevant) to the work of literature was to concentrate attention on the work *in itself*. This has yielded us splendid results in the techniques of close reading and in the appreciation of formal structure. But the effort to eliminate historical irrelevance and personal idiosyncrasy from literary interpretation has ended up in a kind of estheticism that is frequently just as far from commitment to human values as is the production of the chemist and of the logician. What

[7] "Literature—Our Untamable Discipline," *College English*, 28 (Feb., 1967), 351–58.

literary studies need now is in the first place a New Historic-
ism that will put its elegantly analyzed artifacts back into the
living stream of the history of culture. In the second place,
those of us who profess to teach literature need to accept the
special role that comes with the territory. Handling stuff that
is itself alive with feeling and with moral significance, we
cannot afford to be always detached.

As professionals it is we who have the most direct responsibility to keep Criticism alive in the university. Our relative
failure is partly the result of a long and misguided attempt
to make literature into a discrete science. We have resisted
our natural role as humanists and generalists, for fear that
in the competitive university environment we would be
thought to be lacking a professional "field."[8] The same fear
has now infected even the secondary school teaching of
literature. Competing with "new science" and "new math,"
and propelled by the reaction against progressivism—which
is now resulting in uncritical hostility to the cultivation of
sensibility in any form—high school curricula are filling up
with professional Literary History and Critical Analysis of
Texts at the expense of the education of judgment and
feeling that should be their prior aim.

The recent creation of a National Endowment for the
Humanities may ultimately help transform the stance of our
academic humanists. At least it gives them the kind of
recognition that may free them to be their best selves. At
the same time we must recognize that the Endowment and
the National Council for the Arts and Humanities under
which it is organized have been created under the impetus
of men who speak largely from the old, well-upholstered

[8] *Cf.* the whole drift of R. Wellek and A. Warren, *Theory of
Literature* (New York: Harcourt, Brace & World, 1962); and the
excellent remarks of Richard Ohmann, "The Size and Structure of an
Academic Field: Some Perplexities," *College English*, 28 (Feb.,
1967), 359–67.

positions.[9] Early reports of the Humanities Endowment projects seem largely to favor conventional scholarship. We can freely grant that support of scholarship is essential: it provides us some of the major materials of Criticism. But it is not enough. We have nothing to indicate that more direct contribution to human values will result except the rather grand but cloudy pronouncements of the humanities establishment. If, as we hope, humanistic study makes people more humane and sensitive to human problems, we should perhaps be bolder in looking among those who show conspicuous effects of such study when we award humanities fellowships and recruit humanities professors.

But, as the *Bulletin of the Atomic Scientists* regularly testifies, men are not humanists exclusively by profession; the university community can practice Criticism without regard to the branches of learning. (In this respect the scientists— particularly the physicists and mathematicians—come off well in proportion to their numbers.) Professors have led public debate on the issues of technology and public welfare, and they are conspicuous in the groups currently debating the morality of American domestic and foreign policy. But the numbers engaged on either side of such issues are small, and the generally beleaguered tone of critical faculty groups indicates how far even these men feel from their normal calling. Some of their diffidence and their vulnerability comes from trying to fill the moral vacuum left in the curriculum by others. Mathematicians do not feel comfortable doing the

[9] See, *e.g.*, Howard Mumford Jones, *One Great Society: Humane Learning in the United States* (New York: 1959); and the *Report of the Commission on the Humanities*, American Council of Learned Societies (New York, 1964). An exception is Henry Allen Moe, briefly chairman of the National Endowment, who said to the ACLS at its 1966 annual meeting that "the curse of humanistic scholarship in my time has been pedantry." *Cf.*, in agreement, Eric Larrabee, "Saving the Humanities," *Commentary*, 42 (Dec., 1966), 53–60; and William Arrowsmith, "The Future of Teaching," in *Improving College Teaching*, C. B. T. Lee, ed. (Washington, 1967), pp. 57–71.

work of political scientists, and physicists are unhappy substituting for historians. But mostly the uneasiness is recognition of their estrangement from the majority of the faculty itself. The majority simply do not feel it their proper business to become "involved."

The trouble is not merely an excess of scholarly detachment; our universities are overrun with men who have no roots in the university tradition of critical thought at all. They are most of them, ironically, our own alumni, graduated as technicians from our own technical curricula (and I do not except history, philosophy, and literature). They have about the same attitude toward the university as do those other, nonacademic, alumni from Yale to Berkeley who see nothing wrong with academic freedom until someone exercises it. For generations, too, our administrators have been "selling" the university to alumni and general public alike. They have sold it simply as an economic advantage to the graduate and the community and have been content to appeal to alumni loyalty on the most puerile level. This easy salesmanship becomes a terrible liability when the issue is the preservation of the university as a source of Criticism.

The future of *university* education, as opposed to the standard product of the knowledge factory, depends less on specific curricular innovations than on a reform of the stance of men. In their present attitudes, today's faculty, administrators, and alumni do not promise more than feeble resistance to the tides of power and interest rising on all sides. There is more hope in some of our students, who have lately become the truest spokesmen we have for the university idea. The student movement has its unattractive elements; it has its share of intolerance, tastelessness, and sheer hostility. Yet beneath the special political motives, beneath the posturing and slogan making of some student leaders, there is a strong current of genuine thought and feeling for the welfare of the university. Students across the nation have already shown by their general unrest that something is terribly wrong with university education today. Thus far they have not been conspicuous in presenting constructive changes. But their specific complaints are instructive enough: their demands for relevance, involvement, moral guidance, and social responsibility point to just those defects in the curriculum and in the personal conduct of university men which have been mentioned above. To these they add defects of personal warmth and of human sympathy. Of course they are asking the university to make up some of the defects of the society as a whole, and there is no reason why they should not. If the traditional sources of sympathy and of moral exercise—the family, the church, the community—seem to be failing in influence, the university as yet does not. With its growth, its prestige, its still lofty affirmations of purpose, it remains a likely resort for student idealism.

Where this fierce idealism comes from is something of a mystery, but we should be thankful for it. There is little of it in the educational system itself. Yet, one hopes that what little there is has had its effect. It is as if for years we had taught Freedom, Democracy, the need for Criticism—for years had been assigning Plato, Voltaire, Jefferson, Thoreau, Emerson, Mill—and suddenly there appeared a generation of students with the temerity to take it all literally! Either that, or through some collective instinct for survival the young have received from their environment the message that their future as free men is bound up with that of the idea of the university itself.

What I have been calling the idea of the university has not always in the past been *in* the university. For much of its history, in fact, the university has no more been a stronghold of Criticism than it has been at the forefront of new learning. It would be fatuous of us to imagine that without the university as we know it, freedom of opinion in our society would perish. The few "free universities" that have recently sprung up outside the walls are limited by their biases and by their lack of resources, but they will do to illustrate that the established institution is never the last resort. Yet the established institution, the university, *is* now at the forefront of learning, and it would be a great pity if it were not also to become the great critical agency in our society. For freedom of opinion is valuable in proportion as the opinion is informed. Somewhere beneath the newly appreciated idea of knowledge-as-power, the American faith in education still draws strength from the notion of knowledge-as-virtue, that somehow if a man knows more he has a better chance to be wise. Either the university of the future will take hold of the connections between knowledge and human values, or it will sink quietly and indistinguishably into the noncommittal moral stupor of the rest of the knowledge industry.

3

THE FUTURE OF LEARNING IN TROPICAL AFRICA*

ERIC ASHBY
University of Cambridge, England

"SALT FROM THE NORTH, gold from the south, and silver from the white man's country; but the word of God and the treasures of wisdom are to be found in Timbuctoo." So runs a Sudanese proverb. Four centuries ago the mosque of Sankoré, near the banks of the Niger, was the center of learning in tropical Africa. It attracted scholars from as far afield as Fez and Cairo. The mosque of Sankoré still stands in Timbuctoo, a squat structure of stones and red-baked earth under a blazing sky; but today it is only an echo of Africa's past. Africans now seek "the treasures of wisdom" in Europe and America, or in African universities that are facsimiles of European or American models. The University of Nsukka displays a striking family likeness to a Midwest land-grant college; Lovanium University in the Congo is a scion of Louvain; Makerere in Uganda is an unmistakably British export. Even the ancient strongholds of Muslim higher education in Fez and Cairo are now westernized. The intellectual life of Africa has been diverted into new channels by three forces: Christianity, trade, and technology. The Brothers of Ploermel in Senegal, the Church

* See p. 66 for Bibliographical Summary to chapter.

[55]

Missionary Society in Nigeria, the Basel missionaries in the Gold Coast, brought the Cross to replace the idol; but they brought also writing to replace oral tradition, and hygiene to replace magic. The traders replaced barter by a money economy. And technology has sucked Africa into the contemporary world; today it is the most compelling force of all: the printing press, the automobile, the aeroplane, the transistor radio, and the television set have lifted Africa suddenly into the Broadway of the Western world. Today the tropical African countries stand fascinated by the sudden dazzle and din of technology, at times doubtful and suspicious of it, but certain they cannot now turn back. That Africa will continue to acquire the material equipment of the Western world there is no doubt. The whole range of the white man's civilization, from his high achievements in literature and science to his shameful indulgences in frivolity, reappear in African societies, just as a dominant factor reappears in the breeding of animals and plants. There is something very touching about the African graduate whose eyes light up as he confesses that his research problem is the poetry of Dryden and Pope; or about the delegation of students in Uganda who urged me to persuade Makerere College to introduce the teaching of Latin; or about the tense shining faces of Yoruba children watching an American cowboy film. But this acceptance of the Western intellectual style, this patina of European culture, this social mimicry of a different race—are they firm foundations for an indigenous African civilization in the future (as similar manifestations in American intellectual life a hundred years ago were for an indigenous American civilization)? Or are they too superficial to support anything but a false and alien way of life? In the words of the Haitian poet Leon Laleau (translated by Samuel W. Allen), for the African, Western culture can mean:

> This beleaguered heart
> Alien to my language and my dress

On which bite like a brace
The borrowed sentiments and customs of Europe.

Yet he covets the culture and embraces it eagerly.

It is not sufficient for Western countries to leave Africans to reflect on these problems. Many Western countries are giving massive intellectual aid to Africa—teachers, scholarships, money for buildings and books. They are pumping American or British or French civilization into the forests and savannahs between Cancer and Capricorn. To what end? With what ultimate design? Only the French, I think, have tried to answer these questions. Their answer is to create an élite of black Frenchmen and, among the rest, a sufficient respect for French language and institutions to ensure a stable community in the French style, a policy of cultural imperialism which started at the turn of the century and was consolidated by Albert Sarraut in the 1920s. It has been surprisingly successful. What better testimonial could an imperial power want than this assertion (about the founding of a university in Dakar) made by a Guinean representative at the French Assembly in 1950:

> We want to have higher education at home, but we want it to be exactly equal to that of the Métropole. We want a Metropolitan curriculum . . . and the same diplomas as in France, for we are as French as are the French of the Métropole.

The superficial consequences of this policy are evident; anyone who has crossed the border between western Nigeria and Dahomey notices an astonishing contrast between the imperfect English of the anglophone Yoruba and the elegant French of the francophone Yoruba. But its deeper consequences are less easy to interpret. The most nostalgic movement back to African indigenous culture is *négritude*, expressed in the French language but protesting against the dominance of French culture. And it was a group of French-

speaking intellectuals in Leopoldville who published, in
Conscience africaine, the cry: "We wish to be civilized
Congolese, not black-skinned Europeans."

History is on the side of *Conscience africaine*. Even similar
races, despite a millennium of traffic between them, develop
characteristic and indigenous cultures. The Latin people
have been in England since A.D. 43 and are still constantly
intermixing with the British. Barely more than a century ago
Latin was the common language among scholars from Scotland to Sicily (as late as 1830, examinations for medical
degrees in Edinburgh were still being held entirely in Latin).
Yet the British and Italians have an utterly different style of
life. The North American people are not just Europeans
living under central heating; in less than two centuries there
has developed something one can call American culture. It
would be surprising, therefore, if the countries of tropical
Africa remain indefinitely no more than intellectual colonies
of one or other of the aid-giving Western nations. But the
future of learning in tropical Africa does depend on attitudes
and policies in Washington, Paris, and London, as well as on
policies in Nairobi, Lagos, and Dakar.

Tropical Africa provides a paradigm of a problem common
to all developing countries and to all countries dispensing
intellectual aid. The problem can be compressed into a
sentence: The countries dispersing aid have shown more
generosity than wisdom, and the countries receiving aid have
been more concerned with short-term opportunism than long-
term consolidation. Hundreds of gifted and dedicated teachers
from many nations have brought higher education to the
developing countries. They have brought it as the early missionaries brought Christianity to these same countries: in the
firm conviction that this—unchanged—was the unique key to
prosperity, just as the gospel was the unique key to salvation.
And leaders in developing countries have welcomed universities with even more enthusiasm and less criticism than their

grandparents displayed toward churches. Indeed, if a handful of enlightened West Africans had had their way there would have been a university on the west coast in the 1860s.

The three forces, Christianity, trade, and technology, all conspired to persuade Africans that their own past was contemptible and useless as a foundation for the future. Therefore their first reaction to the importation of Western learning was a euphoric welcome to it. The early results of accepting it were highly encouraging. From Dakar in Senegal to Dar-es-Salaam in Tanzania, Africans found that they could master Western learning as successfully as Europeans could. The examinations they took allowed no softening of standards and no concession to the deficiencies of their schooling. The degrees awarded to them were from the University of London or were moderated by the universities of Louvain, Bordeaux, or Paris. At the same time, under schemes such as the African Scholarship Program of American Universities (ASPAU), Africans were brought to some of the best American universities, and their academic performance was substantially above the American average! By 1960, when one African country after another was securing independence, Africans had demonstrated to the world their capacity to absorb and digest the intellectual diet offered to the best students in Cambridge, Cornell, or the Sorbonne.

"To absorb and digest" . . . but there is more to the intellectual life than this. Learning has no future in a developing country if it remains just learning; it has to become self-reproducing, inventing its own techniques, propagating its own values, becoming not just a recipient, but a donor, of world knowledge. In a word, there must be indigenous scholarship and research in Africa; and if these are to become anything more than mere outposts of European and American learning, Africans must not only preserve their loyalty to a Western tradition, they must also rediscover and proclaim a loyalty to some indigenous values in African society.

Let us now examine this proposition more closely. The universities in Nigeria, Ghana, Senegal, East Africa, and the Sudan are already lively centers of scholarship. Every one of them produces every year a respectable list of books and articles in learned journals. Some of the research is done by Africans and is on African themes. In certain fields, notably the use, in historical research, of oral tradition and archaeology to supplement the written word, Africans are certainly becoming donors to world knowledge. But something is lacking, not only from scholarship in tropical Africa but from scholarship in countries with a much longer tradition of inherited learning, such as India. What is lacking is the fertile soil of public appreciation, the stimulus of audience participation in the intellectual life of the country. In modern technological jargon, the intellectual life of developing countries lacks feedback.

It is very difficult to pursue learning without feedback. Consider the difficulties that confront a university professor in tropical Africa as he does research in, say, chemistry or history. His audience is the scholarly world of chemists or historians. The nearest colleague in his specialism may be thousands of miles away. His articles will go unread by his countrymen. The very journals in which they are published are edited across the ocean. If he is an expatriate, all his roots are overseas; he may be dedicated to African education, but he draws his sustenance from Oxford or Columbia. If he is an African—and this is the point made so vividly for Indians by Edward Shils in his book *The Intellectual Between Tradition and Modernity*—his family roots are at home but he still has to draw his sustenance from overseas. As an African his loyalty is to his people and his country; as a scholar his loyalty is to the international community of historians or chemists. This dual loyalty is, of course, shared by all scholars; the peculiar difficulty for the scholar in a developing country is that the two loyalties scarcely overlap; for one of them, on which the future of learning depends in his country, the scholar is obliged to look beyond his own people. His only hope of survival as a scholar is to have his intellectual roots in an alien land.

This difficulty is not peculiar to non-European races. Even Australia, even North America in earlier days, were Europe-centered. It would not be an exaggeration to say that although Australia was freed from Britain politically sixty-seven years ago, it was still dependent on Britain intellectually up to World War II. Indeed, as late as 1960, when the University of Sydney celebrated its centenary, about half the nonmedical professors in the university had taken their first degrees outside Australia. It is only in the last twenty years that Australia has become a distinguished self-sustaining intellectual community.

This, then, is the first difficulty. The future of learning in a developing country depends not only on a small élite of active scholars; they must work in a soil that nourishes them. There must, for example, be an intellectual press, such as *Harper's* and *The New Republic* provide in the United States. There must be listeners as well as speakers at seminars and conferences. There must be reasoned constructive criticism of ideas from within the country. No one familiar with developing countries doubts for a moment that these countries can produce men of the highest intellectual caliber, capable of the most distinguished scholarship. What is missing in the developing countries is the matrix within which these scholars can work fruitfully.

The universities of tropical Africa are the centers from which this matrix can spread to schools, government departments, the press, and publishing houses. It is an essential task of the university in Africa to create the urbane society from which learning can draw its sustenance. Therefore extension work, which plays a greater part in the American state university than it does in British or French universities, becomes in developing countries an activity absolutely vital for the future of learning. This has not been sufficiently recognized in some of the universities of tropical Africa, with the result that the intellectuals have become dangerously isolated from the people. The taunt of "ivory tower," so commonly leveled at some African universities, is a symptom of this; no one would call a Midwest land-grant college an ivory tower, whatever other weaknesses it might have. Therefore—to come back to the questions asked at the beginning of this essay—let us face the fact that intellectual aid to foster scholarship and research in developing countries is likely to fall on stony ground unless it is accompanied by a massive program of extension work deliberately organized to create an intellectual community; the nation giving aid must prepare the soil as well as transplant the seedling.

But extension work, even if it is rapidly successful, will not by itself assure the future of learning in any developing country. Scholars must have communication with minds as good as or better than their own, as well as with an appreciative audience in their own country. And these superior minds are inevitably abroad. How can aid-giving countries bring the African (or Asian) scholar in contact with his peers? Already there are generous arrangements for faculty members from universities in developing countries to spend study leave in the mainstreams of academic life; there are arrangements, too, for European and American scholars to go on secondment to African and to Asian universities. But this infrequent, spasmodic experience is not enough. Sustained scholarship requires sustained sustenance. Some better solution than the sabbatical year, or the eight-week summer visit to Britain, is needed; and it is the aid-giving countries that ought to find the solution. Already there is one promising experiment, the International Centre for Theoretical Physics in Trieste. A small band of scientists of international repute is always to be found at the institute, and alongside them, financed by grants from international agencies, are workers from developing countries who spend from one to four months a year at the institute. Here is an idea worth very serious thought. If we in the aid-giving countries are to make the most effective contribution to the future of learning in developing countries, could we not encourage, and finance, arrangements that would bring scores of *active* scholars (not scholars who have fallen into administration or scholars who have become perpetually airborne on government missions) for three months a year to international centers (some in existing universities, some on their own as in Trieste), where they will spend full time on research? Each scholar would come to regard his center as his intellectual home. His bench, his table in the library, would be there, awaiting his return year after year; but (an essential part of the contract) he would return to his own country, year after year, to teach and to build up an indigenous school of research and scholarship. Of course universities that allow some of their faculty members to spend three months a year elsewhere will need a richer staff-student ratio than otherwise would be necessary; but this, too, would in the long run be a good investment in overseas aid.

The future of learning in developing countries is at present very hazardous. Aid-giving countries, by redeploying their resources, might greatly reduce the hazard; and the two most promising avenues for redeployment are, one: a massive campaign designed to create, through special kinds of university extension work, self-sustaining intellectual communities; and two, arrangements that would enable the most productive scholars in developing countries to immerse themselves in the mainstream of scholarship for three months of every year.

But what about the assumption that underlies these proposals for the future of learning in developing countries? It is the assumption that the studies appropriate for universities in Manchester, Bordeaux, and St. Louis are *ipso facto* appropriate in Bombay, Tananarive, and Nsukka. In some areas of study the assumption is plainly correct. Science and technology are supranational; the laws of nature and the properties of matter are everywhere the same. Not only the methods of research but its actual content are common to all mankind. But the range of humanistic studies appropriate for an African, an Indian, a Brazilian, and a Japanese are patently not common to all mankind, even though there are common elements in the techniques of scholarship in these humanistic studies. And when one digs below the level of the purely intellectual life, and reaches strata of values, one has to ask whether it is possible for a developing country to enter the stream of Western civilization without adopting the social philosophies of the West. Is technology (for instance) inseparable from a competitive society? If an African accepts an American education and pursues scholarship in the American style, does he inevitably have to adopt the criteria for success common in America, or even to submit himself to an un-African obedience to the clock?

This essay leaves these questions unanswered. Any attempt to answer them would be disingenuous. But the long-term future of learning in developing countries depends on the answers. It is unlikely that any Westerner would now be so arrogantly parochial as to suggest that Buddha and Mahomet can be neglected because of Christ, or the *Mahabharata* rejected in favor of *Paradise Lost*. Even tropical Africa, although it has no written literature, is acknowledged as a rich source of original music and sculpture and folklore, and anthropologists have accumulated a fascinating literature on the religious and cosmological ideas and the social and ethical values that for a thousand years have given coherence and meaning to the lives of Africans. In a remarkable and important book, *The Primal Vision*, John V. Taylor, who was a missionary in Africa, has paid tribute to the indigenous value systems of the pagan African—the placid disregard for the passing of time, the sense of obligation to the extended family, the "tranquillity of human relationships." And he quotes from an account by J. B. Danquah of the qualities expected in an elected chief among the Akan:

He had married and been given in marriage with honour; he had bought or sold in open or private market with honour; he had been a member of the company of fighting men with honour; he had sowed and reaped with honour; suffered famine or enjoyed plenty with honour; brought up children with honour; worshipped at the shrines with honour; had suffered bereavement with honour; and, above all, had joined with others, or acted by himself, to settle family and other disputes, bringing peace and increase to the family with honour.

It will be a sad day for the future of the humanities in tropical Africa if traditions and values such as this passage describes are buried beneath the trivia of imitative studies of Western literature and philosophy. It is sometimes said that we shall have to leave the Africans themselves to decide what to accept and what to reject from Western tradition, and to blend what they accept with their own traditional cultures. I cannot agree with this view. Those who designed models of Western education for export must be willing to continue to cooperate with Africans in the adaptation of these designs to incorporate African indigenous values. (The same is true, of course, with even greater emphasis, for countries, such as India, which had a splendid literature centuries before Virgil, and a sophisticated philosophy centuries before Plato.) Indeed, the most valuable contribution that scholars from aid-giving countries can make to the future of learning in Africa is to apply the rigorous techniques of Western scholarship to African problems so that there is no doubt about the respectability of these problems for research. And the most valuable contribution that the African professor can make to the future of learning in Africa is—apart from his own research—to ensure that *all* African undergraduates are introduced to the scholarly approach to these problems, so that there grows up in these very fragmented societies, from Niger to the Zambesi, a common core of culture not entirely derived from outside Africa.

Bibliographical Summary

THE main sources of information on African higher education are E. Ashby, assisted by M. Anderson, *Universities, British, Indian, African: A Study in the Ecology of Higher Education* (Cambridge, Mass.: Harvard University Press, 1966), and E. Ashby, *African Universities and Western Tradition* (Cambridge, Mass.: Harvard University Press, 1964).

The difficulties of life as a scholar in a country with no self-sustaining intellectual community are brilliantly analysed by E. Shils, *The Intellectual Between Tradition and Modernity: The Indian Situation*, Comparative Studies in Society and History (The Hague: Mouton, 1961).

The proposal for bringing scholars from developing countries every year into the mainstream of world scholarship springs from the experience of the International Centre for Theoretical Physics in Trieste, described in *Minerva*, 3, 1965, 533–36, by M. J. Moravcsik, "Some Practical Suggestions for the Improvement of Science in Developing Countries," *Minerva*, 4, 1966, 381–90; and by Abdus Salam, "The Isolation of the Scientist in Developing Countries," *Minerva*, 4, 1966, 461–65.

The complexity and sometimes sophistication of African ideas and values and institutions are well described in three collections of articles: *African Worlds*, Daryll Forde, ed. (London: Oxford University Press, 1954); *African Political Systems*, M. Fortes and E. E. Evans-Pritchard, eds. (London: Oxford University Press, 1940); and *Continuity and Change in African Cultures*, W. R. Bascom and M. J. Herskovits, eds. (Chicago: University of Chicago Press, 1959).

A sensitive and beautifully written book, *The Primal*

Vision, by J. V. Taylor (London: Student Christian Movement Press, 1963) is a vivid assertion of the depth of thought and feeling in African society as seen by a Christian missionary. Another equally illuminating book is Adam Curle's *Educational Strategy for Developing Countries* (London: Tavistock Publications, 1963).

4

THE FUTURE OF INTERNATIONAL POLITICS

HARLAN CLEVELAND

A N INQUIRY INTO the future of international relations must start with a guess about what kinds of international political communities will be most in evidence, what issues will be featured in their politics, and who the actors will be.

The community-building stimuli are predictable; what cannot be foreseen is the reaction of men and nations to them. But recent history suggests that when science and technology make possible a new or extended form of cooperation, national frontiers are readily set aside and national governments are pushed by their own interested constituencies to make the necessary international agreements. The United States, which went to one international conference a year in the nineteenth century, attended nearly seven hundred of them in 1966.

As examples, here are some of the developments that will call into being new international structures or force the adaptation of existing ones:

• Man will reach the moon and won't stop there. The farther he gets from Earth, the more irrelevant will seem the national frontiers, the more necessary and natural an international approach to the exploration of outer space. If evidence is found of another intelligence with which man can communicate, the drawing together of Earth's inhabitants will be all the more rapid.

• Meanwhile, the use of outer space will bring about another revolution in communications and transportation around our little globe. The nearness of nations to one another will force them to think seriously about forms of cooperation which have never before been more than academic.

• Earth satellites, cloud photography, and fast computers will enable man for the first time to watch the whole of the world's weather at once. His forecasts will improve in quality and stretch out farther into time. And he will start *changing* some kinds of weather, in some places, at human command.

• Nations with great arsenals of nuclear and other "sophisticated" weapons systems will contemplate the futility of possessing more than enough destructive power to wipe out whole societies—and turn seriously to designing international controls over the level and deployment of such armaments.

• Ways will have to be found to erode, and in time erase, the division of Berlin, Germany, and Europe. The arrangements will have to be somehow guaranteed internationally by the powers that enter into them.

• Ways will have to be found to regulate the small-power arms races and inhibit the spread of weapons of mass destruction to nations that cannot afford them. Yet small wars will persist, and ways will have to be found, also, to provide armed peacekeepers to prevent conflicts and police cease-fires and agreements. As one near-term example, the war in southeast Asia will have to lead to some form of settlement— and some kind of peacekeeping machinery—by which the conquest of some nations by others can be prevented without the enormous input this now requires from the outside.

• The nation-based ideologies with which we are now familiar will wear out as more and more national leaders adapt social theory and political polemic to the insistent demands of increasingly complex technological societies with increasingly international ramifications.

• The gap between the rich countries and the poor countries will widen. All economies will grow, and many poor economies will prosper in time, but the most developed countries will control a disproportionate share of the total growth. This state of affairs will sooner or later become politically intolerable; pressure from the poor and a sense of missionary obligation among the rich will require a massive transfer of resources. How these resources are transferred, and what mutual obligations their transfer creates, will be a prime object of the politics of the future—though the basic approach of "self-help and mutual aid" will prevail.

• World population will grow, perhaps to six billion by the turn of our century. Most of the growth will be urban and will occur in the developing societies, especially in Asia and Latin America. The growth may not be so explosive as the demographers are now predicting, because the combination of knowledge, chemicals, and women's instincts may be explosive in their own way. But the biggest increases may well come in this next generation, and the international community will somehow have to cope with the resulting economic (food, employment) and social (urban living) problems.

• The penetration of "outsiders" into the internal affairs of nations will grow, not decline. In the "new," "developing" "nations" of Africa and Asia, the atavistic nationalism so characteristic of the post-colonial 1960s is bound to be as shortlived as it is nonfunctional. Outsiders are needed to provide technical aid and military muscle, and sometimes even to furnish convenient political scapegoats for necessary but unpopular decisions by weak governments; but their selection, the regulation of their behavior, especially the control of the political use of their power, will increasingly be regarded as an international problem.

• The social problems of urban growth and congestion,

seriously tackled by no nation so far, will be increasingly regarded as international in scope. The pollution of air and the shortage of clean water; delinquency and the slum fringe; how to reconcile the need for growing productivity with cradle-to-grave security; the creation of city jobs for marginal farm workers; the unwillingness of people to stay at the "village level"—these problems are universal in the urbanizing societies, and all societies are urbanizing.

• Man's capacity to manage large human events will be put to the test as more and more activities can be managed only on a worldwide, or at least intercontinental, scale. In the generation just past, the big discovery was long-range planning by public institutions. We can guess from American experience that in the next generation, the new discovery about large-scale international management will be not "planning" but creative and pluralistic improvisation on a general sense of direction. But that requires an unprecedented sense of freedom in "leaders" that begin to be counted in the millions.

• For this and other reasons, the next stage in the history of freedom is likely to feature, not the rights of ethnic and racial groups, but the rights of individual men, women, and children. The revolutions of national independence and racial equality have led to new opportunities and also to new evidence that man's inhumanity to man does not disappear with colonial rule and enforced discrimination. How the international community organizes to protect individuals against the nations and groups to which they "belong" may prove to be the most explosive of all forms of international politics.

These are but a dozen of a hundred possible examples of trends that will stimulate international organization. In every field of science and technology (including "social" sciences and technologies), breakthroughs are common; more and more intensive forms of international cooperation are therefore commonplace. Biologists have yet to learn what life is, what really goes on inside a cell; psychologists have only begun to observe the mind systematically, let alone explain or predict its behavior. In almost every field of scholarship, the men and women closest to its frontiers are those most impressed with the paucity and the limited relevance of our knowledge so far.

So the only safe assumption for an institution builder is that new scientific discoveries, new theoretical perceptions, and new technologies will continue, at an accelerating rate, to require us to build new international institutions so that the new technologies can work for, and not against, the future of man.

II

A technological imperative thus makes greater international cooperation likely in every department of man's destiny. Some pundits and politicians see the growing need for international actions causing the nation-state to wither away; the requirement for man's survival, they think, will turn out to be some form of world government. But while the writers of ideal constitutions have been writing, the nation-state has been showing—again—an astonishing resilience and adaptability.

In our own time the nation-state has survived the internationalism of world religions, of corporate business, and of Communist ideology. Indeed, the striking thing about all three of these forms of internationalism is that they have had to clothe themselves in national trappings—and bend their doctrines to match—in order to win acceptance.

The "Christian" parties in Europe are reinforcements, not challenges, to the nation-state. The political urge of Islamism, Hinduism, and even Buddhism is increasingly fulfilled by direct participation in national struggles for secular power. Most Christian missionaries, especially in their three hundred Protestant incarnations, have shown a willingness to promote and assist parochial nationalisms which is astonishing in salesmen of supposedly universal values. Priestly endorsement of short-term secular national aims has traditionally come cheap, even from the Universal Church; Cardinal Spellman's pep talk to the Americans fighting in Vietnam, which occasioned some controversy at the time, was merely one incident in a long and distinguished Christian tradition.

Capitalism and communism, while likewise professing a doctrinal universality, also have found that their successes come mainly from operating not against but for, not outside but inside, the framework of national economies and national governments. Communist parties have succeeded in establishing themselves in those few places where, as in Stalin's Russia, they concentrated mostly on building socialism in one country; and have failed where as in western Europe and America and Africa and most of Asia, the national Communist parties could not help looking like agents, or at least stooges, of a foreign *national* power. Big corporations operating across international frontiers have found that the best formula for business success is to stop looking "foreign" and start looking like an indigenous piece of the national landscape.

The success of the nation-state in absorbing its internationalist invaders has led in our time to grotesque caricatures of national sovereignty. Just when the Atlantic peoples were seeking answers to their market and security problems in wider and closer associations of nations, the new young leaders of subject peoples, educated mostly in Western schools, were insisting on national independence and on calling their development efforts "nation building." Once again the political energy generated by the universally valid Greek idea that citizens of a polity should make their own laws rather than receiving them from priestly or royal authority—and the universally valid claims for racial equality and better living standards—were applied within, rather than against, the nation-state.

III

Experience does not therefore enable us to write off the nation-state as a dying object of relevant loyalties or a withering form of political organization. Indeed it suggests that for the rest of this century we will be reckoning with the nation-state as a basic building block in every form of international community.

Yet there *are* these new internationalizing trends, the consequence of scientific invention and technological innovation, to which the nation-state itself is having to adjust. To maintain itself as a primary object of its citizens' loyalty, the government of a modern nation must give them the feeling that it has a "say" on their behalf in decisions that affect their destiny. And if these destiny decisions—the ones that make the difference between ignorance and education, inequality and equality, poverty and prosperity, war and peace—are increasingly taken in and enforced by international organizations, every "national" government will be spending more and more of its time and money trying to qualify as an influential participant in the politics of those organizations.

It is clear enough that even the most influential nation-state can exercise its national influence most effectively from inside—not from outside—international organizations.

What is not clear is how, and how soon, and to what degree, the practical needs for international organization will lead the nations away from overfascination with their conflicts and toward a new preoccupation with their expanding areas of common interest. The degree of world order and international progress which we shall know between now and the end of this century will depend heavily upon the answer to that question. When it comes to the forecasting of weather, the progress is already swift; when it comes to the forestalling of war, the evidence is less persuasive.

As things stand now, the world is fragmented into scores of mostly small and mostly weak nation-states, each trying to pursue its own national interests as it sees them—these plus a handful of "major powers." As things stand now, only these last could qualify as truly influential participants in the international organizations; for to so qualify, a participant must be *big enough* and *rich enough* to contribute significant resources, *willing enough* to see its destiny entangled with that of other peoples, and *skillful enough* to practice effectively, on behalf of its constituents, the new politics of international organization.

Of the world's existing nation-states, only one already comes even close to meeting all these rigorous tests of relevance. The United States of America is big enough and rich enough to bring its resources to bear anywhere in the world —alone or in cooperation with others; most Americans are willing to assume that our destiny is necessarily linked with that of other continents and other peoples; as a consequence, Americans are already major contributors to, and among the most skillful leaders in, half a hundred international organizations. The efforts of other nations, and troupes of nations, to participate with the United States in the making of destiny decisions will be the story of international relations during the rest of this century.

Of the world's other sovereignties, only two are certainly big enough to qualify under present circumstances. Communist China may make up in size and potential what it still lacks in gross national product, but its leaders are still so parochial in their outlook and so clumsy in their international operations that mainland China does not yet meet the other two tests of effectiveness in world politics. The Soviet Union is surely big enough, by any measure, and its leaders certainly see their destiny in international terms; but despite the alleged internationalism of Marxist theory, in practice the Soviet leaders yield to none in their addiction to nationalist dogma and their devotion to "sovereignty"—and so they are, by and large, ineffectual in the politics of international organizations. The Soviets still think that if a nation is big enough and strong enough, it can go its own way. On the basis of their own postwar experience, Americans are justified in coming to the opposite conclusion: the bigger you are, the more you are drawn into everybody else's affairs.

A few other countries might be considered as coming close to qualifying as direct participants in destiny decisions in a world lineup in which the average size of nations is small —and getting still smaller. The United Kingdom has the will and the skill but no longer the economic power required for global influence; Japan and Germany are still inhibited by their history and the lingering resentments of their neighbors from translating growing power into growing international participation. France, which is positioned by its history to lead, is constrained by the notion that the destiny of each nation can be reserved for decision by its leaders without advance international engagements. India and Brazil have the potential but not yet the internal cohesion to wield more than a regional influence.

Beyond these nation-states and a very few others, a hundred nations or more are too wanting in the ingredients of national influence to enable their peoples to feel their governments make a crucial difference in decisions about peace and prosperity. A good many of the smaller states in every continent—from Scandinavia and the Low Countries around to Thailand, the Philippines, Australia, and New Zealand— certainly try to make up in international outlook and hearty participation what they lack in economic size and military power. Insofar as the votes in UN assemblies are crucial to their destiny, the Africans as a group are vigorous participators. And if effective participation in destiny decisions were measured by the noise-level of verbal contributions to international discourse, then a good many nonaligned leaders would certainly qualify. But real decisions are still likely to be made by contributors, not by observers, however vocal.

IV

A key problem for most of the world's peoples, therefore, is how to organize to operate effectively within big organizations, in which the destiny decisions are made: that is, how to make sure they are effectively consulted on nuclear affairs, on arms control, on trade and monetary policies, on the more equitable distribution of the world's resources, on the politics of weather control, on the benefits accruing from atomic energy and space exploration, on arrangements for peace-keeping and peacemaking, and on the growing volume of international rules that guide the penetration of outsiders into matters that used to be regarded as "national" preserves, such as economic growth, social development, and the protection of the inalienable rights of man. The first need of the smaller nations is to be taken seriously on big questions.

In the decades ahead, two trends will operate to modify the present gross disparities between national power and national influence of the great and the small nation-states.

One is that the "major powers" will discover that their own national interests converge more and more with the national interests of others on the great issues and great tasks of our times—that national interests can be pursued most effectively through international organizations, and national purposes can be pursued most effectively through international cooperation. Learning that, they may even come to appreciate more the values that nations and peoples without "power" can contribute to the world's well-being, and to be more grateful for the pluralism of human society and culture. They will see, too, what Americans are beginning, perforce, to understand: that if one or more of the great powers gains too much influence by the contribution of too great a proportion of the resources of the international community—even in the form of development aid—the basis for cooperation is eroded and the character of international organization is blurred.

So the great powers, in their own interests, will increasingly have to identify those interests with the interests of others and seek to draw them into more robust forms of partnership.

The other trend that will tend to narrow the "influence gap" in the international community is that the smaller, and particularly the smallest, nation-states will somehow have to combine into larger units with firmer voices. In the foreseeable future we may still see existing nation-states split into ministates by the divisive passions of tribalism. But the net trend will be the other way—for such reasons as resources development, industrialization and trade, and also—perhaps even more so—to add to their "influence" in the world community.

This is why the trend toward regional unity, already much in evidence, will certainly continue strong. In the three decades I am presuming to call the foreseeable future, Western Europe will probably be forced, by its own urge, to participate in wider matters of vital interest to Western Europeans, to continue the amalgamating trend that already finds expression in advanced forms of economic cooperation and a common market, and to widen the constituency to include the British and Scandinavians to the north and west, and perhaps other peoples to the south and east. (Because participation in wider world decisions requires a certain degree of likemindedness, there is a necessary limit to "Europe's" eastern expansion without profound political change.)

Economics is also the first-stage booster for Latin American unity. But in welding the Latin Americans together, the major influence is likely to be the political need to deal on a more nearly equal basis with the North Americans. In Africa and the splintered Arab world, some sense of racial likeness may speed the development of two or three sub-continental units; even today, the fragmented sovereignties of Africa are internationally effective on economic develop-ment, trade policy, and security matters only when they suc-ceed in acting together. In Asia and the Pacific, the regional cooperation is likely to be slow in developing, but India and Japan are two cores of potential strength, and the truculence of the Chinese Communists is already hastening the trend toward regionalism.

During this "foreseeable" period, then, the nation-state will not be withering away. But two other things will be happen-ing. First, small nations, by combining into larger ones, will be redefining what it has to mean to be a nation-state in the third third of the twentieth century. And second, the smaller number of larger "nations" will be internationalizing a growing proportion of all the decisions they make, includ-ing nearly all the really important ones.

V

What issues will predominate in the new politics? Judging by the considerable experience of twenty postwar years, the nation-states or nation-groups will argue and negotiate, agree and disagree, about issues of *function* and of *control*.

As the technological imperative brings more and more subjects into "international relations," the ever widening definition of what is appropriate for international agencies to do will create a great deal of trouble. Most national govern-ments today would resist my conclusion, earlier in this article, that there is anything inherently international about the pro-tection of citizens from aggression by their own government or racial group. But setting standards for other people's be-havior in matters of human rights is an international prospect of growing urgency, and what starts as an effort to influence other people's behavior is more than likely to end by agreement to standards that constrain one's own behavior as well.

Nobody can predict how controversial any particular extension of jurisdiction will be in each of the fifty-three organizations we already belong to, or in the many more that presumably will be established in the remaining years of this century. What does seem to be predictable is that the area of international jurisdiction will grow at something like the speed of scientific and technological change—because the one is a function of the other.

What limits the rate at which public tasks and public policy issues are internationalized? Essentially the "governor" on international systems seems to be the enormous difficulty of deciding who should decide to govern them.

It is these "constitutional issues" that produce the great debates and defections that characterize the life of any lively international organization. The recurring issue over the use of the Security Council veto has regularly enlivened the proceedings of the UN. In recent years the classic battle over the power of the General Assembly to assess its members for peacekeeping operations moved to the UN's center stage; but the issue was the same: could a major power be forced by the votes of other nations to approve a UN operation it regards as contrary to its own interests—or to do itself something it decides it does not want to do?

In the North Atlantic Treaty Organization, still by a wide margin the world's largest peacekeeping force, the recent defection of France from NATO's integrated military organization was touched off by a similar fear that France might be made to do something it might not want to do. There is less automaticity in NATO's response to aggression than is generally believed: each member still has to make its own decision precisely what to do in any given emergency. But peacetime cooperation in establishing an integrated command does create a strong presumption that the allies will act and react together if attacked; it was from this presumption that the French government withdrew in 1966.

The control of international military forces creates hard enough political dilemmas. But some of the civil forms of internationalism are going to present even more excruciating choices between the nostalgia for unfettered independence and the need for international executive operations that impinge deeply on the vital interests of nation-states.

It is easy enough to agree that radio frequencies should be allocated by an international authority—otherwise the confusion on the air waves would be intolerable for all. But when men of one nationality have it in their power to change the weather that controls other men's agriculture and air defense, it will be far more difficult to decide who should decide what. And in the tortured field of disarmament, the end question is: Who keeps peace in a disarmed world? What kind of executive—with what punitive powers—under what form of legislative control—should have the power to bring major nation-states to heel?

As a final example, the poor nations seek a constantly widening international control over the transfer of resources from the rich nations. Taken together, the international funds and banks are now the world's biggest aid program. As they grow, the concerted effort by the net recipients of benefits to dominate the system will create a widening constitutional crisis with the net contributors. The international executives will have to be far-sighted enough to serve as the "liberal center," preventing either recipients or contributors from "winning" the battle for control.

By and large, two ways of making collective decisions have been worked out by mankind to make cooperation possible where no person or group can be trusted to make the ultimate decision. One is the UN way—to count national noses, sometimes weighing the count because the noses are of varying shapes and sizes. Large countries often get permanent seats, or special voting rights, on governing bodies —precisely to prevent the sovereign equality of nations from producing actions that are ridiculously out of touch with the realities of power. (Where the "action" is merely an expression of opinion, as often in the UN General Assembly, the big nations have learned to swallow and smile when they do not agree.)

The other method is that of consensus, as practiced for example in NATO. The North Atlantic Council never votes. If everybody agrees, the Council acts; if everybody does not agree, the Council often creates some formula whereby those who want to act can act together without unanimous consent. Thus when France withdrew her military cooperation but stayed in the Alliance (and thus in the fifteen-nation North Atlantic Council) the other members set up a four-teen-nation council called the Defense Planning Committee to make all decisions affecting the integrated defense of the NATO area and went right ahead with plans to modernize NATO strategy.

Neither the UN nor the NATO solution to the dilemmas of international governance is "best," and there are dozens of conceivable variants of each. The new politics will have to produce tailor-made solutions to each puzzle as it appears. If more and more international decisions are a technological "must," the ingenuity of man is equal to the task of contriving decision-making systems that most people think are fair, most of the time.

5

URBAN PROBLEMS AND
GROUP RELATIONS

ROBERT C. WEAVER

Secretary of Housing and Urban Development

URBAN GROWTH is an inevitable consequence of contemporary population growth. Men have nearly always lived in communities but never before to the extent that they do now, and by all accounts and projections the pace of urban growth will accelerate and continue to set precedents as far in the future as men can see.

The accelerating pace of urbanization since the beginning of this century is unmistakable, and it is a worldwide phenomenon. In these years, the world's population has grown 50 percent, its urban population has grown 240 percent, its largest cities 260 percent.[1] There is nothing to indicate that the pace will not continue. In the United States, the population, presently nearing 200 million, is projected to reach 400 million in half a century, with 320 million of our people living in urban communities.

The future of man is therefore largely an urban future. There is little reason to question the quantity of urbanizing that will take place. There is every reason to be concerned over whether men can gain the knowledge and the skills

[1] The White House Conference on International Cooperation, Report of the Committee on Urban Development, Nov. 28–Dec. 1, 1965, Exhibit II.

to shape events in such a way as to preserve and enhance the quality of urban living.

Typically today in urban problems, as in many problems, there is a widespread yearning for some single or simple solution, no matter how complex or diverse the elements may be. No matter how stubbornly intertwined the forces may be, the search goes on, by some at least, for the single strand that would, when given the proper pull, unravel even a seamless web.

But among thoughtful observers, the urban condition is increasingly recognized for its multiplicity of problems. They are the problems of people and their needs for satisfaction in shelter, employment, education, health, transportation, entertainment, culture, and many other factors. Their very delineation is a step toward a strategy of solutions. It is a step toward gaining an understanding that while each is a field for specialization in itself, the interrelationship of all is still another field worthy of specialization.

To view them as an interrelated whole, nevertheless, presupposes an understanding of each, the complexities, subtleties, paradoxes—and the heritages containing both good and ill. Among the ills, poverty and racial discrimination are but two factors in the cantankerous and individualistic histories of urban communities, but they are so important among all aspects that they are sometimes confused with the whole of urban problems.

There are, of course, other problems in the urban environment of the United States than the problems of the nonwhite in the city. There are problems of governmental organization, adequate provision of community facilities, bringing open space and beauty to the city, training professional and technical personnel, and a great many others.[2] It is well to keep in mind that even where poverty can be eliminated and

[2] For a fuller discussion see "Cities in Crisis," by the author, in *The Troubled Environment*, a symposium sponsored in 1965 by Urban America, Inc.

where racial discrimination can be overcome, serious urban problems remain.

It is also true, however, that the elimination of poverty and the overcoming of racial barriers will involve nearly every aspect of the urban condition. It will require an understanding of their interrelated characters. Their solutions would be perhaps the most important actions that could be taken to preserve and restore the human values of urban settings and to create healthy and thriving communities.

The future of the city is inextricably related to the future of the urban poor. At this moment in time, the single most striking fact about the American city is that its fate is indivisible from the fate of the American Negro. The ultimate test of the American city is whether it can achieve a balanced growth that provides full and equal opportunity and participation for the Negroes. They are the most sizable minority grouping that does not share freely in American social and economic life. But this condition applies in commensurate degree as well to such smaller minority groups as the Mexicans, Puerto Ricans, Indians, and migrant laborers.

It should be made clear that a reference to the city in this context means not only the central or inner city but the suburbs, the metropolitan regions surrounding cities, and the urbanizing fringe areas beyond. There are no solutions for any of them that do not affect the others and do not depend on the others.

Parenthetically it might be said that the ecology of urban regions, that is, the interrelated character of the central city, metropolitan region, and the newly urbanizing areas, is not well understood and that it represents one of many subjects among urban problems where knowledge is still as yet at a frontier.

II

Many efforts are under way to extend and broaden knowledge in urban affairs, particularly in the area of group relations in urban settings. These are attempts to penetrate the surfaces, and they often pose challenges to conventional wisdom. An example is a recent attempt to learn more about the actual conditions of the people who are being supported, in part at least, by welfare programs assisted by the federal government. There are, this study showed, some 7.3 million Americans now on federally assisted welfare rolls. On the basis of traditional thinking, it would have been a typical guess that some number of millions of these persons could be made employable and self-sufficient by a suitable combination of job training and education programs.

What the study actually revealed, however, is that only 50,000 males were capable of benefiting from such programs. Of the others, 2.1 million, mostly women, are more than sixty-five years old; 700,000 are blind or otherwise severely handicapped; 3.5 million are children whose parents cannot support them; the remaining 1 million are the parents of these children, including 9,000,000 mothers and 150,000 are fathers, and two-thirds of the latter are also incapacitated in one way or another.[3]

It is significant that we are only now beginning to get the kind of knowledge revealed by this preliminary study. But the important point to be made here is that this knowledge raises new questions about how the traditional thinking on making the poor self-sufficient needs to be reevaluated in terms of actual conditions revealed by new knowledge.

Similarly, it raises questions about how to motivate the people who live in slums and racial ghettos, wherever they are in the world, who feel lost and alienated from the rest of society but who are capable of full participation in the larger environment. Clearly, exhortation alone would not be effective. Certainly, the approach must be one that involves these

[3] Reported by Joseph A. Califano, Jr., special assistant to President Johnson, address to Washington chapter, Sigma Delta Chi, Apr. 19, 1967, unpublished text, p. 6.

people in a meaningful participation. This is not done simply, and it will require modification of attitudes, values, and behavior, as well as perfection of techniques in communication.

Much has been written about the subculture of the slums and racial ghettos. My own contribution began twenty years ago with the first comprehensive analysis of racial residential segregation.[4] The reformulation of the problems twenty years later does not involve any basic reversal of philosophy or any retreat from the goals expressed. It does of course involve changes in strategy, tactics, and priorities resulting not only from the dramatic events of these years in the pursuit of civil rights but also from new knowledge that has been attained by a variety of research.

Still, there is a widespread tendency to look upon the residents of a ghetto as a homogeneous group though the civil rights movement and the social sciences have clearly demonstrated the fallacy of that simplistic view. The ghetto has many elements among its residents. They range in values from what might be called the "respectable poor" who are often vehemently middle class in their values to another extreme element that repudiates middle-class concepts and middle-class behavior. And there are many variations between.

We do know that there is a subculture in the ghetto and that its values are significantly different from the dominant ones. We shall have to take this into account, examining the nature, incidence, and peculiarities of the subculture, and the various shades of difference in values and behavior patterns.

It is clear then, in my view, that here are two areas where further knowledge is vital: the characteristics of the urban poor, their physical, mental, and social capacities for full participation in society; and their attitudes, values, and

[4] Robert C. Weaver, *The Negro Ghetto* (New York: Harcourt, Brace & Co., 1948). Reissued in 1967 by Russell & Russell.

behavior patterns toward the whole of society. Without attempting to assert that these exhaust the list, I will move on in this selective discussion to observe that personal traits must be viewed in relation to the movements of people and their mobility.

III

There has been particular concern in the United States for some years now that the population of core areas of many cities has been declining while the immediate suburban populations are rising rapidly. Increasingly also the poor and disadvantaged are becoming concentrated in central cities, while the suburbs are inhabited almost exclusively by the middle class.

In a nation in which the general level of affluence is unprecedentedly high, enclaves of poverty in the cores of cities are increasingly visible to all but especially to their virtual prisoners, to whom they are intolerable and a source of tension and explosion.

There is, in one sense, contained within the United States an underdeveloped nation consisting of thirty million poor persons, about a third of them nonwhites. Among the poor, a principal and significant difference between whites and nonwhites, for this discussion, is that the nonwhites are relegated to a segment of the housing market. There can be no true equality of opportunity so long as that condition remains.

The limited choice of housing shapes a number of problems. It artificially inflates the cost of shelter in the slums. It mandates *de facto* segregation of public schools. It limits job opportunities. It erects the barriers within which a subculture of tension festers.

The desire to equalize opportunity and to foster residential integration does not require, however, that these areas of nonwhite concentration be abandoned, nor does it require that those who elect to live in them be denied the opportunity to do so. We cannot espouse freedom of choice and simultaneously deny it to any group. There are, in many cities, large ethnic neighborhoods that are maintained on a wholly voluntary basiṣ.

What is required is the eradication of artificial barriers to free movement in the housing market, and concurrently, the upgrading of life in the neighborhoods that have been so long neglected. As a consequence of action in both directions, not only will nonwhites have greater residential mobility but they will also enjoy improved capabilities and status whereever they reside.

Laws alone, however effectively enforced, will not bring this about any more than wishing for it, however piously, will make a change. To change racial residential patterns will require motivation and action across a broad range of fronts, and I believe the decisive factor will be economic mobility. The effort to press for a public policy of free and open occupancy must be joined by a variety of efforts to expand nonwhite participation in all other phases of American life but particularly in jobs and education as well as political action.

Improvement of the conditions in the slums and freedom of movement out of them are not inconsistent. They are mutually supporting. The ghettos cannot be made livable and attractive unless there is an appreciable increase in mobility for nonwhites. The sheer pressure of numbers from population growth will eventually damn the ghettos, and further in-migration confounds the situation.

Economic pressures equal the physical pressures. There will never be enough, or sufficient diversity, of jobs in the ghetto to meet the requirements of its residents. The majority of nonwhites now employed find jobs outside their areas of residence. It is well documented that the incidence of unemployment among Negroes is far higher than among whites. And the unfortunate truth is that segregated schools perpetuate color distinctions no less than they respond to them. The traditional function of the public school to enhance mobility has broken down in the slums.

Programs for job training, job availability, improved education, and all types of human rehabilitation will be involved over the long range. A short-term solution can be employment and apprenticeship programs in the physical rehabilitation of the ghetto itself. However, a time will come when a great majority of those engaged in rehabilitating the ghetto will have to find other work. It is important to recognize the temporary nature of ghetto employment and the corresponding necessity to expand job opportunities.

On-the-job training programs are vitally important, but they are presently few in number inside the ghettos. Much of this type of work is not only outside the ghetto but outside the central city, and often it is not accessible by public transportation. If there are to be—as there must be—greater employment opportunities for nonwhites, they must have access to housing beyond the central cities, too. Job mobility requires residential mobility as well.

IV

The ultimate goals for urban areas are easily stated in broad terms: equal opportunity and maximum freedom of choice; the highest possible standard of living; the most attractive and economically viable environments; reduction of substandard housing, crime, delinquency, and human want; assurance of human dignity and a high sense of personal worth; reestablishment of free public education as an effective instrument for economic and social mobility as well as psychological health.

Ghetto patterns are sooner or later inconsistent with most of these goals. They complicate the achievement of all of them. Yet it is crucial not to confuse ultimate goals with intermediate steps. There are those who hypothesize that nothing can be done to move toward the goals until the ghetto patterns are eradicated. This is unrealistic, and for the simple reason that there is literally nowhere else for the ghetto residents to go while the eradication takes place.

There are others—the Black Nationalists—who consciously or unconsciously believe that enforced segregation and submerged status cannot be changed, and they retreat to an untenable position that a closed, self-sufficient black society can be maintained. Finally, there are those who assert that any attempt to improve the ghetto merely perpetuates it, and they therefore oppose any such efforts. They, too, are unrealistic. Few of them have felt the pulse of immediacy that haunts most disadvantaged nonwhites, whose concern is for a decent home, a good school, better municipal services, a more attractive environment, assistance in getting a good job, and effective aid in social problems.

Between now and the time that they have free access to housing throughout the urban complex, the mass of nonwhites want action. Without being economists, they know that there is little low-income housing in suburbia. They realize that access to hotels, theaters, restaurants, and the like is a meaningless right so long as they have insufficient money for admission. Many are not sure that their children are best served by being bused to schools in hostile neighborhoods. And many of them appreciate that their ghetto areas are often so well situated near the center of cities that they now inhabit potentially valuable urban real estate.

To say to them that nothing substantial can or should be done in the ghetto, or to insist that no low-income housing should be built or rehabilitated where they live, is to articulate a position they will not accept. They are committed to doing something about the ghetto. They resent the limitations now imposed. They want equal opportunity. But they won't wait for housing integration—which means little in the present housing market because of their incomes—before changes are made.[5]

There are substantial efforts underway, or being planned, to move beyond long-continuing efforts to improve cities by public housing and urban renewal—to move to a posture of preserving and improving entire neighborhoods that have been neglected. These efforts involve governments at all levels, private industry, universities, and a variety of non-profit interests. These efforts extend both to physical facilities and to human welfare.

One of the newest prospects for augmenting the supply of low- and moderate-income housing in suburbia is the development of entirely new communities planned from the beginning to embrace housing for many income levels. This presupposes strong public policy and participation, for otherwise, new communities will generally cater to higher-income families.

The new communities, however, can be effective instruments for racial integration. They are much like the concepts of educational parks for central cities, these parks being planned from the beginning to be large enough to draw students from so much of the community that they will inevitably be integrated. Until recently, the articulation of such a possibility was tantamount to destroying public support for it. Today, however, both of these concepts are freely and widely discussed. In the concept of new communities, it is possible to require a multi-income and a multi-ethnic participation as a condition for federal involvement.

V

There is no paucity of prophets of doom on the urban scene. But this is not new. Cities have been abused and

[5] For a discussion of this problem in greater depth, see the author's *Dilemmas of Urban America* (Cambridge, Mass.: Harvard University Press, 1966), Chap. 4.

relegated to destruction by myopic foreseers since their beginnings. In this nation there are those who hanker for a rural past and still equate urbanity with evil. There are others who observe urban deficiencies and cannot see any other solution than abandonment. All of the naysayers ignore the investment of the city, its markets, its diversity of services, and its unique capacity, as August Heckscher has put it, to be "the home of the arts" as well as "a work of art itself."[6]

American cities have a particular tradition. It was to our cities that waves of immigrants moved, and it was largely in them that the acculturation of newcomers occurred. In the process, these new Americans were prepared to enter the full potential of American society. Thus, the city has been, in this and every nation, as Charles Abrams phrased it, the "concourse of the various—in faces, in trade, in the exchange of thought, and in the potentials for leadership."[7]

Cities are the creation of man, and since most of their problems are man-made, man also has the capacity to deal with them. Three basic ingredients will be required—additional resources, additional knowledge, and additional trained personnel.

What the total cost will be cannot be determined now. It will vary in response to our successes in developing technology, modifying institutions to permit application of new approaches, increasing and redistributing incomes, learning how to deal effectively with social and human problems, and improving the quality of administration.

Research and development still have not produced a basic foundation in urban knowledge or a systematic inquiry into new techniques, materials, and methods in home building or urban transit systems or other community facilities. It is my hope that a major research program will be funded by our

[6] August Heckscher, "A New Universe of Creativity," *The General Electric Forum*, Jan.–Mar., 1967, pp. 7–8.

[7] Charles Abrams, "Downtown Decay and Revival," *Journal of the American Institute of Planners*, Feb., 1961, p. 9.

national government in these areas. At the same time, American manufacturing firms generally have far surpassed the home-building industry in research.[8] If the building industry followed the general pattern, it would devote 2 percent of receipts to this endeavor, and if it did, this would mean $300 million by 1975—far beyond the present level of effort.

The third basic need—for trained people—is a fairly universal deficiency, involving a lack of generalists as well as specialists and including operating personnel at all levels, within government and outside it. Today it is difficult to recruit the talent required to administer existing programs at their relatively low level of funding. It is inconceivable that we could successfully operate an effort of much greater magnitude without a much larger component of administrators, research workers, operators, and consultants.

The American city today is both witness and participant as massive social and economic changes cause a drastic alteration of our society. But, as noted in the beginning, the process of urbanization is worldwide. No two cities anywhere are identical, but all have their individual components of economic, political, and social problems. The tensions between economic classes are universal, and those tensions are becoming increasingly urban tensions.

This nation attempts to meet its troubles through the joint efforts of private enterprise and government. This is neither the easiest nor the most direct approach. But it does contain the potential for ultimate efficacy and maximum freedom. In the end, this approach, with all its detours, will have been worthwhile only if the freedoms become available to the least advantaged as well as all others.

[8] Leonard A. Lecht, *Goals, Priorities, and Dollars* (New York: The Free Press, 1966), p. 202.

6

ART FOR A CHANGING SCALE

GYORGY KEPES

School of Architecture and Planning
Massachusetts Institute of Technology

THE NINETEENTH CENTURY came to its end in an
explosion of human knowledge and human energies
overwhelming in its consequences. A new world rapidly took
shape as the physical environment became transformed.
Agriculture and industry underwent enormous expansion.
World population multiplied. Cities became giant spreading
tangles of soaring buildings, roaring traffic, and bustling
humanity. Space shrunk as the upper air became a realm of
superfast transport. Time grew enormously as the origins of
the universe were put further, further, and further back, and
measured intervals of time became fantastically minute slices.
Rapid advances took place in every field of technology. Social
relations were disrupted by a cycle of wars and revolutions.
The unprecedented scale and speed of the new events were
major factors in the inevitable disorientation as people endeavored to face and solve their problems.

Thus the advent of the twentieth century did not resolve
the conflicts of the nineteenth century; it exacerbated them.
Our century still faces the same problems that early industrialization left in its wake, and on a tremendously exploded
scale. Slums and machine-regimented human work are ruth-

lessly invading the most distant corners of the globe. Indus-trialization, urbanization, mechanization, westernization, and mass production have reached into India, China, Africa, and the South Seas. As in the past, the process of alleviating material misery generates toxic by-products, and the degree to which the harmful by-products, can be avoided or neutral-ized depends upon the quality of our life. We cannot, like Ivan Karamazov, return our entrance ticket to life because it was bought by the suffering of the innocent. We have to accept twentieth-century conditions, but we also have to learn how to make optimal use of them. The intensity of life, the splendor of solidarity, the faith and wisdom of age-old customs, the pride in making things expressed in folk art, folk songs, the dignity of a fully lived life, all are clearly endangered by the invasion of our half-understood, potent technical tools. Can we translate these qualities of the smaller-scale life to the new amplified scale? No doubt each scale has its own structural solution, its own pattern of values. To retain the values of the past without recognizing the structure of the present is to undertake sentimental adventures that will surely falter. The poetry of our new scale, the faith, the order, the pride and splendor of today, come only from a full grasp of what makes our age.

Whatever the magnitude and complexity of the world, the artistic imagination still feeds back information to the central scale of human values. The individual is still dependent on the work of his hands for biological and psychic health. It is still through those hands that he is materially involved in his world. The nineteenth century increasingly emphasized work as a justification of existence, an inner guide and compass, the raw material of social progress. Leading nineteenth-century scientists and social thinkers recognized the propell-ing force of work in the evolutionary process, both biological and social, and based their essential argument about society on the premise of a conflict in the distribution of the values produced by labor. As early as 1831 Carlyle was able to recognize the constructive aspects of the industrial world and accept productivity as the key to existing and forthcoming values:

> Hast thou heard, with sound ears, the awakening of a Manchester, on Monday morning, at half-past five by the clock; the rushing off of its thousand mills, like the boom of an Atlantic tide, ten thousand spools and spindles all set humming there—it is perhaps, if thou knew it well, sublime as a Niagara, or more so. Cotton-spinning is the clothing of the naked in its result; the triumph of man over matter in its means. Soot and despair are not the essence of it: they are divisible from it.

As the division of labor grew, the greater grew the cleavage between work as a creative process and as drudgery that corrodes man's confidence in his role in life. When the individual was no longer able to participate in all the steps of the metamorphosis of raw material into created object, work lost meaning, honesty, and basic significance. Blake, Ruskin, Morris, Tolstoy, and Rodin were only a few among the passionate voices that rose against distortion of human work. As Ruskin hoped:

> It would be a part of my scheme of physical education if every youth in the state, from the king's son downwards, should learn to do something finally and thoroughly with the hand, so as to let him know what touch meant; and what stout craftsmanship meant.

William Morris commented:

> There is no square mile of the earth's surface that is not beautiful in its own way if we men will only abstain from willfully destroying that beauty; and it is this reasonable share in the beauty of the earth that I claim is the right of every man who will earn it by due labor.

In the ever growing complexity of the industrial world, the attenuation of the creative aspect of human work has increasingly taken away basic nourishment. The farther away we get from a fully lived, productive life, the higher rises the heap of roadblocks to health and true self-realization. In the nineteenth century most of the courageous spokesmen against these ills were Utopians—unrealistic and sentimental in the ways they suggested for reducing inner tensions. Like the aging Tolstoy, they were willing to sacrifice the technological base of the modern world for a sentimentalized primitive life as direct and simple as the Sermon on the Mount. But no matter whether they sought redemption or social therapy, they understood that it is humanity's birthright to work. The birthright of labor, as Morris put it, is the joy of labor.

Domestication of the most obvious dynamics of the twentieth-century world had its earliest and strongest hold in Italy. Lagging behind industrially, the restless young Italians glorified the dynamic new wonders, which were, for them, a dream. Their glimpses of the new technical life were tempting; and, in addition, history made advanced techniques supremely welcome to life-hungry Italian intellectuals. Italy was the country of museums, the guardian of past richness, richness with no immediate relevance for the twentieth-century man seeking his own identity. One can hardly imagine a more acute contrast than a racing car tearing through the narrow, beautiful streets of medieval Siena. Electricity, the airplane, the motor car, and the many other emblems of twentieth-century technical power hardly seem comfortable alongside the memories of the more climactic richness of past artistic efforts.

To the generation of Italians at the beginning of the twentieth century, it seemed that the two worlds could not coexist and that to live and to live up to the twentieth-century potentials it was necessary to blast away all the inhibiting memories of the past. "Let's kill the moonlight," declared one of the futurist manifestos. The violence, vitality, and brutality of the technical tools and the beast in man became the new ideals. Painters and sculptors hero-worshiped speed and motion. They dreamed of a complete rebirth, a new strength, completely divorced from the past. Boccioni, a gifted and sincere artist, commented in one of his letters, "Our primitivism should have nothing in common with that of antiquity. Our primitivism is the extreme climax of complexity, whereas the primitivism of antiquity is the bubbling of simplicity."[1]

The artist-poets felt that their task was to find ways in which to structure a new scale of the world. Boccioni's "climax of complexity" expressed the new scale and the concomitant task of bringing the new wealth and dynamics into meaningful order. The old walls, the old spaces, the old motives and reminiscences of antiquity seemed only handicaps. Again, to quote Boccioni, "I have tried for a great synthesis of labor, light and movement."[2]

The nineteenth-century dreams of Turner and Constable to return light and movement to the dark, smoke-ridden industrial towns, and William Morris' dream of restoring human dignity to human labor were reformulated in twentieth-century terms. In certain ways these were reduced to mere acrobatics of the explosive spirit of ennui. The nineteenth-century dreams of light, color, motion, and work had an ethical overtone, an ideal behind it. The futurist hero worship of dynamics was basically a technical enterprise to record and absorb the new perceptual task of the twentieth-century industrial world but without any clear inner compass of what to do with it or how to use it. Though their limitations and the inherent traps in the material with which they

[1] Letter to Vicco Baier, 1913.
[2] Letter to the director of the Galeria d'Arte Moderna, Venice.

worked led some of them to the Fascist worship of power, still their work prepared a climate of awareness. They pioneered in a new visual language that could express the intensity of experience of the dynamic new technical world. The road from the first motor car to the first visual turmoil in the cities, to airplanes and present supersonic flight, has been uninterrupted.

The Italian futurists were not alone in responding to the technical world. Observing eyes in France and Russia also read the promise of the new visual environment. Each country and cultural background brought forth its own interpretation and emphasis.

In France, under the influence of the Italians, Guillaume Apollinaire, the poet, led an aggressive attack on the past, beginning with the inherited structure of language. Like the Italian Marinetti, he wished to destroy syntax, get rid of adjectives and punctuation, leaving only the most elementary patterning of sound and words. The two men held the belief that the new quality of intensity of their age could not be presented with the outdated tools of language, and therefore an essential first step was to chop away all unnecessary historical barnacles.

The Russian futurists, including Mayakovsky and his friends, started with the same wild destructive spirit. They, too, rejected all memories of the past and acted on the words of their manifesto that "the Academy and Pushkin are more unintelligible than hieroglyphs." But quite soon their personal intensity and the background of a fermenting social world gave them a purposeful direction. Mayakovsky aimed also at a new simplicity and at strength, but in his confidence and exuberance he wished to shift the focus from the machine to man. His dynamics had, as a goal, to spur mankind to a fast conquest of physical power geared to human needs. Man, nature, and technical power were to be brought together in a broadening scale that would enrich human life.

The sunbeams we shall tie
In radiant brooms, and sweep
Clouds from the sky
With electricity.
We shall make honey-sweet the rivers of the worlds.
The streets of earth we'll pave with radiant stars.[3]

The creative energies of liberated man would open up a new scale of life in which friendship with nature would be deepened.

The romantic dreams of Shelley, the all-embracing luminous space of Turner, had echoes as short-lived as the original dreams themselves. The expression of life exalted aggressive movement, noise, and speed; as Marinetti put it, "The racing space, the acrobat somersault, the slap in the face and the blow of the fist . . . war, the bloody and necessary test of the people's force." The new challenge of a bigger, faster, and potentially richer world found its caricature in the cult of crude sensation, in a bombastic journalistic hero worship of twentieth-century dynamic hardware—the car, the machine gun, the airplane.

The challenge of the new cannot be met by merely giving in to what is new, by a sheer mirroring of novel kinetic excitement. Without a sense of the deepest roots and a total, broad awareness, the menacing power of the man-created world is treated with the same respect that a child gives to a firecracker or roller-coaster ride. To face the new scale there must be an acceptance of both the old and new, the immediate and the distant, the inner and outer world, and an awareness of their interconnections.

A simultaneous awareness of dimensions on a multiple scale is essential if the moment of today and the projected

[3] Vladimir Mayakovsky, *Mystery-Bouffe*, trans. by George Rapall Noyes and Alexander Kaun, in *Masterpieces of the Russian Drama*, ed. George Rapall Noyes (New York: Dover Publications, 1961), II, 879. Reprinted through permission of the publisher.

purpose of tomorrow are to coexist. Saint-Exupéry, a sensitive observer of the challenge of our broadening vistas commented, "If the traveler, climbing a mountain toward a star, becomes too absorbed in the problem of climbing, he may forget which star is guiding him. If he moves only for the sake of movement he will reach no destination." Our age is characterized by the disjunction in our awareness of the immediate and the subsequent. We seem moved by a tremendous kinetic inertia that pushes us ahead without forethought of where we are going or willingness to check our directions. We have inherited concepts of order belonging to a smaller scale of existence; these are becoming increasingly useless in the explosive new scale of events. We have been accustomed to making ordered relationships by mapping objects and even individuals in their positions relative to one another. Now we are forced to recognize that objects do not have final, unchangeable positions, that human relationships are among the things in the man-created environment that have direction and velocity. The world is energies in interaction. We have to recognize that a description of position tells only half the story. If we see a still photograph of a heavily trafficked street, we find it difficult to tell which cars are in motion and which are standing still. Our information must include velocity as well as position if we are to order the situation. Similarly, in the kinetic situation of today, changing social forces in hitherto neglected areas of the world are posing the demand for an understanding of the dynamic new economic processes. Our understanding can be meaningful only if position, direction, and velocity of the processes are related.

To structure our chaotic environment as well as our knowledge and values, we have to accept the conditions of the new scale and learn to use the tools that have grown from it. Both the world we create inside our heads and the world we create outside our bodies have one basic objective: to preserve the condition of life. We ourselves and our tremendously extended feelers of sensibilities, tools of observation, structures that shelter and give us physical comfort, have, in the final analysis, one objective—to preserve the condition of life in our internal environment, not only in the biological-physiological sense but in the deepest human sense. Our human system, if we may so call it, is a network of interacting variables that has some power of regulating itself in its own experiences. Life and death depend upon our power to regulate the forces that we create.

The artistic sensibility and imaginative act are key factors in regulating the interacting variables of our man-created inner and outer worlds. Artistic sensibility is now seeking new images that will give us our bearings. As the nineteenth-century creative vision projected the images of health and fullness, light, space, and color, and the inner richness of a fully lived life, so twentieth-century artistic sensibility is trying to read the signs between life as it is and life as it could be, and to create vigorous images of order that can domesticate the centrifugal forces of daily life.

The opening of new scientific vistas has widened the physical dimensions of our environment through new forms of transportation and new modes of communication. The implication of these new dynamic dimensions and the potential structure of the new scale of things was the essential theme of the creative imagination. One of the great visionaries of the nineteenth century, Friedrich Nietzsche, put it clearly when he said, "He who one day teacheth men to fly will have shifted all landmarks; to him will all landmarks themselves fly into the air; the earth will he christen anew—as 'the light body.' "[4]

To find one's way in the new dimensions, one has to rename the paths of the universe and set new frames of reference and orientation. The twentieth century brought with it great

[4] *Thus Spake Zarathustra*, Discourse LV, No. 2, in *Complete Works*, Oscar Levy, ed., X (New York: The Macmillan Co., 1911), 235.

promises not only to secure safer conditions for human existence but a greater range for the human spirit through un-
obstructed vistas and new freedom of vision. But the vistas
began to increase faster than vision could encompass them.
It can happen in nature that the woods grow so abundantly
that all sunlight is cut off from the struggling seedling. In
the same way the tremendous growth of knowledge threw a
deepening shadow on many of the early attempts at orientation in this new world.

To use a simple illustration from our daily life, the
increasing number of people whom we meet and with whom
we are acquainted through picture magazines, television,
newsreels, photography, and the new tempo of traveling has
made it increasingly difficult to keep sufficient intimacy in
our contacts to develop true friendships. In fact, in certain
strata of our society, the density and complexity of the daily
routine have made almost a farce of the meaning of friendship. In a similar way, our relation to the environment, to
the city we live in, has become thinner and thinner. So has
the intimate sense of belonging that gave some ages civic
pride in civic achievements.

The many things we know and the many things we know
about suggest a similar situation in knowledge. Our orientation is affected by the tremendous number of possible vistas
that man has opened through conceptual and perceptual tools.
Things hitherto unseen by the unaided eye now offer, through
new instrumentation and such new aids to memory as photo-
graphic emulsion, a vast, complex perspective.

On a more fundamental level we are able to produce and
release energies on a scale that keeps us in fearful suspense.
The tools of preserving life and the tools of destroying life
are terrifying in magnitude. The population expansion, with
all its unresolved future dangers, or "overkill," a term with
devastating implications, implies that there is a power within
human hands that must now be keyed to a meaningful scale

of values. There is no doubt that, given the present pace of inventive power, we have been losing our perspective of knowledge, our bearings, our sense of belonging, our discipline of vision.

From whatever direction we observe the contemporary scene, its most obvious characteristic is incredible acceleration in scale of magnitude, rate of change, and complexity of interrelationships in scientific, technical, and social realms. Just as the political sphere is expanding its areas of interconnection, so every region of the globe is becoming touched by some economic tie from another distant region. This interpenetration of economic spheres is underscored and amplified by vast improvements in techniques of transportation and communication.

The common problem that arises in the attempt to readjust to the increased dimensions is the need to read the characteristics of each level without losing sight of the connecting links among the many levels. To take an everyday example of this problem, we change space context and speed of motion in abrupt, unconnected ways when we move in a big city. To step from an automobile into a subway is to shift not only vistas but dimensions of awareness and scale of orientation. In this and in all similar daily experiences, there is a confusing fabric of response to the surroundings. In an automobile one may sit next to a friend, while at the same time images of the surroundings race past the perceiving eye like a wild motion picture. In the subway one is in close physical proximity to an array of strange faces and unknown lives, all traveling in the same direction but without any obvious visual signals to mark the path. The continual change of scale is further accented by sudden shifts in the spatial setting, from the intimacy of the home to the turmoil of a busy street or the impersonal pattern and segmentation of office space.

These simple, everyday experiences give only a faint hint of the multidimensional kinetics of other scale changes that we hear and read about. The astronaut who sits in a closed space capsule becomes quickly invisible to the naked eye and relies on instrument communication as he races through space. The instruments by which his flight is maintained, guided, and observed are, to a great extent, reduced to a microscale beyond the ability of the unaided eyes to decipher. The span of distances, the velocity of travel, the visible vistas are in a continuous mobile field, shifting from one range to another. These dynamic scale changes could lead to complete disorientation if we did not have tools to master them. And the great significance is that most of the new scientific concepts and technical invention are instruments useful in gauging the new scale of knowledge and existence. It was observed a long time ago that each scale level has its own structure of perception and meaning, but only our century has formulated the knowledge into usable conceptual tools.

Locke, in his *Essay on Human Understanding*, commented that

> . . . were the senses acute enough to discern the minute particles of bodies, and the real constitution on which their sensible qualities depend, I doubt not but they would produce quite different ideas in us . . . and that which is the yellow color of gold, would then disappear and instead of it we could see an admirable texture of parts of a certain size and figure.

We know today that qualities of our sense experience—soft, sweet, sour, bright, or dark—are projections of certain scale events in other scale regions. We have to accept the substances of our environment in their proper scale, meaning that our conceptual grasp of observable events in the physical world has to be recognized as the result of scale orbits of knowledge. "The accuracy of prediction is proportional to the knowledge of the totality in which an event occurs (which surrounds an event)," as Heisenberg, a leading physicist, observed. In fact, as he recognized, it is impossible to make an accurate survey of a particle or set of particles of atomic or subatomic sizes. That is, our tools cannot reach beyond certain minute magnitudes, and this limitation also limits our observation of scale interaction. The "uncertainty principle" of Heisenberg is not just a negative principle; it is also a tool attuned to scale levels. In a burst of events, the first few years of this century formed connecting links between the physical environment on the one hand and different ranges of knowledge and feeling on the other. There were new discoveries relating the unaided senses, new bridges built between hitherto unconnected concepts of the inquiring mind and between the creative imagination and the new tools of machine technology. Cézanne's famous letter to Emil Bernard in 1904 from Aix-en-Provence underlines this development:

> . . . my project of doing Poussin entirely from nature and not constructed piecemeal from notes, drawings and fragments of studies; in short, of painting a living Poussin in the open air, with color and light instead of one of those works imagined in a studio where everything has a brown color of feeble daylight, without reflections from the sky and the sun . . .

Here, Cézanne indicated an essential task of his time: to find continuity with the great intellectual achievements of the past and at the same time to readjust those achievements to direct contact with the present, even in the level of "the little sensations of the eye," tapping rich sources of visual joy and strength. He wished not only to correlate the past and present but to weave the intellect and the senses into a single fabric.

Some of Cézanne's great contemporaries touched upon this same theme of tying together artistic response and a broad intellectual questioning of the world. The potent new tools of industry were first feared and rejected by the intellectual Luddites. Ruskin and Morris more than doubted the possibility of making the machine a successful creative tool and rejected any hopes of domesticating the new beasts. But in 1902 Frank Lloyd Wright, with clear and courageous vision, declared a new union of art and technology in a lecture at Hull House:

> Is it not more likely that the medium of artistic expression itself has changed and broadened until a new definition and a new direction must be given the art activity of the future, and that the machine has finally made for the artist, whether he will own it yet or not, a splendid distinction between the art of old and art to come? A distinction made by the tool which frees human labor, lengthens and broadens the life of the simplest man and thereby the basis of the democracy upon which we insist.
>
> If the art of the Greek, produced at such cost to human life, was so noble and enduring, what limit dare we now imagine to an art based upon an adequate life for the individual?[5]

The hopeful visions of the artist and the architect were able to accept the broadened scene. They were able to connect the past and present order of life, the power of the new technology and creative vision. But they were not alone in their confidence in the new tools of industry. Some of the scientists at the turn of the century were more than ready to expect from the vistas of their own field rich new resources for creative vision.

In 1902, the same year in which Wright wrote "The Art and Craft of the Machine," Michelson, the first American to receive the Nobel prize in physics, accepted the new scientific and technical dimensions of the twentieth century as legitimate tools and goals for artistic image making:

[5] "The Art and Craft of the Machine," Frank Lloyd Wright, *Writings and Buildings*, ed. by *Edgar Kaufmann and Ben Raeburn* (New York: Horizon Press, Inc., 1960), pp. 60, 70.

Indeed, so strongly do these color phenomena appeal to me that I venture to predict that in the not very distant future there may be a color art analogous to the art of sound—a *color music*, in which the performer, seated before a literally chromatic scale, can play the colors of the spectrum in any succession or combination, flashing on a screen all possible gradations of color, simultaneously or in any desired succession, producing at will the most delicate and subtle modulations of light and color, or the most gorgeous and startling contrasts and color chords! It seems to me that we have here at least as great a possibility of rendering all the fancies, moods, and emotions of the human mind as in the older art.

These beauties of form and color, so constantly recurring in the varied phenomena of refraction, diffraction, and interference, are, however, only incidentals; and, though a never-failing source of aesthetic delight, must be resolutely ignored if we would perceive the still higher beauties which appeal to the mind, not directly through the senses, but through the reasoning faculty; for what can surpass in beauty the wonderful adaptation of Nature's means to her ends, and the never-failing rule of law and order which governs even the most apparently irregular and complicated of her manifestations? These laws it is the object of the scientific investigator to discover and apply. In such successful investigation consists at once his keenest delight as well as his highest reward.[6]

Confident vision read the expanding scale and perspective as a challenge rather than an obstacle. With mounting speed, new territories were opened and scientific links discovered among seemingly disparate fields. Einstein and Minkovsky were among those who constructed a common fabric from hitherto separated territories of human understanding. It is evident that there are new ways in which to control the pace

[6] A. A. Michelson, *Light Waves and Their Uses* (Chicago: University of Chicago Press, 1907), p. 2.

and scale of changes. On the one hand, the continuing human explorations have to be interlocked and interconnected in a common legible structure. The new vistas of knowledge, the new powers of energy, the new complexity of relationships have to find a new level of ecological balance. An uninhibited will to fly will only lead us to the fate of Icarus. The twentieth century has to find the wisdom of Daedalus if it is to learn its own measure, map its direction, and set its ecological limits. To domesticate the tremendous forces will require new ordering principles geared to the continuous dynamic changes of scale. If the twentieth century offers a basically different human environment it does so primarily because of the rapid expansion and contraction of its scale. If we move from the individual to global interdependence or back from group conditions to individual happiness, so do we move continuously from the scale of our senses to the atomic scale of events to the cosmic scale of space travel.

7

ENVIRONMENT AS PROGRAMMED HAPPENING*

MARSHALL McLUHAN

Fordham University and the University of Toronto

IT HAS BEEN SAID that the present time offers us such immediate access to the entire range of cultures of other times that the architect can orchestrate different spaces, with their differing sensuous involvements, with the same freedom as the composer and the conductor. The architect can, in this electric age, modulate the forms of space of many other cultures much as the poet can shape his rhythms by free choice among a great diversity of words. T. S. Eliot's celebrated observations in *The Use of Poetry and the Use of Criticism* about the activity of the "auditory imagination" seem now to be relevant to the architect in his shaping of spatial form:

> What I call the "auditory imagination" is the feeling for syllable and rhythm, penetrating far below the conscious levels of thought and feeling, invigorating every word; sinking to the most primitive and forgotten, returning to

* Some of the material in the present essay was used by the author in the Purves Memorial Lecture for 1967 sponsored by the American Institute of Architects. It is here published for the first time.

the origin and bringing something back, seeking the beginning and the end. It works through meanings, certainly, or not without meanings in the ordinary sense, and fuses the old and obliterated and the trite, the current, and the new and surprising, the most ancient and the most civilized mentality.[1]

To say that we live mythically today while continuing to think conventionally may help to draw attention to the technological gap in our ordinary experience. Electric technology, simply because it is all at once, is also discontinuous. It tends therefore to create exterior situations that have all the structural characteristics of the human unconscious. To the rational observer who seeks to find connectedness and uniformity in the spaces of his world, the new situation presents an extreme form of the irrational.

When the inner spaces of our lives go outward, the result is a structure like Habitat at Expo '67. This is a mosaic form of composite spaces which in effect presents an X ray of our entire culture. It is really very much like any page of the telegraph press during the past century. The mosaic of items on a newspaper page are connected only by the dateline above them. There is no other connection. The mosaic arrangement of multiple items of daily news creates not a picture of the world but an X ray in depth. A picture has a vanishing point related to a fixed position from which the picture is taken, but a mosaic, like a total field of energy or relationships, does not present the means for a point of view or a fixed position. It is an all-at-once or mythical structure in which beginning and middle and end are simultaneously present.

T. S. Eliot explained in his essay "Tradition and the Individual Talent" that all literature and art from Homer to the present constitutes a simultaneous order that is totally modi-

[1] London: Faber and Faber, 1933, pp. 118–19.

fied by the advent of any new work. A new work creates new space for itself and for all the preexisting space, yet this is quite different from shifting one's point of view. A point of view depends upon a pictorial space that is uniform and continuous and connected.

The Western world discovered visual or pictorial space when the phonetic alphabet was invented. The unique property of the phonetic alphabet as contrasted with all other forms of writing is its power to translate sounds into visual space. The resulting stress and prominence given to the visual sense above the other senses increasingly created for Western man an environment built on the visual assumptions of uniformity, continuity, and connectedness. Such spatial assumptions scarcely existed in cultures based on acoustic patterns, for example. What appears to us as the irrationality of the preliterate world is in fact the result of structuring forms on perfectly consistent auditory assumptions from which visual continuity and connectedness have been abstracted.

A century ago, in 1868, Claude Bernard, the French pioneer of interior medicine, was elected to the French Academy. His phrase *le milieu intérieur* came at the same time that the French Symbolists were inventing *le paysage intérieur*. This interior landscape, the successor to the external landscape of the Romantic poets, was deliberately programmed as a teaching machine, as it were, as appears in the very opening lines of Eliot's "Love Song of J. Alfred Prufrock":

> Let us go then, you and I,
> When the evening is spread out against the sky
> Like a patient etherised upon a table;

These lines wittily summarize both the first and second Romantic movements. The outer world of the setting sun is juxtaposed with the inner landscape of the patient's interior.

In his *Background of Modern Poetry* J. Isaacs has some relevant things to say about these two kinds of space. He considers them as two waves:

> . . . The first wave is a romantic notion, and belongs to the Pre-Romantic age of the middle of the eighteenth century, when poetry was sought in primitive poetry, in ancient poetry, in ballads and in archaic writing, much as modern art sought its inspiration in archaic sculpture and African carvings. The second wave is in the Symbolist movement of the end of the nineteenth century. If we like to attach names to the two waves, we can call them Ossian and Mallarmé. In both there is a striving beyond mere statement in order to gain a special effect. The earlier movement was a movement *against* something. The later was a movement *towards* something, and only incidentally against the moral and the didactic in poetry.[2]

The first movement is concerned mainly with Euclidean and Newtonian space. The second one takes us "through the looking glass" into the space-time world of modern physics. The first space is continuous and connected and uniform. It is a visual space. The second space is discontinuous and not uniform and not connected. It is auditory space or tactile space or kinetic or proprioceptive. As D. H. Lawrence wrote of it:

> Still, and sensitive, and active,
> Audile, tactile, sensitiveness as of a tendril which
>   orientates and reaches out,
> Reaching out and grasping by an instinct more delicate
>   than the moon's as she feels for the tides.

The first space is one that permits detachment and objectivity. The second kind demands empathy and involvement. The second Romantic movement naturally concentrated upon the *effect*.

[2] New York: E. P. Dutton & Co., 1952, p. 19.

As the Western world separates itself from a 2500-year devotion to visual space, it naturally rediscovers the characteristics of the spaces generated by the other senses. I vividly recall an occasion when I made my first encounter with acoustic space as a concept. Professor Jacqueline Tyrwhitt, now at the Harvard School of Design, was a member of our Toronto seminar on Culture and Communications. She had been explaining some of Siegfried Giedion's recent findings in which he discriminated between enclosed and unenclosed spaces. Since that time his study of *The Beginnings of Architecture* has brought these matters into a luminous focus. As Professor Tyrwhitt followed his exploration of Egyptian as contrasted with Roman space, she stressed the point that a pyramid did not enclose any space since darkness is to space what silence is to sound. In the same way, an Egyptian temple does not enclose space since it, too, is dark. Even the Greeks never achieved true closure of space. This remained for the Romans. At this point psychologist Carl Williams (now President of the University of Western Ontario) intervened. He observed that unenclosed space could best be considered as acoustic or auditory space. Williams had long been associated with E. A. Bott, who has spent his life studying auditory space. Bott's formula for auditory space is simply that it has no center and no margins since we hear from all directions simultaneously. Structurally, it tends to be the space of all preliterate societies since the auditory sense has much primacy over the visual sense in preliterate cultures.

Structurally, auditory space tends also to be the characteristic form of an electronic culture. Instant movement of information creates a configuration of space-time in which no point of view is possible and no single plane perceptible. Electronic configurations, in short, are in a structural sense remarkably acoustic. All-at-onceness abolishes uniformity and continuity, and it also demands that the environment will be considered as an art form. "We have no art," say the Balinese. "We do everything as well as possible." The instantaneous movement of information itself creates a total environment, as witness the satellites that now encompass the planet itself in an information environment. It is only the sense of sight that possesses the properties of uniformity and continuity and connectedness. And it is only in those cultures in which phonetic literacy is salient that we can find visual values of rational connectedness to be pervasive.

At the present time, therefore, the Western world, long based on visual values of rational continuity, finds itself cut adrift from these sensory ground rules. The electronic age, if given its own unheeded leeway, will drift quite naturally into Oriental modes of cosmic humanism and total involvement of everybody in everybody and of all spaces and all cultures converged into a kind of mosaic without walls. We have already moved into this dimension, and the resulting panic is to some degree compensated by enthusiasm for the disappearance of many of the barriers, private and corporate, that had been carefully erected by our visually oriented forebears.

This visual world is one of matching, of fragmentation, and of classification. The new multisensuous world is one of making in which space is not a cavity to be filled but a possibility to be shaped. Even when put in these terms the advantages seem to be all on the side of making rather than matching. However, in a tribal and amorphous world of interacting resonances, the discovery of new means to private identity and private space naturally appeared Utopian, as we can see from Plato's *Republic*. But the *Oedipus Rex* of Sophocles reports the inner terrors that accompanied that achievement of detribalizing man into private visual space.

We, too, experience similar terrors today as we go through the reverse process of retribalizing and of yielding up our private visual structures to the resonance of acoustic space. Our children are born into a total electric environment of information only to find themselves inserted into a very different kind of environment at school. Quite naturally, the educational establishment represents a blueprint of classified information and fragmented time that were designed to instruct by imprinting data and disciplines upon the growing child. That is to say that the educational establishment is a faithful reflex of visual culture.

In recent decades the establishment has become enveloped in a new information environment that causes a kind of reversal within. The new need is to direct the educational enterprise toward discovery rather than instruction. As the environment becomes richer in information than the classroom, the student's genuine role becomes diverted toward involvement and discovery rather than focused on the acquisition of classified data.

A similar reversal takes place in the business world. As the information environment gets richer and richer, job holding yields to role playing. A role tends to be created when several jobs converge. A surgeon has a role rather than a job, as does a top executive or a mother. Each of them has several jobs to perform simultaneously. An artist has a role rather than a job because he must use all his faculties at once.

In the older fragmented and mechanized world of specialisms we tended to use only a part of our faculties at any one time. This was called "work." When, like the artist, we use all our faculties at once, we are recognized to be playing and are at leisure. A man must work very hard at his hobby, but because he uses all his faculties when playing, he is thought to be at leisure.

The electronic information environment tends to create this new configuration of leisure via total involvement. Looked at in the rear-view mirror, this leisure takes on the illusory form of unemployment and joblessness and vacancy. In point of fact, leisure is a space-time dimension that must be shaped and created by the individual user. Such leisure is not a goal but a kind of total field of relations. It is nothing less than social communication. A child of the electronic age, looking around him at the job holders, cannot help but feel that they are pathetic holdovers from some other age. When a child assumes similar postures and activities he feels rejected and alienated.

The first and second Romantic movements illustrate the eighteenth-century discovery of the external environment as a natural teaching machine. This discovery was made possible by the advent of the new man-made environment of mechanical industry, just as the mechanical environment became an especial object of attention with the advent of the environment of electric information.

Any environment has the property of being mainly invisible. This is a theme of *The Hidden Dimension* by Edward T. Hall. His earlier study of time as *The Silent Language* is complementary to this new book on space. Whatever involves us or totally surrounds us acquires the property of being imperceptible. It has been observed that "we don't know who discovered water but we are pretty sure it wasn't a fish." Robert Ardrey has developed the concept of territoriality to account for the environments that envelop different cultures. My own concept of technologies as the physical extensions of man is somewhat akin to Ardrey's concept. However, it is easier to demonstrate the physical times and spaces created by radio or motor car than it is to explain why bird song or physical odor should constitute a space boundary that might be regarded as impenetrable by other creatures.

There are reasons why we should in our time have become aware of the environments created by ourselves. For one thing, the mere speed of change in these environments has made it possible to shift from one to another in such a way that discrimination by comparison and contrast becomes perfectly natural. Elias Canetti has written of *Crowds and*

Power, discussing the various structures and patterns of psychic space created by various types of crowds. For example, a football crowd has little in common with a symphony crowd. Most crowds are simply invisible except statistically. Yet statistics represent a new means of X-raying crowds of money and data which were impenetrable before the present age.

The same speed of access to many kinds of data has given us the power to X-ray all the cultures and subcultures in the world. We no longer approach them from any point of view or for the purpose of taking a picture of them. The new approach is the X-ray approach of penetration in depth to achieve awareness on many levels at once. It is natural that we should adapt this approach to our own condition. The psychiatrists have done so for the individual, and comparable analysis is now available for the corporate or group condition.

The habit of avoiding the present or the new which has been immemorial human tradition tends to yield to this X-ray approach of the structures that shape and surround human perception. *The Myth of the Eternal Return* by Mircea Eliade discusses in detail the age-old human habit of hiding from the present by cyclic images of repetition. Just as the ordinary person finds comfort in the repetitive routine of the daily round that prevents direct confrontation of the immediate situation, so have most preliterate societies, including the great cultures of Asia, protected themselves from pressures of the eternal present by assigning the entire show to a spinning mechanism.

The need for a rear-view mirror as preferable to direct confrontation is omnipresent in preliterate societies as much as in our own. In the same work, Eliade reports:

> . . . Each time that life is threatened and the cosmos, in their eyes, is exhausted and empty, the Fijians feel the need for a return *in principio;* in other words they expect the regeneration of cosmic life not from its restoration

but from its recreation. Hence the essential importance, in rituals and myths, of anything which can signify the "beginning," the original, the primordial (new vessels and "water drawn before sunrise" in popular magic and medicine, the motifs of the child, the orphan, and so forth).[3]

The perpetual presence of the dead in preliterate societies creates an abiding terror. They are the enemy, much as in our own world the artist is enemy because of his insistence that we look at the present. He is somewhat in the position of the small child at the exhibition of the Emperor's new clothes. The artist has little inclination to look at the old clothes and is fascinated by the new manifestations of form and sense.

In the present time, the artist has shifted his attention from the private to the corporate scene and space. A happening as a programmed art form expresses the need to deal with the total environment as a work of art or as what Daniel Boorstin would call "pseudo-event." In the age of electric information the service industries take over the total human environment as their responsibility: everything from government and education to entertainment networks is involved in creating "happenings," as it were, or in transforming the environment into a work of art. Town planners report that during the past thirty years more space has been enclosed architecturally than in the preceding six thousand years. The next thirty years will see a great escalation of this process. In other words, without even looking beyond architecture it is possible to see the world as a happening today.

Siegfried Giedion was one of the first to train perception in these matters. His book *Mechanization Takes Command* is subtitled *A Contribution to Anonymous History*. At the outset he mentions how a split had occurred between thought and feeling in the nineteenth century. This break had come about through mechanization. One could add that the gap

[3] *The Myth of the Eternal Return* (New York: Pantheon Books, 1954), p. 81.

between mechanical culture of the nineteenth century and the new organic and integral culture of the present electric age was also a means of making us aware both of the nature of the mechanical and of the nature of the electrical.

The mechanical proceeds by fragmentation of all processes, including the process of perception. The mechanical enthroned the "point of view," the static position, with its vanishing point. The electric age favors a total field approach, a kind of X ray of forms in depth which not only avoids a point of view but avoids looking at situations from any single level. Giedion's opening section on "Anonymous History" asserts the importance of this X-ray approach to the most ordinary forms:

> For the historian there are no banal things. Like the scientist, the historian does not take anything for granted. He has to see objects not as they appear to the daily user, but as the inventor saw them when they first took shape. He needs the unworn eyes of contemporaries, to whom they appeared marvelous or frightening. At the same time, he has to establish their constellations before and after, and thus establish their meaning.
>
> History writing is ever tied to the fragment. The known facts are often scattered broadcast, like stars across the firmament. It should not be assumed that they form a coherent body in the historical night. Consciously, then, we represent them as fragments, and do not hesitate, when necessary, to spring from one period to another. Pictures and words are but auxiliaries; the decisive step must be taken by the reader. In his mind the fragments of meaning here displayed should become alive in new and manifold relations.

This passage is a kind of manifesto of the mosaic approach that has supplanted the pictorial. For, paradoxically, pictures are opaque, whereas the mosaic lets light through in depth and transforms the entire environment of artifacts into a teaching machine. Perceptually, any environment whatever is a teaching machine in so far as it adjusts our sensory levels until they are accommodated to that environment. The "Anonymous History" approach, however, accepts the entire world as an organized happening that is charged with luminous and exciting messages. To read the language of forms, anything from a Cadillac to an ash tray renders the book of the world an inexhaustible source of insights and discoveries.

William Butler Yeats once observed that the emotion of multitude results in a poem or a play when more than one story line is present. When there is both a plot and a subplot, there is an effect of depth and richness out of all proportion to the components of the poem or play. Something like this seems to have happened to us on a planetary scale. When we put the man-made environment of the satellites around our planet, Nature itself becomes the content of a man-made environment.

The natural tendency when one environment goes inside another is for the contained to become an art form. While our electric technology tends to put the human unconscious outside as a sort of discontinuous, mythic environment of forms that coexist and are simultaneous, the putting of Nature inside a man-made satellite environment results in substituting our human rational responses for the old irrational nature. The human dialogue used to be carried on with Nature, as it were, and is now carried on with the man-made environment that has supplanted Nature. This situation puts artists and architects in a totally new role of making and generating values, where previously we had been spectators. Of course, we could be as deluded as the two fish in *The New Yorker* cartoon who were pictured as having climbed out of the water onto the shore. One says to the other: "This is where the action is!"

8

THE DOCTRINE OF CREATION AND HUMAN RESPONSIBILITY

JOHN MACQUARRIE

Union Theological Seminary

THE TITLE of this essay brings together two notions that are not perhaps very obviously related. One is a mythological or theological idea concerning the origins of the world. The other is the idea of the advance of man through the expansion of knowledge and through his growth in experience. The expression "education of the human race" is borrowed from the title of Lessing's famous work, and although we do not propose to discuss Lessing's specific views, the whole context of ideas lying behind this expression belongs typically to the Enlightenment and to the modern world that has emerged from it. When we attend to this, it becomes harder than ever to see how such a progressive, humanistic conception can be related to ancient stories of the creation. Of course, we often hear nowadays from some biblical theologians that the Judeo-Christian doctrine of creation, by abolishing the notion of an animistic universe, made possible the secularization of nature and so laid it open to scientific investigation. As we shall see, this is much too simple a statement of the relation between the doctrine of creation and the rise of modern knowledge, but there is a measure of truth in it. However, it would seem to suggest that the doctrine of creation, though it may have been important in the past in giving encouragement to the scientific enterprise, has served its purpose and is no longer of any more than historical interest. But I intend to argue in this essay that the doctrine of creation has a continuing importance for the education of the race. I do not think we want to fall back into the deism of former centuries—though some contemporary theologians seem to be in danger of this—and suppose that although God set things going in the beginning, he is now an absentee landlord who leaves us to manage as best we can.

Almost every race and religion have their stories of creation, but we shall concern ourselves only with the biblical doctrine. Creation is a pervasive idea of the Old Testament, for it meets us not only in the creation stories at the beginning of Genesis but also in the Psalms and in the writings of the prophets. The idea is taken over into the New Testament and is indeed used to interpret the distinctively Christian belief that God has acted decisively in Jesus Christ, for the result of this act is seen as a "new creation."[1]

We would go far wrong if we supposed that creation stories, whether those of the Bible or other ones, were concerned primarily with speculations about the beginnings of the world. Disinterested questions about the origins of the universe come only much later. Though the early stories of the creation do in fact tell how things began, their interest is obviously an existential one. They are not trying to answer the merely curious question of what happened in the beginning but are rather seeking to answer a question that lies much nearer to man and is much more urgent—the question of his own identity. We first begin to understand the creation stories when we see them as answers to the question: "Who are we?" To this extent, Bultmann's existential interpretation of mythology is justified. Regin Prenter is essentially correct

[1] II Cor. 5, 17.

in his judgment of the Old Testament witness to the creation: "The concern of the Old Testament is not to explain how the world came into existence; its concern is that the life of the world may be preserved."[2] There is striking confirmation of this point in the current situation, in which we now realize that the question of cosmic origins is an empirical one, to be decided by such techniques as radiotelescopy which reaches far into the past, and that this has nothing to do with the theological meaning of creation.

We are saying then that the doctrine of creation is to be understood primarily in existential or anthropological terms. It tries to answer man's question about himself, that is to say, to give him a self-understanding; and perhaps it could be argued that self-understanding or self-knowledge is both the most difficult and the most important item that goes into the education of the human race.

Yet the interpretation of the doctrine cannot remain narrowly existential or anthropological. Man does not exist as an isolated subject. He is always a being-in-the-world. Thus he is inseparable from his environment and unintelligible apart from it. He is, moreover, a social being, a being-with-others, so that he is to be understood also in a social context. But any society, in turn, lives within a history and can be understood only in the stream of history. But history belongs within a cosmos, and we find ourselves asking about its status and significance there. Is history the clue to the whole, or only a by-product? Where do these questions stop?

The answer is that we must carry them as far as we can go. Man is the ontological entity, whose very being leads him into the question of being. To understand himself, he must also try to understand the wider being within which his own specifically human being is set. And there are no limits that can be set to the questions he asks. In vain would the positi-

---

[2] *Creation and Redemption*, trans. by Theodor I. Jensen (Philadelphia: Fortress Press, 1966), p. 193.

vist erect barriers and ask man to be content with understanding himself as the cooking animal or the featherless
biped or whatever. So that although we say that the creation
stories have primarily an existential and anthropological
interest, this interest inevitably broadens out into an ontological and cosmological one. Yet this has to do not with
origins but with meaning, and any ontological or cosmological dimension of the stories (and of the doctrine based
on them) is inseparable from the existential interest.

These points are surely well established from a brief
examination of the two creation narratives at the beginning
of Genesis. Much the older of the two stories, the so-called
Yahwist account of creation, now stands second.[3] Its overwhelmingly anthropological interest is apparent. God first
of all makes man. Then he provides a background and environment for him, by planting the garden and by providing
in it such plants and animals as are useful to human life. In
this story, everything is seen from the human point of view
and any cosmological interest is strictly secondary to the
central interest of providing man with an identity and a self-
understanding. The later and much more sophisticated story
of creation from the source P, now standing first in the
biblical text,[4] is very different and in its ordered account of
the work of creation is remarkably similar to modern theories
of emergent evolution. First, God creates the light in a blind-
ing initial flash of energy. Then heaven and earth, land and
sea take shape, the vegetation and the animals appear, and
finally man himself is created. Here the cosmological interest
is much more pronounced, but the creation culminates in
man, and he is given dominion over the earth. So one can
still say that the story is designed to provide a self-understanding, but the self-understanding is less narrowly circum-
scribed, for to answer adequately the question of man is to

[3] Gen. 2, 4–25.
[4] Gen. 1, 1–2, 3.

be drawn into all the questions that man himself, as the ontological entity, raises.

What, then, is the self-understanding that is conveyed in
the biblical stories of creation? In the Yahwist account, man
is said to be constituted by the dust of the ground and the
breath of life. Under these symbols, the basic tensions of
human existence, in both its facticity and its possibility, come
to expression. As dust of the ground, man understands himself in his solidarity with nature, in his finitude and earthi-
ness. Yet as the bearer of breath or spirit, he has a unique
place in creation. He is not just another item in the world of
creatures but may be said even to transcend the world. He is
tied to it and belongs within it, yet at the same time he rises
above it and stands in an openness of possibility that is unique
among the creatures. The same polarity appears in the later
creation story. Man comes along at the end of the work of
creation and is obviously part of the series. Again, his earthi-
ness is fully recognized. But he alone is made in the "image"
of God. Early Christian theologians tended to think of this
"image" as man's rational nature. Man is the rational
(*logikos*) being because he has a share in the divine Word
(*Logos*), through whom the worlds were made. Modern
scholarship would consider the emphasis on reason as too
narrowly intellectualist a way of representing what is meant
by the divine image in man. A more existential interpretation
of the *imago Dei* is required, and perhaps we find it in the
notion of the openness of the human existent, for it is this
openness that lets him be transcendent and creative, and it
is in these respects that the likeness to God manifests itself.
But of course this understanding was present in the older
theology also, because of the association of the *Logos* with
creation. In any case, the mention of the divine image in the
P account of creation and the subsequent command to man to
subdue the earth marks him off as the creature with a
unique status.

The biblical stories of creation are far from a dualistic account of man. Here they may be contrasted with Gnostic and Manichean myths, in which man is compounded of radically different and incompatible elements. While the Bible recognizes the polarities of human existence, it conceives these to be embraced within a unity. In spite of his uniqueness, man belongs within the world. He is not an angel or some spiritual being that has fallen away and become entangled in an alien matter. Yet it is just because the unity of man is asserted that the tensions within that unity present such an urgent problem. These tensions threaten to tear man apart: possibility in conflict with facticity, aspiration in conflict with impotence, rationality contradicted by irrationality, the freedom of spirit tied down to the fate of the dust. As man began to reflect and to question, there was no problem more urgent or more difficult than simply the problem of identifying himself.

These biblical writers expressed their solution to the problem in their use of the word "God." Although men's ways of thinking about God have varied greatly, I believe there is a constant strand of meaning expressed in the word. It is a far cry from the mythologically conceived God of whom one could use language like "walking in the garden in the cool of the day" to the subtle concepts of God that are current in twentieth-century philosophy and theology, and yet in the discourse of religion the word has fundamentally the same use. Schubert Ogden put the matter very well when he wrote: "I hold that the primary use or function of [the word] 'God' is to refer to the objective ground in reality itself of our ineradicable confidence in the final worth of our existence."[5] It is this use that has remained constant through the changing images of God. The word "God" is used to express faith in being—faith in human existence but also, beyond that, in the ontological context of our existence. When men say "God,"

[5] *The Reality of God* (New York: Harper & Row, 1966), p. 37.

they are affirming that in spite of its polarities and in spite of the distortions into which these polarities can push us, human existence does make sense. The opposite point of view, the denial of God, regards human existence as fundamentally absurd or senseless. We may, according to this view, be able to construct limited areas of meaning and value, but in the end, man is absurd in the universe. His uniqueness is the uniqueness of a freak, a wild accident. This view finds classic expression in Sartre's famous description of man as the "useless passion." This does not prevent Sartre or anyone else who shares his view from pursuing worthwhile ends, but there is a fundamental pessimism in it all. One may sometimes wonder whether (as Ogden suggests, and as writers such as John Baillie and Karl Rahner have also contended) the professed atheist who devotes himself to moral aspirations is not an implicit or anonymous believer. But for my part, I hesitate to say anything of the sort, for it might seem to place in doubt the very integrity of the man whose moral commitment is being admired.

The doctrine of creation, then, aims at providing man with a self-understanding. It brings him to understand himself in the fundamental polarities of his being and goes on to assert that these polarities are not to be interpreted as a senseless and frustrating dualism but that they make sense and provide man with the raw material, as it were, for a great destiny. How do we link this doctrine with the education of the human race, understood as man's growth in knowledge and experience?

I have already alluded to the view that the biblical doctrine of creation was a major factor in the encouragement of scientific investigation, though I also indicated that this is a limited thesis. The ancient Hebrews, after all, though they had a doctrine of creation, were hardly distinguished for their scientific or technical prowess. They were inferior in war to their neighbors who had iron chariots, and in the arts of peacetime they had to call in foreigners for such projects as the building of the Temple. Christianity all but smothered the incipient science of Greece. Aristotle's accurate descriptions of animals were replaced by the medieval bestiaries, which were interested more in spinning out the alleged moral and spiritual "significations" of the animals than in giving information about their observable characteristics. There follows the sad story of the Church's repeated clashes with the men of science, astronomers, geologists, and biologists in turn. This opposition between the men of biblical faith and the men of science was not merely accidental, though contemporary theologians try to forget it. There is certainly no simple explanation of the immensely complex rootage of the Western scientific outlook, as those who have tried to write the history of the West have shown.

But if we avoid exaggerations, we can nevertheless acknowledge that the biblical doctrine of creation made its contribution. However, there are different opinions on how this contribution was made. There seem to be at least four ways of understanding it.

1. The first way focuses on man's special status in the scheme of creation and on the command to him that he should subdue the earth. This self-understanding contains within itself the drive toward the exploration and utilization of the earth's resources. Man becomes aware that he is not just a part of nature but has a unique power and dignity through which he can bring the earth and the phenomena of nature more and more under his control and more and more into his service. If one were to use the contemporary terminology of Teilhard de Chardin, one could say that, on this first view of the matter, the creation doctrine expresses the idea of "hominization." Within the created sequence there appears a being who, although belonging to that sequence, nevertheless transcends it in such a way that the control of the world, hitherto vested in impersonal laws of nature, is now being

transferred to the personal being who stands out from the world. Man stands out from the blind and passive system of nature as the transcending being in whom nature has become self-conscious and self-directing, so that even if one can still speak of a human "nature," one has to acknowledge that this nature has acquired an openness that does not belong to nature below the human level. Perhaps one could express precisely the same idea by saying that the biblical doctrine of creation points to the contrast between nature and history. Man does not have his being as part of a natural process but as one who makes and is made by history. It is well known, of course, that the biblical stories of creation were not unconnected with the Hebrew experience of history, and this indeed was implied in our earlier contention that the interest of these stories is anthropological rather than cosmological. In the words of Walther Eichrodt, "there was a deliberate linking up of creation with history."[6] One may contrast this view of man, which takes him out of nature and places him in history, with the Greek understanding of him as part of the cosmos. Yet even to say this is to be reminded of the complexity of these problems and of the inadequacy of any simple or one-sided answers, for it was the Greeks who advanced much further in science than ever the Hebrews did.

2. A second way of looking at the relation between the doctrine of creation and the rise of science stresses rather the profane character of the world. In pantheism, the world itself is divine; in polytheism, many beings within the world are either divine or demonic. So man feels himself inhibited in his handling of the world, and we all know how, in various countries, ancient superstitions can have a very oppressive effect on the people and may hinder the use and development of scientific methods in medicine, agriculture, and other fields. But in a doctrine of creation, the world is external to

[6] *Theology of the Old Testament*, trans. by J. A. Baker (London: Student Christian Movement Press, 1961), I, 231.

the Creator. God has become transcendent, and the world itself is cleared of divinity and left open to exploitation for the sake of man. The argument is well summarized by an eminent physicist of our time, Carl von Weizsäcker, who has himself been influenced by the Protestant theologian, Friedrich Gogarten:

> The gods of nature have been vanquished by the God whom Christians call "Our Father." Therefore man, as God's son, has received power over nature. As he is son, and not servant, he is free, and his freedom includes the freedom to act against the will of the Father, the God of love. He can now subject the world to himself, and secularism does precisely this.[7]

The last two sentences of the quotation, however, make it clear that the author considers the secular scientific outlook to have a decidedly ambivalent character, and to this we must return.

3. I must now draw attention to a somewhat different reading of the situation, found, for instance, in Karl Jaspers, and this reading is not easily harmonized with the one just expounded. On this third view, the stress is upon the dignity and worth of the world rather than on its profane character. God made the world and pronounced it to be good. It is therefore a worthy object on which man can bestow his thought and work. To say that the world is made by God and is therefore good separates the biblical doctrine of creation from all Manichean and dualistic views, according to which the material universe is essentially evil. If the physical universe is considered evil, then indeed there would be little incentive to scientific investigation. But something of this dualism was present in the Hellenic understanding of the world. Greek science failed to develop further than it did not because it lacked theoretical foundations but because it was not sufficiently empirical. The Greek scientist did not want to soil his

[7] *The Relevance of Science* (London: Collins, 1964), p. 178.

hands, so to speak, by getting immersed in experiments, so he dealt with the ideal objects of the mind. (This is a generalization to which there are obvious exceptions, such as Aristotle's observations of animals, mentioned above.) But when the world was understood as God's creation, it acquired a new dignity and the way was opened for empirical science. The point is perhaps best illustrated by contrasting Greek physics with modern physics.

4. There is still another way of looking at the matter. We mentioned that when they introduce the word "God," the old creation stories are declaring their fundamental faith that man's being-in-the-world makes sense. Although we thought of this primarily from the anthropological point of view, it clearly implies that the world makes sense, as does man's existence, as well. There is a *Logos* in the world as well as a *Logos* in man. Only the confidence that there is an order in the world could sustain the endeavor to discover this order. This faith in the orderliness of the world was called "cosmic religion" by one of the greatest scientists of modern times, Albert Einstein. "The most incomprehensible thing about the world," he declared, "is that it is comprehensible."[8] Einstein moreover thought of this "cosmic religion" as standing in historical continuity with the Old Testament.

But is all this merely of historical interest? Does it show that, among many other factors, the doctrine of creation contributed toward the rise of scientific inquiry in the West but that we have now outgrown that doctrine? It encouraged man to seek knowledge of natural phenomena, and this knowledge in turn allowed him to gain control over them. But now that man has taken over, is the doctrine of creation still of any significance or has it served its purpose?

Many writers who acknowledge the usefulness of the doctrine of creation in the Western tradition do in fact seem to think that this usefulness belonged only to the past and

---

[8] *Albert Einstein: Philosopher Scientist*, P. A. Schlipp, ed. (New York: Harper & Row, 1959), I, 248.

that today the doctrine is effete. But we have made it clear at the beginning of this essay that our own conclusion would be different and that we would try to show that the doctrine of creation has a continuing importance for the education of the human race.

A pointer in the direction in which we wish to move was already given when we noted Carl von Weizsäcker's reservations about the ambivalence of secularization and the rise of science. Actually, in the four points outlined above, we have presented a somewhat one-sided interpretation of the biblical material. Certainly, in the Bible, the shift from nature to history is not intended to eliminate God from the picture, for although history is constituted by man's free choices, it is still supposed to be under the providential control of God; and the history of the Old Testament is presented as the story of God's dealings with his people and the fulfilling of his purposes for them. So we have here something much more complex than simply a contrast between heteronomy and autonomy. It is not a question of a disjunction between man's being part of a cosmic system and his exercising an unrestricted freedom. Rather, the kind of history envisaged in the Bible implies a dialectical relationship between the freedom of man and the providence of God; or, to express this differently, man's freedom is set in a context of grace and judgment. But this dialectic is implicit also in the manner in which man is presented in the creation stories, for it is again one-sided to dwell on his transcendence of the world and to forget that he is also part of it. While man is indeed said to be made in the image of God, he is quite definitely assigned to the creation, and there is no merging of the human into the divine, in Hebrew thought, as there is in the classical conceptions of demigods and heroes. Indeed, in the story of the fall of man, it is the desire to be as God that is represented as his undoing.

These biblical ideas, I would claim, are not simply old-

fashioned remnants of the creation story which can now
be dispensed with. They belong integrally to that self-understanding that found expression in the creation narratives, and
we go wrong if we think that the import of these stories for
modern man is to be seen only in the handing over of the
world to man for his exploitation.

The important point that has also to be borne in mind is
that man's freedom is not an absolute, and that his position
in the world is not that of absolute sovereign but rather that
of steward. One contemporary philosopher who has expressed
very clearly in the context of a secular philosophy what is the
essence of the biblical insight is Martin Heidegger, who
writes in one place: "Man is not the lord of beings; he is the
guardian of Being."[9]

Man then is considered the steward or guardian of Being.
Perhaps the word that best expresses his relation to the world
in which he finds himself is "responsibility." He does not have
the world at his absolute disposal but is made responsible
for it. The terrible danger of the technological age, as already
hinted at by Carl von Weizsäcker, is that it may become
dominated by the subjective will-to-power. But man, who is
creaturely as well as self-transcending, must learn to understand himself as freely cooperating in an enterprise much
bigger than he knows about. He has to handle the creation
and make use of its resources with responsibility—not only a
responsibility toward other men, of his own generation and
of generations to come, but a responsibility toward the cosmos
as a whole, and a responsibility toward the mysterious creative source whom we call God. The development of such a
sense of responsibility is surely one of the most urgent needs
in the further education of the human race, and the biblical
doctrine of creation is very relevant in helping us toward
such a self-understanding. A doctrine of responsibility is a

[9] *Über den Humanismus* (Frankfurt-am-Main: Vittorio Kloster-
mann, 1947), p. 19.

reminder that there are no rights without corresponding duties and that talk about the rights of man must be correlated with an understanding of his obligations. Perhaps it is no accident that at this very time the idea of responsibility is apparently assuming a more important role in Christian thought. This idea is obviously a key one in the contemporary Catholic moral theology of Bernard Häring; while among Protestant thinkers, Fritz Buri makes the idea of responsibility central in his theological exposition. A responsible self-understanding is a major need of our contemporary world, and it may well be asked whether such responsibility can maintain itself apart from that vision of man and the world which found its classic expression in the biblical doctrine of creation.

II

AREAS OF KNOWLEDGE

9

THE SPIRIT OF SCIENCE AND MORAL INVOLVEMENT

JERROLD R. ZACHARIAS
Massachusetts Institute of Technology

T HE EDUCATIONAL POLICIES COMMISSION of the
National Education Association published, in 1966,
a booklet called *Education and the Spirit of Science*.[1] I read
it eagerly, because for many years I have found it so hard to
explain what is the spirit of science to someone who is not
himself a scientist or who has not spent many years in a
science laboratory or working with scientific theory.

It was, however, this very difficulty that aroused my
objections. As I wrote to I. I. Rabi, a member of the Commission and one of my oldest friends, who had sent me a
copy:

Thank you for sending me *Education and the Spirit of
Science*; I am very glad to have it. Surely it was written
by someone whose heart is on the right side of the issues,
but the account itself I consider to be repetitious and
mushy. It is hard for me to believe that it would be understandable to anyone who was not already convinced by
his own experience. . . .

I will try to send along some specifics in a few days,

[1] Washington, D.C.: Educational Policies Commission, National
Education Association of the United States, 1966.

specifics which might make the spirit of science more comprehensible.

My reactions were aimed primarily at a list of values "on which science is everywhere based" and that "characterize the enterprise of science as a whole." As cited in *Education and the Spirit of Science*, they are:

1. Longing to know and to understand
2. Questioning of all things
3. Search for data and their meaning
4. Demand for verification
5. Respect for logic
6. Consideration of premises
7. Consideration of consequences[2]

I have no objection to these statements, except insofar as I believe that one cannot understand them unless one has in mind specific examples. I believe that professional scientists, while they are exercising their profession as scientists, always work from specific examples, however simple or complex, to the awesome generality. And I believe that the only way to clarify this notion is for me to wallow in some specific examples so that you know what the discussion is about.

Longing to know and to understand. The spirit of science . . . seeks to understand because it accepts knowledge as desirable in itself. It expresses its curiosity endlessly, recognizing that questions are infinite, answers finite.[3]

What bothers me about this is simple. I do not believe that longing to know or understand is unique with science or scientists. Man is surrounded by an endless amount of mystery. And those of us who work in science content ourselves with trying to understand only a small part of this infinite mystery.

Let me give a specific example. Several years ago at the

[2] *Ibid.*, p. 15.
[3] *Ibid.*, p. 17.

beginning of the Kennedy Administration, the members of the President's Science Advisory Committee were discussing the advisability of endorsing a program to put a man on the moon. I was very much opposed to it. I thought that the expenditure of billions of dollars for that project would make the public content that it was indeed supporting science. But having a man·on the moon is only a very, very small part of what we hope to achieve scientifically in this century.

Finally it occurred to me that once we had satellites surrounding the earth, the public, including the scientific public, would become more curious about the physical laws that govern the behavior of a satellite. I remember thinking with pleasure that someday we would have, twenty-three thousand miles above a point on the earth's surface, a satellite that would be used as a transmitter and retransmitter of television and radio. People would wonder how man could put an object into space and hold it stationary with respect to us, without a skyhook, defying the law of gravity, and not falling into us.

The public, however, has not been aroused. To be sure, they are interested in the television and other communications that are transmitted and retransmitted. But Isaac Newton's very simple laws of motion, which explain how an object can remain poised as do the satellites, never seems to have affected the public, or even in fact the scientific public, except those people who happen to be interested in satellites or who need an example to teach a certain area of physics.

Why are so few people, with that supposed "longing to know and to understand," interested in an explanation of why the satellite stays there? I satisfy myself with a hypothesis pretty much as follows: a man is so accustomed to an infinite amount of mystery that understanding one little piece doesn't change that infinity at all. It's the nature of infinity that subtracting or adding doesn't change it.

My statement, then, about "longing to know and to understand" is that those of us who are professional scientists feel that just the experience of understanding, even though it be about something seemingly trivial, something simple, something not very deep, is enough to content us momentarily. We feel that one has to understand something simple in order to learn the nature of understanding itself. So we are content with some piece of understanding, whether or not it affects our entire structured understanding of everything. We feel it is better to understand something than to understand nothing, even though we cannot understand everything, or even very much.

> *Questioning of all things. Search for data and their meaning. Demand for verification.* There is no perfect knowledge and no perfect knower. Certainty, as a concept, is replaced by probability. All conclusions and decisions are more or less suspect; science rides on a preference for the less over the more.[4]

Again using examples, let me elaborate on certainty versus probability. I believe that the air I breathe, which is a mixture of gases, consists of molecules that are relatively far from one another, say ten molecule-diameters apart. They are as far apart as two people in a theater with ten seats between. And if you consider a theater so sparsely populated, a gas is not a very condensed substance.

One gets a little better feel for this if one condenses a gas. Whether nitrogen, oxygen, water vapor, or carbon dioxide is condensed into a liquid or a solid, the density changes by about a thousand. This means that the gas molecules are juxtaposed by a factor of about ten. The reason that the density is increased by a thousand, not ten, is that there are three dimensions. There are ten empty seats to the right and left, ten empty seats forth and back, and ten empty seats up and down. And ten times ten times ten is a thousand.

I further believe that these molecules in the gas of the air around us are moving roughly at the velocity of sound in air,

4 *Ibid.*, p. 17.

a thousand feet a second, or about thirty times as fast as a man can run. Going at all kinds of velocities in the neighborhood of this velocity—some faster, some slower—these molecules collide with one another and with the walls of the vessel and then bounce back. When they hit, they push on the wall, and the wall has to push on them to make them bounce back. It's turn and turnabout. The faster they move, the more momentum they carry; the heavier they are, the harder they push; and the harder they push on the wall, the harder the wall has to push back. The whole notion of gas as consisting of a chaotic collection of particles can be set up mathematically into what is known as the *kinetic theory of gases.*

If I ask students why they believe the kinetic theory of gases, they say, "It works, doesn't it?" or "It's accepted theory." And I say, "Yes, but on what experimental bases? How do you know? Why do you believe it? What's there?"

And we start. We start with some simple gas law such as, "The pressure of the gas times its volume is equal to the amount of gas and to its temperature ($PV=NRT$)." The hotter the temperature, everything else remaining constant, the higher will be the pressure. Everyone knows this. Just measure the pressure in your tires after driving at the speed limit on a hot summer day. Compare it with the pressure in that same tire before it's heated and after, to check.

In the equation $PV=NRT$, N is a measure of the amount of gas; T is the temperature; and R is a proportionality constant which, when measured for any gas, turns out to be 2 calories per gram molecular weight, or per *mole*. It's the same for all gases—already a miracle! You can measure this no matter what the gas—carbon dioxide, H_2O, H_2, argon, neon, and so on—and you keep getting the same constant, R, or 2 calories per mole.

For an entirely different kind of measurement, measure the amount of heat necessary to increase the temperature of a gas by 1° centigrade. Gas is an elusive thing. One can measure the amount of heat required to increase its temperature by holding its volume constant in a container that will not expand as the temperature rises, or one can try a similar experiment in an ordinary room in which the gas is free to expand so that its pressure, rather than its volume, remains constant. Obviously, in such experiments one must keep either the pressure or the volume constant.

Thus, the professionals have come to work with specific heat at constant volume, C_v, and specific heat at constant pressure, C_p. One can also measure the difference between C_v and C_p and lo and behold! what appears is that constant 2 calories per mole, the same constant, the same number for any gas, despite entirely different kinds of measurement.

Gases do more things. They are viscous; they resist the motion of something. For instance, the water droplets of a cloud are continually falling, but they're falling very slowly because of the viscosity of the air. Watch smoke coming out of a chimney, even on the most windless day. There it hangs. It has been going up because it was hot. But by the time it cools off, it just hangs in the air. It doesn't really "hang"; it is falling But it is falling slowly because of the viscosity of the air.

The kinetic theory of gases predicts that the viscosity of a gas is independent of pressure or density. For instance, if the air at high altitude, where the atmospheric pressure is low, were at the same temperature as sea level, smoke would fall at the same rate at high altitudes as at low. Your intuition would say that the denser the fluid through which the droplets fell, the more resistance there would be to the motion of the drops. What the theory predicts and what experiments support is against your intuition. If one measures the velocity of fall of smoke at pressure of one atmosphere, half an atmosphere, or a tenth of an atmosphere, the rate of fall is exactly the same in accordance with theory.

The theory predicts something else that is intuitively backward: as a gas becomes hotter, the viscosity gets higher rather than lower. Whereas your automobile engine is harder to start at lower temperature, because oil becomes more viscous, the opposite is true of gas. The kinetic theory predicts that the viscosity of a gas gets higher with higher temperature. I could provide all sorts of detailed support from actual measurements and actual observations. You can see that things fall at the same rate; you can see that something is more or less viscous without a lot of fancy measurements. Whenever you do this, the kinetic theory of gases is borne out.

For me, the molecular notion of a gas is a deep conviction. It is so deep that I don't feel that it can be just a probability. My conviction is so strong that I would bet everything I own, have, or could get on its veracity.

You might say, "That's a safe bet. What else could it be?" Well, just feel the air around you. Does it feel like a bunch of molecules colliding with you? Doesn't it feel rather like some kind of continuous, gauzy, vaporous, structureless, expansible fluid? After all, you can pour a heavy gas into a light gas. Gas does have many of the properties of fluids. But no one has ever found any evidence that disagrees with the kinetic theory of gases or any predictions that have not been verified.

That is the nature of a deep conviction. Not all notions in science have that particular depth. I've picked that specific one because to break or to overthrow it would require changing the results of already performed experiments that indicate that this belief is correct. This conviction is so deep that I would be willing to call it absolute, contrary to the caveats of *Education and the Spirit of Science.*

To be sure, there are some theories about which my conviction is considerably less solid. So let's go to the opposite extreme.

Astronomers often state that the distant galaxies beyond

ours are retreating from us with velocities that are proportional to their distances from us. This sounds incredible at first. It gives the feeling that we must be at the center of something. That is not, however, a necessary consequence. Imagine, for instance, that you are inside a large assemblage of things and that the whole assemblage is expanding. Then everything would be moving away from you, no matter which member of the group you were.

The theory of the behavior of galaxies goes even further. It says that the farther away the galaxy, the faster it is moving. We don't have much evidence for this. There is some in the form of the spectra of some of the atoms, which we believe are like atoms here on earth. The spectra of those atoms are shifted toward the red, indicating that their wavelengths are longer or their frequencies are less. And this can be interpreted as an indication that they are moving away from us. But the lack of much additional evidence leaves a weak belief.

When I suggested to a friend how improbable it is that the galaxies are moving away from us at speeds proportional to their distances away, he countered, "How would you like to have them? Fixed? Is that any more probable? Does that satisfy you any more?" I admitted that it did not.

But its still a weak belief, and if some notion came along such as the peculiarities of the space between us and the galaxies, I would not be surprised.

Respect for logic. Consideration of premises. Logic is the science of valid inference.[5]

Let me get to basic difficulties here right away. When all of us were younger and in secondary school we learned about a logical structure with Euclid. Euclid set up axioms and ways of operating with these axioms which resulted in theorems.

I remember how strange it was to go through a page or

[5] *Ibid.*, p. 19.

so of proof of something that seemed perfectly obvious. I remember explicitly one theorem that we were supposed to prove: *If you consider a point remote from a circle and draw two tangent lines from the point to the circle, the lengths of those tangent lines from the point to their tangency are equal.*

I don't remember the proof anymore, but I do remember my reaction: that it was a silly thing to do, to go through a lot of equations to prove something that was obvious. That object with the two tangent lines was symmetrical: all you had to do was turn it over. You couldn't say which tangent line was which; therefore, they must be equal.

I've confronted mathematicians subsequently with this very fundamental objection of a child to the nature of Euclid. They say very simply that the notion of using symmetry to prove something of this sort is powerful, clean, clear, and useful. But Euclid's axioms in this case were restricted to a plane. He could not invoke symmetry; he could not turn something over because he could not get out of plane. By turning something over, even in your head, you are getting out of the plane.

Logic, in other words, can be very constraining. So we must be sure to use not just *restrictive* formulations of logical representations of nature, but we must use formulations as *general* as man can think of. Not just for shortcuts, but because we have no sureness that our intuitive notions, which would help us set up our axiomatic system, are the right ones.

For an example I shall pick special relativity. Everyone is accustomed to thinking of space as space and time as time. They are not in the least confusable. Who would ever dream of measuring how far it is from here to there with a watch, or measuring how much time has passed by measuring the distance? Our intuitive notions are really straight on this. The only trouble is that they are wrong.

Even to define a space or a time, one has to use notions of simultaneity. When two simultaneous events are at the same point in space—right at the observer—simultaneity is simple to state and to understand. Consider, however, two events like a flash of lightning ten miles away and a flash of lightning one mile away. The signals, the flashes of lightning, take time to get to us. And so, if you ask, "Were the two lightning bolts simultaneous?" the answer depends on where the observer is. If the observer is halfway between the two lightning flashes, he might see them at the same time. But if he's off to either side, he sees them at different times. So simultaneity itself is relative and depends on space.

Now the reason I go into all these particulars of this particular point is that logic with people who work with nature is only partial. We live with a great many half-baked notions. Even our "logical" notions of space and time are half-baked. So the sentence, "Logic is the science of valid inference," leaves out that whole and most important notion that for the study of nature logic is a very "iffy" business.

> *Consideration of consequences.* Awareness of implications can, like the rest of knowledge, at best be incomplete. But a rational person does not accept a value or decide upon action without trying to be aware of its implications.[6]

It is so tempting to believe that a physicist should be selfless and valueless, that he should not make moral judgments because he cannot substantiate moral judgments in the same scientific way that he validates his belief in simple and direct affairs of nature. But there is more than this. A professional scientist lives an ethical life, in the science at least, for a very simple reason. If he were to publish something that he thought was not correct, he would know perfectly well that his conclusions would not last long. Nor would his reputation last long with his fellows.

It bothers me very much indeed that C. P. Snow, who claims to have been a physicist, has written a novel in which

[6] *Ibid.*, pp. 20–21.

the leading character, a physicist, falsifies some photographs. It just doesn't happen, except in those peculiar cases when the man becomes no longer a scientist but insane. There have been several cases in the last century of professional scientists who have gone out of their minds. And in a couple of those instances they falsified data.

Once more I cite an example. A few years ago, when scientists in the Soviet Union took photographs of the backside of the moon and distributed them to the world, a friend asked me, "Are they not just possibly faking? After all, none of us knows what the other side of the moon looks like. Couldn't they just say they went there and then send us a photograph?"

I laughed and said, "No. They may be Russians, but they are scientists. And they know they can't fake. It would hurt them if they did; it would hurt their souls."

At this point, instead of talking about moral consequences, I am switching to the education of children. I believe one can let children learn science, not only for its own sake, but also as a way to develop intellectual strength, intellectual integrity, and intellectual agility.

There are two questions here: (1) Is it possible to bring up children in a way so that they do not fall prey to dogmatism? (2) Besides listening to the precepts, guidance, knowledge, and prejudgments of their elders, can they understand —in their "guts," not just in their heads—that it is possible to learn about evidence by working with nature?

The nature with which they work must be uncomplicated enough, repeatable enough, simple enough, manageable enough, so that the children can close an experience within a finite number of weeks. If one takes the behavior of human beings as the subject on which to operate, the natural perversity of people who are sensitive to being watched makes it very difficult to find a clear piece of sociological data, uncolored by the reactions of the observed.

Two or three years ago in a meeting devoted to a study of medical education, one surgeon pointed out that psychiatry was so difficult because human beings are not predictable. I said, "Nonsense. It's just that we believe that what is predictable is trivial. For instance, I predict with almost complete certainty that of the forty people at this meeting, no one will appear naked at the breakfast tomorrow." Quick as a flash, two psychiatrists retorted, "Don't make the stakes too high."

On the other hand, let us look at how Roger Payne handled a study of seedlings with a class of elementary school children while he was developing a science unit for Educational Services Incorporated. The children had viewed a time-lapse film that showed bean seedlings raising and lowering their leaves in time with the day-night, darkness-light cycle. An observation that the plants grew upward rather than at an angle led to a discussion of whether or not a plant needed light to decide which way to grow. This question brought others and finally a decision to experiment with seeds, which the children themselves planted in varying conditions of light. Light from varying angles, absence of light, and light in different colors were tried on oat seeds planted in all sorts of containers. The teacher did not need to know any answers. In fact the children were better off and happier if the teacher professed ignorance and let them learn directly from the plants—from the stuff of nature itself. And their observations raised more questions—about the effects of gravity, temperature, moisture, and so on—questions the children themselves asked and sought answers to.

One aspect of science is that every time you ask a question, you almost always raise more questions than you answer. Science, then, is not an endless frontier but an expanding frontier. The more we understand, the more we see the tenuous nature of our innocent assumptions, as I mentioned before in talking about space and time.

Now I think I'm ready to say why I think science—not as a discipline but as something you've been brought up in, "a way of life"—has something to do with moral values. Let us use an example that strikes close to home. Some ten or fifteen years ago I was in a smoking compartment of a Pullman car, talking to a friend about control of atomic weapons. Rather casually I asked, "How many deaths and casualties do you think the United States could stand and still survive? As many as a few million? Or could we stand the slaughter of even twenty million?"

A man who seemed to be asleep sitting near us jumped to attention. "My God!" he exclaimed. "Do you realize you are talking about the possible extermination of 10 percent of the population of the country?"

I looked him squarely in the eye—he was still a bit shocked—and said, "No, sir. We're probably talking about the extermination of all of it, and every other man, too. One has to figure out where the limit would be."

The purpose of saying this kind of shocking thing here—and it shocks me, too, if only because it is possible to say—is to indicate the kind of person who has lived a life of trying to obey the Ten Commandments. So long as the world is in such a condition as to make it almost impossible to live by any particular moral law or precept, we must regard morality and the study of it as a living subject, just as alive as the forefront of any intellectual activity we engage in.

Why do I believe that living a life associated with scientific attitudes is beneficial to the understanding of moral issues, to trying to formulate moral principles? I guess it's because it comes natural for someone brought up with scientific attitudes to reject dogma or at least to look at dogma with a skeptical eye. Every time some scientific idea is taken for granted, we find we have to look further. Sometimes the agreement between nature and the dogmatic formulation is far from satisfactory. So naturally those of us who are professional scientists look at moral values in much the same way.

A few years ago I was one of many people who were frightened when the antipolio vaccine of Jonas Salk was introduced to the public in a wholesale way. I would have been more content to have taken our chances with the introduction of this radical vaccine to some fraction of the population. Validating a vaccine or medication of any sort does not require a sample as large as the total population. Ten or 20 percent of the population—a large sample—would have been enough. But polio is such a dreadful disease that it seemed to a great many professional physicians that the country was not taking too big a risk. Delaying the general application of the vaccine long enough to evaluate it fully would almost certainly have cost the lives of potential polio victims. Some group of people had to make a value judgment. They had to take their chances, and they took them with their eyes wide open.

It was a success story, but it need not have been. And what would we have thought then? "Those hard-boiled professional scientists don't care about human life." But it was exactly about human life that they were caring. It took a tremendous lot of thought, investigation, and weighing of evidence in order to reach a conclusion.

The method of handling large issues demands very careful weighing of all sorts of evidence, weighing one man's evaluation of human life against another's. Take, for instance, the now controversial issue of the bombing of North Vietnam. Many people have studied the problem of the bombing of the North, or they've studied the reasons for our involvement in Vietnam. But I have never heard of a study of this problem in which the primary aim was to determine the *moral* issues.

I propose that we go at moral issues explicitly but in a very substantive way. I believe that one doesn't understand moral issues without saying that moral issues are what you are going to work on. I am not saying that you can understand the moral problems in the Vietnam War without understanding the war itself, why we are there, what the involvement of other countries might or might not be, or what our emotional reactions to communism are or should be. One cannot separate his actions from practical issues. Moral judgments that are independent of practical issues are most likely to be unsound.

Every time scientists pull together groups that are man enough, strong enough, diverse enough, committed enough, and willing to spend time enough to understand something, we advance understanding. Sometimes we come to a very sharp decision and act on that. A scientist is explicit; he doesn't merely listen to somebody's statement. Those of us involved in science know perfectly well that every idea, no matter how simple sounding, is in fact very complex. It takes a lot of thought and study. And moral issues deserve just as much care as scientific issues.

Someone will reply, "But moral issues have been studied over the centuries by all sorts of extraordinary people. Take St. Augustine, or this man, or that man. . . ." The world is different now. They did not have atom bombs to worry about, or biological warfare, or machine guns, or the population density that we have, with its broken families or its particular form of racial violence and oppression, and so on and so on. It all has to be done again, and it will have to be done over again. One has to *continue* to do it to keep morality a living subject, as science is.

There is no special magic to the method of science. There is, however, a strange kind of humility that states simply, "Pay only small heed to the dogma; just remember that every question is more difficult than you think."

When do you make a decision on a moral issue? Anytime; you *constantly* have to make decisions. At what point do you know? There is no sharp way. A scientist decides to "finish" an experiment when additional time doesn't change the values very much. He says, "I could improve this with another two weeks or so, but I wouldn't improve it very much. In fact, it might go downhill." And when you're dealing with a moral issue, you say, "We have gone just about as far as we can go in our thinking, and now we must act." It's a good question: How do you know when to stop?

10

BIOLOGY AND HUMAN VALUES

JOHN T. EDSALL
Harvard University

The Inherent Values of Science

T HE PURSUIT OF SCIENCE, considered as the search for
the deepest possible understanding of the universe and
all that it contains, represents one of the supreme values of
life in our civilization. In an era so filled with turmoil,
hostility, and destruction as ours, such achievements as the
development of quantum mechanics and the unraveling of
the genetic code are among the few events of the modern
world of which our descendants may be unreservedly proud.
A deep appreciation of the value of science as such does
indeed require prolonged and arduous discipline; the value of
a deeper insight into the world, for the sake of the illumination that insight brings, is acknowledged by many but fully
appreciated by relatively few.

Science today, as a body of coherent knowledge, is certainly
one of the supreme creations of man. It differs from all, or
nearly all, of the great intellectual constructions of the past in
being coherent yet tentative, based in experimental fact but
subject always to modification by new discoveries. There are
branches of science that for many of us have a profound
aesthetic appeal, comparable to that of the greatest works of
art. I remember when, after many painful struggles as a

[157]

learner, I began to master the fundamental concepts of thermodynamics and to see the power of their application to solving vast numbers of special problems by the guiding light of a few great principles. It was like the vision one attains from the top of a great mountain after an arduous climb, an abiding vision that no one who has experienced it will forget, though he may forget all the details of what he has learned. But science is also messy and confused; it is full of unexplained, puzzling bits of information that do not yet fit into any coherent scheme; of experiments that go wrong, and of constant alternations of discouragement and elation for the investigator. No scientist today, even after a lifetime of devotion to the subject, can clearly see more than a few corners of its vast structure. Indeed it is no static structure but a growing organism, growing indeed at present with fabulous speed and extending pseudopodia in all directions.

This slightly grotesque image, however, scarcely does justice to the beauty of the subject or to its appeal and fascination for the scientist. The broad vistas of science are for me, as I think they are for many others, a constant source of inspiration. Whether one's own work is going well or badly at the moment, it is good for the scientist to live in the constant presence of the great visions that science offers.

In what follows,[1] I lay particular stress on modern biology, its inherent value, and its influence on the general life of mankind. Biology, especially in its relations to physics and chemistry, is the science I know best. Moreover, I believe that biology is now at the very center of scientific activity, and that its recent and probable future discoveries have the profoundest human implications.

[1] Parts of this chapter are drawn from the Seymour Korkes Memorial Lecture, which I delivered at Duke University on April 6, 1967. I wish to thank my colleagues there, and in particular Dr. and Mrs. Philip Handler, for the hospitality shown to me during that visit.

Some Effects of Science in the Modification of Ethical Values

What I have said hitherto applies largely to science as seen by the scientist himself, but the relation of science to human values extends far beyond this. The great vistas of space and time which modern science has opened up, the perspectives of evolution, and the interrelation of all living creatures—these affect the outlook of vast numbers of people throughout the world today. I am tempted to say "of most people," but this would be untrue, since hundreds of millions of people in the world today live completely without knowledge of these conceptions that modern science has introduced. Nevertheless such knowledge, rapidly or slowly, spreads and permeates the thought of people everywhere and modifies their outlook and their aspirations.

Some scientists and philosophers have said that science is ethically neutral, without influence on human values—that it is significant only as a tool, enabling us to realize our aims more effectively but in itself without influence on the nature of those aims. This I do not believe. In doing experiments and recording results, of course, it is essential to guard against our own desires and preconceptions, and to do everything we can to avoid letting them distort our findings. But in the larger sense, as science grows, as our broad picture of the world and of man is enlarged and deepened by it, and as its consequences for the world become ever more apparent, it becomes one of the major forces that modifies and remolds our concepts of what is good, what is tolerable, and what is intolerable in human life and conduct. These are not abstract issues; they involve many of the deepest personal and social conflicts of our time.

The relation between the progress of science and the change in our sense of values is obvious in many things. A polluted city water supply was at one time an unpleasant but tolerated nuisance; when it became known that it was also a carrier of typhoid fever and other diseases it became in effect a crime to tolerate such things. After these achievements of modern public health, which came toward the beginning of our century, or even earlier, we are again threatened by pollution on a far wider scale than before—a pollution that threatens the whole environment. To this grave problem I return later.

In matters of still deeper human import, also, such as the institution of slavery, the progress of science and technology has led gradually to a profound change in moral attitudes. For centuries a few sensitive and high-minded men denounced the practice of human slavery, but it persisted because it was woven deeply into the economic structure of most earlier societies. As technical advances made new sources of energy available, the compelling need for slave labor grew less and approached the vanishing point; in Europe and America hardheaded businessmen joined the humanitarian idealists, and practical politicians rallied to support the antislavery movement. I do not mean, of course, that the progress of science was the only reason for the abolition of slavery—the world is far too complex to be explained by any such simple theories—but the scientific advances were an indispensable component of the whole change in moral outlook.

One of the most profound changes in general outlook in our time—a change common to East and West, though manifested in different ways—is the rising general conviction that a good life is possible for most men on this earth. Men are discarding the past attitude of resignation to a world predominantly characterized by suffering and want, in which they looked to a better world to come, having few hopes of this one. Now increasingly their desires and hopes are centered in the present world. One may approve or disapprove this trend; that, for the moment, is not the point. These new hopes may prove to be illusory, in view of the grim realities of the world today. My point is that the trend exists, that it represents a fundamental shift in the value judgments of mankind, and that it is a direct consequence of the progress of pure and applied science.

The very temper and attitude of mind that permit science to flourish must in themselves produce conflicts with many traditional values. The scientist is forced to guard against his preconceptions, to be on the watch for them and eliminate them whenever possible, to regard all his conclusions as in some degree tentative and subject to further modification in the light of experience. This attitude may remain limited; the scientist may apply it only to the particular range of problems that he deals with in the laboratory; but inevitably it tends to spread and becomes the basis of our approach to broader issues. Inevitably it is disturbing, for it clashes with traditional ways of thought and dogmatic belief, which are deeply rooted; these are the product of generations of men, and they are charged with powerful emotions. These traditional attitudes are generally the product of instinctive wisdom; they have grown up without logical foundation, as useful beliefs generally do, but with profound relevance to human needs in the society in which they arose. As the world changes, these beliefs may become irrelevant, sometimes dangerously irrelevant; and in our time such changes are brought about predominantly by the progress of science and technology. The scientist generally sees these changes and their implications sooner than most other people; this is not surprising, since, generally, scientists have helped to bring them about.

I see three great areas today in which the clash between the traditional wisdom and the forces that compel a revision of our outlook is particularly acute—first, in our attitude to war, aggression and resistance to aggression; second, in human fertility and the command to be fruitful and multiply; and third, in the need to guard and improve our natural resources rather than squandering them. All three are intimately related. The most precious of all our natural resources is the biological and social inheritance of mankind, and this is threatened by modern war, in a manner totally unprecedented. One of the major pressures that can lead to war, now as in the past, is the pressure of expanding and hungry populations; and this has increased, and is increasing, with a speed hitherto unknown. Population growth is likewise the great devourer of natural resources. Science and technology have shown that it is possible to make the world a pleasanter place for the ordinary man than he could ever have dreamed in the past. When there are more people than ever before, and each man asks more of the good things of life than ever before in history, we consume more food, more metals, more fuels, in fifty years than in all the previous history of mankind; and even this is small compared to what we may expect in the next fifty years.[2]

I return later to these themes, after turning first to some of the major advances in modern biology and their implications.

The Revolution in Biochemistry and Molecular Biology: Achievements and Prospects

In 1923 J. B. S. Haldane, one of the most versatile scientists of our time, published a small booklet called "Daedalus: or Science and the Future." In this he predicted that, although the center of scientific interest at that time lay in physics, our century in science would be preeminently the era of biology. Haldane began his scientific career as a biochemist; he became an eminent geneticist; and it is significant that

[2] I have spoken here necessarily in broad general terms; the detailed evidence is to be found in many places. See for instance that fascinating and disturbing book by Harrison Brown, *The Challenge of Man's Future* (New York: The Viking Press, 1954).

the most dramatic advances in modern biology have come in the fusion of these two fields of research. However, Haldane's prophecy appeared to remain unfulfilled for some twenty years after he made it. In spite of many brilliant advances in biology and biochemistry, the period from 1920 to 1945 was predominantly the period of great advances in nuclear physics. Since the end of World War II, however, events have abundantly verified Haldane's prophecy. A great turning point in biology came, indeed, in a paper published in the midst of the war. Avery, MacLeod, and McCarty in 1944 demonstrated that the "transforming factor" of pneumococcus, which brought about the transformation of this organism from a form without a capsule to an encapsulated form, was deoxyribonucleic acid (DNA); thus DNA was indeed the essential material for transmitting hereditary information. For some years the full significance of this epoch-making discovery was unappreciated; indeed it was not until 1953, when Crick and Watson deduced the two-chain structure of DNA, coiled in a double helix, that a clear-cut chemical basis for understanding the transmission of hereditary information emerged.

These achievements launched the prodigious development of what is now commonly called molecular biology. However, we must remember that the recent rapid advances were made possible by a long previous period of solid but less spectacular developments, in genetics and in biochemistry, extending over a period of a century or more. The patient laborious investigations of the chemists who investigated proteins from about 1840 on, and nucleic acids from 1870 on, laid the essential foundations of structural knowledge that were necessary for the rapid flowering of molecular biology in the last twenty years. Classical genetics, beginning with Mendel, and continuing with William Bateson, T. H. Morgan, H. J. Muller, and many others, had built up a magnificent and largely self-contained theory of genes and their manifestations in organisms, solidly based on a vast number of experimental facts.[3] Shortly after 1900, proof was obtained that the genes were located in the chromosomes, within the cell nucleus; but their chemical nature remained obscure until the work of Avery *et al* and of Crick and Watson.[4] Each of the two complementary strands of the DNA helix is a chain with many links, perhaps tens or hundreds of thousands; but there are only four different kinds of links. These are the four purine and pyrimidine bases, which for short we may designate as A, G, C, and T. Of these, G in one chain is complementary to C in the other, and conversely; similarly for A and T. Thus a short section of the double helix might be represented diagrammatically by a pattern such as:

$$\text{-G-T-T-C-A-A-A-C-G-}$$

. . . .

. . . .

. . . .

$$\text{-C-A-A-G-T-T-T-G-C-}$$

Here the upper and lower lines of letters represent short segments of the two complementary chains of the helix. The vertical dotted lines connecting the upper and lower lines are symbols for the hydrogen bonds which chemically determine the complementary relations. Note that G in one chain is always opposite C in the other, and A is opposite T; thus the sequence in either chain completely specifies that in the other. Each chain has thus a pattern complementary to the other; on replication, each guides the formation of a chain complementary to itself, and thus both are reproduced. In proteins there is nothing like this sort of complementarity,

[3] See T. H. Morgan, *The Theory of the Gene* (New Haven: Yale University Press, 1925).

[4] For a further historical account of the development of ideas concerning the nature of the genetic material, see for instance B. Glass, "A Century of Biochemical Genetics," *Proceedings of the American Philosophical Society*, 109 (1965), 227.

thus proteins are not suitable as the transmitters of heredi-tary information. It is the pattern of the sequence in the four bases in each chain that contains the information transmitted to the next generation, by replication of the DNA. By another process, known as transcription, the DNA chains of the cell nucleus form, complementary chains of ribonucleic acid (RNA) containing the four bases G, C, A, and U (the latter in RNA corresponds to T in DNA, and is closely related to it). These pass from the nucleus into the cytoplasm, attach themselves there to the structures known as ribosomes, and thereby serve to guide the formation of proteins.

Proteins are synthesized, like nucleic acids, in the form of long chains with many links. In this case these links are the twenty amino acid residues that are found everywhere in nature, from bacteria to man. It is now clear that a triplet of successive bases in the nucleic acids determines a single amino acid residue in a protein chain: for instance, the triplet sequence UAU or UAC determines the amino acid tyrosine and AAA or AAG determines lysine. The mutation of a single unit in one of these triplets can lead to the ap-pearance of a different amino acid residue in the protein whose structure is determined by the gene in question. Such changes indeed are the fundamental units of biological mutation.

This set of relations between the base triplets and the amino acids constitutes the genetic code, which specifies the relation between the nucleic acids and the proteins whose structures they specify.[5] The proteins, in turn, play the central

[5] The best general survey of modern molecular biology is probably J. D. Watson's *Molecular Biology of the Gene* (New York: W. A. Benjamin, 1965). It is written with great lucidity but requires a basic knowledge of chemistry. On a more technical level the sym-posium on *The Genetic Code* (Cold Spring Harbor, N.Y.: Cold Spring Harbor Symposia in Quantitative Biology, 1966), Vol. XXXI, presents an impressive array of recent discoveries. One may partic-ularly recommend the opening article by F. H. C. Crick, "The Genetic Code—Yesterday, Today, and Tomorrow."

part in almost all the other activities of the organism. They constitute the structural framework of tissues like muscle, tendon, and hair; and in their myriad different forms they become enzymes that catalyze every biochemical process.

Proteins are molecules of such complexity that for a long time it seemed an almost hopeless task to decipher their structure in detail. During the last twenty years, however, the structures of a substantial number of proteins have been completely worked out. Not only do we know the exact order of the amino acid residues in many proteins, but in several instances—as with the oxygen-carrying protein myoglobin and the enzyme lysozyme, which attacks bacterial cell walls —we know with high precision the three-dimensional architecture of the molecule and the arrangement of the active site where the enzyme attacks its substrate. Moreover, the synthesis of proteins by the organic chemists, which seemed an impossible dream a few years ago, is now becoming a reality. Insulin, one of the simpler proteins, has now been made synthetically by three groups of researchers, one of them in China. There is every prospect that, within a generation, chemists will create synthetic enzymes to catalyze reactions not promoted by any enzyme found in nature. Thereby they may produce in industrial chemistry a revolution that will permit many processes, now proceeding only at high temperature and in poor yield, to run smoothly and with high yield at ordinary temperatures.

Regulation of Biochemical Activity

In recent years we have gained new insight into the factors that regulate and control the operations of living organisms. That organisms require such regulatory mechanisms has been apparent since the time of Aristotle, and probably since long before. In modern times such concepts were emphasized in the nineteenth century by Claude Bernard, who pointed out that the constancy of the internal environment—*i.e.*, primarily the circulating blood, in higher organisms—is an essential condition for the freedom of the organism. Walter Cannon expanded the concept of homeostasis, including the regulatory controls involved in the interaction of the hormones and the organs on which they act; and the integrative action of the nervous system had been manifest long before Sir Charles Sherrington published a famous book with that title just over sixty years ago.

In recent years, biochemists have discovered the existence of regulatory controls at a deeper level. Not only does the genetic material contain the regions that direct the synthesis of specific proteins; these regions are under the control of other genetic factors, the operator genes, that determine whether the biosynthesis of specific proteins under the control of a given operator, shall or shall not proceed. The synthetic processes cannot be allowed to run at full speed all the time; that would be intolerably wasteful. The proteins manufactured under the guidance of the genetic material are not wanted all the time or in unlimited quantities. Much of the time—indeed most of the time, for many genes—the operator gene is held in check by the attachment of a repressor; this "turns off" the synthesis of the specific enzymes that are under the control of a particular operator. If the cell lacks the molecules on which these enzymes act, there is no need to produce the enzymes. If such molecules then enter the cell, they may act as "inducers," combining with the repressor and thereby causing it to release its grip on the operator gene, so that the synthesis of the necessary enzymes can proceed. Thus, in the economy of the cell, these enzymes are manufactured only when needed.[6] There is now decisive evidence, due primarily to very recent work of Walter Gilbert and Mark Ptashne at Harvard, that the repressor molecules are proteins. Although these genetic mechanisms have been established most clearly in bacteria, it seems almost certain that similar processes operate in all higher organisms also.

Another form of control, feedback inhibition, operates, not to prevent formation of the enzyme, but to regulate its activity after it is formed. Many biochemical processes involve sequences of reactions which lead to the synthesis of some essential chemical substance, from the starting materials that the cell has available. Starting with a substance A, for example, the sequence may lead to an essential biochemical substance F by a series of intermediate steps, each catalyzed by a specific enzyme:

$$A \rightarrow B \rightarrow C \rightarrow D \rightarrow E \rightarrow F$$

If substance F accumulates, beyond the current needs of the organism, it is obviously economical to shut down the whole process, partially or completely. In feedback inhibition this is indeed what occurs: F combines with the enzyme that converts A to B, and the F-enzyme combination thereby loses its capacity to catalyze this process. If B is not being made, all the later steps in the process automatically shut down also, since the starting material is no longer available. If the concentration of F falls, the F-enzyme complex dissociates, the free enzyme becomes active once more, and the whole process resumes. Such processes beautifully regulate the flow of matter and energy in the cell; they serve to insure that there is enough but not too much of each of the various essential metabolic substances. It is a beautiful piece of biological engineering, which makes exacting demands on the design of the enzyme that catalyzes the conversion of A to B. This enzyme not only binds molecule A, in the process of converting it to B; it must also bind F, a very different molecule, at some other point of attachment on the enzyme surface; and the binding of F must somehow alter the enzyme reversibly so that its capacity to convert A to B is temporarily diminished or abolished. In spite of these stringent specifications, enzymes that fulfill them have evolved again and again, and they are of the utmost importance in biology.[6]

These advances in our understanding of biological regulation foreshadow future advances in areas still uncharted. Perhaps the domain of our greatest ignorance in biology today is in the field of development. How does a complex organism, with its many different organs and with complicated interactions between them, emerge from a fertilized ovum? The anatomical patterns in the development of the embryo have been known in detail for a long time; but the underlying nature of the processes involved, on the molecular level, is still most obscure. The great advances of recent years in biochemical genetics, and in the processes of regulatory control—so briefly sketched above—offer suggestive clues that may lead to a future revolution in our understanding of development and differentiation. No one can forecast the time and character of a scientific revolution before it occurs, but there is a pervading belief among biologists that such a revolution in our knowledge of development is sure to come, and that it is not very far away. When it comes, it will certainly throw floods of light on matters and problems now obscure—on the nature and control of cancer, for example, and on other problems that may be of still greater importance to mankind.

Some Effects and Implications of Modern Biology

What now of the direct effects, on mankind at large, of the revolutionary new knowledge in biochemistry and genetics? As yet the intellectual excitement this new knowledge has generated has far outrun its practical effects; but such effects

[6] Much of our insight into these phenomena is due to J. Monod, F. Jacob, and their collaborators. For further information, see, for instance, J. Monod, J.-P. Changeux, and F. Jacob, "Allosteric Proteins and Cellular Control Systems," *Journal of Molecular Biology*, 6 (1963), 306; D. E. Atkinson, "Regulation of Enzyme Activity," *Annual Review of Biochemistry*, 35 (1966), 85; J. T. Edsall, "The Organization of Protein Molecules for Regulatory Processes in Biology," *Proceedings of the American Philosophical Society*, 111 (1967), 59.

are sure to follow, as they have from other great fundamental discoveries.

One practical effect is to emphasize a major aspect of the conservation movement—the conservation of the most precious of our natural resources, our genetic heritage. The integrity of the thin delicate threads of the nucleic acids, with their encoded patterns of base sequences, is essential to the future of mankind, as to all other living creatures. Consciousness of this responsibility has led to greatly increased care in the medical use of X rays. It has also influenced public policy, for public awareness of the genetic dangers of radiation was certainly one of the factors that led to the limited nuclear test ban treaty of 1963. (Personally I would rate the slowing of the nuclear arms race as a far more important reason for the treaty, but that does not affect the point made above.) And it has implanted widely the conviction that a nuclear war, for whatever cause it might be fought, would be an unprecedented crime against mankind—in the most literal sense, a betrayal of our inheritance, on a colossal scale. Apart from the hundreds of millions of deaths, the vast social disruption, the desolation of the land, and the ecological changes that such a war would bring, there is the consciousness that the descendants of the survivors would pay a terrible price—exacted by us—for countless generations to come. Insofar as knowledge of genetics is widely diffused and deeply understood throughout the nations of the world, it can act as one influence toward sanity and restraint in the effort to prevent nuclear war.

What of the hopes for more positive aid to mankind from genetic knowledge? I am as yet mistrustful of programs for positive eugenics; I believe that we still know far too little about human heredity to offer wise and practicable plans for improving the quality of the human race. Social policies that encourage the intelligent and able to have children, and discourage the incompetent and shiftless from having them, should do some genetic good and are unlikely to do harm;

but in view of our present ignorance, one should not exaggerate the possible good. Nor should we concentrate too heavily on intelligence as a quality to be promoted by genetic selection; kindheartedness and generosity of spirit are at least as important for a good world, and the best parents do not always have the best brains.

The great recent advances in genetics have come chiefly from the study of bacteria and viruses. However, there is, I think, some reason to hope that our knowledge of human heredity may increase profoundly in the next generation. It is now readily possible to examine the chromosomes of man or any other species, quite rapidly and simply, and to detect abnormalities that before could have been overlooked. Moreover, with modern tissue-culture techniques, we can propagate cells from human tissues and study them in culture. In such cultures it may be possible to make a far more detailed genetic analysis of the constitution of a particular individual than is possible today, and perhaps to detect recessive genes, not apparent in the phenotype of the individual himself, that would otherwise remain unknown until they might appear in homozygous form in some of his descendants. One may even imagine a file of such genetic data for each individual, and a computer program in which prospective mates could combine their personal data and receive in reply an evaluation of at least some of the characteristics of their possible children. Clearly this is at present a flight of fantasy, but I believe that it is nevertheless a genuine possibility.

Some eminent biologists, notably Joshua Lederberg, have proposed programs of "genetic engineering" whereby undesirable genes could be modified in, or lacking genes introduced into, people suffering from genetic abnormalities.[7] In bacteria this can be done by transformation, as in the studies

[7] See, for instance, J. Lederberg "Biological Future of Man" in *Man and his Future*, A Ciba Foundation Symposium (London: J. & A. Churchill, 1963), p. 270; also E. L. Tatum "The Possibility of Manipulating Genetic Change" in *Genetics and the Future of Man*, J. D. Roslansky, ed. (New York: Appleton-Century-Crofts, 1966),

of Avery, MacLeod, and McCarty, but also by transduction, in which new genetic material is introduced into the bacterium by way of a bacterial virus. One cannot copy these techniques in any simple way when dealing with man or any higher organism. Nevertheless, with the aid of tissue-culture techniques, and their genetic manipulation, it may be possible to introduce modifications, or replace missing genes, by some form of transfer, in human cell cultures and reimplant the modified cells in the person who needs them. The actual achievement of any such treatment is still not a practical prospect; no one yet knows how it may be done. However, the possibility of doing it is very real indeed. How such things may be done wisely, and without harmful side effects, if indeed we do learn to do them at all, is a matter for earnest and careful thought. The possible may become the actual sooner than we think.

Multiplication of Mankind and Deterioration of the Human Environment

The recent advances in molecular biology and the genetic code represent a great triumph of basic science, with many implications for the future of man. However, the applications of biology with the most far-reaching effects on man in our time arise from earlier advances in fundamental science. Public health measures and applied microbiology have reduced infectious disease from the major preoccupation of physicians to a relatively minor role; the general run of problems that a doctor encounters in his practice is now quite different from what it was in 1900. I would not join those optimists who claim that infectious disease will soon be a thing of the past. Man will continue to live in a world full

---

p. 51. Several of the other articles in this volume are also of great interest in the present connection; I would mention particularly those by Bentley Glass, Paul Ramsey, and Kingsley Davis.

of bacteria and viruses, most of which are harmless to him or indeed beneficent. Some, however, will continue to cause disease and to develop resistance to antibiotics; we may achieve a biological balance between man and the micro-organisms at a much lower level of infection than in the past, but I do not expect infectious disease to disappear.[8] However, the decline in infectious disease, partly from the use of antibiotics and pesticides, but largely from fundamentally simple public health measures like the purification of water and pasteurization of milk, has shifted the whole center of gravity of the world's major problems. Mankind, instead of struggling to maintain its numbers in the face of disease and early death, is now overwhelmed by population increase, with the prospect of doubling the world's present population within twenty-five to thirty years. Over most of the world, in Asia, Latin America, and Africa, where the rates of increase are the greatest, population increase is running ahead of food supply. A recent study[9] shows that, throughout Central and South America, population growth runs well ahead of the growth in gross national product per capita. These facts mean that sheer hunger is one of the most terrible medical and human problems of today. Hunger not only kills; it can stunt and cripple its victims for life. The most widespread form of malnutrition, the protein deficiency kwashiorkor, afflicts countless millions of children throughout the world. If they survive, they are likely to have suffered permanent damage, both in body and mind. It is a grim fact that we live in a world where more people than ever before are prosperous and well fed; yet it is also a world where more people than

[8] For a detailed and searching discussion of the points briefly mentioned here, see René Dubos, *Man Adapting* (New Haven: Yale University Press, 1966).

[9] See *Population Bulletin XXIII*, No. 3, June, 1967 (Washington, D.C. [1755 Massachusetts Ave., N. W.], Population Reference Bureau, Inc.) Earlier issues of this bulletin contain much valuable information on population problems.

ever before are in hunger and misery. Both statements can be true, because there are more people.

Even apart from the problem of hunger, population growth threatens the livable qualities of the world. Living space disappears, noise increases, forests are cut down, rivers, lakes, and air become more polluted. As these trends progress, most people are losing what was once the birthright even of the poor—space, some sense of quiet, clean air, and water.

It is tragic that an era of supremely great discoveries in biology should also be an era of unparalleled destruction of animal life. All over the world, as human population multiplies and industrialization proceeds, species after species of animals and birds have become extinct or are threatened with extinction. With modern mechanized equipment, whales can be killed at rates incomparably greater than ever before. The modern whaling industry appears to be hunting the whales to extinction and thereby of course destroying itself. Whether human restraint and foresight can avert this tragic end remains to be seen. In the desert country of Arabia and North Africa, hunters with modern motorized equipment can hunt down game animals with ease, and many of these are apparently on the way to extinction also. The widespread use of chemical pesticides has almost certainly wrought immense destruction of birds and fishes, and perhaps of some animals also.[10] And of course the spread of human population has devoured much of the habitat of many animal species. The rich variety of living creatures that our ancestors knew may be a thing of the past, just as many of our rich and varied landscapes are being reduced to dull uniformity by the highway and the bulldozer. Our descendants may be compelled to live in a world that has lost irretrievably much of its color and variety, although they will perhaps have the consolation of not knowing what they are missing.

Modern science has endowed us with immense powers.

[10] See for instance the pesticide report of the President's Science Advisory Committee, 1963; summarized in *Science*, 140 (1963), 878.

We can alter the world, on a vast scale, more rapidly than ever before; and we can do so without realizing the ramifications of the forces we have set in motion. The use of chemical pesticides is a striking example: they killed noxious insects, improved crop yields dramatically, and nearly wiped out malaria and some other diseases in certain areas. It took time to discover their widespread toxic action and the damage they did to the ecology of many regions, and then to begin restricting their use within well-defined limits, eliminating altogether some of the most dangerous and developing new and specific pesticides directed against particular classes of insects and not toxic to organisms in general.[11]

If we are to avoid future disasters that could arise from misuse of our great powers to change environment, it is imperative to think of the world as a complex interrelated system in which a modification introduced anywhere produces, not only the effect immediately intended, but other effects that flow from the interactions within the system. The physicians and public health officers who did so much to wipe out infectious disease did not foresee the terrible problems of population growth that would follow. The trained experts who introduced DDT and other pesticides knew what they wanted to achieve, and for the moment at least, they largely achieved it; but surely they failed to foresee the gravity of the complications that followed. As troubles arise, corrective steps are taken, sooner or later, and the damage begins to be corrected. In future, however, we cannot afford to wait for the damage to be done; the situation cries out for more foresight, for a searching and detailed analysis of the whole interacting system into which we propose to introduce some new modification.[12] Analogous to the type of analysis

[11] See C. M. Williams, "The Third Generation Pesticides," *Scientific American*, July, 1967.
[12] A relatively simple but still somewhat complex system that illustrates such interactions is the blood in its interactions with oxygen and carbon dioxide. See L. J. Henderson, *Blood* (New Haven: Yale University Press, 1928).

developed at such places as the RAND Corporation, to deal with problems of military strategy, might well be employed on a larger scale to deal with the great problems of the interaction of organisms, including man, with their environment. Foresight, of course, will never be perfect; in our analysis of problems we must work with simplified models of the actual world. Even after the most careful analysis some of the results of introducing any major change into the world will be unexpected. But with constant vigilance we can incorporate the causes of the unexpected findings into our model, correct initial forecasts, and adjust policy accordingly. With power must go restraint: we can change the world so fast, and often so dangerously, that we shall increasingly be compelled to think deeply before taking new major actions if we are to survive.

In his book *The Next Million Years* Sir Charles Galton Darwin suggested that our descendants might look back upon the present era as the Golden Age of human prosperity. He portrayed a future in which the pressure of population on resources would continue unremittingly in devastating fashion, with profound unrest and the constant threat of war. For us who are here now it is hard to think of the present time, with all its fears and horrors, as a Golden Age. Nevertheless, for people like myself, who live in a wealthy and fortunate country and have taken part in the great adventure of modern science, it has been an inspiring time to live in. It remains to be seen whether we can disprove the validity of Darwin's somber forecast for the generations to come. Even if we are wise enough to avert the catastrophe of nuclear war, the rich countries may slowly drown in the pollution produced by the consequences of their own affluence, and rich and poor alike might eventually be overwhelmed by failure to solve the great problems of food, space, and natural resources.

Modern biology has achieved deep new insight into the

nature of all living creatures, from bacteria to man, with prospects of still more important discoveries following in the next generation. The wise use of applied science and technology for the benefit of man, however, is a problem whose full dimensions we have scarcely begun to envisage; and few as yet appreciate its urgency. It involves not only the scientists but also the politicians and all other people of the world and we must face it adequately if we are to have hope for the future of man.

11

FROM SOCIAL ENGINEERING TO
CREATIVE CHARITY

JOHN T. NOONAN, JR.
University of California, Berkeley

I T IS THE DISCOVERY of every first-year student of law
that there is no law written down anywhere which he
can look up and apply to solve the problem before him. The
hundreds of books of statutes, the thousands of case reports,
the multitudinous volumes of learned legal treatises which line
the shelves of the law library may be relevant to the problem;
they do not answer it. The answer, the response of a living
human being to a fresh human question, is given only by a
human being himself, analyzing the present facts, testing,
selecting, and combining the answers to past problems, and
reacting in the light of this new synthesis to the situation
before him. It is thus that the student, discarding the preconceptions of the layman, learns that law for him is not the
words of statutes to be memorized or the precedents established by predecessors to be revered but a process in which
he is to be a vital and creative participant.

Prophets of the future may foresee mechanization as the
most measurable change that technological development can
bring to law. But the view of law as process is so firmly
engrained in student and practitioner that mechanization of
the technological kind predicted holds no special significance

for them. It will be possible to feed statutes, cases, treatises, into a great computer that will then do the work of identifying and compiling "governing law" and analogies.[1] Such a computer when perfected will mean a considerable reduction in the work of junior lawyers. Its effective use, however, will depend on analysis of the case before computerization occurs, and what the computer provides will be only the raw ingredients of law. The lawyer's essential task of deciding the law of the situation before him will remain. Enabled to collect past relevant data more swiftly, the lawyer as a person trained in the process will still have to respond to the matter at hand.

Law is a process, and it is because this is so that I would view as foolish any attempt to foretell the substantive rules that may govern American business, family life, or use of the automobile or narcotics fifty years from now. Stability of rule is not characteristic of the common law.[2] Great change in legal rule occurred in the course of nineteenth-century industrialization in an underpopulated and relatively isolated United States. It would not seem that a denser population and closer relations with other countries would lessen the rate of change. How particular statutes and precedents may survive could only be a guess. The rules may be expected to change in response to technological innovation, to population rates,

[1] See William B. Eldridge and Sally F. Dennis, "The Computer as a Tool for Legal Research," *Law and Contemporary Problems*, 28 (1963), 78–99. A commercial company based in New York, Law Research Service, Inc., already provides computer research to law firms and law libraries throughout the country. Citations are given by teletype immediately, excerpts from opinions are given within a day; the charge is twelve dollars per query.

[2] Dean Pound wrote in 1936, "Even in a reasonably modified form it is not easy to maintain a doctrine of identity or continuity of rules of law for the common-law world. . . . As we look back over our legal history, we cannot but be struck with the relatively short life of rules of law, *i.e.*, of legal precepts affixing definite detailed consequences to definite detailed states of fact." Roscoe Pound, "What is the Common-Law?" in *The Future of the Common Law* (Cambridge: Harvard Tercentenary Publications, 1936).

to shifts in theological and moral beliefs, to all the other factors affecting the physical and social environment. For example, the rules on negligence have been elaborated largely in response to the introduction of machinery into daily life. The technological development asked for a legal response. As the most familiar of mechanisms, the automobile, continues to be put to lethal use, it is not improbable that at some future point, absolute liability for injury resulting therefrom will be imputed to the manufacturers on the theory that they make an instrument that is inherently dangerous.[3] Such a result will be more likely if the automobile death rate mounts with an ever increased use of cars and it becomes evident that much safer cars are technologically feasible. For another example, the rules governing the origin of life will have to respond to the possibilities of banks of stored spermatozoa, of the transplantation of ova, of the existence of embryos outside the uterus. It may be guessed that legal protection for the rights of the child produced by artificial insemination will be extended.[4] It may be guessed that the rights of the embryo in any form will receive even greater legal recognition[5] and that this development of tort law will counteract the strong pressures to extend the legalization of abortion. But all these surmises are speculation. The wisdom of the common law is not to decide cases before they arise; only when cases are argued are the major consequences of decision graspable. It is to follow this wisdom not to predict what specific rules will be adopted. All that may be expected is substantial change.

[3] In short, what may be expected is an application to automobile manufacturers of the classic torts doctrine of *Ryland v. Fletcher*, 1868, *Law Reports*, 3 House of Lords 330. See, in general, on the impetus to impose strict liability, Harry H. Ognall, "Some Facets of Strict Tortious Liability in the United States and Their Implications," *Notre Dame Lawyer*, 33 (1958), 239, 272.

[4] See Note, "Social and Legal Aspects of Human Artificial Insemination," *Wisconsin Law Review*, 858 (1965), 884.

[5] David A. Gordon, "The Unborn Plaintiff," *Michigan Law Review*, 63 (1965), 579, 627.

Plunged into the flow, the lawyers will respond to the changing environment with a thousand shifts, expedients, improvisations, and these in turn will become the statutes and precedents of a more remote day. What will be law will be the process of response.

Yet law is not only a process in the sense I have suggested of trained persons responding to their environment. It is a process in which the lawyer interacts with other human persons. The observation may appear obvious, but it seems necessary in view of the emphasis often placed by lawyers on the process without reference to persons. The most influential example of a process-oriented approach is the *Report on Professional Responsibility*, prepared in 1958 by a joint conference of the Association of American Law Schools and the American Bar Association. This states, "The lawyer's highest loyalty is at the same time the most intangible. It is a loyalty that runs, not to persons, but to procedures and institutions."[6] In context, this statement may be read as only a laudable rejection of the view that loyalty to a client is the measure of a lawyer's duty. The superior loyalty the report proposes, however, seems not only intangible, like all virtues, but abstract, lacking in concrete substance, and purposeless. Why should a lawyer be loyal to process? Is the spinning of the wheels of a court more sacred than the spinning of the wheels of a mill? Process here seems to be proposed as an end in itself, removed from the life of the lawyer and the lives of other persons his acts affect. Such a view of the law is too unreal to provide a basis for prediction of law's development. Process invokes loyalty because it serves persons, and persons are the realities by which the lawyer's conduct is measured. The law is process by which a lawyer acts and affects himself and other human beings.

What may be said of the future of law must be said of this process related to persons. Here one ventures on no easy

[6] "Professional Responsibility: Report of the Joint Conference," *American Bar Association Journal*, 44 (1958), 1161.

guesses about the future of a rule but on a sounding of broad philosophical tendencies as these tendencies are reflected and, in turn, shaped, in the special world of lawyers. The course of American legal history has been to pass from an emphasis on law as the assertion of individual rights in the nineteenth century to an emphasis on law as social engineering in the twentieth century.[7] The lawyers' view of their function has made this change possible. What will the lawyers' future concept of their function be?

I would answer this question with a paradox: individualism will decline, personalism will increase. The paradox is resolved by identifying individualism in this context as the doctrine that any single individual who has the economic ability may hire a lawyer and may expect him to carry out orders so far as law permits; while personalism in this context is the belief that each person has a right to the aid of a lawyer in case of need, a right that is qualified by the requirement that respect must be accorded the conscience of the lawyer. I shall give two examples of declining individualism. First, consider the evolution of the concept of the trial. A trial, according to the individualists, is designed for the satisfaction of the parties. Its purpose is not to discover truth but to satisfy the participants' combativeness. It is a substitute for physical combat.[8] In the course of it, violence and such peaceful means as bribery, forgery, and some forms of perjury are excluded; yet nondisclosure of evidence, half-truths, and perjurious self-serving by one's client are permitted. Open appeal to the emotions of the jury is acceptable. Cross-examination to discredit a truthful witness is desirable. A lawyer must fight for his client with the utmost zeal.[9]

---

[7] Roscoe Pound, "Fifty Years of Jurisprudence," *Harvard Law Review*, 50 (1937), 557 and 51 (1938), 810–12.

[8] The most perceptive presentation of this view is Charles Curtis, *It's Your Law* (1954), pp. 17–21.

[9] See Monroe H. Freedman, "Professional Responsibility of the Criminal Defense Lawyer: The Three Hardest Questions," *Michigan Law Review*, 64 (1966), 1469–84.

This concept of a trial still has its defenders, and it corresponds to the practice of many advocates today. However, the concept is in transition. It has been rejected by the important statement of the American law schools and the American Bar Association referred to above. The new concept of the trial is that it is designed for the discovery of truth, and the adversary system is justified only as it serves this end. In this view, the adversary system is defended because it prevents a tribunal from coming too quickly to a conclusion, from too readily stamping a particular view on facts, because it preserves a heuristic tension in the minds of the triers of the case. It provides a "social framework within which one's capacity for impartial judgment can attain its fullest realization."[10] The adversary system itself is not likely to disappear. But this rationale of the system will exclude all the lying means, the irrelevant attacks on the opponents, and most of the rhetoric that has been dear to the defenders of the individual's right to a fight.

There are clear signs that the view of the trial as rational investigation is gaining ground. One such indication is the shift in what is considered good technique in arguing a case to a court. There will always be some element of emotional appeal in advocacy, for men are not pure intellects, and emotion may properly be employed to aid the response to truth. But the harangues of the past, the efforts of a Charles Choate or a Clarence Darrow, seem curiously old-fashioned,[11] and they seem old-fashioned because of their resort to emotional irrelevancies. It would seem likely that the advocate of the future would place even less reliance on the art of the orator.

Beyond the changing style of argumentation, another sign is the use of the procedures known as discovery and pretrial.

[10] *Op. cit. supra*, note 6, p. 1161.
[11] For an example of Darrow, see Arthur Weinberg, *Attorney for the Damned*, p. 139 (1957); for an example of Choate, see Robert Swaine, *The Cravath Firm*, 2, 60–62.

By discovery, information known to the adversary is forced to disclosure before trial. In pretrial a hearing is held before the trial; it is the apex of discovery; an experienced judge describes it as "an indispensable tool in assuring a fair trial."[12] The federal courts have here set a standard that will be followed eventually by laggard localities. By these devices of reason, trials are already being rationalized.

A third index of change is the increasingly strict standards of rationality imposed on the government in criminal prosecutions. The prosecutor is now compelled to respond to the broad discovery rights of the accused, is prohibited from suppressing evidence helpful to the accused, is required to make available to the accused the names of material witnesses, and must call the accused's attention to the doubtful credibility of the prosecutor's own witness.[13] A trial "no longer can be properly considered a game of wits and skill."[14] It might be argued that these restrictions on the prosecution can be regarded only as restrictions on the disproportionate power of the government, not as milestones toward rationality. But on July 1, 1966, the Supreme Court put into effect a rule conditioning the accused's right of discovery upon the defendant's giving the government a limited right of discovery.[15] This was the first step to establishment of a

[12] Irving R. Kaufman, "The Philosophy of Effective Judicial Supervision over Litigation," in "Proceedings of the Seminar on Procedures for Effective Judicial Administration," *Federal Rules Decisions*, 29 (1961), 214.

[13] The cases establishing these four propositions are, respectively, *Campbell v. United States*, 373 United States Reports (1963), 487; *Brady v. Maryland*, 373 United States Reports (1963), 83, 87; *United States ex. rel Meers v. Wilkins*, 326 Federal Reporter 2d 135 (2d Circuit 1964); *Curran v. Delaware*, 259 Federal Reporter 2d 707 (3d Circuit 1958), *certiorari denied* 358 United States Reports (1959), 948.

[14] *Curran v. Delaware, op. cit. supra*, p. 711.

[15] *Federal Rules of Criminal Procedure*, 16c. For what could well serve as a rationale for the change see William J. Brennan, Jr., "The Criminal Prosecution: Sporting Event or Quest for Truth," *Washington Law Quarterly* (1963), p. 293.

rule of candor for both prosecuting and defense attorneys. In the future it may be expected that standards will be imposed on the lawyers defending criminals as on the lawyers prosecuting them, and that eventually the same rules will be laid down for lawyers in civil litigation as those that now govern a federal prosecutor. The irrational is thus being gradually eliminated. In this process, what remains of nineteenth-century individualism's view of the lawyer as a fighter for his client will vanish.

My second example of the trend from individualism is the development of the group practice of law. Canon 35 of Professional Ethics of the American Bar Association, accepted in 1928, stated, "The professional services of a lawyer should not be controlled or exploited by any lay agency, personal or corporate, which intervenes between client and lawyer. A lawyer's relations to his client should be personal, and the responsibility should be directed to his client."[16] In the spirit of this canon the courts forbade the employment of lawyers by such groups as trade unions, real estate associations, and automobile clubs that desired to hire lawyers to serve their members.[17] A lawyer could have only an individual as a client; he could not be hired by a group to act for individuals in the group. In the 1960s, however, the principle of Canon 35 gave way before the twin pressures of the racial crisis and the desire to provide legal service to the poor. In 1962 the Supreme Court held that the National Association for the Advancement of Colored People could not constitutionally be prevented by a state from providing lawyers to parents who wanted to be plaintiffs in

[16] American Bar Association, *Canons of Professional Ethics*, Canon 35.

[17] E.g., *Chicago Bar Association v. Chicago Motor Club*, 362 Illinois Reports 50, 199 Northeastern Reporter 1st (1935); *In re Brotherhood of Railroad Trainmen*, 13 Illinois Reports 2d 391, 150 Northeastern Reporter 2d, 163 (1958); *Chicago Bar Association v. Friedlander*, 24 Illinois Reporter 2d 130, 164 Northeastern Reporter 2d, 517 (1960).

school desegregation cases. In 1964 the Court held that there was similar First and Fourteenth Amendment protection for a union that chose a particular lawyer and recommended him to its membership, thereby effectively channeling the legal business of the individual members to the approved lawyer.[18] In addition to civil rights organizations and trade unions, other groups such as teachers' associations, shipowners, and the Armed Forces now provide lawyers.[19] In California, where the fullest study of the need has been made, a committee of the Bar Association recommended in 1964 that a general rule be adopted permitting group legal services, provided that "the group has bona fide purposes other than providing legal services" and that there is "no group control over the lawyer in areas usually reserved for the attorney or the client."[20] Congress has permitted the Office of Economic Opportunity to support group legal practice, and it has provided federal backing for the establishment of neighborhood legal offices.[21] These offices are governed by nonprofit agencies and administered with "the maximum feasible participation of residents of the area and members of the groups." Cutting between lawyer and ultimate client, these local agencies determine basic policies and hire lawyers to serve the poor who qualify for help under the federal and local standards. Given constitutional protection and already exemplified in a variety of forms, group legal practice exists, and it may be expected to multiply enormously.

There has been and will be opposition. The Committee on

[18] The cases are respectively, *N.A.A.C.P. v. Button*, 371 United States Reports 415 (1962); *Brotherhood of Railroad Trainmen v. Virginia State Bar*, 377 United States Reports 1 (1964).

[19] Standing Committee of the California State Bar on Group Services, "Report on Group Legal Service," *California State Bar Journal*, 39 (1964), 652, 670–689.

[20] *Ibid*, 723.

[21] Economic Opportunity Act, Title 2, Section 202 (1964); *United States Code* 42, 2782.

the Unauthorized Practice of Law of the American Bar Association opposes the sweeping California proposal.[22] The reason is that group hiring of a lawyer works a revolution in the individualist's image of the lawyer's relations to his client. Between the lawyer and the individual he serves there now stands the group. Whatever area of tactical decision is left to the lawyer and the individual, it is likely that the policies of the group that pays him or recommends him will operate as a powerful influence upon his decisions. There is no longer a one-to-one lawyer-client relation but at least a triangle of lawyer, hiring group, and ultimate client. The lawyer can no longer single-mindedly consider the interests of his client but must take into account a body of men, some of whom may conflict among themselves. The ideal of service to a single individual is no longer useful as a guide for the lawyer's acts.

If my examples are persuasive in indicating that the individualistic view of the lawyer's function is declining, they might suggest that an increase in personalism is unlikely. The very development of scientific trials and group law might seem to threaten any form of personalism. What evidence supports the belief that a personalist view may become dominant?

Personalism, as here defined, does not permit the client in a trial to ask anything of the lawyer that the lawyer could not conscientiously do for himself. It thus strikes at the shield for personally demeaning conduct, the shield consisting in the belief that vicarious responsibility justifies, or that one may nobly do for another what one would be ashamed to do for oneself. The rhetoric, artifices, and evasions of the old-style trial are instances of what vicarious responsibility permits. Their decline liberates the lawyer to be himself. Free to proceed rationally, the lawyer may be

---

[22] *American Bar Association News*, p. 5 (Feb. 15, 1965).

expected to act as a person, not a tool. He will no longer rationalize his conduct by a doctrine, analogous to *raison d'état*, of "necessity of the client."

Can there be predicted such a development of free, responsible activity that if a lawyer would not defend himself when charged with a crime of which he is guilty, he would refuse to defend a client known by him to be guilty? On the one hand, since it is common practice in the overwhelming number of criminal cases for lawyers to plead guilty clients who are guilty (usually after bargaining), such an absolute standard might not destroy the process of criminal justice. On the other hand, as no one is compelled to incriminate himself, a lawyer might reason that to refuse all clients known by him to be guilty would be to do a disservice to the trial system accepted by society and to create a system in which the lawyer would become in effect a witness for his client's innocence. A sense of personal responsibility by the lawyer would seem to include a respect for the social value of the availability of trials to determine guilt. At all events, with the acceptance of personalism there will be no basis for the lawyers actually conducting criminal trials to permit their clients to use means in which connivance so frequently demeans the advocate.

Moreover, the acceptance of lawyers for groups will provide legal service based on need. The old view encouraged lawyers in charity to give their legal services to the poor, especially in criminal cases, and gradually the Supreme Court made counsel in serious cases a constitutional requirement.[23]

---

[23] The evolution here is from *Powell v. Alabama*, 287 United States Reports 45 (1932) holding that in a capital case involving ignorant, youthful defendants the state had the duty to provide counsel, to *Gideon v. Wainwright*, 372 United States Reports 349 (1963) holding that in all cases where a serious punishment is involved the defendant must be given counsel. Doubtless, evolution here will eventually extend the requirement to cases where the penalty is small.

But the old view failed to stimulate lawyers to give legal service to many poor and middle-income persons who needed it.[24] The new approach will be more effective in providing lawyers to all members of the community, and this quantitative enlargement of the lawyer-using public will be an expansion of legal service to persons.

The development of group law also will have a liberating effect on the lawyer. What will happen is suggested by what sometimes happens now when corporations have wise counsel; here is the one established precedent for the practice of law for a group. The precedent is disguised because the fiction has been maintained that to serve a corporation is not to serve a group but a single entity; the corporation has been imagined as an individual to whose welfare the lawyer's loyalty singly runs. But "corporation" is only an arrangement of certain persons—the chief executive, the directors, the stockholders, the employees. In representing this arrangement of persons a lawyer is representing a group.[25] In the ordinary case the interests of the group are not in open conflict. But where does the lawyer's loyalty lie in case conflict breaks out within the group? Ultimately, it is the stockholders' money that pays him, and orthodox theory on corporations would identify the stockholders as the owners to whom his loyalty is given. Yet in many cases of conflict some of the stockholders are contesting the action of others of the stockholders. In such cases the current prac-

[24] See especially Jerome E. Carlin and Jan Howard, "Legal Representation and Class Justice" in Symposium on Group Legal Services in *UCLA Law Review* 12 (1965), 381, and this symposium generally; see also Elliott E. Cheatham, *A Lawyer When Needed* (1963), p. 40; Patricia Wald, *Law and Poverty* (1965), ed. by Abram Chayes and Robert Wald, pp. 64–67.

[25] See *Otis and Co. v. Pennsylvania R. Co.* 57 F. Supp. 680, 681, 684 (E. D. Penn. 1944); *Radiant Burners, Inc. v. American Gas Association*, 207 Federal Reporter Supplement 771, 774 (Northern District of Illinois 1962), *reversed* 320 Federal Reporter 2d, 314 (7th Circuit 1963).

tice is for the lawyer to look to the board of directors representing the stockholders in control at the last election.[26] The lawyer is then conceived of as lawyer for the majority or at least for the group that once had been in control. He is still expected to act with some fairness to the adversary stockholders. In these circumstances it is not unusual for a lawyer to have a certain amount of discretion, to act, within limits, as arbiter of competing forces. The lawyer emerges as a person, whose wisdom determines policy. This emergence is dramatic in the case of conflict, but even in the ordinary pacific situation the interest of the president as employee is not identical with that of the stockholders as investors; the interests of the controlling stockholders do not necessarily coincide with that of all the stockholders; the directors view their work and rewards from a different perspective from that of the salaried employees. In all these instances of submerged conflict, it is the lawyer who today guides the directors, executives, employees, and stockholders to equitable results. It is not because he has a single client, the corporate entity, but because he has an arbiter's sense of justice that the lawyer is able to serve the different persons comprising the group. It may be argued from the generally excellent service that lawyers furnish their corporate clients that men of integrity will be found to do as well for other mixed groups of persons. The expansion of the lawyer's use as arbiter and conscience for a group can only enhance the lawyer's own personality, his awareness of his creative function.

The examples of declining individualism then embody emergent personalism. The personalism of the future will require of the lawyer fuller consciousness of his humanity. The virtue of the lawyer today is justice; the paradigm for

[26] See *Marco v. Dulles*, 169 Federal Reporter Supplement 622, 630 (Southern District of New York 1959), *appeal dismissed*, 268 Federal Reporter 2d, 192 (2d Circuit 1959).

his behavior is the court, and its virtue of fairness is his. Yet if the lawyer will not be a tool of a client, neither will he be the simple instrument of justice. Justice is only one of the virtues. There is reason to believe that at one time justice was so hard to attain that lawyers did well to specialize as its defenders. Yet there seems little reason that these specialists, like statues of the goddess, should be forever blinded to other considerations of humanity. There are other virtues besides justice, and to be a human person the lawyer of the future will embody them in his practice of his profession.

Already, in the canons of the American Bar Association, there are glimmerings of the future. However cross his client is at his adversary, a lawyer is not to engage in personalities with opposing counsel: he "should never minister to the malevolence or prejudice of a client in the trial or conduct of a case. . . . Improper speech is not excusable on the ground that it is what the client would say if speaking in his own behalf."[27] What is already a standard of charity in litigation will become the standard in other areas where a lawyer must treat other persons on behalf of his client. Toward all of them, his client's adversaries, victims, creditors, and debtors, he will act with charity. It is now recognized that vicarious responsibility is no excuse for a lawyer's incivility. It will be recognized that it is no excuse for a lawyer's participation in harsh overreaching, avaricious exploitation or disingenuous negotiation. If, as seems likely, harsh, avaricious, or disingenuous clients will have few lawyers to choose from, this result cannot be deplored.[28]

Personalism will profoundly affect one area where now in a special way lawyers act toward some persons as if they

[27] American Bar Association, *Canons of Professional Ethics*, Canon 18.

[28] An exploration of the notion of vicarious responsibility as a defense for uncharitable conduct is made by Curtis, *It's Your Law*, pp. 27–29.

were things. This area is the punishment of crimes. Already the present system is under direct attack. The criticism is as old as Socrates that it makes no sense to do evil to a man to make him better.[29] It has been repeated for our age by the dean of living jurisprudents, Giorgio del Vecchio. He says:

> The truth is, that evil can only be compensated for by good. If the proverb "An eye for an eye, a tooth for a tooth" has been repudiated in its crudest form by the conscience of civilized nations, and one no longer cuts off the hand of a thief or tears out the tongue of a slandermonger, yet the false idea still obtains that the evil of a criminal action must be met with a corresponding evil in its punishment. But does the desire to cause pain to a human being, even though he be guilty, mean that his personality is respected? Or is this not a sort of duplication of the wrong done . . .? Is it just for a human being to be denied the possibility of developing his own spiritual and intellectual powers, and of communicating with his fellow man over long periods of time, even for life? And is it just that such punishment be the motive for grief and serious damage, not only to the culprit, but also to his innocent family?[30]

These sentiments are the sentiments of the present age. They take concrete form in the general decline of capital punishment and in its abolition in eighteen countries and eight American states.[31] Beyond this tangible symptom, it may be speculated that much of the increased sensitivity to the

---

[29] Plato, *The Republic*, 1. 9. 335 d.

[30] Giorgio Del Vecchio, "Equality and Inequality in Relation to Justice," *Natural Law Forum* 11 (1966), 44.

[31] Clarence H. Patrick, "The Status of Capital Punishment: A World Perspective," *Journal of Criminal Law, Criminology and Police Science* 56 (1965), 397. Thirty-six countries, in addition to those that had abolished the penalty had not had executions in the period 1958–62 covered by Patrick's study (p. 405). He observes: "Actually the yearly total of executions in the world today appears to be less than the number which took place in some single countries at an earlier time." (p. 409).

rights of defendants in a criminal trial results from a sense of unease about the system to which convicted defendants are subjected. In the future, two developments may be expected: prosecutors and judges alike will realize that they are rational agents cooperating in the process by which other men, the criminal defendants, are killed or psychologically injured, that they cannot rid themselves of responsibility by saying that their function is solely to convict or to sentence. At the same time they will recognize that no human person has the right to kill or maim another human person except in self-defense. Retribution may no longer be asserted to be the right of human beings. Nor may a man convicted of a crime be treated as a thing, to be freely used to deter others from criminal behavior.[32] Criminal sanctions then will be seen as possible only as restraints of men actually likely to injure other humans. All other treatment imposed by a court will be genuinely medicinal, directed to rehabilitation in an environment likely to promote rehabilitatation. Cooperation will be refused to any system of criminal justice which, giving lip service to rehabilitation, employs measures that can only further disfigure the criminal. The lawyers as participants in the process of criminal law will insist that they not be participants in the denaturing of human beings.

The questions may be raised: Will such a system of personally responsible lawyers be produced? Can it survive? To the first question a confident answer comes only with confidence in the education of lawyers. The lawyers of the future will have had much more formal education than any lawyers of the past. As recently as 1948 only 37 percent of lawyers in practice had college degrees; as recently as

[32] See e.g., the demand for reform already advanced in Puerto Rico, Helen Silving, "A Plea for a New Philosophy of Criminal Justice," *Revisto Juridica de la Universidad de Puerto Rico* 35 (1966), 401, 406, 409.

1963, 63 percent had such degrees. It is likely that in another generation 90 percent will have such degrees. Already almost 90 percent of practicing lawyers have law-school degrees as compared to only 61 percent in 1948.[33] If the kind of college education the lawyers receive is broadly humanistic, if the law schools follow the pattern of the leading schools in educating for responsible leadership, it seems probable that the lawyers of the future will have the intellectual resources to be masters of themselves. Any general failure of moral nerve, any general loss of purpose by the culture, must, of course, have its effect on lawyers too; they may, in disbelief in higher values, turn the law into a game for profit or amusement as do many of the lawyers fictionally created by Louis Auchincloss. But there is one factor in the lives of lawyers which will continue to check the easy acceptance of all lack of purpose; they are intimately involved by their work in the realization of human intentions; it is hard for them, though not impossible, to suppose that human creativity is random, chaotic, and without end in view beyond the moment's impulse.

The second question, the viability of a profession composed of such men, requires some consideration of what eats at the present system. One destructive agent is what is preemptively called "corruption" in the way some translators of the Bible preemptively designate sexual sins as "immorality." Corruption in this narrow sense of bribes, favoritism, and profiteering in public office is a major problem of the present. It is least corrosive in the higher judiciary, most corrosive in those areas of administrative action where the government is dispensing favors as small as liquor licenses or as large as television channels. It is unlikely that any governmental system has ever been totally free from

[33] American Bar Foundation, *The 1964 Lawyer Statistical Report* 30 (1965).

these evils,[34] and the peculiar dangers of the present rest in the size of the governmental favors available through corruption and the passive acceptance often found toward it. In part, the tolerance extended to it in America is a survival of group thinking at the ethnic tribal level; in part, the tolerance is based on respect for aggressive individualism. Both these bases will disappear. It would be plausible to predict that the self-directing lawyers of the future will be less willing than some client-oriented lawyers today to earn fees as conduits for bribes or influence.

Another class of destructive agents are the bureaucrats. By bureaucrat in this pejorative sense I mean the man who knows all the rules without understanding any of their purposes. He views his job as the mechanical application of whatever his manual prescribes. He presently thrives on the legal staffs of many federal, state, and municipal agencies. He is often a lawyer, but he is the enemy of the true lawyer. It is likely that the creative, purpose-oriented lawyer of the future will effect his radical diminishment.

A third element affecting the present system is its concern with the rich. Probably the best talent of the profession is devoted to the law of the financing, taxation, and regulation of corporations and to the trusts and wills of the wealthy.[35] Even if the assumption is made that those with the most money have the greatest need for legal services, it may be argued that a wider dispersion of legal talent would be healthier. Again, it would seem that the lawyers of the projected future will be more likely to achieve this distribution of services to persons in need.

It may be pressed, however, would lawyers of the kind described be employed? Would they not be such in-

[34] See, for example, the many instances of corruption of judges in the Roman Republic and classical Roman Empire, analyzed by John M. Kelly in his book, *Roman Litigation* (1966).

[35] See Cheatham, *op. cit. supra* in 24 at 3.

dependent, nagging, self-willed obstructionists to the realization of entrepreneurial dreams that no one would hire them? The brusque answer is that, whatever lawyers the future produces, they will be sought, because business would come to a standstill without them. Given the present complexity of governmental regulation and taxation, neither of which is likely to diminish, lawyers must be used. The kinder, and no less compelling, answer is that such lawyers already exist and are far from being shunned: they exist in those private counselors like Grenville Clark and Harrison Tweed, who are the consciences of the corporations they serve and the guiding spirits of many churches, universities, and charitable trusts; in those attorneys in government like Henry Stimson and Dean Acheson, who invigorated whole departments of government; in those law professors like Austin Scott and Warren Seavey, who rationalized and reshaped the domains of common law they cultivated. The only sound basis for confidence in the future is to observe that the present is not without its resplendent representatives.

It is one of the curiosities of Utopian thought to imagine a world without lawyers as a better world.[36] Lawyers will always exist in any advanced civilization because human hopes must be expressed in words, and words are inherently ambiguous, fragile, open to interpretation and so to argument. Apart from the ambiguity of documents, lawyers are required by the nature of human problems: in any dynamic environment, conflicts are not such that one side is always obviously right; logic and clear ideas are of little help in resolving them. Resolution comes through argument and decision, and a lawyer marshals the facts and posits the values at issue. Resolution comes through compromise, and a lawyer negotiates it. Resolution comes in advance of con-

[36] Ch. Perelman remarks critically on this phenomenon in "What a Philosopher May Learn from the Study of Law," *Natural Law Forum* 11 (1966), 1.

flict, and a lawyer constructs the forms in which human energies are harmoniously channeled. In any real society of opening possibilities, there are tasks that can be done only by the man skilled in words, sensitive to human purposes, knowledgeable of the ways by which human beings are led to cooperate: by the lawyer.

The lawyer will be a participant in the future. It is not, however, Utopian to suppose that the lawyer of the future will be more consciously his own master, less his client's tool; that he will be seeking the truth in disputes; that he will not shelter behind his responsibility for another; that his virtues will not be exhausted by fairness; that he will serve many groups besides the corporation and many persons besides the rich; that he himself will be a charitable creator of values.

12

TECHNOLOGY, BUSINESS
AND EDUCATION

JAMES R. BRIGHT

*Graduate School of Business Administration
Harvard University*

Technology today is interacting powerfully with business and society and apparently will continue to do so with growing intensity through the foreseeable future. Recent history and current events suggest that technological progress will be the most powerful factor in the future environment for many business firms and other institutions. Although technological change has been with us for many ages and has been a pronounced element in the economic and social environment since the early 1880s, there are at least five reasons why its importance is at present growing.

1. The performance of new technological devices is being improved at a sharply accelerating rate. For example, the atom bomb was thousands of times more powerful than TNT, and the H-bomb was far more powerful than the A-bomb. The first computer had a computing speed two hundred times that of man; recent computers operate many millions of times faster.

2. Successive advances in a given field are introduced more frequently. Consider that, since the coming of the transistor in 1948, there has been a major development in electronic component design about every two and one-half to three years. Each time the industrial leadership and for-

tunes of firms have been severely affected. The tin can was a product that belonged to the steel industry since the days of Napoleon; but, since 1957, the tin can has had at least four new competitors—the aluminum can, the composite fiberboard–aluminum-liner can, the plastic can, and new forms of thin-tin containers. During this time, steel has lost as much as 80 percent of its position in some parts of the tin-container market.

3. The size of the resources needed to bring about many of the new technological innovations (meaning usable hardware and not just the invention itself) is growing to a staggering degree. The U.S. Government spent some two billion dollars to create the atom bomb. IBM is now "betting" more than twice as much—five billion dollars—on their new 360 computer system. And no longer do firms propose the next advance in air transport. The cost is so great that only governments can underwrite the effort. Even consortiums of governments are required, as in the case of the British-French effort to produce the Concorde Mach 2 transport.

4. The impact of new technology on existing institutions is severe and promises to be equally or more severe in the future. Thus, in about twelve years the diesel locomotive wiped out steam locomotive business. In about seven years television played havoc with profits in the movie industry, which is only now struggling back to economic health. In some three years the missile replaced the bomber as the main strategic military weapon. With this replacement went a net loss of close to three hundred thousand jobs in the aviation industry and the displacement of hundreds of thousands of other jobs. Suppliers of equipment, materials, and components had to reorganize drastically. Profitability of many firms fluctuated severely.

5. New technology is creating new communities such as Cape Kennedy, the community around Huntsville, Alabama, and the science-oriented industrial complexes of Boston and

California. New institutions also result, such as NASA, which has a budget larger than almost any other government agency. On the horizon is an oceanographic equivalent of NASA, which will undoubtedly receive similar financial support and result in other new institutions.

New associations also have sprung out of technological progress, such as multination efforts to cooperate in space, to operate communication systems, air transport systems, massive irrigation systems, and water and power distribution projects.

Every institution, corporate and other, faces a high probability that technology will bring a major change to its mode or sphere of work within the next twenty years. The firm, its employees, and its managers inevitably are going to be affected. Technological progress is most assuredly a major element of our world. It is no longer adequate to think of the environment in which we live and work as merely a political, economic, and social environment. This environment now has a technological dimension of increasing significance. Educators dare not neglect this dimension.

The Directions of Technological Progress

Technological change is too broad a notion to be useful, and "automation" is much too narrow to reflect the full technological state of affairs. We must teach ourselves and our children, as well as our institutions, to analyze technological progress for its components and to anticipate the consequences of each type of technological progress. As one such attempt, I offer these eight directions of technical change, with some suggestions of their effects.

INCREASED TRANSPORTATION CAPABILITY

The mastery of distance in less time and/or cost is the result of such devices as the jet transport, the hydrofoil boat, the helicopter, and the less spectacular but very influential developments in container ships, pipelines, piggy-back trailer trains, the unit train, and the superhighway.

Man's ability to move himself and other things has also been affected by resort to new media. Work in space has led to commercial operations—Communication Satellite Corporation—within eight years of Sputnik's launching. Activities under the oceans include such sports as skin diving; and now we see the first two national underwater parks and the beginning of underwater laboratories and submarine tourist activities, such as that which the Swiss operated in Lake Lucerne in 1964, when some ten thousand tourists paid for deep submarine voyages.

INCREASED MASTERY OF ENERGY

Through atomic energy greater magnitudes of power are available for war and peace. Through new control techniques energy is monitored and directed with increased precision. Improved techniques for energy storage, such as nickel-cadmium and other types of batteries as well as fuel cells and nuclear fuel, are making energy portable, divisible, and applicable at very distant points, and on almost any scale. Most striking is the generation and transformation of energy by new sources and devices that did not exist twenty years ago.

INCREASED ABILITY TO ALTER MATERIALS

New properties are given to old materials, making them more durable, stronger, or giving them other special properties. Synthetic materials, especially plastics, are challenging natural materials. Foods and medicines are increasingly being synthesized through industrial chemistry. Progress in materials is changing product design, product life, sources of supply, and therefore the economic health of industries and of regions.

THE EXTENSION OF MAN'S SENSORY CAPABILITIES

Radar and television have broken through limits previously enforced by distance, darkness, and fog. Radio and high fidelity systems, which multiply, amplify, record, and project sound, have expanded beyond measure the ability to speak and hear.

Man's sense of touch has been extended in two ways: (a) his "reach," meaning his ability to control and manipulate things beyond arm's length, has been lengthened indefinitely by progress in remote control, and (b) his power of discrimination has been extended by new instruments for identifying and measuring with minute precision.

The senses of both taste and smell are given new range by chemistry and instrumentation. And it is especially striking that man's memory, meaning his ability to reconstruct what has passed, has been vastly augmented by various types of recording and duplicating mechanisms such as audio-visual tape, magnetic tape for sound, Polaroid photography, and copying techniques such as xerography. Major industries arise around each of these new capabilities.

THE GROWING MECHANIZATION OF PHYSICAL ACTIVITIES

This aspect of automation has been discussed thousands of times (and perhaps overemphasized). It is clear that the mechanization of production tasks will continue. Less appreciated is the entrance of mechanization into the field of distribution. Storing, shipping, and warehousing of goods, order picking, loading of common carriers, and the movement and control of goods passing through the distribution system into the hands of the customer are being mechanized to an ever increasing degree. An integrated, machine-like system is emerging in distribution just as it did in production.

The functions of inspecting and testing also are being

automated, speeding the production process (and incidentally reducing one type of skilled job).

THE GROWING MECHANIZATION OF INTELLECTUAL PROCESSES

This is the other form of automation that has been so widely discussed. Two distinct technical phenomena are involved. The spectacular one is the use of the computer to collect, store, manipulate, and display data or dispatch signals according to its analysis. However, we should not ignore the development of *programming* devices such as magnetic tapes, punched cards, and electronic circuitry. The program control of machine tools, typewriters, and other devices means the direction of long and intricate machinery actions with less human intervention (and less operator skill).

INCREASED CONTROL OF THE ENVIRONMENT

Steady progress is being made in modifying the growth of crops and herds and in controlling their reproduction, their anatomical structures and metabolism, their chemical content, and their usefulness to man's purpose. Organisms also are being adapted to growth in difficult environments. This progress is far from over.

Now we are facing a new activity on a vast scale—the control of temperature, humidity, the chemical content and structure of the water, air, and the types of organic life that will be allowed in the environment.

Environment control is being further realized by the growing ability to alter the earth's surface through techniques of earth moving, dam building, river control, and irrigation. Much of this activity implies infringement on someone else's preferences or property. Political actions thus will affect technological progress to a strong degree.

THE GROWING CONTROL OF HUMAN LIFE

The reduction of disease is an ancient goal, now growing closer. Malaria has almost disappeared; polio is no longer such a terrible threat. We can expect one disease after another to be gradually eliminated.

The second area of technical activity is the increasing ability to control growth, including the generation of life itself. Control of emotions and of body functioning is now commonplace.

It is obvious that we are just at the threshold of major progress in providing mechanical parts for the human body. While artificial limbs are an old story, new versions of artificial kidneys, veins, larynxes, and now the heart itself are accelerating. They will be the basis of significant businesses someday.

Some Economic Consequences

These trends each could be described in greater detail, but for our purpose, what we have noted is enough to suggest the approach we must take and to project the types of effects we can anticipate for economic activity. In the summation that follows, I am withholding judgment on "merits" of continuing technological progress. Let us first simply point out some business consequences and then alert ourselves to some of their social implications.

1. Geography is losing its significance as a barrier to war, to trade, to travel, and to the exchange of cultural ideas and knowledge. A given idea or practice cannot be protected by insulation. Markets and competition will take form at greater distances. It follows that regions of the world will tend to make optimum use of their resources and to specialize in the things they can do best. The barriers to movement are becoming largely political.

2. Therefore, there will be more intense competition between different materials, foods, fuels, transportation systems, and even between recreational areas and different sports. The general trend is increasing competition for every kind of activity. Furthermore, this competition often will come from nontraditional sources.

3. Another kind of competition is growing. I will call this competition through displacement of technological function. Thus, the railroad that hauls coal to power plants finds its business threatened by extra-high-voltage power systems, which make it more economical to ship electricity from the mine mouth than to ship coal to a local power plant. Communications systems providing two-way sight, sound, and facsimile transmission tend to eliminate the need for business travel. Transportation systems are therefore coming into competition with communication systems. Similarly, the speed and cost of transportation are improved, and the need for local warehousing is thereby reduced. The coming of the one-hundred-ton C_5A jet freighter will change stock locations and inventory levels. As a material is made corrosion proof, the need for paint is reduced. And in similar manner, many established activities will be eliminated because their functions become unnecessary.

4. The competitive life span of most products will decrease. Technological developments are coming so rapidly that the superior performance of the latest model obsoletes a product far more rapidly than in the past.

5. The cost and time for generating each next major product improvement are increasing.

6. Major industries will arise around each new major technical capability or technological discovery. A prime example is medical activity, which will grow in cost, complexity, and industrial content. The proliferation of special devices and materials in all fields will offer many opportunities for small firms.

7. There will be less and less labor content in carrying out most routine activities, including both production and distribution. Because of a higher machine content, with more capital input required, fixed costs will grow and variable costs decline. The result is that businesses are less able to weather a great variation in demand, especially on the down-side.

8. The government is and will be an even greater prime mover in many of these technological advances. In some instances this is because the cost is so great, in others because the government has the need, and in others because it has the span of control necessary. Sometimes the government simply feels the pressure or desire to bring about a major change. Governments, it must be noted, are sensitive to forces that are not always economically rational. Consider how an inflammatory journalistic effort, distorted though it was, forced auto-safety legislation.

9. Many of these technological developments have power-ful interactions with other parts of society; *e.g.*, a decision to control water pollution as this decision impinges on towns, communities, individuals, industrial processes, and com-panies. It follows that we must become sensitive to the "levels of causality" arising out of a technological advance.

10. Because of the variety of technical resources required, there will have to be more consortiums and combinations of companies and institutions to explore and to provide the components needed for technical innovation.

11. There will be more risk and failure in business be-cause of technological uncertainties and technological com-petition added to the already complex business environment.

12. Technology trends that improve communications, transportation, collection, storage, recall, and display of in-formation will combine to make more and more events and knowledge instantly available from distant points. Education and entertainment will be handled more and more by elec-

tronic-based systems, and the knowledge resources available to every institution and home will grow enormously.

13. Population growth will place great demands on the economy and on society. While food for Americans does not appear to be a problem, the growth of population in developing countries is something else. As Dr. E. E. Howe of Merck Institute for Therapeutic Research recently reported:

> . . . it is useless for our country to institute any program, in a developing country, to increase the food supply without first assuring that there is a major program on population control. To do so will almost certainly increase the sum total of human suffering in the long run.[1]

The anticipated increase of U.S. population to some three hundred million by 2000 A.D. will, however, place us under many other serious economic and social pressures. Transportation, education, medical support, recreation, urban affairs, waste disposal, and many similar areas will be affected. Technology will be called upon to provide solutions.

14. Technology will assure America of more health, wealth in material matters, and vast new industries rising around new technologies; from these, better jobs and economic opportunities will grow.

Social Problems Arising Out of Technological Progress

It is relatively easy to foresee the economic-technological trends and interactions, and it is not too difficult to identify some of the social consequences. But it will take many imaginative and energetic efforts to deal with these problems.

A technological advance, generally, means the creation

---

[1] E. E. Howe, "World Protein Needs and How They May Be Implemented," *Proceedings* (Washington, D.C.: The Technology of Food Supply, Dairy and Food Industries Supply Association, Inc., 1967).

of superiority and some resulting displacement. Existing devices, products, materials, services, and even industries are superseded by something new. Firms that are blind or inflexible to this type of change will gradually meet economic death. And this means the loss of jobs.

Apparently, and most frequently, new technology builds greater economic activity than it destroys. Whatever jobs aviation might have cost railroading, it has certainly more than made up for by providing as much as twenty times more jobs in building and operating aviation enterprises. Perhaps this is an underestimate. However, as with so much technological change, (1) there is not a one-to-one correspondence between old and new activities; (2) it is almost certain that the new jobs will not be in the same geographic locations; (3) the new technology will not require the same mix of skills and facilities; and (4) there will often be a serious time lag in economic activity while the adjustment is made. While the net effect on total employment throughout society is extremely difficult to state, and undoubtedly will vary from time to time, there is no doubt whatsoever that many individuals will lose present jobs and, thus, that in some manner they must find new ones.

As a corollary, the economic worth of many traditional skills is destroyed because they are no longer needed by society or because a machine does the job faster and better than a person. The destruction of the economic value of existing skills by technological progress is an old, old story in industrial history. Strangely, it has been sadly neglected by many sociologists, labor relations specialists, politicians, and even engineers and managers currently concerned with automation. It is often casually assumed that new and highly complex equipment requires highly skilled *operators*. The opposite is more the case: modern equipment commonly demands of operators almost no skill. A little review of the relative skill required by the modern housewife in contrast to that of her great grandmother is a simple but everyday illustration of the point: many household tasks have been reduced to a matter of reading instructions or pushing buttons. Precisely the same thing has happened with the great bulk (but not all) of industrial jobs as they have become "automated."

However, although *operating* skills frequently are reduced, there is a very distinct increase in the skills (education) required to *design* the new machines and processes and perhaps to perform associated services such as *installation*, *startup*, and *maintenance*. We face the dichotomy of lowering skill requirements in some parts of society and raising them drastically in parts of the planning-designing-controlling-maintaining activities.

Another consideration is simply the number of jobs needed in a new skill. For example, programming of computers was claimed, ten years ago, to require a highly skilled person. With progress in computer languages, and other software, the bulk (but definitely not all) of industry's programming needs can be served by a high school graduate trained in, say, a special two- or three-month programming course. However, the fantastic growth of the computer (now being built at a rate of thirty-five a day by IBM alone, with more than twenty thousand now in use) means that programmers are still in very short supply. Skilled machinists for large, heavy machine tools also are in very short supply because of the sheer volume of demand in certain industries, such as those producing electrical generating equipment.

My purpose is not to insist that a certain end condition will result but only to point out that the effect on skill requirements (and hence education needs) can be quite different in different parts of society, at the same time and because of the same device. We must examine the total mix of effects before we jump into new programs for adjustment.

This leads to the question of the availability of education.

If technological advances are going to come more rapidly, be more severe, and differ widely from what has gone before, it follows that education and reeducation must take place at frequent intervals. The factory worker will need to be taught a new skill. The manager and engineer must acquire a working knowledge of new technology and analytical approaches. Therefore, the need to return to an educational posture from time to time will become more frequent. But American society has not organized its educational institutions to update knowledge and skill in an efficient, systematic, and socially acceptable way. This we must learn to do.

The destruction or decline in the value of assets is another real problem. When a technological advance reduces the value of a given production machine or even a factory, society may be able to accept the disruption without too much upheaval. But when an industry is hit, as when the automobile and airplane destroyed the passenger railroad business or when atomic fuel threatens to reduce coal mining, society has a much more serious problem on its hands.

Some effects on assets are more subtle. They flow out of secondary consequences of a technological advance. How do we respond to the way that the automobile, leading to suburban shopping, may have reduced the value of a downtown store location or a railroad passenger station? And consider the effect of technological progress on the very existence of communities. In California about 40 percent of the wage earners receive their living directly or indirectly from government work in aerospace or defense products. The city of Seattle and its surrounding areas are heavily dependent upon the fortunes of the Boeing Airplane Company.

In the past, regional areas have been badly hurt when their local business has been reduced for economic reasons. It is apparent that now not only may economic factors put an end to given types of activity in a given area, but technological events may also wipe out work. How shall the state or the nation deal with this problem?

Perhaps a wise and energetic government may be able to spur additional economic activity in new fields, but is it possible that these new jobs can be created in factories and industries dedicated to old technology? I think not. It is impossible to provide coal miners with aerospace jobs in coal-mining towns. And this highlights a new need—the *need for mobility*.

Mobility implies that people must be moved into the places where new jobs are available, for new jobs cannot be moved to them very often. Now consider the host of problems that follow from this. First, we have the natural reluctance of people to move from old familiar places and friendly associations. Second, who will provide the cost of relocation and retraining? Must the individual bear this cost? his old firm? his new firm? the new technology? or the government?

Indeed, how shall we find out where new jobs and new skills are needed and match them with skills, or at least aptitudes, of displaced employees? Clearly we need some kind of a national job-information system.

And then what about the continuity of job benefits, and what about attitudes of people who now find no security in years of service and a job well done through a patiently learned skill?

It seems to me that there are two responses that we must structure into our society:

1. We must increase mobility of employees; and this implies knowledge of opportunities, "portability" of job benefits, assumption of retraining and relocation costs, some minimum job security, devices to ease social shock to the family, and probably a change in attitudes. This last point may be the most difficult of all to achieve.

2. We must improve institutions for updating education and providing retraining and new, specialized knowledge

and skill. (This also requires a change in attitudes and procedures toward continuing education.)[2]

One could list a number of other problems growing out of technological progress: as work hours diminish and leisure time grows, where is the virtue in activity? Must we learn a new definition of work?

If constant change, mobility, reeducation, and new locations, activities, friends, and duties can be accepted, what do they do to an individual's life, which now has become highly fragmented? Furthermore, life becomes an activity without roots in places and environments. Does this not do serious damage to the emotional stability of many people?

Let us close with a last concern—the growing gap between the intellectually *élite* and the average worker. It is striking that outstanding managers, scientists, and engineers, and other types of professionals, seem to have an intense interest in their jobs. They are absorbed by them, and they willingly give frantically long hours to "work." Meanwhile, the blue-collar worker seems to get less and less satisfaction out of a more highly automated task. Here he

[2] It is rather interesting to note that the military deal quite successfully with both these problems. Both officers (managers) and workers (enlisted men) move frequently to widely different activities throughout the world. One might argue that they have to take orders. True, but they do not have to spend their careers in such service, as hundreds of thousands choose to do. Why is the military successful in handling mobility? I surmise that it is because (a) *movement is accepted* as part of the job from the moment military personnel are "employed"; (b) moving is *not a financial cost* to the individual; (c) *the receiving community is quite prepared* for the newcomer physically and socially, and (d) *everyone else* in the community *is going and has gone through the same experience* over the years.

On retraining—it is anticipated that the average Army officer spends almost half his career going to schools at various professional intervals. After his basic branch school (*e.g.*, artillery), he can expect, in later years, to attend the Command and General Staff Course (general management), then later the Army War College (policy) or the Industrial College. From time to time he may be tapped for special short courses, such as logistics management, chemical warfare, counterinsurgency, and so on. He readily accepts the notion of continual retraining for new responsibilities and special needs.

has little opportunity to contribute originality of output or differentiation of results. His hours become fewer, more mechanistically controlled, and (I hypothesize) less satisfying. "Work" is something he seeks to reduce. Thus, we are in the peculiar position of reversing the traditional pattern. For the first time in history, workers have free time and sufficient affluence for leisure pursuits, but now the intellectually élite (the professionals) are frantically paced. Shall we deplore the worker's lack of interest in his occupation, or the intellectual's excessive interest in work? There is a disturbing gap here—and a very puzzling one. Moreover, the communication gap between the professional and his family, his employees, and other professionals is growing because of high specialization.

The reader will sense that this little essay has moved from the study of technology to its resulting social problems, and with this shift I for one, have become increasingly less confident of my assessments. Surely, we are leaving future generations of scholars, managers, political leaders, students, and educators ample opportunity to become absorbed in *their* work!

13

DEVELOPING PATTERNS IN PHILOSOPHY

JAMES D. COLLINS
Saint Louis University

PHILOSOPHY IS FULLY involved in the surge of new knowledge and the problems coming in its wake. Quantitative description of the philosophical activity in all countries shows a burgeoning increase of teachers and societies, journals and books, in the period since World War II. The bibliographies of philosophy sponsored by UNESCO and Louvain University have a wide and well-ordered coverage by period and subject matter, but they are unable to record the entire flood of publications in all the specialized areas of interest and are bound to overlook even some outstanding general results. Philosophical societies are organized along national and international lines, in terms of specific periods of thought and special areas of research, and even around individual philosophers of commanding importance or new interest. Predictably, the plethora of meetings, symposia, research programs, editions, and commemorative volumes has resulted in a communications crisis and in some plans for unifying the information flow and achieving a retrieval system. In these respects, the situation in philosophy fits the common description of the rapid expansion of research and communication in the latter part of our century.

Yet just as clearly, philosophy retains its own manner of sharing in the accelerated growth of knowledge. The socialization of philosophical work proceeds according to a distinctive rhythm, determined in part by the close correlation of this work with the other modes of human research and in part by the aims and attitudes of philosophers themselves. The latter are dealing with problems that have a long maturation span, that develop in and through the enlivening diversity of viewpoints, and that require a generalizing judgment about the human significance of the cooperative findings of many minds. And however close and stimulating the integration may be between the philosophical and the other modes of investigation, a certain delaying freedom for reflection and for trying out alternate interpretations is always essential to philosophical study. Perhaps for this reason, it *cannot* be said that over 90 percent of the major thinkers and concepts in philosophy have appeared only in our century. This is not due to an occupational nostalgia for some golden age in the past, or to any disaffection with the advances being made in other fields, or even to a dramatic atrophying of philosophical powers today. Rather, the negative observation serves to underscore that philosophers seek to contribute in their own fashion to the knowledge tide, whose main impact upon philosophical life is more likely to be implosive than explosive in nature.

My aim here is to examine some recent work done in philosophy, in order to discover some patterns of noetic growth that they may manifest. There are three areas in which these patterns will be sought: in historical studies, in the specializing doctrinal fields denominated as "philosophies of" this or that, and in the efforts to achieve some convergence between the general interpretations being offered by phenomenology and analytic philosophy. These domains contain a vast number of findings and embody a number of countertendencies concerning the meaning and goals of philosophy. My limited purpose is to analyze a few outstanding achievements that may well indicate the kind of influence that contemporary philosophical inquiry is having upon the course of mankind. At least it is essential to understand that this influence is being determined jointly by the philosophical energies expended in all three fields: historical, special doctrinal, and general interpretative.

The Relevance of History

Like every other theme in philosophy, that concerning the importance of historical studies is open to radical questioning and must be reconsidered in each generation. There was a period (roughly from the mid-thirties of our century until the mid-fifties) when the history of philosophy seemed to be doomed as a creative discipline and element in the formation of the philosophical mind. This was the time when many logical positivists and phenomenologists felt that they could go it alone, that the analysis of common sense and scientific statements or of present attitudes could dispense with historical perspectives, and even that the latter were inhibiting factors to philosophical creativity. This criticism of historical studies was partly a means of overcoming the dominance of idealism which had appropriated history of philosophy for its own ends, and partly a way to foster original thinking against the weight of fact and argument pressing in from the past. Historical research seemed to be incompatible with the new philosophies, both because of its idealistic categories and because of its stifling effect upon any bold thinking in the present.

Although such suspicions are still present in the philosophical community, they have had to become adjusted to other considerations that effectively alter the situation. For one thing, there is no need to continue supporting the attitude that historical studies consist in piling up further facts on an already insufferably heavy pile, without discrimination or judgment about their philosophical significance. Like literary critics and artists, the philosophers can take heart from Ben Jonson's remark that we should regard the great minds of the past as guides but not as commanders, as well as from T. S. Eliot's concurring observation that we study the past for fertile comparison and not for the amputation of our own thoughts.[1] Another reason for withdrawing the moratorium on the history of philosophy is that the analysis of human statements and attitudes cannot be carried very far without recognizing that the materials in question convey many levels of significance in an implicit form. A really competent analysis requires that the historical sources of such meanings be investigated and explicitly placed at our disposal. In the study of such historically rooted meanings, neither idealism nor any other philosophy enjoys a monopoly, unless it be that of default through the absence of other working perspectives.

Perhaps the most decisive factor in the new lease upon historical research is simply the actual participation of a significant portion of the philosophical community in such work, as well as the proven usefulness of the research to the rest of us. This is clearly the case with the remarkable developments in the history of Greek thought (especially the research on the pre-Socratic thinkers and on Plato and Aristotle) and in medieval philosophy (a grasp of whose development and continuity is truly a twentieth-century accomplishment), as well as the first steps being taken in East-West comparative philosophy. But I would like to con-

[1] T. S. Eliot, "Tradition and the Individual Talent," in his *Selected Essays* (new ed., New York: Harcourt, Brace & World, 1960), p. 5. The role of history of philosophy is explored by H. R. Smart, *Philosophy and Its History* (Lasalle, Ill.: Open Court, 1962), and by J. H. Randall, Jr., *How Philosophy Uses Its Past* (New York: Columbia University Press, 1963). The effect of the knowledge implosion upon philosophical originality is described by G. J. Seidel, *The Crisis of Creativity* (South Bend, Ind.: University of Notre Dame Press, 1966).

centrate upon three case studies in modern Western philosophy, where we can discern several features of the dynamism of philosophical knowledge in the historical mode. These instances concern skepticism, the Locke-Berkeley complexus, and research on Hegel.

1. A good indication that fresh winds are blowing in the history of modern philosophy is found in the new emphasis being placed upon the role of skepticism. As it was taught a few decades ago, modern philosophy began with some skeptical remarks by Montaigne and their overcoming in the certitude of the Cartesian Cogito, after which no significant role was played by skeptical thinkers. This neat dismissal of the skeptical problem might have satisfied historians of philosophy, had their discipline remained isolated from the rest of the world of learning. But since that discipline was kept deliberately open to other influences, the restriction of skeptics merely to the initial moment of modern philosophizing could not be maintained for very long. For a jarring element was introduced by historians of French culture in the seventeenth century. They noticed that, far from dwindling to a mere rivulet after the criticism of Descartes, the skeptical tradition grew in strength and boldness. From the standpoint of the history of literature and religion, the skeptical movement remained important and kept the initiative, long after 1650. Otherwise, one could make little sense out of Pascal and Bishop Huet, Bayle and the monstrous counterattack on skepticism mounted early in the eighteenth century by Jean-Pierre de Crousaz.

A study of these borderline figures between philosophy and other fields was not enough, by itself, to make a major difference in our way of viewing the early modern years in philosophy. The history of ideas could not transform the history of philosophy solely through its own findings but only by mediation of a philosophical judgment that these findings basically affect our interpretation of some central modern philosophers.[2] The need to take a second look at the skeptical trend became undeniable as soon as it became evident that Descartes, Malebranche, and Leibnitz were much more fundamentally and continually engaged with skeptical issues than was previously suspected. The eventual breakdown of Cartesianism, the difficulties over causality, and the eruption of theodicies and antitheodicies could not be properly understood apart from a more explicit and detailed reference to the skeptical thinkers. Moreover, the full strength of their tradition could be measured only by crossing centennial divisions and geographical lines. Just as skepticism had to be traced backward from Montaigne and into Renaissance Italy, Spain, and Portugal, so did its later fortunes have to be followed into the eighteenth-century Enlightenment in France, Britain, and Germany.[3] To fail to do so would mean losing a basic dimension in our philosophical understanding of Berkeley and Hume, Diderot and Rousseau, Lessing and Hamann. Only when the vital center of pre-Kantian philosophy was seen to be deeply affected by the course of skeptical argumentation, did the cross-fertilization of knowledge from other sources achieve a noticeably different emphasis in the history of modern philosophy.

As often happens, the total effect of this cooperative research is much greater than the summation of the individual projects. For we are now able to recognize the difference between a *distributive* treatment of particular skeptical writ-

[2] On the differences between the two disciplines, consult P. O. Kristeller, "History of Philosophy and History of Ideas," *Journal of the History of Philosophy*, 2 (1964), 1–14.

[3] The trend of this research can be followed in: R. H. Popkin, *The History of Skepticism from Erasmus to Descartes* (New York: Humanities Press, 1960); J. S. Spink, *French Free-Thought from Gassendi to Voltaire* (London: Athlone Press, 1960); H. G. Van Leeuwen, *The Problem of Certainty in English Thought, 1630–1690* (The Hague: Nijhoff, 1963); R. A. Watson, *The Downfall of Cartesianism* (The Hague: Nijhoff, 1966); and P. P. Hallie, *The Scar of Montaigne* (Middletown: Wesleyan University Press, 1966).

ings and a *thematic* presentation of the skeptical outlook, as furnishing one of the general and constant motifs in modern philosophy. To seek out the meaning of being and human values, in the presence of a persistent skeptical challenge, is an essential defining note of philosophizing in the modern manner. That is why Hegel treats skepticism as one of the permanent phenomenological formations of the human spirit, why Kierkegaard paradoxically invokes Hume and Hamann together in preparation for the life of faith, why Husserl returns to the Cartesian situation as an archetypal source, and why Santayana weaves his philosophy out of the interplay between animal faith and skepticism. Lucidity concerning the latter's abiding role as a goad to inquiry is a condition for attaining full awareness of the modern philosophical spirit. And in the degree that philosophy is an essential component in man's future, a grasp of the skeptical theme is also a general condition for the attainment of maturity by modern man in his many other cultural modalities.

2. It is always dangerous to say that one has the thought of a past philosopher completely pinned down and dissected. For such an assertion fails to reckon with the nature of historical inquiry, which receives its orientation from *an always changing present situation* in philosophical discussion and in cognate disciplines. What assures our interest in a philosophical source is the proven presence there of pools of meaning, which remain unsuspected or unemphasized until they are found to respond to some current problem in philosophy or some line of research developing in other fields. This delicate correlation between contemporary questioning and the exploration of historical sources is well illustrated by recent studies in Locke and Berkeley, especially their views on science and language. The two topics bearing out this point are best observed when these British thinkers are considered together in dialogue, rather than taken in their separate universes.

A look at the histories of philosophy will show how widely shared was the venerable tradition of dealing with Locke's way of ideas and Berkeley's critique of the concept of matter quite in isolation from the current state of scientific thought. It was considered sufficient to quote Locke's graceful reference to the incomparable Mr. Newton and to hint that Berkeley went in over his depth in his discussion of mathematics and motion. It was possible to retain this attitude of incuriosity about the precise relationship between the two philosophers and the growth of science only up to the time when the nascent disciplines of history of science and philosophy of science began to focus upon the period in question. But then the findings made in these latter areas proved to be so relevant for the better understanding of Locke and Berkeley that a shift of perspective was clearly advisable for historians of philosophy. In turn, their own research is having a reciprocal effect upon the history of science itself, owing to the interlocking relationship among the several disciplines involved.

There is a much broader sharing of concepts and problems (especially on the skeptical issues revolving around knowledge claims about substance and modes) among the continental rationalists and British empiricists than was previously recognized. Yet some definite philosophical differences persist between the two traditions, determined partly by differences in the scientific setting of their respective speculative efforts. It is no more profitable in philosophy than in science to think solely in global terms about the scientific revolution of the seventeenth century. Especially for appreciating the direction taken by British philosophy, it is necessary to distinguish carefully between the pre-Newtonian and the Newtonian phases of scientific thought.

In the main, Locke's fundamental work was done in the pre-Newtonian scientific milieu dominated by Boyle and Sydenham, that is, by experimentalists in the chemical, biological, and medical fields. Hence the *Essay Concerning Human Understanding* made a uniquely tempered synthesis between the interpretative activities of reason and attention, the dynamism of the material world, and the restricted range of our knowledge.[4] Diagnostic probability was assigned a large role in both theoretical and practical issues, thus giving Locke a middle path between systematic rationalism and skepticism. Perhaps only on the eve of Newton's triumph was it possible to attain precisely this blending of epistemological factors and to regard it as a satisfactory solution of the issues.

To view Berkeley as coming in the wake of the *Principia* and indeed in the full tide of the Newtonian popularizers is to realize that his intellectual position is something more than a conceptual *tour de force*. He is not simply drawing paradoxical conclusions from statements made by Locke but is wrestling with changes induced by Newton's conception of natural philosophy and the contributions made to it by mathematics and experiment. Yet we have been able to grasp Berkeley's problem only as a result of the confluence of three factors in the current growth of knowledge: the editing of his own early *Philosophical Commentaries;* the comparisons, made by philosophers of science, between Berkeley and Ernst Mach on the constructive and interpretative elements embodied in scientific laws; and the aforementioned prolonga-

---

[4] The Lockean synthesis of science and epistemology is the central theme in two books: C. A. Viano, *John Locke: Dal razionalismo all' illuminismo* (Turin: Einaudi, 1960), and Maurice Mandelbaum, *Philosophy, Science, and Sense Perception* (Baltimore: Johns Hopkins Press, 1964). Special aspects of this correlation are studied in a remarkable series of articles published in *Journal of the History of Ideas*: R. M. Jost, "Locke's Rejection of Hypotheses About Submicroscopic Events," 12 (1951), 111–30; D. A. Givner, "Scientific Preconceptions in Locke's Philosophy of Language," 23 (1962), 340–54; P. Romanell, "Some Medico-Philosophical Excerpts from the Mellon Collection of Locke's Papers," 25 (1964), 107–16; G. A. J. Rogers, "Boyle, Locke, and Reason," 27 (1966), 205–16; L. Laudan, "The Nature and Sources of Locke's Views on Hypotheses," 28 (1967), 211–23.

tion of studies of skepticism into the British sphere. Only when they are all drawn together do these lines of investigation enable the historian of philosophy to make a more appreciative reading of the text of Berkeley. His immaterialism is now seen to be, not a wild Gaelic fancy, but a shrewd and well informed attempt to defend a minimal coherence of thought and language at a time when the Newtonian world picture was providing further grist for the skeptical tropes.

On a closely related issue, our conception of Locke and Berkeley is being modified in the light of another contemporary focus of scholarship. This time, the revision is stimulated by the joint implications of language studies and the linguistic approach in philosophy of science. These tendencies make the historian of philosophy specially sensitive to a deficiency in his treatment of the two British thinkers, namely, his relative slighting of their remarks on the nature and functions of language. The linguistic turn in philosophy is having deep repercussions on the entire history of philosophy, making a prime topic of the doctrine on language in all the historical sources. Berkeley is a clear beneficiary of this new interest. In the course of exorcizing all meaning from the term "matter" and of bringing everyday usage in line with his immaterialist outlook, he becomes quite reflective on the several uses of language. He examines its role not only in communication of theoretical knowledge but also in evocation of moods, in persuasion of assent, and in the fine tactics of obfuscating another mind. As for Locke, his correlation between words and representative ideas by no means constitutes the sum of his theory of language. To appreciate its real complexity, however, this theory must be studied in conjunction with his account of active reflective reason and his scientific preconceptions.

Both literary critics and comparative philosophers are interested in the dominant metaphors that distinguish one art work or one philosophical standpoint from another. Until recently, analysis in terms of the distinguishing root metaphor was applied mainly to broad philosophical positions and concepts, such as hylemorphism, monism, and organicism. But this approach is now being extended to the study of individual thinkers, including Locke and Berkeley. Both men are dissatisfied with the metaphor of the machine as a model upon which to organize their reflections about the knowing process and the nature of the universe.

Without fully anticipating Dewey, Locke the medical man and civil servant does modify the mechanistic account of knowledge by viewing the relation of man to the world in more organic and practical terms. In a living, practical intercourse with the world, man does not have to claim that his definitions give a sharply etched and essential insight into the nature of things. It is by subordinating the machine metaphor to a more humane one, drawn from the practice of the chemist, the physician, and the statesman, that Locke is enabled to describe with equanimity the flickering candle of practical human intelligence at work in the world of everyday affairs.

In Berkeley's case, the machine metaphor is not only subordinated but replaced by the metaphor of language itself.[5] Since he is not encumbered by a theory of ideas as representatives of states of matter, he can establish a direct relationship between ideas, or sensible things, and the realm of mind. Berkeley conceives of the pattern among the ideas constituting nature to be a kind of language: it is the manner in which God communicates His presence to men, and which

[5] A full scale interpretation of Berkeley in terms of the plurality and elusiveness of the metaphors required for understanding the natural world is made by C. M. Turbayne, *The Myth of Metaphor* (New Haven: Yale University Press, 1962). The function of metaphors in scientific thinking is set forth historically by T. S. Kuhn, *The Structure of Scientific Revolutions* (Chicago: University of Chicago Press, 1962), and in logical terms by M. B. Hesse, *Models and Analogies in Science* (South Bend, Ind.: University of Notre Dame Press, 1966), especially pp. 157–77.

enables men in turn to acknowledge the divine reality in their practical activities. Instead of being an autonomous machine, remorselessly grinding out its operations and frustrating our efforts to relate with it, the sensible world is to be viewed as a divine-human linguistic pattern. Its function is sacramental and expressive: to manifest the reality of the divine spirit to men and to give orientation to the tendencies of the human spirit in its search for interpersonal values.

What these researchers in Locke and Berkeley suggest is that our comprehension of modern philosophers will be increased by making a twofold comparison, as a matter of deliberate policy. We should try to illuminate a particular philosophy by examining the *scientific matrix* within which it develops, and also by looking for its *guiding metaphor* on how to conceive the universe and man's function therein. As the instance of the British empiricists shows (and this theme could be pursued in Hume's imaginative variation of mechanical and organic models of the world), the reflective originality of a philosopher vis-à-vis the predominant scientific conception of things is often discovered in his use of a slightly different central metaphor than the one underlying the scientific theorizing. In long range terms, the example of Locke and Berkeley also suggests that the philosophical component in the growth of human knowledge will continue to be closely responsive to the current phase of scientific thought and yet remain somewhat critically related to it. One facet of the philosophical vocation is to keep searching for more adequate metaphoric guides than the reigning one. This methodic dissatisfaction furnishes one intellectual condition enabling both the philosopher and the scientist to make further creative advances beyond a given state of research. To resist the sealing-off process of a ruling world view (whether picturable or not), there must be an opportunity for philosophical self-interrogation as well as for scientific hypothesizing.

3. As late as thirty years ago, it would have been a safe prediction that Hegel would lose his power of fascination for the philosophical community and that investigations into his thought would dwindle to an inconsequential trickle, more philological than philosophical in import. And yet the present horizon is filled with research works and popularizations, journals and congresses (in both Eastern and Western Europe), dedicated to Hegel's philosophy. In scope, intensity, and competence, this new tide of interest is unsurpassed by previous contributions in that area.[6] The renascence of Hegelian studies is a cautionary lesson that no historical assessment, especially a negative judgment of obsolescence, concerning a major philosophical mind can be regarded as utterly definitive. More than likely, such a judgment means, not that the primary source itself has run dry and lost all attraction for men, but that a particular line of interpretation of the primary source has now petered out. New methods of releasing the intellectual riches have to be devised, but the history of philosophy is like that of literature insofar as there is never a total abandonment of the effort to reawaken the primary texts.

In examining the phenomenon of Hegel's rebirth among us, we can at the same time improve our self-comprehension. There was no arbitrary way in which an enthusiast could convince people about Hegel's actual relevance. That evaluation could result only from a remarkable convergence of many directions of inquiry upon a common focus in the thought of Hegel.

One such contemporary motivation rises from the world-wide need to understand the intellectual roots and genesis of

[6] Hegel research is reported extensively in *Hegel-Studien* (1961 ff.). Its international character, correlation with many fields, and philosophical sweep, are evident from three symposia: "Studies in Hegel," *Tulane Studies in Philosophy*, 9 (1960); D. C. Travis, ed., *A Hegel Symposium* (Austin: University of Texas Press, 1962); "Hegel Today," *The Monist*, 48 (1964), 1–132.

Marxism.[7] Unavoidably, the effort to grasp the outlook of Marx, especially as expressed in his humanistically oriented early economic-philosophic manuscripts, leads men back to a fresh reading of Hegel. The ambiguity of the Right and Left Hegelian schools invites scholars to trace that ambiguity to its fountainhead and thus to make a more humanistic and work-centered interpretation of Hegel. Especially the Hegel of the *Phenomenology of Spirit* and *Philosophy of Right* shows a modern awareness of social strife and historical development of attitudes which is useful not only for appreciating Marxism but also, more directly, for grasping the conflicts and aspirations of our developing century.

The reappraisal has gathered further momentum from the effective use of the Hegelian heritage made by existentialists and phenomenologists. They have dissociated the idea of dialectical method from the construction of a ponderous system and restored it to the function of discerning the formation and interplay of complex meanings within the self and in society. In so doing, they have brought into relief the twin Hegelian themes of freedom and concrete thinking.[8]

[7] The Hegel-Marx relationship looms large in: A. Cornu, *The Origins of Marxian Thought* (Springfield, Ill.: C. C. Thomas, 1957); R. Garaudy, *Dieu est mort: Étude sur Hegel* (Paris: Presses Universitaires, 1962); K. Löwith, *From Hegel to Nietzsche* (New York: Holt, Rinehart & Winston, 1964); J. Hyppolite, *Études sur Marx et Hegel* (new ed., Paris: Rivière, 1965); N. Rotenstreich, *Basic Problems of Marx's Philosophy* (Indianapolis: Bobbs-Merrill, (1965); L. Dupré, *The Philosophical Foundations of Marxism* (New York: Holt, Rinehart & Winston, 1966); and S. Avineri, *The Social and Political Thought of Karl Marx* (New York: Cambridge University Press, 1967).

[8] These topics dominate the expert general presentations made by J. N. Findlay, *Hegel: A Re-Examination* (New York: The Macmillan Co., 1958); W. Seeberger, *Hegel oder die Entwicklung des Geistes zur Freiheit* (Stuttgart: Klett, 1961); and G. R. G. Mure, *The Philosophy of Hegel* (New York: Oxford University Press, 1965). A good place to begin the study of cultural and moral alienation is in these works: Findlay, pp. 119–31; Seeberger, pp. 416–45; Mure, pp. 93–102. Also A. W. Levi, "Existentialism and the Alienation of Man," in *Phenomenology and Existentialism*, ed. by E. N. Lee and M. Mandelbaum (Baltimore: Johns Hopkins Press, 1967), pp. 243–68.

These themes are never properly developed within the extreme settings of individualism and totalitarianism. For Hegel, the achievement of human freedom and concrete values is essentially a social and interpersonal task, one that sets goals for society in the very act of maturing the quality of personal intelligence and decision. This is one reason why the existentialist and phenomenological analyses are pitched at the intersubjective level. To penetrate the human situation, these analyses must respect our essential openness to the world, temporality, and social history. Hegel's actuality can be measured by his influence in determining these latter points of reference for the study of man.

We also come to acknowledge Hegel's germinating presence whenever we probe into the historical springs of the basic themes of *alienation* and the death of God. Here is a striking confirmation of the claim that philosophy has its own rhythm of maturation and that several disciplines usually contribute to the process as soon as human nature in its broadest aspects is involved. From his earliest manuscripts to his most finished treatises, Hegel's writings are filled with a sense of the dislocations in the psyche and society. He develops a theory of man's alienation and thingification—his loss of spiritual self-possession and union with natural processes— as a means of interpreting such universal phenomena in our lives. One of the chief expressions of alienation is found in the feeling that we are cut off from the divine life and that, in fact, God is no longer a living actuality among us.

But it has taken a century and a half for these thoughts to seize hold upon our general outlook. For this widespread awareness of the implications of alienation to grow, much more has been required than the philosophical reflections of Feuerbach and Marx, Nietzsche and Sartre. Their leading ideas have had to be integrated with the specific work done on the problem in the framework of psychiatry and theology, sociology and literary criticism. What we now call the pervasive sense of alienation is a complex and slowly developing signification and practical attitude. Into its formation and elucidation have gone the joint efforts of men working in all these fields, with their appropriate methods and concepts.

One of these co-contributing disciplines is the history of philosophy, which does not specify its activities in a cultural vacuum. In serving the needs of philosophical reflection, it also serves the broader demands of humanity in our age. The historical findings on the philosophical sources of the themes of alienation and God's death are being put to many uses by scholars and reflective minds of all sorts. This is a sure sign that we have only started to plumb these interpretations of our existence and to make them somehow operative in our social and religious life. Our future relationships with our fellow men and God will be deeply marked by our prolonged experience and examination of alienation in all its modes.

Into the Special Fields

A characteristic tendency among many philosophers today is to dedicate oneself to some special doctrinal field. Whereas a Kant or a Hegel dealt with art, religion, and history as parts of a general systematic investigation, some philosophers are now inclined to concentrate their entire inquiry in one of these regions. The philosophy of science is so vast and complex an enterprise that the individual thinker feels barely able to keep abreast with its main currents and to contribute to some specific issues. Owing to the vast influx of materials, the philosopher of art finds generalization difficult within the world of art, let alone the achievement of integration with the rest of philosophy. Moreover, there are journals and associations, technical vocabularies and research instruments, devoted exclusively to the philosophy of history or the philosophy of religion. The pressures of research and competency often induce a man to restrict his professional work to but one of these worlds of meaning, even though he has to abandon the traditional image of the philosopher as one who maintains a universal concern for the problems of mankind.

Thus it would be misleading to depict philosophers as a uniform group of partisans of generality confronted with the world of specializing tendencies in all other sciences and arts. Philosophy is thoroughly a member of this world of knowledge increasing through the pathways of specialization, and hence it experiences at its own intimate center the tension between a general humane concern and the drive toward specialized types of research and judgment. Yet it belongs within this world of accelerating research in its own way and has its own way of responding to the internal tug toward *both* general wisdom and specializing competence. Since it belongs to the philosopher's vocation to become as reflective as possible about his condition and methods of work, it may be instructive to examine some features of this domestic tension in philosophy today. The manner in which philosophers are meeting this problem may have some analogical significance for other investigators as well.

Instead of approaching this question directly from the standpoint of the philosophical generalist in methodology and theory of knowledges, however, I would like to show how the question formulates itself within the perspective of the philosophical specialist himself. This can be conveniently observed in the philosophy of history, although some adjustments would be required to fit other areas of special doctrinal speculations. And in order to grasp the operative pattern, it is advisable to focus upon the common conditions and tendencies of the work being done in this field of philosophy of history, rather than upon individual motivations.

There is a significant absence of a wall of isolating indifference between the working historian and the philosopher of history. The two manage to maintain an operational zone of interrelation, not indeed between history and philosophy taken in block form, but rather between certain mutually relevant phases of active discussion in these two disciplines. This *phasic operational* relationship is one of the firm, actual modes of communication found in our universe of rapidly separating galaxies of knowledge.[9] Some professional historians regard it as important for their research and the formation of students to consider general questions about the meaning of history and the nature of historical knowledge, just as some philosophers deem it necessary to specify their own treatment of these same questions by a study of the actual practice of historians. An added inducement toward gaining mutual clarification exists because persuasive interpretations of history and historical judgment have already been introduced into the public forum by a Voegelin and a Toynbee, neither of whom can be categorized strictly as a historian or as a philosopher of history. Thus one valuable area of intersection among the knowledges of man is being supported by the recognition of some common interests and problems among otherwise differently orientated investigators.

However, diverse their theoretical positions, philosophers of history agree in practice today upon a very broad threefold division of their problems. Most philosophical discussion can be grouped around the three areas of internal patterns and trends in history, the nature of historical statement and expla-

[9] This interchange is encouraged by the examples of a philosopher (B. Croce) doing professional historical work and of a historian reaching a reflective generalization about his field (E. H. Carr, *What is History?* [New York: Alfred A. Knopf, 1962]). The open door policy prevailed at the conference for historians and philosophers presided over by Sidney Hook: *Philosophy and History* (New York: New York University Press, 1963), as well as in two philosophical anthologies: *Theories of History*, P. Gardiner, ed. (Glencoe: The Free Press, 1959), and *The Philosophy of History in Our Time*, H. Meyerhoff, ed. (New York: Doubleday Anchor, 1959). This cooperation is placed upon a permanent editorial footing in the journal *History and Theory*.

nation, and the relationship between such pattern and explanation and the basic historicity of man.[10] Although there is a
close connection between these three types of philosophical
theory of history, they do help to define different aspects of
the meaning of history and even of the philosophical work
being done in this field. Roughly speaking, the contributions
of the classical tradition of philosophers of history from Vico
and Hegel to Comte and Dilthey center around the speculative determination of patterns and trends; recent Anglo-
American inquiry is concerned mainly with the critical and
methodological analysis of historical explanation; and the
phenomenological and existential stress is laid upon the
anthropological aspect of history, as expressive of our historical mode of being. This division is one of emphasis rather
than of exclusive interest, since most philosophers of history
refuse to take a narrowly reductive view of the tasks in their
field, whatever restrictions they may place upon their personal range of work.

Looking now at the problem of doctrinal specialization
from within the threefold structure of the theory of history,

[10] W. H. Walsh's *Philosophy of History* (New York: Harper
Torchbook, 1960) and B. Mazlish's *The Riddle of History* (New
York: Harper & Row, 1966) exploit the first two categories: the
speculative theory of the meaning and mechanism of history, and
the critical theory of how we come to know what happened. The third
approach in terms of philosophical anthropology and transsubjective
time is developed metaphysically in three groundbreaking books: N.
Rotenstreich, *Between Past and Present* (New Haven: Yale University Press, 1958); E. L. Fackenheim, *Metaphysics and Historicity*
(Milwaukee: Marquette University Press, 1961); Paul Weiss, *History
Written and Lived* (Carbondale: Southern Illinois University Press,
1962). From the phenomenological and existentialist side, one may
consult: Edmund Husserl, *Phenomenology and the Crisis of Philosophy* (New York: Harper Torchbook, 1965); Karl Jaspers, *The
Origin and Goal of History* (New Haven: Yale University Press,
1953); Karl Löwith's two works, *Meaning in History* (Chicago: University of Chicago Press, 1949), and *Nature, History, and Existentialism* (Evanston, Ill.: Northwestern University Press, 1966); and
Paul Ricoeur, *History and Truth* (Evanston Ill.: Northwestern
University Press, 1965).

we can see that there is no sheer closure of this specialized field. In the degree that a contemporary philosopher of history draws sustenance from the previous philosophical tradition, he recognizes the powerful continuity between the general theories of knowledge, action, and value in a Kant or a Hegel and their respective treatments of progress and freedom in history. Reflection upon such a correlation between the broad philosophical framework and the specific conception of historical trends and patterns in these classical instances is a spur toward making explicit whatever similar correlation may be used by today's specializing philosopher of history. A scrutiny of his own operative presuppositions not only makes his treatment of history more straightforward and rigorous but also keeps it permanently open to the integrating principles and to the other specific domains in philosophy, in the degree that their relevance to his procedures can be shown.

The fact is, however, that much contemporary theorizing about history moves from the first-level study of patterns to the second-level study of the kinds of statement and explanation that yield historical knowledge. This shift of interest to the epistemology and methodology of historical discourse (from discourse *in* the historical mode to that *about* the historical mode) is not an isolated phenomenon peculiar to workers in the field of philosophy of history. It corresponds to a more general trend toward an analytic study of groups of statements made in several modes of discourse: scientific and esthetic, moral and religious. Here is another indication that the philosopher of history is not so lost in his specialization that he does not respond to, and make effective use of, methodic approaches working more generally throughout the regions of philosophy.

We have a case here of that sort of specialization which does not sunder all relationships with the rest of philosophy. This is evident from the treatment of even some quite specific issues. For instance, differences concerning the use of causal language in historical explanation can be traced to some general differences among philosophers over the nature of the causal relationship, the need for adaptation to human action as a subject matter, and the comparison between scientific and historical description of the course of events. Far from being a sealed-off compartment, the philosophy of history often serves, along with the philosophy of science, as a testing ground for the explanatory reach of a general theory of knowledge and reality.[11] Just as there is open intercourse between positions taken in philosophy of science and those taken in the theory of historical statements, so is there a channel of communication between these zones of inquiry and and the central themes in any philosophy of human experience.

The purpose of contemporary metaphysical and phenomenological studies of history is precisely to explore this fundamental channel and to make it an actually traveled route for understanding the meaning of history. That meaning is not exhausted by determining some internal trends within the historical process and some structural limits of statements and acts of comprehension concerning such process. We also have the opportunity of following these two approaches to their point of unification in human reality and, hence, of inquiring how it is that we live historically and engage in historical inquiries at all. To ask about the historical nature of human existence and thinking in this general way is to

[11] The complementarity between theory of knowledge and theory of history can be seen in three analytic works: P. Gardiner, *The Nature of Historical Explanation* (London: Oxford University Press, 1952); W. H. Dray, *Laws and Explanation in History* (London: Oxford University Press, 1957); A. C. Danto, *Analytical Philosophy of History* (New York: Cambridge University Press, 1965). Carl Hempel's application of his philosophy of science to historical explanation is a central point for discussion in the essays edited by W. H. Dray: *Philosophical Analysis and History* (New York: Harper & Row, 1966).

bring the philosophy of history explicitly within the matrix of one's central philosophy of man in relation to his world. It is to raise the question of the distinction between the temporality and historicity of nature and that of the specifically human mode of existing in natural reality. Such generalizing of the interpretative basis of history is not the privilege of any one school of philosophy, even though at present it is cultivated most steadily by the phenomenologists and existentialists. One task for future dialogue is to stake out the common ground that these philosophical approaches occupy along with the Marxist, naturalist, and idealistic conceptions of man's temporality and historicity.

As it turns out, then, the philosophy of history provides a meeting place for diverse intellectual interests. It evokes a flow of phasic operational communication between historians and philosophers; it furnishes a challenge to general theories of method and knowledge to test themselves in a concrete portion of human life; it offers a significant variation of problems for workers in the theory of science or art or religion; and it encourages the different philosophies of man and nature to compare their accounts of how the historical mode of being develops within the natural world. A regional theory that includes such generalizing functions within its proper scope is not actually opposed to the philosopher's vocation of seeking wisdom but provides one path toward obtaining wisdom within the context of our world of expanding knowledge. It is not the prelude to fragmentation, but rather it generates a new integrating level of human cognition and values.

This suggests that the trend toward specialization in philosophical studies should be viewed in function of the life of *the entire philosophical community*. As Charles Peirce once remarked, philosophy no less than science profits from the modern requirements of the division of intellectual labor. This or that individual line of motivation may be quite separatist and isolationist, but the impact of the specialized work as a whole responds to a more open and integrating spirit. The healthy growth of the philosophical community requires that intensive efforts be made to penetrate each area of human activity, to master the methods used in each field, to show the need for adaptation and analogical application of all general principles of method, knowledge, and being, and thus to generate a constant interflow of philosophical intelligence between the foundational and the specializing types of inquiry. Without imposing its own pattern upon the other arts and sciences, philosophy can offer some encouragement to the specialist that he is not tearing the world asunder, and to the generalist that he is not committed to an airy realm of unity devoid of the hard diversities of life.

The Phenomenological and Analytic Convergence

It is a widely acknowledged trait of philosophy since the midcentury that well-planned efforts are being made to break through the barriers separating the two most widespread positions—phenomenology and analytic philosophy. They can no longer be assigned to different geographical homes, since in America at least there is a growing acquaintance with the phenomenological method and source materials, while conversely several continental thinkers are making good use of the analytic and linguistic procedures. As a result of such mutual explorations, it has been found that the two traditions share many more problems and basic concepts than was originally suspected. Since this pattern of convergence is likely to become more pronounced in the coming years, it is fitting to conclude the present analysis of basic patterns with four considerations relevant to the tendency in question. They concern the meaning of convergence, the contribution of historical studies to this tendency, the contribution to it made by some specific doctrinal topics, and the image of the philosopher which emerges from the whole process.

1. It is important to retain the distinction between a

movement of *convergence* and one of *identification*. There are no indications that analytic and phenomenological philosophies are being related in such fashion as to bring about their ultimate fusion and identification. This would be a goal of questionable worth in any case, since it would entail the rubbing-out of certain differences that enable thinkers to perceive different meanings and values, all of which must be cultivated by mankind. Instead, the convergence tendency has a restricted, yet quite important, aim that can be expressed in negative terms and then in more positive ones.

The negative goal is to remove entirely the stultifying preconception that only one of these approaches incorporates a genuine philosophic method and that the other one is the expression of some extraphilosophical cultural condition. The general applicability of the one philosophic method does not necessarily entail the reduction of the other to the status of being either a latent variation of the first or else a psychic and cultural condition, requiring a technique of therapeusis rather than argumentation. Since both the analytic and the phenomenological methods are characterized by their quite general range of operation and by the use of therapeutic techniques, a rather severe intellectual self-disciplining is required for removing the exclusivist imputation. This means that the discovery of elements of similarity between the two philosophical procedures is not to be construed as building the case for their eventual identification or for the total subordination of the one to the other.

More positively expressed, once the two philosophies are brought within hailing distance and encouraged to enter discussion on the footing of mutual integrity, then the differences can be recognized and encouraged. Each one will retain its own manner of achieving rigor and experiential content. Philosophers within the two traditions can learn to converse together and accept insights from each other, without permitting the conversation to become transformed into a total merger and blurring of distinct perspectives.[12] If this meaning for philosophical convergence is appropriate for the relations between analysts and phenomenologists, then it may also guide us in the far more complicated task of strengthening the philosophical discussions between East and West.

2. A further point of relevance for the previously considered work of historical investigations can now be established, namely, the bearing of historical studies upon the phenomenological-analytic convergence. The potentialities for convergence contained in the historical order are only now beginning to be realized, and we may expect that this instrument for broadening the basis of philosophical communication will be used with increasing effectiveness. Its likely fruits can be predicted by indicating just one line of pertinent research, that concerned with Husserl's central concept of intentionality.

Whenever Husserl himself recounted the historical origins of the theme of the intentional directedness of human acts to an objective world, he acknowledged a special debt to Descartes and Brentano, Hume and Kant. Considerable attention has been paid to his first two predecessors on this topic, but at least in the English-speaking world his relationship *with*

[12] An opening toward the values in Continental philosophy is detectable in two cooperative volumes: *Clarity Is Not Enough*, H. D. Lewis, ed. (New York: Humanities Press, 1963), and *British Analytical Philosophy*, ed. by B. Williams and A. Montefiore (New York: Humanities Press, 1966). The editors of the latter work call attention to "the development of a certain underlying tension in contemporary British philosophy. On the one hand, the mood and intent are still predominantly empiricist; on the other hand, the implications of many of the methods used and of the insights attained are not but are moving in a phenomenological and even a metaphysical direction" (pp. 6–7). Conversely, there is an opening toward British and American traditions from the side of phenomenology, as testified by two further collections: *Realism and the Background of Phenomenology*, R. M. Chisholm, ed. (Glencoe: The Free Press, 1960), and *An Invitation to Phenomenology*, J. M. Edie, ed. (Chicago: Quadrangle Books, 1965). In the same spirit, see the issue of *The Monist*, 49 (1965), 1–164, devoted to "Linguistic Analysis and Phenomenology."

Hume and Kant on the constitution of objective meaning has not been sufficiently emphasized.[13] And yet it is precisely from a historically enlightening comparison with the two latter thinkers that we can measure the depth of Husserl's engagement with the same basic problems and sources nourishing the analytic tradition and thus that we can hope to remove the aura of strangeness still persisting around him. The Husserlian doctrine of intentionality is one way of responding to Hume's question of how we can maintain the identity of a perceptual object, amid all its variations and in the face of so much incompleteness of actual perception. And it is also a response to the difficulties engendered by Kant's attempt to account for the objectivity of statements in the scientific, moral, and esthetic modes of discourse. Historical probing into these roots of the problem of intentionality shows that there is a much closer confrontation of the same abiding issues of perception and reasoning, plurimodal discourse and the human context, than the cultural, terminological, and temperamental differences between twentieth-century phenomenologists and analytic thinkers would initially suggest.

A better understanding of the development of American philosophy is promoted also by a broadened historical study of intentionality. This is not surprising in view of the common sources studied by Husserl and the generation represented by William James, Royce, and Peirce. All these men

[13] A good start can be made by consulting the accounts of intentionality given in: H. Spiegelberg, *The Phenomenological Movement* (2nd ed., 2 vols., Hague: Nijhoff, 1965), 107–17 (with references to William James); Q. Lauer's two books, *Phénoménologie de Husserl: Essai sur la gènese de l'intentionnalité* (Paris: Presses Universitaires, 1955), and *The Triumph of Subjectivity* (New York: Fordham University Press, 1958); and Aron Gurwitsch's influential *Studies in Phenomenology and Psychology* (Evanston, Ill.: Northwestern University Press, 1966), pp. 124–74 (valuable comparisons of Husserl with Hume and Kant). It would help to have in English a thorough analysis of Husserl's relations with Hume and Kant, comparable to Iso Kern's *Husserl und Kant* (The Hague: Nijhoff, 1964).

had to wrestle with the theories of Hume and Kant concerning the relationship between the surging life of consciousness and the objective meanings that develop and persist in our world. Both the German thinker and the Americans were also sensitive to the radical psychologism proposed by Mill and Wundt, as well as to several forms of evolutionary and historicist explanation of the human mind in bio-causal terms.

As we increase our historical understanding of these shared sources, we can better appreciate why James should do more than write another version of German laboratory psychology.[14] He engaged in a phenomenological search for the sedimented meanings incorporated in our everyday experience and in scientific concepts, as well as for the persistent aims of man the agent and evaluator, who organizes his several worlds of meaning. Royce (who read Fichte early in life and Husserl in later life) elaborated his own theory of intentionality, relating human meanings to the will activity of an absolute center of life and thought. For him as well as for Husserl, an intimate bond holds between intentional activity and the human self's existence in a community rather than in a solipsistic shell. Peirce also bore the marks of a thinker who had delved into the same sources as had Husserl. He focused on the patterned growth of the community of scientific investigators as one major form of intentional activity and was just as concerned as Husserl to show that such activity is more ultimate than the Cartesian notes of clarity and distinctness of evidence.

3. The tendency toward intellectual convergence, but not coalescence, among the philosophical traditions of our century receives increasing impetus from the philosophical study of *language*. Until now, the phenomenological and the analytic

[14] See Gurwitsch's essay, "William James's Theory of the 'Transitive Parts' of the Stream of Consciousness," in *Studies in Phenomenology and Psychology*, pp. 301–31, as well as J. M. Edie's essay, "Notes on the Philosophical Anthropology of William James," in *An Invitation to Phenomenology*, pp. 110–32.

examinations of the language phenomenon have been conducted in quite separate cubicles. This is understandable, owing to the great complexity of the subject, the many ramifications it has within a particular philosophy, and the rapidity with which general linguistics has developed. In addition, one's own language and literature provide such a rich source of reflection that one's philosophical horizon can easily be made coterminous with them. As a consequence, the two philosophies have followed separate paths in their investigation of language. But there are some factors presently at work which make it difficult to convert a situation of factual separation into a principle of isolation or even into an evaluative judgment about work done elsewhere. Hence such comparative factors are potent means of opening the cubicles and encouraging some cooperative research.

The strong emphasis upon linguistic topics within the analytic group has had the good effect of compelling contemporary phenomenologists to pay closer formal attention to the work done in this area by Husserl and Merleau-Ponty, as well as by the existentialist Heidegger. These philosophers regard language, especially the speaking word and the word being heard, as a basic way in which man keeps open to reality and develops his community ties with other men.[15]

---

[15] Merleau-Ponty's theory of language is the basis for R. C. Kwant's exposition: *Phenomenology of Language* (Pittsburgh: Duquesne University Press, 1965). The distinction between original speech (personal speaking) and objective or second-level speech (organized discourse on facts and theories) is stressed by G. Gusdorf, *Speaking (La Parole)* (Evanston, Ill.: Northwestern University Press, 1965), and in the comparison made between the phenomenological and analytical conceptions of language by M. Dufrenne, *Language and Philosophy* (Bloomington: Indiana University Press, 1963). As he moved into the areas of ethics, esthetics, and religion, Ludwig Wittgenstein had to wrestle with the translinguistic, experiential reference of language, as it speaks in the personal form of witness to reality. See Wittgenstein's "A Lecture on Ethics," and F. Waismann's "Notes on Talks with Wittgenstein," *The Philosophical Review*, 74 (1965), 3–16; also, L. Wittgenstein, *Lectures and Conversations on Aesthetics, Psychology and Religious Belief*

This view of the language activity is not so very far removed from the position of the later Wittgenstein, who sees language also in its humanistic import. The more we probe into the developments on language in the two philosophical traditions, the more we find the creative minds coming to interpret language in terms of man's opening to, and constant practical engagement with, the living world. Differences that immediately crop up between the more dramatic and metaphysical interpretation made by the phenomenologists and the more subdued and restricted interpretation made by the analysts cannot obscure the discovery of some firm common ground of inquiry.

One specific question where the two groups can be observed facing the common human evidence is that of usage involving the language of bodiliness. Both traditions have mounted severe critiques of Cartesian dualism, taken not only metaphysically but also as a careless application of thing-terms to the reality of man. But it is the experience of both groups that, once we are placed on guard against dualistic category-mistakes, the problem still remains of making some discerning use of the language of bodily being and that of reflectivity. Distinctions are still needed in speaking significantly about our own body, both in function of our individual reality and as distinct from the nonhuman bodily world. The precise relationships established by man with the rest of the natural world, in virtue of his capacity for inquiry and for technological reshaping, have to be examined in reference to his talk about embodying human meanings in his conduct and in the environment. Not only naturalism but also phenomenology and analytic philosophy in their attentiveness to the significances of language are thus held together within

(Berkeley and Los Angeles: University of California Press, 1966), pp. 53-64. The comparative theme is developed by P. Ricoeur, "Husserl and Wittgenstein on Language," in *Phenomenology and Existentialism*, pp. 207-17.

the shared domain of human problems. They cannot spring apart from one another on any sure grounds of irrelevance, and the likelihood is that their joint concern about the nature of language will henceforth increase the degree and quality of mutual discussion.

4. Finally, is there any mutuality in their respective conceptions of the philosopher's task? Whether they accept or reject the grand style of earlier types of philosophizing, in practice they are involved in a converging movement because of a minimal, yet basic, agreement about what the philosopher should be doing. Whether he be conceived as elucidating our concepts and modes of talk or as probing into the genesis of our meanings and unifying contexts, his work is essentially that of exploring man's ways with himself and his experienced world. The active modes of human experiencing and acting are manifold and complex, so that they are best investigated by following several paths in philosophy. Nevertheless, there is a center of reference, in human meaningful reality, for both the phenomenological and the analytic ways of reflection. And indeed, the footing in human experience and the discipline of reflectivity may prove to be a sufficiently comprehensive basis for the gradual convergence of other modes of philosophizing in East and West.

14

COMPARATIVE RELIGION:
ITS PAST AND FUTURE

MIRCEA ELIADE
University of Chicago

T HE BEGINNINGS OF comparative religion as a discipline took place during the middle of the nineteenth century at the very height of the era of materialistic and positivistic propaganda. Auguste Comte published his *Catéchisme positiviste* in 1852 and his *Système de politique positive* between 1855 and 1858. In 1855 Ludwig Buchner brought out his *Kraft und Stoffe*. The following year Max Müller published his *Essays in Comparative Mythology*, which can be considered the first important book in the field of Comparative Religion. Darwin's *Origin of Species* appeared three years later, and in 1862 Herbert Spencer issued his *First Principles*.

The new discoveries, hypotheses, and theories that the learned world took up from these works with passionate interest rapidly became very popular. One of the best sellers of the epoch was Ernst Haeckel's book, *Natürliche Schöpfungsgeschichte*. Issued in 1868, it went through more than twenty editions before the end of the century and was translated into a dozen languages. While Haeckel's book was furiously reprinted and translated, and Herbert Spencer was elaborating his *System of Synthetic Philosophy* (1860–96), the new discipline of the history of religions (or comparative religion) was making rapid progress. In his *Lectures on the Science of Language* (2d ser., 1864), Max Müller introduced his theory concerning solar mythology among the Aryans—a theory grounded in his belief that the myths were born from a "disease of language." In 1871 Edward Burnett Tylor published his *Primitive Culture*, brilliantly trying to reconstruct the origin and evolution of religious experiences and religious beliefs. Tylor identified the first stage of religion with what he called animism: the belief that Nature is animated, that is, has a soul. From animism evolved polytheism, and polytheism finally gave way to monotheism.

I do not intend to recall all the important dates in the history of the scientific study of religion during the second half of the nineteenth century.[1] But this new discipline followed the general pattern imposed by the *Zeitgeist:* the positivistic approach to the "facts" and the search for the "origins," for the very beginnings of religion. Max Müller thought that the Rig-Veda reflects a primordial phase of Aryan religion and consequently one of the most archaic stages of religious beliefs and mythological creations. But already in the early 1870s the French Sanskrit scholar Abel Bergaigne proved that the Vedic hymns, far from being the spontaneous and naïve expressions of a naturalistic religion, were the product of a highly learned and sophisticated class of ritualistic priests.

Scholarly discussion about the Vedas was only an episode in the long and dramatic battle to identify "the origin of religion." A brilliant and learned writer, Andrew Lang, contributed decisively to the demolition of the mythological reconstructions of Max Müller. Two of Lang's most successful works, *Custom and Myth* (1883) and *Modern Mythology* (1897) were drawn up from articles in which he discredited

---

[1] Cf. Mircea Eliade, "The Quest for the 'Origins' of Religion," *History of Religions*, 4 (1964), 154–69.

Max Müller's ideas with the aid of E. B. Tylor's theories. But a year after the publication of *Modern Mythology*, in 1898, Andrew Lang brought out another book, *Making of Religion*, in which he rejected Tylor's view that the origin of religion is to be found in animism. Lang based his arguments on the presence of a belief in High Gods among some very primitive peoples, such as the Australians and the Andamanese. Tylor held that such a belief could not possibly be original, that the idea of God developed from the belief in nature-spirits and the cult of ancestor ghosts. But Andrew Lang found among the Australians and Andamanese neither ancestor worship nor nature cults.

This unexpected and antievolutionistic claim, that a High God was not at the end of the religious history but at the beginnings, did not greatly impress the contemporary scholarly milieu. It is true that Andrew Lang did not master his documentation thoroughly and in a discussion with Hartland he was compelled to surrender portions of his earlier thesis. Besides, he had the misfortune to be an excellent and versatile writer, the author of a volume of poetry, among other works. And literary gifts usually arouse the scholars' suspicions.

However, Andrew Lang's conception of the primitive High God is significant for other reasons. In the last years of the nineteenth century and the first years of the twentieth, animism ceased to be considered the first stage of religion. Two new theories were proclaimed in that period. They might be called preanimistic, because both of them claimed that they identified a more archaic stage of religion than that described by animism. The first theory is that of Andrew Lang, postulating a belief in a High God at the beginnings of religion. Though almost ignored in England, this hypothesis, corrected and completed, was later on accepted by Graebner and a host of Continental scholars.

Unfortunately, one of the most learned ethnologists of our

time, Wilhelm Schmidt, elaborated the hypothesis of the
primitive belief in High Gods into a rigid theory of a primordial monotheism (*Urmonotheismus*). I say unfortunately
because Schmidt, though a very able scholar, was also a
Catholic priest, and the scientific world suspected him of
apologetic intentions. Furthermore, Schmidt was a thorough
rationalist, and tried to prove that the idea of God had been
grasped by primitive men strictly through causalistic thinking. As Schmidt was publishing the monumental volumes of
his *Ursprung der Gottesidee* (1912–1955), however, the
Western world witnessed the irruption of quite a number of
irrationalist philosophies and ideologies. Bergson's *Élan
vital*, Freud's discovery of the unconscious, Lévy-Bruhl's investigations of what he called the prelogical, mystical mentality, Rudolf Otto's *Das Heilige*, as well as the artistic
revolutions of dada and surrealism—these mark some of the
important events in the history of modern irrationalism.
Thus, very few ethnologists and historians of religions could
accept Schmidt's rationalist explanation of the discovery of
the idea of God.

On the contrary, the epoch running roughly from 1900
to 1920 was dominated by the second preanimistic theory,
that of *mana*, that is, the belief in an indistinct and impersonal
magico-religious force. It was especially the British anthro-
pologist Marret who insisted on the preanimistic character
of the belief in *mana*, showing that this magico-religious
experience does not presuppose the concept of a soul and,
consequently, represents a more archaic stage than Tylor's
animism.[2]

What interests us in this vivid opposition of hypotheses
on the origin of religion is the preoccupation with the "primordial." Both preanimistic theories—that of the primordial
belief in a High God and that of an original experience of

[2] Cf. Mircea Eliade, "The History of Religions in Retrospect: 1912–
1962," *The Journal of Bible and Religion*, 30 (1963), 98–109.

the sacred as an impersonal force—maintained that they had reached a deeper level of religious history than Tylor's animism. As a matter of fact, both theories claimed that they had disclosed *the very beginnings* of religion.

Freud also thought that, with the aid of psychoanalysis, he had reached the "primordial" phase of human culture and religion. As is well known, he identified the origin of religion and culture in a primeval murder, more exactly in the first patricide. For Freud, God was merely the sublimated physical father who was slain by his expelled sons. This astonishing explanation was universally criticized and rejected by all responsible ethnologists, from Kroeber to Malinowski and from Boas to Schmidt. But Freud neither renounced nor modified his theory.

While Freud was correcting the proofs of *Totem und Tabu*, to be issued in book form the following year (1913), Émile Durkheim published his *Formes élémentaires de la vie religieuse*. Durkheim, too, was certain that, applying the sociological method, one can grasp the "origin" of religion; for him, religion was a projection of social experience. Studying the Australians, he noticed that the totem symbolizes sacredness and the clan at the same time. He concluded that sacredness (or "God") and the social group are one and the same thing. Durkheim's explanation of the nature and origin of religion was emphatically criticized by a great number of outstanding ethnologists.

Schmidt, Freud, and Durkheim were the last authors to claim that they knew how religion originated and for what reasons and purposes. Such a belief is no longer shared by the historian of religion. He knows by now that he is unable to reach the "origin" of religion. What happened in the beginning, *ab origine*, is no longer a problem for the historian of religion, though conceivably it might be one for the theologian or the philosopher. Almost before he was aware of it, the historian of religions found himself in a cultural milieu quite different from that of Max Müller and Tylor, or even that of Frazer and Marret. It was a new environment nourished by Nietzsche and Marx, Dilthey, Croce, and Ortega, and later on by Heidegger and Sartre; an environment in which the fashionable cliché was not *nature* but *history*, not "origin and development" but temporality and historicity.

The discovery of the historicity of man helped the historians of religions to get rid of the last remnants of angelism and idealism. We now take more seriously the fact that man belongs to *this* world, that he is not a spirit imprisoned in matter. To know that man is always conditioned is to discover that he is equally a creative being. He responds creatively to the challenge of the cosmic, psychological, or historical conditionings. For that reason we no longer accept the naturalistic explanations of human cultures and religions. To give only an example, we know now that primitive man did not—and, as a matter of fact, could not—have a naturistic religion. In the time of Max Müller and Tylor the scholars used to speak of naturistic cults and of fetishism, meaning that primitive man adored natural objects. But the veneration of cosmic objects is not "fetishism." It is not the tree, the spring, or the stone that is venerated *but the sacred that is manifested through these cosmic objects*. This understanding of the archaic man's religious experience is the result of the broadening of our historical consciousness.

In sum, a religious phenomenon cannot be understood outside of its "history," that is, outside of its cultural and socioeconomic contexts. There is no such thing outside of history as a "pure" religious datum. For there is no such thing as a human datum that is not at the same time a historical datum. Every religious experience is expressed and transmitted in a particular historical context. But admitting the historicity of religious experiences does not imply that they are reducible to nonreligious forms of behavior. Stating that a religious datum is always a historical datum does not mean that it is reducible to a nonreligious history—for example, to an economic, social, or political history. We must never lose sight of one of the fundamental principles of modern science: *the scale creates the phenomenon*. Henri Poincaré asked, not without irony: "Would a naturalist who had never studied the elephant except through the microscope consider that he had an adequate knowledge of the creature?" The microscope reveals the structure and mechanism of cells, which structure and mechanism are exactly the same in all multicellular organisms. The elephant is certainly a multicellular organism, but is that all that it is? On the microscopic scale, we might hesitate to answer. On the scale of human vision, which at least has the advantage of presenting the elephant as a zoological phenomenon, there can be no doubt about the reply.

The *homo religiosus* represents the "total man"; hence comparative religion must become a total discipline, in the sense that it must use, integrate, and articulate the results obtained by the various methods of approaching a religious phenomenon. In other words, it must become a *total* and *creative hermeneutics*, since it is called to decipher and explicate every kind of encounter of man with the sacred, from prehistory to our days. We do not doubt that this "creative hermeneutics" will finally be recognized as the royal road of the history of religions. Only then will its role in culture begin to show itself to be important. Such a "total discipline" can open new perspectives to Western thought, to philosophy properly speaking as well as to artistic creations.

Western philosophy cannot contain itself indefinitely within its own tradition without the risk of becoming provincial. Now the historian of religions is able to investigate and elucidate a considerable number of "significant situa-

tions" and modalities of existing in the world which are
otherwise inaccessible. It is not just a matter of presenting
"raw materials," for the philosophers would not know what
to do with documents that reflect behavior and ideas too
different from those familiar to them.[3] The hermeneutical
work ought to be done by the historian of religions himself,
for only he is prepared to understand and appreciate the
semantic complexity of his documents.

But it is exactly at this point that certain grave misunder-
standings have occurred. The rare historians of religions who
have wanted to integrate the results of their researches and
meditations in a philosophical context have contented themselves with imitating certain fashionable philosophers. In
other words, they have compelled themselves to think according to the model of the professional philosophers. And
that is a mistake. Neither philosophers nor men of culture
are interested in second-hand replicas of their colleagues
and favorite authors. In deciding to "think like X" about
archaic or oriental thought the historian of religions muti-
lates and falsifies it. What one expects from him is that
he will decipher and elucidate enigmatic behavior and
situations—in brief, that he will advance the understanding
of man by recovering or reestablishing meanings that have
been forgotten, discredited, or abolished. The originality and
importance of such contributions reside precisely in their
exploration and illumination of spiritual universes that are
submerged or that are accessible only with great difficulty.
It would be not only illegitimate but ineffectual to disguise
archaic and exotic symbols, myths, and ideas in a form
already familiar to contemporary philosophers.

This is the reason we have said that a historico-religious

[3] It suffices to examine what some rare contemporary philosophers
interested in the problems of myth and religious symbolism have done
with the "materials" they have borrowed from ethnologists or historians of religions in order to renounce this (illusory) division of
labor.

creative hermeneutics would be able to stimulate, nourish, and renew philosophical thought. From a certain point of view, one could say that a new *Phenomenology of the Mind* awaits elaboration by taking account of all that the history of religions is capable of revealing to us. There would be important books to write on modes of existing in the world or on the problems of time, death, and dream, based on documents that the historian of religions has at his disposal.[4] These problems have passionate interest for the philosophers, poets, and art critics. Some of them have read the historians of religions and have utilized their documents and interpretations. It is not their fault if they have not profited from these readings as they expected.

In brief, the history of religions affirms itself as both a "pedagogy," in the strong sense of that term, for it is susceptible of *changing* man, and as a *source of creation* of "cultural values," whatever may be the expression of these values, historiographic, philosophic, or artistic. It seems difficult to believe that, living in a historical moment like ours, the historians of religions will not take account of the creative possibilities of their discipline. How to assimilate *culturally* the spiritual universes that Africa, Oceania, and Southeast Asia open to us? All these spiritual universes have a religious origin and structure. If one does not approach

---

[4] There is, above all, urgent need to get rid of many clichés still encumbering contemporary understanding—for example, Feuerbach's and Marx's celebrated interpretation of religion as alienation. As one knows, Feuerbach and Marx proclaimed that religion estranges man from the earth, prevents him from becoming completely human, and so on. But even if this were correct, such a critique of religion could be applied only to late forms of religiosity such as those of post-Vedic India or of Judeo-Christianity—that is, religions in which the element of "other-worldness" plays an important role. Alienation and estrangement of man from the earth are unknown and, moreover, inconceivable in all religions of the cosmic type, "primitive" as well as oriental; in this case (that is to say, in the overwhelming majority of religions known to history) the religious life consists exactly in exalting the solidarity of man with life and nature.

them in the perspective of the history of religions, they will disappear as spiritual universes; they will be reduced to *facts* about social organizations, economic regimes, epochs of precolonial and colonial history, and so on. In other words, they will not be grasped as *spiritual creations;* they will not enrich Western and world culture; they will serve to augment the number, already terrifying, of *documents* classified in archives, awaiting electronic computers to take them in charge.

15

CHRISTIANITY AND THE
NEW EARTH*

KARL RAHNER, S.J.
University of Münster

T HE BASIC imperative running through the whole of the
*Pastoral Constitution on the Church in the Modern
World* issued by the Second Vatican Council is the sum-
mons to the people of the Church to work together to bring
modern human existence in all its dimensions to a form more
worthy of man. This imperative arises—the point is crucial
—out of the Council's ultimate Christian understanding of
human existence, not because the people of the Church are
Christians and men *besides*, but precisely because the people
of the Church are Christians. The task they share with all
men of good will (including even atheists) is to be accomplished out of their properly Christian faith, their eschatological hope, and their love for God and man—a love given to
them by God.

This Constitution does not purport to say—or at least
so it seems in many texts that will have to be considered
more exactly a bit later—that this basic Christian attitude
represents merely some sort of special motivation for seeing
through the already given task, that Christianity furnishes an

* Translated by Francis J. Goetz, S.J., with the collaboration of
Clyde Lee Miller, S.J.

ideological driving force or a new, additional, yet merely formal obligation, while the concrete actuality of the task remains untouched by this motive and these new obligations. The basic Christian attitude would then be fashioned from knowledge that is purely within the world, based on philosophy and the natural law, knowledge of a concrete, practical character. Hence such knowledge would at most have to be protected from error by revelation—with moral necessity in the sense of Vatican I. Rather the Constitution states, for example—to anticipate more exact references—that Christians are to imbue the fabric of secular life with their eschatological hope. Thus the characteristically Christian way of taking up the secular task does not consist solely in a Christian's so shaping the world in accord with principles based on the natural law that Christianity has enough room to develop its properly religious, "other-worldly" mission. Such an aim could be achieved by no more than a philosophical pluralism that assured tolerance and freedom in a society.

How can the task of fashioning a world more worthy of man be the common task of all men of good will? How can any consensus regarding this task be reached among all men if the Christians of the Church still interpret the task as calling for action by Christians which is directed to ends materially different from those of other men? Or is this materially different Christian character of the secular task—a secular task whose exact nature is itself not yet clear or determinate—denied again by the Council's Constitution when this Constitution states, more explicitly than the social encyclicals of the popes from Leo XIII to Pius XII, that the Church can furnish no neat recipe for the concrete shaping of the world and of history and that working out concrete plans and directives is rather the common task of all responsible men? Do we find in this Constitution a veiled and unresolved ambiguity? Or is it simply a matter of fact that there are concretely a great many common tasks and preliminary moves toward a "better world" necessarily shared by Christians and non-Christians alike, even if the initial concept of a this-worldly goal and the more or less ultimate tasks concluding the work are materially different for Christians and non-Christians in meaning and deed? In such a case the distinction marking off the Christian's task from that of others could be left to be worked out at some later time.

The difficulty, which still needs clarification, does not derive simply from postulating a common task that Christians share with non-Christians as such. Indeed, one could think that perhaps such a common task can exist, since in the case of non-Christians too the final dynamism powering their historical actions and decisions is, of course, grace, even if they do not know this. One could say further that in every pluralistic society (which is recognized by all as favoring common action) cooperation is to be secured through the interaction of divergent historical drives. So it should not be astonishing if Christians stake their own notion of the future on competitive open dialogue.

II

The difficulty lies rather in the matter itself: do we have, indeed can we as Christians have, a properly Christian, this-worldly ideology regarding the future? Insofar as the question does not refer to general "natural-law" or "Christian" principles—which do exist—but to a concrete program, to clear, concrete imperatives (for today and tomorrow, even though they always remain open to the larger future), the official Church clearly cannot proclaim such an absolute, concrete program.[1] It is not authorized to do this, it is not capable, and makes no claim to be so. Such observations,

---

[1] Karl Rahner, "Grenzen des Amtskirche," *Schriften zur Theologie*, VI (Einsiedeln: 1965), 499–520.

however, do not simply answer the question in the negative. For it is at least still conceivable[2] that the Church find and choose such a concrete program, acting as the concrete people of God in a concrete, as it were, "political" decision, even if this is not at all a mere deduction from natural-law and Christian principles.

What such a choice would mean for the individual Christian can remain an open question here, that is, whether as an individual he has to be "for" the declared choice. Open, too, are the questions of how such a "politico"-historical decision of the Church is concretely brought about and how it functions to form the will of the whole profane society, of a state, of a group of nations, or how it fails so to function. It might also be conceivable that the official Church would later more clearly articulate such a basic decision—at first hit upon almost instinctively and held unreflectively—regarding the concrete, earthly future of mankind, and that the Church would proclaim it in the form of a "directive" to be clearly distinguished from doctrine and commandment. If something like this is considered fundamentally possible,[3] that is, if some middle ground is recognized as occupied by neither the Church in its officially constituted authority nor by individual Christians acting only as individual members of profane society though under Christian "inspiration," in this case there would be place for such a specifically Christian, this-worldly program and decision for the future,

[2] With regard to the following distinction see the *Pastoral Constitution on the Church in the Modern World*, Nos. 43, 74, 75, 76. References to this document will be quoted simply by number hereafter. Other conciliar documents will be quoted with their respective titles.

[3] For more detailed treatment, see Karl Rahner, "Zur theologischen Problematic einer Pastoralkonstitution," in *Volk Gottes*: Zum Kirchenverständnis der katholischen, evangelischen und angliskanischen Theologie, R. Baumer and H. Dolch, eds.: (Freiburg: 1967), pp. 683–703.

however much the program might or might not be carried out in fact.

Is there such a future that Christianity itself can concretely project out of the present? When the pastoral Constitution says[4] that the future and its world must be "more humane," "more just," and "more peaceful" than the present, that it must be penetrated with the justice and love that make possible the free development of every man, must allow the unity of men as a family of brothers to grow, that it must strive harder against the spirit of egoism and other sinfulness, when such basic principles are also detailed for more concrete areas—to promote a just and humane policy toward families, structuring of the economy, efforts for peace, and so on—then of course we are presented with a goal that Christianity, that is, Christian faith and God's command, calls for. But these principles still do not proclaim any specifically Christian content for this desired future.

This is also the case when it is stated that the future shaping of society must be penetrated by the Christian spirit. Again, little more is clearly added when the unity of love for God and for one's neighbor is emphasized or when the significance of revelation for the effective recognition of human dignity is praised. One could well think that the stress on the idea that Christians share the earthly task with all men of good will (for example, *Pastoral Constitution*, Ch. i, No. 21 and *passim*) points to a negative answer to our question as to whether there is a specifically Christian earthly future. And the same negative answer is suggested because the "integral" (otherworldly) vocation of man is distinguished from his human tasks (No. 11) when the "building of the world" "serves the whole vocation of man" (No. 35), because the growth of God's kingdom and

4 With regard to the following see the *Pastoral Constitution*, Nos. 11, 15, 21, 23, 24, 26, 37, 38, 40, 41, 43, 55, 57, 58, 61, 63, 76.

earthly progress are distinguished as two separate things
(Nos. 36, 38, 39, 42, 43), because the relative autonomy of
the order of creation (Nos. 34, 36, 39, 41, 59, 67) is stressed
although its otherworldly connections are emphasized, and
because response to the world and striving toward the native
city of heaven are distinguished and the duality of the orders
of knowledge is underlined (No. 59), and so on.

III

But now the other side of the evidence must also be considered. What does it mean to say that there exists a unity
of mankind which on the one hand Christ founded (No.
32) and which has to grow until the day of fulfillment (No.
32), but which on the other hand does not seem to be
strictly identical with the Church as such since mankind
as a whole is to be brought to the unity of the family of
God?[5] What does it mean when the kerygma of the Gospel
is said to be already rooted in the human situation to some
extent before this fact becomes manifest through verbal
creativity (No. 62)? What does it mean to emphasize that
mankind strives toward a future in which humanity itself
will become a sacrifice pleasing to God (No. 38), and to
say that the earthly service rendered by men prepares the
"material of the kingdom of God" (No. 38)? Several times
at the Council there was talk of the "new earth" and the
"new heaven." Of course this "new earth" is represented as
the eschatological gift of God himself and thus is not merely
the result of earthly progress ("progressus terrenus," No.
39). Yet it is also not simply something to replace what

[5] See Nos. 40, 43; *Lumen gentium*, No. 28. There is no talk here
of the desired extension of the Church to the whole of humanity and
in this sense of the unity of God's family ("unitas familiae Dei"),
since the "growing body of the new human family" is not only to be
thought of quantitatively nor is it identical with the Church, and yet it
is a foreshadowing ("adumbratio") of the future world (*cf.* No. 39).

has gone before. It does not merely push this aside and do away with it, but is a transformation of the previous world ("transformatio mundi," No. 38; "universi transformandi," No. 39). However, this world that is to be thus transformed does not seem to be only the one that God himself has created (taken in its simple, substantial existence). For it is stated (No. 39) that not just love will remain but its *work* ("opus") as well and that we will "find again" the results of our labor ("industriae nostrae fructus"), the consequences of human activity (for they are thought of as "purified.") So the world is conceived as something to be transformed, something man himself has created in the "carrying forward of creation" (Nos. 34, 57). This "carrying forward of God's creation" is frequently referred to, even if it is viewed as the execution of God's creative will somehow distinct from his supernatural, salvific will.

The divine love is also the law of the "transformation of the world" (No. 38), and to it a universal brotherhood ("fraternitas universalis") pertains which apparently does not consist simply of the Church as such (*ibid.*). Eschatological hope is to be impressed into the structures of secular life itself (*Lumen gentium*, No. 35). If the "renewal of the world" is thus already irrevocably established and is already anticipated in this age ("in hoc saeculo") in a real way (*Lumen gentium*, No. 48), then this anticipated presence of the eschatological "renewal of the world" is not given merely in the Church, its kerygma and cult alone, but also in the structures of secular life. Only thus can mankind at present devise a sketchy notion of the world of the future (No. 39). The hints found in the Constitution should certainly not be overinterpreted. The Constitution does not clearly resolve the alternative between what we can call "a secular shape for the future influenced by the Christian spirit but of a purely earthly and passing kind" and "a Christian shaping of the future created by men and possessing ultimate significance." Nor is it really clear how to respond to these alternatives. Yet the Constitution, itself groping and hesitant, brings us to face the question the alternatives raise.

IV

Perhaps the real question has now become clear: Is the world that man himself creates only the "material" for his moral testing, remaining in itself morally indifferent? Will the world simply disappear when the definitive kingdom of God arrives? The thrust of this question becomes clearer when we note that this world is no longer the milieu provided by God himself for man's moral activity, but it is a world raised to the second power: man himself creates it in the course of history as the fulfillment of God's creation committed to him. Can this world, thus understood, still be compared to the rush baskets that the old monks of the Scythian desert wove during the day and unwove in the evening in order to pass their time without sinning while they awaited the eternity of an anticipated but as yet totally unrealized future? Or does this second world, the world of man's creation, enter into the eschaton proper, even if it be unimaginably "transformed"? Does the "new earth" come down from heaven (even though to a virtually neutral "ground" that God once created and that will be constituted by the identity in substance of man's original mortal body with his glorified body and because the material world thereby constituted is no more given up than man's original mortal body is)? Or will the "new earth" be constructed here in time by men? Should we understand "new" earth or an earth that is "renewed" (of course, in the infinity of the eternally young God)?

Earlier man could not put the question so clearly. For this world of which we speak did not exist earlier. Early man lived in a world of "nature" that was merely given. What man created himself was small and frail—from the body, which died, to the relatively few products of cultural activity. All this seemed merely fuel for the coming world conflagration that could leave behind only ashes. The real eschatological outcome of history could be glimpsed beforehand only in the ethical quality of the immortal "soul" taken along into the "beyond." The "resurrection of the body" was expected, of course; one could picture the wounds of Christ's glorified body remaining as the victory marks of his life history. Somehow near the edge of consciousness—and only there—the question we have posed was alive. As the pastoral Constitution indicates, the question has not yet been clearly worked out as a question even today. Nor is it merely a scholastic subtlety, as when De Broglie racks his brains over whether resurrected bodies can still eat. For this question is—though in a pointed form—a question about the more exact relation between Christian eschatological hope and the modern ideology of the future, that is, of a future Utopia (in a neutral meaning of the term). Are we accomplishing our ultimate end if, just, loving, and obedient to God's commission to us regarding this world, we have fulfilled his creative design? Is fulfillment such that the moral element[6] of history remains meta-empirical in its deepest foundations? Will such a morality constitute the final stage of men and matter, which have been created solely by God himself? Or does material, corporal history also help constitute this definitive state,[7] even though by means of death and radical transformation?

This question is not without importance for the relationship of Marxism and Christianity, for the Christian inter-

[6] The ultimate moral quality of history, as it exists before God, cannot be read by us from history with certainty.

[7] This holds as a positive Christian view in any case and was always clearly known by Christianity.

pretation of history, and for many other matters in the Christian understanding of man's existence. As Christians, we are not struggling with a naïve form of Marxism which simply exploits the individual as material for a future society and history. It would indeed be a kind of Marxist faith either to consider oneself able directly to complete "the kingdom of God" by oneself, or to view the future only as the lure of history, a lure always unattainable, receding into the indeterminate, leading to an unfinished whole grasped by no one.

We Christians—even granted the proviso that one can take something too seriously and so ruin it—have to allow ourselves to be asked by Marxism how seriously we really take the world that is committed to our making. Is it ultimately only indifferent material on which we exercise our virtues? Would this be to take it seriously enough? Does it not become in fact indifferent insofar as one could also exercise the same virtues in a world that is kept reactionary—especially the virtue of patience vis-à-vis a mean, annoying, unjust world? If we Christians were to respond to this question, we could not invent our own situations for protecting the kingdom of heaven, but rather we would have to test our heavenly virtues, which alone are "abiding," on the "material" that is sent to us now in the course of the world. And since this world changes, we must ask ourselves once more why it should be that in dealing with change the definitive virtues to be exercised are those whose "material" and "objective" results fall back into transiency, into what is no more. This question is not meant to be clever or overplayed. For it remains true in any case that concrete history in its corporeality is the place where the definitive stage of existence and the absolute future is actualized. In any case, too, all that the Council said holds true about Christians' responsibility for the world and about the error in an artificial opposition between the Christian's integral (and hence "otherworldly") vocation and his task in the world. But perhaps it will be evident that the question we have posed is also not without import in view of the intellectual situation today, in which Christianity has to make its message intelligible.

V

But can this question be answered at all and how is it to be answered?

First, the following is clear: The kingdom of God, the definitive stage which ends and "cancels" history, is something of itself due really to come about. This stage is not just a constant lure for history, its merely asymptotic goal which would simply function to keep history moving. This definitive stage will not be present as a simple last state and end result of history planned and effected by man but will be the act of God. And this act is of course to be regarded— here just as in the history of nature and the world—as the self-transcendence of human history (divine, free, quite incalculable from the starting point of our action). History and its completed final stage are always distinct and separated from one another by that which is experienced in each individual's history as death and entails a radical "transformation"; this last affects the whole of history just as death does the history of the individual. "The time of the consummation of the world and of mankind is unknown, as is the manner of transformation of the whole world" (No. 39). Therefore the statement about the permanence of history—not only in its meta-empirical ethical quality but also in its historical result—is not presented on quite the same terms as the statement about the radical transformation of history into the unknown and into the openness of the absolute future which is God himself. It is impossible to form a concept of history in its permanent definitive state. Every description—we are warned in Matthew 22:30 ("At the resurrection they will neither marry nor be given in marriage . . .")—would be a pseudo-Christian apocalyptic and not a Christian eschatology. Even the attempt to imagine a glorified body as it will be leads to contradictions; this would be all the more the case if one wished to make the same attempt with respect to the body of mankind, which is gradually forming in its own history.

On the other hand, one may not take the opposite position, holding that, besides having eschatological validity and permanence, the end point of mankind's history also would have absolutely *no* concrete reference to mankind's history itself. For the same objection could be made regarding the corporeity of an individual's history. No single time of life can be *the* model of the definitive state of the body, and yet Christian tradition has considered this ultimate state as bringing one's whole concrete history to a glorified manifestation when it becomes actual.

The two propositions about the ultimate validity of history and about its radical transformation for the present remain unresolved for us in a fundamental dialectic that keeps the future open and allows the present to retain its basic importance. Both propositions are hermeneutical principles as well as statements of fact. But, given these presuppositions, what more can be said? History itself constructs its own ultimate fulfillment. What is permanent is the work of concrete love in history; love remains as what is done by men and not merely a moral distillate that history leaves behind as its exhausted "residue." History itself enters into the fullness (*Endgültigkeit*) of God himself, not only of man, who acts once in history and then after his role has been played (as in Hugo Von Hoffmannsthal's "Everyman") leaves it behind as what has become unreal.

Why can it be said that history enters into God's own fullness? Because the Word of God has himself both made and endured history. Were our thesis entirely false, then he would have had to do away with his "role" entirely. But he remains forever the God-Man, and his humanity is not merely rewarded with glory but remains above all his own, which would be really superfluous if this thesis were not true. The opposite contention basically leads to an intolerable division of "soul from body" and of noumenon from phenomenon. True human "history" in freedom constructs of its very nature its definitive stage and is not merely rewarded with it. The conclusive stage is not placed "behind" the history in which events occur for which we are responsible, even if this conclusive stage is not evident on the surface of reality and can never be judged by us. The correctness of our thesis is also suggested by a positive answer to the question whether the ethical—without prejudice to the fact that it has to be done as the work of freedom—*is* not just what becomes more concrete in history, whether it does not have its significance in and from history. So history itself must have an ultimate meaning if the ethical is to have it as well.

VI

If then the history made by man has ultimate significance as event and as result, then the basis and presupposition for this fact become apparent. Even this "worldly world" that as such remains profane still basically manifests in itself a hidden Christian element. The mandate of creation and its completion appear as an inner moment of the single, complete, redeeming, and divinizing will of God for a world in which his self-communication takes place, and they get their final meaning and concrete shape from this whole. So they are fixed precisely in their proper worldly character until their consummation.

All this, however, still says nothing with regard to what makes up the concrete Christian character of the this-worldly realization of the future. Because the answer to this question is so difficult, one should not think that it cannot be ascertained. As was mentioned earlier, however, because the historical action of non-Christians regarding the future is also under the dynamism of grace, this more precise question cannot be posed in face of the unresolved dilemma confronting us, which demands that we either point out some Christian feature in this future which is advocated only by the "explicit" Christians, or that we recognize what is sought after as merely "human." For that reason (and over and beyond it) it is possible that the Christian "significance" and the final Christian root of a historical reality that is to come (social, political, and so on) will first manifest itself when it is already present and thus can be interpreted reflexively. Such a reality manifests itself for example in the growing unity of mankind which is frequently referred to in the pastoral Constitution and which is in fact presupposed for a Church that is really worldwide. Another example might perhaps be the obviously growing openness to the future and its planning—the dialectic of increased planning and of unplanned contingencies that as such are formally and explicitly anticipated. In this dialectic—insoluble for us —God's absolute future perhaps shows itself in silent presence. The Christian shaping of the this-worldly dynamism of the future thus ultimately does not depend on Christians setting up concrete societal, political, social, and other demands special to themselves and to no one else. Such a conclusion would make it clear that at heart the Christian does not have two tasks that would be held together only by a "moral" bond effected by one's obligation to both and thus only by the abstract, moral significance that his secular task would have for eternity.[8]

[8] For further clarification of what is set forth here, see the author's treatment of these problems: "Marxistische Utopie und Christliche Zukunft des Menschen," *Schriften zur Theologie*, as cited *supra*, pp. 77–88; also his "Experiment Mensch," "Christlicher Humanismus," and "Zum Problem der genetischen Manipulation," *ibid.*, VIII (1967).

NOTES ON THE CONTRIBUTORS

SIR ERIC ASHBY, master of Clare College at Cambridge University since 1959, is former chairman of the Nigerian Universities Commission. Born in London, he earned his doctorate in science at the University of London and did research in experimental botany and held professorships in Sydney, Australia, and Manchester, England. During World War II he served as counsellor and acting minister at the Australian Legation in Moscow, and from 1950 to 1959 was President of Queen's University, Belfast. A member of the Central Advisory Council for Science and Technology and the University Grants Committee, he has had fifteen years of experience in advisory work for universities in tropical Africa and was President of the British Association for the Advancement of Science in 1963 and Godkin Lecturer at Harvard University in 1964. He is a Fellow of the Royal Society and holds honorary degrees from fourteen universities. His published works include *Environment and Plant Development* (1931), *Technology and the Academics* (1958), *African Universities and Western Tradition* (1964), and *Universities: British, Indian, African* (1966).

JAMES R. BRIGHT is professor of business administration at the Harvard University Graduate School of Business Administration and a specialist in the relations between technology and business. A native of Pittsburgh, Pennsylvania, he studied at Lehigh and Columbia universities. After holding a position as test engineer for the General Electric Company, he served five and one-half years in the Army and then as an editor for the McGraw-Hill Publishing Company and the Cahners Publishing Company for eight years. He joined the faculty at Harvard in 1954. He has been editor of *Product Engineering* and *Modern Material Handling* and is the author of *Automation and Management* (1958) and *Research Development, and Technological Innovation* (1964), as well as many papers.

HARLAN CLEVELAND, United States Ambassador to the North Atlantic Treaty Organization, is known the world over as one of the most articulate and informed scholars and writers in the diplomatic corps. Born in New York City, he studied at Princeton University and was a Rhodes scholar at Oxford University. He has served as publisher of *The Reporter* magazine, dean of the Maxwell Graduate School of Citizenship and Public Affairs at Syracuse University, as Assistant Secretary of State for International Organization Affairs, and as a member of the board of trustees of Experiment in International Living. During World War II he was decorated with the U.S. Medal of Freedom and Order of the Crown of Italy for his work as vice president of the Allied Commission in Rome. His books include *The Overseas Americans* (1960), *The Promise of World Tensions* (1961), and *The Obligations of Power* (1966).

JAMES D. COLLINS, professor of philosophy at Saint Louis University, is an internationally known historian of modern philosophy. Born in Holyoke, Massachusetts, he received the degrees of B.A., M.A., and Ph.D. from the Catholic University of America and was a research fellow at Harvard University in 1944–45. He gave the Suarez Lecture at Fordham University in 1953 and the Aquinas Lecture at Marquette University in 1962. In 1963–64 he held a Guggenheim Fellowship. His many scholarly studies on both European and American thinkers include books on *The Existentialists* (1952), *The Mind of Kierkegaard* (1953), *A History of Modern European Philosophy* (1954), *God in Modern Philosophy* (1959), and *The Emergence of Phi-*

losophy of Religion (1967), this last being the Thomas More Lectures, which he gave at Yale University in 1963, now published in enlarged form by Yale University Press.

JOHN T. EDSALL is professor of biological chemistry at Harvard University, where he received his A.B. and M.D. degrees and in 1928 began his teaching career as tutor in biochemical sciences. He was born in Philadelphia, Pennsylvania. A Guggenheim Fellow, he has also been a Fulbright lecturer at Cambridge University and the University of Tokyo and visiting professor at the Collège de France and has served as consultant to many foundations and research groups. Since 1944 he has edited *Advances in Protein Chemistry* and since 1958 has been editor of the *Journal of Biological Chemistry*. Known especially for his own research on proteins, he is the author of a large number of scholarly publications, including *Biophysical Chemistry* (with J. Wyman, 1958).

MIRCEA ELIADE is Sewell L. Avery Distinguished Service Professor of History of Religions at the University of Chicago. He was born in Bucharest, Romania, where he received his doctorate from the University of Bucharest. He subsequently studied at the University of Calcutta. He has lectured at the universities of Bucharest, Rome, Lund, Marburg, Munich, Frankfurt, Strasbourg, Padua, and Paris and has served as cultural attaché at the Romanian legations in London and Lisbon. His many books include *Techniques du Yoga* (1948), *Le Chamanisme* (1951), *The Myth of the Eternal Return* (1954), *Patterns of Comparative Religions* (1958), and *The Forge and the Crucible* (1962).

GYORGY KEPES is a painter and since 1946 has been professor of visual design at the Massachusetts Institute of Technology. He became the first Director of the Center for Advanced Visual Studies when this center began operation at the Massachusetts Institute of Technology in the fall of 1967. He is a native of Hungary, where he studied at the

Royal Academy of Fine Arts. His paintings have been exhibited in Budapest, Berlin, New York City, Chicago, San Francisco, Cleveland, London, and elsewhere, and he has written widely on man's visual environment and its effects on consciousness and culture. He is editor of *Visual Arts Today* and of the six-volume series entitled *Vision and Value*, and the author of *Language of Vision* (1944), *The New Landscape* (1956), and many other works.

MARSHALL McLUHAN is director of the Graduate Center of Culture and Technology at the University of Toronto and was named in 1967 to the Albert Schweitzer Professorship of the Humanities, the State of New York Regents chair assigned to Fordham University. Born in Edmonton, Alberta, Canada, he studied at the universities of Manitoba and of Wisconsin and received his doctorate in English at Cambridge University in 1942. He was instructor in English at Saint Louis University from 1937 to 1944. Well known today to all students of the communications media throughout the world, as well as to a large television audience and to many professional groups to whom he has lectured, he was editor of the pioneering periodical *Explorations* from 1953 to 1959 and is the author of *The Mechanical Bride* (1951), *The Gutenberg Galaxy* (1962), *Understanding Media* (1964), *The Medium Is the Massage* (1967), and other works. *The Gutenberg Galaxy* received the 1963 Canadian Governor General's award for expository prose.

JOHN MACQUARRIE is an Anglican priest and professor of systematic theology at Union Theological Seminary in New York. A native of Scotland, he obtained his degrees from the University of Glasgow, where he also taught theology for nine years before coming to Union Theological Seminary in 1962. He gave the Hastie lectures at the University of Glasgow and the Cooper lectures at Swarthmore College in 1962 and was the John M. English lecturer at the Andover-Newton Divinity School and Birks lecturer at McGill University in 1963. He is author of *An Existentialist Theology*

(1955), *The Scope of Demythologizing* (1960), *Twentieth-Century Religious Thought* (1963), *Studies in Christian Existentialism* (1965), *Principles of Christian Theology* (1966), *God-Talk* (1967), and other works.

CHARLES MUSCATINE is professor of English at the University of California, Berkeley. He was born in Brooklyn, New York, and received his B.A., M.A., and Ph.D. from Yale University. He has held research fellowships from the American Council of Learned Societies and the John Simon Guggenheim Memorial Foundation as well as a Fulbright research fellowship. Known as a distinguished medieval scholar, the author of *Chaucer and the French Tradition* (1957), *The Book of Geoffrey Chaucer* (1963), and other works, he was chairman of the Berkeley faculty's Select Committee on Education and editor and co-author of the Committee's epoch-making report, *Education at Berkeley* (1966).

JOHN T. NOONAN, JR., until September, 1967, professor of law at the University of Notre Dame, is now professor of law at the University of California, Berkeley. Born in Boston, Massachusetts, he studied at Harvard University (B.A., LL.B.), at Cambridge University, and at the Catholic University of America (M.A., Ph.D.). From 1955 to 1961 he practiced law in Boston. He is editor of the *Natural Law Forum*, published at the University of Notre Dame, and has been director of the Notre Dame Natural Law Institute, and a Guggenheim Fellow. His many works include *The Scholastic Analysis of Usury* (1957) and the definitive study *Contraception: A History of Its Treatment by the Catholic Theologians and Canonists* (1965). He has served as chairman of the Brookline Redevelopment Authority, as a member of the Special Staff of the National Security Council, and as consultor to the Papal Commission on Problems of the Family, Population, and Natality, 1965–66.

WALTER J. ONG, S.J., is professor of English at Saint

Louis University. A native of Kansas City, Missouri, he studied at Rockhurst College (B.A.) and worked in commercial positions two years before entering the Society of Jesus (Jesuit order), continuing his studies thereafter at Saint Louis University (M.A., S.T.L.) and Harvard University (Ph.D.). He was ordained a priest in 1946. Twice recipient of a Guggenheim Fellowship, he has also been a Fellow at the Center for Advanced Studies at Wesleyan University (Connecticut). He has served as visiting professor at the University of California and Indiana University, visiting lecturer at the University of Poitiers in France, Macdonald lecturer at McGill University in Canada, Terry lecturer at Yale University in 1963–64, and Berg Professor of English and American Literature at New York University in 1966–67. His many publications include the books *Frontiers in American Catholicism* (1957), *Ramus, Method, and the Decay of Dialogue* (1958), *Ramus and Talon Inventory* (1958), *American Catholic Crossroads* (1959), *The Barbarian Within* (1962), *In the Human Grain* (1967), and *The Presence of the Word* (1967).

KARL RAHNER, S.J., is professor of dogmatic theology and the history of dogma at the University of Münster and was a consultant (*peritus*) at the Second Vatican Council. He was born in Freiburg-im-Breisgau, Germany, and after entering the Society of Jesus (Jesuit order), studied at Pullach, near Munich, at Valkenburg, Holland, at Freiburg, and at Innsbruck, Austria, where he received a doctorate in theology in 1936. He was ordained a priest in 1932. After the Nazis disbanded the Innsbruck Faculty of Theology in 1938, he was engaged in pastoral work in Vienna and Bavaria. He has also been professor of Christian thought and philosophy of religion at the University of Munich. In 1964 he was decorated by the government of Tirol, Austria, for his contribution to learning, and in 1965 received the Reuchlin Prize from the city of Pforzheim. Since 1957 he has been editor, with Joseph Höfer, of the *Lexicon für Theologie und Kirche* as well as editor of the series *Quae-*

stiones Disputatae. His numerous works, many of which are now being translated into English, include *Zür Theologie des Todes* (1958), *Free Speech in the Church* (1959), *Inspiration in the Bible* (1961), and *Amt und Charisma in der Kirche* (1962).

ROBERT C. WEAVER, educator, economist, and author, became the first United States Secretary of Housing and Urban Development in 1966. He had been administrator of the predecessor Housing and Home Finance Agency since 1961. He is a native of Washington, D.C., and holds his B.S., M.A., and Ph.D. degrees from Harvard University, with honorary degrees from more than twenty other institutions. Dr. Weaver entered government service in 1933 and has held many federal posts in national housing, defense, and manpower fields until 1944, when he began an extensive nonfederal career in human relations in Chicago and subsequently as lecturer at Northwestern University. He has been visiting professor at Columbia University Teachers College and New York University and has served as an officer or consultant to a large number of foundations and public agencies. His many publications include the books *Negro Labor: A National Problem* (1946), *The Negro Ghetto* (1948), *The Urban Complex* (1964), and *Dilemmas of Urban America* (1965). He is former chairman of the National Association for the Advancement of Colored People and in 1962 was recipient of its Spingarn Medal.

JERROLD R. ZACHARIAS, Institute professor and professor of physics at Massachusetts Institute of Technology, has enjoyed a double career as a research scientist and as a reformer and vivifier of science teaching in the United States and around the world. He was born in Jacksonville, Florida, and studied at Columbia University (B.A., M.A., Ph.D.). He was a staff member of the Radiation Laboratory at Massachusetts Institute of Technology from 1940 to 1945, divisional head at the University of California Los Alamos laboratory in 1945, and director of the Massachusetts Institute of Technology Laboratory for Nuclear Science and Engineering from 1946 to 1956. He has published papers on science and science education, has been a member of the United States President's Science Advisory Committee, is chairman of the Panel on Educational Research and Development of the President's Science Advisory Committee, and is vice president of Educational Development Center, Incorporated.

EST FRISIAN ISLANDS
LAUWERSZEE
THE DOLLART
Emden
Dokkum
GRONINGEN
Franeker
Leeuwarden
Groningen
FRIESLAND
DRENTE
edemblik
Enkhuizen
Hoorn
maar
ZUIDER
ZEE
Koevorden
Kampen
Vecht
Zwolle
BENTHEIM
dam
erdam
LLAND
OVERIJSSEL
Deventer
GUELDERLAND
TRECHT
Ijssel
Enschede
Utrecht
Zuthphen
Wijk-bij-Duurstede
Arnhem
Tiel
Neder Rijn
Waal
Maas
Nijmegen
Kleve
Rhine
's Hertogenbosch
RABANT
burg
Geldern
Eindhoven
Venlo
GERMANY
N
Roermond
LIMBERG
Meuse
UM
Cologne
Maastricht
Tongres
Aachen
STEPHEN J. VOORHIES

EVOLUTION
of the
DUTCH NATION

EVOLUTION

OF THE

DUTCH

NATION

By

BERNARD H. M. VLEKKE

*Professor of History and Secretary General
of the Netherland Government
Historical Institute in Rome*

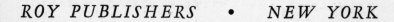

ROY PUBLISHERS • *NEW YORK*

FOREWORD

In writing this history of the genesis and growth of the Dutch nation, I have assumed that the American reader would prefer to a mere narrative of Dutch history, an interpretation of the events and forces that brought the Dutch nation into being and determined its world-embracing activity in past ages and the present time. I have taken it for granted that the main facts of Dutch history are known to the American public. Many works of reference published in this country contain excellent chapters on the Netherlands, and P. J. Blok's "History of the People of the Netherlands" gives all the essential facts. Thus it is that many details familiar to the average reader or to be found in the works of John Lothrop Motley—the great American historian of the Netherlands—have been omitted.

An interpretation, as presented in this book, necessarily gives a personal view of historical events. Strive as we may to be objective, our vision of the past remains largely subjective. For my facts I have borrowed freely from modern Dutch historians, and in many cases I have adopted opinions already expressed by fellow countrymen. But, taken as a whole, the interpretation of Dutch history given in this book is mine and mine alone. This I would emphasize, for many of my colleagues may disagree with some of the opinions presented here, all the more so as I have often deviated from tradition.

My connection with the Department of Education of the Royal Netherland Government lends no special authority to my statements which are nothing but the personal opinions of a Dutch historian who, in time of war as in time of peace, has the right to express himself freely on his country's past. This personal note will not, I trust, deter the reader but rather arouse his interest in Dutch history and create a demand for further knowledge. If this should lead to the publication in English of other historical works on the Netherlands, the author will feel amply rewarded for his labors.

B. H. M. VLEKKE.

Cambridge, Massachusetts.
On the Day of the Liberation of Maastricht.

CONTENTS

INTRODUCTION

$\mathbf{A}$ HISTORY of the Netherlands must first explain how and why a Netherland nation came into being. It seems strange that in a tiny corner of the great plain of northwest Europe, open to invasion from all sides, there should exist a nation quite distinct from its far more powerful neighbors. It is even more remarkable that this small nation has proved strong enough to maintain itself as a separate political entity and to carry its own civilization to the far corners of the earth.

The European territory of the kingdom of the Netherlands covers only 13,700 square miles, an area about equal to that of Massachusetts, Rhode Island, and Connecticut. The country derives its name from its geographic location: "Nederland" is the *lowland* as opposed to the *"overland,"* the high land of the interior. Originally the term was used in a vague sense. Siegfried, the hero of the Nibelungen epic, is called the "helt von Niderland" by a German poet of the early XIIIth century. Here, "Niderland" stands for the great plain of the lower Rhine, which the poet distinguishes sharply from the mountainous area of the middle Rhine, the scene of his hero's chief exploits. Gradually the meaning of the term was restricted to the delta of Rhine, Meuse, and Scheldt, and in Dutch medieval chronicles these lands are referred to as the "low lands along the sea," our "Low Countries."

The medieval scribe who, around 1350, styled himself the "cleric from the low lands along the sea," recognized as his fatherland only the country of Holland, a narrow strip of land from the mouth of the Scheldt to the Zuiderzee. Even a century later, the name applied solely to the western coastal provinces of Belgium and of the Netherlands. Flanders, Brabant, Holland, and Utrecht were included, but the northeastern districts from Guelders to Groningen were considered definitely foreign. To the coastal inhabitants these districts were part of the "Overland" or "Oostland"—the great eastern plain between the Zuiderzee and the Oder—and their inhabitants spoke, not the vernacular "Dutch," but a foreign tongue, the "Low Saxon" or "Overlandish." In the XVIth century the union of the present states of the Netherlands and Belgium was realized. From then on, the name of "Netherlands" or "Low Countries" is applied to the whole of that area, and the latter term even now indicates the *combined* territory of *both* states. The name "Netherlands" was first used politically in 1539. As at that time most historians wrote in Latin, a classical form had to be devised.

The name "Belgica," once applied by the Romans to the lands that lie between the Seine and the Rhine had remained in ecclesiastical use until late in the Middle Ages. Humanistic studies brought revived interest in the pre-medieval history of the northern countries and from Caesar's narrative of his bitter battles with the "Belgae," the name "Belgica" was re-introduced, to indicate the Low Countries.

In the century that saw the union of the "low lands" and the "overland" a religious and political conflict broke out and led to the separation of the northern from the southern half of the Low Countries. *The northern section retained the historical name of the Netherlands.* Latin writers gradually replaced the name "Belgica" by that of "Batavia," introduced from Tacitus. For another two centuries the southern section remained officially nameless, but it received the political denomination "Belgium" after gaining its independence in 1830. In both countries there was a tendency, however, to substitute the name of one province for that of the whole. During the Middle Ages in the southern section, the province of Flanders so exceeded the others in trade and wealth, that "Flemings" became for a while the common name of all traders from the Low Countries. Italian historians called the eighty-years' war, the "guerra di Fiandra." *After the separation of the northern and southern Low Countries, "Flemings" remained the common term for all Dutch-speaking people in the southern part and during the XIXth century they adopted this name as their own.*

In the northern section, the province of Holland far surpassed the others, especially in commerce and shipping. Thus the northern Netherlanders became known among foreign nations as "Hollanders," and from abroad the term found its way into the Netherlands. Napoleon Bonaparte, whose geographical terminology was always loose, gave the title "King of Holland" to his brother Louis. Thereafter the name Holland was commonly used among Netherlanders themselves, but on the restoration of Dutch independence, the historical term Netherlands, in its traditional plural form, was revived for official use.

As has been said, the Netherlands have no geographical boundaries to the south or the east. There is little racial difference between the Netherlanders and their neighbors either on the continent or in Britain. The Dutch language holds an intermediate position between English and High German. In Friesland, a language is spoken that has close affinity to old Anglo-Saxon. In other districts the local dialect approaches the Low German of the adjacent provinces of Germany.

So the name Netherlands indicates that the genesis of the Netherland nation must be sought in the districts bordering the sea, and that their political and cultural characteristics were gradually extended to the east. Accordingly, the first part of this book will retrace this initial development and dwell upon the basic elements that made it possible. The second part will show how the Netherland nation, once it had found adequate political organization, extended its cultural and commercial activities over a large part of the world. The third section will describe how this same nation ceased to be a great power, and even was temporarily deprived of its political independence. Finally, how it asserted its right to free national existence and resumed its historic role of mediator between western and central Europe and even between the Occident and the Orient.

Geographic terminology concerning the Netherlands tends to be confusing and consistency in the use of words is essential to any clear statement of historical development. In this book "Low Countries" will be applied only to the combined territory of the present kingdoms of the Netherlands and Belgium. The noun "Low Countries" badly needs an adjectival form, which unfortunately does not exist. The form "Lowland" seems the only possibility. The familiar adjective "Dutch" will never be used for the earlier period except to indicate the language of the western coastlands both of Belgium and of Holland. After 1600 it may serve as a supplementary adjectival form to "Netherlands." "Netherlands" noun and "Netherland" adjective refer always to the northern part of the Low Countries, that is to the present kingdom of the Netherlands. "Holland" indicates the *province of Holland,* never the whole of the Netherlands. The same is true of "Flanders" and "Flemish." These indicate the province of Flanders, except when used for the history of the last century. In the latter case they refer to the "Dutch" speaking people of the kingdom of Belgium.

"Batavia," the Latin name for the Netherlands, was given in 1619 to the capital of the Dutch East Indian empire. To avoid confusion between the inhabitants of that city and the Netherlanders in Europe when referred to by their Latin name—as was usual at the time of the French revolution—the form "Batavi" will be used for the Germanic tribe of Roman days and that of "Batave," philologically more correct than "Batavian," for the republic in Europe. "Batavian" always indicates a connection with the capital of the East Indies.

CHAPTER I

The Genesis of a Country and of a People

NAPOLEON BONAPARTE, whose inaccuracy in matters of geographical terminology has already been alluded to, once said that the Netherlands were nothing but "an alluvium of some of the principal rivers of his empire." Were it not for the silt carried down from the mountains by the Rhine and the Meuse, he asserted, Holland would not exist. This warping of geographical fact to serve an Imperial policy, is even more absurd than the widespread belief that the Netherlanders won their place on earth by forcing back the ocean and turning the sea into habitable land.

Yet both stories contain an element of truth. The rivers did contribute to the building of Netherland soil; and when that soil seemed doomed to disappear in the tremendous floods of the early Middle Ages, the engineering skill of the early inhabitants saved at least part of it from destruction. Little by little the Netherlanders made their sea-battered land into a well fortified bastion from which time and again they have sallied forth to reoccupy lost positions. The greatest of these counterattacks was the twentieth century draining of the Zuiderzee. The truth is that the Netherlands were born of the sea. Nature not Man made it and later sought its destruction.

At the beginning of the Pleistocene a slight elevation of the land caused a withdrawal of the waters of the North Sea, which covered all of the Low Countries, to a line running north of the Doggerbank from what is now the mouth of the Humber in England to Cape Skagerrak. Britain and the Continent were then one. The Rhine, of which the Meuse, the Scheldt, the Thames, and the Humber were mere affluents, pursued its course in a general northwestern direction. Upon this barren ground the Rhine and Meuse began to build the soil of the Netherlands. Then came the third European glacial period which was the only one that affected the Low Countries. It moulded parts of the Netherlands soil into shape. Enormous masses of ice, descending from the mountains of Scandinavia, Scotland, and northern England, covered the present area of the North Sea as well as the northern section of the Low Countries, and extended to a line running from a point south of Haarlem, over Utrecht and Nijmegen, to Krefeld in the Rhineland. Moving to the southwest the ice carried stones and sand from Scan-

I

dinavia, supplying material for the sandy plains of the Dutch provinces of Guelderland, Overijssel, and Drente. Ice pressure moulded that material into its present form and built the ranges of low hills later covered by forests, which now provide recreation areas for the crowded population of Holland. The ice caused a still more momentous change in the geography of the country. It acted as a dam to the waters of the Rhine and Meuse, forcing them to flow west. Thus the parallel rivers in the central Netherlands came into existence, and we shall see how deeply this geographical formation has influenced the fate of the Netherland people. A third result of the glacial period was the formation of a long narrow strip of loess along the southern rim of the ice. This belt of loess soil, which passes through the modern kingdom at its southernmost point, well provided with water in the valleys, has a prairie-like plateau. It provided a natural highway along which primitive man moved from east to west. In modern times, it has served as an invasion route for great armies.

In the era following the third glacial, colder and warmer periods alternated. In the colder ages, the sea withdrew to its old shores far to the north, and the Low Countries merged again into the huge plains that spread from Wales to Russia, while in the warmer ages the sea reoccupied its lost territories and submerged the northern Netherlands up to the sandy hills of its eastern districts. In both cases nature continued to build, slowly but surely, the soil of the country.

The *fourth* glacial period in Europe, which is supposed to have reached its lowest line about 20,000 B. C., never touched the Low Countries, but turning the northern European plain into an endless tundra, caused a gradual shifting of animal life to the south. The mammoth herds which had grazed on the steppes of northeastern Netherland made place for the reindeer, which alone of all animals could find its food on the tundra. Where the mammoth went, the most primitive type of man, the "Neanderthaler," usually followed. So far there is no evidence that he ever lived in the Netherlands; but his tools have been found in the southern Low Countries on the outskirts of the sandy plains of Brabant and Limburg.[1]

With the reindeer came reindeer-hunters, men of the Cro-magnon race. Their presence in some parts of eastern Netherland seems well established. They too, made their homes at the edge of the sandy areas, on the outskirts of the Veluwe and the plains of Drente, high enough to be protected against floods, yet close to fresh water. There is no reason to assume that they ever left the country, and they may be counted as the earliest ancestors of the present people of the Netherlands.

After the last glacial period the climate of northwestern Europe grew steadily warmer. The melting of the ice freed enormous masses of water,

the sea-level rose, and an extremely slow but steady sinking of the land began. It continues in our day at the rate of one millimeter, say the twenty-fifth of an inch, every year. That seemed to doom the as yet unborn country of the Netherlands. Then nature intervened to provide defenses against the dangers it had created. Around 5000 B. C., if we may accept the word of some geologists, the sea again covered the whole of the present provinces of Zeeland, Holland, Utrecht and part of Friesland and Groningen. It may have flooded part of the low, sandy plains of Brabant and reached the sites in Belgian Limburg where prehistoric man was living. Vague reminiscences of the event may be traced in the medieval legends that describe Tongeren, far inland in Belgian Limburg, as having been a coastal village in the remote past. This same flood caused a momentous and lasting change in the geography of western Europe by opening the straits of Dover and turning the low valley between the chalk cliffs of Kent and Artois into an arm of the sea. Once currents of the ocean had found their way into the North Sea, they swept everything in their path. Sand was taken up in the middle of the channel and deposited, in long soft curves, along its eastern bank. Here the prevailing west winds massed it along the shore of the sea in a long, uninterrupted line of dunes. Holland's Westwall had been created.

The sea behind the row of dunes became a lagoon. This rapidly filled with peat after the salt water had been changed into fresh by influx from the rivers. The Rhine and Meuse sought new outlets. Their many branches, winding through the moor, provided the routes along which the inhabitants of the eastern sands traveled to the western dunes. Instead of an unidentifiable fragment of the vast plain of the northwest, the future Netherlands had become a corner of the continent, and a stepping stone for migrating peoples. With Britain an island on the other side, the North Sea was no longer a barrier, but a broad highway continued to the east by the rivers Rhine and Meuse.

The frequent changes in the formation of the soil must have made the northern Low Countries a rather difficult place for the primitive peoples of Europe to settle. The southern part, present day Belgium, was full of life in the later palaeolithic and the early neolithic ages. The northern part seems to have been desolate and deserted, although it is probable that remnants of the older population still clung to the higher portion of the partly drowned land. In the south prehistoric settlements existed where medieval towns later rose to fame, conclusive evidence of continuity of habitation and culture. In only one place did this early neolithic population spill over the present Dutch-Belgian boundary. In the extreme southeast, around Maastricht, an abundant supply of flint is found; and flint was to neolithic man what iron is to us. Traces of shallow mine pits and enormous quantities of flint fragments show that a regular industry of stone tools was located here.

Archeologists have identified two main groups of inhabitants in the Netherlands during the second millennium before Christ. One center of habitation was the plains of Drente, now a rather desolate province of modern Netherland; another, the fertile loess soil of southern Limburg, one of the most favored districts of the country. The two groups were racially distinct—the men of Drente were dolichocephal, the men of Limburg brachycephal. That distinction persists to this day and the boundary between the two racial groups roughly coincides with the belt of parallel rivers in the middle of the country. More interesting is the difference in civilization between the two peoples. These ancient "Netherlanders" were by no means totally barbarians. They were agricultural peoples and had fixed residences. Those of the south built their cabins close together on elevated spots and surrounded their settlements with walls and moats. Those of the north left the only megalithic monuments preserved in the northern Low Countries. Two rows of large stones were placed upright to form a narrow passage, covered by other stones placed on top. One end was closed by a huge boulder, the other left open. But a small wall of stones kept the space immediately in front of the entrance free. Then the whole structure, except for the narrow space before the entrance, was covered with soil. Thus an artificial rock chamber was built. Like the chambers excavated in the hillsides of Egypt and North Africa, the megalithic constructions of Drente served as burying places for the dead. To these monuments the name "Hunebeds," or "giant beds," has been given.

The tools and ceramics of these two groups and a comparison of their buildings with those in other European areas suggest that both found their origin, if not racially at least culturally, in the lands around the Mediterranean. In both cases, the facts suggest a limited migration of individuals as well as a current of civilization. From their earliest homes on the plains of Drente, the Hunebed-builders moved to the range of dunes beyond the marshes of the lagoon. Evidence of habitation, only slightly later than that in Drente, has been found near Alkmaar, in the northern sector of the dunes. It is quite possible that this same people also spread to the southwest where the borderland of the Veluwe, close to fertile and rich river valleys, provided excellent living conditions. From the sea to the eastern corner of the present provinces of Overijssel, huge peat marshes extend along the present Netherland-German boundary. Farther south, a wide gap between the moors and the great rivers leaves the way free for invaders. There is ample proof that in prehistoric and early historic times, constant immigration from the east took place. If our interpretation of the archeological evidence is correct, hunter tribes of the later neolithic period—say around 1500 B. C.—migrated from the plains of southern Russia over Hungary and Czechia to the upper Danube and from there moved west to the Low Countries. Through the gap in the natural boundaries, they penetrated into the Low Countries to settle on the sandy plain of the Veluwe, whence some of them continued their wanderings to Britain across the yet shallow Straits of Dover.

A dryer period followed the moist era in which the rising sea level and the opening of the Straits of Dover had successively submerged the Netherlands and provided for their protection by creating the western shore line. For several centuries, the moors behind the dunes, formed when the lagoon filled up with peat, were covered with a hard dry surface that gave more freedom of movement to the inhabitants. The sea, its level perhaps ten feet lower than at present, was not yet a threat to the new land. The western dunes, then several miles farther west, enclosed an area thousands of square miles larger than modern Netherland.

The traditional picture of man's progress presumes a gradual evolution of culture from that of the stone age through a bronze age to the iron age. The bronze age is missing in the history of the Netherlands. Only a very few bronze tools and weapons have been found. Apparently the advent of the new material did not interfere with the continued use of stone for the same purposes and in the same areas of habitation. So we may assume that bronze came by a peaceful exchange of goods, and was not brought by a migrating horde or a conquering people of a higher cultural level.

There was also a change in religious customs, and for their funeral rites the ancient inhabitants of the Low Countries gradually adopted cremation instead of inhumation. There is no definite proof that the change in burial rites was accompanied by a change in population, but it was an innovation of great importance, for the burial of the dead near the homes of the living points to a belief in the survival of spiritual force within the body after death, while cremation obviously aims at the immediate liberation of the spirit from the body.

The introduction of the new burial rite is often placed around 1200 B. C. about the time of the first bronze tools. Around 1000 B. C., iron was introduced—again, it would seem, by way of peaceful trading though our evidence is of the scantiest. Thus, the principal cultural changes had been initiated even before the great immigrations of the last centuries before Christ that definitely shaped the racial character of the Netherland people. To the three racial groups already mentioned, two new elements were added. From the northeast came Germanic tribes, from the southeast

Celtic clans. The river belt of the center formed a barrier which, for a century or more, kept Celtic and Germanic tribes apart. Contrary to tradition, the Germanic invaders were the first to settle in the Low Countries. They did not appear until several centuries after the beginning of the Iron Age— how *many* centuries is uncertain. In the five centuries preceding the birth of Christ, three great waves of Germanic immigration swept over the Low Countries. The oldest, which some archeologists name the Proto-Saxon, extended only over the sandy plains of the east and center. It preceded the invasion of the south by Celtic tribes. The second wave, far stronger than the first, belongs to the fourth and third centuries, and spread over the lowlands of the former lagoon as well as over the plains of the east. It crossed the river belt into the southern part, where it absorbed the earlier Celtic population. Thus the tribes of the Belgae, Germanic peoples with Celtic elements and Celtic culture, who were to be Caesar's most ferocious foes, appeared in the Low Countries. The third Germanic immigration took place in historic times, and is connected with the history of the occupation of the Low Countries by the Romans.

These four waves of immigration—one Celtic and three Germanic—within four centuries or less, justify the assumption of a marked increase in the population of the Low Countries. There are indications that the first two immigrations, the first Germanic and the Celtic one, were not very important as far as numbers are concerned. The earliest Germanic inhabitants settled in exactly the same districts as the primitive inhabitants of the Netherlands, to whom they were closely related racially. An increase of population may be assumed from the wide extent of their burial grounds, but there was little if any change in customs or civilization. The Celts did not penetrate into the western part of the country. They settled on both sides of the Meuse, as far north as the present town of Nijmegen, and in eastern Brabant.

The climate period of the sub-Atlanticum had begun. This, combined with the effects of an increase in rainfall, a rising sea level, a gradual sinking of the soil, tended to make the former lagoon behind the dunes once more uninhabitable. As long as there was room in the eastern part of the country, the west did not have any settlers. Indeed, the fact that there *was* room in the eastern section, although it had been inhabited from the earliest times, is sufficient proof that the number of early Celtic and Germanic invaders can not have been great. As regards the Germanic invasion, we can imagine small clans of agricultural people coming in quest of new farm lands; as regards the Celts, they were bands of proud warriors, seeking to extend their rule over less civilized tribes. The civilization of the Netherland Celts was that of the Halstatt period. The ornaments and weapons found in some of their burial mounds suggests wealth and craftsmanship far above that of their northern neighbors.

More important was the second Germanic invasion, that must have taken place in the third and second centuries before Christ. Its route can be traced back to Central Germany. They were so numerous that, in dire need of land, they invaded and conquered part of the lands of the Celts in the southeast and settled in the marshy land between the higher ground in the east and the dunes in the west. Their civilization was lower than that of the Celts though slightly higher than that of their Germanic predecessors. They were the first to take up the struggle with the sea—which, helped by climatic changes, had begun its assault on the Netherlands from the west. In the northern part, the present provinces of Groningen and Friesland, the marshy land behind the dunes provided excellent meadows in summer time. To safeguard themselves and their cattle against the treacherous floods, the new inhabitants threw up large low mounds, flat on top, to serve as places of refuge. With the increase of population, reinforced perhaps by immigration from the northeast, these mounds or "terps" made permanent settlement possible. As the threat from the sea became more alarming in the course of time, the height and size of the "terps" were increased. For a thousand years and more, until the first dykes were built, they were the only safe places of habitation in that part of the country. Because of the periodic raising of the terp-level, the various strata of habitation have been perfectly preserved, and these artificial hills have become veritable treasure-troves for archeologists. Before it was leveled in modern times, the largest of these terps was twenty feet high and covered an area of thirty-seven acres. Like the hill of ancient Troy, some terps contained seven layers of archeological evidence.

These settlers of terp-land were the ancestors of the Frisians. As they settled in uninhabited territory, they preserved a far greater degree of racial purity than their fellow tribesmen who migrated into the central and southern section of the country where they strongly influenced but did not supersede the older population. In Belgium, the invasion of these tribes caused a cultural decline. Roman historians stress the fact that the ancient Belgae were of low culture and more barbarous than all other inhabitants of Gaul, and the contents of their early burial grounds confirm that view.

Thus, Germanic tribes occupied nearly all the Netherlands at the beginning of the second century before Christ. A second Celtic migration, often connected with the spreading of the La Tène civilization of the later Iron Age, touched the Netherlands only in some districts of the southwest and at the extreme southeastern point, in southern Limburg where the loess lands provided a natural highway. For the most part the lowlands of the present province of Holland were still uninhabited. Along the dunes, on the loam ground in the north, and on the sandy plains of the east, fishermen, cattle-breeders and farmers made their living as they do today, and even the dwellings of the wealthier among these early inhabitants of the Low Countries were probably not unlike those still seen in the poorer part of the country half a century ago. This was the situation in the Netherlands when they were "discovered" by the pioneers of Mediterranean civilization.[2]

About 325 B.C., a Greek navigator, Pytheas of Marseilles, undertook the exploration of the western coast of Europe which was then virtually unknown. A century before, Herodotus had given a vague description of these far western lands, renowned for the tin and amber they produced. The Carthaginians had traded on the west coast of Europe, but the geographical information they possessed was not available to the Greeks, their constant rivals and relentless foes. Aristotle knew northwestern Europe only as the "Keltika"—the land of the Celts—for in his time the Celtic expansion was at its peak and the Celts controlled all trade routes from the Baltic and North Sea to the Mediterranean. Pytheas' exploration of the sea route to the northern countries was intended to neutralize Celtic predominance and to wrest from them the amber trade. Had he succeeded in opening a practicable sea route around western Europe, he would have been able to divert this entire trade to his native city of Marseille. But his attempt proved premature, as the distance and dangers of the voyage were too great to permit regular trips. Pytheas reached the coast of Britain, whence he proceeded to the Netherlands. Passing the mouth of the Rhine, he followed the coast to northern Germany. He penetrated beyond the area of farthest Celtic expansion, and described the country as inhabited by "Skuthai"—the Scyths—a general term used by the Greeks to designate all peoples of northeastern Europe, from Scandinavia to the Caucasus.

Pytheas' work of exploration was not continued by later generations. The name of the river Rhine is first mentioned in ancient literature by Cicero in his oration against Lucius Piso. Caesar's expeditions to the land of the Belgae marked the beginning of direct contact between the still backward peoples of the Netherlands and the highly civilized Mediterranean world. Caesar himself never visited the northern part of the Low Countries. In his war with the Menapii, probably one of the few remaining Celtic clans on the lower Meuse, he partially penetrated a densely wooded marshland, which some identify with the moors of the Peel in northeastern Brabant. Caesar left the conquest of the northeastern section of Gaul uncompleted, the boundary only vaguely defined and nowhere defended. To finish the work of his predecessor was one of the tasks of Octavius Augustus, the first emperor.

Drusus, the stepson of Augustus, came to the lower Rhine to take command over the armies that had been assembled for the conquest of Germany as far as the Elbe. The valleys of the affluents of the Rhine formed natural invasion routes through the wild, heavily wooded country; and by sea, the Roman galleys could reach the Elbe and thus penetrate into the heart of the enemy country. Drusus worked methodically. Large forces were gathered in fortified camps at points of strategic interest. The defenses between these camps were strengthened by settling German mercenaries on the left bank of the Rhine. These mercenaries migrated to their new homes with their families. With the assistance of the Romans they brought large tracts of wild land under cultivation. One of these tribes, the Batavi, was destined to become famous in Netherland history. This settlement of mercenary tribes constituted the third wave of Germanic immigration. The Batavi owed their land and most of what they possessed to the Romans. Remains of their dwellings and implements found in modern times confirm the references of Roman authors who pictured this Germanic tribe as deeply influenced by Roman civilization. Until their arrival, the districts between the rivers had been avoided because of the marshy nature of the soil. Drusus built a highway along the lower Rhine, and this served as a rude dyke sufficient to resist at least the minor floods. Scattered through the country along this road, the Batavi threw up low mounds not unlike the terps of the north, but less high. Upon these they built their farmhouses and, as a last refuge for men and beasts in times of floods or wars, they raised a primitive castle on one of the hills near Nijmegen.

The fortified "island of the Batavi"—as the land between the rivers was then called—formed a secure basis for Roman military operations. The Frisians of the terp-land, well provided with cattle and familiar with the creeks and inland waters of the north, were also pressed into service. Once these preparations were completed the Roman navy began to explore the dangerous shores of the North Sea. The Roman galleys, however, were ill-suited for navigation on its rough waters, and although the attempt was repeated several times, the fleet hardly ever succeeded in penetrating farther than the mouth of the Ems.

The northern Netherlands continued to serve as an operational base for the Romans until 16 A. D., when Tiberius ordered these wars brought to an end. At once the Roman hold over the tribes north of the great rivers weakened. The Frisians became restless, and in 28 A. D. drove the Roman tax collectors from their country. The authority of Rome was temporarily restored twenty years later after a vigorous campaign in preparation for which new fortifications and camps were built. One of these is now the city of Utrecht. The troops were again withdrawn south of the Rhine by order of the emperor Claudius, and thus this military event would not be worth mentioning were it not that the elder Pliny served with the Roman legions. Later, when he wrote his *"Naturalis Historia"* and the "Chronicles of His Own Time," he could describe the Netherlands and their inhabitants from personal observation, and from him Tacitus derived much information on the history of the Batavi. The end of the Germanic wars did not lessen the strategic value of the "island of the Batavi" to the Romans. Shortly thereafter, the conquest of Britain was undertaken; and in this enterprise the Batavi again took a great part. New military works, thrown up immediately behind the dunes, served to secure safe and easy communications between the great military centers on the Rhine and the ports of embarkation at the mouth of the Scheldt.

The Romans set little store by the marshlands of the west and the north of the Low Countries which held no allure for them. They preferred to tread on more solid ground. Even for maintaining communications between Britain and the lower Rhine, the land route from Boulogne to Cologne seemed to them safer than the sea route by the mouth of the Rhine. One great highway they built in the Low Countries, running from Cologne through Aachen and Tongeren to Bavai in northern France, and on to the sea coast. This road partly followed the stretch of loess land already mentioned as the great thoroughfare of northwestern Europe. North and south of this road, thousands of Roman veterans settled. With the Romanized nobility of the Belgae, they formed a class of landowners, residing on large estates on which they kept numerous bondsmen, probably poorer members of the Belgian tribes or descendants of the aboriginal population. On these estates they built spacious and luxurious villas, often provided with central heating, a current of hot air circulating under the floors and inside the walls of the rooms. The smaller of these estates covered about 650 acres. Numbers of Roman villas were excavated in the last century; and the "tumuli" of the lords of these estates, high burial mounds resembling flattened cones still stand southwest of the Belgian town of Tongeren. That town was the metropolis of the southeastern Netherlands and adjacent Belgium during the first and second centuries of our era. Far outside its present precincts, remnants of Roman walls indicate that in those days it was a large city some three and a half miles in circumference. Of the modern kingdom of the Netherlands, only southern Limburg formed part of the Romanized area.

The highway from Tongeren to Bavai crossed the Meuse close to the spot where a fortified village had stood ever since the neolithic age. That village may have been razed and ruined by Celtic and Germanic invasions but the place remained inhabited, and at the crossing of the river a new village always rose and finally grew into the town of Maastricht. Farther east, the highway followed roughly the valley of the Geul, a small affluent of the Meuse. Still farther east, the road bent to the northeast, passed by the place where now the mining center of Heerlen flourishes.

The building of this highway and the Roman colonization along its track was one of the most important events in Netherland history. It determined the farthest extent of Germanic influence in the northwestern corner of the European continent, and fixed for thousands of years to come the dividing line between Romanic and Germanic peoples in this area. The inhabitants of present Flanders, Brabant, and Holland continued to live under Roman rule in the same condition of culture as in the centuries before that rule was instituted. A trickle of Roman relics, found along the banks of some of the small rivulets that wind through the moors and heaths of Flanders and Brabant, reveals the occasional visits of itinerant traders. A bag of Roman coins found in the "Haarlemermeer" when this inland sea was drained in the nineteenth century suggests the shipwreck of a Roman vessel. A high burial mound on one of the northwestern islands, close behind the dunes, indicates that here a Roman naval commander met his death and was buried by the sailors of his squadron. Isolated finds tell of minor dramatic events; but with the sole exception of the island of the Batavi, the area northwest of the great highway was a no man's land for the Romans. Along the road and south of it they stretched forth their authority and imposed their customs and finally their language. Later Germanic invasions pushed the dividing line a little farther to the south in southern Limburg, but could not alter the general picture.

Only one center of Roman civilization was established north of the highway in the Netherlands, the present town of Nijmegen, founded close to the ruins of the older castle of the Batavi. This is associated with the extension of the line of fortifications from the Rhine to the sea after the great revolt of the Batavi. In the general history of the Roman empire, this revolt is of slight importance, nor did it alter or even influence the course of Netherland history for the extension of Roman military occupation along the banks of the Netherland rivers was without lasting effect. Yet it has become one of the great traditional events of Netherland history. Our only source of information about the revolt is Tacitus, who based his narrative on the writings of the elder Pliny, and tells the story in great detail.

The Batavi, who had fought for the Romans in numerous wars, grew weary of constant military service. At first their loot from vanquished Germanic and Britannic foes enriched them. Later, even in times of peace, military service kept them away from home for years without sizeable profit. Claudius Civilis, a Batave officer of high rank in the Roman army, conceived the idea of organizing the scattered forces of the less civilized Germanic warriors around men of his own tribe who had been trained in organized warfare. He believed that Roman power on the lower Rhine could be broken and a confederation of Germanic tribes established under the Batavi. The opportunity came after Nero's death, when civil war was devastating Italy.

The initial success exceeded all expectation. The Batavi serving in the Roman army supported their national leader and marched home to join the revolt. The fortified Roman camps of Xanten and Cologne were taken, some of the Belgian tribes forced into cooperation, and a national revolution fomented in eastern Gaul. The Romans, commanded by Petilius Cerealis had to fight every inch of their way back from Trier to the shores of the North Sea. Tacitus tells how the castle of the Batavi was set on fire by order of Civilis when all seemed lost, and archeological evidence corroborates his story. The ultimate fate of the crafty Batave leader is unknown. From that time, the Romans no longer trusted their allies, who seem, nevertheless, to have regained their privileges. Roman hold over the country was strengthened by the construction of a large fortified camp close to the spot where the castle of the Batavi had stood, the beginnings of the city of Nijmegen. This was the only lasting result of the revolt.

Civilis and his Batavi were completely forgotten during the Middle Ages, when the manuscripts of the works of Tacitus lay hidden and unheeded. After their re-discovery, Tacitus rapidly rose to fame among the Humanists of the XVIth century as a teacher of the way of life and the art of politics. Civilis and the Batavi shared in his fame. Humanists from the Netherlands eagerly grasped the opportunity to enhance the glory of their people and their country with the exploits of the adventurous officer and his clan of Germanic mercenaries. Gerard Geldenhauer of Nijmegen was among the first to write a panegyric of the ancient people, whom he proudly designated as the founders of his city and the defenders of his country's liberty. Erasmus liked to call himself a "Batave," the descendant of a more cultured and Latinized nation, whenever his colleagues from over the Rhine sought to appropriate him for the Germani. But the Batavi owe their *real* fame in Netherland history to Hugo Grotius. The great jurist of Delft was the first to interpret the revolt of the Batavi as the earliest Dutch war of freedom against tyranny. Thus, Civilis and the "leading men of the Batave tribe" of whom Tacitus had spoken, became the precursors of the burgher-aristocracy of the XVIIth century.

This version was soon adopted by the leading republicans of seventeenth-century Holland. Civilis and his "Batave liberty" became the watchword of the anti-Orangist movement of that period. The burgomasters of Amsterdam adorned the City Hall with paintings of the ancient hero and his war with Rome. Rembrandt received a commission to paint the Batave leaders when they met to plan the uprisings. The artist, who had his own version of the story, pictured Civilis as a crafty and ruthless old man, arrayed with semi-barbaric splendor, scheming as he feasted among his knavish satellites. The burgomasters indignantly rejected a painting that departed so far from their own conception. What they wanted was a civilized Civilis of aristocratic mien, defying Roman tyranny, a noble character in a heroic attitude, un-historic perhaps, but politically more acceptable.

This official view of the Batave uprising became part of Dutch traditional historiography after 1754 when Johan Wagenaar, the historiographer of the burgher-aristocracy, inserted it in his monumental "Vaderlandsche historie." By the end of the XVIIIth century the burgher-aristocracy had lost all credit with the people; but Tacitus' description was sufficiently flexible to perpetuate the hero-worship of Civilis in the character of a democratic leader! Friedrich von Schiller glorified him in his "Abfall der Vereinigten Niederlande." "One single man born for the opportunities of his time," he writes, "revealed the dangerous latent power of popular hatred against tyranny." Sixty years later a Bostonian, John Lothrop Motley, deplored the fact that "the brave Batavi distinguished themselves in the (Roman) expeditions to crush the liberties of their Germanic kindred." Civilis, he says, although he had received a Roman education, "retained an unconquerable love for liberty and for his own race, and the spectacle of a brave nation inspired by the soul of one great man and rising against an overwhelming despotism will always speak to the heart, from generation to generation." For Schiller and Motley, the uprising of the Batavi foreshadowed the Eighty Years' War against the kings of Spain. Later textbooks of Dutch History, mostly condensations and revisions of Wagenaar's history, have made Civilis just as well known to Dutch school children as Rembrandt or Admiral de Ruyter.

After the large fortified camp near Nijmegen and a number of smaller forts along the southern bank of the Rhine had been built, a group of Roman traders settled near the river under their protection. No further colonization took place in the northern sector, but the presence of soldiers and merchants in the "island of the Batavi" during one hundred and sixty years of peace sufficed to imbue its population more deeply with Latin culture. Latin words, mostly household or building terms and names of plants or animals, entered the Germanic dialects spoken in the Low Countries. Roman examples were followed in the construction of farmhouses and in the manufacture of tools and implements.

This period of peace and quiet progress in the outward forms of civilization came to an end long before the total collapse of the Roman empire. In the turmoil of the barbaric invasions, which continued in the Low Countries from the early third to the sixth century, the people of the Batavi, and most of the other tribes mentioned by Roman historians, were overwhelmed. The Batave regiments of the Roman army survived, but fewer and fewer natives of the Low Countries served in them. About 250 A. D. the Rhine defenses were disrupted by a wild attack of Germanic invaders, plunderers and adventurers of many tribes. Where these bands passed— and some of them followed the highway from Cologne to Bavai—Latin civilization came to an end. The villas of southern Limburg were burned down, and archeologists have found the charred remnants of their substructure. In the first period of the invasion the heavy walls of Tongeren provided a sanctuary for refugees from the countryside; but about 275 A. D. this city too was looted and laid in ashes. On its ruins a new town was built, better fortified but only one-third as large. After this invasion the island of the Batavi was given up by the Roman army. Some inhabitants may have followed the withdrawing troops south of the great Calais-Cologne highway, but many preferred to stay in their own country although exposed to constant danger. Here the gravest threat to the inhabitants was not that of foreign marauders, but the growing violence of the waters.

Aggressors who lusted for plunder preferred the rich districts of Gaul to the marshlands of Holland, and they left their victims at least subsistence. The sea threatened to destroy the soil itself. Geographical evidence shows that around 300 A. D. the effects of the gradual elevation of the sea level began to affect the security of the lowland of Holland. The Straits of Dover had gradually widened and deepened so that larger masses of water flowed into the North Sea. Swept on by western winds, they battered the shorelines of the Low Countries. The dunes slowly gave way, pushed back by the pressure of the wind. In what is now the province of Zeeland, the shoreline was broken in many places, and the wide estuaries of the Scheldt were formed. Here the loss of land continued until a few centuries ago. From 300 A. D. until 900 A. D., the attack of the sea increased in violence. Whole districts east of the dunes became uninhabitable.

It is difficult to move a people from the land of its forebears, even if that land is in danger of being submerged. The inhabitants of Walcheren, Zeeland's most exposed island, for instance, are definitely the descendants of prehistoric people who settled on the same spot. The motto of Zeeland's coat of arms, "Luctor et emergo,"—"Through struggle I survive"—is no idle boast. The Frisians, by raising the level of their "terps," weathered the storm. The Batavi may have been less fortunate. The rivers that enclosed their land no longer found easy outlets. To the danger of submergence by the sea was added the curse of yearly floods. Many Batavi were forced to seek new homes, either with the Romans south of the highway, or outside the military boundary of the empire on the sandy and marshy plains of Brabant.

So far this open space had attracted but few settlers. It was now occupied by groups of immigrants from the northeast. Some may have belonged to the Batavi; others came from over the Rhine. Together they are called "Franks" by the Roman historians, who distinguished them from the Franks along the lower Rhine by calling the former "Salian Franks," while the latter were known as Ripuarians. The inhabitants of the northern districts, because of the increased violence of the floods and of a small but constant influx of settlers from the east, were apparently forced to extend their settlements over the less desirable land between the Meuse and the Scheldt. These Salian Franks were at times a danger to the Roman empire, at times valuable allies. Against them Emperor Diocletian ordered the strengthening of the fortifications along the Calais-Cologne highway. Later these same fortifications were garrisoned by Franks who apparently served well and faithfully until the collapse of Roman authority. Where the Meuse crosses the highway, a strong bulwark was built and its remains can still be seen in the center of Maastricht. Beneath the walls of the bastion, a settlement of traders and peasants formed the beginning of that city.

Around these new fortifications Latin civilization survived for another century. Here, where Roman legions passed regularly on their way from Britain to the Rhine, where merchants from the Mediterranean ventured to barter with the barbarians, the first Christian communities of the Netherlands were organized. It is difficult to find traces of Christianity prior to 313, but excavations in Tongeren suggest that here as in the cities of the Rhine Christianity was professed long before it gained public recognition. Immediately after the decree of Constantine allowing public worship, the Christian communities of the lower Rhine and Meuse were organized under bishops, who took an active part in the theological controversies of their time, an indication that large communities existed before the decree was issued and were in close contact with the center of Christian life in Italy and the Near East. This latter connection is suggested by local legends attributing to the first bishops of the Rhine and Meuse districts an Armenian or Syrian origin.

One of these legends tells how Servatius, first bishop of Tongeren, sought safety from the barbarians within the walls of Maastricht where he died and was buried. Servatius defended anti-Arian doctrines at the Council of Rimini in 359, and local tradition and archeological evidence both corroborate the main substance of the legend. Most townspeople accepted Christianity rapidly after the church had gained official recognition, while the people of the countryside remained pagan three or four hundred years longer.

At the time when Servatius ministered to the religious needs of the population, Julian, later emperor but then commander-in-chief in Gaul, fought the Frankish tribes along the Meuse. He won control of the whole valley and rebuilt the fort of Nijmegen. Peace was restored and according to Julian's panegyrists, the Franks were graciously granted imperial permission to settle between the Meuse and the Scheldt, a polite way of saying that Julian was unable to prevent Germanic expansion to the southwest.

The period of the "Great Migration" had begun, though this term is ill-suited to what took place in the Netherlands. From the confusing references to northwestern Europe found in late Roman literature, the older Netherland historians vainly sought to reconstruct the history of the period between 300 and 600 A. D. Modern scholars, relying more on archeological and philological evidence than on written sources have reconstructed those events in a way that differs widely from the assumptions of XVIIIth and XIXth century compilators. Three major events occurred in the Netherlands during the three centuries of transition from the Roman to the Carolingian period. One of these, the settling of the plains of Brabant and East Flanders, is described above. It represented a shifting of population and a spreading of settlements rather than an immigration.

In the extreme southeast, Roman authority disappeared in 400 A. D. without a last struggle, when the emperors withdrew their troops to defend Italy. There was no destruction or interruption of such meager culture as existed. Even the Christian communities survived, and on Christian graves Germanic names gradually replaced the Latin. The epitaphs bear witness to a constant deterioration of Latin. It seems that when the Roman authorities were no longer able to maintain themselves, the Franks who had settled around their forts, quickly took over the task of government. Nevertheless, a new immigration of Germanic elements must have taken place. Along the road between Tongeren and Cologne numerous villages with Germanic names are found, while in the narrower gorges opening towards the main valley, the villages still bear Celtic names.

The last and historically the most important of the three events referred to, occurred in the north of the Low Countries. The Frisians had remained undisturbed in possession of their "terp-land" until the beginning of the fifth century.[3] Archeologists have discovered that around that time a sudden change took place in the outward form of the civilization of the terpbuilders. The new culture, as revealed in the models of pottery and tools, is perfectly well known from northwestern Germany, where it has been found in the coastal districts of northern Hannover and Schleswig. There it ceased to exist abruptly at the same time it appeared in Friesland. The same type of culture has been found in the oldest Anglo-Saxon settlements in Britain. If we add to this archeological evidence that of philology, which proclaims close affinity between the old Frisian and Anglo-Saxon languages, and that of anthropology, which indicates an immigration into Friesland from the northeast, we can picture for ourselves the complete story. Tribes from northwestern Germany, among whom were the Angli, moved to Friesland, which they conquered. They were less numerous than the Frisians, upon whom they imposed some outward forms of civilization, and extended their authority all along the coast of Holland, subduing the people there and the remnants of the Batavi. The name Frisian, however, remained; and from that time was applied to all inhabitants of the coast north of the mouth of the Scheldt. Farther south, the conquerors occupied the small strip of territory behind the Flemish dunes. Shortly after they had occupied the Netherland coast warriors from this Anglo-Frisian-Saxon group invaded Britain and there founded the Anglo-Saxon kingdoms.

This was the situation in the Netherlands at the dawn of the sixth century. After that, individual immigration still took place, and small groups of refugees have continued to add new elements to the population until our own time. This has not affected the general racial composition of the people. The population of the Netherlands is of mixed origin, some descending from pre-historic settlers and the Alpine race, a few from Celtic conquerors, the majority deriving from Germanic immigrants, who were by no means all of a single racial type although they spoke kindred dialects. Little is known about the density of population in the ancient Germanic Netherlands. The total population of all countries inhabited by Germanic peoples around 400 A. D. has been estimated at about three million. If this is near the mark, there may have been a few hundred thousand in the whole of the Low Countries. In "Terp-land"—Friesland and Groningen—there are still about one hundred and eighty terp-villages and about three hundred other smaller terps. The latter usually provided room for three to five farm houses. Some of these terps were thrown up after 400 A. D., others were perhaps not permanently occupied. Taking all this into consideration, we may assume that the famous nation of the Frisians did not count more than a few tens of thousands in all. At that, "Terp-land" was rather thickly settled in comparison with the sandy plains of the eastern districts. In the western part, the population was certainly less dense, for here large areas were uninhabitable because of the increasing fury of the floods.

From such modest beginnings the Netherland nation was to grow. The population was there. Next came the establishment of a political organization for the whole of the area and the spread of Christianity that remoulded the culture of the people. Both were achieved under the Frankish kings of the Carolingian dynasty in the four hundred years that followed the fall of the Roman empire.

CHAPTER II

First Political Organization of the Netherlands

FEW indeed are the written records of Netherland history that date back to the fifth and sixth centuries. Gregory of Tours, the historian of the Merovingians, relates the legend of Servatius, the patron saint of Maastricht. He adds that Monulfus, then bishop of that See, built a magnificent church in honor of Servatius. Gregory apparently collected this information when passing through Metz on one of his trips to eastern France. It is characteristic that the only contemporary story we have of the sixth century Netherlands comes from their most Romanized part along the devious route usually followed by pilgrims wandering from sanctuary to sanctuary on their way to Rome. There was little or no intercourse between Frankish territory in Gaul and the pagan Germanic peoples of the Low Countries.

Chroniclers like Gregory were interested chiefly in the deeds of saints, kings, and prelates. Of these there were few representatives in the old Netherlands, except in Maastricht. There a line of bishops, respected by their flocks during their lives, were venerated as saints after death. Of the people, we hear nothing at all. Traditional historiography, based on scanty information provided by eighth and ninth century hagiography and on occasional references in the Carolingian chronicles, divides the inhabitants of the Low Countries into three groups: Franks, Saxons, and Frisians. It paints them in dark colors with all the evil instincts of murderous savages. The biographers of saints are rather unreliable, however, since they wrote for the edification of the faithful and excelled in contrast, picturing the pagans as fiends to bring out more clearly the godliness of their Christian heroes. To obtain an idea of the old Germanic Netherlands, we must turn to other sources, we must discover what remains of old customs and institutions. When we have gained a general idea of the facts, additional information may be gathered from the occasional remarks of hagiographers and chroniclers.

The fifth and sixth century Netherlanders were peasants. As in all primitive societies, man had to struggle with both nature and his fellowman. He tended to associate closely with his neighbors, or rather, he insistently maintained the ties that from time immemorial had bound him to his clan and his clan to him. The village community was the basic social unit and the only organization at all closely knit. Tribes were little more than loose associations at village units. An uncertain number of these constituted a district, a *gouw,* the members of which elected a local chieftain. The total of the *gouws* formed the nation, but the national territory had no well-defined boundaries. In emergencies the *gouws* adopted a common leader. If this chieftain, duke or king—whatever title the chroniclers gave him, wanted the support of reliable followers, he had to recruit them from the young men who preferred adventure to hard work in the fields. The mass of the tribesmen followed their leaders to war only when they felt like it and returned home as soon as they had had enough. The village unit provided nearly all their needs and beyond it they recognized little authority.

The arable land of each village was divided among the inhabitants, while the pasture, heath, and forest around the village were common property. This entailed close cooperation by all members of the community. Regulations were made and transgressors punished. Thus a social unit existed with an administrative and a judicial organization. Later, when their regulations had become well anchored in custom, these communities were known as "mark-associations" and the agricultural unit as the "mark." The last traces of these institutions disappeared only in quite recent times. In the Netherlands the last real estate held in common was liquidated by law in 1866, while old local customs, especially in the eastern Netherlands, show the persistence of tradition. A glance at a detailed map of the province of Drente, for instance, reveals the outlines of the old settlements, surrounded by the common of heath and pasture.

These "mark associations" existed among all western Germanic peoples. Among them the same class distinctions existed between nobles, and free men, and between free men and bondsmen. A fourth class, the slaves, was unimportant socially and numerically. Nobility was hereditary. This rank carried greater influence in tribal affairs and a higher social standing and thus a better chance to acquire the lion's share of conquered land and booty. Some of the nobles were of royal rank, which meant that the military leaders, dukes or kings, might be chosen from their families. The mass of the people belonged to the class of the free men. The bondsmen, the *liten* or *laten,* were bound to the soil but were in all other respects not unlike tenants on a great landed estate. In the eighth century a slave trade existed between England and the Continent and it is assumed that prisoners of war were usually sold into slavery. The social and economic conditions prevailing in the primitive Germanic society left little place, however, for the maintenance of large bodies of slaves like those possessed by the Roman aristocrats of the second and first centuries before Christ.

It may be that the "mark association" never existed in its ideal form. In the Netherlands, it was found in its purest form in Drente and Overijssel.[4] By the sixth and seventh centuries, the "mark associations" in the Netherlands had become a restricted group of farmers—landowners who predominated over non-members of the mark, such as tenant-peasants, wage earners, and craftsmen. Even in those districts where the mark institution prevailed longest and in its purest form, there was a strong class sentiment among the associates, who only grudgingly admitted new members and tried to prevent the partition of member-farms. New marks were formed as long as there was land available that could be rendered productive, but in most districts the supply ran out quickly. Thus from the beginning there existed a class of wealthy landowners, with a following of dependent free men, bondsmen and slaves. Hagiographers mention this class as the people whose conversion Christian missionaries sought as it entailed that of all their dependents.

Three other factors determined the development of the wealthier class in the old Germanic Netherlands: the geographical features of the land settled; the period in which the settlement took place; the presence of pre-invasion inhabitants. The first factor was strong in "Terp-land." Here cattle breeding, not wheat growing, was the main occupation. This branch of agriculture suited the estate owner better than crop raising. The conquest of the land by the Anglicans may have fostered this tendency. Although large estates in Friesland and Groningen are often mentioned by writers of the eighth and ninth centuries, they never completely ousted the small landowners. South of the river belt, and still further south on the heaths of the Campina, which spread from the lower Scheldt to the moors of the Peel, where the Germanic settlers came relatively late and where they found an older population, large estates became the rule. Some traits of the village communities north of the rivers existed here too, but lost their significance more rapidly.

Thus agrarian institutions were basically the same in the whole of the Netherlands and, while showing regional or tribal differences, were mainly determined by geographical and historical factors. In this light, the traditional division of the old Netherlanders into the three nations of the Frisians, Saxons, and Franks loses much of its significance. In matters of religion, of which we know but little, in customs, and in social organization, there was little difference between them. The points of resemblance were always more important than the points of difference. All three followed western Germanic law. Disputes—crimes were just disputes between the criminal and his victim and family—were judged by all the free men of the *gouw* or tribe together. The content of the customary law was largely identical in the three sections of the population.

There was and still is, of course, great diversity in the dialects spoken in the various parts of the territory. Because we base our classification of modern dialect groups on historical tradition, we usually distinguish one Frisian, one Saxon and three Frankish dialect groups in modern Dutch. The transition is gradual, however, from the Frankish dialect of the southwest to the Saxon dialects of the northeast. The Frisian tongue distinguishes itself more sharply from its neighbor dialects but covers nowadays a far smaller territory than that which unquestionably belonged to Frisia in the eighth century. The modern dialect-studies neither prove nor disprove the tripartite division of the early Netherland people. It is possible that this classification came into use because of a confusion between *political* and *tribal* distinctions. There were, indeed, Franks, Frisians and Saxons in the Low Countries. Two rudimentary states were organized between the sixth and eighth centuries, one by the Franks, the other by the Frisians. The Saxons never reached that level of political organization before losing their independence. By counting all the people ruled by the kings of the Franks around 700 A. D. as Franks, and all the people ruled by the Frisian kings as Frisians, and by figuring the others as Saxons, the traditional classification was established. This method emphasized political divisions at the expense of tribal distinctions.

Around 500 A. D. King Chlodovech, or Clovis, who ruled the Franks in northwest Gaul, conquered most of the land between the Pyrenees and the Rhine. Because the Franks were mentioned in the days of Emperor Julian as being settled along the Scheldt, and because the Franks of Clovis lived not far south of that area, traditional history will have it that the Franks expanded from present Flanders and Brabant to northwest Gaul and finally over the whole of France. Clovis, however, may possibly have been the leader of a band of Roman mercenaries of Germanic origin who had no direct relations with the inhabitants of northern Belgium. Certain it is that northern Belgium and the southeastern Netherlands—the province of Limburg—were conquered by Clovis *after* he had gained supremacy in Gaul. For a long time that conquest remained superficial. There was only one district in the Low Countries where the Merovingian kings definitely established their authority, and that was the southeastern corner, the land around Tongeren and Maastricht, with its old pre-Frankish Christian community. Maastricht was at times the residence of the king. Scattered findings of Frankish objects along the rivers indicate that like the Romans, the Merovingians tried to establish a military boundary along the Rhine. Frankish government was not well organized in the Netherlands, however, until the end of the seventh century, when the Carolingians came to power.

The Anglo-Frisians of the west and north coast had also begun to organize a primitive state. This may have been a reaction against the rising power of the Franks; or it may have been instigated by the example of the Anglo-Saxons in Britain, with whom the Frisians always maintained close contact. Around 700 A. D. such progress had been made that the rule of their kings extended from the northern tip of Flanders, over Holland, as far inland as the town of Utrecht, over Friesland and the coastland to the Weser, including the island of Helgoland. Frisian power was maritime and strong enough to defy the northern Saxons and Danes and even, when opportunity offered, to invade the Rhineland as far as Cologne. It owned its importance not only to the military prowess of the Frisian kings and their warriors, but also to trade and shipping. The gold coins discovered in the terp-levels of the eighth century originate from many countries and mints. The Venerable Bede was one of the first writers to report on Frisian affairs, and the close association between Frisians and Anglo-Saxons is further shown by the resemblance of their gold and silver ornaments and the similarity of the runic script used on both sides of the North Sea.

The political organization of the Anglo-Frisian kingdom was rudimentary, and the personal prestige of the king probably its most important factor. That is why the only records we have deal with the reign of King Radbod, many times victorious over the Franks. We should know more of this kingdom if the epics that glorified the martial exploits of its leaders and which were still sung by Frisian bards in the days of Charlemagne had been written down and preserved. Nearly all our present knowledge is derived from hostile Frankish sources. In half a century of incessant wars, between 720 and 776, the Carolingians broke the Frisian power and destroyed its independence.

How far did the establishment of political states modify the social organization of the people? The Carolingian conquest first gave significance to monarchical institutions in the Netherlands. Hitherto "kings" had been local leaders. The Carolingian monarchy was the first to control the whole of the Low Countries. Theoretically, relations between ruler and ruled remained for a while what they had been, but in practice the whole situation was changed. Charlemagne's military and civil administration directly affected the character of local government and the judiciary. Besides, the Carolingian monarchy introduced a new factor into the old social structure by the adoption of Christianity and the establishment of the Roman Catholic Church. Christianity was imposed under the direct guidance of the kings, so much so that we may call the Church a part of the new administration.

The Church of Merovingian Gaul never had had much expansive force.

Deteriorating rapidly because of the meddling of barbaric, yet despotic kings with ecclesiastical affairs, it needed a spiritual rejuvenation. A religious revival was begun by Irish monks who came to Gaul to set an example of true monastic life. They commanded the respect of the kings and eventually inspired the Frankish clergy to take its duties more to heart. Saint Amand, the great missionary of Flanders was their disciple. Thanks to him the conversion of the southern Low Countries preceded that of the northern part by three-quarters of a century. But the only Christian church in the Netherlands, that of Tongeren-Maastricht, had fallen so low that Saint Amand, sent to reorganize it, left the diocese in despair within three years.

Whereas in the southern Low Countries religious work had been carried on by itinerant Irish priests or by Frankish bishops inspired by the Irish example, the conversion of the northern Low Countries was the work of Anglo-Saxon missionaries. The close affinity of the Frisian and Anglo-Saxon languages made this task easier for Englishmen than for Franks. Commercial relations between the two peoples provided easy access to the country and assured the missionaries of a friendly reception. Even so, the efforts of the Anglo-Saxon priests remained fruitless until Frankish power secured them a willing audience among a subdued people. The story of Saint Willibrord, the "apostle of the Frisians," bears this out. Upon his arrival in Friesland in 690 Willibrord crossed the country from one end to the other, vainly preaching the Gospel to King Radbod as well as to the common people. On a second trip he traveled as far as Helgoland, then a Frisian sanctuary, where to the dismay of the pagan inhabitants, he desecrated their holy places and killed some of their sacred cattle. Apparently the people were tolerant and even his actions on Helgoland failed to provoke the violent reprisals he probably expected and for which he perhaps hoped. Discouraged, he withdrew to the territory south of the great rivers where, with the support of Pepin (the second major domus of that name), he devoted himself to converting the people of northern Brabant and to preparing for a future mission.

Willibrord saw that he would have to win over the leading classes of the people he sought to convert. His chance came when the rudimentary Frisian state was shattered by the Frankish monarchy. The Frankish and anti-Frankish factions among the Frisians, necessarily became identified with Christianity and paganism. We find evidence of the same party strife in the story of the martyrdom of Saint Boniface. When attacked by an armed band of Frisian pagans, he refused to allow his Christian followers to defend him, preferring to suffer death. Later, when the report of his death spread through the country, the Christians gathered a strong force, over-

whelmed the murderers and carried off their women, children and servants—a rather unchristian act in which the hagiographer apparently saw
just punishment for the ruthless murder of a defenseless missionary. It
clearly suggests a conflict between two factions of the nobility.

This close relation between political and religious penetration of the
Frisian and Saxon districts led to the rapid if superficial adoption of Christianity. The oldest Frisian law code, promulgated in the time of Charlemagne, provides a penalty for the desecration of the sabbath but permits
the killing of a new born baby by the mother, an old pagan custom. In
supplements to the code, we even find penalties for the violation of pagan
holy places. More than two centuries were needed to complete the conversion of the Netherlands which, after 800, were outwardly part of the Roman
Catholic Church. As late as 896, the bishop of Utrecht received donations to
"make it possible for him to instruct and support converts from paganism."
Successful as the close cooperation between secular and ecclesiastical authorities proved, it was pregnant with grave danger for the Church. Willing to support the Church, the Carolingians were still more determined
to dominate it. The whole Church of Gaul was in process of being absorbed
by the state—not only its estates, but even its offices, bishoprics and abbeys.
The bishops, being Frankish noblemen, were unavoidably drawn into the
political quarrels of the aristocracy. Lambert, last bishop of Maastricht, a
contemporary and friend of Willibrord, was first driven from his bishopric
and then murdered by his political opponents. Bishops were obliged to be
lavish with the property entrusted to them for religious purposes.

As an Anglo-Saxon, Willibrord was not involved in the feuds of the
Frankish aristocracy and could accept the support of the Carolingians without fear for his Church. To maintain the integrity of his clergy and to
revive religious fervor among his missionaries, he founded the monastery
of Echternach, in present day Luxemburg. The center of his missionary
activity was Utrecht, then a small Frankish fortress donated by Charles
Martel to the See of Frisia, founded in 695 for Willibrord by Pope Sergius
in Rome.[5] After his death in 739, the episcopal see remained vacant for
fourteen years until another Anglo-Saxon, Saint Boniface, the apostle of
central Germany, took up the task where Willibrord had left it.

After the death of Boniface, the diocese of Utrecht was established, no
longer as an independent Frisian archbishopric but as a bishopric subordinate to the archdiocese of Cologne. In due time its boundaries were determined. To the south, they were the rivers Waal and Meuse. The bishopric
included, however, the delta islands of the Scheldt, the present province of
Zeeland. Its eastern limits coincided with the existing Netherland-German
boundary over about one-third of its extent, a fact of the greatest interest.

Here in this ecclesiastical delimitation we have a foreshadowing of the later political division between the Netherlands and Germany, that cut straight through the originally homogeneous Low-Germanic country. East of Utrecht, the See of Muenster was founded at Charlemagne's behest by the Frisian missionary Liudger. The emperor called him away from his missionary work in the eastern Terp-land and on the banks of the IJssel, to organize the newly established Church in the half-conquered Saxon land. At that time the eastern Terp-land, the lowlands of the present province of Groningen, and the parishes founded by Liudger east of the IJssel, became part of the diocese of Muenster, while all the rest of the Netherlands north of the Waal, formed the diocese of Utrecht. Nijmegen, south of the Waal, belonged to the archdiocese of Cologne, a connection which may indicate that all through post-Roman times not only a trading village but also a small Christian community continued to exist in the old town of the Batavi. South of the rivers virtually all territory now belonging to the Netherlands was incorporated in the diocese of Liége, which succeeded that of Maastricht.

To the Anglo-Saxons the Netherlands owe if not their first schools at least their oldest center of learning. Willibrord had founded a school at Utrecht which was carried on after his death by monks of the Utrecht monastery. Boniface fostered the same ideals. Wherever he went he carried cases of books. His biographer, when relating the murder of the saint by the pagan Frisians in 754, laments the wanton destruction of the books hardly less than the death of their owner. The school of Utrecht provided the first Netherland writer, Liudger the Frisian, later first bishop of Westphalia, who around 800 wrote a biography of Gregory, abbot of the Utrecht monastery. The second Dutch writer, the biographer of Boniface, was also connected with the Utrecht school.

From the Anglo-Saxon missionaries the Frisians and Saxons acquired a fervor for distant pilgrimages. They had already formed a colony in Rome, near the Church of Saint Peter, at the beginning of the IXth century. In 846, when Rome was threatened by Mohammedan pirates, the Romans granted to these Frisians, Franks, and Saxons the painful honor of sallying forth to Ostia to meet the enemies of the faith, a task of which they acquitted themselves with valor but without success.

This brief review of the early Catholic Church in the Netherlands shows that the introduction of Christianity affected not only the religious but also the social institutions of the people. No less important were the changes caused by the political administration of the Carolingians. The latter were powerful enough to establish their authority upon a new basis, making services compulsory that hitherto had been occasional and voluntary. Duties were now imposed upon the people where previously consent and cooperation had been asked. Taxes and tithes were levied, military service had to be rendered regularly and without default. To enforce his demands, the king appointed a count as his representative in each given district. Although the count presided over the courts, the people continued to decide civil and criminal disputes according to their old customs and could not be obliged to apply the royal laws. Regal authority however found other ways of interfering with popular jurisdiction.

One of the simplest was to grant so called "immunity" to ecclesiastical institutions, to monasteries, to the clergy in general and to subjects of the Church. In the days of the Carolingians, the "immunities" were still of minor scope and importance, but they grew with the progress of Christianity and the increase of church property. Another class of people made independent of the old social organization were the personal followers of the king, his "vassals" entitled to special protection. Where he so desired, there were various ways in which the king could bring matters before his own "court," the gathering of the noblemen who followed him. Even in this case it was not the king himself, but the peers of the accused who rendered justice. The natural shortcoming of popular jurisdiction provided the monarchy with good grounds for interference with the custom. The nobles and free men gathered in the "ding" usually appointed some of their own number who were experts in customary law to formulate and pronounce their judgments. The kings encouraged this tendency to transfer the essential part of the judicial function to experts. Thus benches of *scabini,* or jurors were formed and with the support of the counts rapidly superseded the popular courts in most criminal cases. In the southern Low Countries these benches had wholly replaced the older institutions before the end of the Carolingian period. In the northern section ancient custom proved far more tenacious; and here when eventually the rendering of justice was entrusted to experts, they were elected by the people.

New classes were created within the early Netherland society, but for the masses old institutions remained predominant. The authority of the counts was restricted and most officials were chosen from among the leading classes of the nation itself, only rarely being foreigners. Charlemagne took care to have the local law of custom written down and had it not been for the destruction wrought by the Vikings, we might still have the national epics of the Low-Germanic peoples that were recorded by order of the Emperor. These measures show clearly enough that any fanatical leveling of the hills and filling up the valleys of cultural life was foreign to the greatest of the Carolingians.

Far more effective than direct interference with the customs of the people were the indirect consequences to the agrarian communities in the purely Germanic territory of a new principle introduced in the ownership of the soil. From Merovingian times the Frankish kings had claimed the right to all wild lands in their kingdom and also to all fishing that was not private property. There was no cadastre of landed property, however, and there were no maps. The king rarely used his right over uncultivated soil except to make grants of land to his followers. The usual procedure, especially in a distant corner of the kingdom like the Netherlands, was for the aspirant to call the attention of the monarch to the existence of certain forests or heaths and then to receive the ownership or the usufruct thereof. The result was that wild land was appropriated first in those districts where the power of the kings was strong. In other places and where perhaps the wild lands were of less value the appropriation was postponed for a century or more. When royal authority weakened the right of appropriation was assumed by local counts who had become virtually independent. The exercise of this royal prerogative greatly increased the number and size of the large estates. It deprived the peasantry of the reserves of land on which an eventual excess of population might have settled—not that these lands were definitely closed to colonists, but in settling there, they had to accept the conditions of the owner which in practice meant becoming his bondsmen.

There was a close connection between the development of political administration in the Carolingian period and the rapid expansion of the large estates. To organize an administration, the monarchs needed officials; and to pay these officials, they distributed portions of the royal domain. To avoid the complete draining of the royal exchequer, they made use of their right to all public lands. In the long run it made little difference whether the estates of officials were held by them in fief or given to them outright. How did this system, common to the whole of northwestern Europe, affect the Netherlands, placed between the Latinized countries of the southwest and the Germanic countries of the northeast and with close ties with the Anglo-Saxon world over the sea?

At the close of the period of Netherland history dealt with in this chapter, that is, around 825, the country showed considerable homogeneity of culture and population. Its social institutions were slowly evolving towards feudalism, with its sharp class distinctions. The wealthier class of landowners was increasing in power and entrenching itself in an unassailable position above the masses. In this it was strongly supported by the monarchy. The Church too was broadening its power but in doing so was rapidly becoming part of the political machinery. In the Netherlands these tendencies were counteracted by the numerical and economic importance of the surviving class of free farmers. Slavery had virtually disappeared by the end of the Carolingian period. The number of bondsmen was rapidly increasing, and their social security grew with the legalization of their status. All along the coast, in the marshlands of Holland and Friesland which had little attraction for the aristocracy, a free peasantry maintained itself. Here where fishing and trading offered additional sources of income, the people were naturally less dependent on agriculture and less subject to feudalization. The consequences of this will become apparent in the following chapter.

A foreshadowing of the future prosperity of the Netherlands might be seen in the flourishing trade carried on in Carolingian days, from the port of Dorestad, now Wijk-bij-Duurstede. It is true that this "emporium" has lost much of the fame it owed to Carolingian chroniclers and their copyists, as a result of modern excavations. These have revealed a village of skippers and small traders, the houses spreading in three successive rows along a single street, the whole protected by a primitive fortress of earth and wooden palisades. Though primitive, it was the first of the Netherland trading cities and in its time enjoyed a reputation for wealth that won for it the unwelcome attentions of the Vikings.

The Vikings began their incursions during the reign of Charlemagne. To penetrate into the Netherlands, they needed only to follow the sea, the onslaughts of which were more violent than ever and made deep inroads into the land. During the five centuries prior to 800, the west winds had pressed the Netherland dunes back as much as three miles. Buildings inside the dunes constructed in earlier days and obliterated by the retreating masses of sand, reappeared outside the dunes only to be submerged by the sea. The openings in the "Westwall" widened; the lower-lying peatgrounds, slowly built up by nature through hundreds of years, were rapidly dissolved and destroyed. In the north, the openings widened so far that the wall of dunes was cut in pieces and the remaining sections reduced to small islands in the expanse of sea and shoal. Farther to the south, the inland lakes widened and began to form the "Zuiderzee" which was then turned into a salt water basin. It took another six hundred years for the Zuiderzee to gain the dimension it had before the gigantic reclamation of our day was undertaken.

Thus three factors mainly determined the further development of social and political institutions in the Netherlands. The first was political, especially the invasions of the Vikings and the partitions of the Frankish monarchy. In a coastal country like the Netherlands, these events were of special interest. The second was the peculiar character of the soil, which attacked by the sea had to be reclaimed and protected from further inroads. The third was the geographical position of the Netherlands which, with the spreading of Christian civilization and the progress of political organization in northern Europe, became more central.

CHAPTER III

The Origin of the Provinces

FOR nearly sixty years the Netherlands were merely a part of the undivided Frankish monarchy. In 843 the unity of that monarchy was broken, never to be restored. It fell apart into its cultural components: Romanic-Gallic, Germanic, and Ultramontane. In course of time these grew into the states of France, Germany, and Italy. As a borderland between the Romanic and the Germanic sections, the Low Countries unavoidably became an object of rivalry between the kings of the West and the East. By the Treaty of Verdun in 843 all territory between the Scheldt and the Rhine including Frisia, with Utrecht and other districts along the Rhine and IJssel, were given to Middle Francia, the ephemeral realm of Lothar I. With the second partition in 870 at Meerssen, this middle kingdom was divided between its neighbors of the East and West. The new boundary ran from north to south straight through the Netherlands, cutting the territory into two nearly equal parts. This arrangement lasted only ten years. Then, after a series of conflicts during which the local leaders repeatedly changed their allegiance, the whole of the middle kingdom was annexed to the kingdom of the East. From 925, the boundary between Germany and France followed the Scheldt, separating the territory of Flanders politically from the rest of the southern Low Countries.

The history of these partitions is of little interest. Who ever of the Carolingians ruled in the Low Countries quickly discovered that his authority rested solely upon his military prowess; not that the vassals had to be compelled to obedience, but because the king alone could afford protection against the Vikings. None of the Carolingian princes was able to provide that protection. On the contrary, some of them even granted parts of the territory to Norman chiefs, to set one pirate against another. This was not effective and the royal authority remained of slight importance. The inhabitants, abandoned by their sovereign, suffered terribly. Dorestad was bled to death by the pirates. Utrecht was destroyed, and its bishop driven from his diocese. Of all Carolingian and pre-Carolingian monuments in the Netherlands, only one, a small church in southern Limburg, survived the general destruction.

Left by their kings to their own devices, the once war-like Frisians and

Franks were singularly unable to defend themselves. The progress of civilization was interrupted, but so was the development of feudal institutions
in the Netherland coastlands. In this respect the Norman period may have
been of great consequence, but we lack the evidence to determine its exact
significance.

As the partitions did not coincide with ecclesiastical or linguistic boundaries, they were of no political or cultural consequence. In the eastern
boundary of the Middle Empire, one may recognize the present German-
Dutch boundary; but soon we find that it is only because it followed the
contour of the diocese of Utrecht. The latter alone has historical significance. The western boundary continued to exist for many centuries, but
was without historical consequence, hardly perceptible to the mass of the
people. The boundary was not as today a sharp dividing line between two
linguistic areas or two distinct economic and political systems. It denoted
a difference in the allegiance of the fiefholders—nothing more—and this
was of no great importance. Many medieval Netherland nobles held fiefs
from both the German and the French kings, and owed allegiance to both.
They and the masses of the people were far less aware of the separate
political existence of the French and German kingdoms, than of the unity
that bound together all the princes, potentates, towns, and peoples of western Christendom. If the kings of France and Germany had early succeeded
in establishing a strong central government, this conception might have
been modified, but history shaped it so that the kings of France did not
score any success in this direction until after the kings of Germany had
definitely failed. Thus, in the early Middle Ages, the Low Countries were
never subjected to strong political pressure from both sides at the same
time.

It did not much matter to which kingdom the Netherland potentates
owed allegiance. Whether they paid homage to Charles the Bald or Charles
the Fat, to any of the Louis or Lothars, they learned to act for themselves.
They regarded their native lands as hereditary possessions, and took to
themselves much of the royal prerogative. Within two centuries, the Low
Countries, north of the riverbelt, fell apart into five feudal states: the counties of Holland, Zeeland, Friesland, and Guelders, and the episcopal state
of Utrecht, composed of two territorial units: the "Nedersticht" and the
"Oversticht." South of the rivers, Brabant became the principal feudal
state, flanked to the west by Flanders, theoretically part of France, and to
the east by the principalities of Liége, Limburg, and Valkenburg.

The kings of Germany, who were the first to seek a strengthening of
royal authority after the downfall of the Carolingian empire, came close
to attaining their goal. Otto I, Henry II, Conrad II, and Henry III, all

attempted to create some order in the political chaos of the Low Countries. To keep down turbulent local rulers, they strengthened the power of loyal supporters of their regime, the dukes of Lorraine in the south and the bishops of Utrecht in the north. Had this plan succeeded, the bishops of Utrecht would have become secular as well as ecclesiastical lords within their diocese. It is idle to speculate what course Netherland history might have taken if at this early date, the major part of territory had been organized into one feudal ecclesiastical state. The attempt failed mainly because of the stubborn resistance of the "Frisians" of the coastal districts. From this conflict between monarchical power, represented by the bishops of Utrecht, and the stubborn coastal people, were born the western and northern "provinces" of the Netherlands.

The details of this struggle, which lasted from the middle of the Xth to the end of the XIth century, are of little interest. Our knowledge is of the slightest. Suffice to say that in the western coastal districts a dynasty of petty potentates, possibly deriving their origin from one of the Norman pirate chiefs, succeeded in creating a miniature feudal state including the area around Leiden and the domains of the old monastery of Egmond. These "water-counts," petty lords of the dunes and marshes, gradually extended their rule over the thinly inhabited and desolate swamps between the dunes and the lower Meuse. The marshes were their chief protection against the punitive expeditions of the German kings and their faithful followers, the bishop of Utrecht and the duke of Lorraine.

Even so, they might have succumbed in the unequal struggle, had it not been for the assistance of the count of Flanders. The inhabitants of the western marshland were still called "Frisians" by contemporary chroniclers. The Flemish count who saved their primitive feudal state from untimely destruction is accordingly remembered in history as Robert the Frisian. His interest in the northern neighborland was primarily dynastic, but the close association of the various western districts of the Low Countries under a prince who was more deeply involved in the political problems of England and France than in those of Germany is suggestive of later events.

The newly formed coastal principality had no name. Chronicles of its fierce struggle for survival, refer to its rulers as the "Frisian counts," or the "marquesses" of Vlaardingen. Vlaardingen was then a small fishing and trading village near the mouth of the Meuse, where the Imperial troops had suffered one of their worst defeats. When the counts, having firmly established their authority over the marshy country, were accepted as members of the princely aristocracy of the Holy Roman Empire, we find them called "counts of Holland." The origin of the name Holland, first used in 1054, is uncertain. In the Middle Ages Holland was believed to be derived from Holt-land, which means woodland; modern authorities think it came from "Hol," a marsh, and meant "marshy land." [6]

Count Robert of Flanders had helped to save Holland, and naturally his own country gained by the adventure. The Flemish counts had already extended their authority over several districts north and east of the boundaries of the Empire. From the XIth century, we find them in possession of the islands formed by the branches of the Scheldt. Soon the whole island group, then more extensive than now, became known as the county of Zeeland. As long as feudal rulers existed in the Netherlands, it was united politically first with Flanders and from the end of the XIth century with Holland, as a fief of Flanders.

Official recognition of the "water-counts" was due to the fact that in the great struggle within the Empire at the end of the XIth century, they had sided with the victors. Popes and emperors had become involved in a conflict over the lay investiture of ecclesiastics. Discontented groups among the German feudal aristocracy rallied around the pope. One center of opposition was the duchy of Saxony, and it is significant that the counts of Holland maintained close relations with the Saxon nobility. The bishops of Utrecht, on the other hand, were the natural defenders of the Imperial power which had made them secular rulers. Naturally, the Netherland episcopal state shared the fate of its Imperial masters and emerged from the struggle with great loss of prestige and domain.

To the inaccessibility of their marshland and to the political troubles of the Empire, the counts of Holland owed the strengthening of their position. The same causes produced the most remarkable phenomenon of Dutch medieval history—the free or rather anarchical republican institutions in the northern Netherlands, in Friesland and the lowlands of Groningen. After the withdrawal of the Vikings, the old Terp-land had been left to its fate. The German kings occasionally invested one or other of their vassals as count of Friesland, but to bear the title and to rule the country were two different things. The fief was so often bestowed or confiscated that we may assume the fiefholders rarely exerted their authority. Certainly the stubborn and self-willed Frisians felt no obligation towards them. They followed their own way of life, settling their own affairs, caring not at all what German potentate bore the title of count of Friesland. The problem became acute around 1130, when the counts of Holland obtained the investiture, but even then there was no change in the larger part of the territory. Such central administration as had ever functioned in Friesland ceased to exist by the end of the XIth century. In the XIIIth century political anarchy had become so much a national institution that Frisian writers boasted of it. They sought legal confirmation of their existing freedom; and as this could not be obtained from the ruling kings and princes, they found it in tradition which they subsequently claimed as of right. From this to the assertion that the ancient Frisian freedom had been guaranteed by Charlemagne, and from that to the "restoration" of "lost" charters of freedom, was only a few steps.

Gradually, the extent of free Frisian territory shrank in the Middle Ages. Holland, known prior to 1100 only as part of Frisia, had become a separate feudal state. The rise of the Saxon principalities in Germany reduced Frisian territory in the east. For a century or so longer, Frisia extended from Alkmaar in north Holland to west of Bremen.

In the XIIIth century, the Frisian territory was divided by the ever-growing incursions of the sea. Until that time the central part of the Zuiderzee had existed as an inland lake. Then under pressure of northwestern storms, the waters broke up the solid wall of dunes and formed the Frisian islands. The channels and river outlets from the former inland lake to the North Sea widened until they formed one vast inlet of the ocean. Thus the western Friesland was separated from the main body. Cornered between the forces of the counts of Holland and the sea, these West Frisians, after a fierce struggle, were forced in the late XIIIth century, to capitulate and accept the counts as their territorial lords. From that time the Zuiderzee formed the western boundary of Friesland.

The territory was still further reduced as the lowlands of Groningen gradually fell under the influence of the city of that name. Here, in the XVth century, even the Frisian tongue was replaced by a Saxon dialect. By the end of the Middle Ages Frisia, the far flung sea-land of the Frisians, was reduced to the limits of the present province of Friesland.

Thus the territories of Zeeland, Holland, Friesland, and Groningen took form along the sea coast. As we have seen their political development was shaped by continuous resistance to the encroachments of German monarchical power. It was a revolt of the borderlands against the central government, and represents in a way the beginning of an independent Netherland. Of course, the XIth and XIIth century counts of Holland did not undertake this struggle as a "fight for freedom" or to secede from the Holy Roman Empire. They resisted the central authority of that Empire, in the persons of the bishops of Utrecht, just as other feudal princes sought to make their domains hereditary and to secure their rights against monarchical authority. However, the geographical position of the Netherland coastland and their close association with Flanders and across the North Sea strengthened the independence of the county of Holland and its western ties, thus loosening its bonds to the east.

The bishops of Utrecht succeeded no better in organizing political unity in the eastern than in the western half of the Netherlands. From the oldest Germanic times, the plains of the east had been divided into *gouws*. These districts organized as counties during the reign of Charlemagne, tended to become petty feudal states in the confusion of the IXth and Xth centuries. The elimination of the more unruly of these self-created principalities was no easy task. Ancient chroniclers tell in vivid terms of many acts of violence and cruelty committed by the ruthless rebels. After their destruction the monarchy gave the conquered land to other and more trustworthy vassals. Most of the land expropriated north of the Rhine was given to the bishops of Utrecht, while between the Meuse and the Rhine a secular principality arose under the Wassenbergs.

From this dynasty sprang several ruling families between the Rhine and the Meuse. In the extreme south were the counts of Valkenburg, whose tiny territory extended east of Maastricht on that stretch of loess soil already referred to. To the north the counts of Guelders, now Geldern in the Rhine province, controlled both banks of the Meuse from Roermond to Venlo. Still farther north, the counts of Cleve were firmly established astride the lower Rhine, west of Wesel. Thus the descendants of this one family controlled all the routes connecting western Germany with the North Sea ports, the land route along the old Roman highway from Cologne to Maastricht and Tongeren, as well as the rivers Meuse and Rhine. Their power was apparently more firmly established than that of the bishops north of the river. In the crucial years of the early XIIth century, when the political position of the bishopric was buffeted by the Investiture storm, the episcopal dignity was for a while held by a member of the Wassenberg-Guelders family. When the northern ecclesiastical state collapsed shortly afterwards, the counts of Guelders were the chief gainers. The bishops' authority over the lands in the riverbelt had been uncertain. Their power over faraway Drente, the ancient Hunebed country, depended upon the loyalty of vassals they had installed in their castle of Coevorden to control the gap in the peat moors that formed the entrance to Drente's sandy plains. Their position east of the IJssel river seemed more secure, but without royal authority to support them, the bishops could not prevent their secular rivals from encroaching upon their territory. The counts of Guelders soon succeeded in obtaining possession of various pieces of territory and several independent lordships which they organized into a new state, now the province of Guelderland. A purely artificial political structure, it was admirably located in control of the Rhine just where it branches into its delta. The episcopal state was divided in two. One area immediately surrounding Utrecht, became the province of that name. The other beyond the IJssel, was known as the "Oversticht" and encompassed the modern provinces of Drente and Overijssel with the town, but not the lowlands, of Groningen.

Thus, the provinces of the Netherlands, which were to gain world-wide renown in the XVIIth century, came into existence. Originally, there were numerous small lordships enclosed in the larger territorial units. Some were gradually absorbed by their more powerful neighbors, others survived until the French revolution swept them away. At the end of the XIth century the area south of the riverbelt, between the Scheldt in the west and the moors of the Peel on the east, formed part of the duchy of Brabant, but was separated from that state in the XVIIth century, and at the end of the XVIIIth became the province of Noord Brabant. There is no need to describe in detail the dynastic history of the Netherland principalities nor to follow their territorial and political vicissitudes. John Lothrop Motley rightly says: "Even the most devout of genealogists might shudder to chronicle the long succession of so many illustrious obscure." Only the development of the social institutions of the people inhabiting these multifarious states is of interest.

As we have seen, the feudal system had been introduced in the Carolingian period. It did not permeate the whole social structure as in other countries, for geographical conditions hindered its growth. The rapid increase of the population during the Xth and XIth centuries caused an expansion of the area under cultivation. In many parts of the country ancient popular institutions were still strong enough to prevent the benefits of this expansion to accrue to a single class of the population. By the XIth century, the ancient Germanic nobility had virtually disappeared by the killing off of families in clan-strife, the splitting up of estates, the resulting impoverishment of the various branches and other factors. Few of the noble houses of the later Middle Ages could boast of descent from pre-Carolingian or even Carolingian aristocracy. A new nobility deriving its title from the service of territorial lords, took the place of the families of ancient lineages. These were the "ministeriales," the men at arms, retainers and esquires of the provincial counts, their professional soldiery. Besides these, a number of "mayors" of princely manors also rose to the rank of nobility. From this class the gentry of the later Middle Ages sprang in the whole of western Europe.

Where the power and wealth of the territorial lords was small or nonexistent, no class of "ministeriales" could arise. In Friesland, where all central authority disappeared after the XIth century, the old clans of hereditary nobles became extinct. Slavery had disappeared after the Carolingian period. Two hundred years later "bondage," also was virtually a thing of the past in the coastlands. Custom continued to distinguish between bondsmen and freemen, but the only real difference between them was that bondsmen were subject to certain personal taxes from which freemen were exempt. In Friesland bondage vanished completely. In Holland the only lords who had power over bondsmen were the count himself and the abbot of Egmond. In Zeeland, there were only two classes: nobles and commoners. In these countries the term "nobleman" simply meant "fiefholder" or "vassal" of the prince, quite regardless of the origin of the family.

This early abolition of bondage, a development widely different from that pictured in our traditional historiography, was caused among other reasons by internal colonization whereby the provinces of Holland, Zeeland, Friesland, and Utrecht made land and homes for their rapidly increasing population. From the XIth to the XIIIth centuries the coastal Frisians toiled to convert the marshes behind the dunes into arable land.

We do not know with certainty in what century the first dykes were constructed. The Romans had built them as substructures for their highways along the lower branches of the Rhine, but the protection of the low land was a secondary, even incidental, aspect of their work. We know that the technique of dyke building was well advanced in the XIth century, but we can only guess at the date of its origin. The VIIIth century has been mentioned in this connection, though the IXth has perhaps better claims. In Zeeland, where the protective dunes had been broken into small fragments at an early date, and where the impact of the southwestern storms combined with the effects of the Gulfstream to cause abnormal tides—at some places the normal rise is fifteen feet—all ramparts were broken during the VIIIth and IXth centuries. The wide marshland through which the Scheldt had formerly broken its course to the sea was reduced to a number of scattered and precarious islands. While in Holland regulation of the rivers was the first necessity, Zeeland had to build heavy sea-dykes to protect the few relatively safe spots on the islands. Once this was done, its people slowly began to reclaim the lost ground, throwing up new dykes around shoals and shallow water immediately in front of the old ramparts. An initial mistake was made of pulling down the old dyke as soon as a new outer bulwark was built. The results were disastrous as the lower strata of the soil in the shallow inlets of the sea kept moving, and suddenly for no apparent reason, part of the dyke would melt into the sea, leaving a wide gap through which the waters poured to reoccupy the ground they had lost. Thus the aspect of the Zeeland islands was constantly changing. Some of the existing islands were literally built by the age-long efforts of the people; in other places, the sea not only regained its own, but even destroyed old settlements.

The islands of Flakkee and Tholen, for instance, were constructed in the late Middle Ages by the relentless efforts of the people. The island of Walcheren was patched together from a number of smaller islands. That of South Beveland literally moved westward, for while large tracts of land were being reclaimed west of the oldest dykes, the sea broke off equally large sections on the east. The island of North Beveland, one of the oldest of all, even disappeared only to emerge again from the sea sixty-six years later.

The problems of Holland were different. Here the dunes had remained unbroken and the country was fairly well protected from the sea. The danger of flood sprang from the extremely low and constantly sinking level of the soil, which was in danger of submersion at every excessive rainfall and at every spring thaw. The Rhine, dividing into many branches, never formed a deep river bed, and this increased the danger of floods. Once the principal rivers were banked with strong dykes—the bishops of Utrecht deserve credit for the part they took in this work—the inland area was relatively safe. It was still exposed, however, to the dangers arising from excessive rainfall and the low fall of the rivers. After the main dykes along the rivers and the Zuiderzee had been built, the lowland of Holland and Utrecht formed a broad hollow plain surrounded by dunes and dykes, but whenever the outflow of the smaller rivers was interfered with, the situation became critical. Obviously, the next step was to close these natural river outlets and to replace them by sluices to prevent high tides outside the dykes from affecting the level of the inland waters. The construction of dams and sluices began in the XIIth century and was completed a hundred years later. These dams naturally hindered shipping but the small size of the river boats made it possible to haul them over the dams. That called for more hands than the boats carried, and resulted in small settlements of skippers, traders, and craftsmen, which later developed into towns. Hence the names of so many cities in Holland ending with—dam, like Amsterdam, Rotterdam, Zaandam, and many others. Right in the center of Amsterdam, the old dam through the river Amstel still exists.

The third step in the development of the soil, the systematic drainage of the land by ditching, by collecting the water in canals immediately behind the dykes, and by pumping the surplus into the sea was not undertaken until the end of the Middle Ages. We hear of the first windmills in 1408, when one was built near Alkmaar, and officials of the "polders" of southern Holland traveled north to study the new technical marvel. Until that time the "polders," dyked-in tracts of land where the water is kept at low level by artificial means, depended for drainage upon a clever use of the tidal difference in the outside waters, but this course provided no security. By the end of the XVIth century, the whole of Holland and the island area was divided into polders.

In Friesland the situation was different, for here, once the main dykes were built, the sea itself contributed to the reconstruction of the land. The tides deposited enormous masses of silt in the inlets of the sea and along the shore. The main task of the people was to wait for the moment when the filling in of the shallow areas had progressed far enough to justify the building of new outer dykes. The "Middelzee," an inlet nearly twenty miles in depth had already been turned into fertile fields by the end of the XIIIth century, and a century later the sea was pushed back another five or six miles.

The work of converting the old marshlands into arable fields made such progress between the XIth and XIIIth centuries that at the end of that period the area under cultivation—if we except Zeeland and a number of inland lakes in Holland which were drained off later—was not much smaller than at the beginning of the XIXth century.

This enormous task of internal colonization called for the full use of all available man power. There was a constant demand for any surplus labor that existed in the older cultivated areas. This created a freedom of movement which forcibly loosened the stricter social and economic ties holding the various classes of society each in its appointed sphere. In this sense the slogan, "Only free men can undertake such a monumental task," is true. Social and political freedom was not an essential postulate of the great work undertaken in Holland's marshlands, but it was certainly the inevitable outcome. The fact that the feudal system had never really taken root in the coastlands made the development even more natural.

Although the geographical and political development of Holland, Zeeland, and Friesland are fairly easy to follow, we know less about economic conditions during these centuries of internal expansion. However, the struggle against the floods and marshes aroused such boundless energy in the people that soon the reclamation in the Low Countries was too little for them, and a number of emigrants set out for distant and less populated regions where new tasks awaited them. From the end of the Xth century Low-German potentates, the bishops of Bremen, the marquesses of Brandenburg, the dukes of Saxonia, the counts of Holstein and Luebeck sought the assistance of the coastal Dutch in the reclamation of wild lands conquered from the Slavs, especially of those regions where the conditions were similar to those in Holland and Flanders. The first to contract with an enterprizing Hollander for such work was Bishop Frederick of Bremen. Some of the colonists acted as contractors, undertaking to build a definite number of farms on a certain tract of land, and themselves enrolled volunteers willing to migrate to the East. The new settlers always became wholly free farmers, subject to tithes and certain taxes, but without any bond of personal servitude or obligation. This colonization of northeastern Germany continued for more than a century, and the importance of the Dutch-Flemish element in the composition of its German population is attested by the survival for centuries of Dutch-Flemish customary law in that region.

German chroniclers specifically mentioned among the pioneers of what was then the "Far East," "large groups of Flemings, Hollanders, and people from the diocese of Utrecht." The traditional explanation of this exodus is that frequent floods "drove the poor unfortunate peasants of Holland from their native country." Strange indeed for at that very time the people of Holland were feverishly expanding their fields, constructing dykes, building churches in the new villages and primitive towns that sprang up all over the country. On several occasions the coastlands were severely damaged by violent floods, but in spite of these the country and the people became more and more prosperous. It is probable that only excess population that could not find land and work even in the growing Dutch community emigrated. Probably the natural effects of national prosperity and activity, the greater number of marriages, more and better food for everybody, led to an increasing population and lower mortality. The population of the coastlands must have risen by leaps and bounds, even faster than the arable soil could be expanded.

From the foregoing, it is clear that medieval Holland and Friesland do not fit the traditional framework most historical textbooks provide. Serfdom did not exist, and by the XIIth and XIIIth centuries, only the faintest traces of bondage remained. The influence of the people in the administration of justice and in many matters of government persisted despite all political vicissitudes. In Friesland, where no central administration functioned after the XIth century, the villages and small districts became independent political and social units. With the extinction of the old Frisian nobility, the greatest influence in political and judicial matters fell to the principal landowners, regardless of the origin of their families. The country, so to speak, fell apart into thirty small territorial units, the *grietenijen,* each ruled by a *grietman* who was responsible for order and acted as public prosecutor, head of what administration existed—and who represented the *grietenij* at the meetings of his *gouw*. The office of *grietman* was always filled by one of the principal landowners of the district, and a member of the same class held the post of *asega* or judicial expert. In each case the office-holder had to be confirmed at a meeting to which all householders were summoned in order to accept or reject the nominees. This was true of ecclesiastical as well as secular offices, for in most Frisian parishes even the parish priest was elected by the householders of the community.

In this curiously democratic rural society, the springing up of small towns and the founding of large monasteries threatened to disrupt the established "order." The problem was met by the fiction that a town was another *grietenij,* though with a rather dense population. The town administration originally organized like that of a rural district, later followed the example set by towns of Overijssel and Holland. There was no such legal distinction between town and countryside as existed elsewhere in medieval Europe. Here the towns did not receive a privileged status from the lord of the land, but the townspeople governed themselves as their free ancestors had done.

The monastic orders of Citeaux and Prémontré became important in Friesland because of the share the monks took in reclaiming the land. As the owners of large territories and several villages, the abbots and priors of these monasteries held positions like those of the most powerful secular land-holders. They attended the diets of Friesland, and in the second part of the Middle Ages, took an active part in the political quarrels that set the whole country afire and nearly caused the loss of its political independence. In mentioning the "diets" of Friesland, the plural must be used because the old Terp-land did not form a political entity, not even a political federation. Each *gouw* or *go,* the ancient district, remained separate, and until the present day the old names of Oostergo and Westergo are used by the people of Friesland as those of Fivelgo and Hunzingo are used by the people of Groningen. A late medieval attempt to group some of the *gos* for judicial purposes, the alliance of the *Upstalbom,* never ripened into political federation. The organization sprang up during the XIIth century in East Friesland, now the extreme northwestern corner of Germany, and around 1325 the other Frisian districts joined the group. As soon, however, as the Westergo of Friesland sought to transform this loose judicial organization into defensive alliance, and into a political federation for the defense of Frisian freedom, the group fell apart.

In Holland the presence of a territorial prince made the political organization of that province widely different from that of Friesland. It would be a great mistake, however, to overestimate the power of that prince and his fellow rulers in the Low Countries, the counts of Guelders, the dukes of Brabant, and the bishops of Utrecht. The presence of a ruler secured within these territories a certain tranquillity that was lacking in Friesland, but in the early Middle Ages it did not prevent feuds among vassals and the arbitrary levying of tolls on skippers and traders. As a rule, the princes of a coastland like the Netherlands were too well aware of the

importance of trade to obstruct the free movement of merchants. Moreover, the power of the prince was limited. His authority never superseded
the rights of his subjects. In the principalities of the XIIth and XIIIth centuries, the rights of the prince and of the people were pretty well defined.
In territories like Holland, where the large majority of the inhabitants were
free men, the lord's opportunities of encroachment were few.

The prince had some of the prerogatives of sovereignty. Charlemagne
had installed "counts" in all districts to preside over the popular assemblies
and to regulate their judicial proceedings. It had also been the task of the
Carolingian counts to lead the militia of the district to the meeting place
of the royal army. The counts of the XIIth and XIIIth centuries still exercised this right, but for their own benefit. At times they summoned inhabitants of their territory to take part in their quarrels with neighbors, but
local custom regulated the obligation of military service and greatly reduced its scope. Usually it extended only to the personal vassals of the
prince, except in emergencies. Outside these quasi-sovereign rights, the
local ruler disposed only of his own domain, that is his personal estate, his
share in the fines imposed by the courts, certain tithes acquired with property which was once ecclesiastical, and other sources of income granted by
the king or ceded by others. Modern democratic states, and of necessity the
dictatorships into which some have grown, are sovereign in the full sense
of the word. Their authority knows no limit, provided the majority of the
voters accept it. Nobody would concede greater rights to a medieval prince
than he possessed by the law of custom or had acquired by royal patent in
the days when royal authority was still strong. But even the king's own
fiat often failed to make the people bow before an authority they did not
consider legitimate.

Indeed the people expressed their views on this subject most clearly and
unceremoniously. Several counts of Holland—one of them a "King of the
Romans," aspiring to become emperor—died ignominiously with hundreds
of their knightly vassals under the clubs and swords of the Frisian peasants
upon whom they sought to impose their rule. A bishop of Utrecht shared
the same fate at the hands of the peasants of Drente, who slew him in the
peatmoor bordering their land. The occasions on which bishops of Utrecht
had to flee their residence are too numerous to be recorded here. It happened at the end of the XIIIth century, when the peasants of northern
Holland joined the inhabitants of Utrecht in a general revolt against their
lords. It happened again a few decades later when the townspeople of
Flanders and partisans from Zeeland nearly conquered the whole eastern
half of the Low Countries. In most of these uprisings the final outcome of
the military campaign was in favor of the lords, but the political result was

the maintenance or extension of popular rights, the princes being wholly unable to strengthen their sovereignty.

Within his hereditary "domain" the authority of the lord was absolute. Beyond it he could accomplish nothing without the consent of his subjects. After the middle of the XIIth century, after the death of Frederick Barbarossa who had temporarily restored the authority of the central government, the princes of the Netherlands were able to ignore with impunity the sovereignty of the kings of Germany. They could never ignore the remaining elements of popular authority, dating back to ancient Germanic times. The territorial counts, either in person or through representatives, continued to make the rounds of their territory, presiding over the meetings of the people to render justice or to deliberate on administrative affairs. It is true that old forms of popular government were gradually modified, that the mass meetings of the people either lost all meaning and went out of use, that they became meetings of vassals and principal landowners with a purely feudal character; but new forms of self-rule sprang up to take the place of the old ones. There was a direct connection between the late medieval institution of the States Assembly and the ancient gathering of free men.

The counts of Holland, who at the traditional time and place still gathered around them the people of the countryside for the discussion of special questions, had profoundly modified the judicial system by reserving all important criminal cases to their own court, composed of their leading vassals and servants. Thus the higher courts of the county became instruments of the central administration, although it would be wrong to assume that the personal influence of the ruler was predominant in matters of justice. The members of the court nearly always belonged to a class with a strong sense of personal independence, and would not have brooked arbitrary interference. Minor misdemeanors continued to be dealt with by the local courts, of which there was one in nearly every parish. Here the appointee of the count, the *Schout,* was the prosecutor. Until the end of the XIIIth century, judgment was pronounced in the old Germanic fashion by some expert of customary law, and at least theoretically approved by the people. Later, from the days of Count Florent V (1256–1296) the bench of *Scabini* or jurors which had functioned in the southern Low Countries since the Carolingian period, replaced the traditional local court.

This undoubtedly strengthened the authority of the central administration. Originally members of the bench were appointed either by the count from among the principal landowners of the village or elected by the people. For a while the counts hesitated between these two systems, anxious to obtain control, yet loath to provoke the anger of their turbulent people. A compromise resulted in the formation of an oligarchic regime, the retiring jurors presented two lists of candidates to the prince from which he elected the new appointees.

In a rapidly developing territory like Holland, old customs and institutions could not be maintained permanently. Where the constant struggle against the waters, the construction of dykes and dams required the personal attention of the ruler, a public administration grew up much faster than in the poor and conservative eastern districts. The counts began to appoint bailiffs, who presided over the higher courts and administered the princely domain. On the other hand marshland reclamation created new local forms of self-government. Responsible for the maintenance of the dykes the prince delegated that duty primarily to those whose land was immediately affected. Each village, therefore, became responsible for a definite section, and all the inhabitants were obliged to do their share of the common task. So, in practice, the administration of these works was in the hands of the villagers. Their representatives, the jurors where such officials existed, decided all questions pertaining to the dykes. They made regulations, drafted the inhabitants of their village for work, imposed taxes to meet expenses, and punished the recalcitrants and all who neglected their duty. The counts never interfered with the decisions of these dyke-administrators. The long, heavy sea-dykes, stretching along the coast of the Zuiderzee or along the rivers, made cooperation among villages essential. It was organized in the same democratic way.

If the dyked-in area was new land reclaimed from the sea or marshes and recently settled, the organization was slightly different. Here the maintenance of the *polder,* the technical unit of drained land, was naturally entrusted to the owners and cultivators of the newly won soil. In such cases too, the officials of the count acted as supervisors, but the actual administration was directly controlled by the farmers who, more often here than in the older villages, elected their own representatives. These were the beginnings of the *waterschappen,* the self-governing bodies for the administration of the *polder-*land which have continued to function to this day.

The people of the eastern plains, living on firmer soil than their neighbors of the north and west, clung tenaciously to old customs and liberties which in other districts had given way to more modern institutions. They were also slower to break down the social barriers dividing the various classes of the population. The amount of arable land was strictly limited. The villages of Drente were hemmed in by far-flung peatmoors, still unsuitable for colonization. The wind-swept dunes and the pine forests of the Veluwe offered slim inducement to new settlers. For a while the expanding population found homes by draining the lowland near the mouth of the IJssel and by clearing land east of that river, but this possibility was soon exhausted. If the power of the territorial lords had been greater, even this small outlet for excess population might not have existed; for the local rulers claimed title to all wild land, as heirs of the royal prerogative. The tradition of freedom was too strong however, among the Saxon agrarian communities, to permit this. The people of Zwolle and other communities of Overijssel fought and won a centuries-long lawsuit against their lords, the bishops of Utrecht, for the ownership of the "Mastenbroek," a stretch of reclaimed land at the mouth of the IJssel. The scarcity of new land tended to stabilize existing conditions, to restrict the economic freedom of the newcomer by making the "mark association" a closed community of hereditary shareholders, and to strengthen feudal ties. In the west and north there was space in which to move and to expand, and this loosened the social structure. In the east, the lack of space tightened the bonds of the people. This lack of social change militated against any early development of new forms of administration. At a time when the counts of Holland already administered their territory through bailiffs, removable officials appointed for a limited term, the bishops of Utrecht still followed the old custom of traveling through the *gouws* of their territory to meet the free men at the *ding*. Drente, the free districts which now form the province of Overijssel, the *gouws* of Salland and Twente, and the district of Vollenhoven were visited in turn. As social institutions became more stiff and narrow, the gatherings of the free men shriveled into meetings of estate owners among whom, by the end of the XIIth century, ministeriales formed the great majority. The people were no longer represented except through the principal landowners of each parish, Drente the least accessible and the poorest of all the episcopal possessions alone excepted. Here the nobleman, almost as poor as his peasant, a mere pauper compared to the prosperous fiefholders of Holland and Zeeland, never rose much above the general level.

In all these territories the old customary law prevailed, and seems to have sufficed, when in the more progressive territories of the West the need had long been felt for codification and adaptation to new conditions. In Holland and Zeeland, around 1300, every rural district had its *keur,* its local code of private law, based wholly upon ancient traditions but more or less adjusted to circumstances and formally promulgated by the count. The East was almost a century later in codifying its traditions, and Drente did not receive its *landrecht* until the Middle Ages had well nigh passed. It is noteworthy that geographic conditions alone, and not political factors, determined the difference between East and West. The western part of the episcopal state of Utrecht, the *Sticht,* geographically one with Holland, followed the social development of that country step by step, while the episcopal lands beyond the IJssel remained distinct not only in institutions but in natural conditions.

South of the riverbelt, the effect of feudal institutions on social conditions was much greater than north of that dividing line. To put it more accurately, the resistance of ancient traditions to feudal institutions was weaker. The southern part of Limburg formed a section by itself, for as early as the VIIth century, under the Carolingians, large estates had been characteristic of the social system and Roman influence had created conditions quite distinct from those of the purely Germanic North. The vast plain between the Scheldt and Rhine, stretching north and south some twelve miles west of the Meuse, divided by the moors of the Peel, presented still other aspects. West of the moors, where the soil was poor, and most settlements dated only from the Frankish period, the villages were but small strips of cultivated land along the rivulets that ran through the vast heath. The powerful dukes of Brabant who, at the end of the XIth century, became lords of this district, firmly secured their seigneurial rights over the waste lands, the usufruct of which they sometimes granted to the villagers for a yearly quit-rent. In other cases they granted the land itself to monasteries or to secular and ecclesiastical landowners. In this area, where feudal institutions took deep root, bondage lasted no longer than in other parts of the country. It was less important in the south of the Netherlands than in the east but a class of free farmer-owners could not develop. In Brabant the peasant was and remained a tenant. The lords of the soil, whose returns were meager enough, sought to acquire extra income by serving as mercenary knights for foreigners or for their own dukes in the endless princely feuds of the Middle Ages.

Here again the influence of the monastic orders of Prémontré and Citeaux was of great importance. As in Friesland and Groningen their monasteries contributed greatly to the reclamation of land, the only instances of monastic influence on the social order of the Netherlands. Even so, their influence was limited and there is no reason to assume that without them agrarian and social institutions would have developed differently than they actually did. The ancient order of the Benedictines was only sparsely represented in the Netherlands, and its most important monastery, Egmond, was virtually the property of the counts of Holland. Here as elsewhere it pursued culture and learning, while the monks of Prémontré and Citeaux took an active part in the ministry. Only in a few Netherland provinces did the clergy vote in the states assemblies which, from the XIVth century, were associated with the councils of the princes.

In this curious society, with its blending of old Germanic and feudal institutions, the average individual continued to enjoy great personal free-

dom and independence. This explains the rapid rise of small communities
of traders and craftsmen, the continuation in some cases of ancient Roman-
Germanic towns such as Nijmegen and Maastricht. In Nijmegen, the
palace of the emperors, founded by Charlemagne and gloriously rebuilt
by Frederick Barbarossa, reminded people of the town's ancient origin.
In Maastricht the churches of Saint Servatius and the Holy Virgin, with
their monasteries, provided a direct link with Roman times. The settlements themselves were hardly distinct in outward appearance from other
communities with a less illustrious past. Among these, Utrecht was first,
proud of the traditions of Willibrord, first bishop of the Frisians, and of
its position as an episcopal see, even though the burghers constantly rebelled against their lord. Then there was Deventer, the town of Saint Le-
buinus, already a small port in Saxon times that grew in prosperity. To
the north, at the end of the sandy ridge which protrudes into the Frisian
lowlands, an old royal estate developed into a trading village and then into
the prosperous town of Groningen. Politically, the Groningers were subjects of the bishops of Utrecht but, protected in the rear by the rebellious
peasants of Drente, they turned east and north to take a brisk part in Frisian affairs and Hanseatic trade. So did Stavoren, a small open fishing village on the Zuiderzee. In the XIIth century Holland, rich in cities as it was
to be, boasted only a few villages such as Leiden and Dordrecht which
might by courtesy be called towns. Its trade was still unimportant and, until the end of the XIIth century the small town of Tiel, situated inland on
the river Waal, was the main emporium of the Netherlands, a position it
had inherited from Dorestad when that town was destroyed by the Vikings.

All these towns were open places without walls or fortifications. In 1150
the selfwilled Groningers were obliged to promise that they would not
fortify their town, and there are numerous other instances of this tendency
on the part of princes to prolong their control over urban communities. It
is completely wrong, however, to envision the towns as "squalid abodes of
ignorance and misery," the inhabitants of which could only with difficulty
tear themselves free, to quote John Motley once more, from "the wolfish
protection of some little potentate." If we turn to the medieval chroniclers,
we obtain a different picture. A chronicler of the XIth century described
the merchant people of Tiel on the Waal as follows:

> "These men are rough and not accustomed to discipline. They do not
> render justice according to law, but they follow in this matter their own
> free will and pretend that the emperor has confirmed this right to them in
> a charter. They simply deny the debts they have contracted and even if
> guilty of public perjury cannot be convinced of their faults. If one of

them holds something in his left hand and if it is so small that he can hide it in his fist, he will lift the right hand to swear that he has not got it. They do not consider adultery a crime. Better than anything else, they love to drink and he who cracks the dirtiest jokes and makes the others drink gains the greatest praise. They even collect money to buy up all the good wines they can find during the year and with these, celebrate the great feasts of the Church, as if there were solemnity in drunkenness."

The democratic character of medieval Netherland society was strikingly revealed in the Crusades. In general, the Crusades were an undertaking of the nobility and, from the beginning, there existed some concern among the leaders that out of general enthusiasm for the good cause, a popular movement might rise and eventually get out of control. When the first Crusade was preached, thousands of simple people marched out to the East without waiting for the guidance of the nobles. We need only recall how scornfully the chroniclers of the Crusades speak of the "rabble" which found a miserable and not undeserved end in the deserts of Anatolia, to know how disgusted the nobles, professional fighting men, were to see others intrude into their sphere. They did not always preserve this haughty attitude and at times their disdain for the common fighting man changed to deep gratitude. When, exhausted and in dire need of supplies, the knights of the first Crusade reached the coast of Syria and undertook the siege of the Arabian strongholds, they were overjoyed to receive unexpected support from small fleets of North Sea ships of whose presence they had not the slightest idea. Sometimes these audacious sailors are called "pirates" by our sources, sometimes they are recognized by them as comrades in the holy war. Among them are Scandinavians, Englishmen, Flemings, Normans, Frisians and at least in one case the men of Tiel are specifically mentioned. They had made the long voyage to the Levant without difficulty or hardship, which had cost the knights endless exertion and sacrifice.

In no Crusade was the role of the North Sea skippers and merchants more important than in that of 1147, after Bernard of Clairvaux had traveled through the southern Low Countries and the Rhineland preaching the holy war. Once more the kings of France and Germany led their knights overland to Anatolia. The merchants of Cologne, the skippers of Friesland, the men of Flanders and England organized a Crusade of their own. Their ships gathered at Dartmouth, where each crew elected its representative to the common council of war. The rules of discipline were settled by common consent. Headed by their elected leaders, the force, with only a few noblemen among them, sailed for the coast of Portugal to seek entrance into the Mediterranean. The king of Portugal besought them to take part in the siege of Lisbon and the majority of the Crusaders assented in the hope of adequate reward for their services. They conquered a capital for the young Iberian kingdom, but there were constant quarrels between the selfwilled Flemings and the not less stubborn English, and between the Crusaders and the Portuguese king, who prudently held his soldiers in reserve and allowed the northerners to take the risk and gain the glory. Several times Crusaders from the North Sea stopped on their way to Palestine to assist the Portuguese kings against their hereditary foes. Flemish and English settlements were founded in the reconquered districts, some of them only to be destroyed again when the Moors recovered most of the territory they had lost. Count William of Holland assisted the Portuguese in the siege of Alcacer in 1218, but many of his Crusaders, independent Frisians, ignored his leadership and pushed on to the East where they took part in the invasion of Egypt.

The long voyages of the Frisians during the Crusades seem quite out of proportion to the then modest sea trade of the Netherlands. The great period of shipping and trading was still to begin, as we shall see in the next chapter. The Crusades were rather the cause than the result of the Netherlanders seafaring, but it must not be forgotten that in the XIth century the reputation of the Frisians as sailors was well established. Adam, archbishop of Bremen, relates how Frisian sailors had penetrated into the arctic seas and had been driven by storms to an unknown land where the inhabitants lived in caves and possessed great quantities of gold. From such scanty evidence, XVIIth century Frisian historians, seeking to glorify their homeland over the more powerful province of Holland, asserted that as far back as the XIth century their ancestors had visited Mexico and even Chile. The story is characteristic of the megalomania of a certain class of Frisian authors after the Middle Ages, when the real glory of their country, their republican freedom, had been lost and their ancient institutions debased by oligarchic rule. The real contribution of the seafaring population to the growth of the Netherlands is too evident to need such gross exaggeration. One fact is clear however, from this fantastic story and from the true stories of the Crusades: the economic position of the Netherlands in relation to neighboring countries had changed considerably, a most important factor in the development of the Netherland people into a nation with its own character and organization.

CHAPTER IV

The Origin of the Netherland Nation

THE frequent use of the name "Netherlands" in the preceding chapters was inevitable. It would have been more accurate, however, to use some other designation. Until the XIIIth century, the Netherlands did not exist either as a political or as a cultural unit. The area now included within the boundaries of the Netherland state was in no way distinct from the adjacent territories. We have discussed its peculiar geographic aspects and their effect upon social organization. It developed some remarkable local institutions like those in Friesland and Holland. Similar development might be found in parts of northwestern Germany along the North Sea. The difference in social structure between the eastern Netherlands and Westphalia was the slightest. In the XIth and XIIth centuries, as in the days of Charlemagne, the Netherlands were still a forlorn corner of the great empire of West-European Christendom. Culturally, the lowlands at the mouth of the Rhine were wholly dependent upon the great centers of civilization in the Rhineland and in France.

The churches and monasteries of the Netherlands in the early Middle Ages—only few of which still exist—never presented the splendor of their prototypes in the Rhineland, Burgundy, and central France. The peculiar architecture of the Romanesque churches of Maastricht, Roermond, Utrecht, and Deventer shows that their builders followed the great tradition of the Rhinelandish school. The early sculpture of the Netherlands reveals a thin stream of cultural influence from the southeast, along the Meuse valley, where Liége was one of its main centers, to Utrecht and the Lowlands. The same current may be discerned in the development of literature. The only books written in the Netherlands before the middle of the XIIth century were Latin textbooks and Latin chronicles. In this respect, Utrecht and Maastricht were centers of activity. Here too, the connection of Utrecht and Maastricht, via the Meuse and Liége, with upper Lorraine and eastern France is easily noticeable. The old pilgrims' route still linked the tombs of Servatius of Maastricht, Lambertus of Liége, Stephen of Metz, and Lupus of Troyes, to a chain of shrines the pilgrim visited on his way to Rome.

In literary production, Maastricht and Utrecht, where the German kings of the XIth century found ardent supporters in their struggle with the Papacy, preceded the other cultural centers of the Netherlands by more than a century. The first weak attempt at historiography in the coastal district of Holland dates from 1125, and for nearly a century after that neither Holland nor Friesland produced a single literary work, while in southern Limburg, as early as 1170, Hendrick van Veldeke created his "Legend of Saint Servaes," the great epic of the patron saint of Maastricht and of his town and church. This poem of more than six thousand lines was written in the native tongue and is thus the oldest Dutch literary monument that has come down to us. It represented the Imperial tradition and Veldeke himself enjoyed the protection of the Imperial court where he became one of the standard bearers of medieval German poetry. Yet his work at Maastricht marks the beginning of a new period in the history of the Low Countries.

In the same decades in which Veldeke's art flourished, Flanders produced a number of literary works in the vernacular. It may well be that there existed older monuments of Dutch letters that have been lost.[7] Even so, the preservation of a number of Dutch writings, all dating back to the close of the XIIth century, definitely indicates that only from that period did Dutch literary activity really become intense. Flanders and southern Brabant were its centers. The northern Low Countries followed in the XIIIth century, first with new Latin historical works, then with the first chronicles composed in the vernacular. The southern provinces, meanwhile, had produced some of the greatest achievements in old Dutch literature, the mystic writings of Beatrijs of Nazareth and Hadewijch of Antwerp, composed in the first half of the XIIIth century.

This is not the place for an extensive review of XIIIth and XIVth century medieval Dutch literature. There was one outstanding literary figure, renowned rather for the number of his works than for their artistic qualities. This was Jacob van Maerlant, a Fleming who spent part of his life in the territories of the count of Holland. Maerlant started his literary career with the translation of French romances, but then turned to scientific, religious, and historical poetry partly adopted from the French, partly from the Latin. Whatever our opinion of the quality of his art may be, it contained very little that was original. The authors of *Van den Vos Reynaerde,* a Flemish adaptation of Reynard the Fox, showed far greater originality and their work is a real masterpiece of realistic narration. That same realism is illustrated by another of the very few original literary works in medieval Dutch, the story of *Karel ende Elegast,* the saga of King Charlemagne turned thief by divine inspiration. The XVth century was to see a fuller development of original Dutch literature.

By that time, however, a new civilization with its own peculiarities had grown up in the Low Countries. As soon as the Low Countries ceased to be a forlorn corner in a great continental kingdom, and became the cross-roads of European trade and the meeting point of strong currents of civilization, they were to produce a national art, inspired by the traditions of their people and conditioned by the nature of the country. This change did not occur overnight, of course. The trading centers on the lower Rhine branches, Dorestad and Tiel, foreshadowed the later importance of Dordrecht and the IJssel towns. The Vikings in their piratical excursions from the north, were the grim pathfinders of the later Scandinavian trade. The Flemings, who joined the great Norman enterprise of 1066, and acquired estates in conquered England, re-established the ancient connections between the two countries bordering the North Sea.

Politically too, the kingdoms and feudal states of northwestern Europe were drawn closer together. The growing strength of the French monarchy clashed with the feudal rights of the Angevin lords of England and the French coastlands; and Flanders automatically became a central pivot of English, French, and local Netherland interests. The first dramatic expression of these new tensions occurred at the beginning of the XIIIth century when the allied English-Flemish and Saxon-German forces, supported by Count William of Holland and Friesland, met the army of King Philip Augustus of France on the battlefield of Bouvines (1214). The crushing defeat of the allies not only decided the fate of the possessions of the English crown in France, but also determined the future development of the Low Countries. From that day the feudal states of the lowlands were subjected to constant political pressure from the south. The defeat of the Imperial troops, followed in Germany by the reign of a prince of the House of Hohenstaufen who was more Italian than German, and the consequent decline of the Germanic monarchy, further loosened the ties of the border-states with the central government. At the end of the century a king of Germany who came to the Netherlands to assert his suzerainty over the counties of Holland and Zeeland, was ignominiously driven from the royal castle at Nijmegen and forced to flee to Germany by the prince he sought to dispossess.

The internal weakness of England and the peaceful reign of Louis IX in France retarded the political reorientation of the Low Countries. In the economic field, also, the XIIIth century seemed one of preparation for the sudden outburst of energy that the XIVth was to bring. This lull left the princes of the Low Countries free to strengthen the structure of their small states. It gave the Netherlands town-communities time to develop their social and political institutions, a task which was completed, however, without many dramatic incidents. Textbooks often have it that as a rule the feudal lords of western Europe opposed the development of town-communities and that the freedom of the burgher class was won in hard and bloody conflicts. This is by no means correct. In northern France, where the cities dated back to Roman times and had to regain their autonomy after centuries of decay, these struggles were frequent; but in the Netherlands, where towns sprang up under the supervision of the feudal princes, the situation was totally different. It is significant that some of the older towns (Tiel, Utrecht, and Deventer) had to struggle with their overlords for autonomy, while more recent communities, which had originated under the aegis of feudal princes, developed freely. Special factors intervened. In Utrecht, the conflict with the prince was also a collision between a purely secular and a predominantly ecclesiastical organization. The towns of more recent origin, which included nine-tenths of the Netherland communities, did not find princely authority an obstacle to self-government; on the contrary they received strong support from it. We have seen that initially some princes objected to fortification of the towns, but most of them quickly saw the great advantages they would derive from the building and garrisoning of fortresses at the expense of the citizens. Against the case of Groningen, mentioned above, we have that of 's Hertogenbosch, founded and fortified by order of the duke of Brabant for the protection of his northeastern frontier.

Local potentates everywhere fostered the growth of markets and trading places. They readily understood that an increase of population and of income must result in an increase of wealth and power for themselves. Like 's Hertogenbosch in Brabant, Alkmaar and Medemblik in Holland were organized as frontier posts, here against the still-turbulent West-Frisians. At Haarlem, where the coastal road behind the dunes passed over a narrow neck of land between the North Sea and the deep inlet of the IJ, a community formed itself around the castle which controlled that strategic spot. At Leiden, an old fortress on a dead branch of the Rhine saw a group of traders gather around its walls. At Dordrecht, a toll house and a fishing hamlet were the beginnings of Holland's oldest city. At Middelburg in Zeeland, a village of traders and fishermen rapidly gained importance through its contacts with England and Flanders. Utrecht still derived lustre from the court of the bishop, the spiritual leader of the whole territory north of the riverbelt. Nijmegen, whose existence as a river port dated from Roman times, had no overlord but the Emperor himself and for nearly two decades, from 1230 to 1248, was a free Imperial city, the only one of this type that ever existed in the Netherlands. Kampen, Zwolle, and Zutfen entered into competition with the older town of Deventer as trading centers, linking the Zuiderzee trade with that of the Rhine. In the same way Roermond and Venlo on the Meuse competed with ancient Maastricht. Far to the north, Groningen, at first one of the most important centers of trade in the Frisian sector, became the principal market place of the rich coastal districts. Many small towns grew up around the castles of minor nobles. Of them, Breda, Bergen-op-Zoom and, greatest of all, Amsterdam rose to prominence. These communities which later became important towns were not the only ones, and in many cases not the first to receive charters from their princes. Among the earliest places to receive autonomy were Domburg and Westkapelle, fishing hamlets in Zeeland, and Muiden, a small village at the mouth of the Vecht on the Zuiderzee. The charter of the village of 's Gravenzande in Holland is half a century older than that of Amsterdam. Het Gein and Eembrugge, now as in the Middle Ages obscure hamlets, have held the rank of town since the latter half of the XIIIth century.

The policy of the feudal princes was to grant limited autonomy to all places which might eventually become trading centers, either as local markets or as sea and river ports. Few Netherland towns were *founded*—in the strict sense of the word—by a local ruler, but the princes were lavish in granting privileges wherever they believed there was a chance of communal development. The bishops of Utrecht, in spite of their attitude towards their residential town, made strenuous efforts to raise the villages of Rijsen and Ommen, small communities on the eastern sandy plains, to the status of self-governing towns. Neither the protection of a prince nor the legal establishment of freedom, however could change a rural community into a town. The decisive factors were economic. Amsterdam and Rotterdam, among the latest places recognized as towns, were the only ones to become great cities.

The charter rights granted to these communities included jurisdiction over their inhabitants and the power to issue ordinances in special matters. Their charters never provided complete constitutions but only stipulated the extent to which the laws of the towns might deviate from the law of the land. The same classes of people can be found in the rural districts and in the towns. The common rule that "the town made free" was not strictly adhered to, for a number of bondsmen paid personal taxes to their overlords even after taking up residence within the walls of a town. Seigneurial monopolies did not always cease before the gates of all towns. Within the walls of Maastricht the two overlords of the place maintained their seigneurial mills. Many such instances could be given to prove that initially the towns remained part of the larger social community and that only gradually, as their power increased, were urban communities distinguished sharply from the surrounding rural area. With their increase of power, a reverse action started. The towns began the economic penetration of the rural districts around their walls. The definition mentioned above, formulated by one of the best Netherlands historians of the Middle Ages, explains also the great local differences in communal organizations.[8] Nevertheless, the charters can be grouped into a number of "families"; for the advisors of the prince did not always go to the trouble of drafting a new instrument, but took an existing charter as a model.

One may speak of a western and an eastern group of charters. Middelburg's laws were given to all the towns of Zeeland. The towns of Holland mostly followed the model of Haarlem, which in turn derived its institutions from 's Hertogenbosch and indirectly from Louvain. The eastern towns had as their models either the laws of Aachen, Nijmegen, and the towns on the Meuse or as in Guelderland the laws common to the free cities of Germany. Deventer was the mother city of a number of towns east of the IJssel. The Frisian communities grew out of the popular institutions of their province. In the West, the laws of the towns originated either in Brabant or locally, in the East they were closely related to common German forms of organization.

The amazing activity of local princes in promoting institutions of self-government, such as the towns and the *waterschappen,* could bear fruit only under a favorable political and economic constellation in northwestern Europe. Some of the economic factors were internal; others were of more general character. The reclamation of land and improvement of the soil wrought a considerable change in agricultural conditions in the Netherlands. The imperfectly drained marshlands and coastal strips of the early Middle Ages had provided good sheep runs and encouraged wool production. Widespread weaving of woollen goods was practiced in the homes. In those days Frisian villages produced woollen goods for export all over northern Europe. This surplus production stimulated overseas trade. Until the XIIIth century, Frisian merchants peddled their goods from Britain to eastern Germany. Men from Groningen were present in Smolensk in 1224 when a number of German traders concluded a trade agreement with the prince of that city.

With the progress of reclamation and drainage, the coastal marshlands could be put to better use than sheep raising. Cattle breeding and wheat growing took its place. More hands found work on the land while the manufacture of woollen goods declined. It concentrated more and more in the county of Flanders where raw wool was provided from England. These factors help to explain the diminishing importance of the Frisian sea trade. Groningen retained its connections with England, but not with northeastern Europe. Instead, it gained in importance as the principal market for the fertile lowlands to the north of the city. An identical development took place in the western Netherlands. Utrecht, in the XIth century an emporium for the northern trade, declined in commercial importance. Holland, prospering through the increase of its natural resources, had but few foreign trade relations. In all these respects, the XIIIth century is a period of transition. The old ties were gradually loosened. New ones were to be made in the XIVth century.

Such were the internal economic developments. Their importance can not be compared to that of external factors, the greatest of which was the "opening" of the Baltic Sea. In the early XIth century the then important countries of Norway and Denmark still looked west. It was the age of Canute the Great and the Danish invasion of England. Sweden was not yet a united state. A century later, Denmark had turned to the east and begun her expansion along the Baltic coast. At the same time, Sweden was constituted as a kingdom and expanded over Finland. The dukes of Saxony founded Luebeck in 1143, and then began the rapid march along the Baltic coast which culminated in the crusades of the Teutonic Order in the XIIIth century. By the middle of that century, the main objects of the expansion had been achieved, and German trade began to profit from this rapid spread of German culture and settlements. The Wendic League, the alliance between Luebeck and Hamburg, and the German merchants' guild of Wisby were formed, creating the foundations for the greater Hanseatic League. The "opening" of the Baltic Sea and the way in which it was accomplished were important factors in determining the fate of the Netherlands. Had the Baltic not gained the great importance it held from the XIIIth to the XVIIIth century, the Netherlanders would never have become the nation and state they now are. When the Scandinavian countries adopted Christianity and were drawn into the orbit of West-European civilization, when the Baltic Sea became a center of trade, the geographic position of the Low Countries underwent a fundamental change.

In the early Middle Ages the Low Countries had acted as intermediary in the trade between Britain and western Germany. The volume of the trade was modest. As it increased in importance, the German Rhine cities formed direct connections with England. In the XIIIth century this led to the gradual decline of the river trade of Tiel and Deventer in favor of Cologne. The direct outlets of the Rhine into the sea favored communications between Cologne and London. Only Dordrecht, advantageously located at a crossing of waterways, derived real profit from the Rhine shipping, largely because the counts of Holland strongly supported its staple-rights. With the opening of the Baltic and the concentration of wool manufacturing in Flanders, the picture changed radically. Once these two economic centers were brought into direct contact, the Low Countries as a whole found themselves on the crossroads of international trade. The complement of this new economic connection was trade with southern Europe. The gradual shifting from the land to the sea route between northwestern Europe and Italy further improved the position of the Low Countries. Flanders, Brabant, and Holland learned to look west instead of east, towards the sea instead of towards the Continent. This was the basic difference between the XIIIth and the XIVth century Netherlands.

It is remarkable that the various parts of the Netherlands shared unequally in the new development. As we have seen Friesland and Groningen lost importance, and Utrecht too, declined. The towns of Flanders entered upon a period of lasting glory. The role of intermediary between Flanders and the Baltic, and between the Baltic and the Rhineland, was taken by the "IJssel towns," Kampen, Zwolle, Zutfen, and Deventer. To the northwest of these trading centers, the counties of Zeeland and Holland, were left out of the combination. This peculiar situation was reflected in the organization of trade. The IJssel towns, and in fact, nearly all Netherland towns east of Utrecht, belonged to the Hanseatic League which also had a "factory" in Bruges. The towns of Holland and Zeeland, however, never belonged to the Hansa. The geographic location of these two counties, kept alive the seafaring traditions of the inhabitants, however. Though the sea trade of Holland and Zeeland was of little importance until the XIVth century, around 1350 it began to increase rapidly. Middelburg, close to Bruges, enjoyed its share of Flanders' prosperity. Amsterdam and some of the smaller towns began to take part in the Baltic trade, the "mother-trade" of all Netherland commerce. The marvelous expansion of this trade during the next hundred years became the main source of Holland's later wealth and glory.

It was only at the end of the XIVth century that the cornerstone of Holland's economic structure was laid by a technical invention, a new method of salting herring, which permitted the preservation of the fish over a long period and its export to distant territories. In 1384, Willem Beukels of Zeeland discovered that by cutting and gutting the fish immediately after the catch, and depositing it in barrels in alternate layers with salt of good quality, the product could be safely stored.[9] From that time the herring fisheries north and west of the Doggerbank were a gold mine for the Netherland coastal area. The XVth century saw a further technical improvement when, in 1416, a citizen of Hoorn on the Zuiderzee knotted the first large fishing net, making possible the use of larger ships and mass production of the new export. In another chapter we shall see how these inventions transformed the economy of Holland and thus wrought considerable changes in northwestern Europe.

The growing economic power of Holland and Zeeland, outside the Hanseatic League, but in the same field, foreshadowed a conflict the outcome of which was to determine the fate of the Netherlands. The cooperation between the towns of Holland and those of the Hanseatic League could last only as long as Amsterdam's trade was of minor importance.

The change in economic relationships and the growing importance of the western coastland were naturally accompanied by a corresponding change in political relations. As soon as the Low Countries acquired a central position in the economy of western Europe, the neighboring monarchies began to take a lively interest in their political status. This sudden international concern in the fate of the Lowlands was just in time to prevent a one-sided penetration of the area. In Chapter III, it was pointed out that the national evolution of the Netherlands would have been thwarted if France and Germany had both developed into strongly organized monarchies at the same time. Fortunately, the German kings had already met with defeat in their attempt at centralization before the French monarchy began to consolidate its position. In the XIIIth century, after the battle of Bouvines, French influence grew rapidly. King Louis IX and King Philip IV intervened in the quarrels of Brabant, Hainaut, and Guelders. Constant pressure weakened the power of the counts of Flanders. This political penetration unhindered from the east because of the disruption of the German monarchy, threatened to bring the Low Countries within the French sphere of influence.

Economic as well as political reasons forced the kings of England to intervene. Edward I sought to establish an anti-French league of Netherland princes, a policy which had its most dramatic results in the well known revolt of Bruges and the battle of the Spurs at Courtrai in 1302. The murder of Count Florens of Holland, a partisan of France, and the subsequent popular revolt against the murderers, form part of this episode. Though less important for general history, it has become part and parcel of the Netherland tradition because three and a half centuries later it formed the subject of dramas by Hooft and Vondel, two of Holland's greatest authors. In the conflict between the two great powers, the feudal princes of the Netherlands played a rather miserable role. They actually served as mercenaries of both kings and readily betrayed their momentary ally for a higher bribe from the enemy. Only the part taken by the people, the momentous uprising of the Flemish peasants and townspeople and the reaction of the people of Holland who rose to drive out foreign invaders gives color and interest to the story. To these popular movements the Low

Countries owe the fact that the political defeat of England and her princely allies left the existing social order, with its freedoms, undisturbed.

For three decades after this war, French influence was predominant throughout the Low Countries. Flanders was independent again, but humbled. Hainaut, Holland, and Zeeland were united under the dynasty of the Avesnes, who had distinct pro-French leanings. By them free institutions of Friesland were threatened for the first time in several centuries. Utrecht, to which the Avesnes had no claim, virtually became part of their possessions. Brabant alone for a while stood aloof, but was well-nigh crushed by the combined forces of the princes in the pay of France. To all this, England under Edward II could not offer the slightest opposition. A prince of the House of Avesnes accompanied the military expedition across the North Sea by which the unfortunate English king was dethroned and sent to his death.

The whole French network of diplomatic relations was roughly torn apart when Edward III of England decided to claim the continental inheritance of his ancestors. War broke out again, the first of the endless series of conflicts and campaigns usually grouped together as the Hundred Years' War. There is no need to follow in detail the diplomatic intrigues by which King Edward sought at great expense to make the Low Countries into an English bridgehead on the Continent.[10] The results were decidedly discouraging. The only important event of this first phase of the war was another revolt by the people of Flanders. This revolt, led by James of Artevelde, did not further the English plans but its final result was the neutralization of Flanders, which precluded further assistance to Edward from the side of the Netherlands.

The importance of the Low Countries in a general political combination had been proved beyond doubt. By the middle of the XIVth century they had become an economic force and a keystone in international relations. To gain a foothold in the Low Countries was the aim of the three competing powers of northwestern Europe. Violence and bribery had been tried by all and failed. There was another method—the more tender approach to power and influence through marriage. William III of Avesnes, count of Holland, and brother-in-law of the king of France, became father-in-law to kings and emperors, a distinction he owed probably more to geography than to the charms of his daughters. Count Reinold II of Guelders, raised to ducal rank, married a sister of the king of England. Louis of Bavaria, emperor and king of Germany, took one of Count William of Holland's daughters to wife. These exceptional family ties gave the feudal lords of the Low Countries a prestige far greater than they could have won for themselves. The full import of this matrimonial policy was only apparent when the direct lines of the princely houses of the Netherlands became extinct.[11]

The war clubs of the Frisians established a foreign dynasty in Holland and Zeeland. William IV, son of William III, who took his title to the lordship of Friesland seriously, was defeated and killed by the staunch republican peasants, an ignominious death for one who had always endeavored to excel in chivalry. His sister, the wife of Louis of Bavaria, emperor of Germany, succeeded to his inheritance. But before the emperor could consolidate his position in the West, he died, leaving a branch of his family firmly established in the Low Countries. This was a great success for the Bavarian dynasty which was now drawn into western European politics. It led to a counter move by their rivals, the kings of Bohemia-Luxemburg who in the person of Charles IV, assumed the Imperial crown after the death of Louis.

When Wenzel, the brother of Charles IV, married the heiress of Brabant, the Luxemburg family greatly strengthened its position in the Low Countries. As duke of Brabant, Wenzel controlled the important trade route from the Scheldt to Cologne. At the beginning of the XIIIth century the dukes of Brabant had gained partial sovereignty over Maastricht; by the end of the century they had acquired Limburg and by the middle of the XIVth the county of Valkenburg. Thus, they dominated the ancient Roman highway between Cologne and Tongeren from which a new route branched off to Antwerp. The possession of Brabant with its mercenary chivalry which served in all the armies of western Europe and had gained immortal if rather lugubrious fame, was a coveted prize; and the Luxemburg dynasty rejoiced to have secured it. But here the same phenomenon occurred as in Holland: the Luxemburgs had acquired new lands, but in point of fact Brabant took a member of the dynasty to itself.

The Netherland territories had too much individuality to be passed like household objects from one member of a family to another. German princes transferred to the west coast were irresistibly drawn into the orbit of western politics and separated from the main body of Germany. On the other hand, the efforts of Edward III of England succeeded no better. Twice he tried to secure a stronghold on the Continent, first when during Artevelde's administration, he sought to have his son recognized as count of Flanders; again when he demanded Zeeland as his share in the inheritance of the Avesnes. Flanders refused to leave its "natural" prince, and Zeeland to be separated from Holland. This was not due to successful resistance by princely rulers but to the opposition of the people. The time when the fate of Netherland provinces could be decided by the whim of a feudal lord had gone forever.

Relations between the rulers and the ruled had been profoundly modified. Some of the causes of this change are of a general character. In the Netherlands, as everywhere else in western Europe, the revenues of the princes were no longer sufficient to meet their expenditures. The cost of administration, rudimentary as it was, gradually increased; and continuous warfare absorbed a disproportionate amount of treasure. The desire of the Netherland princes to figure prominently in international politics deepened their financial plight, as "selling-out" to France or England could fill their coffers only temporarily. If a prince followed the rules of chivalry, if he considered it his duty as a Christian knight to ride to Spain or to Baltic lands to hunt the Moor or the pagan Prussian, he usually ended in bankruptcy; and there were not a few of these chivalrous warriors among the Netherland feudal lords. Money had to be borrowed to carry on the administration, and the prospect of repayment always remained dubious. The inevitable result was that the debtor was obliged to hand over his regular sources of income to his creditors until his debts were paid. If the creditor was a foreign prince, this might mean the end of the territory's independence. Once the bishopric of Utrecht was nearly divided between the bishop's creditors, who unfortunately happened to be the counts of Holland and Guelders. It escaped from these dangerous creditors only to fall into the clutches of a group of wealthy citizens, who virtually forced Bishop John of Arkel to leave his principality so that they might rule alone and exploit the episcopal domain to their hearts' content.

Financial backers were usually found among a prince's subjects. In Brabant the towns had provided large sums since the end of the XIIIth century. They continued to provide their duke during the XIVth century but only on condition that they be given permanent control of the financial administration. This demand must not be interpreted as a deliberate attempt to wrest political control from the princes. It was a normal business policy. A banker does not lend money without security, and the towns of Brabant wanted control over the administration of the funds they provided. The prince might use his own money—when he had any—for whatever purposes he thought fit, but had to account for every penny he spent of his subjects' money. Moreover, he was not allowed to dissipate his "domain," from which eventual repayment was to come. So his financial backers restricted his right to mortgage part or whole of his estate. This had important political consequences.

For the first time in Netherland history, representative groups of the people expressed their will to stay together, to form a political unit. The desire to safeguard the principality against division or foreign control was the main point in the many charters which the dukes of Brabant, like other princes of the Netherlands, were obliged to grant their subjects. By these charters, of which that of Cortenberg (1312) was among the earliest, the state of Brabant became a social unit, with a political character distinct from the status of its prince. Brabant provides a classic example of this new development of joint administration by a prince and his subjects. In each province the development showed characteristic features.

In Holland, Utrecht, and Guelders, an important part was played by a group of noblemen who, through princely favor or otherwise, rose above the ranks of the common gentry and served as the special advisors and financial supporters of the rulers. The rise in rank and power of one noble family above its former peers naturally led to party strife and civil war. The history of the XIVth and XVth century Netherlands is full of outwardly meaningless conflicts.[12] A number of prominent families were exterminated in these wars and others elevated so that by the middle of the XVth century there arose a new aristocracy, having estates in several provinces and therefore no longer bound to the interests of anyone. Together with the town this group gained a prominent place in the councils of the local princes.

All these new elements in political life—the rise of a provincial "national" sentiment, the limitation of the power of the prince by his financial backers, the evolution of new social groups inside and outside the nobility —combined with the old customs which obliged the ruler to consult with his vassals, created a new institution, that of the "States," the meeting of a number of individuals and delegates of groups who, because of their social standing, represented the main political and economic forces of the country. Hugo Grotius, defending the sovereign rights of the States Assembly of his own age, tried to prove that this political organization was a direct continuation of the gathering of the ancient Germanic nobility, of the "leading men of the tribe" mentioned by Tacitus. More recent historians paint a totally different picture. For them, the States Assemblies started with the meetings of the vassals and clergy of the State, to which in due course, a third estate in the persons of representatives of the towns was added. The subject has recently been exhaustively studied, but the results are still far from clear.[13]

It seems evident that the Netherland States Assemblies grew out of the privy council of the prince. Customary law and his own interest obliged him to summon his principal fiefholders whenever important matters were discussed. The fiefholders were not so much great landowners as hereditary officials, holders of the *schout-ambt* in their *ambacht*—in other words, the chief officials and executives in their parishes. Thus, when all fiefholders were present, all parishes were represented. The prince, of course, summoned his principal councilors and financiers (whom he nearly always provided with some estate or fief in order that they might take their place among his vassals), and also town councilors and other people of influence whose help he might need. In most Netherland provinces, this meeting of the enlarged council, though later called States after the French "Etats," did not originate as a representation of the classes of society. Otherwise it would have been impossible to exclude the clergy as was done in Holland, Guelders, and even in parts of the bishopric of Utrecht beyond the IJssel. In other provinces, a few ecclesiastics attended the meetings—the abbot of Middelburg in Zeeland and the abbots of the Brabant monasteries. The clerical hierarchy as such was nowhere represented. In the "Sticht" of Utrecht, where the chapters of the main churches were very influential, they really acted as a separate political and economic body, not as an ecclesiastical group. The monasteries in Brabant, built on land granted by the dukes and with their money, were taxed by the prince without being represented in the States until late in the XIVth century, when the abbots finally threatened to assert their privilege of tax-exemption under canon law, by appealing to the Pope, unless they were given a share in the financial control of the duchy.

If the States were not really representative of all classes of society, they were still less representative of the people, even of the people of the towns. Everywhere, in the rural districts as in the towns, there was a tendency to oligarchy. The village jurors were originally elected from the wealthier farmers, as were members of the boards controlling the drainage districts. As always—the same thing happens in modern democracies—people of social standing who are in a position to judge public affairs, secured a dominant influence. In many instances this was done by substituting cooptation of the council members for election, even long after election had become a merely nominal function. In 1400, Amsterdam received a new charter, under which members of the town council elected their own successors under limited control by the count of Holland. This and similar privileges laid the foundation for the oligarchic regime that characterized the Dutch republic in the seventeenth century. Briefly, the States Assemblies were enlarged councils to which all social-political entities within the state, that were important enough to make a real contribution in the common weal, had access, if they considered attendance worth while; if they did not, they rapidly lost their places as regular members.

With the great political change of the middle of the XIVth century the States rose to unprecedented prominence and power. The same thing happened in France and England; but it is remarkable that while in France the power of the States General was crushed within a short time, while in

England Parliament gained power only to be devested of it a century later, the States Assemblies of the Netherlands enjoyed unbroken progress in power and influence. This change came when the ruling families of the Low Countries became extinct and were replaced by foreign dynasties.

When the Bavarians succeeded the Avesnes in Holland, the nobles and towns of Holland and Zeeland forced the legal heir, the Empress Margareta of Avesnes, to cede the two counties to one of her younger sons, making it plain that they wanted a prince of their own. For the first time the people of these provinces spoke out in the matter of succession and virtually designated their own ruler. Seventy years later, they did the same thing again, only more drastically. Even so, they were moderate compared to the people of Brabant. In 1356, when Wenzel of Luxemburg succeeded on the ducal throne, the States of Brabant forced their ruler to grant a great charter, the *Joyeuse Entrée* so called because every duke had to swear to respect it before he was recognized as prince. This *Joyeuse Entrée* was a formal contract between the prince and the States with clearly defined rights and duties of the former. The prince swore to preserve the integrity of the state and its "national" character, to refrain from appointing foreigners to offices and from alienating any part of the ducal revenues, and to recognize the authority of the States in matters of taxation. Finally the charter gave the States the right to revolt if the prince broke his oath and violated the agreement.

Thus was established the constitutional function of the States Assemblies. From a board of advisors and financial backers, they had become a representative body that took its place by the side of the central authority, the prince. The importance of this political organism depended wholly upon the strength or weakness of the two parties. When a weak prince like Wenzel of Brabant ruled, practically all power fell to the States.

The XIIIth century had been a period of preparation. The XIVth saw the re-orientation of the Netherlands and the first economic expansion of Holland and Zeeland. Its last quarter marked the beginning of a new era in the history of the Low Countries, during which a distinctly Netherland culture and art came into being. Until the fourteenth century, the Low Countries were hardly different from their nearest neighbors with whom they formed a social, political, and cultural unit. Earlier in this chapter reference was made to differences between the lowlands on the Rhine and the neighboring territories: early and wide-spread social and political freedom, with the popular institutions of Friesland as its most characteristic expression; the multiplicity of free communities, of which only some could grow into cities. In the development of liberal social institutions, the Netherlands were ahead of their southern and eastern neighbors, partly because of the rise in the Netherlands of new institutions conditioned by the character of the soil, and partly because of the preservation of their ancient liberties.

Modern nationalism has a tendency to project the history of each nation into the distant past, when such nations did not even exist. Although it is necessary to go back to the earliest times to discover the elements from which particular peoples were later formed, one must guard against taking for granted national differences long before they came into being. Yet, dimly discernible in the thirteenth and clearly visible in the fourteenth century, are factors to justify the title of this chapter: "The Origin of the Netherland Nation."

We find but little evidence of this thesis in the history of medieval Netherland literature and art. Learning, always international in character, was more so in the Middle Ages when a belief in the basic unity of civilization still prevailed, and when the use of an international language was a prerequisite to recognition in learned circles. For the Low Countries, Paris was the center of intellectual life, not because French culture was admired but because until the XIVth century the University of Paris was the only important one in continental Europe north of the Alps. There is nothing in the works of the earlier medieval historians, theologians, and writers born in the Low Countries, that reveals their Netherland origin.

Gothic forms of architecture were imported from France, although Rhineland influences are discernible. Two major churches were built in the new style in close imitation of foreign models: the cathedral of Utrecht and the parish church (now also cathedral) of 's Hertogenbosch. In nearly all other cases where the Gothic style was tried, adaptations to specific Netherland requirements were made. Materials were lacking for the construction of the huge and imposing buildings so common in northern France, and the marshy soil of the western coastland could not sustain heavy monuments. Brick, the native building material, was less suited to Gothic forms, so the plan and structure of Netherland churches was simplified. In many cases, a timber roof took the place of the stone-ribbed vaulting. The profuse sculptural decoration of the French Gothic churches could not be imitated. Netherland architects reduced the height and extended the width of their churches which thus lost some of the outward characteristics of Gothic. The character of Dutch art was being determined by the nature of the soil and the materials it provided. The character of "the people" (supposing that this abstraction corresponds to any reality existing at the time we are discussing) had little to do with it.

Literature was dependent upon French and Latin models though some works show a realism that is often considered a typical Dutch trait. As in

Maerlant's later work, French examples were deliberately rejected in favor of Latin ones. This might be called the beginning of spiritual independence, though of a rather negative character. German influence was traceable in many mystic writings of the XIIIth and XIVth centuries and in the poetry of the later XIVth. The presence of Bavarian princes in Holland and Zeeland was not without effect in this respect, though French and Latin models predominated. Both the subjects and the forms of literary art are essentially international. Historians of literature have made many attempts to discover "national" characteristics in literary works of a period when no corresponding national sentiment existed. "A sense for crude comical situations seems to be part of our national character," wrote a distinguished Netherland professor of literature when discussing the vulgar yarns written in medieval Dutch. If so, the Netherland people share this trait with many other nations. The negroes of central Africa, sitting together in the tropic nights, or the people of southeast Asia, gathering to tell stories after a hard day's work, indulge largely in the same pastime. The only thing "characteristic" about medieval Dutch literature seems to be a rapid loss of interest in tales of chivalry and the growing popularity of subjects of more general interest. This, like the development of Netherland social institutions, may well have been influenced by the weakness of the feudal system. In a society where a ruling class, with its standards of chivalry, its nice distinctions, its fashions, its rules of "what is done and not done," did not dominate the more primitive, natural and spontaneous traits of human character, subjects of more general interest, religion and morals, were bound to be more popular. The sympathy for the lower classes revealed in many medieval Dutch works is characteristic. It is true of Jacob Van Maerlant, the one medieval Dutch poet of whom we have more than a dim perception. He apparently had a special sympathy for the lower classes of society. Many literary authorities ascribe to him the *Heimlicheit der Heimlicheden,* a Dutch translation of the *Secreta Secretorum.* This treatise, a Latin version of an Arabic original, was written as a manual on the art of life and of government. The Dutch translator made a few remarkable additions to his model when he translated the Latin verses:

"The prince, who is the people's pastor,
Is by his nobles well protected."

His own lesson actually reverses the sense:

"The prince, who is the people's pastor,
For he protects his poor subjects,
The people of the lower classes,

> Who, humble though they are,
> Are those providing all the world
> With everything it needs."

A few lines like these do not prove much, but there are further examples of the same trend of thought in other literary works.

It is not so much the *subject* or form of literary composition that attracts our attention in respect to the origin of the Netherland nation, but the language, the *means* by which it was expressed. It is unnecessary to repeat here that the dialects of the Low Countries formed part of the West Germanic linguistic group, with a gradual transition from Flemish in the southwest to Low German east of the present boundaries, and with the slowly retreating Frisian dialect as a distinct feature. The exact position of these medieval Dutch dialects in the general linguistic group as judged by modern philologists, is unimportant for our purpose, what we have to consider is how contemporary writers considered it. Their name for the language they wrote was *Dietsch*, the Flemish form of the common Germanic term of *Duitsch, Deutsch,* or *Dutch,* generally used by continental Germanic people to indicate the vernacular. So the term has no special meaning except when used to indicate a special West Germanic tongue in contrast to some other. Maerlant, in the thirteenth century, spoke of *Dietsch* as the common language of the inhabitants of the coastlands, a language of which he apparently considered the spoken language of Flanders, Brabant and Holland to be dialects. *Duitsch,* too, is used with the same significance, appearing in Flanders in 1360 when the Bible was *verduitscht*—i.e. translated into the vernacular.

The chronicle of Melis Stoke, concluded in 1305, refers to the northeastern districts of the present Netherlands as the Low Saxon country, in which he includes the Frisians. Here is an important contrast between the Germanic western coastlands and the interior. It is evident that the difference between *Dietsch* and French, the *Walsch* language, was strongly felt. The remarks of Stoke seem to indicate an identical, if far weaker, differentiation between the coastal Low Germanic and that of the interior. Combining this scanty evidence with that provided by the XVth and XVIth centuries, it is apparent that by the XIIIth century the Low Countries began to feel linguistically different from the greater West Germanic community but that the new linguistic boundaries by no means coincided with these of the present Netherland and Belgian states. They included only Flanders, Brabant, Holland, Zeeland, and perhaps Utrecht. In other words, they encompassed exactly the same territory as was drawn into the orbit of the western powers through the influence of economic and political factors.

Fourteenth century Netherlanders, though they had many traits and interests in common did not feel themselves politically or nationally related in any way. When traveling abroad, they never claimed any "nationality" other than their citizenship in the local community. Students who traveled to foreign universities inscribed their names in the registers as "citizens of Ghent, of Antwerp, or of Dordrecht." A citizen of Dordrecht laid the foundation for the Santa Maria dell' Anima pilgrim hospital in Rome destined for the "natio almanorum," the nation of the "Dutch" (i.e. *dietsch, duitsch,* or *deutsch*).

There is one exception to the rule that the medieval Netherlands recognized only local nationality, and that is the case of the Frisians. Throughout the Middle Ages, all natives of Friesland continued to call themselves *Frisones,* with an evident pride in their provincial nationality. Throughout the early Middle Ages, the Frisians had their own national church in Rome, San Michele in Sassia, whose tombstones and monuments still tell the story of Frisian pilgrims.

Nevertheless, inevitable political and economic cooperation among the province fostered a sense of common destiny. By the XIVth century, drainage works and flood protection had made close collaboration between Holland and Utrecht necessary. Wars between the two states never interfered with the combined effort against the forces of nature. This, with common language, common law and common customs convinced the Utrecht chronicler, Johannis de Beka, that the peoples of Holland and Utrecht were essentially one. He dedicated his work jointly to the Count of Holland and the Bishop of Utrecht and in his dedication he wrote:

> "From this history you may learn how good it is that you and your peoples live in mutual peace. Your people formed one nation and belonged to one state before Holland was divided into two parts by the Frankish kings. Keep yourselves as well as your people united in indissoluble unity."

In 1339, when Artevelde came to power in Flanders, an agreement was concluded between the towns of this province and those of Brabant, emphasizing the necessity for cooperation, especially in the economic field. Plans were laid for the issue of a common coinage. They came to nought, but the convictions that gave them birth grew stronger and stronger. More and more the western provinces came together. The leading nobles no longer had estates in one of them, but in all. Drawn into the conflict of Anglo-French interests, the coastal provinces refused to be absorbed by either, and this independence found expression in the declaration of neutrality issued by Flanders under Artevelde. This political act was of the greatest interest as it foreshadowed the future policy of the states that were to arise in the Low Countries. It shows that the modern policy of neutrality was not merely a result of weakness or lassitude, but the outcome of an age-old development. The five provinces of Flanders, Brabant, Holland, Zeeland, and Utrecht became the cradle of a new national unit in western Europe. The final demarcation of this new entity was settled by political events in the coming centuries. Friesland still stood aloof. Since the end of the fourteenth century, Guelders had been closely tied up with the Rhineland, with Cleve, Juliers, and Cologne. For hundreds of years it remained doubtful whether the new nation would have its eastern boundary just outside the town of Utrecht, or on the Weser and Moselle. Fate decreed otherwise and two states, not one, rose out of the new unit.

CHAPTER V

Political Unification of the Low Countries

IN the second half of the fourteenth century, the political status of the Low Countries underwent a profound change. Foreign dynasties had replaced the native ones. In Brabant, Duke Wenzel of Bohemia-Luxemburg weakly represented the German Imperial tradition. The strength of his position depended on friendly relations between his brother, the Emperor Charles IV, king of Bohemia and Charles V, the king of France. They died in 1378 and 1380 leaving incompetent successors, and the power of the House of Luxemburg collapsed. Wenzel's nephew, Sigismund, eventually restored it in part, but its position in the Low Countries was lost forever. A new power arose, surging up from Flanders and spreading rapidly over such feudal states in the Low Countries as had once acknowledged allegiance to the German kingdom. Its progress was halted only at the boundaries of the duchy of Guelders. There the Juliers family had temporarily replaced the ancient Wassenberg dynasty, causing the federation of a number of principalities along the banks of the Rhine: of Juliers, Berg and Mark, and later Cleve. This coalition, stretching from the Zuiderzee to the Moselle, tended to become a permanent political unit and seemed destined to counterbalance the new western group of states.

The kernel of the new western power was Flanders and its bulwarks, Holland, Zeeland, and Hainaut. Louis II of Flanders, last prince of the House of Dampierre, left only one child, a daughter, the wealthiest non-royal heiress in Europe. For years the astute Count Louis had maintained neutrality between the warring kings of England and France. The hand of his daughter was his best political asset, and he used it without scruples. When he consented to her marriage with a French prince, it was under conditions that seemed to safeguard forever the territorial integrity and security of his principality. Duke Philip of Burgundy, son of the late King John of France, became the son-in-law of Louis II and later count of Flanders, but his marriage contract stipulated that he renounce his rights as a French prince to become the independent ruler of Flanders. Political, economic, linguistic and cultural factors imposed this demand though the personal sentiments, education, interest and whole nature of Duke Philip rebelled against it. His acceptance of the marriage conditions was an act of duplicity that could have only tragic consequences. Deliberately, the stipulations to which he and his royal brother, King Charles of France, publicly assented, were annulled beforehand in a secret agreement. Duke Philip wanted both the county of Flanders and his privileges as a prince of the royal blood in France. History forced his successors to choose.

In 1383 Count Louis died. His daughter Margareta and her husband the duke of Burgundy succeeded to the throne. One of the first moves of the new prince was to seek matrimonial alliances for his children which would further extend his power in the Low Countries beyond the boundary that theoretically still separated the French from the German fiefs. By the double marriages of their children, Duke Albrecht of Bavaria-Holland and Duke Philip of Burgundy-Flanders brought their families into the closest of blood relations. These personal ties, the fame to be won, the estates to be gained by participation in the wars of the Royal House of France made the Bavarian counts of Holland and Zeeland, the firm allies of Burgundy. The Romanization of the princely Netherland families progressed rapidly.

Duke Philip's marriage with the "daughter of Flanders" welded close family ties with the duchess of Brabant, wife of Wenzel of Luxemburg. That unfortunate prince died in 1381. The relatives immediately entered into the most unscrupulous competition to gain the good graces of the widowed, childless, but well-endowed old lady, Johanna of Brabant. No service was considered too great to win her favor. When it came to offering men-of-arms or cash, the rich Duke Philip backed by the knighthood of France, the wealth of Flanders, and all the resources of Holland and Zeeland, was in a far better position than the destitute, confused and ill-fated Luxemburgers. For a while a dispute between the helpless old duchess of Brabant, rich in resources but lacking the art to employ them, and the dominant prince of the Rhineland, Duke William of Juliers and Guelders, an ambitious and reckless young man, threatened to involve the French and German kingdoms in war.

Duke William of Juliers and Guelders harassed the Duchess of Brabant until her devoted nephew, the duke of Burgundy, organized the noble enterprise of a French crusade in defense of the bereaved widow. With due regard for the old lady's feelings, he refrained from marching through the plains of Brabant, the natural highway to the Rhine, but led the young king of France and his knights, with their endless train through the rough and well nigh impassable Ardennes. The situation, an anxious one for the dashing duke of Juliers who could not collect sufficient troops to defend himself, was even more anxious for the invaders who wondered how, with the approach of winter, they would be able to withdraw with the wilderness of the Ardennes behind them and the passage through the territories of Duchess Johanna and Duke Philip forbidden. A timely and face saving peace permitted the French to withdraw, and Duke William to vent his military fury on the luckless people of Lithuania.

The main object of the French expedition was achieved. Duchess Johanna was confirmed in her decision to disinherit the relatives of her late husband in favor of her niece, Margareta of Flanders, and her consort. Cession of the duchy of Limburg was the first step she took. By 1400, Burgundian influence was supreme to the Zuiderzee in the north and to the Meuse in the east. Through the possession of Limburg it extended even beyond that river. Duke Philip left Flanders and Burgundy to his eldest son John. His second son, Anthony, inherited Brabant. In Holland, Zeeland, and Utrecht, William of Bavaria, a cousin of the Burgundians, succeeded his father Albrecht.

The matrimonial policy of the Burgundians was a deliberate attempt to create a "sphere of influence" in the Low Countries. But Duke Philip could never have expected, although he may have hoped, that all these alliances, instead of creating a dynasty of many branches, would result in the merging of the three families into one within the short space of one generation. He may have cynically hoped that death would strike in the right places and thus serve the interests of his direct male heirs, that marriages threatening the unity of his estate would fail, and others would be blessed with the right offspring; but he could hardly have dreamed that this was exactly what was going to happen. When he died the chances for a concentration of all the family estates into one seemed remote. He left three sons, each of whom acquired part of his territories. His son-in-law in Holland had offspring of his own and was still young. Within fifteen years, death aided by the unruly character of the Burgundians themselves had accomplished the task.[14]

Duke Anthony of Brabant perished on the battlefield of Agincourt (1417). In the same battle John's youngest brother, Philip of Nevers met his death. His brother-in-law, William, duke of Bavaria-Holland, was badly wounded in the French civil wars and died of infection. His only child was a daughter, Jacqueline of Bavaria, the heroine of much romantic literature. Duke John eagerly grasped the opportunity. Jacqueline was married into the Burgundian family. If the poor girl had had children, the great hope would have been frustrated. But luckily for the Burgundians, Jacqueline was of a difficult character, a consumptive constitution, constantly pursued by bad luck. Her first husband, heir to the French throne, was poisoned. Widowed at seventeen, she remarried into the Burgundian clan. Her next husband, John of Brabant, was impotent and a moron. She deserted him. Her third marriage with an English prince was annulled after her new husband had left her. Her fourth matrimonial adventure with a nobleman of Zeeland was in violation of a contract concluded with her powerful cousin, Duke Philip II of Burgundy. She was allowed to keep her husband, but lost her principalities. Three years later (1436) she died at the age of thirty-six. To this extraordinary sequence of events, add that both Duke John of Brabant and his younger brother died childless (1430) and left their lands to their cousin, the same Duke Philip II of Burgundy and Flanders; and the political unification—or better the federation in a single dynasty—of the western coastlands of the Low Countries was complete. The bankruptcy of the count of Namur offered a welcome opportunity to round off the Burgundian possessions. Both the bishoprics of Liége and Utrecht were secured for relatives of Duke Philip II who thus effectively controlled the Low Countries. Burgundy, a buffer state between France and Germany, had come into being.

From this brief sketch of dynastic causes and their political effects, it is obvious that the federation of the Netherland provinces was primarily due to accidental circumstances. If death had struck left instead of right, the future of the Low Countries might have developed quite differently. Accident played so great a part that some historians are satisfied to explain the whole as a trick of Fate. Fate would have it so! When the result was achieved, even the promoters of this curious political growth did not know exactly how to deal with it. The dukes of Burgundy, bent upon creating a buffer state, barely managed to tear themselves loose from the older unit, the kingdom of France, to which they originally belonged. Against their will, political necessity forced them out of the French political community. A troubled European world provided no place for their new state nor its logical policy of expansion. Again Fate it was, through the hand of death and the accidents of marriage and birth, that led Burgundy to its destiny. The dukes could not even devise a *name* for their new principality.

In opposition to this view, some historians point to the common ties already existing among the various provinces long before the arrival of the Burgundians and contend that the unification of the Low Countries was more or less pre-determined by history. If so, which of the provinces were "pre-determined" to be included in this new unit? The linguistic difference between Dutch and French was not of political importance in this period, that between Dutch and German hardly existed. Moreover, was the later separation of the northern and southern Low Countries equally pre-determined, or did the element of accident enter in again through the fortunes of war? [15]

History can never prove that a particular political development was inevitable. Attempts to project existing Netherland nationality into the dim past or to assume a broader Netherland-Flemish nationality underlying the political growth of the XVth century must be rejected. To ascribe the whole process to fate and accident would be equally wrong. Returning to our conclusions in the preceding chapter, a definite and growing linguistic and cultural connection existed among the five western provinces. The growth of interdependence is expressed politically in the solidarity between Holland and Utrecht, between Flanders and Brabant. Economically the interests of these two groups may have been opposed, yet both derived their prosperity from the same source, their share in the northeast, southwest trade. Linguistic uniformity grew from the moment the Dutch language became a means of literary expression. All these factors militated for eventual unification in a single state, but did not predetermine it. Unification was political. Once it was achieved, cultural factors could but hasten the development of a common nationality, unless economic antagonism destroyed what political and cultural forces had been building.

The main factor of national unity however, is the will to be united. There is no better example of this than the Swiss Republic. The administration of the Netherland provinces was the concern not of the prince alone, but to an even greater extent of the States Assemblies. A most important factor therefore, was the attitude of the States Assemblies when one province after another passed to the Burgundian dynasty. The acquisition of Brabant, Holland, Zeeland, and Hainaut was realized by the Burgundians only by overcoming strong opposition from forces, partly within and partly without the principalities. But everywhere the majority of the States Assemblies sided with the Burgundians. In Brabant they proved sympathetic to the arguments of Duke Philip I who promised them peace and economic cooperation with Flanders. In Holland the majority of the towns and many nobles supported Duke Philip II in a three years' struggle against their "natural" princess, the ill-fated Jacqueline of Bavaria, who offered heroic if useless resistance at the head of a group of nobles and a peasant army. When the younger branch of the Burgundian dynasty became extinct in Brabant, the States, after ripe deliberation, acknowledged Duke Philip II as their prince, giving him preference over two other candidates. The wish to remain provincially independent was strong. Nowhere was there any conscious desire for unification but, with internal autonomy guaranteed, federation seemed to meet the wishes of the great majority of the representative inhabitants.

So the provinces of the Low Countries were not merely thrown together by fate. Neither was it merely accidental that federation started from Flanders under strong French influence, although dynastic factors alone led to unification under the Burgundians. It was the constant advance of French influence that helped to make the national individuality of the Low Countries distinct from Imperial Germany. The political evolution corresponded to an internal development that had been in progress for nearly two centuries, helped by the people. That Burgundian success in the west was facilitated by popular consent becomes apparent when we compare it with the sequence of events in the northeastern sector of the Low Countries.

Philip II was the first to intervene in the affairs of Guelders. His intrigues laid a basis for further political penetration carried out with excessive violence by his son, Charles the Bold. Here every advance of the Burgundians was vigorously opposed by the people. Guelders, subdued by the military force of Duke Charles, fought itself free immediately after his death. It took his grandson, the Emperor Charles V, twenty years to force the northeastern districts into submission. Here, resistance was supported by the people. In the west, it was popular support for the Burgundians, especially in the towns, that made such resistance as was offered futile.

By 1433, the five western provinces were united under a Burgundian prince. Ten years later Luxemburg was added to this domain. The tie that now connected these provinces was merely personal allegiance to a common prince. In accepting Burgundian leadership, each province stipulated most clearly that it would remain a perfectly independent administrative unit, and that it would not be obliged to share in any of the duke's political or military undertakings without the consent of its States Assembly. The instances in which one or more of the provinces refused to provide troops and money for ducal campaigns are numerous. All through the reign of the Burgundians and of the Habsburgs who succeeded them, the States never wavered on this point. It was one of the underlying causes of the great Netherland revolt of the late XVIth century against King Philip II of Spain.

However strongly the States might defend their provincial autonomy, the very fact that there was no longer a resident ruler within the boundaries of each province but that all were governed by *one* prince from an arbitrarily chosen capital—Ghent, Brussels or any other place of importance in Burgundy or the Low Countries—created a political situation different from that of former times. The individual provinces were governed through representatives of the prince. The office of *stadhouder,* a literal translation of the French *lieutenant,* came into existence. The *stadhouder* was supposed to take the place of the prince, to exercise all his prerogatives, to administer the "domain," to command the troops, to preside over the States Assembly, to preside over the judiciary, and to enforce whatever other rights the prince might have. For obvious reasons, the prince was reluctant to place such power in the hands of one man, a powerful noble who usually had considerable resources and following of his own, and might be tempted to revolt against his overlord. With the rather loose Burgundian federation, such a revolt might have been disastrous. Consequently, the dukes tried to build a central administration with branches in the provinces.

The administrative organization of the Burgundian federative state—for it would be incorrect to speak of "Burgundy" or a "Burgundian" or even "Netherland" state—was modeled on that of France. This was natural. The Burgundians never forgot that they were princes of the Royal House of France. John, Philip II, and Charles the Bold fought the kings of France mainly to vindicate the place in French politics they believed to be theirs. Through the Burgundians, a number of French conceptions and institutions seeped into the political organization of the Low Countries, causing tensions which lasted until the end of the XVIth century and were then among the underlying causes of the Great Revolt. The territorial princes of the XIVth century had governed with the assistance of privy councilors and, when need arose, enlarged their council by adding prominent men of their country. The enlarged Council became the States Assembly and an institution in its own right. The privy council, composed of a few men who happened to have the confidence of the prince, remained a vague institution without clearly defined functions. Even so, it played a real and very useful part in provincial administration. The Burgundian dukes, who followed the same system, could not take the combined provincial councils with them wherever they went, nor could they do without a privy council in matters for which they were personally responsible. The result was a duplication of councils, one going with the prince and attending to inter-provincial and personal affairs, the others staying within each of the respective territories and attending to local affairs. The consequence was the subordination of the latter to the former and now that a hierarchy was introduced, the necessity of defining the functions of each of them. This development completed the constitutional organization of the principalities. In each province there was, besides the States Assembly representing the influential social groups, the *Hof* (which literally translated means the "Court") or the *Raad* (the Council) representing the authority of the prince.

Above these councils, the "Great Council" officiated with the duke in the central administration. At its head was the chancellor, virtually the duke's Prime Minister. Soon Duke Philip found it impossible to take his councilors, men no longer in the prime of life, with him wherever his restless nature prompted him to go. He dispensed with the long train of noblemen, officials, priests and lawyers with their servants, horses, wagons, and mules bearing heavy cases of books and legal documents, and took with him only a few of his most trusted advisors for the immediate discussion of matters of high policy. Thus he restricted the movements of the Council. To part of it, with special judicial functions, he assigned a residence in Malines. Thus the "Grand Council" also became a fixed administrative organization.

The institution of these councils was not so important as the spirit behind the innovation. From now on the administration of the provinces became impersonal. This fostered the idea that the territories had an individuality of their own, apart from the person of their ruler. The princely "domain" had become a state, though still a provincial state. Of necessity the administration came into the hands of professional administrators, men trained in legal affairs. This meant study of Canon and Roman law, and Roman law had never been in force in the Low Countries. No other laws than those based on national customs and derived from old Germanic legal principles were admitted in the courts. But Roman law was widely studied. For a time the remote university of Bologna was the main center of legal studies but in the XIIIth and XIVth centuries, Paris, Orleans, and Angers attracted scholars from the Low Countries. These lawyers sought to permeate the higher courts of justice and the higher organs of administration with their legal conceptions. In matters of government this would have meant a complete revolution of the relationship between prince and subjects. In matters of justice it would have meant that the whole judiciary organization and the handling of all legal matters would have to be turned over to lawyers with a knowledge of Roman law. But there is far from theory to practice. The subsequent rules of the "Hof van Holland," when acting as high court of justice, emphatically required that justice should be rendered according to customary law. Only in the XVIIIth century was Roman law officially introduced as an alternative authority, to be used when customary law provided no rule that could be applied. In the other Netherland provinces, the same thing took place. Roman law was cited, was consulted in difficult cases by trained lawyers, but was never enforced.

The towns, confronted with this new central authority and feeling the necessity of a paid expert in their local administration began to appoint pensionaries, i.e., salaried officials. This provided further opportunities for the increasing number of graduates from law schools, although in such offices they had to apply their legal training in defense of the customs and freedoms which were under sharp attack from their colleagues in the provincial government. In 1477 the States of Holland began to discuss the appointment of a permanent attorney for their own affairs, a *landsad-*

vokaat. This did not take place until 1525 when the first official of this rank, the predecessor of the grand pensionaries of the seventeenth century, was appointed.

From the foregoing it will be seen that a permanent if latent conflict existed between the legal experts employed by the Burgundian administration and the representative groups of the people. The constant pressure of the lawyers who, in their contempt for native judicial and legal forms and in their admiration for Roman law, tried to impose foreign legal conceptions on a self-willed people, created permanent tensions. Local outbursts took place, for instance in the Dutch speaking section of the bishopric of Liége. Here the peasants rose in 1461 and, taking a heavy club for their emblem, hunted down and killed all lawyers of the district, accusing them of sucking the life blood of the people through foreign laws that delayed justice.

Popular opposition to the Burgundian reforms was stronger than the attempted reorganization of the judiciary. During the whole of the XVth century, a conflict raged over the judicial authority of the Great Council. This increased after Duke Charles divided the Council into two sections and, in 1473, established one of them in Malines as his "Parliament." In name and function it was but an imitation of the Parliament of Paris, with the difference that the Malines Parliament was created by the sole will of the prince and thus had no tradition behind it that could make it a legal curb on the will of the ruling monarch. Of necessity, the language of the Parliament was either Latin or French, and an order was issued by Charles the Bold to the provincial courts that all documents written in Dutch should be translated into one or the other of the official languages. Procedure would then follow "written law," which often if not always meant Roman law. Centralization of the judiciary as in France, inevitably led to the introduction of this foreign form of law which was never accepted by the people. The provincial States Assemblies violently resented the interference of an inter-provincial Court of Justice in their affairs and compelled its abolition after the death of Charles. Resentment proved so strong and lasting that as late as 1673 the rural districts of Waterland in Holland imposed a fine of two pounds on anyone who "used foreign or obscure terms of law without translating them into plain Dutch," which made the use of the Justinian code rather expensive.

Federation, though not accepted by all and violently resented in judicial matters, was nevertheless favorably received by large sections of the population and especially by the towns that were to play an increasingly important role in the future. With a view of saving time and money, Duke Philip II called the States Assemblies of his territories together for joint sessions. Instead of traveling from province to province to obtain the consent of his subjects to special taxes, he had them convene at a generally accessible place. The first of these meetings was held in 1463 at Bruges. This was not without precedent for the counts of Holland of the House of Avesnes had done the same, but the Burgundians gave these joint sessions a new significance. Here again rivalry between the Burgundian Valois and the reigning French branch of that family forms the background. The king of France used to summon his nobles, clergy and towns to joint assemblies, and the Burgundians just could not bear to be without a similar institution. But in the French States General, the three social groups formed horizontal units, whereas in those of the Low Countries, the six provinces formed six vertical units. No insinuating phrases used by the ducal chancery in summoning "clergy, nobles, and towns" could induce the provincial assemblies to renounce their individuality in favor of a general reclassification. Thus in the Low Countries, the assembly of the States General remained a mere formality. Power of decision lay with the individual provincial assemblies alone. Usually the demands of the duke were presented to the general meeting, and actual negotiations afterwards conducted with the individual States Assemblies in their respective provinces. Geographic circumstances and tradition limited the effects of the innovation, even in this mitigated form. The duke could hardly summon the representatives of *all* his territories, those in eastern France—the duchy and *Franche Comté* of Burgundy—and those of the Low Countries. Only the five provinces of the western coast, with Namur as an unimportant sixth member, conformed to Duke Philip's wish for outward unity, though reserving their individual rights. Here geographic, cultural and historical considerations, assisted the innovation. Here provincial representatives, accustomed to inter-provincial organization, showed willingness to adapt the practice to their own purposes, by maintaining correspondence on matters of general interest. An inner ring of more closely related provinces was thus discernible within the Burgundian union. The greater Burgundian combination apparently did not respond to any normal political growth, and a more national limited federation did not suit the political views of the Burgundian rulers. This was the great weakness of the new state. If the Burgundian dukes had concentrated their efforts on the stabilization of their power in the Low Countries, they might have succeeded better in their policy of state building, though on a limited scale. But their dynastic tradition, their political conceptions, and the implacable opposition of their enemies prevented this. Indeed, the dukes of Burgundy occupied a most difficult position in Europe because of their ill-defined legal status.

Philip I, the founder of the dynasty, never considered himself anything but a French prince. Duke John was the first to separate himself from the French national policy towards England. Beyond that, he played a part as chief of a faction in the French civil wars. Thrown into an alliance with England by his father's assassination, Duke Philip II was the first to oppose France as if she were a foreign power. Nevertheless, he maintained the fiction that he was not fighting his lawful king but a usurper to the throne. Until his death, he was proud of his position as a prince of the Royal House of France. It was his dream to create a second France, between the Channel, the Swiss mountains, and the Rhine. He dreamed of becoming its king, and acquiring equal rank with the kings of France. His institutions were imitations of those of France. The refined civilization of his court was modeled after the French example. The language of the court was French. He had his panegyrists in the writers of Burgundian history, in Georges Chastellain and in Olivier de la Marche. His courtiers called him the "Grand Duke of the Occident." Not to be outdone by the kings of England who had founded the "Order of the Garter," he created the "Order of the Golden Fleece," which was to be a brotherhood of nobles who indissolubly linked their fate to that of the House of Burgundy. He contemplated a Crusade against the Turks, assuming a role the kings of France had neglected to fill since the death of Louis IX.

This dream of building a new France in non-French territory rendered the whole Burgundian foundation vague and unreal. The Burgundian dukes themselves had no clear conception of their aims. They did not plan a state with well-chosen geographic boundaries, they merely grasped at every opportunity to extend their domain. Their personalities alone decided whether their policy of expansion would be carried out with prudence and due regard to geographical and political considerations. Duke Philip II, always cautious beneath an outward display of passion, advanced step by step and allowed the fruits of his policy to ripen before he picked them.

Cautious in his policy of expansion, Philip was not less prudent in his endeavors to safeguard his hastily and loosely built political structure. He knew that, even if he succeeded in uniting the provinces into one state, his work would lack stability unless it was confirmed and legalized by the proper authorities. This was the weakness of his position. No Emperor was strong enough to force the French Burgundians from the soil of the Empire, but only the Emperor could legally confirm their power. Duke Philip sought such confirmation. He was willing to make great concessions and to leave his French fiefs, like Flanders, outside the political unity he wished to constitute as a kingdom under the sovereignty of Germany. On the other hand, and this demand is most significant, he wanted his new kingdom to include the overlordship of numerous feudal states in western Germany—Guelders, Cleve, Berg, Mark, and Lorraine, for instance. This was the first attempt to determine an eastern boundary for the developing Flemish-Hollandish state, and it betrayed the ambitions of the new power. Frederick of Habsburg, then ruling Emperor, knew Philip's anxiety to secure a legalization of his position and to it he opposed a cautious policy of evasion. Duke Philip, too good a tactician to show impatience, avoided pressing the issue. His state remained nameless. "My lands over here" was all his chancery could call his possessions in the Low Countries.

Philip's son, Charles, rash and reckless, was impatient to secure a royal title and equal rank with the kings of the west. With brutal strokes of his sword, he sought to cut down the barriers separating his lands "over here" from those "over there" in the duchy of Burgundy. He failed and in 1477 died insane on the battlefield of Nancy. His frantic efforts to create an independent buffer-state brought out all the weaknesses of his position. He was forced to give up all pretense of being a French prince of the Royal House. The new king of France, the wily Louis XI, bent upon centralizing his monarchy, left Charles no choice. From now on, vassalage was to mean obedience, and disobedience to the king was to be treason to France. The people did not see things in that light; and the nobility definitely refused to accept such an interpretation of sovereignty, objecting to this novel conception because of their ancient traditions as semi-independent vassals. The kings of France finally prevailed although it took them two hundred and fifty years and a series of energetic rulers from Louis XI to Richelieu to drive the point home to the very last of the recalcitrants.

Charles of Burgundy was the first and most tragic of the victims of the new political theory. His bitterness at being outcast from France is reflected by his chroniclers, and in his wild, immoderate actions. Whenever his political schemes were opposed by the king of France or by French intrigues, he lost all sense of moderation. No longer recognized as a prince of the House of Valois, Charles seeking to repudiate what he could no longer call his own, resorted to the strangest devices. Being no longer a "Frenchman," he sought another nationality. Strangely enough he adopted the denomination "Portuguese," from the nationality of his mother, to make it clear to the world that he was independent of France, England, and Germany. Though fighting to create a sovereign state of his own, Charles evidently could not think of that state as a separate national entity. At the time of his death the position of the Burgundian princes was still as vague as when they began their momentous career.

With Charles's death, the Burgundian state seemed doomed to collapse. It was not yet legally constituted, and King Louis of France sought to make the most of his opportunity. The duke's only daughter, Mary of Burgundy, had to face a host of enemies. Threatened by a French invading army, she saw her subjects rise against her authority in resentment of her father's arbitrary proceedings. Yet the Burgundian creation survived. The home of the dynasty, the duchy of Burgundy, was lost. In the Low Countries, however, the dukes had given political form to existing, but vague tendencies, and there they survived.

They had created a dynastic bond among the provinces, and through their court and administration had fostered French civilization all over the Low Countries. They had sought to make their territory independent of France and Germany by giving it a high court of justice, a standing among European principalities, and in 1425 had even made it self-supporting in the field of learning by founding the university of Louvain. They had fostered the growth of an inter-provincial aristocracy by lifting a number of families—the Nassaus of Breda, the Croys and Lalaings from Hainaut, the Bergens from Brabant, the Egmonts from Holland, the Ravesteins from Guelders, and many others—above their former rank and position, while adding to the nobility their own numerous illegitimate offspring. They had developed a financial policy which has never been adequately studied but is remarkable for its attempts to establish a uniform currency throughout the provinces. All this, significant as it is, did not suffice to offset the reaction that followed the severe government of Duke Charles.

It was primarily the will of the leading classes, of the representative States Assemblies, that kept the Low Countries together. The individual provincial assemblies sought new charters to guarantee their complete regional independence; at the same time they sought a common charter for the "Generality" of all the provinces. They asked explicitly that the States General be allowed to convene whenever it pleased them, without being summoned by the prince. They further demanded that appointments to the Grand Council be brought under their control and a definite number of its members be taken from each province. They no longer objected to the central government but sought to make it their own. The "domain" of the princes had developed into a federation of autonomous provinces. Thus the defeat of 1477, by reducing the domains of Burgundy, and momentarily checking the aspirations of its rulers, contributed to its inner stability. The marriage of the young Duchess Mary to Maximilian of Austria, son of the emperor of the Holy Roman Empire finally provided the long desired legalization of its status.

Important as was the political evolution of the XVth century, the social evolution was far more so. This century brought an efflorescence of Netherland civilization, this time with characteristics of its own, which inaugurated the great economic development that was to give affluence and world power to the Netherlands. In this social evolution we discern the opposing tendencies of north and south that a century later, contributed to the splitting up of the Low Countries into northern and southern sections. Cultural life remained centered in the provinces of Flanders and Brabant. The northern provinces, Holland and Utrecht, followed in the wake of their more advanced southern neighbors, with one remarkable exception.

In Flanders and Brabant, the art of painting reached a level so high that it became a permanent part of the great European cultural inheritance. The work of the brothers Van Eyck suddenly revealed the vigorous growth of artistic traditions barely perceptible in the Low Countries a few decades before. Their disciples and successors, coming from all parts of the country, were automatically drawn to the bustling centers of life in Brussels, Antwerp, and Bruges, where princely protection and the patronage of wealthy merchant families enabled them to earn a handsome living. Here, too, they found opportunities for an exchange of ideas with Italian artists from which both parties profited. In their desire to be true, to represent the world as they saw it, their ideas as they conceived them, their love of detail that, however flimsy, nevertheless reflect the true atmosphere of the scene, these painters created the tradition of the really native, wholly and indubitably Netherland art, the great, unquestionably unique contribution of the Netherlands to the civilization of mankind. In the XVth century, this art flourished in the southern provinces, but was never their exclusive product. From the different corners of the Low Countries painters flocked to the centers of cultural life in Flanders and Brabant, but although individual masters left the more backward provinces, artistic potentialities remained. As circumstances changed, art triumphed wherever social conditions gave it a chance. The Burgundians fostered this glorious development but they did not create or determine it. It was the product of a popular, not a princely civilization.

The same was true in music. The Burgundian court with its international relations provided an excellent medium for Netherland musicians and composers. In the XVIth century their fame was at its peak. Here too, the Burgundian court merely drew on the artistic talents of the people. The great masters, Johannes Okeghem and Jacob Obrecht, built their polyphonic music on folk tunes. These songs, in their pure beauty and the tender melancholy of their melodies are perhaps the most perfect expression of Netherland spiritual life of the XVth century. The dukes of Burgundy gained more glory from Netherland arts than they could contribute to the civilization of the country. Cultural life did not fluctuate according to the degree of interest shown by various princes as in some cities in Italy, and it was never concentrated in one single town.

The folk songs were naturally in the vernacular, and the few important literary products of this eventful period were also written in Dutch. That language, the *thiois* or *dietsch,* was looked upon by the courtiers as an "uncouth tongue." As Chastellain said, "the peasants' talk," fit only for the "people of the pastures, the ignorants, rough of mouth and palate, of poor appearance, as suits the nature of the land." [16] Nothing shows more clearly the cleavage between the court and the people, between the superficial refined life of the Burgundians and the real civilization of their peoples, as revealed in their folk songs, their painting and their dramatic literature.

The northeastern provinces, still outside the orbit of Burgundian influence and less stimulated by direct contact with the non-Germanic world of western Europe, seemed backward in comparison with rural Holland. Nevertheless, they too contributed to the cultural life of the Low Countries, for it was in the towns of IJssel that there originated the religious movement known as the *Devotio Moderna.* It is not within the scope of this work to evaluate the significance of this movement in late medieval religious life. It produced one of the most widely read books ever written, the *Imitatio Christi* which was compiled, composed or arranged, as scholars will have it, by Thomas à Kempis. Thomas, born at Kempen in the Rhineland, then part of the duchy of Guelders, lived and worked in the monastery of Mount St. Agnes near Zwolle from 1399 until 1417. His compilation, written by one intimately acquainted, either personally or through their works, with all the prominent leaders of the *Devotio,* represents the true tradition of his community and the spiritual inheritance of its founder, Geert Groote. Groote belongs to the XIVth century like his teacher, the great mystic, John Ruysbroeck of Groenendaal near Brussels. His personality was wholly medieval, the best the Middle Ages had to give. His work, however, bore fruit only after his death in 1384. Thanks to the openmindedness of Groote and his disciples, their work became a great force in the cultural life of the XVth century. It coincided with a growing desire for knowledge among the upper classes and in their willingness to serve their people and with clear insight into practical needs, the followers of Groote showed what the critical, soberminded, burgher-type of Lowlander could achieve when moved by high ideals.[17]

It is difficult to gauge the effect of their work on religious life. Perchance intensification of religious life, especially among the burgher class, and an emphasis on the inner understanding of Christian ideals at a time when often an appalling disparity existed between the outward form of ecclesiastical institutions and their inner meaning, contributed to individual criticism of the Church and its practices. The burgher class eagerly grasped this opportunity for greater independence, though certainly with no deliberate intension of opposing the established Church. In this way the movement of the *Devotio Moderna* may have helped unintentionally to prepare the way for the Reformation, especially as the prestige of the Church suffered in the same period from the Great Schism. In the Netherlands the hierarchy was further degraded by the shameless way the Burgundians used the episcopal dignity for their political ends.

For princes of the Church installed by Burgundian armies and yet supposed to be their spiritual rulers, the people could have little respect. Real religious movements avoided the bishop's palace and the cathedral. In the revival of spiritual life, the "Brethren of the Common Life" (the loose religious association into which many of the adherents of the *Devotio Moderna* had been organized) took a prominent part, but it was by no means confined to Groote's followers. Identical efforts were made by some of the older religious orders, especially the Franciscans. The eloquence of their great preacher, Johannes Brugman, whose sermons rivaled in dramatic effect those of his better-known contemporaries in Italy, is proverbial in the Netherlands to this day. A similar religious renewal took place among the Dominicans and Cistercians. The latter in their Frisian monastery of Aduard, provided a place of rest for the renowned Wessel Gansfoort, one of the earliest Netherland Humanists and a theologian considered by Martin Luther as one of his precursors. It is impossible to pass judgment in general terms on spiritual conditions prevailing in Netherland monasteries and convents of the XVth century. Some were deteriorating, others were flourishing and striving to attain Christian ideals. In some cases the revival of idealism lasted for half a century; in others a relapse into indifference followed the death of a great leader. Erasmus, whose witty and mordant criticism was the fruit of resentment, led later generations to condemn institutions that ought to be judged according to their individual merit.

The same is true of the work of the "Brethren of the Common Life." They also were branded by Erasmus as spirits of darkness, notwithstanding their unceasing labor for the improvement of education. Recent historical works point out that the significance of the Brethren and their work in the revival of learning in northwestern Europe has been greatly overestimated. It is true that originally the Brethren did not teach, that only gradually they took up teaching and founded schools, that their institutions were not progressive and only became so under the influence of Humanism. Nevertheless, the Brethren assumed the care of pupils (previously one of the most neglected groups of society) boarded them and supervised their morals. This could not be without influence upon the educational system in general. Schools patronized, if not run by the Brethren, saw their attendance increase four- or fivefold. The fame of the schools of Deventer and Zwolle was intimately connected with the work of the *Devotio Moderna.*

It is well established that these schools did not originally favor the revival of classical learning and did not share the appreciation of literary form so characteristic of the age. Nevertheless, they later became foremost among institutions spreading the new ideas; and among the friends and pupils of the Brethren many like Roelofsen (Agricola), Gansfoort, Hegius, and Erasmus himself, were the standard bearers of Humanism. The devotion to learning fostered in their schools necessarily resulted in excellence in the new studies. The evolution of education from the XVth to the XVIth century in the Netherlands is typical. Thoroughness of elementary and secondary instruction was and still is, the pride of Dutch education. Even Erasmus, for all his disparagement of his native land, its "barbaric" customs, its monasteries and schools under the control of the Brethren, acknowledges that a high standard of public education existed among the Netherlanders, though few of them attained the highest rank in the world of learning. This thoroughness was the result of the combined influences of the XVth century spiritual and XVIth century literary revivals.

The *Devotio Moderna* and the institutions that emanated from it, spread east and southeast from the IJssel towns. Thus the cultural contacts between the eastern Netherlands of today and western Germany—Westphalia and the lower Rhineland—became closer than ever. Their institutions had branches along the Rhine to Alsace, and through the Low German plains to Rostock and even Prussia. They also penetrated into Holland and northern Brabant; but in the southern Low Countries they touched only the most prominent places, big trading centers like Antwerp. In fact, this XVth century movement foreshadowed a development that was to come early in the XVIth: the formation of a Low German cultural unity, independent of the western Lowland unity and of the High German one of Franconia, the middle Elbe and the South. New forces were moving, along the coast of the North Sea, as well as in the lowlands of Germany, and in the mountainous area of the South. The spheres of influence around these centers overlapped. The future was to decide which influence would survive and where the boundaries between them would be drawn.

The rapid spread of knowledge among the middle classes was conditioned by their increasing wealth. The prosperity of the towns had grown with expanding trade and industry, and had reached a level where at least a certain luxury was permitted. People outside the Church had means to live at leisure and thus devote their time to artistic and spiritual matters. Nowhere in the northern Netherlands did the merchant class equal the prosperity of the bankers of Bruges, the traders of Luebeck and of Antwerp. The general level of welfare was rapidly rising, however; with it further characteristics of Netherland society became apparent.

Around 1377, the Hanseatic League reached the peak of its power. It had humiliated the king of Denmark and Norway, and dictated stringent terms of peace. More and more Luebeck dominated the League, with close support from Hamburg and the "Wendish" towns. Competitors were driven out of business. Frisian coastal shipping had been eliminated since the XIIIth century, and Holland's trade was closely watched by the mercantile lords of the Elbe and Trave. As long as the sea captains from Holland sailed for Hanseatic merchants, they were allowed to visit the ports of the Baltic. On the point of Skonen they might have their "fitten," reserved sites where they pitched their tents during the summer fair and the season of herring fishing. They were also allowed to carry less valuable merchandise along the all-sea trade route, around Jutland to the Baltic towns. But the main part of the east-west trade, the handling of valuable merchandise like Flemish cloth and Russian furs, was strictly reserved to the Hanseatic merchants who followed the overland route from Hamburg to Luebeck. This was shorter and safer than the route around Jutland, but more expensive for it involved excise taxes and more middlemen.

It was certain that once the Hollanders were acquainted with the Baltic trade routes, they would try to cut out the Hanseatic intermediaries and buy direct from Polish and Russian producers. The Luebeck merchants were quick to realize this. Shortly after 1400, they saw that it would require force to prevent the merchants from Holland trading with Russian and Polish wheat producers. The Hollanders cleverly exploited the growing rift between the Wendish and Baltic towns in the League, and the resentment of the Baltic princes, the kings of Denmark, the Grand Masters of the Teutonic Order, and the Russians against the economic tutelage of Luebeck and its allies. The struggle was between vested interests and economic upstarts. Flanders, interested in maintaining itself as the great textile center sided with the Hansa. The Prussian and Livland towns rallied half-heartedly around Luebeck when they realized that the new competition might endanger their own positions as well as that of Luebeck's. The Hollanders were not easily baffled. Avoiding the Estonian and the Livland port, they sought to base their trade on Åbo in Finland. Evidence of this "evil" intent was discovered in the fact that some of them were studying Russian. They deserted the fairs of Skonen and began to make their own connections along the shores of the Baltic. Within half a century the friendship that united Amsterdam and the Hansa when they joined hands in 1370 to make war on Denmark-Norway, changed into open hostility.

Luebeck decided upon a policy of repression. It enacted a series of Hansa decrees excluding Hollanders from trade with the interior of Germany. In 1417, strict regulations were made for the control of all trade by foreigners—i.e., non-members of the Hansa. In the same year, the import of low-quality Leiden cloth, with which the Hollanders competed against expensive Flemish woollen goods, was stopped. All this did not daunt the intruders. Early in the XVth century, we find ships from Holland selling herring and salt from the Bay of Biscay to Novgorod, but they could no longer trade with the interior of Germany. In the development of the Low Countries, these prohibitive measures, cutting off the western coastlands from the interior economically, were naturally an important factor. The Hollanders, then and there, were branded as foreigners by the same northern Germans with whom they had been so closely associated in past centuries.

Luebeck was not satisfied with excluding Hollanders from the German markets. In 1426, their rivals entered into what Luebeck considered an inadmissible combination with Denmark, always restive under Hanseatic supervision. Luebeck responded with a draconic decree: the closing of the Sund to all non-Hanseatic ships. In a few years, war flared. The struggle for the *Dominium Maris Baltici,* control over the Baltic sea, had begun. It was to last four hundred years, to quiet down in the nineteenth century, and to be renewed in our own time. As all discontented elements tended to side with Holland, the war from 1430 to 1441 cracked the Hanseatic system. The conflict took the form of a series of piratical raids. The two opponents inflicted considerable damage upon each other, but could not bring about a decision. The Hansa then resorted to the familiar twentieth-century expedient of economic sanctions. By prohibiting all trade between members of the League and the Hollanders, they sought to starve their enemies into submission and actually did cause endless misery through famine and unemployment in the coastal villages and small towns of Holland. Although the sea captains of Holland drove Hanseatic shipping from the North Sea, the financial wounds they inflicted on the rich merchants of Luebeck were far less fatal than the dearth and starvation caused in Holland by the Hanseatic blockade.

This war was fought privately by the ship captains and sailors of Holland. Duke Philip of Burgundy, their otherwise highly respected lord, sought vainly to intervene in a conflict that disturbed his political combinations. The sea-farers and townspeople disregarded his requests and threats, just as a few years before they had ignored his declaration of war against England and had continued to trade with their duke's enemy despite his angry protests. Not Burgundy but Denmark settled the conflict. King Eric of Denmark, who owed his throne to the Hanseatics, turned against his overweening protectors and with his help, the Hollanders, in a last desperate effort carried the war into the estuaries of the Weser and Elbe, even into the Sund itself to decide the issue. Their victory was by no means decisive—hardly a victory at all in the military or political sense; but it raised the morale of the townspeople of Holland whose ships had managed to hold their own against the powerful Hansa. Under the stipulations of the peace treaty, the ships of Holland were readmitted to the Baltic. After a short breathing spell, they started upon the marvelous expansion of their trade which within half a century made them the equals and finally the superiors of the Hanseatics. In 1476, 168 Luebeck ships visited the port of Danzig, as against 156 from Holland. Twenty years later, the merchantmen from Holland outnumbered those of the Hansea in the same port.

Nothing contributed more to the prosperity of the Hollanders than the growth of their fishing industry. For some unknown cause, the herring changed their yearly migrations from the narrows between the North Sea and the Baltic to the waters east of England and on the Doggerbank. The ship owners of Holland exploited this favorable event to the full and obtained a virtual monopoly of the North Sea fisheries. The handling of the catch required large quantities of salt, which was brought to Holland on her own ships from the Bay of Biscay and later from Portugal. By the second half of the XVth century, the Low Countries has thus become a maritime and commercial power.

Bruges had lost its importance as a seaport, but for a long time remained the principal money-market of Northern Europe. Trade had shifted to Antwerp, now the greatest port north of the Alps. Spanish, Portuguese, and Italian ships brought merchandise to be exchanged for the products of the North. English wool manufacturers, freed from their industrial dependence on Flanders by Flemish weavers who brought their art to England, made the same town their headquarters. Middelburg, favorably situated at the entrance of the Scheldt, had its share of this prosperity but also took an active part in shipping. More to the north, the maritime and fishing interests of Holland, now free to compete with the Hanseatics, spread their commerce, fan-like, along the Atlantic coasts. The Portuguese discovered the shores of Africa and the Atlantic islands, but Flemish capital and the sailors of Holland had their share in this success. When the Azores were discovered and their colonization decided upon, Flemings provided the money and the men. The old familiar Dutch name of van der Haaghen, one of the entrepreneurs, long persisted in the islands in its Portuguese version of Guihermo da Silveira; and the islands themselves are marked on XVIth century maps as the "Flemish Islands."

The XVth century was the period in which Europe became nationally conscious. In Italy, split up into many petty states, a desire for political unity or at least cooperation was a reaction to foreign aggression. "To drive the foreigners from our native soil" became a slogan in the Italian wars around 1500. In France, the English invasion of the early XVth century was repelled by the spiritual and military heroism of Joan of Arc. Even in the hopelessly divided Empire, German feeling tended to unite under the shock of foreign penetration, military and ecclesiastical. The onslaught of Duke Charles the Bold of Burgundy against the German cities on the Rhine, provoked a general reaction to the East. In both France and Germany, attempts were made to set up "national" churches as quasi-autonomous branches of the Roman Catholic Church.

The old tribal sentiments which had prompted earlier chroniclers to extol the feats of their own people and to deride the "cowardice" of foreigners, now developed into a new national consciousness, as yet vague and undetermined, that borrowed its terminology from the classics. The Italians dwelt upon the glory and the glamor of ancient Rome to inspire the hopelessly torn Italy of their own time. The French began to see themselves the *Galli* in recollection of Gauls and boundaries on Pyrenees and Rhine described by Caesar. The rediscovery of the works of Tacitus in the middle of the XVth century lent glory to the previously less esteemed name of *Germani*. North of the Alps, however, there remained a certain incongruity between the precision of classic terminology and the vagueness of national political formulations. England alone had the advantage of natural boundaries. There the political superstructure corresponded to the national entity. In other countries they were but distantly related.

What place did the Low Countries take in this new Latinized political geography? In politics, they were officially partly *Galli*, partly *Germani*. Erasmus used these expressions in one of his letters. He wrote that geographically not only Flanders but also Holland tended more towards France than towards Germany. It was the cultural dependence of Holland on France that made him say so. Caesar, in his *De Bello Gallico*, had provided an alternative in the name *Belgae* for a people he described as part Germanic and part Gallic. His *Belgica* extended from the lower Seine to the Rhine. Most of this territory had retained its name under Roman administration as the province of *Belgica prima*. The dioceses of the Roman Catholic Church corresponded to the *civitates* of the Roman administration, and the term *Belgica* had survived as the designation of the Archdiocese of Rheims, to which Flanders, Hainaut, and most of Brabant belonged. Forgotten in the XIIth and XIIIth centuries, the name reappeared in a Hainaut chronicle of the XIVth century. Its geographical meaning was vague until the Low Countries began to form a political unit of their own. Then it came into use as the Latin term for their inhabitants. Because Latin was familiar only to the more cultivated world, *Belgae, Belgica,* and *Belgium* were terms applied *post-factum* to political formations. They did not indicate national or even well-determined geographic areas distinct from political considerations.

The same was true of the term *Batavi*. Tacitus' narrative had unexpectedly revealed the military glory of the ancient inhabitants of the land between Meuse and Rhine. Humanists, filled with pride when reading of the war-like exploits of Civilis, sought to establish a direct historical connection between the Low Countries of their own time and the Batavi. Some claimed them as the ancestors of the people of Holland; others, as the ancestors of the people of Guelders. This provincial patriotism caused an interesting archaeological discussion of the classic texts referring to the Batavi, the first critical interpretation of ancient Netherland history. The Batavi, according to Tacitus and other historians, belonged to the Germani. And so Erasmus was claimed as a compatriot by his German colleagues, and the great humanist taxed all his ingenuity to avoid acquiescence. Though otherwise he followed the ancient adage, *Ubi bene ibi patria,* and referred to England, France, and Germany as his fatherland whenever he happened to feel at home in any one of those countries, he definitely refused to see his native land, which was to him a distinct part of Western Europe, included in Germany.

The High Germans themselves were among the first ones to see the Low Countries as an individual entity in the European world. The term *Nederland,* originally applied to the whole area of the Low German plain, was more and more identified with the *Dietsch*-speaking part of the Burgundian monarchy. The differentiation between the *Dietsch* of the coastlands and the *Overlandish* of the eastern plains became more pronounced. *Dietsch* and High German were then already different languages, too far apart for the one to be commonly understood by the speakers of the other. An envoy from the Elector of Saxonia to Philip of Burgundy, in the middle of the XVth century, needed an interpreter to be understood by Flemings. The Hanseatics spoke of the towns of *Netherland,* opposing them to those of Nether Germany. When Archduke Maximilian of Austria went to Flanders to marry Mary of Burgundy, it was according to the words of his panegyrist, a voyage into *Niderland*. Ten years later, in 1497, the French version of the names appeared in a significant form when Maximilian was recognized as *le mambour de tous les Pays Bas,* the protector of all the Low Countries. The geographic term had gained political and national significance. The poets of the Burgundian court, as well as their French opponents, styled Duke Charles the Bold "the Lion Rampant of the Lowlands adjoining Germany." The "Lion Rampant" was an apt name for a prince all of whose provinces, united under Burgundian rule, carried the lion rampant in the coats of arms—black on gold for Flanders, gold on black for Brabant, red on gold for Holland.

Cultural influence from France, economic antagonism to the Hansa, political and linguistic cleavage from High Germany, political hostility to the French kings, vigorous cultural and economic developments at home had united to create the core of a new nation, to which the hybrid Burgundian state gave inadequate political expression. It found a purer interpretation in the endeavors of the provincial States Assemblies, after the death of Duke Charles, to reorganize his monarchy along popular, federative lines. The XVIth century was to fulfill the promise of the two preceding centuries.

CHAPTER VI

The Great Crisis of the Sixteenth Century

MARY OF BURGUNDY was only nineteen when her father, Duke Charles, fell in the battle of Nancy. Helpless and alone, she faced the joint threat of French invasion and of internal revolution. Although forced to relinquish the arbitrary authority her father had assumed, and mortally insulted by the people of Flanders who murdered her most trusted councilors before her eyes, she remained the sole arbiter of the future of the Low Countries. By her marriage, the inheritance of the extinct Valois-Burgundian dynasty must pass into the hands of one or other of the ruling families of Europe. King Louis XI of France coveted her lands for his seven-year-old boy, the future Charles VIII. The duke of Guelders, a prisoner of the Burgundians in 1477, nourished hopes of exchanging his cell for the palace of the young duchess. King Edward IV pondered a matrimonial alliance between the Low Countries and England. Philip of Cleve, the playmate of Mary in her childhood, dreamed of life-long companionship and joint rule with the friend of his youth. Frederick of Habsburg, the third Emperor of that name, who twice had received the pledge of Duke Charles for the marriage of Archduke Maximilian with the heiress of Burgundy, had not given up hope of securing her glorious inheritance for his dynasty. Mary, desirous of personal as well as political support and unwilling to seek an agreement with France, turned indeed to the Habsburgs for protection.[18]

Maximilian, a romantic nature, lacked the strength of character to carry through the schemes his fertile imagination conceived. As a dreamer he was not unlike his father-in-law, Duke Charles, but although his ambitions were greater he was far more aware of his limitations and the extent of his power. He looked upon the Low Countries not as the center of his political fortunes but only as one of several pawns in a wider European game. As archduke of Austria and, later, ruler of the Holy Roman Empire, as well as prince of the Lowlands, his attention was constantly diverted from one corner of Europe to another, from Brittany to Hungary, and from England to Italy. The beginnings of his career in the Low Countries were glorious. At the battle of Guinegate, he defeated the French invaders and stopped the open attempts at conquest of the French king. Admired and loved by the people, apparently happy with his young wife—though he no more understood her French than she his High German—he seemed destined to play a brilliant role in Netherland history. With his support, Duchess Mary could ignore the concessions she had been forced to make in the revolutionary years after her father's death. The new rulers resolved to take up where Philip II had left off, and to rebuild the central administration after French models. Under the Habsburgs as well as under the Burgundians French conceptions of political administration guided the court of Brussels. Coming from Germany, where their authority was most limited, the Habsburgs found the French system a marvelously efficient means of government.

However, the glory of Maximilian did not last. He was one of those princes whose intemperate character, perhaps even more their bad luck, spells failure to their most cherished plans. Mary of Burgundy died after only five years of married life and reign. The people who had once revolted against her would never have deserted her, for she always and under all circumstances was their "natural princess." Maximilian was merely a foreigner and his subjects made him feel it, not only the rebellious Flemings but even more the higher aristocracy, the numerous and powerful bastards of Burgundy, Philip of Cleve and many others. Mary's four-year-old son Philip was now the "natural" prince. Maximilian, although appointed regent and guardian of his child by Mary on her death bed, was roughly pushed aside.

The States General, after some hesitation, decided to recognize him as Regent, but—they made it perfectly clear—only to carry out *their* political views. It was *they* who made peace with France and in so doing disregarded Maximilian's feelings and delivered his little daughter into the hands of his mortal enemy, King Louis, while *they* decided that the duchy of Burgundy was not worth fighting for. They warned Maximilian that they would fight no wars and pay no taxes for the benefit of the Habsburg dynasty or for the Regent's political schemes. They accused him of "plundering the country and carrying off its wealth to Germany," an accusation which to Maximilian, poor and penniless as he was, must have sounded like a derision. The higher he rose in Germany, where in 1486 he was elected "King of the Romans," the more suspect he became in the Low Countries. The States General strengthened their connections with France, even to the extent of giving the wily old Louis XI undue influence in Lowland affairs. Returning from Germany with the royal crown, Maximilian was hailed by the court poets as the successor of the Caesars but was jailed by the guilds of Bruges. Before his eyes, his friends were executed, and he himself, the Emperor-elect, was forced to kneel before an altar in the mar-

ket place at Bruges and swear that he would never take revenge for the
insults suffered. Once free, he broke his oath and revolt flared up all
through Flanders, Brabant, Holland, and Utrecht.

There was a great deal of provincialism behind these uprisings. The
power of the central government was to be curbed. Yet nobody, except a
very few of the nobility of Holland, wanted it abolished. The Burgundian-
Lowland state might well have fallen apart had it not been for the determination of the States Assemblies to stick together as a Lowland federation. Nobody except Maximilian was interested in the recovery of the
duchy of Burgundy, the native state of the dynasty which was conquered
by Louis in 1477. With the interests of their prince in Artois and some other
French-speaking territories the States dealt lightly. Those of Flanders even
considered giving up all the Walloon country to the king of France. But
they were willing to fight for the independence of the other provinces, and
they were determined to keep them free from France as well as outside all
Imperial authority. After Maximilian's betrayal of his solemn pledge to
the people of Bruges, Philip of Cleve organized the rebels and became
their leader. He called all Lowlanders to join the national cause against
the Habsburgs, who planned to "incorporate" the Low Countries into
their "Austrian" empire. Young Philip was to be the ruler and the native
aristocrats his advisors, to the exclusion of all foreigners. The Netherlands,
the prince of Cleve proclaimed, "were subject to God and the Sun alone,"
not to any king or emperor. Here the centuries-old political aspirations of
the western coastlands were brought to their logical conclusion: complete
separation from both France and Germany.

Philip of Cleve met with support all through the provinces, in the northern marshes of Holland, as in the southern plains of Flanders. Yet he was
doomed to fail. The success of his "national" revolution depended on too
many kinds of local issues and social conditions. He had set an example by
joining the revolt, but most of his peers, members of the new upper-
aristocracy created by the Burgundians, refused to break definitely with
the king-archduke in whose service they could win fame and estates.
Philip's soldiers were the guildsmen of Flanders, irritated by the decline
of Flemish industry and trade, and some of the minor nobility of Holland
and Utrecht, who had been reduced to secondary rank when their provinces became part of the Burgundian state. The forces of the future, the
prominent merchants of Antwerp, offended by the economic particularism
of the Flemish towns, the traders of Holland, the rural weavers and industrialists of Hainaut and Walloon Flanders, after some hesitation sided
with the central administration, not out of sympathy for Maximilian but

because they hoped to see the obsolete economic prerogatives of the Flemish towns broken.

Philip of Cleve might have been more successful if foreign support had not failed him. The Low Countries were now in a peculiar international position. For two centuries Flanders had been a political pivot in the long series of French-English conflicts. Now Flanders had lost most of its industrial importance and the kings of England had not the same economic hold over the merchants of Antwerp and the shipowners of Holland as they had had over the weavers of Ghent and Bruges. The French-English antagonism itself no longer held first rank in western European politics. It had been replaced by the growing French-Spanish rivalry for leadership in Italy. This left the Low Countries a chance to withdraw into a policy of neutrality best suited to their interests and for the time being in accordance with the wishes of the new king of France, the inexperienced Charles VIII. As yet the Habsburgs wielded no great power and a little unrest in Flanders and Holland was enough to neutralize the danger that might otherwise have threatened France from that quarter. Hence the French king's lack of interest in Cleve's national revolution. At first supported he was left to his fate when it became clear that, whatever the outcome of the struggle, Maximilian could never mobilize the recalcitrant Lowlands for a large-scale attack on France's northern frontier.

In 1492 the last strongholds of the rebels fell before the onslaught of Maximilian's army under Duke Albrecht of Saxonia-Meissen. The war had cost the Habsburg dynasty one province, that of Guelders where, with the help of France, Charles of Egmont had been restored to the ducal throne. It left the Habsburgs deep in debt to the Saxon duke to whom they were unable to refund the cost of the campaign. In 1494 Maximilian's regency came to an end; his son Philip was declared of age and assumed the reins of government.

Duke Philip was wholly influenced by his Netherland surroundings. Through him—a boy sixteen years old—the higher aristocracy ruled. Their policy aimed at peace with France and the re-establishment of good trade relations with England. It ignored completely and deliberately the ancient feudal ties of Holland, Brabant, and other provinces with the German empire. It was indifferent to the recovery of the Burgundian inheritance. When Duke Charles of Guelders, supported by France, fought the troops of Maximilian, the government of Brussels refused to support the soldiers of their prince's father. Not to be drawn into any great European conflict was their principal maxim of policy. Their aim was to preserve the limited Lowland state as created by the early Burgundians and to maintain its form of government as a moderately centralized monarchy in which authority would be divided between the prince and the States Assemblies. The promoters of this policy were the Croys, the Bergens, the Nassaus of Breda, the Burens, the Egmonts, the higher aristocracy whose members sought to assume the role of spokesmen for both the people and the States Assemblies. That young Philip was heir to the throne of Vienna and perhaps to the Imperial Crown, caused these nobles no satisfaction, only anxiety. They wanted him to be their "national" prince, but fate ordained otherwise.

The history of the reigns of Maximilian and Philip definitely proves that by this time the people of the Low Countries had become conscious of their national individuality. With the reign of Philip national sentiment gained political expression. The boundaries of the new national unit were still undetermined. The political aspirations of its princes usually outstripped the wishes of the aristocracy or wealthy burgher class. The latter were not interested as were the former, in Guelders or Friesland. The existing popular tendency to confine the new state to the western coastlands and Flanders involved great risks. Holland was not yet the strong economic power it was to become and Flanders, no longer what it had been. Antwerp, the brilliant center of the coastlands, was bound with chains of gold to Italian-Spanish interests on the one hand and to the Baltic towns on the other. However, it did not develop a shipping of its own. The Lowland federation was still weak and this explains the almost excessive diligence with which its leaders sought to cultivate relations with France. Sometimes it seemed that the Low Countries would reach the longed-for goal of national independence only to fall, thereafter, under the control of their southern neighbor.

Accident, pure accident, suddenly changed the course of events. In 1496 Duke Philip married the Infanta Johanna, third child of Ferdinand of Aragon and Isabella of Castile. Four years later, death had removed all other heirs to the Spanish throne and opened to young Philip, himself ruler of the Low Countries and heir to the Austrian principalities, the magnificent prospect of becoming prince consort to the queen of Spain, Naples, Sicily, and America. Overnight his outlook on world politics changed. With grief, his subjects saw him abandon his national policy of neutrality and peace for the pursuit of dynastic interests. His first care was to secure his promised Spanish inheritance, threatened by the intrigues of his father-in-law, King Ferdinand. His relations with France and England were no longer determined by the interest of the Low Countries but by the necessity of countering the moves of the king of Aragon. A favorable commercial agreement with England, secured in days of national policy, was voluntarily abandoned for another, more advantageous to English interests, in order to bring the English king into a common front against France. Heir to the Spanish-Austrian empire and future lord of many millions, Philip would no longer tolerate the independence of the poor duchy of Guelders, which he himself, when local ruler at Brussels, had permitted to be revived. The change of policy was significant and of evil omen, as was the change of attitude among his subjects. The States General, which had not complained of the abrogation of many privileges they had extorted from Mary and Maximilian and seen rejected by Philip, suddenly closed their purse to the prospective ruler of many kingdoms. "No money for dynastic wars" was the immediate reaction of the representative classes of the provinces. Philip had but a dim conception of the difficulties that were to mar the glory of his new position when he died at Burgos in 1506.

His son Charles inherited all his titles and claims.[19] During his minority, the Low Countries were governed nominally by Maximilian as regent, but actually by his daughter Margareta, as "governess." Margareta understood the peculiar problems of Lowland politics, and carefully sought to promote the Habsburg dynastic interests without openly affronting the national tradition which insisted on maintaining a balance among the western powers and avoiding conflict with France. Even so, she encountered strong opposition from the aristocracy. The early recognition of Charles's coming of age, when he was only fifteen, was one of the master strokes of the leader of that aristocracy, William of Croy, Lord of Chièvres, who thus secured control over the destinies of the principality for himself and his colleagues. For a few years more they were allowed to enjoy their power and to follow their traditional policy, years in which even the turbulent Duke Charles of Guelders was permitted some respite from his endless wars with the Habsburgs. Then Destiny resumed its course, and Charles, king of Spain, Naples, and America at sixteen and emperor at nineteen, started his momentous career in which the Low Countries were automatically reduced to a secondary position.

Emperor Charles V was the last "natural" prince of the Low Countries. Born in Ghent, speaking French as his mother tongue and well acquainted with Dutch, educated by the high nobility of the Lowlands and, originally at least, beloved by the people, he could rely on the loyalty of his Netherlanders even though world-politics kept him out of the country for nearly the whole of his life. From the higher aristocracy he had little to fear for, unlike Maximilian, Charles had something to offer them—estates in Spain (where Chièvre's son became archbishop of Toledo), fame in the endless wars (by which the glory of the House of Egmont was established), and rich marriages, such as linked the Nassaus of Breda with the princes of

Orange in southern France and elevated them to the rank of sovereign rulers. Finally one of his trusted advisors, his former tutor Adrian of Utrecht, became Pope Adrian VI, the only native Netherlander to occupy the See of St. Peter.

Charles's reign, his struggle with France and with the Reformation in Germany, have often been described. We are concerned only with his actions in the Low Countries where his rule was of decisive importance. Under his administration the international legal status of the United Provinces was adjusted to the national development of the last century. An eastern frontier was established which persists almost unchanged to the present day. He it was who gave definite shape and form to the still somewhat amorphous Lowland state. In a long and often pitiless struggle, his troops conquered all the territories to which Charles held unsatisfied claims: Friesland (he pretended as count of Holland) and Guelders (he claimed by right of purchase as well as conquest). The bishopric of Utrecht, already under the indirect control of the Burgundian-Habsburg family, was incorporated into Charles's principality thanks to a fortunate coincidence in Italy and in the Low Countries.

In this forty years' war for the possession of the northeastern provinces, Duke Charles of Guelders headed the anti-Habsburg elements. Rough, selfish, even brutal, obsessed by a fixed idea that grew into anti-Habsburg mania, this indomitable prince carried on a destructive war against an overwhelmingly superior enemy for four decades, supported only by the sympathy of his people and the intermittent assistance of the king of France. Although this war must have exhausted the already poor duchy of Guelders, Duke Charles retained the loyalty of his subjects who were united with him in their dogged resistance to the "French" government of Brussels and its attacks on their "Germanic" liberties, and against the "foreigners" from Holland and Brabant. These terms "French" and "Germanic" are found in the writings of the time and have a definite national meaning. Holland, Brabant, and of course the Walloon provinces, once forming part of the Empire, had long since been estranged from Germany. Guelders, Groningen, the "Oversticht" of Overijssel, Drente, and even Utrecht were not, however, and with the growing national consciousness east of the Rhine, they were on the point of being drawn into the German national group. They were separated from Nether-Germany before their ties with the East had become too strong. But it was a close call.

To understand the significance of this fact and the reasons for the defeat of Guelders, one must bear in mind conditions in the fastly decaying German Empire. Its real name, the "Holy Roman Empire," was so typically medieval and so reminiscent of extinct forms of thought that its use was limited to official documents. The territory of the Empire had been slowly reduced until it contained mostly German-speaking lands and the terms "Empire" and "Germany" had become almost synonymous. The conception of "Germany" as a country with its own nationality and the "German" language as the tongue of a greater Germanic group, developed at about the same time. The use of the native tongue in literature and documents naturally led to the gradual introduction of a common literary language in large parts of the Empire. High German developed more quickly than Low German, but around the middle of the XVth century, with the intensification of trade relations, the increase in prosperity, and the establishment of institutions for higher learning in Northern Germany, Low German also became a recognized medium of literary expression and communication.

The invention of printing naturally promoted the use of Low German. Printing made possible an appeal to larger masses of readers; and since these masses were acquainted only with their local dialects, it also made imperative the use of words commonly understood. In learned publications the use of Latin bridged the linguistic gap, but if a writer wanted to deal with problems of popular interest he was obliged to use a more popular medium. Thus, the great religious controversies of the early XVIth century not only promoted but were dependent upon the use of the vernacular. High German did not meet these requirements in Nether-Germany. As later events proved Dutch could have done so in large parts of the area, but it was only natural that Low German as a literary language gained wide recognition in the first half of the XVIth century. Westphalia and the Low Countries were the center of the Anabaptist movement, and the Mennonite sect originated in Friesland. It was natural therefore that the voluminous literature advocating these religious trends, should be written in Low German. The Hanseatic League whose influence extended as far west as Utrecht, was another force promoting the use of the same language. Guelders, Friesland, and Groningen fell within this new linguistic sphere of influence.

For a while it seemed that two German languages instead of one would develop and one of them gain a firm hold on the eastern provinces of the present Netherlands. Such an evolution might have changed the course of history in central Europe. Actually, Low German gave way to High German after a century of struggle in which it was exposed to constant pressure from the west where the Dutch tongue pressed eastward, and from the south where the High German pressed northward. By the second half of the XVIth century, this evolution had made considerable progress. The question then arose, where would the future demarcation between

High German and Dutch be established? Obviously the linguistic boundary could have formed along a line quite different from the present political boundary. Although usually ignored this is self-evident. Once we grasp its meaning we understand the importance of the conquest of the eastern provinces by Charles V. It was this that assured the extension of the Dutch language and culture as far as the present political boundary.

Assimilation of the western "Overland," i.e. Low German districts was not difficult, but Charles never saw the present boundary as the final limit of Netherland expansion. Contacts with Cleve, with Bentheim, a small country southeast of Drente, with East Friesland, and even with Muenster were numerous. Some of these territories fell definitely within the sphere of interest of the Low Countries. In the XVIIth century, Dutch political influence and the Dutch language penetrated beyond the present boundary. The subsequent political evolution and the linguistic victory of High German over its competitors, finally made national and political boundaries coincide. *Post factum* this gave to the conquests of Charles V, the appearance of a final unification of the Netherlands. The latter expression, found in every textbook of Dutch history, is a perfect example of the interpretation of the past through the present.

Thus the desperate struggle between Charles of Guelders and the heirs of the Burgundians was more than an episode in the internal development of the Netherlands. It represented the first deliberate attempt to wrest a section from the vague Low German block of land and people. The Duke of Guelders showed some understanding of the peculiar character of his position. Besides mobilizing against the Habsburgs all discontented elements in Utrecht and Friesland, and assuming the leadership over the powerful city of Groningen, he turned constantly to the east to secure the support of Low German powers. He was active in the free cities of Bremen and Hamburg, as well as in Brunswig. Yet a purely personal conviction, to which he clung stubbornly, proved fatal to him. Nothing could have been more profitable to his cause than help from the new power of Lutheranism. Most of the North German cities, the princes of Saxonia, Hessen, and Lueneburg, and not a few episcopal princes had joined the Reformation. If Charles of Guelders had done the same, his cause would have become that of Protestantism, which the Emperor might defeat but could not conquer. But, even as leader of the anti-Burgundian faction, the duke of Guelders, educated in France and inclined to follow French examples, would not hear of turning Lutheran. He persecuted the Reformation in his own land even more savagely than did Emperor Charles in his part of the Low Countries. Naturally, the attempt of Guelders to side with the Imperial faction in religion while fighting it in politics was doomed to failure. It is of historical interest that French influence, which had helped the separation of the western Low Countries from Germany, was just strong enough to prevent Guelders from drifting to the German side in times to come.

In this last, desperate struggle for provincial independence, the ancient Frisian freedom was doomed. The "seven Frisian sealands," split into three units, two of which fell to Charles's Lowland principalities while one was thrown back into the orbit of the Empire. In vain the Frisians invoked their great charter, allegedly granted by Charlemagne himself. Even the confirmation of these supposed liberties by the Emperor Sigismund in 1417 proved of no avail. "Charlemagne's charter was sealed with a seal of butter and could not bear the sunlight," the enemies of Friesland mocked. The Frisians themselves contributed more to the downfall of their ancient free republic than their enemies. Continuous party strife during the XIVth and XVth centuries had brought in foreign elements. The counts of Holland of the Bavarian dynasty, the city of Groningen, and then Duke Albrecht of Meissen, general in Maximilian's service, had successively held control over Friesland in the name of one party or of another.

East of Lauwers Bay, the civil war strengthened the position of the village headmen to such an extent that from this chaotic period emerged a new aristocracy, involved in constant feuds. The treacherous waters of the Dollart Bay formed a natural hiding place for pirates with whom many of the local aristocrats agreed in their conception of good and evil and the best way to make a living. The trading centers of the neighborhood, Groningen, Bremen, and Hamburg could hardly look on idly while their merchants were despoiled by these lawless elements. Hamburg intervened in the region of the Ems, east of the Dollart. By political and economic measures Groningen extended its influence over the *Ommelanden,* the districts west, north, and east of its city walls. Thus, the land on the Ems, garrisoned by Hamburg troops, became a separate political unit under the leadership of the Cirksena family of Grietseel. In 1469, Emperor Frederick granted this family the title of count of East Friesland and rank among the princes of the Empire. West of the Dollart, Groningen extended its influence as far as Lauwers Bay. Thus, the Frisian lands were once more partitioned and the name Friesland finally restricted to three districts between the Lauwers and the Zuiderzee. Here, the language of the Frisians survives until today. Some of the ancient institutions too, retained sufficient vitality to remain in force under the new Habsburg administration.

By his war with Guelders, Charles not only made good his claim to Friesland but also acquired the territory of the bishopric of Utrecht to which he had no right whatever. The ecclesiastical principality was unable to defend itself against the constant incursions of Guelders troops. In 1528 the last prince-bishop ceded his secular possessions to the emperor, an unheard-of thing, for the lands of the Church could never be alienated. In 1527, Imperial troops had conquered and sacked Rome, taking the Pope prisoner. This made Pope Clement VII for a while a meek instrument in the hands of the Emperor, and Papal approval was readily granted to the cession of Utrecht. It remained to be seen whether the bishop's subjects were willing to acknowledge their new lord. The city of Groningen readily accepted the overlordship of Charles who supported its economic interests against those of the *Ommelanden*. City and countryside were united in a new province, *Stad en Landen,* a mésalliance of the worst type which for two centuries suffered from ceaseless family quarrels. The province of Drente, peasant country without a single town, was a union of six districts each divided into village communities in which the head of every family voted without regard to descent or rank. Although a few noblemen, so poor that for generations they provided the stock type of the aristocratic beggar, took part in all judicial and administrative affairs of the diet of their own right, the influence of the peasantry was predominant. The acceptance of Charles as lord of Drente changed nothing in the ancient form of local self-government of this faraway territory, hidden in the moors and off the main trade routes. All these provinces—Friesland, Groningen, Drente, and Overijssel—accepted Charles with relief born of freedom from constant warfare, but not without stipulating in formal deeds the full preservation of their liberties.

The same was true of Guelders, where before his death in 1538, Duke Charles saw his will flouted by the refusal of the States Assembly to accept his heir designate, the king of France. Instead they elected the duke of Cleve, Juliers, and Berg. This reformed the traditional Rhineland federation. Emperor Charles could not further postpone the conquest of Guelders, as the new duke was inclined to Protestantism and might introduce the Reformation in his states, thus bringing his predecessor's anti-Habsburg policy to a logical conclusion. In 1543 the Emperor attacked Juliers with superior forces and compelled the cession of Guelders by the treaty of Venlo which also contained explicit guarantees from the new prince to the States of Guelders for their freedoms. The Guelders episode in XVIth century Netherland history is of great interest because it established what proved to be the final boundary between Dutch and German territory and also because it throws light upon XVIIth century and XVIIIth century problems of Netherland history, especially the lasting contrast between the so-called "sea-provinces" (Holland and Zeeland) and the "land-provinces" (incorporated into the Netherland state through the war of the two

Charles'). After the subjugation of the northeastern provinces, the older and more natural federation of the coastal provinces remained distinct within the new combination of the "Seventeen Netherlands."

The Emperor sought to impress upon the outside world that the Low Countries now formed an indivisible political entity. The first step was a readjustment of their relations with the Empire, for which the Diet of Augsburg, convened after the defeat of the Protestant German princes, provided a favorable opportunity. A decision was reached by this Diet in 1548, providing that all the Low Countries under the rule of Charles V— by this formula Liége was excepted—would form a separate "Kreis" or administrative unit within the Empire, enjoying its theoretical protection in return for a modest annual payment. The States General saw to it that the payment remained as hypothetical as the protection. Moreover and this was far more important, the Low Countries were no longer subject to the jurisdiction of the Imperial Chamber of Justice—the Reichskammergericht. Brabant had been exempted as early as 1356. Flanders, after 1529 politically separated from France and incorporated into the Empire, had never been subject to it. Holland had assiduously ignored it. Nevertheless the judicial separation of the Low Countries from Germany was a most important step towards the recognition of their complete independence.

By securing the consent of all the provincial States Assemblies to a new law of succession, Charles provided against the possible partition of his new state. He still wanted to make a kingdom of the Low Countries, but he understood the aversion of his subjects to political innovation too well to press the point. He had made good all the legal claims he had inherited from the Burgundian dukes, and for the time being he was satisfied, although his government remained alert for the eventual openings that might lead to further expansion eastward. East Friesland could be claimed as a part of the original Frisian coastlands. The county of Lingen in Westphalia was actually acquired for the House of Habsburg but not incorporated into the union of the "Seventeen provinces." [20]

Charles who only occasionally visited his Lowland domains, was satisfied to leave a good deal of liberty to his representatives in Brussels, his aunt Margareta of Austria and later his sister Mary of Hungary. Besides these governors, members of the higher aristocracy served as *stadhouders,* lieutenant-governors in the provinces, as councilors and as military commanders. One man usually held several such offices. The technical work of administration was carried on by members of the gentry and of the burgher class, trained lawyers or members of hierarchy of the Church. Tedious and complicated questions of administration and finance were not to the taste of the higher aristocracy who in turn resented the influence of lower-class people in matters of high politics. The difficulty was solved by Charles in a decree of 1531, dividing the "Great Council" into two parts, the "Secret Council" for administration, and the "Council of State," a small group of personal advisors of high rank, for matters of general policy. This was a necessary reform, but it tended to create the impression that the high nobility had a right to the direction of political affairs and were the natural spokesmen of the people. They already considered themselves the defenders of the country in their military capacity as commanders of the *bandes d'ordonnance,* a cavalry militia recruited from the gentry and maintained at the expense of the States General. This extraordinary power concentrated in the hands of the high nobility was not to be surrendered without a struggle.

After 1543 the inter-provincial wars which had been the curse of the Low Countries during the Middle Ages, came to an end. Peace reigned and prosperity increased. Contemporary writers like the Italian Ludovico Guicciardini in 1567, could find no words to praise the prosperity of the Low Countries, the wealth of commerce and agriculture, the numbers of their cities, the butter, the cheese, the horses, the cattle, the trees along the roads. "Though Holland produces no wine," he said, "its inhabitants drink more of it than the people who grow it." "The butter and cheese," he continued, "represent a value equal to that of the spices brought by Portugal from the Indies." But visitors, once taken with admiration for a foreign country, tend to exaggerate. Our knowledge of the social and economic conditions prevailing in the Netherlands in the XVIth century, is still far from complete.

There is little doubt that the northern Low Countries suffered heavily from the civil wars during Maximilian's rule and from the wars with Guelders. The peasantry saw their crops destroyed on the fields. Many small cities were looted. For decades the Zuiderzee was unsafe for shipping because of Frisian partisans who plundered any merchantman with a valuable cargo. However, the general trend of social development was not interrupted. Free peasants working their own soil still predominated in the western coastlands and in Friesland. Tax records going back to the beginning of the XVIth century, permit a fairly accurate computation of land ownership. In Groningen one-seventh of the soil belonged to the monasteries and convents, while all other ecclesiastical institutions together possessed a little less than one-eighth. These Church lands were leased out to tenants whose position was more secure than that of modern tenant farmers. Of the remaining three-quarters of the soil, the majority was in the hands of free peasants. In Friesland, where the Church also possessed about one-fourth of the land, the nobility held only one-twelfth. In Hol-

land, the situation was much more complicated, for there the burghers of
the towns competed with the Church and the nobility in the acquisition of
land. Even so, the farmers were for the most part the owners of the land
they worked. We know that in the district of Rijnland 40,000 acres were
tilled by the owners as against 24,000 by tenants. The Church holdings
were only moderately large. In Uitgeest the Church possessed 3,500 out of
a total of 14,000 acres, which was a very high percentage, for usually its
landed property in this county amounted to no more than a tenth of the
total acreage.[21]

There were some two hundred noble families in Holland who possessed
ambachtsheerlijkheden, or seigneurial rights in the villages. But these
rights were limited: the levying of a head-tax on descendants of former
bondsmen, the income from highway tolls, fishing and hunting rights. All
these sources of revenue were fixed by tradition, usually at a low sum. The
seigneur was normally the principal landowner in his village, but the average extent of seigneurial lands was not more than four hundred acres.
Moreover, the influence of the nobility was limited and retroceding. In West
Friesland, the feudal system had never taken root. Around the cities great
inroads were made in it by the townspeople. The city of Amsterdam
gradually bought up the seigneuries around the city walls to have freedom
of expansion and control over the economic activities of the village people.

Perpetuation of a number of seigneuries in the hands of a single family
of the higher aristocracy further reduced the influence of the gentry as a
class. Four members of the higher aristocracy had extensive possessions in
Holland around 1550: Egmont, Nassau-Breda, Hoorne, and Brederode,
who together controlled (but did not own outright) 39,000 acres out of
a total of about 309,000 acres in Holland. The gentry of Holland formed
an upperclass without exaggerated pretensions or sufficient power to become oppressive, and had a real function in Holland society. Its members
lived in close touch with the burgher and the peasant class and were able to
represent the latter which as yet could not easily make its voice heard in
public. The gentry handled the more intricate problems of rural economy
and organization. They were usually the controllers of the dykes and
polders and were the entrepreneurs of new drainage systems. In Zeeland,
especially, their efforts in this direction were very assiduous.

The number of farms steadily increased and their average size decreased
accordingly. The countryside of Holland, prosperous as it was, could not
support its population. One means to remedy this would have been to
reclaim land from the sea and the inland waters but the first half of the
XVIth century was not propitious to so constructive a task. Great exertions
were made in Zeeland, where the island of Beveland expanded rapidly to

the west, but as much ground was lost in the east through the extraordinary floods of 1509, 1530, and 1532. The island of Overflakkee was truly created out of hitherto useless shoals. The island of Tholen, which had begun to take shape in the XVIth century—in 1411 the polder of Vossemeer, the traditional home of the Roosevelt family, was dyked in—grew nearly double in size. Gains and losses were nearly equal in this part of the country. Holland lost more than it gained. The first heroic attempt to close in part of the sea, the Bay of the Zijpe at Holland's northern point, an enterprise for which plans had been made as long ago as 1388, seemed doomed to failure, when in 1556, the direct intervention of King Philip II, son of Charles V, brought the work to a successful conclusion. A few small inland lakes were drained, but far larger ones were created by thoughtless peat-digging along Holland's eastern frontier. The chain of lakes and pools stretching from Utrecht to Naarden, east of the Vecht, was thus brought into existence.

It became more and more evident that the task of defending the country against the sea had outgrown the capacity of small local communities. Central, or at least provincial, control was instituted. Special funds were needed and this brought about the curious phenomenon of the "dyke-indulgence" of 1515. While traveling through Holland, Charles V, then only fifteen years old, noticed the bad condition of several important dykes. Learning that an indulgence had recently been promulgated in Rome to collect money for the new church of St. Peter and rightly thinking the dykes more important than even the most marvelous Renaissance architecture, he prevented the proclamation of the indulgence in the Netherlands and obtained from the Pope a similar favor for all who contributed to the maintenance of the dykes. At the same time Rome consented to the levying of a ten percent tax on all ecclesiastical income in the Low Countries for the same purpose. More than 75,000 ducats were received from the indulgence alone but, if we believe Erasmus, not a penny was spent on the dykes. In Holland large scale drainage and land-winning enterprises were undertaken only after a wealthy burgher class, willing to risk large capital in this rather speculative project, had developed in the towns.

The countryside of Holland and Zeeland may have been prosperous and its dairy production already important, but alone it could never give the provinces the exceptional position they gained within a few decades. The States of Holland gave the facts very clearly in a petition to the Emperor Charles:

"It is noticeable that the province of Holland is only a small country, not very long and still less wide, enclosed by the sea on three sides. It must

THE GREAT CRISIS OF THE SIXTEENTH CENTURY 109

be protected against the sea by dykes, which leads to great expenditure for
dykes, sluices, mills and moats. Moreover it contains many dunes, moors,
and inland waters which grow more extensive day by day, barren lands
unfit for fields or pastures. For these reasons the inhabitants with their
wives and children, in order to make a living must devote themselves to
industry and commerce in such a manner that they fetch raw materials
from foreign countries and export to Spain, Portugal, Germany, Scotland,
and especially to Denmark and the countries of northern Europe. From
these they buy enormous quantities of wheat. Consequently the main industry of the country is shipping and related trades, and from this many
people live, like merchants, skippers, sailors, shipbuilders, and carpenters."

The prudent representatives somewhat exaggerated the poverty of their
native soil to impress upon their sovereign how far-reaching the consequences of his foreign and financial policies might be for the welfare of his
subjects. Nevertheless their statement was true enough. A constantly increasing proportion of the people depended on the fisheries and the Baltic
commerce, with their related trades of shipping and handling salt, building ships and importing wood, producing hemp, importing tar, manufacturing naval equipment, and whatever was necessary to support the main
trades. Around 1560 Holland and Zeeland sent nearly 600 ships with crews
of twenty men each to the fishing grounds every year. Thus twelve thousand fishermen made their living from the industry besides numerous
craftsmen and dealers who drew their incomes from the same source.
Including the families of the fishermen and shore workers, more than fifty
thousand people in the two provinces depended upon the fisheries for their
living. Imagine a trade providing for thirteen million inhabitants of the
United States, and it will be possible to understand the full meaning of
Adriaan Coenenzoon's lines written in 1577:

> "This is why in my other great work on the fisheries I named the her-
> ring *Gratia Dei,* for people make this their daily food far more than any
> other fish, also because it brings so great a trade among our Netherland
> people who win their daily bread from it. We might as well call these fish-
> eries the Golden Mountain or the Triumph of Holland. Had Cicero lived
> in this country in the time of the herring, he would have found a more
> beautiful name for it."

The fishing boats spent half a year on the fishing grounds. The rest of
the time they traded as freighters with Norway and Spain and in the Baltic.
In the Baltic trade the Holland ships gradually outnumbered those of the
Hansa. In 1503, 850 out of 1,220 ships passing the Sund came from the
Low Countries, and 455 of these were from Holland. War, acts of piracy

by the Frisian partisans, and a general state of insecurity caused a decrease in the next thirty years. In 1545, 580 out of 934 ships sailing through the Sund were from Holland. In 1560 they numbered a thousand out of 2,730, but in 1565 they were 2,130 out of 3,480. After 1565 the outbreak of the political and religious disturbances caused another short relapse, preceding the era of greatest prosperity. The trade with Spain and Portugal, the counterpart of that in the Baltic, developed as rapidly.

The trade movement to the west is more difficult to follow from the available documents, than that to the east, where by levying Sund tolls the kings of Denmark provided convenient records for future historians. We know that trade with France and Spain had gained such importance by the middle of the XVIth century that a war with France caused to the people of Holland a loss of more than two million guilders in ships and goods at the hands of French privateers. We know also that the Netherland ships sailed far beyond Spain. In 1508, a Zeeland ship entered the port of Veere with a cargo of sugar from the Canary Islands. They did not venture into the Mediterranean until the end of the century. Nevertheless, before that date they did a considerable share of the Portuguese trade. The Flemings of Bruges and the Brabanders of Antwerp had been the principal financial backers of Portuguese overseas enterprises since the XVIth century. As already stated they had taken part in the colonization of the Azores. It did not take the shipping interest of Holland and Zeeland very long to take part in the commercial exploitation of the newly opened regions, first as freight carriers from Lisbon to the north, then, under charter from Portuguese merchants and under the Portuguese flag, for the carrying trade between Portugal and Brazil and the coast of Guinea.

Remarkable as was the steady expansion of commerce and shipping in Holland, it was matched by the economic organization of these trades. The ships and men mentioned in the records are from all parts of Holland. Small towns of the northern sector—Edam, Monnikendam, Enkhuizen, Medemblik, Hoorn—are frequently represented. That did not mean that commercial enterprises were equally scattered over the country. The people of all the coastal villages and towns had their share in shipping and fishing but they were mostly on the payrolls of the merchants of the larger cities, especially Amsterdam. The poor village people could never provide the capital required for these enterprises. Even for the herring fishing, besides the ownership of a boat, an outlay of a thousand to fifteen hundred guilders was required for every trip to the banks. Economically the northern countryside was dependent upon the merchants of Amsterdam.[22]

Here, on the roadstead of the IJ, the deep inlet of the Zuiderzee which nearly divided Holland into two parts, as many as 500 ships were at times anchored. Compared with Antwerp where 2,500 ships were often loading and unloading at one time along the quais of the Scheldt, the number was still small. But nearly all the vessels visiting Amsterdam were built and owned in Holland, while most of the ships plying the Scheldt were owned and operated by Hanseatics, Spaniards, and other foreigners. Amsterdam was a shipping center of importance, but until the wars of liberation, Antwerp remained the economic and financial center of northern Europe.

Holland, as pictured here, was still a country of seafaring folk and peasants, free and relatively prosperous if times were favorable, but not wealthy, with a scattered upper layer of society consisting of well-to-do, self-willed country aristocrats and of enterprising small-scale capitalists in the principal towns. The gentry stuck to their rights in the rural districts, and the city capitalists used all their influence and power to maintain their control over public affairs in the towns. The working classes, both seamen and landsmen, often protested against the growing exclusiveness of the ruling classes but with little chance of success. The central authorities favored oligarchy in city government. Resentment thus stored up played its part in the revolution of the last quarter of the century.

Conditions in the eastern provinces were different. The overseas trade of the IJsseltowns were rapidly declining, and the turmoil of the Guelders wars gave the deathblow to an economic activity which was already struggling without hope against the daring competition of Holland. The inland trade prospered, however, once peace was restored to the Rhine and IJssel lands. Deventer again became the center of the Westphalian export trade. Herds of cattle, oxen, cows, and hogs were driven overland from Holstein and Denmark. The yearly fairs were visited by more than 1,500 wagons from Muenster and Paderborn, from Hessen and Thueringen. Along the Rhine the products of the duchy of Berg and the county of Mark, now better known as the industrial area of the Ruhr, came via Cologne to Deventer, Arnhem, Dordrecht, and Nijmegen. Copper and iron, coal and charcoal were shipped down the river as they were in peace times in our day. Yet, the towns of the eastern Lowlands were far less important in the general economic structure of the Netherlands than those of Holland. In the east the rural nobility yielded greater power both in public affairs and in rural economy. The Veluwe, Guelders' northwestern forest district and the sandy plains of Overijssel, were the only places in the Low Countries where part of the peasantry still lived in bondage. The burden was not heavy and the bondsmen's rights guaranteed by customary law, for, where ancient customs and institutions remained in force, ancient freedom also prevailed.

The incessant and methodical interference of the central administration with local institutions resulted in a latent but ever present conflict between the representatives of the emperor and of the people organized in their social groups. The new monarchy was only a loose federation of autonomous provinces bent on independence, and in turn each province was hardly more than a union of towns and rural districts, with interests more often in conflict than in harmony. Under Charles V, when the prince had become an absentee overlord, it was no longer the ruler's personality but the States Assembly that in the eyes of the people represented the province as a political entity. The States naturally developed into a regular institution, a vital part of the governmental system, with their own officials and their own funds. The officials of the central government, the Council or Court, were regarded more or less as representatives of a foreign power. The conviction that the States not only represented but *were* the province, was nowhere stronger than in the newly acquired northeastern districts. Though conquered by force of arms they took the stand that they had recognized Charles as their prince freely and of their own will, and were his subjects by their own consent. They considered their acceptance of the Habsburg ruler in the nature of a contract, freely entered into and binding both parties by specific obligations. In 1533, Charles tried to institute a Council of Overijssel and to refer a number of cases to the Council as a Court of Appeal. The States of Overijssel declared that such institutions had never been heard of and simply ignored their existence. In Guelderland an identical struggle took place. The States had accepted the Council under their "contract" with Charles, but accused it of gross violations of their privileges. In 1560 the members of the States once more formed an "alliance" to oppose innovations. They even appointed a permanent committee to test the legality of every act of the Council. And whenever the princely councilors dared to mention "written" or Roman law, a storm of protest rose.

A common front formed against the prince did not mean union among themselves. Each province was the scene of conflicts of interest, of such frequency and violence that the country often seemed on the verge of civil war. First there was constant antagonism in the later Middle Ages between the laity and the clergy. The misdeeds of unworthy individual ecclesiastics and their abuse of spiritual authority provided a wonderful arsenal for the laity in their struggle against the privileges of the priests. Yet such abuses provoked the wrath of the townspeople less than the competition of the monasteries and convents in certain trades such as those in wine and beer, and in the manufacture and sale of clothing and household goods outside the guilds and below their fixed prices. The towns became more and more alarmed by the threat to their freedom and from the gradual but steady increase of land in the hands of the ecclesiastical institutions. Laws were passed and enforced for the correction of many of these grievances.

The constitutional position of the clergy was weak. Only in the province of Utrecht were they strongly represented in the States Assembly. In two other provinces, Friesland and Zeeland, they had some voice. All the other States Assemblies were composed wholly of laymen. The clergy reacted weakly, knowing that the central government favored the point of view of the laity. They contended that there was no reason to complain of their judicial immunities which were not respected anyway and declared they had often shown willingness to compromise in matters of trade and taxes. There was not much they could say because the shortcomings of the existing system were self evident. In 1514 a small town like Haarlem had seven monasteries and twelve convents, only a few of which could really justify their existence, even from the medieval point of view. Large monasteries with only a few monks in residence were no exception. The towns, the nobility, the central government in turn assailed the position and property of the Church. The future revealed which of the three was finally to gain from these attacks.

More damaging to general welfare was the antagonism between the urban and rural communities. The villages constantly fought the industrial monopolies of the towns, by manufacturing goods and selling beer and wine outside the jurisdiction of the guilds with their price regulations, and outside the city's power of taxation. The gentry upheld the rights of the countryside. The towns responded by buying up the suburban seigneuries and enforcing their repressive economic policy in the capacity of feudal lords. Life in the XVIth century towns was monotonous, and the citizens spent so much of their time in the taverns within and without the city walls, and drank such amazing quantities, that the taxes on beer and wine provided the towns with a most important source of income. The unrelenting efforts of the towns to repress and destroy all industrial activity in the countryside, made relations between these two sections of the population tense indeed. In Groningen, to quote a contemporary, "the city and its Ommelanden lived in such violent mutual dislike as had never been heard of either among the Turks or among mankind."

Town versus countryside was not the only conflict among XVIth century Netherlanders. Towns opposed towns and these interurban conflicts were matched by dissensions in each town among the inhabitants. It had always been the policy of the Burgundian dukes to foster oligarchy in the towns, to control the councils and the election of jurors and burgomasters. The often unruly guilds had been brought under strict supervision. Municipal finances nearly everywhere were disorganized as a result of the long wars, the heavy demands of the central government, and the rapid devaluation of gold and silver that followed the looting of the Aztecs and Incas by the Spaniards. A difficult period of economic transition ensued during which the ruling classes were naturally blamed for the difficulties. Having no voice in the city governments the guilds were constantly bringing pressure to bear upon the oligarchs, and there were other organizations that could speak for the citizens. Each town had to provide a *schutterij* or city guard for its own defenses. The citizens enrolled in this guard elected their own officers and often had their own buildings for social gatherings as well as for military exercises. When these *schutters* opposed the ruling oligarchy they had the armed force of the town at their back. They might have overthrown the existing system and installed a more democratic government, had not princely authority time and again supported the oligarchs, upon whom it relied for a radical reorganization and the subjugation to central authority of the contending groups and interests.

Against all these social factions with their individual rights stood the professional civil servants of the government in Brussels. They were lawyers trained in Roman law, fully convinced of the legal right of the prince to absolute sovereignty. They despised the traditional institutions and the imperfection of the ancient customary law. They interfered with the rendering of justice by the country gentry, referring as many cases as possible to provincial courts where matters were handled in writing and only a professional lawyer could find his way through the labyrinth of ordinances and statutes. They agitated against the privileges of the provinces, the cities, and the districts. These, however, were jealously guarded and now carefully collected, transcribed and entrusted to the care of officials of the States Assemblies. The State Attorney of Holland thus became, in the middle of the XVIth century, the first archivist of the province.

"It is strange," the States of Overijssel once said, "that our prince has undertaken to institute new officers and new authorities of which the people have never heard before, a practice never tolerated by the States of the province." "It is strange to conceive," the officers of the emperor said about the same time in Utrecht, "that His Majesty the Emperor and His servants are not allowed to inflict punishment on one of His subjects, even though an ecclesiastic, without the consent of His other subjects." These two statements contain the essence of the conflict that burst into open revolt in the second half of the century.

By the middle of the XVIth century there was enough inflammable material in the Low Countries to set the whole country ablaze, even without the great spiritual conflict that divided the people into two violently opposed camps. The Reformation started abroad, but found its first martyrs in the Low Countries. The various forms that opposition to Rome assumed were tested until the particular type of religious thought, best suited to the character of the people was found. Luther had the spontaneous support of part of the clergy, but as soon as Saxon Protestantism became better known in the Low Countries, it was criticized by the large majority of reformers there, finally to be rejected in favor of more individualistic and radical tenets originated in Alsace and in Switzerland. The Anabaptist movement found its most tragic expression in the Netherlands, where also its final creed and morality were determined. Apart from the adherents of the foreign forms of Reformation, a large group of Netherland intellectuals dreamed with Erasmus of a purified Church and shared his dislike of the stringent ties of church membership in its old as well as in its new forms. Reformers finally turned to Calvinism which offered a clear, logical, and democratic ecclesiastical organization with political principles acceptable to Netherland opinion. However, Erasmian trends of thought remained active and largely determined the religious future of the Netherlands. Thus, for their Reformation, the Netherlands turned from Germany to Switzerland and France, putting the final touch upon the separation of the Low Countries from the Empire. Later on in many places, competition between Calvinists and Lutherans coincided with that between the Dutch and High German languages.

The spread of the Reformation in the Low Countries is usually attributed to the ignorance and moral laxity of the Catholic clergy. The higher offices in the hierarchy of the Church were held by members of the gentry who coveted the income rather than the duties of the many offices for which the chapters of the churches provided handsome stipends. The lowest ranks, parish priests, vicars, and monks, were generally believed to be incompetent. Catholic authors themselves deplore the fact that ignorance of the people and other abuses made it easy for Protestantism to win over people otherwise well-disposed to the Church. Protestant authors see in the Reformation the liberation of the laity from the oppression of an almost wholly hypocritical priesthood.

Erasmus with his witty and sarcastic attacks on monks and priests, with his rancor against all monastic institutions, was largely responsible for this picture. There is no doubt that at that time abuses, even great abuses, existed in the Catholic Church, in the Netherlands as in all other countries. But those abuses had long existed and had not prevented the people being devoutly attached to their religious beliefs. As late as 1557, when Protestantism had already spread widely, a Venetian diplomat wrote from the Netherlands, "No other people show so great a devotion in attending the holy services." Those words do not justify the interpretation placed upon them that for practical reasons a large part of the people merely did lip-service to the established Church.

The first adherents of the Lutheran reformation were all priests; and the first Protestant martyrs, Hendrik Bols and Johan van Essen, executed in Brussels on July 1, 1523, were Augustinian monks. To them Luther dedicated the hymn in which he sang of God's miraculous works *zu Brussel in Niederland*. Many priests condemned the abuses of the Church, and people came to hear them which they would not have done had they not been seriously interested in the Church. From the pulpits the defenders and opponents of Rome violently attacked each other and created such unrest that the States of Holland, reluctant to resort to repression, sought to mitigate the prevailing animosity by requiring that all controversial points be omitted from the sermons. Among the people there was intense interest in religious affairs and a yearning for reform, kindled by a true understanding of Christian principles, but at times this interest took forms to which the secular authorities were even more averse than the ecclesiastic. In the very moment when the clergy of the Low Countries provided the first enthusiastic propagandists for reform without Rome, they also provided a Pope of Rome, Adrian VI, who too defended the vigor and integrity of Christian principles, but he fared no better with the officialdom of the Vatican than his religious opponents at home fared with the officialdom of the Emperor. Adrian was by no means, of course, the only devout and learned priest in the Low Countries to defend the Catholic Church. The university of Louvain, often described as a bulwark of brutal reaction and barbaric oppression, became more and more influential in the Catholic world. With all its abuses and its many unworthy members, especially in the higher ranks, the clergy of the Low Countries provided a great number of fervent and deeply religious men who, rightly or wrongly from our point of view, worked steadfastly and selflessly for reform within the Church or for reform without the Church.

No sudden eclosion of evil practices among the ecclesiastics distinguished the reformation period in the Netherlands from former centuries, but the different light in which these abuses were viewed when a better understanding of the principles of Christianity and a deepening of religious sentiment had penetrated to the masses of the people. The influence of the Devotio Moderna has already been mentioned. The printing press also played an enormous role in the dissemination of religious literature, and in the awakening of new and often conflicting views on religious dogma and practice. Where these disputations would lead, nobody knew. A splitting up of the great Christian community was not intended. For a while the whole membership of the Church seemed to be gathered in one great ecumenical council with free oral and written discussion throughout the Christian world. Both sides shared the sincere hope that the whole community would abide by the final outcome of this exchange of ideas among the faithful. The period of the reformation saw the culmination of a centuries old intensification and popularization of Christian religious opinions and theories. Some, however, considered that theological discussions were a wrong approach to the problem. They contended that, instead of clarifying the issue, the discussions merely added party strife to the already existing abuses. They followed Erasmus who had done so much to encourage criticism of prevailing conditions. His refusal to join the religious revolution did not spring from a bookworm's aversion to violent conflict, as has been said often. His views were clearly expressed when he wrote of the first Protestant martyrs:

> "I know not whether I must deplore their deaths or not. Certain it is that they died with great and unheard-of steadfastness, though not for the principles but for the paradoxes of Luther, for which I would not be willing to die because I do not understand them. I know that it is glorious to die for Christ. The pious always have to suffer, but among those who suffer the impious are also found. The skill of building oneself up as an angel of light is widespread, but rare is the gift of a discreet mind." [23]

Did he not mean that the wise and discreet reformer ought to realize that not by changing forms and inciting to violence, but only by the incessant inward and spiritual struggle of each individual could the needed reform of the Church be accomplished? For Erasmus it was the spirit, not the form, that counted. He held that an agitation which would see the established Church overthrown rather than give up one of its peculiar tenets was presumptuous. Separation would only result in the creation of new churches which after a while would present the same abuses as the Mother Church. Practice is by no means as easy as theory, as Erasmus learned when despite his concessions to one aside and another, he finally found himself rejected by both. But in the Netherlands, he had many sympathizers. The States of Holland, in forbidding the public discussion of religious issues, were prompted by Erasmian ideas.

Lutheranism spread everywhere in the Low Countries where contact with Germany was close. Merchants as well as mercenary soldiers spread it, as soon as whole areas of northern and western Germany had adopted it. But the thinkers among Netherland reformers soon turned to Zwingli and Anabaptism rapidly grew in strength among the masses, not only the poorer sections but also among the middle class. The reformers had to face the wrath of Emperor Charles V who as king of Spain and protagonist of Christianity against Islam and as protector of the Church could make no concessions. Moreover, his personal feelings were definitely on the side of Rome, its institutions and its dogma. Worse for the Netherlands, his conception of royal authority influenced by the glorious tradition of Spain, prompted him to make use of the established Church for the furthering of his monarchic interests. The Inquisition was well known in the Low Countries, but as an ecclesiastical tribunal. In 1552, the Emperor boldly decreed that Frans van der Hulst, councilor of the Court of Brabant, a layman and lawyer, would have power to prosecute all heretics, if necessary without regard for existing forms of justice. This innovation broke with all traditions. The decree immediately brought popular sentiment on the side of the persecuted by presenting the fight against heresy as an attack on the chartered freedoms. From the very first the religious struggle became entangled in a constitutional conflict.

Many governments of the cities, many noblemen, rural judicial authorities, and even the principal councils, otherwise loyal and obedient servants of His Imperial Majesty, rebelled against the new institution. The two "commissaries for the suppression of heresy," appointed out of the Council of Holland, soon asked to be relieved of this special duty. They said that they had seen enough misery and were tired of appearing as imperturbable spectators while poor people were put to the question and suffered torture. Reproved for allowing many unfortunates to escape, they replied, "You would have felt inclined to do the same if you had seen the poverty and wretchedness of the prisoners." Officers of the Inquisition who went through the villages to round up suspects usually found the culprits gone. Even so, a number of people were executed. First to die in the Netherlands were Willem Dirks and Jan de Bakker, the latter a priest. They were excuted in 1525 in Utrecht. Protestant martyrologies indicate by name 223 persons executed during the reign of Charles V. This figure is surprisingly low, considering the ruthlessness and extreme severity of the laws against heresy. It may come as a shock to readers who have innocently accepted the figures of excited contemporaries. "Thirty thousand in Holland and Friesland alone," a Venetian diplomat reported in 1546. The difference is partly explained by the fact that the list of 223 did not include the names of those who fell in the revolt of 1535, when in an outburst of frenzied fanaticism thousands of Anabaptists rose to establish the "Kingdom of Zion" on earth. Anabaptism was brought to the Netherlands by Melchior Hofmann who had been forced to flee from Strasbourg and had come to Amsterdam where, under the protection of the liberal city government, he gained many adherents until the Council of Holland could no longer tolerate his activities. After his decapitation, Jan Matthyszoon of Haarlem and Jan Beukelszoon of Leiden (John of Leyden) became the leaders.

In the winter of 1533, these two prophets of revolutionary reformation established an Anabaptist republic in Muenster in Westphalia, afterwards transformed into the "Kingdom of Zion" under the rule of Jan Beukelszoon. The revolution in Muenster was mainly the work of Hollanders and found strong support all over the Netherlands. At the end of 1534, Muenster sent out a call to arms. Four emissaries were sent to plant four "banners of war" in the Low Countries. Along the coastland fanaticism rose to such heights that in Amsterdam a revolt broke out and the Anabaptists occupied the town hall; and in Friesland they tried to convert the monastery Oldeklooster into a fortress. Both positions were stormed and the rebels killed in action or executed afterwards. Loose gangs of revolutionaries, moving aimlessly through the country, were dispersed by troops. Though many hundreds died in this revolt, the number must have fallen far short of the thirty thousand reported by the Venetian diplomat.

The Anabaptist revolt is often explained as a social revolution of the poor against the rich. The poor sought and found arguments for communism in the Bible; and growing impatient to see the millennium fulfilled, they resorted to violence. There is ample evidence of revolutionary social trends in Anabaptist teaching, and there is no denying the fact that the *result* of that teaching was revolution. On the other hand, it is incorrect to associate this whole religious movement with the social revolutionary agitation of a number of its adherents. Before Muenster fell, some prominent Anabaptists had already turned away from the excesses of violence and were trying to bring the new sect back to its original beliefs, the core of which was absolute individualism in the profession of Christianity with complete renunciation of all secular ties. Christianity, for them, was spiritual; and the establishment of an organized Church in daily contact with the institutions of secular power was the first step toward the profanation of all things sacred. Menno Simonszoon, pastor of Witmarsum in Friesland, became the principal leader of this purified Anabaptism.

Nor is it true that membership in the Anabaptist movement was restricted to the poorer classes of society. Among the adherents of the sect condemned by the courts in Holland there were many whose property was valuable enough to make its confiscation a matter of interest to the authorities. The truth may be that as soon as Anabaptism began its revolutionary agitation, many people joined the movement in the belief that revolution could only improve and never injure their position. These elements remained active even after the fall of the Anabaptist sect in Muenster. Professing adherence to the "Batenburger sect," they rapidly became common highway robbers who committed their crimes under religious slogans. Vehemently persecuted by the secular authorities and the Inquisition they were rapidly exterminated. This revolutionary Anabaptism did something to incline local officers of justice toward better cooperation with the hated Inquisition. This is borne out by the fact that ninety percent of the 233 names in the martyrologies are those of Anabaptists. Once the danger was past, however, the towns became as skeptical as ever of religious persecution.

Charles V must have taken the Anabaptist movement as definite proof that Reformation and Revolution were one and the same thing, that Luther's teachings threatened the State and society as well as the Church. Again ignoring local and provincial charters, he issued new, draconic decrees against all innovation in Church and religious affairs. A Protestant exodus resulted. Hundreds left Antwerp and the coastal provinces to find refuge in England. From northern Holland and Friesland other groups went to Emden, where they found an active Calvinist community under a Polish preacher, Johannes a Lasco. Here the Netherland Protestants, never in agreement with Luther and already strongly inclined towards Zwinglian ideas, rapidly went over to Calvinism. Here the printing presses were set in motion to produce hymn books, catechisms, and pamphlets that were to spread the new creed among those who had wavered and stayed at home to do lip service to the state religion. Other groups gathered in Cologne, in Wezel, and in Aachen. Thus were founded the refugee churches in which the Netherland reformation was moulded into definite form. From these centers just outside the national boundaries, some Netherlanders wandered south, to the Palatinate, to Alsace, and finally to Geneva where Calvin himself held sway.

The XVIth century in Netherland history was vibrant with life and full of promise for the future. Before Protestantism began really to spread, humanistic trends of thought had completely conquered the intellectual classes of society. Erasmus was naturally the standard bearer of this movement in northwestern Europe, but we must not be induced by his sarcastic references to the "barbarism" of his fellow-countrymen to believe that but for Erasmus the study of the ancient classics would not have flourished in the Netherlands. Besides Agricola and Gansfoort, who as philosophers and theologians influenced the intellectual and spiritual life of the fifteenth century, New-Latin poets added to the glory of the Netherlands. Peter van den Berg (latinized as Petrus Montanus) never rose above the modest rank of rector of schools in small towns like Alkmaar and Amersfoort, but he wrote audacious satires on the evil effect of monarchical rule. "Nothing is more depraved than royal power with its shameless abuses" is one of his favorite themes and he illustrated it with choice historical examples. Johannes Murmellius, also from the Low Countries and one of Montanus' successors at Alkmaar, wrote the renowned *Pappa Puerorum,* a Latin grammar. This became one of the best sellers of the XVIth century. In fifty years about 30,000 copies circulated in the Low Countries and Germany. The study of Latin was brought into direct contact with daily life. Unlike our modern grammars, which call for endless translations of meaningless little exercises with boring references to the noble character of Aristides or Scipio and the virtues of Roman soldiery, it attempted a direct introduction to the language. "Educators," Murmellius wrote in his preface, "must see to it that texts for the instruction of children are written in a simple and natural style and form. Otherwise the multiplicity of verbs will upset the mind of the pupil, just as too much food upsets the stomach." And exactly as the manuals handed today to American soldiers overseas, his booklet begins with ordinary topics of conversation, the renting of rooms, the teacher, quarrels among students etc. Latin taught in this way became a living language. Janus Nicolai Secundus (Jan Claeszoon in good old Dutch) mastered it so completely that his *Basia,* a classic of lyric literature, has been imitated and translated into many languages. Ronsard and Goethe are among the many indebted to his immortal work.

Sneer as he might that the Netherlands had produced no scholars of importance, Erasmus recognized that the general standard of education was comparatively high. The Netherlands did bring forth a number of scholars who could bear comparison with those of France and Italy. Georgius Macropedius (in Dutch: Joris van Langhveldt) taught for many years in the modest Latin school of 's Hertogenbosch. He was well versed in Greek, Hebrew, and Chaldean literature and wrote twelve Latin plays, comedies and dramas. The acting of Latin plays, usually picturing Biblical episodes or having a strong moral implication, was part of the humanistic educational system. The same kind of literature brought fame to Gnapheus, or Willem de Volker of The Hague, later driven from the Netherlands by the Inquisition. The time soon came when the Humanists were forced to choose between the Reformation and the Church of Rome. Erasmus avoided it as long as possible because he resented the idea that a final choice had to be made. This "Erasmian" point of view was long and tenaciously defended by generations of Netherlanders. Although doomed to failure it permeated Netherland thinking.

The greatest of the appeasers in the religious conflict was George Cassander of Kadzand, in Zeeland Flanders, born in 1513, who devoted his whole life to a vain attempt at reconciliation, only to be finally ousted and condemned by both Rome and Geneva. The prince of Orange and three successive Emperors supported him unavailingly. Cassander died in 1566, before the religious conflict had caused the general conflagration of Europe. Some of the Humanists sought to follow the Erasmian line. Others fervently supported either one or the other side in the conflict. One Netherlander among the early Jesuits rose to fame as the champion of the Counter-Reformation in Germany. This was Petrus Canisius of Nijmegen. Gerard Geldenhauer, secretary of the last Burgundian bishop of Utrecht and historian of the Batavi, whole-heartedly joined the Reformation, as did Gnapheus. Those who were stubborn in their refusal to choose between Protestantism and Roman Catholicism had to revert to subterfuge and hypocrisy. "If only," the famous Justus Lipsius wrote, "I could form my life to my own liking, I would live in solitude, amidst gardens and fields and study my books listening to the murmur of rivulets." Erasmus had also longed to sit in a garden with friends and discuss topics of eternal interest. The time was not ripe. Lipsius wandered from one university to another, from Protestant to Catholic institutions, admired for his knowledge of Tacitus but despised for his lack of moral courage. The time was to come when the educated people of the Netherlands could sit in their gardens studying philosophy and discussing literature, but it would mean that Netherland civilization was on the decline and with it, freedom and prosperity.

Janus Secundus, the greatest of Netherland New-Latin poets, counted among his friends another artist of international reputation, the painter Jan van Scoorl. Like Secundus, Scoorl was one of the artists who secured for the Netherlands their place in the picture of Renaissance civilization. The first native painters of Holland preferred to move south to the cultural centers of Bruges, Antwerp, and Brussels. The second generation produced Geertgen van Sint Jans, who helped to form the Leiden school of painting that a hundred years later gave Rembrandt to the world. By 1500 a number of artists of repute were working in the northern Low Countries. Jan Mostaert lived in Haarlem; Jacob van Oostzaenen in Amsterdam, and in 's Hertogenbosch one of the most remarkable painters of all times, Jeroen Bosch, gave free reign to his fantasy in the allegorical representation of sin and evil. Lucas van Leiden sold his first painting in 1508, when only twelve years old, and became the master engraver of Holland. The seeds that were to grow in the XVIIth century into one of the greatest schools of painting of all ages and all lands, were already sown.

It was a truly native art that flourished in the Netherlands. Few of the early Netherland painters saw as much of the world as Jan van Scoorl who traveled through Germany and Italy and who, as curator of the Papal museum of antiquities, under his fellow countryman Pope Adrian VI, made first hand studies of classic and Renaissance art. Italian models in-fluenced the art of the Netherlands but never so much that they affected its basic elements. Again the contrast between the art protected and sponsored by the court in Brussels and that produced by the people is noticeable. Bernaert van Orley, court painter in the first half of the XVIth century, followed almost exclusively the great models of Italy. The northern paint-ers, not uninfluenced by the same examples, relied mostly for the subjects and the details of their pictures on what they saw in the world in which they actually lived. The Netherland painters learned much from Italy, but only to master and assimilate what the south could teach.

His health gravely impaired, Charles abdicated in 1555, and divided his inheritance between his son Philip and his brother Ferdinand. The Spanish crown and all its possessions fell to Philip, Austria to Ferdinand. It would have been only natural for the Low Countries, organized as a separate entity within the Empire by Charles himself, to have been thrown in with Ferdinand's share. But Charles looked upon the Lowlands as first of all the property of his family. The interests of their people, of the Empire, of the northern branch of the Habsburg dynasty did not count. Spain was the core of his power. Spain would go to his son, and to strengthen her posi-tion, Spain was to have a fortress in northern Europe to outflank if need be both France and England. The holding of an advanced and exposed position sometimes saps the strength of the whole defense. That was what befell Spain in the XVIth century.

CHAPTER VII

"All This For Freedom's Sake"

ONLY a few years after the accession of King Philip, the first signs of the great Netherland revolt were clearly discernible. This most important of all periods in Netherland history began with a political revolution by the high aristocracy. It spread as an anti-Spanish and anti-clerical movement that found its principal adherents among the gentry and the burgher class. Finally, after a short period of repression, it led to a general revolt in which all elements of religious, political or social discontent participated. The numerous conservatives who chose to sacrifice part of their convictions rather than risk their whole position, or who could not conscientiously go the whole way with the revolution, were crushed in the conflict between Dutch Calvinism and Spanish Catholicism, two equally stubborn and equally narrow-minded factions. The outcome of the struggle was quite different from what any of the participants had expected. The Netherlands, instead of being reduced to a mere province of the Spanish Empire, of falling under the control of France or England, or of increasing the number of Protestant principalities within the German Empire, emerged from the struggle as an independent republic of great power, with a strong tradition of freedom and a firm belief in its own strength and ability to maintain itself among the great powers of Europe. In a single generation a group of shipowners and merchants of moderate wealth grew into a political power that seriously resented the slightest infringement of its sovereign rights by ancient and powerful monarchies.

The dramatic character of this struggle for freedom, its unexpected outcome, the liberalism of the principles proclaimed by its leaders, form such a marked contrast to the equally dramatic developments in Spain—the sudden decline of this great monarchy and the intolerant character of its ruler—that the Netherland revolt ranks as a classic episode in European history. Scores of Netherland writers have devoted many folio volumes to its description. Most renowned of these native historians was Hugo Grotius. Numbers of foreign writers too were attracted by the subject. Events in the Low Countries were followed with such passionate interest all over Europe that nearly eighty non-Dutch contemporary chroniclers are recorded. The eighty years' war in the Low Countries left its trace in Spanish literature as in Spanish historiography. Lope de Vega wrote a dramatic play on the siege of Maastricht (1579) and showed a more adventurous interest in the Low Countries by taking part in the expedition of the Invincible Armada. Calderon fought in the Spanish army besieging Breda and made the episode the subject of one of his plays.

Italian Humanists found in the Netherland revolt material and inspiration for imitations of Livy. German authors from Rostock to Basel, from Brunswig to Austria, chronicled events in the Low Countries in the style of modern reporters. Jacques Auguste De Thou was the most prominent of the French historians on the subject. The English contributed less to the historiography of the revolt, perhaps because the intellectual elite in England was satisfied with the Latin and French versions of the story. But that the Netherland leaders attached great importance to the English people's being well informed, is born out by the fact that they had all of their principal political pamphlets translated into English and circulated in the British Isles. It was no mere exaggeration on the part of the Dutch chronicler Reyd to write that even "Turks and Moscovites followed the events in the Low Countries with divided interest."

What was a stirring dramatic episode for contemporaries, became a glorious historical inspiration for future generations who saw in the war between the Spaniards and the *Gueus* a conflict between tyranny and freedom. The Netherlands were represented as the traditional battlefield of the forces of light and darkness, of liberty and oppression, of despotism and humanity. Friedrich von Schiller grasped the dramatic possibilities of the subject in his *Egmont*. He began writing the history of the revolt as the story of a people not born for heroism but magically lifted above their natural selves by the inspiring ideal of freedom. Little fitted for assiduous historical research, he dropped the subject after merely touching upon its beginnings. The same idealistic version of the war, in this case based upon a deep respect for the inherent freedom-loving qualities of the Netherland people, was expressed by the Bostonian John Lothrop Motley, undoubtedly one of the greatest advocates the Netherlands ever had.

In his *Rise of the Dutch Republic,* Motley had left a vivid, sometimes fierce account of the outbreak and the progress of the revolt. His book is an expert English paraphrase of the XVIIth century Netherland version of the history of the revolution, with masses of new material added from European archives. He shares the partisan viewpoint of most of his early Dutch sources and at times exceeds them in partiality, for his XIXth-century liberalism is even more foreign to Spanish ideals and methods than was their XVIIth century Calvinism. Motley's book, though superseded in numerous details by later research and no longer acceptable as an interpretation of the facts, gives a good account of the outward progress of events, and the excellence of its style makes any attempt at improvement hazardous. That more stress may be laid upon interpretation in the light of recent investigations, a summary of the principal occurrences will here suffice.

Philip II, king of Spain, was the fourth prince of that name in the Netherlands, belonging to the Burgundian-Habsburg dynasty. He was born in Valladolid and educated in Spain where he learned to esteem Spanish ideals and the Spanish way of life above all others and became intransigeant towards foreign ideas. Even had he been willing to respect the rights and customs of his non-Spanish subjects, he was unable to understand what their national habits and institutions meant to them. Philip has been described as one of the most sinister characters that ever ruled a monarchy, but modern research and more impartial appraisal have, so to speak, rendered him to humanity. He was definitely no more cruel than many of his contemporaries, let alone earlier and later despots and party leaders. From birth he was associated with trends and policies that mankind was just learning to abhor. Many a year passed however, before the Spanish methods of Philip's day were generally recognized as wrong. That came in the late nineteenth century, and since, Philip's memory was generally loathed.

Philip's administration and policy presented two marked characteristics. One of these, difficult for us to understand, was generally accepted in his time; the other, easy enough for us to understand, was somewhat unintelligible to his contemporaries. The latter was his firm belief in bureaucratic methods, his dislike for oral discussion, his reluctance to leave the handling of all details to his officials. He was a fanatic for files and memoranda, three hundred years before the typewriter and the telegraph. This technique of written administration, destructive of all personal contacts, was perhaps more irritating to the higher aristocracy of his state than his claim to absolute monarchy. The haughty nobles of the higher aristocracy, who persisted in believing themselves the king's peers, were already romantics clinging to the past. They might have been satisfied if only appearances had been kept up, if the writing desk had not been so conspicuously substituted for the conference table.

The other characteristic of Philip's rule was the constant and complete intermingling of religious and political affairs. In his mind apparently the Spanish monarchy as well as the Catholic Church represented Absolute Truth. They were not two but one. His view being the true one, there could be no other truth and no other possible policy than his own. And so he never hesitated to use the Church for political purposes any more than the kingdom of Spain for the defense of the Church. However, being king of Spain before being protector of the Church, he had to strengthen the monarchy before the Church could be defended. To some extent this explains his often apparently hypocritical policy. Self-evident as this policy may have been to the king, it was certainly obscure to every one else from his Protestant enemies to the Pope himself.

With his kingdoms, Philip inherited a war. French armies were threatening the southern frontier of the Low Countries. In two battles, in which Philip's Spanish and Lowland forces fought loyally side by side, France was defeated. The ensuing treaty of peace of 1559 relieved Philip of a heavy burden. The war had strained his financial resources to the breaking point and had kept him in Brussels when he longed to return to Spain. He could not leave, however, before obtaining additional financial support from his provinces in the Low Countries. The negotiations for these subsidies gave the king a foretaste of what was to come. The States General, convened first at Valenciennes then at Brussels, agreed to disburse after the usual tergiversations and remonstrances but only if the money thus provided were considered public funds and not royal property. In token of this, its administration was to remain in the hands of a committee of the States.

This was the first clash between two wholly opposed conceptions of government of the Low Countries. Basically the question was whether the provinces would be self-governing in the fullest sense of the word, or accept the leadership of the monarch? Even if the royal leadership respected all institutions and privileges not wholly incompatible with the general aims of monarchical policy, it would still be inacceptable to the provinces unless those general aims concurred with their own. This meant that the Low Countries, in the opinion of the States, ought to be allowed to follow their own foreign policy within the Spanish empire and to handle internal problems according to their own national wishes. Fundamentally this was the same desire for neutrality in European politics as had been first expressed in the county of Flanders in 1340.

In Philip's war against France, Holland and Zeeland had been left to their own devices to resist French privateering against their merchant and fishing fleets. The interests of the country as a whole demanded a policy of friendship with England regardless of the personal feelings of King Philip, widower of Queen Mary Tudor and rejected suitor-for-political-reasons of Elizabeth. The expanding maritime interests of Holland and the trade of Antwerp could not afford to be subjected to the attacks of English privateers every time King Philip chose to disagree with his selfwilled sister-in-law. Moreover the northeastern provinces, which had reluctantly recognized Philip's father as their territorial lord, could find no mention in the treaties of recognition of using their money and blood to protect His Majesty's Italian possessions against the ambitions of the king of France.

Philip temporized. If he could but obtain the much needed funds, he might disregard further complaints of his subjects. But his subjects insisted that their complaints be heard and decided to prescribe the use of the subsidies just granted and how the defense of the country should be organized. They resolved never to bear the cost of wars for the protection of other parts of the Spanish empire. Then they advanced their views on the attitude to be taken towards encroachments by the State-controlled Inquisition on the judicial prerogatives of the provinces.

All this was radically repugnant to Philip's conceptions of his monarchical power and of his duties as a Catholic prince. He seems to have believed that if he won over the higher aristocracy by generosity and flattered the people by display of clemency, he might gain support that would enable him to strike, as soon as peace was concluded, against the recalcitrant gentry and ruling burgher class. Heavy taxation followed the granting of the new subsidies, but various members of the higher aristocracy were exonerated and even had former tax payments refunded. To appease the people of Antwerp, the intransigent foe of heresy went so far as to restore five Antwerp Protestants to liberty. And yet, when Philip left the Netherlands, he found himself in the almost complete disagreement with both the aristocracy and the States. In vain had he bestowed upon individual members of the aristocracy high honors, large money-grants, great offices in the Council of State, governorships of provinces, even commands over Spanish regiments. As a class the aristocracy refused to yield to his blandishments. Individually they accepted the appointments and the honors, all except the command over Spanish troops. As a class they wanted to know what their real influence in the government would be. The States General, when the king took leave of them, emphasized this attitude, demanding a national government, a national army, a national policy. As Philip prepared to leave for Spain, no specific cleavage existed, only deep discord. Before the king had actually sailed from Flushing, a conflict arose.

Philip's conception of the relationship between Church and State, and the mutual assistance they should render each other in creating the ideal political and religious order, that he believed the only true one, is nowhere more apparent than in his reorganization of the Catholic hierarchy in the Low Countries. In 1559, Philip obtained from Pope Paul IV a Papal decree under which the Low Countries, until then included in the archdioceses of Cologne and Rheims, were organized into the three new archdioceses of Cambrai, Malines and Utrecht and fifteen dioceses. The boundaries of the combined archdioceses coincided with the political boundaries of the Burgundian Lowland State—except Luxemburg. This organization was never carried into full effect, but it did mark a decisive step in the formation of the Low Countries as an independent national unit in Europe. Henceforward all non-Netherland ecclesiastical influence, except that of Rome itself, disappeared from the northern Low Countries. Groningen no longer belonged to the diocese of Muenster, or Nijmegen to that of Cologne. The Netherlands had received a national ecclesiastical organization.

That aspect of the situation was of no interest to contemporary Netherlanders. They were far more concerned with other aspects of the Papal decree, which was virtually a concordat with the king. Besides the new territorial division, the decree provided that the nomination of the bishops would be subject to the king, and that the king provide emoluments for the new dignitaries. This he certainly would not do out of his own funds. The States of the provinces questioned the king's right to make such a covenant. Nothing of the kind had been foreseen in the "Contracts" by which the northeastern provinces acknowledged Charles V, and so those provinces held it to be illegal. Finally the decree called for the incorporation of some ancient monasteries into episcopal domain, thus making the bishops appointed by the king representatives of the monasteries and as such members of the States Assemblies. This was revolution from above. It directly attacked the independence of the States Assemblies. If this reorganization were carried out, the Netherland Church would become a state institution. In a most impolitic way, that showed how far Philip was from understanding the situation in the Low Countries, he emphasized the political aspect of this reorganization by appointing as archbishop of Malines and Primate of the Low Countries, the chief political advisor of the government, Antoine Perrenot, seigneur de Granvelle, former bishop of Arras, an ecclesiastic of worldly inclination.

A greater mistake Philip could hardly have made. Upon leaving for Spain he entrusted the administration of his northern European state to his sister Margareta, Duchess of Parma, and to the Council of State. Within this Council he appointed an inner council or "consulta" of three members, of which Granvelle was the absolute leader. He requested Granvelle to correspond with him directly, thus reducing the duchess of Parma without her knowledge to a secondary role. Although she was the nominal head of the government, decisions were to be discussed and prepared between her king and her prime minister. This same minister was also the head of the Church and was soon honored with the dignity of Cardinal. From Philip's point of view in which Church and State were one and incarnate in the person of the Spanish monarch, the appointment was ideal, for it expressed his great principle of administration. From the Netherland point of view it was proof that the king would never recognize the multiplicity of forms in Lowland political life, and that the Church was not of God but of the world. Within a few years the antagonism between the king and his subjects became irreconcilable. Either the monarchical principle or the constitutional one must triumph.

In the first five years after Philip's departure the conflict took the form of a clash between Cardinal Granvelle and the aristocracy. Against the "prime minister" the seigneurs formed a "league" of mutual assistance. The form and character of the opposition reminds one of France, where exactly the same situation occurred in the late XVIth and again in the XVIIth century. Like the Condés and Bouillons in France, the Egmonts, Lalaings, Nassaus and their associates in the Low Countries, organized a "Fronde." The same causes produced the same reactions in France and in the Low Countries. In its reorganization King Philip's centralized monarchy in the Netherlands, built after the French model, had outdistanced France herself. The reactions that were to shake France in the XVIIth century revolutionized the Low Countries fifty years earlier.

The "Frondeurs" of Brussels showed the same lighthearted extravagance, the same impudent arrogance, the same love for a theatrical display of resentment as the French nobility were to show in their fight against Mazarin. Reveling with their friends and retainers from the lower gentry, they drank to the downfall of the cardinal and coined "bon mots" at his expense. They paid and protected the writers of libelous pamphlets in which the cardinal was mercilessly attacked. They did not trouble to disguise their political schemes and openly sought contact in Germany and France with nobles of the same class, presenting their struggle in the Low Countries as the common cause of the nobility against any restriction of their rights by monarchical power. While undermining the authority of the cardinal, they vigorously opposed all schemes to involve the Low Countries in the great political enterprises of the king. They prevented armed intervention in the French civil wars, which the king had commanded to be made by Lowland troops. Philip, lord of one of the richest countries of northern Europe, had to admit that its power, though legally his, could not be used to further his foreign policy.

In similar conflicts in France at a later date, Richelieu and Mazarin vanquished the aristocratic opposition with the support of their king. Granvelle's position was far more difficult. He received little sympathy from the duchess of Parma, and when she was won over by the opposition and persuaded that all difficulties would vanish if the cardinal were removed, even King Philip could no longer maintain his faithful and devoted minister. In 1564 the king asked him to go to Burgundy, and from there he was sent to Italy. His departure left the duchess of Parma, now the sole representative of the king, dependent on the powerful nobles who claimed to be the leaders of the nation and were now able to make good their promises.

The higher aristocracy, however, was by no means representative of the people. With few exceptions they were all Walloons. Not only were they ignorant of the mother tongue of the large majority of the people, but they sprang from social surroundings entirely different to those prevailing in the northern and western parts of the country. The Walloon nobles excelled in chivalry throughout the Middle Ages. They were hostile to France from whom they feared aggression, but even so they were saturated with the traditional ideals of western chivalry which found its models in France. They knew that they would have to reckon with the interests and wishes of the burgher class of the western provinces, but this did not mean that they respected its members or wanted to be associated with them. They were equally averse to associating with the gentry, whom they might employ as retainers but would not treat as equals. Of those who were not Walloons one, the count of Mansfelt, a German prince in the service of Brussels, had no strong convictions in Netherland politics. Another, Lord Brederode, might be considered a Hollander, although he was born in Brussels. A third non-Walloon member of the higher aristocracy was Lamoraal, count of Egmont, of great military fame and a descendant of one of the oldest families of Holland, but related to the Walloon nobility through his mother. Most of his estates were situated in the southern Low Countries, and his lieutenantship of Flanders linked him still closer to the South. The outstanding figure among the aristocrats was William of Nassau, prince of Orange, of Rhineland descent.

Born in 1533 at Dillenburg in the county of Nassau, the son of Count William and Juliana of Stolberg, he had been designated heir to all the Nassau estates in the Low Countries by his cousin René of Breda and Châlon, prince of Orange. The Nassaus had come to the Low Countries at the beginning of the XVth century when Engelbert I married the heiress of the House of Polanen, Lords of Breda. His grandson Engelbert II, the great friend of Maximilian, largely extended his estates through the benevolence of that prince and acquired the domains of Diest and Sichem in southern Brabant. He bequeathed his lands and titles to his nephew, Henry of Nassau, of the Rhineland branch of the family. The new Lord of Breda rose even higher in the favor of the Habsburg rulers than had his father. He represented the Habsburg interests at the meeting of the German electors in Frankfurt in 1519 to choose a successor to Emperor Maximilian. He was

Imperial ambassador to France and England and commander of the army that invaded France in 1536. He married the granddaughter of another famous commander of the Imperial troops, Philibert, count of Châlon and prince of Orange, who in 1527 under the command of the duke of Bourbon had stormed Rome and stabled his horses in the Sistine Chapel. Through this marriage the Nassaus acquired the principality of Orange in southern France, which gave them sovereign rank. Hendrik's son René, prince of Orange and Châlon, Lord of Breda and Diest, fought and died in the service of Charles V. He left all his estates to his eleven-year-old cousin William, the eldest son of the count of Nassau. As a member of the higher aristocracy of the Low Countries his further education was supervised by the duchess of Parma herself. His patrimony of many families was still further enlarged when young William married Anna of Buren, the daughter of one of the Emperor's most loyal generals. Through this marriage he obtained control over other large estates in Zeeland, Guelders, and Holland.

By 1550 William of Orange was the richest nobleman of the Low Countries. Favored by Charles V, he took part from his youth in all important political discussions. He commanded part of the cavalry at the battle of St. Quentin, and was among Philip's representatives who negotiated the treaty of Chateau-Cambrésis in 1558. The king honored him with the lieutenantship over Holland, Zeeland, and Utrecht, made him marquis of Antwerp and gave him a place on the Council of State. Royal grants of money and tax-exemptions somewhat relieved the prince's financial position, which in spite of his enormous income was strained by careless spending. In 1564 his household alone cost 44,000 pounds and 256 people were on his civil list for personal services. Though one of the youngest members of the higher aristocracy, the prince of Orange was its most prominent leader. He owed this position to exceptional intellectual ability, a quality only too rare among his class. The ousting of Granvelle from the Government of the Low Countries had been largely his work. His opponents nicknamed him "the Silent" meaning to convey that he did not speak his mind, but astutely concealed his real thoughts under pleasant and meaningless conversation.[24]

Leading the aristocracy in constructive work proved far more arduous than rallying them for opposition. The nobles knew approximately what they did *not* want to do, but were completely at a loss when obliged to formulate a constructive policy. They did not want the Inquisition or any religious persecutions. But they were helpless when confronted with the problem of maintaining order after Catholicism and Calvinism, equally unwilling to tolerate "heretic" beliefs, began their struggle for supremacy.

The nobles were willing to obey the king, but they wanted to rule alone. Inevitably the problem arose of what to do if the king disagreed with them? If they submitted, their independence was gone. If they disobeyed his orders, they must be willing to accept the ultimate consequences of their policy—revolt. Of all the aristocrats, Brederode alone never hesitated. Rough and adventurous, never favored by the king and so without any feeling of personal indebtedness towards him, he rejoiced at the idea of armed revolt in the "great tradition" of his ancestors who, anti-Burgundian since the earliest days of party strife in Holland, had fought with Jacqueline of Bavaria against Philip II of Burgundy, and with Philip of Cleve against Maximilian of Austria. Monarchical tradition prompted the Croys and the Lignes to side with the king as soon as they saw in what direction things were going. Egmont, always helpless in politics, refused either to desert the king or to follow him, thus forfeiting everyone's friendship. Amidst this hopeless division, the prince of Orange tried his best to preserve at least a semblance of unity.

Discontent was wide spread in the Low Countries, but there was only one strong and determined opposition group, the Calvinists who opposed the king on political as well as religious grounds. They had what neither the Lutherans nor the Anabaptists had, an organized church well disciplined in matters of doctrine and morals. Again and again their leaders in Geneva pressed upon them that they had to obey God rather than their prince, and laid down general rulings on the rights and duties of the people towards their secular lord, but leaving particular decisions to the consciences of individual congregations. Those rulings included the right to revolt whenever a prince persecuted the Church of God or oppressed his people, provided that not the people or private citizens but someone invested with legal authority took command. Calvinism gained strength rapidly in the southern Low Countries after coming out into the open in France, where it defied the royal authority under the illustrious leadership of the prince of Condé. In England the death of Queen Mary had left the crown to Elizabeth, who tolerated Calvinist refugees from the Low Countries, and even permitted them to practice their religion publicly. These events encouraged the secretly organized Calvinist churches at home, which with the help of returned exiles rapidly propagated the new creed. Once the Inquisition had been stopped, the breaking up of national religious unity could no longer be prevented except by the wholesale slaughter of dissenters.

The majority of the aristocracy still hesitated. Was religious tolerance to be introduced? The prince of Orange declared in the Council of State that an end should be made of "the arbitrariness with which kings determine and direct the religious sentiments of their subjects," but the novelty of this idea shocked even his own colleagues and supporters. Exactly at this moment the Church of Rome further defined its dogma at the council of Trent. Evasion of the dogmatic issue was no longer possible. The introduction of the decrees of Trent was bound to sharpen the conflict in the Low Countries, and Philip ordered them applied. The aristocracy, enjoying the good things of this life too much to be bothered with problems of the life hereafter, failed to grasp the deadly seriousness of the two extreme points of view. By negotiating and compromising they hoped to find some way out of the dilemma. Perhaps permission to worship in their own way would satisfy the reformers; perhaps King Philip would be satisfied with an outward show of religious unity. In these vain hopes they deceived nobody but themselves.

The Council of State decided to send Egmont to Spain to place the views of the aristocracy before the king. This was a marvelous choice indeed. The conceited Egmont with his less than average political intelligence went as special ambassador for a group that had no clear-cut policy. While he traveled, feasted, visited the king in the Escorial, listened to the flattery of the Spanish grandees, every day more filled with pride, others acted. The Calvinist congregations, still hiding from the Inquisition, had managed to form a synod with a few executive officers. They indignantly rejected every compromise in religious matters, reasserting their dogmatic beliefs in the same way the Catholics had reasserted theirs by accepting the decrees of Trent. The policy of the prince of Orange, champion of tolerance, was too vague for them. The Calvinist congregations knew what they wanted and knew they would never obtain it from the king except by force. To gain their point they needed men of the sword. Calvinist leaders of the Walloon nobility approached Louis of Nassau, brother of the prince of Orange.

The prince, concerned by the pre-eminently Calvinistic character of the new agitation, advised moderation. Under his influence the leaders modified their program to make it acceptable to Catholics. In its new form it was circulated among the gentry of the Low Countries where it received enthusiastic support, nowhere more than in the northern coastlands, in Holland and Friesland. Thus the league, or "compromise" of the nobles came into being. On April 5, 1566, hundreds of its members marched in solemn procession through the streets of Brussels to the residence of the duchess of Parma to present a petition against the continuance of religious persecution. This most unusual political demonstration made an enormous impression on both government and the people. The army, the national cavalry militia, by hundreds of its members, was demonstrating against the administration. Actually this was the beginning of a revolt. The helpless duchess of Parma, advised by the Council of State and the aristocracy, hesitated and finally refused to act either one way or the other. The *Ligue des seigneurs,* so harmoniously united in opposition, split immediately when the final issue of obedience or revolt was put squarely before them. Orange and a few of his friends knew full well that support of the gentry might involve them in armed resistance to the government, yet were willing to put loyalty to political principles above personal allegiance to the king and Church. Egmont and the majority of the aristocrats shrank from disobedience to the prince whom they as his vassals, had sworn to follow.

The helplessness of the government immediately brought the Calvinists into the open. All over the southern part of the Low Countries congregations held their meetings, usually outside the precincts of the towns. Large numbers of exiles returned, burning with resentment against the Spanish regime that had driven them from their homes. Funds, collected for seemingly innocent purposes, were really to enable Louis of Nassau to engage thousands of mercenary soldiers in Germany. The watchwords of revolution were coined. Staunch supporters of the regime had given the protesting nobles the name of *gueus*—beggars—not because they were in financial straits as has often been suggested, but because in the eyes of the conservatives, they had put themselves outside the pale "good society" by siding with trouble makers, outlaws and revolutionists, as today people who never dream of sharing their wealth with others are called "communists" by their opponents.[25]

The name was taken up by the opposition and *Vive le gueus* became its slogan. The "Songs of the Gueus" spread from town to town and some of them are still the national songs of the Netherlands. Political tension rose to such heights that the agitation could no longer be controlled. The prince of Orange, anxious to avoid an open revolt for which he felt the country was not prepared, rushed from one danger point to another, from the meetings of the gentry to the city of Antwerp seething with agitation, from conferences with the Calvinist leaders to the Council of State. He gave advice to the duchess of Parma and recruited troops against her all at the same time.

In distant Spain, King Philip, watching Netherland events closely, saw the mistake he had made in recalling Granvelle and leaving the administration to the aristocracy. He refused, however, to do what his father had done in a similar case—rush north and put an end to all uncertainty by personal intervention. He waited. He wanted the aristocracy to involve themselves deeper and deeper in political confusion, so that afterwards the retribution might be more thorough. He left the duchess of Parma in the most impossible position, without support and virtually without instructions. Then the fanaticism of some of the Calvinists suddenly brought all the plans and calculations of the opposition to nought and restored the authority of the regime. In August 1566, working people in western Flanders, inflamed by violent denunciations of the Church of Rome by Calvinist preachers, stormed the churches, breaking the images, destroying liturgic vestments, desecrating all that was sacred to Catholics. With the rapidity of lightning the movement spread northeastward until it reached Amsterdam and Groningen. For a moment the nation and the government were dumbfounded at the audacity of what was after all only a small minority. Realizing that in many towns the magistrates had tolerated if not encouraged the iconoclasts in their destructive work, that part of the militia was in sympathy with the Calvinists and on the verge of revolt, that many of the aristocrats were unwilling to take part in forcible repression, the duchess of Parma decided to grant freedom of worship to both Lutherans and Calvinists. Her concessions were answered by fresh demands. Her attempt to collect a small force caused the Calvinists to assemble a military force of their own, the command of which they entrusted to Brederode. Civil war was inevitable. When it broke out the hopeless weakness of the revolution was revealed in a few short weeks. It was now the duchess who could rally around herself all discontented elements: Catholics who saw that "tolerance" would mean subjugation by Protestants; members of the league of the nobles who mistrusted the leadership of Brederode and Louis of Nassau; aristocrats disgusted with Calvinist radicalism; even Lutherans who feared the intolerance of the Calvinists. Philip, deeply shocked by the outbreak of iconoclasm, provided the duchess with badly needed funds. On the side of the revolution leadership of unity, purpose, funds and troops were lacking. Brederode, more a braggart than a gentleman, proved a complete failure. Orange, seeing the revolutionary cause lost, tried to stop the revolt before it had really begun in the hope of saving thousands from the gallows and from exile. A few minor skirmishes and all was over. Hundreds of prisoners were hanged. Left without pay, most of the rebel soldiers had deserted before going into action. The revolt was crushed and, from all over the Low Countries, endless trains of horses and wagons carried the Calvinists into exile. With them went thousands of non-Calvinists, so deeply committed to the revolution that they dared not face the restored royal authority. With them went William of Orange.

The duchess of Parma had scored a complete success. The decrees against the Reformation were again enforced. It was now her task to pacify the country, re-establish confidence among the people, revive sentiments of loyalty towards the prince. But at that very moment King Philip ordered Fernando Alvarez de Toledo, duke of Alva, to lead a punitive expedition against the Low Countries. Once more the king showed his complete lack of understanding of Lowland problems. He thought the Lowlanders sufficiently humbled for him to complete the task begun by his ancestors of the Burgundian dynasty—the establishment of a centralized monarchy over and above the local autonomies.

In the early fall of 1567, the duke of Alva, with over ten thousand Spanish and Italian soldiers, arrived in Brussels. His commission gave him the title of commander-in-chief of the royal troops in the Low Countries under the authority of the duchess of Parma. Actually it invested him with all the powers of government. The duchess, suspecting the real purpose of his coming and deeply offended that she, under whose leadership the revolt had been crushed, was now deprived of real authority instead of being rewarded for her success, resigned her high office. It was immediately taken over by Alva. The appointment of a Spaniard as governor of the Netherlands was unheard of. Never before had the government in Brussels been entrusted to anyone outside the Burgundian-Habsburg family. By giving it to a vassal, regardless of how prominent he might be among the Spanish aristocracy, Philip deliberately lowered the standing of the office and consequently the status of the Low Countries within his empire. Alva's task was to punish all rebels—the word to be taken in a very broad sense. He was to teach the higher aristocracy that the only reason they were permitted to enjoy wealth and influence was because they were expected to be meek and obedient servants of the royal will. He was to restore respect for the Church among all classes of society, and to teach all ecclesiastics that the king's policy and the interests of the Church were one and the same, that to oppose the former was to harm the latter. He was to reduce the States Assemblies to a secondary role by freeing the royal finances from their control and by garrisoning the principal towns. He was sent to prove to the people of the Low Countries that the only and inevitable cure for religious disturbances was royal and relentless tyranny in the French fashion tinged with Spanish fanaticism. For the people of the Lowlands, Madrid not Rome was to represent Catholicism. Philip haughtily refused to allow a representative of the Pope to enter Brussels, even under the severe supervision of Alva. Pope Pius V, instead of protesting against the overbearing attitude of the Spanish king, meekly applauded the arbitrary proceedings of the new governor, thus making worse the plight of freedom-loving Netherland Catholics.

The duke of Alva organized a new council, the *Conseil des troubles,* the Bloody Council, to serve as a special court before which anyone ever suspected of rebellion could be brought to trial. Nearly all the members of that court were natives of the Low Countries, who from conviction or cowardice fully supported Alva's policy. Ordered to disregard all privileges and immunities, the new court by its first ruthless decisions caused a fresh exodus of Lowlanders to England and northern Germany. The counts of Egmont and Hoorne were the most illustrious among the thousands of its victims, and their case presents the most flagrant violation of law. Their trial and execution were carried out with complete disregard of their privileged status as knights of the Golden Fleece, which exempted them from all judicial power except that of their peers. The humiliation of the higher aristocracy was complete. The majority of its members humbly begged forgiveness for their past misdeeds. Brederode died in exile. Only the prince of Orange had both the will and the resources to continue the struggle against the monarchy, even after he had been deprived of all revenue from his Lowland estates. The humbling of the aristocracy was to be followed by the crushing of local autonomy.

Philip, with faith in Alva's ability, decided to capitalize on his momentary prestige. The States General would be summoned in ironical compliance with one of the principal demands of the opposition, but for no other purpose than to learn His Majesty's wishes in the matter of taxation. Then, after being forced to agree to the royal demands, they would be dismissed never to convene again. The model of the new law that included a sales tax, was taken from Spain. The "tenth" and "twentieth" pennies to be introduced in the Low Countries, were simply a Dutch version of the Spanish *alcabala*.

When the States General convened at Brussels on the twenty-first of March 1569, the people were cowed. Even when outside help was proffered, they dared not make use of it. In the summer and fall of 1568, William of Orange had invaded the Low Countries. By stretching his personal resources to the utmost and with the help of the French Huguenots and the Protestant princes of Germany, the prince had succeeded in gathering an imposing army, but that strong force had been badly handled. The invasion of the Low Countries was planned from three points at the same time, the heaviest blow to be dealt at the center with Brussels and Antwerp as its direct objectives. But each force acted separately and Alva defeated the Huguenots in the south and Louis of Nassau in the northeast before William ever took the field. Then by outmaneuvering the prince of Orange, Alva prevented him from occupying a single town of importance and left him no chance to win over the Netherlands by a successful engagement. The soldiers of the prince dispersed, but their captains followed him from Brabant to Lorraine and Strassbourg, demanding repayment of their expenditures. Ruined, despairing of his own and his country's future, William joined the armies of the Huguenots in France. The campaign was a total failure but it gave the Netherland nation its national anthem. It was in 1568 that William's trumpeters sounded for the first time the *Wilhelmus* for which his faithful friend Marnix of St. Aldegonde had composed the text.

William of Orange had learned one important lesson. For his campaign he had appealed to the Protestant princes of Germany, presenting the cause of the Low Countries as that of Protestantism. Himself a prince of the Empire and married to a daughter of the Elector of Saxony, he regarded the Protestant German princes as the natural defenders of local religious and political autonomy against Catholic authoritarianism. Neither France nor England, he believed, could have the same interest in the preservation of Lowland liberties as the princes of the Empire. He knew the inclinations of Queen Elizabeth towards strong monarchical authority, and he distrusted the exclusively Calvinist opinions of the French Huguenots. The defenders of the *Religionsfrieden,* the religious peace of Augsburg concluded in 1555 in Germany, were in his opinion the natural protagonists of a regime of liberty and tolerance in the Low Countries. Through this policy the ties between the Lowlands and Germany which the Habsburg rulers had striven to cut completely, would be strengthened. In this the prince of Orange saw no danger. He was not working for the subordination of the Low Countries to Imperial authority, but rather for the extension to the Low Countries of liberties enjoyed in the Empire.

To his utter disappointment the Protestant princes refused to see the problem in the same light. From the moment they threw off Imperial supervision by the defeat of Charles V in 1555, they had considered themselves the equals of kings and emperors. Strengthened in their self-esteem by the Lutheran doctrine demanding submission of the individual to princely authority, they seriously objected to assisting "rebels against their lawful prince" as it pleased some of them to style the Lowland patriots. The only exception was the Palatine Elector, but he was a Calvinist and prompted by religious interest.

William of Orange strove desperately to prevent the Lowland revolution from becoming a partisan Calvinist affair. He realized that Calvinism was dreaded by all princes, Catholic and Lutheran, as an anti-monarchical movement which, as King Henry II of France once told him, sought to overthrow all monarchies and to establish republics on the Swiss model. But no choice seemed left. The Lutheran princes of Germany were too "isolationist" to recognize the danger that threatened them if King Philip succeeded in making of the Low Countries a bulwark of Catholic authoritarianism. The Huguenots of France understood the situation better, and Alva assisted in their enlightenment by sending troops to the support of the Queen Regent of France in her war against the Protestant faction.

Returning from France, the prince of Orange wandered through Germany, often obliged to hide from his creditors, but always in touch with the exiles from the Low Countries and with the last remnants of opposition within the country. All he could do was to create some order and give an appearance of regularity to the piratical enterprises of the "Beggars of the Sea." These were a group of nobles and merchants who, with hundreds of exiles from the Low Countries and adventurers from anywhere, had equipped a number of small vessels with which they waged a privateer campaign against King Philip and anyone loyal to him who traded with his lands. This was broad enough to include most other ships that sailed the northern seas, and the Sea Beggars were impartial indeed in their attacks on merchant shipping. They were allies of doubtful value to the prince of Orange and the national cause, unless some sort of order could be established among them, and their "military tactics" brought in line with the general policy of the prince.

The duke of Alva might well feel confident of having overcome the principal obstacle to the organization of an authoritarian regime in the Low Countries. He summoned the States General, advised them of the royal demands for taxation, left them no opportunity to discuss his proposals and compelled their acceptance. Recalcitrant towns were punished by quartering Spanish soldiers in the homes of the citizens. For two years Alva accepted a yearly contribution of two million guilders in lieu of the new taxes, but in 1571 he decided that the time had come to enforce the new law ruthlessly. By that time he had become the most hated man the Netherlands had ever known in their history. The Spanish regime had reunited the national opposition that had been broken in 1566 by the intemperate action of the Calvinists, no mean accomplishment. The iconoclasts had brought the religious issue to the fore and thus prevented a common front of Catholics and Protestants against the authoritarian regime. Alva, by directing his attacks against the ancient institutions of the country, forced all defenders of those ancient rights, whether Protestant or Catholic, to unite regardless of the risk involved for their individual Church. Hatred of the duke, "the tyrant," was general. But from where was help to come?

William of Orange, completely ruined by his disastrous expedition of 1568, had no hope but in France. The purpose of Alva's regime was to make the Low Countries into a bulwark of Spanish power. France was now surrounded by Spanish bastions—in Italy, in Burgundy, in Flanders. The king of France could not tolerate such encirclement of his territory, and sooner or later the traditional conflict between the Houses of Valois and Habsburg was bound to break out again. The moment seemed near in

1571. Admiral de Coligny, the leader of the Huguenots, had gained the confidence of King Charles IX and was inciting that young monarch to war with Spain. Louis of Nassau, brother of William of Orange, was in close touch with Coligny and through this connection sought to make the coming war a campaign for the liberation of the Low Countries. He himself with a number of volunteers was to form the vanguard of the invading force. Coligny and perhaps even the king would follow with the royal army, strengthened by the dashing cavalry regiments of the Huguenot nobility. Orange, at the head of an army recruited in Germany with the support of Netherland exiles and French sympathizers, was to invade the Lowlands from the east, while revolt in the Low Countries would break the backbone of Alva's defense. The revolt proved a success, but the other plans came to naught. They merely diverted Alva from throwing all his forces against the rebels without delay and crushing them before they could consolidate their positions.

On April 1, 1572, a squadron of the "Sea Beggars" fleet appeared at the mouth of the Meuse, near Brill and finding the town ungarrisoned, they captured it. The western coastlands were only thinly occupied, for Alva had withdrawn nearly all his forces to bolster the defense of the southern frontier against French attacks. Too late he realized that leaving the Scheldt, Meuse and Zuiderzee ports unprotected, presented a far greater danger than the evacuation of a few inland fortresses in the south. Troops hurriedly dispatched to occupy Flushing and to keep open the Scheldt and the port of Antwerp arrived too late. The town had gone over to the revolution. A few Spanish companies could have prevented this loss, which in the years to come proved disastrous to the Spanish cause. Alva had no opportunity to retrieve it. Louis of Nassau had crossed the French-Lowland boundary and occupied the town of Mons. The vanguard of the invaders was there, the main armies, more than twenty thousand soldiers under the prince of Orange and a stronger force under Coligny, were to follow. But the ill-paid forces of the prince were unwieldy and difficult to handle. The French army never came. With a single stroke the pro-Spanish faction in France, headed by Guise and supported by Catherine de' Medici, mother of the king, relieved Alva of his worries. Coligny was murdered, the French troops disbanded, Louis of Nassau left to his fate and the prince of Orange obliged to retreat and seek refuge among the rebels of Holland.

The revolution had spread rapidly. Enkhuizen, at the entrance of the Zuiderzee, had followed the example of Flushing. Then, by persuasion or by the joint force of the Sea Beggars outside the walls and their sympathizers within, nearly all the towns of Holland and Zeeland were won over. Middelburg was held for Spain by its garrison; Amsterdam, by the *stadhouder* of Holland with the help of the ruling oligarchy. Most of the towns of Friesland and Overijssel and many in Guelders and Utrecht followed the lead of Holland. A large part of the Netherlands had fallen to the rebels before Alva could turn his attention from the southern frontier. But the revolution appeared more formidable than it really was. The Sea Beggars, partisans rather than patriots, had committed such cruelties that with the spreading of the revolt hundreds of Catholics fled into exile. The defense works of the towns were weak, merely medieval stone walls, unable to withstand bombardment by Spanish artillery. There were few professional soldiers, and the military value of the city guards was dubious. Finally, there were no funds and no administration to collect such funds. This last defect had to be remedied first. The towns of Holland and Zeeland were found willing to recognize the prince of Orange as their leader. The Sea Beggars occupied the country in his name. The town councils gave William's authority a mask of legality by ignoring the fact that he had resigned as lieutenant of Holland, Zeeland, and Utrecht, and by declaring him King Philip's lieutenant in His Majesty's absence to resist the duke of Alva, who was supposed to have abused the royal confidence. Through this fiction the Hollanders sought to quiet their own conscientious scruples and to avoid appearing as rebels against their legitimate prince. Avowed rebels might not have been able to obtain any support from foreign princes who were all very sensitive on this point. Besides the councils were most anxious to discredit the rumor that the triumph of Calvinism would mean the establishment of a Swiss republican form of government.

The representatives of the towns of Holland who on July 19, 1572, met at Dordrecht with the delegates of the prince and the Sea Beggars, reconstituted the Government of Holland. The prince of Orange was chosen as its head, but being wholly without resources of his own, his relation to the States Assembly naturally became that of a prime minister dependent upon the support of a representative body. In theory, the prince, while not possessing sovereignty, represented it; in practice, the powers of sovereignty lay from then on in the hands of the States.

This weak rebel organization had to meet the onslaught of Alva's military power. Once the danger from France had passed, the duke of Alva regrouped his army and sent a strong force northward. The riverbelt in the middle of the country made an invasion from the south difficult. So the Spaniards first moved northeast, crossed the Rhine near the confluence at Lobith, and then invaded the area in revolt from the east. The story of this invasion has been described many times. Zutfen was stormed and its citizens cruelly massacred. The other IJssel-towns meekly submitted. Part of the Spanish army marched north to Friesland and reoccupied most of the position lost to the rebels. The main force marched west, destroyed Naarden, after dreadful scenes of murder and looting, and made its headquarters in Amsterdam which had been held for the loyalists by the desperate efforts of its ruling oligarchy. Haarlem might have surrendered had it not been for the determination of the prince of Orange and the garrison. The Spanish commander, Alva's son, Don Fadrique, after a moment of hesitation, decided to storm the walls. This was the decisive moment of the revolt. Until then the Spanish troops had been a police force on a ruthless punitive expedition; until then the people of the Netherlands had not stood up and fought the king's professional soldiery, arms in hand. More than fifty years later the Netherland historian Hooft wrote: "The Netherlanders are slow by nature and think twice before they act. But once their patience is exhausted, especially if their liberty is being curtailed, no power on earth can hold them back. They will fight with complete disregard of danger or the superiority of the enemy." The same view inspired Schiller's sour remark in his history of the Netherland revolt: "No people is less predisposed to heroism, but circumstances made the Netherlanders heroic." By ordering an improvised attack on Haarlem, Don Fadrique took a grave risk. Had his more experienced father been present, the mistake might have been avoided and Holland reconquered for King Philip. The storm troops were beaten back, not once but several times. The artisans, shopkeepers and clerks of Haarlem were filled with confidence and pride at having found themselves the equals of Europe's best professional fighters. The same pride and confidence filled the hearts of all who fought for the revolution, and inevitably led to an overestimation of their own strength. The small armies of volunteers and Sea Beggars that sought to relieve Haarlem learned to their cost that fighting Alva's troops in the open was a different matter from beating back their attacks from the city walls. The capture of Haarlem took the Spaniards seven months, and its heroic defense raised the hopes of the rebels as much as it depressed the Spanish soldiery.

From Haarlem, Don Fadrique decided to march against northern Holland to open the trade routes of Amsterdam. A naval force, collected in that port was to clear the Zuiderzee of the Sea Beggars. The defeat of that naval force saved northern Holland and the revolution, for it gave the rebels mastery of the sea and of river estuaries, without which Holland and Zeeland could be neither defended nor conquered. Control of the coastal waters provided the revolution with a new source of income—duties on trade with enemy-occupied lands. No ships were allowed to sail to Antwerp or Amsterdam without paying tolls to the revolutionary government, and many ship-captains drew the obvious conclusion that it might pay them to transfer their trade to the rebel towns. The Spanish attacks were by no means ended. King Philip decided upon a change of leadership in the Low Countries and recalled Alva, whose failure had become conspicuous, sending in his place Don Louis de Zuniga y Requesens, former governor of Milan, who was supposed to be a naval expert. This carried considerable weight in his appointment, as Philip now saw that naval forces would be more important than land forces in the reduction of the rebellious provinces. At the same time, Requesens was more likely to achieve reconciliation than had been Alva's strictly military mind. Philip planned to split the opposition, to lure the Catholics back to the royal side by promises of pardon and respect for national liberties, to leave the Calvinists in a helpless minority. He might have succeeded had he come in person. Instead he instructed Requesens to follow a policy of half-hearted concessions which failed completely because of the deep mistrust of all Netherlanders for everything Spanish.

At first Requesens was quite successful. A severe blockade brought the towns of southern Holland to the verge of collapse. Leiden was besieged, while Delft, Gouda, and Rotterdam were virtually cut off from each other. The countryside was at the mercy of the Spaniards. The position of the rebels seemed hopeless. Everything depended upon a few towns. Among the city oligarchs there were always some willing to restore their allegiance to the king if political liberty was assured. When Leiden was besieged, and the States of Holland met at Rotterdam, all precedent was broken by admitting the representatives of the city guards and guilds. The prince of Orange knew that in grave crises, the mass of the people are more to be relied upon than the ruling classes, and he had often insisted on having important ordinances approved by the people as well as by the magistrates. In his desperate attempt to save Leiden, he asked his brother Louis of Nassau to organize another army of German mercenaries and to invade the Netherlands from the east. Again the leaders of the revolt made the mistake of directing their attack against Brabant instead of reinforcing their positions in Holland. Louis of Nassau did not even succeed in crossing the Meuse, and he lost his life and the battle at Mook in April 1574. The revolution seemed doomed. The Sea Beggars had been driven from Friesland. They were losing ground in northern Holland, and their commander vented his rage on the Catholic peasants, thus creating a new danger by destroying all sympathy for the revolution among large masses of the population. Further to the south the Spaniards held Leiden besieged until October 3, 1574, when the countryside was flooded by order of the prince, and they had to abandon their positions. At this, one of the darkest moments in the history of Holland, the University of Leiden was founded in recognition of the heroic resistance of the citizens and as a token of confidence in the future.

The Spanish withdrawal from Leiden was more a moral than a military victory for the rebels, as only a few months later the Spaniards renewed their attacks and conquered a number of small towns in eastern Holland. The real victories of the rebels were won in Zeeland. Requesens, sent to the Low Countries because of his knowledge of naval affairs, had succeeded in arming a number of ships in Antwerp, only to see his squadron utterly destroyed in a furious battle in the Eastern Scheldt. Thereupon Middelburg, which had been valiantly defended against the Sea Beggars for two years, surrendered and joined the revolution. Zeeland, unassailable amidst wide inlets of the sea, was the bastion of the patriots. Their small and easily handled ships controlled the estuaries of the Scheldt where a knowledge of local geography and good seamanship enabled their naval commanders to outmaneuver any Spanish force. Then Requesens decided to show the Beggars of the Sea that even an island could be conquered by the Spanish army without naval support. He ordered General Mondragon to conduct his troops at night and through shallow water to the island of Schouwen Duiveland. This audacious enterprise succeeded. The town of Zierikzee was taken after a six months siege. Its fall separated Zeeland from Holland, but by the time of its capitulation in June 1576, the whole situation had changed, and the revolution was victorious.

The Spanish position in the Low Countries collapsed suddenly, of itself, as if from over-strain. Events justified the advisors of King Philip who had recommended total withdrawal from the Low Countries rather than a costly war for the maintainance of royal authority. The northern outpost of the Spanish empire was absorbing too large a part of the Spanish forces, while adding nothing to the strength of Spain's political position. Spain, the greatest naval power in the Mediterranean, was losing all prestige in northern Europe through her inability to destroy a few hundred rebel vessels. Instead of defending the coast of Italy or the Spanish strongholds in North Africa against the Moors, her army exhausted itself in the cold marshy lands of the north. The result was that both the African fortresses and the Low Countries were lost for King Philip. Gold and silver from the New World merely passed through Spain to fill the coffers of bankers who, at exorbitant rates of interest, provided funds for the Lowland campaign. A delay in the arrival of the "silver fleet" or any disruption of the complicated Spanish political machine, and King Philip would face loss of credit and increasing financial difficulties in the future.

Requesens, obliged to summon the States General in May 1574, met with general stubborn resistance to the continuation of the war. The Wal-

loon provinces finally granted money, but the others demanded that negotiations should first be attempted for the reconciliation of Holland and
Zeeland. Requesens reluctantly consented. This concession, a sign of weakness on his part, gave the rebels some legal standing, an important fact of
which the genius of Orange took every possible advantage. His position
further improved when negotiations were started in Breda under the
auspices of the Emperor. This alone shows how much prestige Philip had
lost. While formerly he had ignored all ties with the Empire, he was now
obliged to accept the mediation of his overlord in a conflict with his own
subjects. The negotiations broke down over the future religious status of
the Low Countries. Philip maintained that he alone was to decide and
that his mercy could never go farther than granting heretics leave to depart
from his territories and take their possessions with them. Holland and
Zeeland, led by the prince of Orange, demanded that the question of
religion be settled by the States General, by the people of the Low Countries
themselves. Philip could never accept this point of view, nor could he
enforce his own.

The success of Requesens' army in Holland and Zeeland was dearly
bought but, instead of concentrating his war effort on Holland, Philip
became increasingly ambitious. This brought about the collapse of the
Spanish military position in the Low Countries. It came suddenly in 1576.
Requesens fell dead at a time when there was not a penny in the treasury.
With some hesitation the Council of State took up the reins of government
until the king should send a new governor. The Spanish commanders
showed little respect for the interim administration. The Spanish soldiery
revolted against their commanders, resolved to get their overdue pay in one
way or another. Towns were occupied and plundered by the troops, Antwerp suffering worst of all. A revolution in Brussels, prearranged by the
prince of Orange, deprived the Council of State of its liberty and forced a
convocation of the States General. The atrocities committed by the Spaniards in Antwerp drove the States General, representing the southern
provinces, into alliance with Holland and Zeeland. At Ghent on November
8, 1576, the States of all the provinces concluded the agreement, known
as the "Pacification." This treaty provided that all the provinces would
join in the ejection of Spanish troops and that all matters of general interest (among them religion) would be settled by a meeting of the States
General to convene as soon as peace and order were restored. The Low
Countries were now united against Spain.

During the ensuing three years, the struggle was concentrated in the
southern provinces. King Philip sent his half-brother, Don Juan of Austria,
as Governor; but this young prince felt helplessly out of place amidst the

political complications of the Low Countries. These three years gave Holland and Zeeland the necessary respite to reorganize their administration, to restore their economy, and finally to recover the towns conquered or never given up by the enemy. Haarlem returned to the side of the rebels and finally Amsterdam itself admitted the troops of the prince of Orange.

In these years the prince could turn his attention to the south. For him the revolution could never be subordinated to provincial considerations. To succeed and have lasting results it must be made national. On this point the States of Holland and Zeeland were far from agreement with their leader. The particularism of the Hollanders and Zeelanders had grown to such an extent in the four years they had fought the enemy alone, that a permanent union even of the two provinces appeared obnoxious to both of them. The States, now completely dominated by the magistrates of the cities and therefore by commercial and shipping interests, were unwilling to sacrifice any of the advantages they enjoyed from their naval control over all Lowland waters. They needed the cooperation of the other provinces in pushing the Spaniards so far back that all danger to Holland and Zeeland would be eliminated, but they would not accept the supremacy or even tolerate the influence of any other province. The prince of Orange did not care which of the seventeen provinces predominated in the federation or where the central administration was established. Tradition made it difficult for him to conceive of any other city than Brussels as the center of government, or even of a purely Dutch administration to replace the old French-Burgundian system.

The States of Holland held different views. They trusted far more in their own strength than in federation and were decidedly averse to receiving orders again from Brussels. Religious divergence further widened the cleavage. In the agreement of Ghent the southern provinces explicitly stated that no religion except that of Rome would be publicly proffered in their territory where, however, the persecution of dissenters was to cease. Holland and Zeeland, while reserving their decision in this matter, continued to give Calvinism a free hand in the gradual suppression of the Catholic Church. It shows the greatness of William of Orange that he was one of the few who realized from the first that this vague temporary agreement would lead to a religious conflict unless some policy of mutual tolerance could be introduced and maintained.

On his return to Brussels after ten years' absence, the prince was met by members of the aristocracy, men of his own class and his former comrades in the service of the king and in opposition to Granvelle. At the outset it was apparent that he was no longer one of them and that they could not or would not understand or follow him. In those ten years the prince had found the common man of more help in his struggle for freedom than the aristocrat. He had passed through years of penury, if not poverty; his habits had become simple compared with his previous luxury. He had mixed with merchants and sea captains, instead of restricting his society to the mighty and had lost his taste for the fashionable life of Brussels. Probably he had also lost caste with his former comrades. During the hard years of desperate resistance, his religious convictions had deepened and although by no means a fanatic, he had become a convinced Calvinist. This widened the gulf that separated him from the Catholic aristocracy. On the other hand, he had become a statesman of international fame and had risen far above the level of the "frondeur" of 1563, the aristocratic party leader who claimed to speak for the people without knowing them. When the aristocracy discovered how high William stood in the opinion of the people, that he alone was the trusted advisor of the States General, they turned against his influence and organized a "Fronde," like the one he and they had once organized against Granvelle. They induced Matthias of Austria, cousin of King Philip, to assume the governorship of the Low Countries in the name of the States General.

The intrigues of the aristocracy, although troublesome, were among the lesser worries of the prince. His most difficult task was to keep the provinces united against Spain. That unity was threatened, not only by the intrigues of Spaniards who sought to win the Low Countries back for their king, but even more by the imminence of civil war between Calvinists and Catholics. The treaty of Ghent was acceptable to King Philip except as regards religion, and it remained to be seen whether the States General—in which the southern Catholic provinces held a majority— would remain steadfast for the sake of the Calvinists in Holland and Zeeland, if their own political demands were granted. As a matter of fact, the States General, against the wishes of Holland and Zeeland, agreed to accept Don Juan as Governor on condition that he would immediately withdraw the Spanish soldiery and respect the liberties of towns and provinces. Restoration of religious unity in all the provinces—including the now Calvinist ones—though postponed for the moment, was agreed to by both sides. Only Don Juan's impatience to regain real authority saved the situation for the prince of Orange and again put the whole of the Low Countries on their guard against Spanish "perfidy." Having strengthened anti-Spanish sentiment in the southern provinces, the prince of Orange sought to secure further internal unity, but the religious problem stood in his way. With the growth of anti-Spanish feeling, anti-Catholic trends also rose rapidly. In Holland and Zeeland, Catholics had submitted to violation of their rights when their liberties were in extreme danger from Spain. There,

the Calvinists had gained easy supremacy by exploiting the religious indifference of large numbers of Catholics and the anti-Spanish sentiments of
the masses. This led them to believe that revolt against Spain would also
bring about an acceptance of Calvinism by the South. But the southerners
did not see things in that light. Feeling strong and united in their opposition
to Spain, they did not want Calvinist soldiery in their towns for whenever
troops or adherents of the prince came to the South from Holland, they
brought religious conflict with them. The leading classes of the South, in
their opposition to Calvinism easily confused the cause of liberty and of
the prince with religious persecution, and this drove them back into the
Spanish ranks.

One thing stands out from the confused history of the crucial years between 1576 and 1579. Wherever the mass of the people, represented by the
guilds and city guards, obtained the upper hand, the revolution continued
even at the cost of Catholicism. It was *not* that the masses everywhere were
strongly inclined towards Calvinism, for the devout Calvinists always remained in the minority, just as were militant Catholics. The small burgher
class cherished their political freedom more than their religion. They were
generally willing to fight for the former, but seldom for the latter. Once
forced to submit to Spain again, the masses found little difficulty in read-
justing their religious convictions to the teachings of the Catholic Church;
but as long as the revolution lasted, they were willing to follow its more
forceful protagonists, the Calvinists. But wherever the city oligarchs and
the higher aristocracy maintained their authority, the prince of Parma
who in 1578 had succeeded Don Juan, was sure to find a more sympathetic
audience than the prince of Orange. Vested interests in the Church and in
secular society turned back to Spain when they saw their authority diminish
in proportion to the progress of the revolution. Personal feelings or family
connections did not weigh heavily once the very existence of a class seemed
threatened. By 1579, the names of Egmont and Lalaing, sons and relatives
of Alva's victims, were again to be found among the loyal defenders of
Spanish authority. The Walloon provinces, less antagonistic to Spain than
the Dutch speaking majority, made their peace with the king in 1579. In
vain had the prince of Orange tried to induce Calvinists and Catholics to
live together by promulgating a decree of religious tolerance. It was nowhere accepted or even put into force; neither by the Calvinists of Holland
and Zeeland nor by the Catholics of the Walloon provinces. Religious
strife became so violent and general that the union of the seventeen provinces was rapidly falling apart, and some provinces like Flanders seemed
almost on the verge of disintegrating into their component parts.

Leaving the internal forces of destruction to do their work in the Low

Countries, Parma, with a strongly reinforced royalist army, concentrated on the siege of Maastricht which he stormed and sacked in 1579. His policy of reconciliation promised to all who were willing to return to allegiance to the king, full liberty according to ancient custom. He was wise enough to adhere strictly to his promises, even when their execution caused him serious difficulties in the prosecution of the war. The prince of Orange, feeling his hold on the southern provinces slipping, sought to safeguard at least Holland and Zeeland by bringing the adjoining provinces, especially those north of the riverbelt, into closer contact with the center of the revolution. He tried to create a stronghold within the Low Countries, in the strategically located northern provinces. This was the origin of the famous Union of Utrecht. It was a weak beginning indeed. When the Union was signed at Utrecht on January 23, 1579, only the representatives of Holland, Zeeland, Utrecht, the Ommelanden of Groningen, and William's brother, John of Nassau in his capacity of lieutenant of Guelderland, put their names to the document. Friesland, Overijssel, Drente, and the States of Guelderland proclaimed their adherence. Fear of Calvinist domination held some of them back for several months, others hesitated for fear of losing even the smallest part of their provincial autonomy.

For fifty years the northern provinces had been kept together in a personal union under the Habsburg dynasty, and with that bond broken it was difficult to substitute a new unifying factor. The only one the founders of the union conceived as workable was negative—common resistance against foreign attack. The means they devised for even this limited end, such as a common system of taxation, could never be put into practice. The Union as concluded at Utrecht did not replace the previously existing central administration, but left merely a vacuum in its place, a deficiency that was to have its effects during the next two centuries. But then, the Union was not intended as a constitution. Its members still belonged to that larger, though badly impaired federation, the Seventeen Provinces of the Low Countries; and that federation sought desperately to create a new administration in the hope of preventing complete disintegration. Some of the Brabant and Flanders towns followed the example of the Walloons and returned to obedience to the king; others, determined to resist Spanish tyranny to the last sought admission to the Union.

In this hopeless situation, the States General led by the prince of Orange, finally decided to discard the fiction that they were still loyal subjects of his Spanish Majesty, resisting only his evil servants and soldiers. Holland and Zeeland had for some time given up all pretense of loyalty towards their former sovereign and urged the States General to do the same. By a decree of July 22, 1581, the States General demanded that all their officials and all inhabitants of the provinces swear loyalty and obedience to the "United Low Countries" instead of to the king of Spain. Their resistance to the Spanish regime had become a formal revolt against the king himself. Before deserting their old sovereign, the States General elected a new one, Francis of Alençon, duke of Anjou, and brother of Henry III of France. The new prince, forced to accept the most stringent restrictions on his executive powers, had no sooner experienced this new type of constitutional government than he sought to overthrow it. The troops of the sovereign fought a brisk battle with his citizens in the streets of Antwerp, ending in the complete humiliation of the French prince. His death was a great relief to his new subjects who disliked his French origin anyway and despised his usurped tyranny even more than that of Philip.

The collapse of the central administration nearly caused the downfall of the new freedom. The cities of Brabant and Flanders, left to their fate, successively made their peace with the king or were conquered by the Spanish army which under Parma's leadership showed its traditional vigor and efficiency. Even the provinces of the Union of Utrecht were no longer safe. Discontented Catholics, incited by the forceful propagation of Calvinism, joined the enemy. Town after town and noble after noble made their peace with the king. The worst defection was that of the governor of Groningen, which caused the loss of half the northeastern provinces. Only Holland and Zeeland seemed to stand like rocks in the raging storm. But only outwardly. Enkhuizen, one of the first towns to join the revolution in 1572, ten years later was the scene of a pro-Spanish conspiracy, and similar disloyalty was noticeable in Amsterdam, Gouda, and even in Delft, the residence of the prince of Orange. In the South a number of cities still held out, but a common defense no longer existed. Holland and Zeeland, feeling safer in isolation than in alliance with uncertain friends, were on the point of raising the prince of Orange to sovereign rank, which would have meant separation from the main body of the Low Countries, when that great leader of the revolution fell a victim to Spanish terrorism. Outlawed by King Philip in 1580, he had been constantly exposed to attacks on his life. On July 10, 1584, Balthasar Gerard, a Burgundian, earned the promised blood money by shooting the prince in his home at Delft.

The cause of the Revolution seemed hopeless indeed. Its leader was dead, the union of the seventeen provinces broken, and the army disorganized. Philip was greatly strengthened by the acquisition of Portugal in 1580, which doubled his naval forces, and the Spanish king felt confident that after all his cause would triumph in the Netherlands and in the whole of northern Europe. One year after William's death, the duke of Parma scored his greatest victory by the conquest of Antwerp in spite of desperate attempts on the part of Holland and Zeeland to save that all-important city.

At this moment, however, the struggle in the Netherlands became truly international. The German princes had proved unresponsive to all appeals from the Low Countries. The Emperor had restricted his interference to repeated mediations between the king and his former subjects. From the east nothing was to be expected. Germany herself, through the inaction of her leaders, and in spite of all the theories expounded at the Imperial Diets, ejected the Low Countries from her midst. In these very years, the Low-landers had grown so foreign to the Germans that they were ousted by the latter from the old common pilgrim hostels in Rome. Conscious of their national individuality, Lowlanders registering in foreign universities no longer styled themselves natives of this or that town, but *Belgae,* meaning inhabitants of any part of the Low Countries. The States of Holland, when preparing to proclaim Prince William count of Holland, explicitly denied the overlordship of the Emperor. Long before 1648, the year of the official separation so often deplored by later German nationalist historians, the bond between the two territories was broken.

While Germany remained indifferent, France and England became more interested in the Lowland conflict, as their fear of Spanish dominion grew. In France, King Philip had now his partisans well organized in the *Ligue* under the leadership of the Guise family. Not only the Huguenots, but the royal authority itself was threatened by the powerful new organization. In England, Queen Elizabeth felt insecure as long as Mary Queen of Scots was alive and the center of continuous intrigues. Once already the rebels in the Netherlands had given her invaluable aid by forcing Don Juan of Austria, then governor of the Low Countries, to send his troops overland to Spain instead of permitting them to embark in a North Sea port for the invasion of England and the liberation of Mary Stuart. At that time, in 1577, the naval forces of Holland and Zeeland had kept the Scheldt tightly closed and prevented an attack on the British coast. Both France and England relied on the continuance of the Netherland revolution to safe-guard their own independence. So far only a trickle of volunteers and an occasional grant of money had come from England, where Queen Elizabeth continued to practice a policy of appeasement. This was doomed to failure as King Philip did not trust her. In his opinion, she was a usurper and an apostate. The Pope had excommunicated her and Philip felt it his duty to lead a crusade for the restoration of legitimate authority and ortho-doxy in the island kingdom. All this was evident to Queen Elizabeth, even before the prince of Orange died, but she had found him so strongly in-clined towards France that cooperation had never been wholehearted.

After William's death, his policy was continued by the States General who, despairing of ever gaining complete independence offered the crown of the Low Countries to the king of France himself. Philip forestalled possible acceptance by strengthening his alliance with the French Catholics. Support of the Netherland revolt by the king of France would have meant a Catholic revolt against King Henry with the support of Spain. This threat was made so plain that King Henry refused the tempting offer. Obliged to turn once more to Queen Elizabeth, the States General received only the promise of an auxiliary army under the command of the Earl of Leicester, and in return were forced to accept English garrisons in the towns of Flushing and Brill.

Leicester came in 1585. Instead of concentrating on the military defense of the country, he turned his whole attention to the internal problems caused by the excessive provincialism of the States Assemblies. While Leicester was quarreling with the States of Holland, Parma conquered town after town. Again Spanish soldiery ravaged the soil of Holland itself. Leicester obtained some support from the lower classes, from the strict Calvinists and regionally, in the old northeastern provinces from Utrecht to Friesland. Against him stood the States of Holland, led by the first great native statesman of the Netherlands—Johan van Oldenbarnevelt.

Leicester's position, hopeless from the beginning because of his own incompetence, became impossible when suspicion arose that his policy was to serve the interests of England rather than of the Netherlands. This charge was first made when he banned all trade with Spain, all export of food stuffs, and ordered strict control over all shipping. The merchants of Holland accused him of deliberately destroying Dutch commerce for the benefit of English competitors. This was not true, but suspicion ripened into hostility when Leicester began to undermine the authority of the States Assemblies, to establish a more democratic regime under the city guards and guilds, with the secret intention of subordinating Netherland foreign policy to that of England. Elizabeth was just then making a final effort to appease Spain and Leicester tried to use the most violently anti-Spanish elements among the Netherlanders to secure a reconciliation with King Philip. This policy failed as it deserved to, for it was basically wrong. Indignantly he left the Lowlands, accusing the people of "ungratefulness," when they had merely defended their newly won freedom against the insidious policy of a selfish ally.

At this juncture, Parma conquered the port of Sluis on the Scheldt thus securing a naval base to receive the mighty fleet which King Philip was sending against both England and the Netherlands. The seamanship and heroism of Elizabeth's naval commanders and their sailors defeated the

Invincible Armada, and the watchfulness of Netherland cruisers prevented it from establishing contact with the troops of Parma on the coast of Flanders. From this moment England became the irreconcilable foe of Spain. After the outbreak of civil war in France, the conflagration spread over all western Europe. Philip had provoked a crisis, the first result of which was to divert his forces from the Netherlands. As in 1576, a sudden and unexpected change in the general political situation saved the revolution in Holland in an hour of dire peril. Again the scales turned, this time for good.

The events that followed would not have been so decisive had not latent forces in Holland and Zeeland come to the surface at the same time. The desperate struggle through the years 1572 to 1576, in which these two provinces were almost crushed, had placed in their hands nearly all the trade and shipping that formerly enriched the whole of the Low Countries. The ten years of internal peace that followed in the Northwest—years of civil war for the South—had consolidated this position. Parma's reconquest of Antwerp and most of the South and Northeast gave the Hollanders and Zeelanders an excuse to treat their competitors as enemies, and to sustain their monopoly of trade and shipping by a naval blockade. The war had not drained Holland's manpower, for the army was composed wholly of foreign mercenaries. It placed a heavy burden upon the treasury, but this was met by evergrowing revenue from taxation and port dues.

Although war funds were available, disorderly management hampered the Netherlanders in their military ventures during the years of Leicester's presence. The departure of this would-be reformer of Netherland institutions left the place free for national leaders. While Oldenbarnevelt, grand pensionary of Holland, shaped the foreign policy and ordered the finances of the new commonwealth, young Maurice of Nassau, son of William of Orange and his successor as stadhouder, reorganized the army.[26] This young man in his early twenties became one of the most famous generals in Europe. He owed his fame to his knowledge of engineering and supply problems, which he had thoroughly studied with the help of his cousin and friend, William Louis of Nassau, stadhouder of Friesland, and of mathematicians like Simon Stevin of Bruges. He understood that a small but well paid force that could be kept well in hand, was far more effective than a large army of underpaid mercenaries who devoted more time and energy to looting the countryside than to fighting the enemy. The canals and rivers of Holland, Zeeland, and Friesland permitted rapid concentration of a fighting force at any point of the front. More and greatly improved artillery, a better disposition of troops on the field of battle and above all thorough training of the soldiers before they were sent into battle made the Netherland army the model of Europe's fighting forces. In a few years Maurice had reconquered Groningen, the towns of Overijssel and Guelderland, and secured the province of Zeeland against future attack by the occupation of a number of small Flemish towns on the south bank of the Scheldt. These "bridgeheads" created the present district of "Zeeuwsch Vlaanderen" (Zeeland Flanders) which until our day forms part of the kingdom of the Netherlands.

These victories greatly increased the prestige of the new Commonwealth. It had proved able to take care of itself without outside help. Not only that, Netherland troops were even dispatched to France to help the new king, Henry IV, against the Catholic League and Spain. The Netherland navy assisted the fleet of Queen Elizabeth in its attacks on the Spanish coast. The new relations between the States General at The Hague and the rulers of western Europe found adequate expression in the triple alliance with France and England concluded in 1596 and directed against Spain. The Netherland Republic was recognized as a sovereign power, *de facto*, if not *de jure*.

Thus, the "fight for freedom" had been brought to a successful conclusion. Spanish tyranny and the Inquisition had been destroyed in the Netherlands. In their place a republican government had arisen in which, it is true, a few thousand city aristocrats and country gentlemen members of the States Assemblies, dominated the masses of the people. A minority of Calvinists, as few perhaps as 10% of the population around 1600, monopolized all public worship. Had the Great Revolt, really been a "fight for freedom"; or was it, after all a partisan revolution, that substituted one tyranny for another? Motley would have indignantly rejected any such doubt of the purity of the rebels' intentions, but criticism of the traditional historical explanation by modern authorities has done much to deprive the greatest of all episodes in Netherland history of its glamor, and to reduce the "fight for freedom" to a hateful partisan strife between two equally selfish, intolerant and tyrannical factions.

The historians of the seventeenth and eighteenth centuries represented the revolt against Spain as lawful resistance by the legitimate authorities of the States Assemblies—against the usurpations of the monarchy. But before the eighteenth century had come to a close, a reaction set in which pointed out that not the States but the monarchy represented legitimate authority and that the revolt of the Netherlanders was nothing but a rebellion of subjects against their lawful king. The closing period of the eighteenth century was not particularly averse to such revolution, but Netherland historiography being on the conservative side sought to justify the revolution as a defense of the "true Reformed religion" against the persecution of

Rome. The liberal period which saw the rise of modern nationalism sought and found a "national" interpretation. Robert Fruin, greatest of Netherland historians, explained both the revolt against Spain and the subsequent cleavage of the Low Countries as a fight for freedom, restricted to their northern section by the strong social, political and historical antithesis between the peoples of present Belgium and Holland. Later authorities on the subject have varied this interpretation by predicating a broader national basis to include, either the whole population of both Belgium and the Netherlands or only the Dutch-Flemish speaking people.

The school of thought which found in unity of language the principal criterion of nationality, accused the Calvinists of the North of having broken the natural unity of the Netherland-Flemish group for purely religious motives. This school assumed such unity to have existed before 1576. Its opponents emphatically denied the "national" character of the revolt, on the ground that no Netherland, "Lowland" or "Dutch Flemish" nation existed before the Republic was constituted. Some pointed out that in point of fact, the monarchy, the central administration in Brussels, represented the "national" element in the sixteenth century Low Countries, and that the rebels were provincial separatists. In this interpretation the revolution was a civil war between provincialists and unionists embittered by identification with the conflict between Calvinists and Catholics. Its exponents labeled the revolt a "conservative revolution," sprung from stubborn local resistance to the introduction of modern centralized administration. They found forces of reaction, not of progress, behind the agitation. Add to these manifold interpretations that of a small group of Marxist historians who ascribed the conflict to purely economic motives, and we have some idea how far we have come from Motley's "fight for freedom." [27]

Yet, the Great Revolt *was* a fight for freedom. It did not substitute democracy for oligarchy in the city governments, nor the principle of tolerance for that of State-religion. But it maintained one great tradition, that of briefed freedom and limitation of the power of government by law and custom. The struggle of the late XVIth century was for the Netherlands, what that of the XVIIth century was for Great Britain. Government, even if concentrated in the hands of a small group of the people, was to be constitutional, not arbitrary. The fact that the revolution hindered the establishment of a well organized central administration does not make it reactionary. Less important aims were simply sacrificed to the more important. Thanks to the revolt of the XVIth century, the constitutional development of the Netherlands in the ensuing centuries was gradual and relatively peaceful, undisturbed by violent convulsions such as shook other continental European nations. Historians sometimes forget that the revolt not only saved the northern part of the Low Countries from arbitrary rule, but also to a large extent the southern part as well. Spain's only means of winning back the southern provinces had been to guarantee their ancient rights and institutions. There too the revolt, if not so fully successful as in the north, nevertheless achieved great results.

Interesting as it is to determine the real character of these stirring events, it is more important to know how the actors in the drama understood and justified their own work.[28] The political justification of the Netherland revolution developed after the struggle had begun. The legitimacy of resistance and the rightful authority of those who led it were always emphasized. Not for a moment did the Netherlanders assert a "right of revolution"; they always claimed to be the defenders of law and justice. For the Calvinists the issue was clear. The magistrates from the king down were in duty bound to defend the purity of the Christian religion. In fighting the "abuses of Popery," the Calvinists claimed to be upholding the authority of the monarch who, if not blinded by superstition, would have been bound to do the same. The magistrates were always expected to lead. Popular excesses like the Iconoclasm of 1566 were aberrations, deplored by the Netherland Calvinist leaders, as well as by Calvin himself, not for their consequences but for their origin. All who resisted the purification of the Church were "usurpers"; if they used force to uphold their opinion, they became tyrants who might be withstood without incurring the blame of rebellion. In this the Netherland Calvinists, like their French co-religionists, stood half way between the extreme views of John Knox, who opposed such tyranny on principle, and of Martin Luther, who preached passive submission to the evil power of oppressive authority. Netherland Calvinist opinion justified resistance for religious but not for political reasons. It helped to relieve the conscience of the rebels, but did not satisfy their political convictions. Moreover, this predominance of religious over political motives contained dangerous implications of Church supremacy over the state, a thing the city aristocrats were not willing to tolerate.

Anti-clericalism had been a strong influence in the early years of the revolt. The towns of Holland would no more permit Calvinist than Catholic theocracy. When Adriaan Taling, minister of the Church in Leiden during the siege, compared the city magistrates to "pigs who look no farther than their fodder" because they had ordered the words *Haec Libertatis Ergo* ("All This for Freedom's Sake") printed on newly minted coins, instead of *Haec Religionis Ergo* ("All This for Religion's Sake"), Jan van Hout, town secretary, grabbed his gun and threatened to shoot down the minister from his pulpit. *Haec Libertatis Ergo* had a definite meaning, first expressed by Prince William of Orange in his manifesto of

1568, when he said: "The liberties of the towns and provinces are not free grants of royal benevolence but contracts binding both the prince and the people." Here for the first time, the "contract" theory which fitted admirably into the constitutional traditions of the Low Countries, was propounded. The great charter of Brabant, the *Joyeuse Entrée,* exonerated the States and the people of that duchy from all obligations towards their prince in case of violation of its stipulations. The northeastern provinces claimed to have accepted the Emperor Charles as their prince freely and by formal contract. The prince of Orange's manifesto was no novelty for the Netherlanders, who more or less arbitrarily assumed that the principles of the *Joyeuse Entrée* applied even outside Brabant. The inhabitants of Holland remembered having voluntarily accepted a Burgundian duke as their prince in preference to their natural princess Jacqueline of Bavaria. Once already they had renounced the allegiance of one prince to accept the sovereignty of another, why not again?

This opinion naturally led to a new theory, in which the rights of sovereignty were restricted by the rights of the people, and finally the authority of the monarch was held to be subordinate to that of the States. This became the Netherland conception of "liberty" for which the struggle against the power of Spain was carried on. It was the right of the people to demand—through their traditional spokesman—that the monarch respect the freedom and privileges of each social group and refrain from interference with their ancient institutions. If the monarch failed to respect their rights, the people were entitled to resist and even to oust him. This was stoutly maintained in the decree rejecting Philip's authority in 1581 in which it was said that all people were born free and that it was their right and duty to fight for this natural freedom against tyranny. Similar political ideas were propounded in France about the same time. The most famous of French treatises on this subject is Duplessis Mornay's *Vindiciae contra tyrannos* written in 1579 by a Huguenot who had just before spent considerable time in the Netherlands. There was definitely an exchange of ideas, but the difference between the French and the Netherland conception is too outspoken to assume copying of the former by the latter. In this and other French treatises the Calvinist theological and political theories of revolution are combined. In the Netherland declaration of 1581 religious reasons were wholly omitted; the Great Revolt was justified solely by political arguments. It was indeed a struggle *Libertatis Ergo.*

This fact had important consequences for the religious development of the Netherlands. In the crucial years between 1572 and 1576 the Calvinists, unflinching opponents of King Philip and the Inquisition, had taken the lead among the revolutionists and gained control over the city governments and thus over the States of Holland and Zeeland. From that time it became the constant aspiration of zealous Calvinists to impress their conceptions upon the state authorities and to re-shape the Netherlands as a second Geneva. Equally persistent as this pressing by the Calvinists, was the resistance to such extreme views by the majority of the ruling oligarchy. "This war," Oldenbarnevelt said, "has been fought for the freedom of the provinces, not for the establishment of one reformed religious creed over all the country." The Calvinist religious leaders demanded the suppression of all non-Calvinist public worship, the expulsion of all Catholic priests, war against popery, everywhere and always, as the first aim of Netherland policy. The political leaders, having seen that Netherland Catholics, after their cruel persecution by men like Lumey and Sonoy, commanders of the Sea Beggars, were all too likely to become pro-Spanish Fifth Columnists, agreed to the suppression of public Catholic worship and ordered all foreign priests to leave the territory of the Republic. But they had no inclination to imitate Philip and Alva and become active persecutors for religious motives. In theory the new Netherland government was intolerant, in practice it was not.

The Union of Utrecht explicitly provided for freedom of conscience and provincial autonomy in matters of worship. As a matter of fact the Calvinists, strongly supported by the armed forces, imposed Calvinism everywhere. The Reformed Church followed in the wake of Maurice of Nassau's conquering armies. Firmly entrenched in leading positions, the Calvinists and their non-denominational sympathizers, who dreaded Catholicism for its connection with Spain, decreed the abolition of all "popish practices" and thus slowly turned the majority of the people towards the Reformed Church. But it took a long time before this goal was achieved, and in many rural districts and among the poorer sections of the population in the cities Calvinism never took firm hold. Not without reason did Theodore Bèze complain of the laxity of the Netherland State in spreading Reformed principles. Calvinism was encouraged, protected, and given a privileged place in the new Republic, but only because it was proof positive of the irreparable break with Spain. The Netherlands became Calvinist because they were anti-Spanish, and this political Calvinism was a constant source of grief to all true believers in Calvin and his teachings.

Thus the policy of religious tolerance, inaugurated by Prince William of Orange, had ended in a tragic failure. His ideal had been that Catholics, Lutherans, and Calvinists should live side by side in peace. He was one of the few who indignantly opposed persecution of the Anabaptists, still suspect because of the upheaval of 1536. The foremost champion of religious tolerance in the Netherlands was Dirk Volckertszoon Coornhert. The story of his life reflects the conflict of opinion then prevailing in the Netherlands. Born in Amsterdam and brought up as a Catholic, he traveled through Spain and Portugal before he settled in Haarlem where he became an engraver, illustrator, and printer. Acquiring knowledge by study of the books he printed, he became a notary and secretary of his town. The Spaniards put him in prison as a Protestant, but at the same time he incurred the wrath of Calvin for supporting the Castillionist point of view, which belittled the importance of dogmatic distinctions. Having escaped from the prison of the Inquisition, Coornhert fled to Germany, returned in 1572, and again was forced to flee because of his courageous denunciation of the cruelties perpetrated on Catholics. In 1576, as things seemed to be settling down in the Netherlands, Coornhert returned to Haarlem. Having resumed his office, he immediately began to advocate toleration and equal rights for both Catholics and Protestants. Once more he was bitterly attacked and driven into exile. Later he was permitted to return to Holland, but never to his own town of Haarlem. Until his death in 1590 he never ceased to maintain the great principle that brotherly love is the first maxim of Christian morality, and that even the most bizarre "heretic" only seeks to serve God to the best of his ability. Coornhert's ideals were never openly accepted by the Netherland Republic, but to the credit of its leaders be it said that they often followed them in practice in days when cruel religious persecution was common in both Protestant and Catholic countries. The same spirit of toleration saved the Netherlands from one of the worst horrors born of superstition, the burning of witches and sorcerers which came to an end in the Netherlands more than a century before its inhumanity was realized in either Massachusetts or Germany.

CHAPTER VIII

Dominating the Seven Seas

IN 1596 the Netherland Republic had entered into the triple alliance with France and England. Two years later King Henry IV made his peace with Spain at Vervins. After another five years, Queen Elizabeth died, leaving her kingdom to the wily James I. The Netherlands continued the struggle alone. Their former master, Philip II, died in 1598, but not before realizing that his sovereignty over the Low Countries, so tenaciously defended, had been a mill stone around his neck and had dragged him from the height of power to the abyss of disaster. Determined to rid the Spanish crown of these burdensome possessions, he transferred the sovereignty over the Low Countries to his daughter Isabella and her husband, Albert, archduke of Austria. Spain with her dependent territories he left to his son, Philip III. The cession to his daughter included his claims to the northern Low Countries where nobody then heeded his wishes or decisions. The archduke's attempt at reconciliation with the rebellious states inevitably came to naught, as the northern provinces were no more willing to recognize his sovereignty than that of their former king.

War continued; but the Republic, now perfectly safe from Spanish invasion, was unwilling to run great risks. Maurice of Nassau undertook an expedition into Flanders, where at Nieuwpoort in 1600 he won his only great battle in the open. In spite of this the Spaniards conquered Ostende, the last stronghold of the Republic in the southern provinces. The war spilled over the eastern boundary and a number of towns in the Rhineland and in Westphalia had to suffer attacks from both parties and to tolerate foreign garrisons. In 1595, the States forestalled a possible attack from East Friesland by occupying several fortresses along the river Ems. Only twenty-five years had elapsed since Netherland Calvinists had sought refuge from Alva's violence in the lands of the count of East Friesland and already that tiny country had been brought under the tutelage of the erstwhile refugees, now leaders of a strong power. In the first decade of the XVIth century when weariness weakened the strategy of Maurice of Nassau, the Spaniards under a new and energetic leader, Ambrosio Spinola of Genoa, won a few spectacular successes in the eastern provinces. After this the archduke concluded a twelve years' truce with the States General.

Both parties were weary of the long conflict, but neither had suffered enough to make it willing to sacrifice its principles. The archduke made the greater concession, for he agreed to deal with the Republic "as he would deal with a free, independent state." It was a roundabout way of recognizing the independence of the Netherlands, but one from which there was no going back.

The conclusion of the Twelve Years' Truce assured the Netherlands a prominent position among the European powers. Achieved after forty years of hard struggle, under the leadership of two members of the dynasty of Orange-Nassau and of the city aristocracy of Holland, this success sanctioned the constitutional organization of the Republic as it had developed during the war. The Union of Utrecht, originally nothing but a treaty of alliance between independent sovereign provinces, now became a sacred constitutional law which during two centuries was never changed, however glaring its shortcomings might be. Of this momentous document, only one article was ever put into full effect though at times violated in isolated instances. It was the first article which provided that the united provinces would present a common front to the outside world, as if they were one state. As far as the internal affairs of the new federation were concerned, the negative aspects of the Union were always stressed at the expense of the positive ones. In other words, the Union of Utrecht was merely an acknowledgment that each of the provinces needed the help of the others to maintain its independence, but so long as this limited purpose was achieved provincial sovereignty might in no way be curtailed. Consequently, the Republic had a national foreign policy, a national army and even to some extent a national navy but it had no national administration.

No wonder that the federal machinery worked with difficulty, indeed it is a miracle that it worked at all. That it did work was due only to certain factors which in themselves were contrary to the basic principle of provincial sovereignty. These factors were the common bond created among the inhabitants of the various provinces by the profession of one and the same Reformed religion (a national church movement in spite of the article of the Union reserving all church matters to provincial authorities); the semi-monarchical position of the House of Orange-Nassau, rather an anomaly in a state that professed to be a federative republic; the predominant position of the province of Holland which when necessary acted if the Union failed to act and often bore the financial burden for all the Netherlands. The constitutional history of the Netherland Republic reveals continuous conflict and compromise among these three forces.

The Republic was ruled by an oligarchy of some ten thousand persons who strove to keep all important political offices in their families. They succeeded in so doing, fairly well in the XVIIth century and almost completely in the XVIIIth, the system being more effective in the towns than in the rural districts. The gentry were supposed to represent the countryside. In Holland they had little influence, one vote against eighteen for the towns—and that one vote was expressed through, although not controlled by the grand pensionary of the province, always a member of one of the city aristocracies. In Zeeland only one nobleman voted, the lord of Maartensdijk, who happened to be the prince of Orange. In the old northeastern districts united with Holland and Zeeland under Charles V, membership in the States Assemblies was dependent upon the possession of certain estates or sites where franchise-holding farmsteads once stood. Not that acquisition of such real estate unconditionally entailed a seat in the representative body. Noble descent and a certain degree of wealth were also required but no list of noble families or of franchise-holding estates was ever compiled. Strange as it may seem, this omission provided exactly the instrument the ruling class needed to maintain its oligarchy, for, in this way, every new claim to participation in the provincial government had to be passed upon by them.

The city aristocrats had little difficulty in preserving the oligarchic form of government, for in normal times members of the town councils decided who should fill any vacancy and they elected the burgomasters and jurors. Certain princely prerogatives, once exercised by the king's representatives, and later by the princes of Orange in their capacity of stadhouder, had hardly any influence on this self-perpetuating system of family rule. The ruling families proved so efficient in excluding new elements from participation in public affairs that within a few decades they formed a separate caste. Neither wealth nor ability could procure a share in the government to outsiders. As time went on, this family rule became more and more selfish, but it was many decades before it became really hateful to the people. On the contrary, for years the system seemed beneficial and well adapted to the peculiar Netherland circumstances. World wide trade had given the merchants of Holland a knowledge of foreign lands and customs. Their children, educated, both in a great business and in a great humanistic tradition and with sufficient means to devote time and energy to matters of state were on the whole better judges of international affairs than the princes of Europe and their aristocratic advisors. There was less corruption in Netherland administration than in that of other countries and, with growing prosperity, the people were in general well content to leave matters of general policy in the hands of the burgher-aristocrats. Only when disparity between profits received and services rendered became too glaring did the people object to the position of the privileged class.

The events of 1581 and later years had led the provincial States Assemblies to assume the sovereignty of which they had deprived King Philip. But the members of these assemblies, though all belonging to the new privileged group, really represented a number of conflicting interests. The divergence between town and countryside, apparent in the XVIth century, continued to exist in a somewhat different form in the XVIIth and XVIIIth centuries. In Holland it presented no problem. There the towns ruled, and their relation to the rural districts, has been aptly described as that of a metropolis towards a colonial dependency. In Friesland the situation was reversed for there the towns held only one vote out of four, the States being divided into four sections, three of which represented the ancient *gouws,* while the fourth was composed of the eleven towns of the province. But in provinces like Overijssel, where three towns opposed sixty nobles, the vote of each town being counted as equal to that of one-third of the nobles, and in Groningen, where the city had one vote and the nobility another, the constitution invited conflict. There the "sovereign authority" exercised by the States Assembly was a relatively novel institution, and ancient Hansa towns like Groningen and those along the IJssel were reluctant to recognize it. An endless series of quarrels ensued—in the States of Groningen they at times developed into brawls among the "Noble and Mighty Lords"—with inevitable delay in deciding matters of higher policy, all of which caused grave concern to the gentlemen of Holland who were eager to get things done.

The same class that ruled the towns and rural districts controlled the judiciary, for the town jurors were elected by the town councils, and all administrative and judicial posts in rural districts were filled through the provincial States, controlled by the same group. The only weakness in the system—a weakness beneficial to the liberty of the people—was the lack of an organized police system in the towns. The officers of justice had a few assistants, but even in a big city like Amsterdam they were too few to maintain order. For this purpose the oligarchy had to depend on the city-guards and the army—that is on ordinary citizens they had haughtily excluded from the city government, and on faithful soldiers of the prince of Orange whose influence they jealously sought to limit. So if the citizens *wanted* to revolt, they could do so with little danger if supported by the prince of Orange. Then the oligarchic system was bound to collapse. The greatest of the oligarchs, John De Witt, the famous grand pensionary, was one victim of this peculiar weakness of the system.

The Seven Provinces forming the Union, Holland, Zeeland, Utrecht, Guelderland, Friesland, "Stad en Landen"—(Groningen), Overijssel—and supposed to present a common front to the outside world and to pursue *one* foreign policy, had no Foreign Office, let alone a Minister of Foreign Affairs or Secretary of State. All matters concerning the "Generality"—the nation as a whole—were handled by the States General, composed of delegates from the seven provincial assemblies. These delegates were not representatives of their provinces, and had no power to act on their own responsibility. They came to the Hague merely to hear what was proposed and then went home to receive instructions from their provincial assembly. If the proposal was something new, the delegates of the towns in the provincial meetings also went home to ask the views of their local authorities. Travel was relatively comfortable in the XVIIth century Netherlands as the canals offered safe and direct connections for the *trekschuit,* a river boat drawn by horse or manpower. Foreigners, used to bumping over uneven roads in heavy carriages, admired the *trekschuit* for its smooth convenience as today we admire the airplane. But a great deal of time was wasted in journeying to and fro between Friesland or Zeeland and The Hague, not to mention the long drawn out proceedings in the States General themselves. To make things worse, decisions had to be unanimous.

Except for the "Council of State," a relic of old times now only a shadow of its former self, the States General were the only national administrative body of the Republic. The constant fear of the provinces lest this central executive organ should gain influence at the expense of their own autonomy caused them to keep it under strict control. Such a system could not work. Some strong man or influential group had to take the lead and then the aristocracy would submit and follow, at times accepting leadership tacitly, at times protesting violently.

There were two centers where such leadership could originate. One was the province of Holland which, in theory, carried 54 percent of the nation's financial burden and, actually, far more and which also provided most of the nation's leaders and most of the nation's ships and sailors. The other was the House of Orange. Whenever one of these forces secured a firm hold on public affairs, the States General usually consented to delegate part of their power to a small committee selected from their number to cooperate with the leadership. The name of this committee, *Secreet Besogne,* shows that its chief purpose was to maintain secrecy in handling foreign affairs. Centralization under the supremacy of Holland would have been a logical national development. The other provinces could in no way compete with Holland and seemed to have no right to equal rank and vote. Therefore, if no counter influence made itself felt, Holland took the lead in foreign policy which it left in the hands of its highest official,

the grand pensionary. This was the basis of the political power of Oldenbarnevelt and later of John De Witt. But usually, there was a counter-
influence, that of the House of Orange.

The constitutional position of the Orange family was peculiar. William I
("the Silent") had been one of the wealthiest land and office holders in
the Habsburg Lowland state and stadhouder or lieutenant of his king. The
king had been deposed but not his lieutenant. This curious and illogical
situation caused no concern so long as the States of Holland were thinking
of electing a new prince. The problem would have been neatly solved if
William himself had been elevated to the rank of count of Holland as was
planned in 1584. But after the whole idea was dropped the States appointed
William's son, Maurice, as stadhouder with certain sovereign prerogatives. In the eyes of the States of Holland, Maurice was their servant for he
was appointed and paid by them; in the eyes of the common people, Maurice was the national leader and therefore put above the States. Originally
each province had its own stadhouder, although cumulative appointments
were not unusual. In addition to being stadhouder of Holland, Maurice
was appointed, in 1589 and after, stadhouder of Guelderland, Utrecht, and
Overijssel. Friesland, Groningen, and Drente had their own stadhouder
in the person of Maurice's cousin, William Louis of Nassau. Thus the chief
offices in all the provinces were in the hands of one family in which the
leadership of the Holland branch was recognized, a family that received
added lustre from the glorious memory of William I, from its enormous
estates and from the military success of Maurice and his position as commander-in-chief of the army and navy.[29] In theory, the prince of Orange
was merely a prominent citizen of the Republic, as John De Witt used to
say, in practice he was a candidate to the throne and recognized as such
by the mass of the people and by foreign powers. Maurice's brother and
successor, Frederick Henry, was addressed by foreign rulers as "Your
Highness," a title usually reserved for princes. The Stuarts of England
even gave a royal princess in marriage to his son, young William II. The
princes of Orange had no claim to sovereignty in any province of the Netherlands but backed by popular approval they did claim the right to act in
the name of the Union and if necessary to curb the self-willfulness of their
rulers the Nobles and Mighty Lords—the States.

Cooperation between these two forces in the Republic—an ideal condition—lasted only so long as the country was in grave danger from the
Spanish army. Holland financed and supported the campaigns by which
Maurice liberated the seven provinces from Spanish rule. As soon, however, as this purpose was achieved (around 1600, after the great victory of

Nieuwpoort), a rift appeared between the two forces in the Union and soon began to widen.

This was the origin of the tragic conflict of the second decade of the XVIIth century in which Maurice of Nassau represented the forces of unification on a national basis and Oldenbarnevelt those advocating the leadership of Holland. The pretext for this conflict was a religious one: the Calvinists had split over the dogma of predestination, accepted in its strict interpretation by the majority under the leadership of Franciscus Gomarus, and rejected by a minority under Jakob Arminius, both professors of theology at Leiden. The States of Holland sided with the minority, as the more liberal conception concurred with the Erasmian tradition, still strong among the educated class which preferred political rather than dogmatic Protestantism.[30] The rift between Arminius and Gomarus led to a demand for the convocation of a national synod which Holland, relying on the text of the Union of Utrecht, stubbornly resisted. Foreign powers intervened in the dispute. The conceited James I of England, proud of his theological knowledge and prejudiced against Oldenbarnevelt, sided with the Gomarists; while the king of France, interested in maintaining the grand pensionary in power, favored the Arminians.

When Maurice entered the lists in aid of the Gomarists, he found his supporters ready. Behind him were the "land provinces," still jealous of the "sea provinces," a cleavage as we have seen as old as Netherland history. Behind him was the army, and with it the orthodox Calvinists, all who wanted Church interests to take precedence of political interests. Behind him also were all who opposed the oligarchy, or, for one reason or another objected to Oldenbarnevelt's influence. Among the latter happened to be the ruling magistrates of Amsterdam. The outcome of the conflict was never in doubt. It was of no avail to the grand pensionary that Hugo Grotius, the greatest genius in the field of letters ever produced by the Netherlands, stood on his side. But the outcome might have been less bloody. The seventy year old pensionary, "a man of great activity, business, memory, and wisdom, yes extraordinary in every respect" (we quote the register of the States of Holland) was beheaded on May 13, 1619, after a mock trial to cover up this political murder. Oldenbarnevelt was one of the few really great statesmen the Netherlands have ever had. Although not unselfish, his patriotic convictions were so deep, his success in the management of internal and external affairs so great, that he may well share with William I, the distinction of founder of the Republic. Twice in Netherland history was such a political murder committed, on each occasion a great man, a leader of the oligarchic party, was the victim. Force was on the side of their opponents who finally after two centuries reorganized the Netherland state after their own conception. Spiritually the oligarchs of Holland, the "Regents" as they are usually called, may well be counted the victors, for it was they who largely shaped national traditions.

The Regents liked to draw parallels between their own state and that of Rome, the ideal republic. Holland, like Rome, had grown from small beginnings; but it had grown fast; and its empire extended to the distant corners of the earth. As in Rome, the creation of the Republic had been the work of the aristocracy who stretched forth the iron hand of unbending authority over the people and alone, directed the policy of the State. As in the Rome of Augustus, a prominent position in the Republic was held by an hereditary leader, commander-in-chief of the army and navy, who constitutionally, was no more than the first of the citizens. The burgher-aristocrats of Holland considered themselves the Romans of Northern Europe, and the humanistic tradition prevailing since the days of Erasmus gave life and color to this conception.

But the men of Holland did not fall into slavish idolatry of ancient Rome. Their spokesmen transposed the Roman epic into the ancient Germanic world to create a surer foundation for their political tradition. Publius Cornelius Tacitus, the great Roman historian from whom XVIIth century political thinkers learned the art of government, provided them not only with a eulogy of their semi-monarchical state controlled by an aristocracy but also with predecessors in old Germanic times, Civilis the Batave and his associates, who fought for freedom against Roman imperialism as they the Regents had fought for liberty against Spanish tyranny. Hugo Grotius, in his *On the Antiquity of the Batave Republic* written around 1610, carefully reviewed what Tacitus wrote on the revolt of Civilis and finding a reference to Civilis and the "leading men" of the Batave tribe as arbiters of peace and war, somewhat lightly concluded that this meeting of the "leading men" was the prototype of the later States Assembly, and that the latter institution dated back to old Germanic times. The States, Grotius contended, had always held the sovereignty of the province and had merely entrusted it to their princes during the Middle Ages to take it back again in 1581. Did not some of the medieval charters provide that the government be in the hands of "the most honorable, most noteworthy, most liberally-minded and peaceful" citizens of the town, and did not these terms exactly describe the ruling oligarchy? Pieter Corneliszoon Hooft, son of an Amsterdam burgomaster and one of the outstanding men of letters of his time, wrote a play Baëto or the Origin of the Hollanders, in which he created a new version of the legend of the Batavi and described the origin of the ancient Batave "state." According to him, the first king did not assume leadership of his people until asked so to do by the soldiers and citizenry and then only with the advice and consent of the most noble and prominent citizens. There was the same idea again: the prominent citizens in control of the community, they might offer actual leadership to a prince, a commander of the troops; but they would not tolerate presumption on his part or admit the mass of the people to a share in the public affairs.

This exalted conception of the high and unattainable character of the oligarchic system seemed to be shaken to its foundations at the beginning of the XVIIth century by the execution of its great protagonist Oldenbarnevelt. Grotius, condemned to life imprisonment, escaped in the well-known romantic way in a trunk from the place of his arrest and spent the rest of his life outside the Netherlands, a sad result of internal strife. But in spite of this rough repression of eminent learning representing the oligarchy, its tradition gained force as time progressed.

The Republic of the United Netherlands thus constituted, derived all its strength from its economic resources. Before the Twelve Years' Truce had come to an end, the provinces of Holland and Zeeland had developed into the principal commercial power of Europe, even of the world. In these two provinces no other city approached Amsterdam in the extension of trade and financial resources. The trade with the Baltic, with southern Europe, with the East and West Indies was largely concentrated in this one town which for three-quarters of a century provided the most spectacular instance of a city-empire the world has ever seen. The whole of the Netherland Republic then numbered about one million five hundred thousand inhabitants, of whom certainly more than half resided in the two coastal provinces and about 100,000 in Amsterdam. This small group of people built a commercial empire and became the leaders of trade in every corner of the world.

One of the strangest fables of history attributes the prosperity of the Netherlands in the XVIIth century as based upon the exploitation of the East Indies. Some textbooks of history even support this legend with the further statement that the seamen of Holland and Zeeland learned the routes of Spanish and Portuguese trade by piratical raids and plunder, finally supplanting the Spanish-Portuguese monopoly with their own, only to be superseded in turn by the economic expansion of England. Historical legends are usually persistent, but rarely are they so damaging to historical truth, as this particular fable which falsifies the whole picture of XVIIth century history.

Before the Great Revolt, Antwerp had far exceeded Holland and Zeeland in commercial importance. There was however one characteristic difference. Antwerp's trade was passive. Its ports received ships from Lue-beck, Lisbon, and Venice which there exchanged their cargoes. Spaniards, Germans, and Italians were numerous among its leading business people. On the other hand, from the very first Holland and Zeeland concentrated on carrying freight in their own ships, and the geographic nature of these provinces furthered such a development. In the Baltic the sea captains of Holland had been fierce competitors of the Hanseatic merchants since the XVth century, and in the XVIth century—long before there was any ques-tion of "preying upon Spanish commerce"—they steadily forged ahead in the important wheat trade from Poland and Lithuania. In 1585 the city of Antwerp fell to the Spaniards. From that time the Scheldt was closed to all shipping. Amsterdam became the center of the Baltic trade which was soon dominated—but never monopolized—by Holland, Spain, at war all over Europe, did not produce enough for her own consumption. Nether-landers and Englishmen were the only people who could transport Baltic wheat to the ports of southern Europe. The English, up to 1588, had the advantage of being at peace with Spain while the Netherlanders, as "here-tics" and "rebels," ran some risk in entering Spanish towns. Nevertheless, the bulk of the trade to Spain was carried by Netherlanders and not by the English.

This success was due to superior seamanship and greater financial re-sources. After 1594 the ship builders of Holland designed a new type of ship, the *fluit,* longer and narrower than the older models, and a good sailing vessel. The length of a *fluit* was normally 125 feet and its displace-ment rarely more than 300 tons. Because it was easier to handle, the new ship was more economic, and this fact alone explains something of Dutch maritime and commercial superiority. But far more important was the strong financial position of the Netherland merchants. Early Dutch capi-tal resources did not originate from treasures captured from the Spaniards in piratical raids as some textbooks seem to suppose, nor were they built from the fortunes of Jewish immigrants as a few serious historians have suggested. They were slowly accumulated by many generations from the fisheries, the river trade, and the Baltic trade. The wealth of Holland was bolstered by the Spaniards themselves when they drove thousands of Cal-vinist merchants and industrialists from Antwerp, Brussels, Ghent, and other southern cities. These merchants were allowed two years to wind up their affairs and were permitted to take their property with them, a lenient policy adopted by the duke of Parma to avoid a last ditch defense of be-leaguered cities. These immigrants from the South added greatly to the financial resources of Holland and Zeeland and were always among the first to engage in new and risky enterprises, although they were by no means the determining factor in the development of northern economic power. Dutch superiority in capital resources was the main cause of Dutch supremacy in world trade. When the Dutch East India Company was organized, a capital of six and a half million guilders was raised without any difficulty. The English East India Company had originally at its disposal only 80,000 pounds, not even a sixth of the Dutch capital. The king of Denmark, who planned an East India Company of his own, collected only a few hundred thousand guilders most of which was provided by Netherlanders. The merchants of Holland ousted the English from the Russian trade by offering higher prices and bribing the officials of the Czar who were quick to see where real money was to be had. The picture was the same everywhere and this was why the economic conflict between the English and the Netherlanders became so bitter. Whatever efforts the English made, however drastic the decrees King James signed, even claiming the North Sea fishing grounds as part of his kingdom, the progress of Dutch commerce backed by strong resources could not be equaled, let alone stopped.

Dutch capital, profitably employed in and steadily increasing because of European trade, made possible the expeditions to the four corners of the earth which caught the imagination of the world. Excess energy and resources found interesting outlets in these distant voyages which, after initial reverses produced sizeable returns. The East Indian and West Indian trade were the natural outgrowth of the rapidly expanding Dutch commercial system. A few facts will bear this out.

The trade on the Baltic had long been established. But up to the XVIIth century it was carried on in competition with the Hanseatics and in cooperation with Denmark. In the first decade of the XVIIth century the Hanseatics ceased to be serious competitors and, in 1611, Oldenbarnevelt reversed Netherland policy by concluding an alliance with Luebeck against Denmark that sought to enforce its control over the Sund. So far, contact with Russia had to take place through intermediaries in the Baltic ports. Temporary Russian control of Narva (until 1581) immediately brought Dutch ships into that port. At the same time Netherland sea captains began to follow the English and sail around Norway to Russia's northern coast. In 1567 Olivier Brunel, the pioneer of Dutch-Russian trade, opened direct relations with the Russians. For a time temporarily their prisoner, he accompanied their explorers along the northern coast of Europe and Asia as far as the river Ob. In 1578 the Dutch maritime interests established a factory at the mouth of the Dwina near Saint Michael's monastery, preferring this location to the landing places used by the English. Around that factory the Russians built the town of Archangelsk. In 1587, Dutch vessels trading on the White Sea outnumbered the British ten to one, according to a statement by Czar Feodor. In 1600 Isaac Massa, a trader from Haarlem, was appointed the first representative of the Republic to the Czar of Russia. Eighteen years later the first Russian embassy came to the Netherlands.

Commerce with northern Russia naturally stirred interest in the navigation of the northern Seas. Desirous of reaching East Asia by a route not under Spanish control, Netherland navigators explored the Arctic Seas. They were perfectly aware of the fact, considered by some a great discovery of our "air-minded" generation, that the North Pole sea route, if practicable, would be by far the shortest between western Europe and eastern Asia. The first expedition to the north sailed in 1594. Two others followed in a few years, exploration being continued even after the first Dutch ships had reached the Indies by the traditional southern route. The only results were the discovery of Bear Island, Spitsbergen, and the northern point of Nova Zembla where Heemskerck and Barendsz were forced to spend the winter of 1596–97. Later expeditions in the XVIIth century brought Netherland ships as high as 83 degrees north, in the seas of Spitsbergen, and 85 degrees north in Strait Davis, where all hopes had to be given up that the Polar Sea could ever be used for commercial navigation. Later expeditions to the north were connected with the whale fisheries which started around 1613. Shipping in the far North occupied scores of vessels, while more than a thousand others sailed to and fro between Holland and the ports of the Baltic. Even more ships were engaged in the trade with England and the countries to the South. English foreign commerce, still in its early stages, was badly hampered by monopolies granted to privileged companies, the Muscovy Company for the Russian trade and the Merchant Adventurers for the cloth trade on the Continent. This system lacked flexibility, and Dutch ships not only carried all freight between England and Germany, but also between England and France, and even to a great extent the coastal shipping from one English port to another.

France was one of the Netherlands' most important customers as early as the XVth century. In the last decade of the XVIth century Dutch capital began to penetrate the whole French productive system. Agents of Dutch companies settled in the principal towns of southern France and by advancing money on the coming wine harvest secured virtual control over the French wine trade. Dutch vessels carried the product from Bordeaux and La Rochelle to Holland and Zeeland. Spain and Portugal depended so much for the import of foodstuffs on Dutch ships that Philip II, although sorely tempted to destroy ships and crews, hesitated to take any action against them. Having done so once or twice, he was forced to allow them to return. We are told, but there may be some exaggeration in the report, that more than 25,000 sailors made their living in the Spanish-Portuguese trade alone. All these trade relations were fully established before a single ship had found its way to Java or the Moluccas. And a few years before the first trip to the East Indies was undertaken, Dutch ships penetrated into the Mediterranean where they found Italy in dire need of wheat. In 1590 for the first time they entered the ports of Genoa, Naples, and Venice, where they became regular visitors. Medieval commercial trends had been reversed: instead of meeting in the Low Countries the merchants of the Baltic and of Italy saw the ships of Holland come to them. Before the XVIth century came to a close, trade connections were established with the Levant and permission obtained from the Padishah of Turkey to trade with all Ottoman ports. Here in the Mediterranean the Dutch were their own worst enemies. The Barbary pirates were a scourge to all shipping, but it is doubtful that the North Africans with their old-fashioned ships could ever have become the menace they were later had not an international gang of outlaws taught them the tricks of navigation. And among these outlaws, Dutch renegades were prominent.

Around 1590 Dutch ships began to sail to the West Indies in search for salt they badly needed for the herring trade. The routes to the Western hemisphere were no secret to them. For many years Dutch masters and their crews, had sailed back and forth between Portugal and Brazil under the Portuguese flag. Dutch capital was back of Brazilian trade as the capital of Flanders and Antwerp had been half a century before. The strict regulations issued by Philip II who, after 1580, was king of Portugal as well as of Spain, made Portuguese-Dutch cooperation more difficult but did not bring it to an end. By a decree of 1585 he ordered all Netherland ships in Spanish-Portuguese ports seized and in 1590 he sent the crews of twenty-one ships on their way home from the Mediterranean to the galleys. These decrees merely incited the Netherlands to further expansion.

On the coast of Guinea, where the Portuguese held a monopoly, Zeeland and Holland interlopers carried on such a brisk trade in the last two decades of the XVIth century that their vessels often out-numbered those of the ruling power. By 1594, Dutch trading was expanding feverishly north and south, and the time was near when those enterprising merchants and mariners would begin to send their vessels around the Cape of Good Hope and through the Straits of Magellan. They were by no means unacquainted with these trade routes, for many Hollanders had sailed on Portuguese ships to the Indies, and though few such adventurers returned, several of them did come back to tell of their experiences. Dirk Gerritsen Pomp visited India and Japan in the seventies and eighties of the XVIth century, and Jan Huyghen van Linschoten who returned from India in 1592 published, a few years later, a detailed description of the country and the course taken. One of the main reasons the Netherlanders did not venture sooner on the Indian route was the exaggerated opinion of the efficiency of Portuguese control over the sea-lanes. As a neutral flag might provide some protection, we find enterprising traders negotiating in 1592 with a petty German prince, the duke of Lauenburg, for the organization of an expedition around the Cape. This scheme came to naught but in 1595 four ships commanded by Cornelis de Houtman set out for the Far East for the account of a group of Amsterdam merchants. Two years later three of the four came back, only half laden; but although the profits were by no means large, the success of the completed voyage provoked general enthusiasm and in 1598 no less than twenty-two ships, divided into five squadrons, each sailing for a different account, sailed on the same mission. Thirteen followed the route around the Cape explored on the first voyage, and of these, twelve came back, some of them with most precious cargoes that brought enormous profits. The other nine tried the western route through Magellan Strait, but of these only one returned to Holland. It was the ship commanded by Oliver van Noort who reached the Philippines by the western route and returned via the Sunda Islands and the Cape, thus completing the first Dutch circumnavigation of the world.

Of these five expeditions and five others that followed in 1599 and in 1600, only one, that commanded by Van Noort, turned to piracy and "preying on Spanish shipping" and that expedition resulted in the bankruptcy of Van Noort and of several of his financial backers. Jacob van Neck, commander of the second expedition to the Indies, proudly stated that his great commercial results were achieved solely by normal and honest trading. The leaders of the early expeditions usually received definite instruction to avoid bloodshed and violence with the natives as well as with the Portuguese. That policy changed after 1600 when the natives of the Moluccas, violently hostile to the Portuguese whom they had driven from most of their islands, requested help from the Dutch to oust their enemies completely. This led to the first clashes around Amboina and Tidore, but the initial military results gained by the Dutch were very meager.

Owing to the disasters that befell the expeditions which took the western route around South America, and to competition of the various companies, the total financial results of the first six years of the East Indian trade were small. Only one expedition gave the shipowners a profit of 100 percent, about 700,000 guilders in cash. Against this and smaller profits made by other expeditions around the Cape, stood a loss of half a million guilders on the voyages to the West. As a matter of fact the first six years enriched a small number of individuals and ruined some others, but did not yield the nation as a whole as much as the herring fisheries earned in two or three months.

This state of affairs was clear to everyone interested in the new trade. How could the East Indian trade ever become profitable if the Portuguese should organize the defense of their monopoly, thus forcing Dutch ship-owners to arm their ships more heavily and to garrison their trading posts in the East? Thanks to the courage of its leader and crews, a small Dutch squadron under Wolfert Harmenszoon, had gained a spectacular victory in 1601 over a Portuguese fleet off Bantam in Java, but it had been unable to exploit this success and the Portuguese had severely punished the people of Amboina for appealing to the Dutch. The East Indies trade could only be continued if it were organized and the States General and the States of Holland, prompted by Oldenbarnevelt, insisted on the amalgamation of the existing companies for Asiatic trade into one commercial body. In March 1602 the United East India Company received from the States General a monopoly for all Dutch trade east of the Cape of Good Hope and west of Magellan Strait.

The charter of the Company granted it the privilege of exercising all rights of sovereignty on behalf of the Netherland Republic in the territories it might conquer and in its relations with Asiatic powers. It received a subsidy from the national treasury to carry on the war against Spain and Portugal in the same regions. The orders issued to the next expeditions explicitly provided that war should be waged against the enemies of the State wherever necessary, without however putting war above trade. The latter interests were to be the paramount consideration. The Company was a business concern, not intended for the creation of an Asiatic empire. The capital of the Company was to be six and a half million guilders. The Board of Directors was to consist of seventeen members nominated by the four chambers of Amsterdam, Northern Holland, the Meuse, and Zee-land. Anyone was free to subscribe to the shares or to buy them on the stock exchange, but the Directors of the individual chambers, except in the case of Zeeland, were not to be elected by the shareholders but to be appointed from among them by the councils of the towns in which the chambers were located. In Zeeland the States of the province controlled new nominations. Thus the influence of the ruling class on the administration of the Company was assured.

The new organization immediately developed amazing activity. In three years it equipped thirty-eight ships for the Far East; and within a decade its vessels were seen off the coasts of Japan, of China, of Indo-China and Siam, of India and Arabia. In the same ten years they had discovered parts hitherto unknown to Europeans, such as the northern coast of Australia. In those ten years the Company distributed dividends only once, in 1610. True it was a large dividend, no less than 162 per cent of the original capital, but in the same period the new enterprise was burdened with heavy debts for the organization of its power in the Indies. Because of the peculiar financial organization of the Company, it is impossible to calculate the real profits derived from this branch of trade in the early part of the XVIIth century. It is a safe conclusion, however, that the shareholders and some of the commanders in the East who were rarely averse to serving their own interests along with those of the Company, earned a great deal of money. The nation as a whole saw a large part of these profits neutralized by the continuous disbursements to keep the war-chests and cash reserves in the East sufficiently provided. In the first decade of its existence the Company always had between twenty and thirty ships and perhaps three to five thousand men in the Far East. The pay of the lower ranks was outrageously low, a common sailor or soldier receiving about ten guilders a month for sailing half way round the world and venturing his life in war. The higher employees were not well paid either, but at least had a chance to make extra income by doing a little trading on their own account.

In comparison with the national income from the European trade, the East Indian undertaking was initially of no great significance. The fisheries alone occupied about twenty thousand sailors and paid about 2,800,000 guilders in yearly wages, bringing an annual profit of 800,000 guilders to the owners of the ships. In this branch of industry alone, six million guilders were invested or only a little less than the capital of the East India Company. The trade with Spain and Portugal, we are told gave employment to another twenty thousand sailors and that on the Baltic to even more. The capital invested in European trade far exceeded that employed in Asia, and the profits although less spectacular, were certainly more regular.

Thus the East Indian trade, which for centuries has fired popular imagination because of the adventurous character of the long sea voyages and of the blunt, open, if somewhat crude narratives left by its principal heroes, was really but one of many branches of Netherland commerce covering a large part of the world. Although the most spectacular, it was not even the most important ramification of Dutch trade. There were others, less noticed by contemporaries but of great consequence. In the early years of the XVIIth century, Dutch traders came to the coast of America to buy beaver skins from the Indians, and in 1609 Hendrik Hudson, instructed by the East India Company to explore the northeast passage to Asia, but obsessed with the idea of finding a route to the northwest, navigated his ship up the Hudson River as far as present Albany. Adriaan Block, ship-wrecked on the coast óf Manhattan, was the first white man to build a ship in New York harbor. Isaac Lemaire, merchant of Amsterdam and orig-inally one of the principal stockholders of the East India Company, de-cided to break the Company's monopoly by evading the terms of its charter and his son Jacques Lemaire sailed to the Pacific by the western route. He avoided the Strait of Magellan by circumnavigating the top of South America. The names of Cape Horn (after the town of Hoorn where Lemaire had found his principal supporters), Staten Island, and Lemaire Strait were then written on the map. All trade with America's east coast and the western shores of Africa was taken over by the West India Com-pany when this body was organized after the Twelve Years' Truce had come to an end in 1621. However, this Western Company was not a com-mercial enterprise. It was actually organized for preying on Spanish ship-ping, for privateering against the enemy's American empire. Its history belongs to that of the war against Spain more than to that of general eco-nomic development.

The economy of the Netherlands would have been unbalanced indeed, if this astounding growth of overseas trade had not been accompanied by a similar expansion in industry and agriculture. Naturally, all forms of in-dustry supplying the fleets were flourishing, and the wharves of Amster-dam, Zaandam, and the Meuse were forever busy building and fitting out ships. The manufacture of sails and ropes was an important industry. Salt, imported from southern Europe and the West Indies, had to be treated before being used by the fishermen. Such industries created work and pro-vided sizeable profits, but they were wholly dependent upon the sea trade. More remarkable was the expansion of the cloth industry of Leiden, favored by the economic decline of the ancient sites of cloth production in the southern Low Countries. During the XVIIth century Leiden's industry flourished only to collapse when France introduced a protective policy, later adopted by most other countries. When Leiden was no longer able to compete with foreign manufacturers, the center of the industry was transferred to Brabant where the poor village people of this terribly im-poverished district were willing to work for the lowest of wages. Amster-dam, Haarlem, and Rotterdam also had their share in the textile industry of the XVIIth century. Haarlem was a great center of linen manufacture while in Amsterdam silk imported from Persia and China was woven into beautiful fabrics. Utrecht surpassed all other Netherland towns in the production of velvet and *velours d'Utrecht* gained a world wide reputation.

Many thousands of people found occupation in these industries, but only a few of them attained prosperity. The same was also true of many smaller industries which, like the manufacture of gin in Schiedam, sometimes gained wide popularity but hardly contributed to the general well-being of the people. It is only too true that the masses of the townspeople received a very small share in the marvelous profit realized by the economic expansion of the country. Women and children were often preferred as workers in industry because they were "cheaper," which means that children six years of age and over were forced to work as long as daylight permitted their exploitation, and then were set free to beg on the streets. In the busiest center of Holland's industry, twenty thousand people—not necessarily unemployed—had to be kept from starvation by charity, and it was truly said that in Amsterdam contagious diseases which took the lives of thousands of poor people, never afflicted "burgomasters, aristocrats, ministers of the Church, or town officials." Apparently pre-disposition for the disease had something to do with under-nourishment and miserable living quarters. The dwellings of the poor were not so neat as the rooms we see in Vermeer's paintings, their clothing not so fine as that of the ladies and gentlemen portrayed by Rembrandt. Under-payment was normal, and vacations were unknown. There was no respite on Sundays, and the previously existing holidays were abolished by the Reformation.[31]

Granted that appeals to charity usually met with generous response from those who were more amply blessed with this world's goods, but willingness to give alms does not make up for a lack of all sense of responsibility towards one's fellowmen. In the East Indies the ruthlessness of Governor General Coen, who did not hesitate to exterminate the people of the Banda Islands to gain control of their clove-production, was opposed by the humanity of Laurens Reael and others who bitterly protested the massacre of the Bandanese who, they said, had "fought for the same cause against Coen as the Netherlands fought for against Spain, that of their freedom." Sailors kidnaped and murdered so-called savages when landing on some forlorn shores in far away Tierra del Fuego or Africa; but others, we are told, had such commiseration for a little negro baby, left behind by his fleeing mother, that they sacrificed their scarves to make it comfortable. These are a few instances of conflicting attitudes which could be multiplied a hundredfold. It was poverty that made the working people both on land and on sea rough and uncouth. In the same way the upper classes, often ruthless in their exploitation of the poor and merciless towards beggars, showed on many occasion a heart for the sufferings of the masses.[32]

All these commercial and industrial activities caused a vast accumulation of capital in the hands of the principal merchants, while the middleclass, although by no means rich also became moderately prosperous. This capital sought investment. Government bonds, issued by all the provinces (those of Holland being naturally preferred) were the most favored form. Because of growing confidence in the stability of the new Republic and the continuous increase in capital, the rate of interest paid by the States of Holland was reduced from 12 or 10 percent to 6 percent a year. In 1650 Holland alone had a national debt of 140,000,000 guilders and nearly all its bonds were in the possession of nationals of the province.

Another more speculative but possibly more profitable investment was provided by agricultural enterprises, in the first place, by the dyking in and reclaiming of swamps, inland lakes, or inlets of the sea. In the twenty-five years before 1590 and 1615, a period when the East India trade had not yet added much to the welfare of the Netherlands, nearly a hundred thousand acres of land were reclaimed. In 1610 the Beemster lake, nearly eighteen thousand acres in extent, was drained. It proved a hazardous enterprise from a financial point of view, for the first organizers lost nearly all their money when the breaking of a dyke and reflooding of the *polder* made necessary a second draining. Once the enterprise was completed it gave enormous profits, nearly a quarter of a million guilders a year. To continue our comparison between the returns from home and continental enterprises, with those from the Indies, the profits from reclaiming land alone must have equaled or exceeded those from the Far Eastern trade during the first decade of the XVIIth century and probably continued to exceed them for the next hundred years. In the years between 1615 and 1640 another 110,000 acres were added to Holland's arable soil. The largest of all inland lakes, the *Haarlemmermeer,* which extended over fifteen thousand acres and yearly extended to destroy neighboring peatlands, was also scheduled for drainage. The famous engineer, Jan Adriaansz Leeghwater, made plans for this enterprise which even in the nineteenth century when the project was completed with the help of steam driven machinery, provoked the admiration of all experts. The risks and the capital involved seemed too great, however, for the seventeenth century and Leeghwater, greatly disappointed at not being allowed to undertake this monumental work, looked for other tasks. His fame was such that he was called to France, to Lorraine, and to Holstein to undertake drainage works. Even so, he remained a simple working-man, the master mechanic and carpenter who, in between the draining of swamps, devoted his time to the construction of clocks for church towers, and felt honored when he was allowed to wait upon His Excellency, the Prince of Orange, and the city aristocrats who had come to "open" the newly reclaimed polder in the Beemster.

If we seek to give the economic system of the seventeenth century Netherlands a name, and many people nowadays insist on pasting a label on every historical or social development, it should be that of imperialistic capitalism.[33] Capitalist it certainly was and its imperialism was by no means confined to America, Asia, or Africa, but sought to penetrate and master Europe as well as distant lands. Everywhere and always the sole concern of XVIIth century Dutch capitalism was "profit making," whether under the Netherland flag or that of some other nation or even under the black flag of piracy. But it must be repeated that in this respect the Netherlands sinned no more than other nations. Gold was their sole aim and many did not hesitate to sell Spain ammunition and war equipment that, a few days later, might be used against Netherland towns and troops. A popular story told of a sea captain who said that "he would sail into hell and trade with the devil were it not that his sails might catch fire."

Netherland merchants had no more qualms about slave-trading than the English, Spanish, or Portuguese; and the Dutch slave vessels plying between the coast of Guinea and the West Indian Island of Curaçao became notorious. But slaves brought to the Netherlands became free the moment they trod its free soil, and worth remembering are the lines the poet Breero wrote on the slave traders of his day in his town of Amsterdam:

> "Inhuman is this practice, a godless knavery,
> For human beings to be sold, like beasts in slavery.
> In this town, too, there are a few, who ply the trade
> But God knows who they are; their sins shall be repaid."

Slave-trading was only one of the more extreme outgrowths of this thirst for gain. The truly capitalistic character of the early XVIIth century Netherland economy was nowhere more manifest than in Scandinavia.

The Scandinavian countries, so long under the supremacy of the Hanseatic League, were as poor in capital as they were rich in natural resources. Norway produced wood; Sweden, iron and copper; Denmark's potentialities were much the same as those of the Netherlands, but financial resources for their development were lacking. From the end of the XVIth century the kings of Denmark and Sweden appealed to Holland for assistance. Denmark sought to establish an East Indian trade of her own with Dutch money, Dutch leaders, and Dutch crews sailing under the Danish flag. In Sweden King Charles IX, endeavoring to promote his country's commercial relations, decided to build a port on the southwest coast of his kingdom. Göteborg arose, largely constructed and settled by immigrants from the Netherlands. Abraham Cabelliau, the leader of this enterprise, formerly a captain in the West Indian trade, became Swedish minister of economic affairs. He formed the audacious idea of competing with the Dutch East India Company and of diverting the Persian silk-trade from southern Persia where the Company had its factories to lead it along the old Viking route through Russia to Sweden. This plan was by no means impracticable. Transportation along the Volga and Newa to Sweden was certainly less expensive and less risky than the long journey around the Cape of Good Hope and over the stormy Atlantic Ocean to Holland. But the Russian czars were not cooperative. Sweden was their potential enemy, the state that kept them from the Baltic. Rather than favor Sweden and her Dutch financial backers, the czars sought to organize their own silk-trade; but in turn they met with little encouragement from the merchants of Amsterdam. However, the trade along the Volga later became important in connection with the Russian export of furs, for during the seventeenth century numerous small colonies of Netherlanders were scattered along the Russian rivers, from Narva and Archangelsk to Astrakhan.

While Cabelliau planned Swedish-Dutch economic expansion in the East, another Netherland promoter dreamed of using Sweden for the realization of a great Protestant American empire that would supplant the Spanish Catholic regime in Central and South America. This man, Willem Usselinx, a rather disagreeable bachelor who was easily offended and believed his compatriots were all in league against his wonderful ideals, left the Netherlands after his proposals for a West India Company had been rejected. Such a Company, he insisted, was needed not only for business reasons but also for the propagation of Calvinism in South America and for the colonization of a new Netherland beyond the ocean. The States General gave him ample opportunity to expound his plans, but finally rejected them as too ambitious, giving their preference to the founding of the privateering enterprise of 1621 which took the name of West India Company. Usselinx, disgruntled, withdrew to Sweden where he sought support for his grandiose schemes from Gustavus Adolphus and where a man, he wrote, "could at least live in peace without being constantly disturbed by women's mania for cleaning and dusting."

Sweden could not provide the resources Usselinx needed for his plan. He went to France, then returned to Sweden; and finally a small Swedish Netherland Company was launched with Dutch money, working with Dutch ships, and former employees of the Dutch West India Company. Peter Minuit, founder of New York, was to be the first Swedish commander in America. The colony was settled within the boundaries of New Netherland on the Delaware River and in 1637, of the twenty-four men garrisoning the Swedish fort Christina, twenty-three were Netherlanders. In all these Scandinavian enterprises, Netherlanders, who resented the monopolies held by the great Companies in their own land competed with Netherlanders.

The position of Louis de Geer, merchant and industrialist from Liége who had taken refuge in Holland was somewhat different. De Geer succeeded in getting control of the Swedish copper trade, and in return for loans and merchandise received a number of mining concessions. Upon this basis he built Sweden's heavy industry. His concern was a trust which controlled the most important Swedish product from the mine to the retail shop. While old De Geer cast guns and equipped armies and navies, his daughters in Stockholm sold copper kettles, knives, and kitchen utensils over the counter. With his industrial enterprises he combined a banking business which enabled him to lend to the Swedish kings the money with which they bought their military equipment in his storehouses. The great campaign of Gustavus Adolphus in Germany from 1630 to 1632 was largely financed by De Geer and supplied from his factories and warehouses. Who knows whether the epic march of Swedish troops from the Baltic to Munich would ever have been made had it not been for the backing of De Geer? Later when Oxenstierna, the Swedish chancellor, continued the struggle for the domination of the Baltic and found Denmark's navy in his way, an appeal to De Geer for help sufficed to bring relief. With his own money the great capitalist assembled a navy in Dutch ports, equipped it with guns from his storehouses, manned it with a Dutch crew, entrusted the command to a Dutch admiral. Flying the Swedish flag this fleet sailed for the Baltic and defeated the Danish navy which by the way, was largely composed of hired Dutch auxiliaries. This campaign of 1645 virtually secured to Sweden the command of the Baltic, a result of supreme indifference to De Geer but not to the States General who watched with grave concern the growth of Swedish imperialism that might well endanger free navigation in the Baltic.

De Geer's career provides one of the most striking instances of XVIIth century Netherland capitalism, but its presence could be noticed everywhere Netherland merchants went. There is no more interesting romance of trade than the development of the East India Company. The traditional picture of Dutch activity in the East emphasizes the crude and merciless exploitation of the inhabitants of the Spice Islands by the rigorous maintenance of a strict monopoly in favor of the Company. Such a system of exploitation existed, it is true, in the Moluccas, although nearly twenty years of hard fighting were required to enforce it. The results were most damaging to the interests of the native people and, therefore in the long run, to the interests of the Company itself. But it is by no means true that the Company depended upon this exploitation for its profits. From the first days of trading in the Far East the Netherlanders had had difficulty in finding suitable merchandise for export to the East. They could not forever continue to bring in "Norembergerie," that was ironware, small utensils, weapons, and other products from the workshops of Nuerenberg and other German industrial centers. A substantial item of the outgoing cargo was bullion, coined silver and gold which constituted a heavy drain on the precious metal reserves of Europe. To reduce this drain and to make the East Indian trade more profitable, the fourth governor general of the Indies, Jan Pieterszoon Coen, planned a new economic system for the Company. Coen was astounded by the enormous amount of international trade going on among the Asiatic countries. Would it not be possible for the Dutch to obtain the same control over the freight carrying trade in Asia as they held over this trade in Europe? If so, the profits from that trade could be collected in the form of precious Asiatic products for shipment to Europe. The Directors in Amsterdam would receive their yearly dividends from the Asiatic trade in merchandise upon which they could make an additional profit in the European market.

In 1619 Coen founded a center for this inter-Asiatic trade, the city of Batavia. Within a few decades the new system, though strongly modified from Coen's original views, was working fairly well. The accounts of the Company clearly bear out that the outlying trading posts in countries where the Company held no sovereignty and did not need to maintain armed forces, normally brought far larger returns than posts in the Malay Archipelago where the Dutch monopoly had to be enforced by ships and troops. Nagasaki in Japan, Ormuzd and Ispahan in Persia, and Suratte in India were among the most profitable factories. By this inter-Asiatic trade the Company not only succeeded in earning large dividends for the shareholders in Europe but also in accumulating in India a reserve fund of about twenty million guilders. In building up this trade, the Directors had burdened the Company in Europe with a debt of about ten million guilders. Thus the Dutch East India Company really owed its success to having ample capital at its disposal, and it was to this backing as well as to the energy of many of the commanders in the field that the Company owed victory over its competitors.

The English East India Company had penetrated into the spice producing areas shortly after the Dutch, and bitter competition ensued that often resulted in bloodshed. A naval battle fought off the roadstead of Batavia was almost a complete Dutch defeat, but the energy of Governor General Coen saved the situation. Driven from the Malay Archipelago the English were giving up hope of obtaining a share in the spice trade when political circumstances in Europe forced the States General to agree to a proposal made by King James that the activities of the two companies should be coordinated. Coen, furious at being forced to work with the English, forced them out of business by the simple expedient of making cooperation so expensive for both sides that only the Dutch, and not the British could afford the burden. The so-called "massacre of Amboina," a rather superficial judicial proceeding against some Englishmen accused of conspiracy against Dutch sovereignty, which ended in the execution of the alleged culprits, further embittered relations. King James expressed the resentment of the British when he said to the Dutch Ambassador in London:

> "Your men have robbed my people of their possessions. You have made war on them. You have killed and tortured several of them. You never considered the benefits you have received from the Crown of England who made and maintained you as an independent nation. You have a man in the Indies who deserves to be hanged. Your people present your prince of Orange as a great king in the Indies while they picture me as a small ruler. You are masters of the sea wide and large and can do what you want."

There was much truth in King James's words, although it is remarkable to see the story of Queen Elizabeth's dealings during the Netherland revolution transformed into a legend of royal magnanimity.

The sudden eclosion of Netherland capitalistic success comes so surprisingly in the general picture of world history, that other and hidden forces are often sought behind it. Already Schiller has been quoted: "There is no people less disposed to heroism than the Dutch but the prompting of great ideals made them play a role far beyond their natural capacities." It is indeed remarkable that in the course of forty years, this small nation should found New York, then New Amsterdam (1625); Capetown (1652); and Batavia (1619); establish the first summer settlement in the Arctic Seas, Smeerenburg on Spitsbergen; discover Tasmania and New Zealand (1642); sail the Pacific from the Antarctic Seas to Kamchatka; trade with the Japanese, the only Europeans so to do; control the coastlands of southern Asia; conquer Pernambuco and northern Brazil; settle a number of West Indian Islands, the Hudson valley, and the southern point of Africa, besides sending small colonies of expert farmers and craftsmen to England, France (La Rochelle), Brandenburg (Potsdam), Sweden (Göteborg, Norrköping); Denmark (Amager), and Russia (Moscow). In northern Europe in the first half of the seventeenth century Dutch was the common language of the sea, and Dutch technical terms found their way into English, German, Russian and the Scandinavian languages. At that time it would have been more likely that an English admiral could speak Dutch than a Dutch admiral English. Dutch was the diplomatic language of the countries on the Baltic. What enabled the Netherlands to make such rapid expansion, what prompted the rather slow and allegedly obtuse Lowlanders to such outstanding achievements?

Those well versed in Netherland history and acquainted with the principal traits of the Netherland people, know the answer. They know that
the geographical location of the country, the sea-faring traditions of the
people, the moderate and nerve-steadying climate all had their share in
this development. They know that Netherlanders are neither slow nor
without temper and ambition. Historians not entirely satisfied with these
natural causes, have sought a special stimulating factor in XVIIth century
Netherland history and found it—some in the predominance of Calvinism,
some in the influx of Spanish and Portuguese Jews. The moral principles
of Calvinism and the rigidity of its tenets may have helped to foster the
qualities of self-reliance and of persistence in a given task so typical of the
Netherlanders; perhaps also a feeling of superiority, of being God's elect
and as such above the masses outside His grace. But Calvinism certainly
was not a dominating factor in the development, for we have seen that
in the few decades in which the sudden upsurge occurred, the dogma of
Calvin had no more than a meager hold on the spirit of the leading Netherlanders. A more likely cause of economic prosperity was that practical but
not superficial way of thinking that made the leading classes in Holland
averse to all extremes in religious controversy.

There is no doubt that Jews, especially *Christãos Novos* and *Marranos*
(Portuguese and Spanish Jews, outwardly converted to Christianity)
played an important part in Netherland economic life. But their importance increased considerably with the progress of time, and was far greater
in the XVIIIth than in the XVIIth century. Simple chronology bears this
out.[34] The first settlement of Portuguese-Spanish Jewish refugees was in
1593, when Netherland commerce was already flourishing. The immigrants
brought some capital with them, but not enough to be of much importance.
Many were moderately wealthy, but none of the heads of the two or three
hundred Jewish families in Amsterdam at the beginning of the XVIIth
century, is mentioned among the prominent empire-builders of that time.
We know of many Amsterdam business leaders of the period; we know
that Calvinist immigrants from the southern Low Countries were always
in the forefront of new and hazardous enterprises. We know also that the
money they ventured was their own, nowhere do Jewish elements appear.
Of the six and a half million guilders needed to start the East India Company, not even five thousand came from Jewish sources. It is said that in
the XVIIIth century one-fourth of the shares were controlled by members
of the Jewish community, but this movement of capital cannot have
begun before 1700. There was never a Jewish director in the Company, and
the silly attempt to attribute Jewish origin to Governor-General Coen—by
deriving Coen from Cohen—only betrays a pitiful ignorance of the Dutch

language.[35] The Amsterdam Jews were more interested in the West than in the East India Company, probably because they continued to trade with that part of the world, through their relatives in Spain and Portugal. Even here they did not contribute more than a third of one percent of the capital of the West India Company. Hardly any Jews moved to the East Indies, but the lands conquered from Portugal in America, where they perhaps hoped to find reminiscences of their former fatherland, held great attraction for them.

The Spanish-Portuguese immigration to Amsterdam added a remarkable element to Netherland society. It increased the picturesqueness of the city, and no one appreciated this more than Rembrandt, who found so many of his models in the growing Jewish quarter. Re-converts to Judaism who, in the time of the Inquisition, had lost contact with Jewish tradition, eagerly sought to master Hebrew and become acquainted with the most recent Jewish religious thinking. Having returned to the creed of their fathers through trial and dangers, they were strict in dogma and in their adherence to ritual. The relative freedom of the press permitted by the States of Holland enabled the new community to print Hebrew texts as well as works on religion and philosophy, written in Spanish or Portuguese by Jewish leaders who had not yet mastered Hebrew. A school for Jewish theology and literature was founded in Amsterdam and the training of religious leaders energetically promoted. However enthusiastic the prosecution of Hebrew studies may have been, the *Christãos Novos* hardly equaled the Christian scholars of Leiden University in penetration of ancient Israelite thought. In the rediscovery of ancient Israel Protestant biblical scholars were a greater help to the Jews than were the Jews to the Christians. Freedom of conscience was guaranteed by the Union of Utrecht, and without much hesitation the Jewish immigrants extended this to include freedom of worship. The authorities of Amsterdam raised but little objection to the opening of synagogues, to the dismay of the Christian minorities who resented the privilege granted to the Jews less than the discrimination that denied to Catholics and other non-conformists what was permitted to the Jews. Yet the general attitude of the rulers and people of the Netherlands towards the Jews remained friendly. More and more refugees came in from foreign countries, and to the small but wealthy colony of Sephardim, another Jewish settlement, the larger and poorer one of Ashkenazim, was added after the outbreak of the Thirty Years' War in Germany.

In the early decades of their "Golden Age" the Netherlands surpassed all other countries in prosperity. They also granted greater freedom to the individual, and the liberal economic policy followed by the States was almost as potent a factor in national welfare as was geographic location. The port and custom duties, very moderate in comparison with those of other states, encouraged shipping and trading. Similarly the willingness of the Government to admit foreigners drew energetic and intelligent members of various other nations to the United Provinces. Although the guilds and the minor trades, remained hermetically closed to these immigrants, the newer industries and sea-faring were always open to them. Englishmen served in great numbers on Dutch ships and some like Hendrik Hudson have remained famous in history because of what they did in this service. Numbers of Germans also came, from petty princes of the Empire who served for high pay as commanding officers in the Dutch army, to those driven by misery or the spirit of adventure to enlist as soldiers of the East India Company. Others came from German Calvinist countries overrun by their enemies, and ministers of the Church separated from their congregations found new pulpits in the Netherlands. Mining and forestry experts found remunerative employment with the West and East India Companies. French Calvinists, insecure at home after the death of Henry IV, also flocked to the haven of freedom. There were so many French officers and soldiers in the Dutch army that French Calvinists congregations were organized, which included refugees from the Walloon provinces.

The excellence of the Dutch army under Maurice and Frederick Henry, drew young officers and future princes to its headquarters to study the new tactics. The Bouillons of France, related to the House of Orange, but soon to separate from the Reformed Church, were there. So was Frederick William of Hohenzollern, later the "Great Elector" of Brandenburg-Prussia, who married one of Frederick Henry's daughters. Thus the headquarters of the Prince of Orange became an academy of military science. The presence of so many who were illustrious, if not by intellect at least in name, formed a magnificent court at the Hague, in striking contrast to the simple princely household at Delft of the first William. French and German scholars came to Netherland Universities. More than any of the other provinces, Holland was a cosmopolitan center, the focal point of divergent trends of thought and culture. Yet, all these elements were blended into one national Netherland civilization.

It is hardly possible to give an adequate description of this civilization in the few lines that can be devoted to it here. Nor does it make any sense to paste a few wornout labels, "Baroque," "Dutch-Renaissance," and others like them, under the multi-colored picture of Netherland life of the "Golden Age." Professor Huizinga, in a series of lectures on the general aspects of this cultural period, has emphasized its "middleclass" character, and explained how in this liberal oligarchy, national culture was the common cement that bound together the ruling and middleclasses. Also that in this professedly Calvinist community all the leading lights of culture, Rembrandt, Vondel, Grotius, were dissenters from the privileged Reformed Church.[36] All the arts, painting, architecture, literature, were strongly influenced by southern Renaissance and Baroque models. There are numerous examples of Rembrandt's direct inspiration by Italian predecessors, from Leonardo da Vinci to Caravaggio. Nearly the whole dramatic literature of the Netherlands is inspired, directly or indirectly, either by Plautus and Terence, or by Spanish, Italian, and French works. English drama, introduced into the Netherlands by English actors in Leicester's day, had far less influence on Dutch authors. But in all these imitations native Dutch traditions so thoroughly transformed the foreign models that true works of art were created.

It is obviously impossible to define the essential characteristics of these native artistic traditions. Realism and a love of small detail, to give individual character and color, were conspicuous. There seems to have been an aversion to abstract distinctions and an attempt to maintain intimacy with varying outlooks on life. The artist usually formed an integral part of his community and did not live on the outskirts of society as often happens in our day. Constantijn Huyghens, aristocrat and shining light of classical learning, is the author of a popular comedy which sometimes shocks our more delicate feelings. Certainly the painters dealt with life in all its aspects from the loftiest to the most vulgar, and succeeded in bringing out the really human qualities of all their subjects. Snobbery in any form was still foreign to Netherland artists in the early XVIth century, and to Netherland society in general. It was soon to follow, however.

Painting was the most popular of Netherland arts. All the great Dutch masters produced and sold a large number of works, and taught scores of pupils. Only a small percentage of these became professional painters. Breero the poet and Jacob van Campen the architect, started life as students of painting. When an Asiatic prince needed a Dutch artist for his court, the East India Company had no difficulty in finding a budding portrait painter among its employees. In the second half of the century some people in Batavia possessed sixty or seventy pictures, and so general an interest in painting necessarily implies a great deal of amateur work. There is no reason to add to these pages a catalogue of famous Dutch masters or their biographies, which can be found in any biographical dictionary or textbook on the history of art. The names of Rembrandt, Vermeer, Frans Hals, Jan Steen, Gerard Dou, Ruysdael, Van Goyen, Van de Velde, and many others are familiar to all visitors of museums anywhere in the western world. Yet it is not without interest to devote a few words to the position of painters and the art of painting in Netherland society as a whole. The art was popular because it was—to use our most familiar label—far more "democratic" than any other of the arts, even literature. Portraits or groups, landscapes or seaviews, still-life or historical and allegorical compositions appealed to the masses, and those who could not afford paintings could at least acquire engravings by the same masters. We know that paintings were sold at open stands at the fairs, and engravings were so popular that their production became an export industry. In the first decade of the XVIIth century the East India Company even tried to sell them in the Far East, but the Buddhists and Moslems of southeastern Asia showed no desire to buy the choice collections of landscapes, nudes, classical illustrations, Madonnas, and scenes of Dutch country life sent out.

The Dutch masters naturally chose their subjects to suit the taste of their patrons. The official predominance of Calvinism meant that they had few orders for large murals and none for huge altarpieces like those which in the southern Low Countries occasioned Rubens' masterful compositions. The court of the princes of Orange, although a little suspect to the more extreme Calvinists because of the carefree social life centered there in Frederick Henry's time, did not offer the opportunities one might have expected to Dutch painters. Frederick Henry ordered a number of paintings, among them several by Rembrandt; and his widow had the great hall of her residence at the Hague, the "House in the Woods," decorated with large pictures representing the great moments of her husband's life. The princes of Orange favored painters from the southern Low Countries who worked in the grand Baroque manner as well as their northern colleagues.

The great artists of Holland fortunately escaped being the protégés of the mighty. To be sure, men like Pope Julius II and the princes of the House of Medici were wonderful animators of art in Italy during the Renaissance, and the world owes much to the support given by Spanish kings to men like Velasquez. But the situation in the Netherlands, where a large number of less wealthy patrons fostered painting not for their own glory but out of real interest in art, was far more desirable. This was responsible for the great variety of artistic production, and created a far more agreeable social position for the artist. The Netherland painter of the XVIIth century was regarded socially as a skilled craftsman, but even so the distance between him and his patron was far less than that between the highly honored artist at a royal court and his Maecenas. The prices paid for paintings were high, if we allow for the fact that the works of a contemporary master can never be valued so highly as when their exceptional value has been recognized for generations and they can no longer be produced. Prices of sixteen hundred guilders paid for the "Night-watch" or five hundred guilders for a portrait are certainly high, as the buying power of the guilder in Rembrandt's day was equal to at least three dollars of our currency.

This did not preclude personal tragedy in the artistic world, for some of the greatest among the Dutch masters found even this semi-independent status incompatible with their artistic sentiments. Vermeer who could never produce in quantity, suffered terribly although his paintings brought high prices. Others failed through mismanagement of their financial affairs, either because temperamentally they never could make ends meet, or because they lived in too pretentious a style even when making good money. Rembrandt's attempt to rise above the level of common painters may have been looked upon askance, but his tragic downfall was by no means due to lack of appreciation on the part of his protectors. After his bankruptcy, he continued to receive many commissions, and in the documents of the time he was always referred to as a "painter of great renown." His individualism, his unflinching determination to picture things as he saw them, and not as conceived by others, inevitably created numerous difficulties, but he could rely on the admiration of many of his fellow countrymen for his art.

That many Netherlanders preferred the less wonderful but more accessible paintings of minor artists to those of the great master was natural enough. They were no mean connoisseurs of art, who appreciated Ferdinand Bol's work, and they never sank to the low level of the twentieth century's gullible masses. When he died, in 1669, Rembrandt did not hold first place among the Dutch masters in the eyes of his contemporaries, but his fame had spread all over Europe. Admiration of the Dutch school of painting rose so high that while formerly Holland had taken lessons from Italy, the reverse was now true. Italy and especially Rome had received many visitors from the Lowlands during the XVIIth century. Many works of Dutch artists—citizens of the Calvinist republic—still adorn the churches and palaces of the Papal City.

Architecture also added to the reputation of Netherland art in Europe. Dutch Renaissance, succeeded by the severe classicism of the middle of the century, set the style in large areas of northern Europe. The persecution of Alva caused the emigration of many Netherland architects. The economic relations of the northern Lowlands with the Baltic countries determined their paths of exile, and we find traces of them in East Friesland, in Denmark, and in Danzig. Increasing prosperity of the towns furthered the desire of town councilors and burgomasters in Holland to display the wealth of the citizens and the grandeur of the town in rich public buildings. This laudable pride on the part of a city government led to the construction of the town hall of Amsterdam. The project, designed and begun by Jacob van Campen, Lord Randenbroek, descendant of an aristocratic family in Amsterdam, and completed by Daniel Stalpaert and Pieter Post, was so monumental that the burgomasters had the work started without revealing its full magnitude to the councilors, lest it be rejected as too costly and ambitious. Begun in 1648, "the eighth wonder of the world" was so far completed after seven years that it could house the magistracy. For a century and a half it remained the seat of Amsterdam's government, to be handed over as a palace in 1808 to Louis Napoleon, king of Holland by the grace of his brother Napoleon. It is still in use as a royal residence, for which it is ill-suited, and a latent conflict over its ownership between the kingdom of the Netherlands and the city of Amsterdam was settled in favor of the former a few years ago.

Jacob van Campen's works were few in number. His successor as the leading Netherland architect was Pieter Post of Haarlem, builder of the Mauritshuis, formerly the palace of Johan Maurits of Nassau, governor of Brazil, and now a museum; of the marvelous town hall of Maastricht; and of the "House in the Woods," built for Frederick Henry of Orange-Nassau. Unlike Van Campen, Post had risen from the artisan class. His father is mentioned in the archives as a glass painter; and like so many architects, young Pieter began his career in a painter's studio. Like Van Campen, he was profoundly influenced in his architectural conceptions by French models, and French architects appear among his colleagues; but Netherland culture was far too vigorous to slavishly imitate foreign examples. Moreover, the commissions of architects in Holland and Zeeland were very different from those of architects of France. Orders for the building of palaces or châteaux were rare in the land of shopkeepers and seafarers, but there were numerous demands by wealthy merchants for the rebuilding of their town and country houses into solid and spacious private residences. The town house, with its gabled façade and its decorations in variegated stone, was the architect's usual subject. Rare were the occasions when a merchant, often more powerful than many a prince, wanted his might and opulence expressed in the scale and design of his dwelling. Opportunities to build churches were also rare. In many towns the Calvinist congregations found ample space in the magnificent churches built in earlier Catholic centuries. Amsterdam, with its rapidly growing population, was an exception. The *Westerkerk* of Amsterdam built by Hendrick de Keyser in 1620, is one of the best examples of this new ecclesiastical architecture, which represents a transition from the traditional type of Catholic church to a new form better adapted to Protestant forms of worship.

Netherland painting of the XVIIth century spread the fame of the country throughout Europe and even to the courts of Asiatic potentates. Netherland architecture did the same on a smaller scale. Here for once, war worked constructively instead of destructively. Maurice and Frederick Henry had made the Netherland army famous, especially for its fortifications. Between them and the Spanish commanders a fierce competition raged in the construction of defenses that could withstand the destructive power of artillery, as also in developing new forces of destruction. Netherland engineers, led by men of genius like Simon Stevin, won and the whole of Europe sought to profit by their work. Friendly Protestant powers asked the prince of Orange for engineers and architects who, sent out for war work, often found more useful employment in building palaces and churches or constructing bridges and improving the public highways of foreign towns. Of these engineers some went to Sweden and some to northern Germany, where Frederick William of Hohenzollern, son-in-law of Prince Frederick Henry, sought to derive every possible benefit from this fortunate family relation.

If painting and architecture, socially speaking, were trades carried on by skilled artisans, literature was a pastime, rarely a profession. There are a few cases in the history of XVIIth century Netherland letters, in which poets were supported by groups of patrons for art's sake. Jan Janszoon Starter was one of these. An Englishman by birth, he grew up in Amsterdam where he moved in literary circles before going to Leeuwarden, capital of Friesland, where he started a bookselling and publishing business, striving hard to promote the art of letters in a petty and rather bourgeoisie environment. Having failed, he returned to Amsterdam, where he received a pension from a group of admirers, on condition that he produce a certain number of poems annually. Such agreements are difficult to fulfill, and Starter finally did what in those days a Netherlander only did as a last resource: he joined one of the many mercenary armies as a quartermaster and died in faraway Hungary.

Starter's life is an exception in Dutch literary history. Gerbrand Adrianszoon Breero, son of a shoemaker and himself a student of painting and lieutenant of the City Guards—ability to hold one's own in a beer drinking bout was more necessary for this function than military experience—was also bohemian in his way of living, but he felt entirely at home in his native Amsterdam and among the co-citizens of whom he drew striking pen pictures in his comedies and poems. He was no artist basking in the favor of society, but the embodiment of the popular spirit of the Amsterdam of his time. As such he provides illuminating historical evidence, most necessary to those who might otherwise see the XVIIth century Netherlands only through the works of Jacob Cats, the most widely read of all the authors of his age and the most satisfied with his own work and the world he lived in. All other men of letters of the time, among them such famous names as Joost van den Vondel, Pieter Corneliszoon Hooft, Constantijn Huyghens—adopted literature as a "pastime" albeit a very serious one to which Hooft at least, devoted most of his time and none of them failed to see a great cultural and national asset.

The goal they set themselves was to adapt the essence of classical literary tradition to Netherland surroundings and to create in their northern, Dutch-speaking republic a narrative tradition equal to that of Rome. The pure Latin of Cicero was to be matched by the purity of their native Dutch; the political wisdom of Tacitus' historical works was to find its counterpart in Dutch descriptions of the Great Revolt; the comedies of Plautus depicting every-day life in Rome were to be surpassed by the picture of Amsterdam's people as they lived and loved and thought. The best of this classical Dutch literary culture was to express profoundly Christian feelings and thoughts, in fulfillment of Erasmus' dream of a world purified from party strife with Christian learning rejuvenated through the critical adaptation of the best classical civilizations had to offer. Netherland men of letters strove earnestly and diligently for this ideal, laboring to perfect their own knowledge and means of expression, training themselves by translating the classics, by paraphrasing the best of ancient comedy and poetry in Dutch verse, by assiduously studying their own language. Modern Dutch is to a large extent their creation. It was they who fought the infiltration of many superfluous French words of the Burgundian period which had threatened to overcrowd the native vocabulary. Not needing to fear German encroachment, they preferred to borrow a word from the Low or High German, if no other way of supplanting the French was possible and if the German word seemed understandable to the masses. They explored the inexhaustible treasures of Amsterdam's popular language and added them to the many expressions already introduced from Flanders and Brabant, which had once held the lead in literature.

Hooft used this new linguistic instrument to set forth, in the form of historical narratives, the political ideals of the oligarchic republic, while Vondel chronicled its greatness, its internal strife, its victories over its enemies in a thousand poems. Late in life he started his Latin studies afresh, better to observe his classical examples. Unpretentious, with deep respect for contemporaries whom he far surpassed in the depth of his literary conceptions and his mastery of the language, this shopkeeper of lower middleclass truly represents the humanistic Netherland civilization of his age. The wide range of his political, religious, and cultural interests shows how great a place the small nation on the North Sea then held in general culture.

In all these fields of art, the province of Holland took the lead. Some literary figures had their homes in other provinces, notably in Zeeland; some painters came from that province or from Utrecht; but in all fields, Holland was easily predominant. And in Holland, Amsterdam, the home of Rembrandt, Breero, Hooft and Vondel was first. Haarlem, where Frans Hals lived and worked, where Van Campen and Pieter Post were born, was an honorable second. Clearly was there a connection between the sudden spread of wealth and the spirit of enterprise in this one province, and the cultural activity there. It was not wealth in itself that caused the arts to flourish, for as Holland grew richer, its artistic productivity diminished in quantity and quality. Vondel survived all of the other standard bearers of the arts; and when he died in 1679, the great days had passed.

The other provinces underwent a cultural conquest by Holland. "Overlandish," the local form of Low German, was the literary language of the northeastern provinces in the last decades of the XVIth century. The representatives of the Calvinist congregations of Drente, when invited in 1618 to the national Synod of Dordrecht, asked to be excused, "the Netherland language not being very well known in their province." Hollandish, in the typical form given to it around 1600, although not unmixed with Brabant forms, became the official language of all the provinces before 1650. In 1619 the Synod of Dordrecht had ordered the Bible translated into Dutch. This was by no means the first Dutch version of the Old and New Testaments, but it was the first to receive official sanction and to be propagated by the Church. The first task of the translators appointed by the Synod was to establish a number of grammatical and orthographic rules in order to ensure uniformity which otherwise would have been sorely lacking in a work composed by natives of different provinces. The committee did not hesitate to create new grammatical and idiomatic forms whenever this seemed desirable, and some of the novelties they introduced became part and parcel of everyday Dutch. In this way the Staten Bible, so called because the States-General sponsored its publication, became one of the strongest factors in the linguistic unification of the small but heterogeneous territory. In Friesland, where the ancient Frisian language was still spoken, the linguistic influence of Holland caused a difference between the language of the towns and that of the countryside, *Stad-friesch* (urban Frisian) and *Land-friesch* (rural Frisian), and with the progress of time, the Frisian tongue more and more adapted itself to the language of the intellectual class of the nation.

In all these aspects of culture, Holland was dominant. In the field of learning the provinces, even the towns, sought jealously to safeguard their independence. Holland had had its university at Leiden since 1575. Originally planned as an academy for the education of Calvinist ministers, its formal purpose became "unhampered, public instruction in theology, law and medicine, also in philosophy and other liberal arts, as well as in the Latin, Greek and Hebrew languages." Several of the other provinces, jealous of the religious independence guaranteed them by the Union of Utrecht, decided to have their own schools of theology. Friesland founded the university of Franckerker in 1585; Stad en Landen, that of Groningen in 1614; Utrecht established its own in 1636; and Guelderland, in 1648 in Harderwijk. Zeeland and Overijssel never had universities of their own. The city of Deventer in Overijssel, like Amsterdam and other cities, maintained an *Athenaeum* or *Illustrious School,* in which higher instruction, not ranking with that of the universities, was given. In these schools and universities, men who have a permanent place in the annals of learning taught students from all over northern Europe. Daniel Heinsius, Gerard and Isaac Vossius (Netherlanders), Joseph Scaliger and Claudius Salmasius (both born in France), Johannes Gronovius (born in Germany) were the standard bearers of the classics. In their classes Latin and Greek were taught not only for the value of the languages and their literature but also as an introduction to the fields of history and political science. The Tacitus courses at Leiden took the place of our courses in government and diplomacy.

One name is missing in the academy of Netherland learning, and that the greatest of them all: Hugo Grotius. Driven from his country in 1619, the great scholar vainly attempted to obtain permission to return. That permission would have been granted if Grotius had been willing to retract his support of Oldenbarnevelt. This he rightly refused to do. Once he came back to Rotterdam in the hope that the authorities would ignore his presence, but within a few days he was forced to flee again. There was no place in the Netherlands for this greatest of its scholars. The author of the treatise on the Freedom of the Seas (*Mare liberum,* published in 1609) and of the *Apology of the Christian Religion,* which ran to one hundred and ten editions and was translated into most European languages, had to do his later work outside his fatherland, under the protection of the kings of France and Sweden. In France he wrote his most important work: *De Jure Belli ac Pacis* (On the Laws of War and Peace), a compendium of learned references to the righteousness of war, a problem that has tortured human conscience throughout the ages. His rational conception of the problem and its basic philosophic principles were new which made his book a standard work for future generations, and provided common basis of reason for people who had drifted apart forever in religious thinking.

Few Netherlanders have added so much to the fame of their homeland as did Grotius, and none enjoyed such a reputation among his contemporaries. At the age of sixty-two he died in Rostock on his way from Sweden to Paris where he had served as Swedish ambassador. The pusillanimity of his opponents kept Grotius out of his native land, but if he had returned from exile his character might have involved him in difficulties that might have shorn him of some of the glory that is his. Although physically separated from his native land, he remained close to it spiritually. Until his last years he worked on his great *History of the Netherland War,* written in the style of Tacitus, and entered into polemics with Netherland authors on matters of theology. Only five years after his death, the political group whose principles he had so tenaciously defended regained control in Holland, and his body was finally brought back and buried with his ancestors in Delft.

Oriental studies occupied a distinct place in Netherland scholarship of this period. To penetrate more deeply into the mysteries of the ancient Hebrew world and the origins of the Christian religion, Aramaean, Syrian, Chaldean, and Arabic were studied. A knowledge of the last language rapidly proved of practical value. Dutch connections with North Africa and the Levant were frequent, and a knowledge of the Arabic language was useful wherever Mohammedanism had spread, in Persia, India, and the Malay Archipelago. Leiden University was the second institution of higher learning to establish a separate chair of Arabic, Paris having been the first. Scaliger, already mentioned as a great teacher of Greek and Latin, was among the promoters of these new studies. Leiden was lucky to have as professor of Hebrew Raphelengius, a scholarly printer who equipped his presses to publish books in Oriental languages. Thomas Erpenius and Jacob Golius continued the work of these men and made Leiden the principal center of Arabic scholarship. To the credit of Holland's burgher aristocracy, so often accused of crude materialism, be it said that through the endeavors of Erpenius and the assistance of the oligarchy, the States General were persuaded to ask the "king" of Morocco, one of their more dubious allies, to send an expert to teach the Leiden scholars colloquial Arabic.

Botany was a part of the study of medicine, for herbs were then the basic material for the preparation of drugs. Charles l'Ecluse (Carolus Clusius) made the Botanic Garden of Leiden University one of the best equipped institutions of its kind. Simon Stevin and Willibrord Snellius, whose name is still connected with the law of optical refraction, taught mathematics and physics. In a country of seafarers astronomy, geography and navigation, as well as all instruments serving any purpose in these fields, were bound to attract special attention. We find Zacharias Janszoon, or Janse of Middelburg, mentioned as the inventor of the spy-glass. A series of great geographers were connected either by birth or occupation with the Netherlands. Gerard Mercator, born in Antwerp, belongs wholly to the southern Low Countries; but Jodocus Hondius, his fellow townsman, was one of the cartographers attracted by the intensity of geographic studies in Amsterdam, and moved there to publish Mercator's Atlas. Willem Janszoon Blaeu founded a map publishing house which produced the Atlas that made his name famous by its careful and artistic execution.

In this world of feverish literary and scientific activity, erratic characters were bound to appear. Over-wrought by the progress made on every hand, they thought the time had come for a final solution of all problems. Among them was Cornelis Drebbel with his fantastic schemes for the manufacture of a *perpetuum mobile,* and his submarine, which according to some reports functioned marvelously well in the river Thames, and according to others only succeeded in diving and never coming up again. The pride of Netherland students in the pre-eminent position of their country in natural science make them "nationalist" even in this the least national of all fields. This led to the development of a more accurate Netherland terminology in mathematics than existed in any other language. It was created by Simon Stevin. Although the high place held by the Dutch language in international intercourse was a source of national pride, a knowledge of French, Spanish, and Italian was quite common among educated people. That of English and German was not so frequent but still rather general. The studying of so many languages bred a vague idea of the relationships existing between them. Raphelengius called the attention of the learned world to this fact. Three Netherlanders, Justus Lipsius, Franciscus Junius, and Isaac Vossius were leaders in the rediscovery of the old Frankish, old Anglo-Saxon, and old Gothic languages. They opened a new field of scholarly research, thus destroying a marvelous legend that was springing from the over-confidence of the young Lowland nation: that Dutch being so beautiful, so easy to handle, and such a good medium for the study of foreign languages, must be the oldest of all languages. Jan van Gorp, physician at Antwerp, a native of North Brabant, had given currency to that legend in the XVIth century, arguing with great weight and seriousness that Dutch had been spoken by Adam and Eve in Paradise.

CHAPTER IX

The Netherlands as a Great Power

THE armistice of 1609 established the international position of the Netherland Republic. The subsequent years of truce strengthened the new state's position, partly because of its increasing economic power; partly because of the decline of adjacent kingdoms. Great Britain, united under King James I, was in the pangs of a long constitutional conflict. France was torn by internal dissension until the reins of government were seized by Richelieu; and for years after his ascent to power he was obliged to act cautiously and to avoid open conflict with foreign powers. Spain was involved in the Thirty Years' War by which the German Empire was torn apart. A rising power like Sweden that owed so much to Netherland capitalism, had to heed the views of a Republic whose navy controlled the entire Baltic area. The general situation in Europe in the first quarter of the seventeenth century was favorable to the United Provinces, but they took no advantage of it to widen their political influence. Trade, not long-range national views, determined the foreign policy of the burgher-aristocracy. The Netherlands suffer to this day from this narrow though explicable lack of vision of their leaders.

In 1609 just as the Twelve Years' Truce was signed, the duke of Cleve, Mark, Berg, and Juliers died without leaving a direct heir. This Rhineland federation had played an important part in Netherland history in the XVth and XVIth centuries. Guelderland had narrowly escaped absorption by it and only the military power of the Burgundian-Habsburg dynasty had saved that province for the Lowland Union. Ties between the Low Countries and Cleve and Juliers had remained close. In the last years before the Truce the war had been carried into this area. Netherland and Spanish garrisons had occupied Emmerik, Rees, Rheinberg, and Wesel. In the confusion created by the extinction of the Cleve dynasty, a strong tendency had manifested itself among the inhabitants for association with the Netherland Republic. The States General were unwilling to listen to any such suggestions. Although forced to intervene to prevent the principalities passing to a pro-Spanish Catholic, they stubbornly refused even to consider the incorporation of part of them into the Republic. The merchants of Holland who at heart considered the "land-provinces" more a burden than an asset and who were over-confident that their financial power would permit them to build up an adequate defense at any time, deliberately neglected this opportunity to strengthen the Republic's eastern boundary. In those days no national or linguistic difference stood in the way of a part of the Lower Rhineland becoming Netherland territory. But the sea-provinces had become one of the western European powers, and the war had so widened the gap between the Netherland sea-provinces and a disintegrated Germany, that the gentlemen of Amsterdam and Dordrecht simply overlooked the possibility of their national boundaries being threatened from the east. The land provinces were there to serve as a protective cushion for Holland and that, in their opinion, was nearly all the land-provinces were good for.

Thus, the Republic let pass the golden opportunity. Instead of heeding the appeal of the pro-Dutch elements in Cleve and Juliers, the Netherlanders backed the Protestant candidate to part of the inheritance, including the duchy of Cleve and the small seigneuries of Huissen and Zevenaar situated east and west of the Rhine, well within Netherland territory on the strategic approaches to the heart of the country. This Protestant candidate was none other than the prince-elector of Brandenburg, duke of Prussia, of the House of Hohenzollern. It was no fault of Holland's burgher-aristocracy if the invaders of 1940 were not able to start their aggression from a even more advanced position than they actually had. Worse, the incorporation of Cleve into an East-Elbian principality created a linguistic and cultural boundary a few miles east of Nijmegen that had never before existed.

One reason why the leaders of the Republic were indifferent, was that they could not think of themselves as a great power in international politics. They realized too well as Oldenbarnevelt said that France and Great Britain had to be treated "respectfully" being "incomparably more powerful" than the Netherlands because of their *potential* resources and their stronger centralized government. Their foreign policy was the logical outcome of their realization of the potential power of their western neighbors. They sought to maintain good relations with France and Britain, but dreaded to commit themselves to close alliance with either. They resisted Spain, but were little inclined to renew the war and fight to the bitter end to drive Spain from all of the Low Countries. If closely scrutinized this policy reveals itself as a return to the cherished neutrality, which had been the ideal of the Burgundian-Lowland aristocracy in the days of Maximilian and Charles V and at the beginning of King Philip's reign. Now, however, neutrality had to be dynamic so that any threat to Netherland independence or to the freedom of her commerce could be anticipated and prevented.

There was little chance for neutrality in 1621, when the Twelve Years' Truce came to an end. The Spanish-Austrian forces had gained their first successes in the Thirty Years' War. The Republic, remaining too much on the defensive saw its outposts south of the riverbelt conquered or threatened. In 1625 the death of Maurice of Nassau, aged beyond his years, seemed another blow to the Netherlands. Actually it proved helpful for it gave free scope to the ability of his younger brother Frederick Henry, who was eager to gain military laurels and more tractable in his dealings with the ruling oligarchy.[37] A new series of victories began: the liberation of the last towns held by the Spaniards in the eastern provinces; then in 1629 the conquest of 's Hertogenbosch, which the enemy could not prevent even though Imperial troops came to the assistance of their Spanish allies and invaded the Netherlands right up to the boundary of Holland. The year 1632 gave promise of even greater successes. A revolutionary movement seemed imminent among the aristocracy of the southern Low Countries, and a revival of the alliance of 1576, the Pacification of Ghent, did not seem impossible. In a few weeks the prince of Orange conquered the towns on the Meuse, including Maastricht. In vain the Spaniards and their Imperial allies under Count Pappenheim, the famous cavalry leader in Wallenstein's army, stormed his trenches outside the town. With the loss of Maastricht direct communication between the Spanish Netherlands and western Germany was cut, but the revolution in the South came to nothing.

This campaign and the prospect of a revolt against Spain in Flanders and Brabant forced the leaders of the Republic to define their attitude towards the possible liberation of the southern provinces. Complete liberation of the South might prove impossible, but the future southern boundary of the Netherlands would depend on the outcome of the campaign. No linguistic or other barriers existed, until far to the south. The framers of Netherland policy had an opportunity to include in the growing Dutch nation as many of the old Lowland inhabitants as reasonably possible. Once more, they let the opportunity pass. Commercial interests might be harmed if Antwerp were freed, and those interests predominated. They even prevented conquered territories from being treated as free members of the republican community. The fate of towns in Brabant and the Meuse districts left no illusion about the egotism of the seven provinces. The population was deprived of self-government in all conquered areas, except the town of Maastricht where peculiar constitutional conditions made this impossible. Deprived of freedom in matters of taxation and religion, they were subject to the arbitrary decisions of the States General. All this created violent antipathy in the South against the North, and the Northerners felt disinclined to burden themselves with large territories which could only be held by military occupation. The South, more Catholic than ever under the influence of the Counter-Reformation, hated Calvinist supremacy. The North, although relatively tolerant in its own territory, could not have proclaimed general and complete freedom of worship without shaking its own state to its foundations.

The problem of the southern provinces became acute in 1635. The war was growing into a world conflict. The fate of Europe was to be decided on the battlefields of Germany, that of America and Asia in Brazil, Ceylon and Malaya. In this gigantic struggle the Republic of the Netherlands was only one, though one of the most important, belligerents. Minor interests had to give way to the needs of grand strategy. The West India Company after an initial failure, had struck a major blow at the enemy in 1628 by the capture of a Spanish silver fleet off Matanzas. The eleven million guilders booty of this successful if somewhat inglorious encounter, made Admiral Piet Heyn the best remembered of all Dutch naval heroes. His glory is sung on the streets today. He himself complained that nobody had paid any attention to victories he had won in hard-fought battles, but that everybody cheered his capture of defenceless merchantmen. He fell a few years later, fighting Spanish privateers, yet few people remember his heroic death. The directors of the Company divided the booty—a bonus for themselves, a nice dividend for the shareholders, a large percentage for the prince of Orange, a very small one for Piet Heyn, a tip for the common sailors. Some of the gains were earmarked for further expeditions, but the war chests of the Republic profited little from the victory. In 1630, Pernambuco was conquered and part of Brazil subjected to Dutch rule. In 1634 Curacao was wrested from the Spaniards, and became a center of slave smuggling to the Spanish Main. Whatever its ultimate result the founding of New Amsterdam (New York) as a center for the Hudson fur trade was unimportant in the eyes of the directors, whose great aim was to crush all Portuguese power in Brazil and West Africa and to dominate the Caribbean. In Asia, the Portuguese were driven from the Persian Gulf; their strongholds in Ceylon and southern India were stormed; and with the conquest of Malacca in 1641, they were expelled from the East Indian Archipelago.

In Europe, King Gustavus Adolphus of Sweden, backed by Dutch capital, had marched against the Austrian-Spanish armies and gained many victories, before he met his death on the battlefield of Luetzen. The Austrian-Spanish combination, unbelievably tenacious in spite of terrific losses and a constant lack of money, recovered from the blows inflicted by the Swedish king; and its armies again swept northward through Germany. To avoid complete disaster to the anti-Habsburg coalition, the Netherlands and

France who for years had been backing this coalition were forced to come into the open and wage all out war. So in 1635, the Netherland Republic and France entered into an alliance directed against Spain. All Spanish positions in northern Europe were to be reduced, and the Austrian armies forced back to southeastern Germany. With some hesitation the States General agreed to a plan for the conquest of the southern provinces by a combined Dutch-French army, and the subsequent division of this territory between the two powers.

This plan miscarried. Against an attempt at subjugation, by people who ostensibly came as liberators, a national movement developed in the South, which may be called the first really "Belgian" movement. Frederick Henry did not conquer a single southern city; but he lost some of the recently captured strongholds along the Meuse, such as Venlo and Roermond. An attack on Antwerp succeeded no better. Again, only the sea power of the Netherlands prevented the Spanish counter-attacks from far outweighing the Netherland assault. A strong naval force dispatched from Spain to Flanders was intercepted by Dutch squadrons, the first command of Maarten Harpertszoon Tromp, the famous admiral of Holland, and annihilated in the battle of the Downs (1639) in British territorial waters over the futile protest of King Charles.

After these years of intense exertion, lassitude overcame the Netherland leaders. Frederick Henry, highly honored by the States General and by foreign powers, wanted to continue the war. Overestimating his influence in affairs of state, feeling himself a member of European royalty through his son's marriage with a daughter of the king of England, he was inclined to follow a personal foreign policy, at variance with the wishes of the Regents and the merchant class of Holland. The burgher aristocrats brought to power by the fall of Oldenbarnevelt, almost imperceptibly drifted back into the policy of the grand pensionary whom they replaced. Gradually a new conflict for supremacy was arising between the province of Holland and the House of Orange, which represented the interprovincial forces. Basically, the question was whether the Republic should take only enough part in European politics to assure the safety of Holland and Zeeland and their maritime trading routes, or whether it should aspire to permanent influence in northwestern Europe, and carry on a war that would lead to territorial aggrandizement, the commercial importance of which was not apparent. To put it plainly, it was a conflict between a policy of limited participation in European affairs merely to secure independence and a policy of active participation in shaping the destinies of Europe. The prince of Orange naturally inclined to the latter; the merchants of Holland, to the former. The prince wanted to give at least moral and financial support to his son's father-in-law, King Charles, in his struggle against the armies of the Parliament. The States of Holland would rather have supported Parliament. If they did not do so, it was to profit by England's temporary weakness and settle other European affairs according to their own commercial interest.

For the first time in 1645, a Netherland fleet policed the Sund to keep the straits open for Dutch shipping while Sweden and Denmark were at war. The merchants of Holland saw no reason to continue a war with Spain that could serve only the interest of France. Austria and Spain were exhausted, the German Empire ruined, Sweden unable to force a decision. France alone was growing in strength and sending her armies ever farther into central Europe. It hardly seemed necessary for the Republic to fight the king of France's war. Spain, well aware of this attitude of the Dutch republic, made great concessions to the Netherlands to separate them from France. During the protracted negotiation, Frederick Henry died in 1647. Immediately Holland took the lead and against the votes of Zeeland, Friesland and Utrecht, and the wishes of the new stadhouder, William II, persuaded the majority of the States General to make peace with Spain and sign the Treaty of Muenster (1648). This treaty recognized the existing boundary between the northern and southern Low Countries, leaving the northern districts of Flanders and Brabant and the town of Maastricht under the control of the States General. This treaty further guaranteed the Netherlands all the possessions they had acquired in the East and West Indies, and permitted them to keep the Scheldt closed so as to control the overseas trade of the southern provinces. The official recognition of the independence of the Republic was a mere formality, as was the promise of Spain to secure identical recognition from the Emperor and the Imperial Diet. The former complied, the latter did not, which altered nothing in the existing situation.

The peace treaty was a triumph for the Republic over Spain and for Holland over the other provinces and over the prince of Orange. In a way it was a triumph for the city of Amsterdam over the rest of the Republic. The treaty re-established the supremacy of the burgher oligarchy, broken thirty years before by Prince Maurice. Thus it inevitably led to a new outbreak of the constitutional conflict. William II, young, ambitious, intelligent and contemptuous of the Dutch middleclass way of life, sought to seize the reins that had fallen from his father's hands. The young prince wanted a bold and vigorous foreign policy by which the Republic would take sides with the kings of England and France against their enemies: Parliament in England, Spain on the Continent. He did not hesitate to resort to armed force to break the opposition of Holland's leaders. Laying siege to Amsterdam, he made the proud burgher-aristocracy bow to the storm, but that was all he achieved. Outwardly victorious in this internal conflict, William moderated his ambitions because he knew that he could never force the towns to provide the money his enterprises would require. In the hour of his triumph he had to permit Amsterdam to strengthen its fortification, for better future defense against the Republic's commander-in-chief. Death prevented an aggravation of the conflict. In 1650, when only twenty, William died suddenly. An heir to the House of Orange was born a few days after his death. His widow, an embittered royal princess, who felt out of place in the bourgeois world, and who, after Cromwell's victory in England, was merely the sister of a pretender, possessed neither the character nor the ability to uphold the great tradition of the House of Orange.

The victory of the burgher-aristocracy was complete, so complete that the Regents of Holland thought the time ripe to draw the logical conclusion of the revolution of 1581. Sixty years previously, the Netherlands had rejected the authority of their king but had left his lieutenant, the stadhouder, in office. The war of liberation had enhanced the office of stadhouder and made it hereditary in the House of Orange. Now the opportunity offered to put this ambitious family of would-be monarchs back where it belonged, in the opinion of the burgher aristocrats, as merely prominent citizens of the Republic. The States of Holland decided to appoint no successor to the late stadhouder, either in his civilian or military offices. The States General were to command the army and navy, which meant in practice that the army fell apart into seven small corps, and the navy into three units. The last remaining institutions of central authority were broken. There was to be freedom and equality for all citizens and for all provinces, which meant that citizens who and provinces which exceeded the others in wealth and power, were to dominate. The theory was beautiful but the practice quite different. The Netherland Republic was transformed into a Hollandish State—the province of Holland with dependencies, some of which it treated respectably, others ignominiously.[38]

The second half of the XVIIth century is in some ways, the most glorious period of Netherland history. It lacks the brilliance of the fifty preceding years; it did not produce such great or so many artists; but it saw the ripening of the fruit that had been flowering. In those five decades the Netherland nation—the product of social, political, and geographic circumstances and of the individual efforts of hundreds of years—took definite shape and character. After 1672, when it had passed through the ordeal of hostile aggression aimed at its total destruction, its permanence seemed assured and its place in the European world determined. Glorious as is the history of these fifty years, it nevertheless reveals definite shortcomings in the social and political structure of the nation. These not only spoil the "artistic" effect of the historical picture, they also had grave consequences which ultimately proved as dangerous to the life of the nation as had been hostility of foreign powers.

After 1650, republican liberty, the "True and Only Liberty," obtained in the Netherlands; but Liberty was rather arbitrarily interpreted. The theory was that all the provinces were allies of equal rank, that all public offices were granted only to "Virtue," to quote John De Witt, never to wealth or rank; that all consciences were free and no one was to be persecuted for his religious opinions, that arbitrary or corrupt officials would not be tolerated. In a word, that "Tyranny" would never again be felt in the Seven Provinces, that Law and Justice would rule. Audacious political writers added that the "True and Only Liberty" (the term was used by the burgher-aristocrats to describe the Netherland constitution after the downfall of the House of Orange) would not be completely realized unless freedom not only of conscience but also of worship were granted, and unless all restrictions on economic activity, such as guilds and privileged trade companies, were abolished. These were extreme opinions, however, never publicly sponsored by the leading group among the burgher-aristocrats. The reality was quite different.[39]

Only "Virtue" qualified for office, De Witt had said. Apparently a very small group of Netherlanders held a monopoly of "Virtue"; for in practice offices were never granted except to relatives, friends, or protégés of office holders. De Witt's father had said, "The burgher is a small fellow, and must be kept small." It was on this principle that the burgher-aristocracy acted. The ruling oligarchy grew more and more self-centered. In these same decades the first "contracts of correspondence (*contracten van correspondentie*) were concluded—agreements by which a few families controlling town governments agreed to secure the benefits of their position to their relatives and descendants and to divide all lucrative offices among the various parties so that each in turn would have a chance to profit from the public institutions. The oligarchies of different towns supported each other and if necessary exercised political pressure to exclude undesirable newcomers from office. The Grand Pensionary De Witt himself controlled the States of Holland largely through his personal connections, especially among the ruling cliques of Amsterdam. The rule of "equality for all" was violated, not only in public administration but even in social life. The ruling caste so far segregated itself from the middle class that it virtually formed a new nobility, hence the somewhat childish endeavors of the oligarchs to buy country estates, titles of which they loved to assume.

Thanks to the Erasmian tradition, the new nobility were liberal minded but their liberalism sometimes seemed more negative than positive. Their policy was based not on the conviction that every individual had certain rights and freedoms, but rather on the determination not to allow any pressure group to dominate in the political field. During the whole of the XVIIth century Calvinist synods lodged complaints against "Popish impudence," the recurrence of secret Catholic worship. The States had officially forbidden this but tacitly permitted it for the benefit of the police who levied a heavy, unofficial tax on the Catholics. As time progressed the States grew more and more resentful of this pressure from the official Church, and finally forbade the Calvinist synods to bring any further complaints. They allowed the Jews to practice their own religion, but as soon as the Jewish communities dared to approach the "Noble and Mighty Lords" of Holland for exoneration from certain rules they considered oppressive, strict conformity to establish regulations was demanded. The States referred a protest by the Synod of southern Holland against the teaching of philosophy, in particular the philosophy of Descartes, to the faculty of Leiden University, but when one of the professors included his "minority opinion," the States indignantly returned the report with the remark that no professor should ever dare offer his personal opinion to the High Assembly without being asked. Having thus put the learned gentleman in his place, and received a purified version of the report, they ordered theologians and philosophers to confine themselves to their own field of learning; they forbade philosophers to enter the field of theology or to make use of arguments taken from the Bible; they forbade the reading or discussion of Descartes' books in the classroom; and last but not least, they ordered all university professors to refrain from exchanging insulting remarks, from criticizing each other's views, from abusing one another's characters. The Noble and Mighty Lords probably knew that their delimitation of the fields of theology and philosophy lacked precision and needed some further elucidation. In their conception of liberalism, the difficulty was easily met by enforcing moderation of opinion on both sides.

Likewise the States, instead of accepting the principle of freedom of worship, as urged for commercial reasons by Peter De la Court, the author of a treatise *The Interest of Holland,* contented themselves with permitting moderate liberty in this field subject to heavy payments for the benefit of the ruling class. The burgher-aristocrats of the second half of the XVIIth century may have been more convinced Calvinists than those of the first half, but even so they dreaded theocracy more than any other form of "Tyranny." Here again, aversion to theocracy rather than sympathy for liberty seems to have been the source of their toleration. However, in one respect, their tolerance was positive and that was the freedom of the press. Without the liberal attitude of the States, Holland could never have become as it did, the center of European book production in the later XVIIth century. Occasionally certain books were banned, but such cases were rare exceptions. Peter De la Court's "Interest of Holland" was banned for its extreme views but this did not prevent its being circulated all over the country. The Church of southern Holland had demanded the suppression of the book, but they would hardly have achieved their aim if De la Court's views on foreign policy had not been just as unorthodox as his opinions on religious tolerance. Baruch de Spinoza's *Tractatus Theologo-Politicus* was not forbidden, until the reactionary days of 1672, although the same Synod called it a "dirty and truly blasphemous book." Freedom of opinion and conscience were fairly secure; freedom of worship was tacitly allowed. Although many Dutch Catholics were inclined by tradition and because of the unjust exploitation of their insecure legal status, to look to the Catholic monarchs of Europe as their natural protectors, the greatest of them all, the poet Vondel, was also the greatest of Dutch patriots. The boasted equality of opportunity did not exist, except in the navy and in commerce. In spite of this drawback, the amount of popular freedom enjoyed in the Netherlands was great enough to make near-by peoples envious.

The second edition of De la Court's book, published in 1669, contains a remarkable chapter in which the author explains that the province of Holland need not fear the possible hostility of the other members of the Union. This could be understood to mean simply that Holland did not *need* the other provinces. It would be sufficient, he wrote, to dig a large, deep moat, separating Holland from Utrecht, or, as Utrecht was an agricultural district bound to live or perish with Holland, on the boundary of Utrecht and Guelderland. This moat, a substitute for a permanent line of inundations, would make Holland forever invincible. The Grand Pensionary De Witt had objected to the publication of this singular theory in the first edition of the book. Actual plans to dig such a moat never existed, but the theory accurately reflects a way of thinking quite common among Holland's aristocracy. To them, the eastern provinces were a financial burden. Holland would have to pay the majority of the troops if an army were needed to protect them. They contributed only a nominal amount to the equipment of the navy. They differed economically and culturally from the western coastland. For the Hollander, the peoples of Overijssel and Drente were *moffen,* a slur applied by Lowlanders in the sixteenth century to German mercenary soldiers and later extended to all Germans or, as in this case, to all "Easterners." The penniless country squire of Drente was the buffoon of the Amsterdam stage. In the opinion of many Hollanders, the cause of the eastern provinces was not that of the coastal lands. Amsterdam protested vehemently when De Witt took this interest to heart and sought to protect Overijssel from aggression by preventing militarist expansion in some of the West German principalities. Not unnaturally, this narrow selfishness of Holland's ruling class, a combination of snobbery and political egotism, caused resentment. For the first time the rule of the burgher-aristocracy was really hated, despite the fact that in general it fostered prosperity. The mere idea that a small group of individuals, mostly related by family ties, could dominate the States of Holland and through them the Republic, sufficed to anger the Dutch middle classes. The fact that they themselves were growing ever more prosperous as a result of the successful policy of the ruling class only increased their resentment at being excluded from political offices. Because of the general antagonism of the masses, of the army, of a large part of the navy, and of many oligarchs in the northern provinces, the domination of the ruling group was never very stable. The slightest reverse on the field of battle, at sea, in foreign policy, brought demands that Prince William III be restored to the position of his ancestors. During the twenty-two years (1650–1672) that the oligarchs ruled without check or competition, they had to be constantly on guard against Orangist movements.

Thus, for twenty-two years, a small group of men decided the policy of the States of Holland and of the Union. Their power was backed by no strong police or armed force obedient to their orders, but only by the prestige of success. So long as trade and shipping kept all hands busy and all minds occupied, their position was secure. But in the ultimate analysis, their position depended upon the ability of a single man, the Grand Pensionary John De Witt. William Temple, the British statesman, called him "the perfect Hollander" and no better description of his personality is possible, for he possessed most of the virtues and few of the weaknesses of his class. Born in Dordrecht of an old family of merchants who had become prominent in the magistracy during the revolution of 1572, De Witt had received the kind of education then common among the aristocracy of Holland. He attended elementary and "illustrious" schools, where he received a sound classical training and was taught the principles of mathematics, a field of learning in which he always showed special interest. He learned French and some English and German; he received lessons in music and fencing. At sixteen he went to Leiden University, where he studied law. Four years later he left for his *Grand Tour,* then considered an indispensable part of a gentleman's education. With his brother he visited Paris and Angers, through southern France he traveled to Geneva, back to Paris, and then, via Calais, to England. Oxford was duly visited in

1645, but more attention was paid to the internal political situation of England, where King Charles had fallen into the hands of his enemies.

Back home, John De Witt began his career as a lawyer at the Hague, then as pensionary of his native town. At the Hague, where his practice of law apparently left him plenty of leisure, he worked assiduously at mathematical problems and composed his treatise on conic sections (*Elementa curvarum linearum,* first published in 1659 by one of his friends), which a modern historian of science has called "the first textbook of analytical geometry." The third section of this treatise showed that he had completely mastered the new mathematical theories of Descartes. Law and mathematics however left him time for poetry. Here art was put to practical use: De Witt's literary production was limited to more or less conventional love poems written for the young ladies of his social circle. In those early years of his public career he did not move in the highest circles at the Hague. The prince of Orange's court still dominated all society and there was no place among the high and mighty members of royal or noble families for the son of a burgomaster of Dordrecht, a stubborn defender of the "liberties" of the burgher-aristocracy. John's father was among the six members of the States of Holland arrested and imprisoned by order of the Stadhouder in 1650; and the death of Prince William II was a triumph for the De Witt family and its political associates. A few months later John De Witt became pensionary of Dordrecht, and in July 1653 was appointed grand pensionary of the States of Holland. His powers explicitly included all the prerogatives formerly enjoyed by Oldenbarnevelt and since the death of that great man strictly withheld from his successors. The highest circles at the Hague, somewhat nonplussed by the sudden eclipse of the glory of the House of Orange, no longer shunned this brilliant city aristocrat, and we find him a member of the "Brotherhood of the Knights of Joy" which counted among its members noble ladies of the Houses of Nassau and of Brederode.

The young grand pensionary, only twenty-eight when he assumed his responsible post, remained the undisputed leader of the Republic's foreign policy until the catastrophe of 1672. Precise and clear in his style, prudent and sometimes over-cautious in his diplomacy, perfectly correct in his personal bearing, cool and even haughty towards anyone who was not his close friend, he impressed his contemporaries by his brilliant intelligence, his perfect honesty, his enormous capacity for work. It seems safe to conclude that without him the predominance of Holland's aristocracy would have lasted but a few years. When internal difficulties arose in some of the provinces, De Witt headed missions from Holland to restore peace. When disunity among the commanders hampered the operations of the Navy,

De Witt was there to take command himself as the representative of the States General. In one famous incident the grand pensionary safely took his fleet from the roadstead into the open sea against the advice of experts who had declared the undertaking impossible. He worked unswervingly to secure unity of opinion and purpose among the States. The difficulties of his tasks were increased by the tradition of the States Assemblies, which required unanimity of decision. There was no actual voting at the meetings, but each town deputation put forward its views, and having heard them the pensionary was supposed to draw a "conclusion" with which every deputation could agree. In the solution of these legal puzzles, De Witt was a master. His prestige grew until it overshadowed that of his employers, the States of Holland. This situation created resentment from which arose the first rift in the closed ranks of the aristocracy, and their opponents made excellent use of the openings thus provided.

The cool haughtiness of the grand pensionary towards all people outside the oligarchic caste, was the one trait that prevented his becoming a popular figure. In this respect his personality was typical of the social development of the Dutch burgherclass. De Witt was the ideal *deftige burger,* an untranslatable Dutch expression, the meaning of which may be clear from the foregoing. To be *deftig* became the ambition of the whole Dutch middleclass of the next two hundred and fifty years, and from this general ambition Netherland society suffered until 1940. This deliberate snobbery impaired the magnificent growth of Netherland culture. This was already apparent in De Witt's career. Here was a leading statesman of the Netherlands, ruling at a time when native art flourished as never before or since, and who apparently hardly realized that such an art existed. His biographer notes that the grand pensionary seems to have been on rather friendly terms with Arthur Quellinus, the sculptor who modeled his bust. Portraits of him were made by second-class painters, and the one surviving letter of his to a painter is painfully haughty and condescending. Vondel, the great poet, admired De Witt and glorified him in verses which could hardly have escaped the grand pensionary's notice, yet he never paid any attention to the man who was merely a minor office clerk.

The Netherland States, as well as Netherland society, were taking definite form in the second part of the XVIIth century. In Europe itself the Republic defended its newly acquired place. In the western hemisphere the ephemeral empire was crumbling, that in the eastern was being consolidated. In the Americas, Netherland power had reached its peak shortly before 1640. John Maurice of Nassau, a cousin of Stadhouder Frederick Henry, had accepted the governorship of Brazil, when that Dutch colony extending from the mouth of the Amazon to Bahia (now San Salvador), seemed to have a great future. John Maurice is the only Dutch empire builder of the seventeenth century who sought to make the style of his administration reflect the greatness of his task. Where the Portuguese had created plantations in a cultural vacuum, he was determined to transplant Netherland arts and sciences. Mauritsstad, the new town that replaced the destroyed Portuguese settlement of Olinda, was his creation. The famous architect Pieter Post accompanied him and built his princely residence, Vrijburg, in Netherland Renaissance style. Scientists such as William Piso and George Marcgraf followed him to his new home and at his behest studied and described the flora and fauna of the country. Such ideals of colonization little suited the wishes of the merchants who ruled the Dutch Atlantic empire from Amsterdam and who sought only profit from an impossible combination of trade and privateering. Part of the Caribbean Islands were controlled by the West India Company; settlements had been formed on the coast of Guyana in the section that now is British; and the colony of New Netherland, extending from the Delaware to the Connecticut Rivers, was giving sizeable returns thanks to the good relations existing between the Dutch and the dreaded Mohawk Indians. After the conquest of the most important Portuguese trading posts on the coast of Guinea and of Angola, the Portuguese Atlantic empire seemed doomed to disappear. The Dutch tricolor ruled the South Atlantic as completely as it did the Indian Ocean. But the whole structure in the New World was inherently weak. By 1670, Dutch authority was reduced to a few Caribbean Islands, to part of the coast of Guyana (including present British and Dutch Guyana), and to scattered trading posts in Africa, where now the British colony of the Gold Coast is found. The whole magnificent Brazilian empire and the promising settlement of New Netherland on the Hudson River had been lost.

Why did the Atlantic empire crumble so rapidly, why did the East Indian empire grow and prosper, although far more money and energy were spent on the former than on the latter? It was not only because the natural resources of the East were more easily exploited than those of the West. The causes of the tragic failure of the West India enterprise were deeper and manifold. First among them was the divided character of the West India Company, to which we have already referred. The needs of a privateering concern differ from those of a business company. Privateering on a large scale called for large sums for the equipment and manning of ships, which in this particular case had to be full-sized men-of-war. To be profitable enormous booty had to be taken year after year, a thing hardly to be expected for the Spaniards and Portuguese were by no means defenseless, and quickly learned to counteract the ways of the Dutch privateers. The directors in Amsterdam fondly believed they could continue to play the role of buccaneers on a large scale. Their ships and crews had all the adventures and all the hard fighting that was the lot of the buccaneer, but the one brilliant stroke of Piet Hein in the Bay of Matanzas remained an isolated case. Not bad luck, but the Spaniards prevented a repetition of that success.

The West India Company wanted both to plunder the Spaniards and to create an empire. The East India Company first established an empire, carefully selecting for that purpose an area where its enemies were weak, and then turned to the attack. The directors of the West India Company, technically an improved edition of its East Indian model, believed they could build up a commercial system in the Atlantic like that of their colleagues in Asia. The backbone of the Asiatic system was the spice and cloth trade between India and the Malay Archipelago. That of the Atlantic system was to be the slave trade from Angola and the Gold Coast to the Caribbean and Brazil. The West India Company actually gained control of the centers of slave export. It never got a hold on the territory into which the "goods" were to be imported. The gentlemen in Amsterdam figured that if they gained control of all the principal harbors from which "black ebony" was shipped to America, the Spaniards and Portuguese would be forced to buy from them in spite of the king of Spain. They partly succeeded in this scheme, but their monopoly did not last long. In the place of the ousted Portuguese, new competitors appeared in the persons of British interlopers. In half a century they had become the principal slave traders; to the Dutch only a few crumbs were left.

Even so, the West India Company might have paid if the directors had not concentrated their efforts on the wrong point and then abandoned the work when it was half done. The strong naval forces equipped by the Company in 1630 and later might have conquered one or more of the larger islands of the Caribbean from the Spaniards. Instead the directors chose to attack Brazil. Why, we do not know; perhaps, as a Dutch historian has suggested, because they believed that the king of Spain would react less forcefully in defense of a dependency of his Portuguese crown than of one of his hereditary Spanish possessions. Perhaps they derived this idea from the history of the East Indies. It was a fatal mistake, for they attacked Portuguese territory only ten years before Portugal was to revolt against Spain and to become the ally of the Netherlands in Europe. Once started on the enterprise, they did not carry it to its logical conclusion but stopped after the conquest of the northern half of the country, leaving the enemy convenient points for a counter-attack in the southern section.

Having begun the conquest of so large a territory, the company had to devise a colonial policy. Years before the West Indian enterprise was begun, William Usselinx, the spiritual father of the undertaking, had suggested a conquest combined with a vigorous policy of colonization and, as he happened to be a convinced Calvinist, of forcible conversion to the reformed Religion. The directors who, in the words of a prominent Netherland statesman of the following century, "possessed the pure shopkeeper's mentality and made consistent negligence their principle of action," executed the first part of this program halfway, the third with remarkable persistance, and did nothing about the second. They seemed to believe that in the thinly populated Western Hemisphere the same commercial policy could be followed as in Asia with her populous empires.

Without difficulty they acquired a large and beautiful country in North America, from the present Hartford, Connecticut, to Albany, New York, and down to the boundaries of Maryland. They began by bringing all the settlers scattered at different points along the Hudson together in one community, New Amsterdam on the southern tip of Manhattan Island. That community was to be the base of the fur trade with the Indians. This system did not work; the Mohawks and their allies controlled the fur trade from the north, and only by accepting them as intermediaries could real results be achieved. A new system was inaugurated, that of the "patroonships," grants of land with seigneurial rights to Netherland capitalists who would colonize their concessions. One of these seigneuries, that of Rensselaer on the middle Hudson, became prosperous; but it owed its prosperity to its location, which permitted it to monopolize contact with the Mohawks. If the Rensselaer family prospered, the Company suffered; for it lost in furs what the Rensselaers gained. A trickle of immigrants moved towards the promised land on the Hudson; more would have come and more would have stayed if the directors had shown better understanding.

The story of New Netherland's vicissitudes, the reluctance with which the directors yielded to popular pressure on the Hudson and at home, and with which they granted more liberty to the colonists, has been told many times. What was gained in concessions was often undone by the misrule of the governors, who received their post because of family relations. All this continued while land-hungry English immigrants were crowding in from the north. In 1635 they occupied the Dutch "House of Hope" on the Connecticut, which they replaced by the settlement of Hartford; while three years later a company under the Swedish flag but with Dutch resources occupied the banks of the Delaware. The latter intrusion was beaten back by the energetic Peter Stuyvesant who, mustering the largest armed forces until then gathered in the white settlements—seven hundred soldiers on ships—forcibly hauled down the Swedish flag in 1655. New Netherland did not prosper. It received only a very meager share of the Company's resources. Money and men poured into the Caribbean, where some of the islands seemed bottomless pits swallowing any number of men and amount of material sent to secure their permanent occupation. The small island of Tobago near Trinidad alone received more than seven hundred Dutch immigrants in twenty-five years. Less than seventy survived, and the island was not yet in the Company's possession. New Netherland might have been saved if these immigrants had been encouraged to go to the Hudson instead of to the Caribbean.

The Brazilian Dutch colony suffered from the same misguided policy. The directors expected the new colony to produce sugar and dye-stuffs without people to produce them. Since the XVIth century, the district of Pernambuco had been one of the richest sugar producing areas of the world. The directors built great hopes on the capture of the Portuguese plantations many of which would be evacuated by their original owners; but they had not figured that the Portuguese would apply a "scorched earth" policy and burn down the sugar mills, plantation buildings, and even the crops on the fields. John Maurice succeeded in getting the sugar production started again by selling plantations on easy terms, by importing negro slaves (some 23,000 of these unfortunates were brought over from Africa in nine years), and by policing the countryside against the raids of Portuguese guerillas.

In this reorganization of Brazil's economic life the Jews played an important role. The baptized Brazilian Jews, oppressed by the Inquisition, had looked forward to Dutch occupation. Apparently they had shown their sympathy with Portugal's enemies too openly, for shortly before the fall of Pernambuco the Inquisition charged some of them with high treason and defection from the Church they had accepted by baptism. Once the Netherlanders were established in Brazil, the colony became a haven of refuge for Jews from many European countries and from Portuguese territory. Hundreds of their co-religionists who had found homes in Amsterdam came over to Pernambuco to live in a Portuguese-speaking world, beyond the reach of the Inquisition. Two-thirds of the plantations sold by the Company were bought by Jews, while other members of the same community devoted themselves to trading. The influence of these Jewish colonists became such that in Brazil—for the first time under the Netherland flag—anti-Semitism developed, doubtlessly fostered by lingering Portuguese ideas.

All the energy of John Maurice of Nassau, all the bravery of his soldiers, all the feverish activity of the immigrants, Jews and non-Jews, could not save the colony. The sugar industry was only partly restored. Brazil formerly exported more than twenty million pounds a year, mostly produced in the North, and this had fallen to not more than seven or eight million pounds. Employers and capital were lacking and labor was scarce. The slave trade could have supplied the labor if guerilla warfare and political unrest had not discouraged capitalists and immigrants. The amount of private capital invested in Brazil can not be computed. The sale of plantations alone brought the company more than two million guilders. In the nine years between 1636 and 1645 the sale of slaves brought nearly seven million guilders. All these were not paid for in cash, certainly not the plantations. It seems safe to conclude, however, that the planters of Brazil and their financial backers at home sank more than ten millions in this South American enterprise, which ended in tragic failure.

Traditional historiography has it that the prosperity of the homeland caused the failure of the Dutch settlements in the Western Hemisphere. The ordinary reasons for emigration, economic distress and religious persecution, were lacking. This seems to provide a perfect and even satisfying explanation of the tragedy of Brazil and the languishing existence of New Netherland. But this theory is not wholly correct. Religious reasons were indeed lacking. In only one case did a small group of dissenters leave the Netherlands because of persecution. This was the exodus of a few thousand Arminians after the Synod of Dordrecht had excommunicated them from the Dutch Reformed Church. Economic reasons for emigration, however, undoubtedly did exist. All contemporary writers complain of the "overpopulation" of the Netherlands. "Our country is overcrowded with people, and there are ten hands for every job," wrote a pamphleteer of 1622, and later writers proposed to make the West Indies a "Home for the Poor" and to refuse charity to all able-bodied unemployed who did not emigrate. There were poor people enough in the Netherlands, but not in the right professions. The weak and undernourished workers of the cities with their starving children, could not provide the right kind of immigrants. Farmers were needed. Zeeland had a surplus of farmers and farm hands, and from there thousands emigrated, but to the Caribbean Islands where sub-tropical diseases, the hostility of the Spaniards, murderous attacks by the Carib Indians exterminated most of them. The truth seems to be that there was a shortage of the right type of emigrant-pioneer, and that such people as presented themselves too often sacrificed their lives in efforts doomed to fail.

In spite of all this, the American settlements might have flourished if the best type of emigrants had not been attracted elsewhere. The single group who left the country to escape religious persecution, moved to Holstein, where they founded Friederichstadt. The princes of northern Germany whose territories had suffered horribly in the Thirty Years' War, sought colonists expert at draining marshes and specialists in dairy production, and found them in emigrants from Groningen, Friesland and Zeeland. Why should these people go to the wild lands on the Hudson where Indian warfare was a constant threat, or to Brazil where they would be exposed to the revenge of the Portuguese, when they could obtain land in Brandenburg, Holstein, the Rhineland, Denmark, Sweden, France (near La Rochelle), or even in England, where they drained the Norfolk fens? Here security and prosperity were assured. Many thousands of such colonists spread over Europe. Compare this situation with that in England, where thousands of the common people were *forced* to emigrate and where religious persecution provided them with strong leadership and the success of English and the failure of Dutch colonization is easily understood.

In the history of Dutch XVIIth century emigration one episode stands apart. In 1662 Pieter Cornelis Plockhoy, who for years had dreamed of sweeping social reforms, received permission from the burgomasters of Amsterdam to recruit a number of men, willing to follow him to New Netherland to found a model colony on the basis of complete equality and democracy. Plockhoy had previously expounded his ideas on the ideal social community in several treatises. No ecclesiastics were to be permitted to exercise authority, private economic interests were to be completely subordinated to those of the community, no man was to be another's servant and all authority was to rest with the citizens in meeting assembled. Plockhoy's plan for his settlement in New Netherland was not quite so radical, yet radical enough to make its ready acceptance by the City of Amsterdam difficult to understand. The burgomasters, officially loyal members of the Reformed Church, permitted the founding of a settlement from which clergymen of all denominations would be rigorously excluded and where no dogmatic Christian creed was recognized! The program for the settlement, circulated by Plockhoy in the Netherlands, may indeed be called one of "the most extraordinary of the early memorials of American colonization" as a New York historian has described it. Plockhoy's colony did not last long. In 1664 English soldiers plundered it and dispersed its inhabitants. Plockhoy died, many years later, in Germantown, Pennsylvania.

The concentration of the West India Company on trade rather than on agriculture, despite its disadvantages was not without beneficial consequences. It created a workable basis for cooperation with the native populations. A superficial survey of Netherland colonial activities in the West leaves the impression that the Netherlanders were more humane than most other European nations in their dealings with the Indians. Some historians have dwelt upon this theory and exaggerated the nobility of the Dutch attitude. The Netherlanders approached the Indians from a different point of view than either the English or the Spaniards. Unlike so many English immigrants, they were not poor land-hungry farmers, whose interests of necessity clashed with those of semi-nomadic natives. Nor did they seek to exploit the riches of the earth by compulsory labor. Coming long after the Spaniards, they resorted to negro slave labor when they wanted such exploitation. They needed the Indians as purveyors of natural products or—as in Brazil—as allies against a common enemy.

In their relations with the native populations, the Dutch followed a consistent policy. There was usually one tribe or group of tribes with whom they cultivated friendship. In the Hudson valley the Mohawks were their allies, on the coast of Guyana some of the Carib tribes, in Brazil the Tapuya Indians, who lived in the mountains northwest of Pernambuco. Two of these Indian nations found their historians in contemporary Dutch writers. Johannes Megapolensis, minister of the church at Rensselaerswijk near Albany, left a description of the Mohawks, whom he vainly sought to covert to Christianity. He sadly acknowledged his impotence when he saw the wild warriors standing in the rear of his church, smoking and laughing at him while he was thundering away at his rough Dutch parishioners. Elias Herckmans, member of the Council of Brazil, gave a far less sympathetic description of the Tapuya Indians, but his observations were long considered authoritative by ethnological experts.

The directors of the West India Company showed less foresight in dealing with their own compatriots than in handling the native problem. The aristocrats who at home followed the theory that the burgher being a small fellow must be kept small, were disinclined to treat the motley group of settlers in their colonies with more respect. They refused to consider the possible effect of self-governing English settlements adjacent to their own possessions. This led to a continuous struggle for greater autonomy by the people of New Netherland. Here at least a limited amount of self-government was wrested from the reluctant gentlemen of Amsterdam. In Brazil the situation was complicated by the presence of Catholic Portuguese colonists. John Maurice of Nassau did his utmost to secure for the inhabitants a modest share in public affairs, regardless of their religious convictions. The stubbornness and narrowmindedness of the directors, combined with the religious fanaticism of some of the ministers of the Church, thwarted all his efforts and led to the catastrophe of 1654, when the capital of the colony capitulated to a victorious army of insurgents, who after eight years of bitter fighting had driven the Dutch troops from the soil of Brazil.

In 1640 the people of Portugal revolted against Spain. The national revolution spread over all colonial territories and in Brazil naturally directed itself against the Netherlanders. The States General, glad of the Portuguese resistance to Spain, could not very well attack these same Portuguese for their support of the rebels in Brazil. Once peace with Spain was concluded, the Republic declared war on Portugal, but only the East India Company benefited through the conquest of Portuguese strongholds in Ceylon and India. Brazil was irretrievably lost. In 1661 peace was restored. The West India Company ceded all claims in Brazil in exchange for a lump sum of eight million guilders.

The great Atlantic enterprise had failed. Not only Brazil but also Angola on the African coast had been reconquered by Portugal. In 1664 King Charles II of Great Britain decided to make good his claims to the eastern seaboard of North America. A British squadron appeared off New Amsterdam and forced the surrender of the colony. Subsequent Dutch-British wars brought a short-lived restoration of Dutch sovereignty on the Hudson in 1673, but the eventual outcome was the restriction of Dutch territory in the New World to the island groups of Curaçao and St. Eustachius, and to the coastlands of Guyana where in 1664 an enterprising Zeeland commander had added the territory of Surinam to that of Demerara, Essequibo, and Berbice, now forming British Guyana. These small countries and islands, and some slave trading posts on the African Gold Coast, were the meager result of fifty years of warfare and colonization in the Atlantic area. No wonder that the West India Company went into bankruptcy in 1674, with a debt of six million guilders, and no prospects to speak of. A new West India Company with a modest capital of 630,000 guilders took over the Company's assets and one-third of its debts. Except for the slave trade, the West Indies were thrown open to private commerce.

The Dutch settlements in the Americas left few traces. Only the Netherlanders on the Hudson vigorously maintained their traditions, of which the Dutch Reformed Church was the main support. Of the colony in Brazil nothing but memories remained, but the national revival provoked by the Dutch invaders of that country contributed greatly to Brazilian national consciousness and the territory of Pernambuco became the cradle of Brazilian nationalism. Thus, unwittingly and unwillingly, the Netherlanders may have contributed to the independence of the largest South American republic. The Jewish communities fled from Pernambuco when it was restored to Portuguese sovereignty. Some of their members returned to Europe; some sought a new home under the Dutch flag in the West Indies where many of their descendants may still be found in Curaçao and Surinam.

The development of the Asiatic Dutch empire was the exact reverse of that in the West. Here expansion and stabilization were continuous. The conflict with Portugal, so disastrous to the West India Company, provided its sister institution in the East with a golden opportunity to finish the job interrupted by the Treaty of Muenster. In 1648 the status quo had been accepted as a basis for the demarcation of Dutch and Spanish-Portuguese colonial spheres of influence. This had left the coast of Ceylon divided between the Dutch and the Portuguese, a situation which benefited only the king of Kandi, who ruled the interior and thanks to this divided control was able to play one European power against the other. The southern tip of India was also under divided control. The second war with Portugal resulted in the establishment of the supremacy of the Dutch East India Company in this whole area. Ceylon became the company's "cinnamon garden," and the king of Kandi its vassal and royal purveyor of elephants. The only use the gentlemen of Amsterdam had for these interesting animals, was as presents to other Asiatic princes.

Control over the ports of southern India gave the Company a monopoly over Asiatic textiles, and cloth from Malabar was one of the principal objects of trade in the Malay Archipelago. Once in possession of all these trading posts (which nowhere included authority over the interior), the Dutch Company definitely superseded the Portuguese empire in Asia. Only the bravery of their inhabitants saved Goa and Macao, which are Portuguese today, from the same fate as Colombo and Malacca. Some Portuguese commerce was still carried on with the connivance of native princes, who now resented Dutch control of the seas as much as they had formerly detested Portuguese supremacy. The sultans of Macassar in southern Celebes were among the principal supporters of non-Dutch trade. In their capital, Portuguese, Danish, and British traders had factories, and the hardy Buginese and Macassar sailors kept up a brisk smuggling trade in cloves and nutmeg in the strictly monopolized area of the Moluccas. In 1661, tension between the government of Batavia and the king of Macassar resulted in war. In two strenuous campaigns the Company's troops, commanded by Cornelis Speelman and aided by Aru Palacca, prince of the Buginese, forced Macassar to submit. Foreign traders were driven from the town, which lost all significance once monopoly had stifled its trade. Some Portuguese merchants continued to intrude from the island of Timor, where missionaries of their nation had established native Christian communities. The Company paid no further attention to this remnant of its rival's empire and eastern Timor has remained Portuguese despite successive Dutch-Australian and Japanese occupation.

Against these gains, and the exclusive right to trade with the people of Japan—through a single factory on the small island of Deshima opposite Nagasaki—stood the loss of Formosa, one of the Company's most promising settlements. The Company's dealings with this island just off the Chinese coast present unusual features, which distinguishes its history from that of other Dutch settlements in the East. When the Dutch went to Formosa in 1624, the island was still definitely outside the Chinese cultural and political area. Its inhabitants, racially related to the Philippine tribes, were more open to western influence than those of the south Asiatic regions, where Hinduism and Mohammedanism opposed European cultural influence and the Company could not promote Christianity without impairing its good relations with the natives and consequently its commercial interests. Formosa provided an opportunity for the "Spanish" method of colonization: converting the native people to the religion and the language of the rulers. The results were most encouraging. Within fifteen years a Christian community of five to six thousand people had been formed. Wherever congregations were organized schools were opened, because knowledge of Dutch was necessary for the new Christians, who were supposed to read the Staten Bible. Several hundred children attended school, and the hope seemed well founded that the whole population of Formosa would be won over to Christianity and Netherland civilization. The Netherlanders did not have the opportunity, however, to indoctrinate the people of Formosa for an equal period of time as the Spaniards had to educate the Filipinos. Thousands of Chinese patriots, forced to seek refuge on the sea from the Manchu invasion of their homeland, lurked around Formosa in the hopes of establishing a foothold on the island. In 1661, the Chinese leader Koxinga landed with a strong force and undertook the successful siege of the principal Dutch stronghold. The negligence of the Government at Batavia contributed as much to the loss of the Dutch fortress as the skill and courage of the Chinese partisans. The Netherland settlers were murdered, the natives ruthlessly punished, and the island occupied by Chinese immigrants. Even so, traces of Dutch cultural activity among the natives lingered on into the XIXth century.

The loss of Formosa, deprived the Company of its base for the China trade and was a major setback. It was the only setback, however, that the Batavian merchant-princes suffered in those years of their greatest prosperity and expansion under the able and cautious leadership of Governor-General Johan Maetsuijcker (1653–1678). For twenty-five years, without once taking a vacation, this shrewd and stubborn administrator ruled the Dutch Asiatic empire from Batavia's sultry castle. He knew how to pick his men from among the crowd of naval officers, employees, and native allies with whom he had to work. His legalistic mind was well adapted to the task of keeping everyone, from the boisterous and extravagant admiral Speelman, the conqueror of Macassar, to the ministers of the Church in

Batavia, in his proper place. His firm policy of never allowing any person or interest to disturb the rigid principles of administration laid down by the Company, truly represented in the Far East the political traditions of the Dutch ruling class. Not being himself a member of the Dutch Reformed Church, he vigorously opposed religious intolerance. Strictly interpreted, the ordinances of the Company, permitted only congregations of the Dutch Reformed Church to worship publicly in the Company's territory. These were not enforced, for the Chinese and Mohammedans continued to practice their own forms of worship. In calling for the suppression of these practices, the Batavian consistory made the mistake of basing its argument on the Law of Moses instead of on an ordinance of the directors, which gave Maetsuijcker an opportunity to rebuke them: "The laws of the ancient Jewish republics have no force in the territory of the East India Company!"

Maetsuijcker was the author of the first code of laws of the Netherlands Indies. Known as the Statutes of Batavia, this code was promulgated in 1642. It is important as the basis of Dutch judicial organization in the East. Dutch law was to be followed in all cases not provided for in the code. Where Dutch law was insufficient, Roman law was to be followed. One important exception was made to this general rule: if a case touching upon a point of Chinese customary law was brought before the court, the court might assign a Chinese judge to sit on the bench and to decide the case according to Chinese law. This was the beginning of the plural judicial system still prevailing in the Netherland Indies.

The directors of the East India Company, whose record as exploiters of native peoples is sufficiently bad, are usually charged with the additional crime of gross cultural negligence. In this respect their reputation is worse than their deeds. It is obvious that they did not promote scientific research or spread knowledge as part of their government in the East. Like modern business concerns, the company showed great interest in discoveries that contributed directly to the financial success of their enterprise. The directors were willing to pay for better methods of combating the diseases that were frequent aboard ship on long voyages; but when asked to submit their ideas on the subject, the professors of medicine found endless subterfuges to avoid answering that they had none. The Company did nothing to discourage the publication of books on the East Indies, their peoples and their natural characteristics, unless they thought some trade "secret" was involved. Abraham Rogerius's description of Hinduism and Rumphius's work on botany are monuments of Indology. Herbert De Jager, one of the greatest linguists of his age, was in the service of the Company when he studied the affinity of the Malay-Polynesian language group. The directors paid for translations of the Bible into Malay and for the education of missionaries, but the results of their endeavors were modest. Like most modern business men the directors did not go out of their way to promote learning or culture, but encouraged it when their help was asked. Business interests predominated. The spread of Christianity usually meant the converting of those already baptized by Portuguese Jesuits from Catholicism to Calvinism. Interference with the internal administration of native princes, allies of the Company, was not tolerated. Wherever Islam ruled (and that was nearly everywhere in the Company's sphere of direct influence), the conversion of the natives and the spread of western knowledge was not to be looked for. Even the field of education was not completely neglected by the Batavian government, too often described as showing no interest in this field, for it opened schools for slave children in its capital.

Shortly before Maetsuijcker took the reins of government in Batavia, a most important decision was reached by the directors in Amsterdam. To lessen the dangers and discomforts of the long sea voyage to the east, a half-way station was founded on the southern tip of Africa. In 1647, the ship "Haarlem" had been wrecked in *Tafelbaai*. The crew succeeded in getting ashore and stayed there five months, during which time they grew vegetables and traded with the natives. The climate, the fertility of the soil, the friendliness of the natives, all seemed to invite a settlement; and in 1651 the directors sent Commander Jan van Riebeeck to South Africa, where on April 6, 1652, he went ashore and built his camp on the present site of Capetown. His instructions were to maintain good relations with the native Hottentot tribes, and he was explicitly forbidden to take part in their mutual wars. His arguments that the Dutch settlers by joining with one tribe against another could easily procure herds of cattle for the colony, failed to change this decision.

The problem at the Cape, as in Brazil and New Netherland, was how to recruit settlers. Riebeeck offered a simple solution which if carried through would have changed African history. The "cheapest" and best colonizers, he said, were the Chinese. He had been in the Indies and knew how Jan Pieteerszoon Coen had esteemed the Chinese for their industry and simple way of life. Batavia could never have flourished as it did but for Chinese artisans and trades. The Batavian Government rejected Riebeeck's idea, and sent out a small number of slaves. Others were brought in from the coast of Guinea, but not in considerable numbers. In 1657 Capetown numbered 134 Europeans and 11 slaves. The new settlement served real needs. In the first seven years of its founding, an average of twenty-five ships a year carrying five thousand men, anchored in the bay. For the crews, the change of diet, from salt fish and biscuit to fresh vegetables and meat, was a relief that saved thousands of lives. The captains, who liked to increase their income by cutting down on the crews' rations, naturally complained of Capetown, where they said, the meat was lean and the roadstead dangerous.

In those years four great modern cities came into existence under the Dutch flag: New York, Pernambuco, Capetown, and Batavia. New York, small as it was in 1660, was already a city of many languages and peoples. Pernambuco had a population drawn from all nations and was notorious for its "night-life," to put it mildly. Capetown was a small hamlet, a street with a church and a fortress, with a tribe of miserable, degenerate Hottentots living beneath its primitive walls. Batavia was the most "magnificent" of the four, with its streets along the canals, just as in Holland, with its Chinese shopkeepers and artisans, its Dutch *burghers* with their numerous slaves, and its *Mardykers,* freedmen, descendants of former Portuguese slaves born in India. They were Christians and aped the Europeans, walking the streets, as a contemporary author says, "dressed up like a quack's monkey at a country fair." They were so many that Portuguese, with a mixture of Dutch and Malay, was the common language of XVIIth century Batavia, much to the disgust of the directors in Amsterdam, who vainly urged the use of correct Dutch. This was the Netherland empire of the middle of the seventeenth century. It was curious that a small nation should wield greater power in the distant oceans than in the sea washing its home shores.

The European position of the Netherlands underwent considerable change in the second half of the XVIIth century. Netherland trade no longer expanded as it had done in the first four decades of the century. As larger ships were used, the bulk of the merchandise carried increased, but not enough to keep Netherland trade at the same high level in relation to international commerce as a whole. Substantial profits were made in the Baltic, the Spanish and Mediterranean trade; but in France and England the predominance of the Netherlanders was waning rapidly. More and more capital amassed in the hands of Dutch merchants. The desire to seek new economic outlets, to exploit every possible opportunity, decreased with the progress of well-being. This accumulation of wealth seemed to ensure to the merchant princes of Amsterdam a firm and permanent hold over a great part of international trade. They did not want to spend all their time and energy acquiring more.

Satisfied with their gains and those of their ancestors, the Dutch merchants were no longer so keen to eliminate competition, especially as they understood the grave risks entailed. The general situation of Europe had changed considerably since 1648. Spain was reduced to a second-class power.

For ten years after the Treaty of Muenster her armies, though continuously defeated, remained in the field against France. France was taking Spain's place as the great military power of the continent. Danger to the land boundaries of the Netherlands could come from that quarter only, and no longer from Spain or any part of Germany. Spain had ceased to be a naval power after the crushing defeat at the Downs in 1639. On the seas the Netherlands found a new competitor in Great Britain, reunited under new rulers, sturdy middleclass men and country squires who at the outset closely resembled the Dutch Regent class. Denmark, in control of the Sund, looked to the Netherlands for protection against the ambitions of Sweden, well on her way to making the Baltic a Swedish lake. The Republic of the Netherlands, obviously satisfied with what it had, seemed a natural defender of weaker powers willing to accept its economic leadership. Such a policy would mean siding with Spain against France, to maintain the southern Lowlands as a buffer state between the Dutch frontier and expansionist France. It would mean supporting Denmark, Brandenburg and Poland against Sweden. Finally it would entail bold and vigorous opposition to England everywhere—in America, in Africa and nearer home in the Channel and the North Sea.

A policy of deliberate opposition to England, France and Sweden seemed sheer madness and national suicide. No serious Dutch statesman could advocate it. John De Witt, cautious and peace-loving, certainly would not involve his country in such risks. Yet, events in 1672 were to prove that the material resources of the Republic were so great that it was actually able not only to withstand the combined attack of these military powers, but to defeat them with the help of weaker states. Even had he favored it personally and been able to win over the States to it, John De Witt realized that an active foreign policy, was bound to bring about internal revolution. Such wars could not be fought without a commander-in-chief, and none other than the prince of Orange was acceptable to the army or the people. For political reasons as for reasons of principle, the burgher-aristocracy was opposed to all forms of militarism, to "wasting" money on soldiers and equipment, even on ships of war. The world being what it unfortunately is, De Witt with his cool judgment knew that certain military forces are needed in peacetime to prepare for inevitable wars. The majority of the States Assemblies lacked all knowledge of military matters; they had faith in the old-fashioned system of equipping merchantmen for naval warfare, which had brought the glorious victory of the Downs and had won the empire; they believed that a navy could be created overnight. They willfully ignored the fact that at the time of the battle of the Downs, the

Netherlands had had an army under eminent leadership and with a great tradition.

The opportunity which had offered itself around 1650, when France could still be stopped in her conquest of the southern Netherlands and Britain could still be defeated, was allowed to pass. Three years after the burgher-aristocrats had gained full control, they were attacked by Great Britain. The royal claim to sovereignty over the "English" Seas was taken up by Parliament. It was preceded by an act of economic war against the Netherlands, the Navigation Act of 1651, which gave a monopoly of British imports to British shipping. Great Britain was on her way to more complete economic nationalism, and other nations were soon to follow. The Act was intended as a serious blow to the Dutch system of trading, but for a time it was less strongly enforced in practice than formulated in law. In itself it could not furnish the essential requirement of commerce: capital. The practical application of these British pretensions to maritime sovereignty caused the outbreak of warfare, in which the Dutch republic despite its greater financial and naval resources, suffered a serious defeat.[40] If it had not been for the genius and courage of the Dutch commanders—Tromp who fell in the battle of Terheide, Witte de With, De Ruyter and others who worked wonders with undisciplined fleets, small and badly armed ships, and a constant shortage of ammunition—the defeat would have been decisive. Not only the North Sea and the Channel, but all European waters were theaters of war. In the northern and southern theaters the Dutch easily remained masters. Their economic influence and the fear of Sweden brought Denmark to their side and permitted the closing of the Sund. In the Mediterranean their squadrons defeated the British and secured control east of the Straits of Gibraltar. But in the main theater of war, the situation was different. Tromp was confronted with a gigantic task. British merchantmen, few in number, could put safely into ports on the western coast of England, only occasionally threatened by Dutch privateers; while the large and valuable Dutch convoys from the south and the west could only reach port through waters controlled by the enemy. Tromp needed his whole fleet to protect those convoys. To carry on offensive operations at the same time was out of the question.

This disastrous war might have served as a lesson to the ruling caste in Holland, had it not been that the ensuing peace treaty suited their particular political interests too well. In England the power of Parliament was broken by Cromwell who, a shrewd diplomat and Calvinist idealist at the same time, saw a similarity between his own interests and those of the ruling oligarchy in Holland. Fearing that the Netherlands, if aroused to energetic action abroad by an ambitious prince of Orange, closely related to the Stuarts, might become the base of a royalist counter-revolution, he decided to sacrifice momentary naval supremacy to security against such an eventuality. In the peace of Westminster of 1654, two regimes, both threatened at home by interrelated oppositions, found each other. By his concessions Cromwell saved Holland's oligarchy from certain defeat at the hands of the Orangists. It was a humiliating success for that oligarchy. The treaty permitted Netherland merchants to continue their temporarily interrupted trade, but that was all. The international position of the Republic had suffered greatly. The king of France, young Louis XIV, was crushing Spanish power in the southern Low Countries. As his share in the booty, Cromwell demanded and obtained with other territories the town of Dunkirk. The Narrows of Dover were now as completely English as the Sund was Danish. Netherland commerce was hemmed in between two gates which could be closed at any time. The policy of active neutrality seemed to have failed. The Republic had become merely a passive onlooker while England and France decided the fate of western Europe.

This political situation did not reflect the existing potentialities of power, as John De Witt well knew. In spite of the heavy cost of war, the credit of the States of Holland was rising. The rate of interest on the public debt was reduced to four percent, an unusually low rate. The States General could raise millions without difficulty and remain financially independent, the bondholders being citizens of the Republic, whereas foreign governments had difficulty in finding a few hundred thousand and even for that had to appeal to Dutch bankers. The leaders of so sound and powerful a state did not need to bow to foreign rulers at a time when armies were for hire, and in a country with more ships and sailors than any other.

In spite of all this, the Republic did not dare to offend either Cromwell or King Louis by openly opposing their ambitious schemes. The situation became critical when Sweden, the third of the new militaristic powers, began an all-out drive for control of the Baltic Sea and the Sund. War flared up again in East Prussia with the Hohenzollerns, in Poland, in Denmark. If the Sund became Swedish, if Poland and Prussia were no longer accessible to Dutch wheat-traders, then the Republic, cut off from the source of its financial strength, was bound to succumb. Necessity forced the Republic to side with the weaker powers. Dutch squadrons protected Danzig and kept the Sund open. Help was promised to Denmark, and the Swedish troops were driven from its soil. Fate assisted the prudent but energetic policy of De Witt. Cromwell's death freed Holland's oligarchy from an overzealous sympathizer. Contrary to all expectation the peace treaty concluded between Spain and France in 1659, left the southern Low Countries as a protective cushion for the Republic's southern frontier.

Cardinal de Mazarin, prime minister of France, had been moderate in his demands, not from conviction but because he hoped to complete the French conquest of the Spanish monarchy through the tender approach of matrimonial alliance, rather than by the crude methods of war. The peace treaty of 1659 merely gave the Netherlands a brief respite. It in no way solved the Belgian problem. Both in the east and in the south, the Netherland frontiers needed greater security. Disdainful of continental affairs the oligarchy of Holland failed to recognize this. Drawing their living from the sea, connected with foreign countries by the sea, they thought of Holland as an island, and of the land provinces as so many bridgeheads on the continent. The grand pensionary knew better, but his hands were tied by the egotism of his caste. He was forced to permit foreign powers to make the areas adjacent to the Republic bases from which to launch possible aggression.

The eastern frontier was the most neglected, yet nowhere had the Republic a better chance to secure itself. After the Thirty Years' War, northern Germany was in a deplorable condition, spiritually and materially. Dutch cultural influence was strong throughout the old Low-German lands. The Dutch language was widely understood. Netherland actors brought Dutch plays, or Spanish plays in Dutch translation, to the stages of Bremen, Hamburg, Berlin, Koenigsberg, and even of Danzig and Riga. Dutch literature was admired and imitated. The Dutch language was the official medium of religious instruction in East Friesland. In that small district the struggle between Dutch and High German lasted for two centuries, from the middle of the XVIIth to the middle of the XIXth century. While the Reformed Church in East Friesland adopted Dutch versions of the Psalms and catechism and all its sermons were preached in Dutch, the Lutherans made High German their church language. Religion and the language of worship became strangely interrelated. To preach in a Calvinist Church in High German or in Dutch in a Lutheran one, verged on "heresy." This relation both strengthened and weakened the Dutch linguistic hold on East Friesland. Its strength was that Dutch became part of a religious tradition among a naturally conservative people. Its weakness was that Dutch was always considered the language of a particular, closed group. By the end of the XVIIth century the civil authorities of Emden, supported by the example of the court of the East Frisian counts, where High German was spoken, began to propagate that language deliberately. Resentment against the subordination of the county's interest to those of the Republic naturally emphasized East Friesland's political and cultural connections with the Empire. The Dutch language was bound to regress even further when in 1744, Prussian authority replaced that of the native princes. In the small principality of Bentheim, east of Overijssel, Dutch was the literary language throughout this period. The States General were even the official protectors of the Calvinist Congregation in the little state. Lingen, somewhat further to the east, belonged to the princes of Orange. The duchy of Cleve had been intimately connected with the Netherlands since the Middle Ages. John Maurice of Nassau, the governor of Brazil, had administered this and other provinces for the prince-elector of Brandenburg and embellished his residence with the assistance of Dutch architects. Dutch was spoken and used as a literary language here until far into the XIXth century. All along the eastern boundary of the Republic Netherland influence was strong.

That fact gained particular significance from the general attitude of the German people towards the United Provinces in the latter part of the XVIIth century. There was much envy, of course, of the extraordinary prosperity of the Netherlands, which contrasted sharply with the poverty of war-torn Germany. The power of Dutch capitalism which fattened on loans to German princes, created bitter feelings expressed in the saying, "Where a Dutchman treads, no grass can grow." "The ancients," wrote a pamphleteer, "said that the crocodile was the only animal equally dangerous on land and in the water. If they had lived in our age, they would have known that the crocodile has its counterpart among the nations." [41] But to many Germans the Dutch republic meant something more than profit-making capitalism. All over western Germany, local princes were struggling with their subjects in a determined attempt to establish absolute sovereignty and to suppress the traditional liberties of the local States Assemblies. In Emden, Muenster, and Duesseldorf, when their freedom was threatened by their respective princes, the representatives of the towns called for "Dutch medicine to cure aching liberty." Even the town of Brunswick looked west for assistance. The philosopher Leibniz was among those who admired the Republic for the moderation of its government. Idealists, scholars, merchants, townspeople usually sympathized with the Netherlands. The princes constantly complained to the Imperial court against Dutch interference.

Holland's burgher-aristocracy did not know how to make use of the brilliant opportunity offered here. They did not *want* to be bothered with West German problems. The town of Muenster, harassed by Bernhard von Galen, its tyrannical prince-bishop, nicknamed "Bombing Barend," sought help from the States General. Amsterdam vigorously opposed intervention.

These inland problems were of no interest to sea-faring Holland, its burgo-masters contended. The grand pensionary knew better and secured per-mission at least to mediate between the town and bishop. A few years later Amsterdam was to find by bitter experience how closely those "in-land problems" affected its own interests.

The problem of the southern frontier was only little better understood than that of the eastern. The Republic wanted the southern provinces to stand as a buffer between its territory and France, but the merchants of Holland stubbornly refused to relax their stringent control over the eco-nomic life of those provinces. In view of the rough disdain with which the representatives of the States General treated the Government of Brussels, it would not have been surprising if the people of Flanders and Brabant had longed for incorporation in France, which would have freed them from the Republic's oppressive economic hegemony. It was only the broad local autonomy they enjoyed in the last decades of Spanish rule, and which they would have had to sacrifice under the absolute monarchy of King Louis of France, that kept them from seeking such incorporation. John De Witt tried to ward off the danger from the south by seeking the friend-ship of Louis XIV and proposing a joint settlement of Belgian affairs, but he himself must have seen that such expedients could not solve the problem.

De Witt sought the friendship both of France and Great Britain. It was the only way in which he could pursue the policy of "most passive possible neutrality," which had become a dogma of the aristocracy. He knew that it could not save his country from grave dangers. England, determined to gain naval and commercial supremacy and encouraged by her success in the first Anglo-Dutch war, waited only for an opportunity to strike a second, more deadly blow. King Charles II, with some of Cromwell's shrewdness but none of his idealism, ascended the throne of his father after the pitiful collapse of English republicanism. From him the Netherlanders had noth-ing to expect. The Orangist party, building its hopes on the relations be-tween the Stuart and Orange families, deceived only themselves when they looked to Charles for an alliance, that would have been the counter-part of the former combination between Cromwell and De Witt. By ask-ing the help of the British king in their struggle against the burgher-aris-tocracy, they merely gave Charles the means of dividing and weakening the Republic before attacking it. De Witt may have hoped that France at least would remain loyal to her promises, but King Louis was waiting only for another chance to expand his northern frontier to include Belgium, and a conflict between the Netherlands and England would provide that op-portunity.

With an administration like that of the Republic, the Netherland State

seemed doomed to be crushed between its powerful and dangerous neighbors. The strangling of Netherland trade by closing the Baltic and the
Channel seemed easy. The southern and eastern frontiers were open. The
frontier strongholds that had withstood Spanish attacks fifty years before
were neglected, and useless against new, improved methods of attack. Yet
in the fifty years following the humiliating treaty of Westminster, the
Republic defeated its opponent in four major wars, strengthened its boundaries, and asserted its place among the nations of Europe. Only De Witt's
devotion and energy made this possible. He laid the foundation for the
work of Prince William III of Orange who in the last quarter of the century became the leader of the great alliance which then saved Europe from
conquest by monarchical totalitarianism.

De Witt organized the finances of the Republic, re-established its credit,
reduced the rate of interest on its debt, and created a reserve which in the
hour of need made possible the rapid building and equipping of a strong
navy. De Witt urged the reorganization of the army, but among the leading aristocrats anti-Orangist sentiment prevailed over national interest.
De Witt with his supporters organized a Dutch diplomatic service, the
like of which has never been seen in the Netherlands. Finally, everywhere
and always the grand pensionary set a personal example; when all seemed
lost, he impressed his colleagues with his cool and calm determination to
carry on no matter how small the chance of success.

What Prince Maurice had done for the army at the end of the XVIth
century, De Witt tried to do for the navy sixty years later. In the first Anglo-
Dutch war, the Netherlands had very few ships built and equipped for
war, and these few were far less powerful than the English. Ships of forty
or at most sixty guns had to fight enemy vessels of sixty to ninety guns.
The guns of the British navy were standardized, those of the Dutch fleet
came from numerous arsenals—from Amsterdam, Rotterdam, Zeeland, the
storehouses of the East and West India Companies—and were all of different calibre. The Dutch navy, fighting for the richest state of northern
Europe, lacked ammunition because the four admiralties lacked credit and
did not receive sufficient funds from the state authorities. Sometimes the
members of the admiralties, aristocrats like all other office-holders, resented
interference by the States, because they feared to lose their private and
illicit profits. The Dutch navy could not find sailors, while the port of
Amsterdam was teeming with unemployed seamen. Contemporary historians assert that sailors went into hiding or fled to Emden or Hamburg
when recruiting for the navy began. "They did not like this business of
shooting off arms and legs," we are told.

They had reason to dislike it. When in 1653, Witte de With inspected his squadron of fifty ships, he found only one medicine chest aboard for all! There were no rewards for the wounded or pensions for the widows of those killed in action. Even the widow of Piet Hein, who had captured Spain's silver fleet, did not receive a cent above six months' salary after her husband's heroic death. As for crippled sailors, they were put ashore to go begging on the streets. If only they had been paid for their services, the situation might have been different; but the wages on men-of-war were lower than on merchantmen, at most eleven guilders a month, and the food was poor. Wages were not paid regularly and when, in the first Anglo-Dutch war, the crews of a squadron mutinied, the States of Holland, instead of sending the sailors' pay, demanded of the admiralty "that the impudence of the crews be properly punished." After rendering eminent services, Admiral Maarten Tromp, received a bonus of two thousand guilders, a mere gratuity compared to the enormous grants formerly made to the princes of Orange for the conquest of a single town. The crews received no bonuses, hardly an extra glass of brandy. Once Tromp was so short handed that he attacked an English fishing fleet to press enemy sailors into his ships. A large percentage of the crews was always made up of "Eastlanders" and "Northlanders," North Germans and Scandinavians. The officers were always Dutch, but that did not mean that they always obeyed orders. Tromp, escorting a huge convoy from France to the home ports, saw many of his captains flee with the merchantmen when the English approached for the attack. They had so stuffed their men-of-war with French merchandise that at the firing of the first broadside their ships would have capsized. Then the old sea-dog, with a few dozen loyal assistants, had to do the work alone. Performing marvels of seamanship, for days he fought a slow rearguard action and brought the majority of the merchantmen safely home. Strict, military discipline could not be applied. Roughness or insolence on the part of the commander was simply not tolerated. Admiral Witte de With, whose passion for the naval service was well known, was so hated for his temper and bluntness that once the crew of a man-of-war on which he was about to raise his flag went on strike when they saw the admiral coming. He stormed with rage, but nothing could be done about it.

The grand pensionary showed an understanding of the problem. At his proposal, Michiel De Ruyter, a Zeelander, was appointed Lieutenant-Admiral of Holland, an extraordinary action for the States, always fanatically provincial. De Ruyter had worked his way up from cabin boy to captain in the merchant service and, having made a small fortune, decided to retire and start business ashore in his native town of Flushing. At the urgent request of the States of Zeeland, he reluctantly consented to accept a commission as captain in their navy. His fame spread rapidly and a few years later, he received the appointment of the States of Holland which virtually made him commander-in-chief of the Republic's navy. The second Anglo-Dutch war had broken out, and the first naval battle off Lowestoff had seemed to augur a disaster greater even than that of the first war. De Ruyter was the one man who could create order and maintain discipline among officers and crews, and inspire them with enthusiasm for the cause they defended.

Under his leadership the fleet, which in the first sea war against England could hardly be held together in battle, was changed into the powerful force that beat off the attacks of the combined English and French navies in the third North Sea conflict. Officers and crews, formerly so recalcitrant, were raised under De Ruyter's command to furious enthusiasm. Yet De Ruyter never became a professional soldier and never ceased to deplore the rough and bloody character of his work. Other naval commanders, like Witte de With and the younger Tromp, were happy in the frenzy of a naval clash at close quarters, firing broadsides from thirty or forty guns pointblank into the opposite ship, or making fast alongside and boarding it cutlass in hand. The latter was a favorite tactic with the Netherlanders, which is somewhat surprising in view of their fundamental loathing for warfare in general. It was De Ruyter's a-militaristic leadership, his simple manner aboard, his solicitude for the health of his crews, that made him popular; and in this respect his individuality has historical significance. It fits admirably into the general picture of the period, demonstrating what valor, what leadership, could spring from the middleclass of Holland and how this type of Netherlander could compete with the greatest in the same field without ever degenerating into a pure militarist. As the perfect citizen-admiral, de Ruyter deserves his place among the heroes of republicanism; and in a way he admirably fits the conception (of which his contemporaries were so fond) of the Netherland republic as the "Northern Rome." [42]

In 1664, English squadrons attacked and conquered the Dutch settlement on the Hudson and the trading posts in West Africa, initiating the second Anglo-Dutch war which started with a crushing defeat, but was brought to a successful end when De Ruyter sailed his ships into the mouths of the rivers Thames and Medway. In the preceding conflict, the Dutch had lost every major battle. In this conflict, thanks to the energy of John De Witt and the leadership of De Ruyter, they were victorious in all the most important battles. France, supposed to assist the Netherlands under an alliance concluded in 1662, stood aside until forced to act by further political complications. Holland was suddenly confronted with the evil results of its negligence of West German affairs. Bishop Bernhard of Muenster, having forced the freedom-loving citizenry of his capital into humble obedience, and encouraged by British promises of financial support, suddenly invaded the eastern provinces. The Dutch army, once so famous under Maurice and Frederick Henry, now hardly even deserved the name. The bellicose bishop marched through Overijssel and Guelderland until he was slowed down by the combined efforts of a weak Dutch corps under John Maurice of Nassau and a French auxiliary division. The best way to offset this nuisance, induced by English gold, was to use Dutch gold to stir up trouble on Muenster's eastern boundary, and accordingly this was done. Brunswick and Brandenburg gratefully accepted a commission to invade the bishop's territory. But the unfavorable impression created by this demonstration of the weakness of the Dutch eastern boundary remained. It spoiled the effect of the victories over England. Of what avail were De Ruyter's victories if the land route to the Hague remained open to hostile armies?

Again De Witt understood the danger, but his position was growing more difficult every day. The miserable condition of the army led to an outcry from the Orangist party. De Witt was accused of responsibility for losses suffered in the English war. Did not the prince of Orange's uncle reign in Great Britain? Why not elevate that prince to the dignity of his ancestors, and so restore peace? The rank and file of the Orangists may have believed in the efficacy of his plan, but their leaders knew better. Nevertheless the opportunity to create difficulties for the opposing party was not neglected. While De Witt had to meet this criticism, France took advantage of the apparent weakness of the Republic and of the war with England to re-open a campaign for the conquest of the southern Low Countries. It met with virtually no resistance from Spain, which was unable to defend her rights. But even King Charles II recognized that complete French control over the Flemish coast would be a threat to the safety of England. Unless Louis XIV was willing to ensure his cooperation by major concessions, England would oppose him. For this the help of the Republic was needed.

De Witt was not eager to act with a king he distrusted, who resented his late humiliating defeat by De Ruyter's fleet, and who was opposed to the rule of the aristocracy. If he did so De Witt would be obliged to oppose his country's ally, France. He would rather have negotiated an agreement with King Louis, but the majority of the States was against him. If followed De Witt's policy could have led to a joint conquest of the southern Low Countries by France and the Netherlands, and a combined last ditch defense against England. The outcome of such a struggle could hardly be in doubt, but such far-reaching views were not in the line of the States. The stabilization of existing conditions, not the strengthening of the Netherlands, was their policy. De Witt, forced to bow to the majority, concluded a treaty with Great Britain which ended the war and created a defensive alliance against France. King Louis was obliged to yield, but from then on, the Republic having wavered between inactivity and intervention, stood alone. The States had refused to side with the weak against the strong or to create the forces necessary for this policy. The alternative policies of siding with Britain and France having failed, the Netherlands now faced the wrath of strong and weak powers alike.

Three years after the victorious Dutch expedition up the Thames, King Charles of Britain seeking revenge, and King Louis bent upon crushing the one power that stood in the way of his conquest of Belgium, concluded an alliance at Dover to destroy the Republic. It was even more than that. The convention of Dover may be called a conspiracy of absolutism against liberty, for had it succeeded, British parliamentary government would have succumbed with Dutch freedom. King Louis next bought the potential support of Sweden, the active participation of that enterprising ecclesiastic, the bishop of Muenster (who swore that his Westphalians now thoroughly subdued would march as long as they got their daily loaf of pumpernickel), and the aid of the archbishop-elector of Cologne and Liége. The prince-elector of Mainz, the duke of Hannover, the prince-elector of Bavaria, even the Emperor himself, were drawn into the scheme by French promises and the lure of French gold. Spain, realizing that the coming war would settle her fate, preferred an heroic end to an inglorious liquidation. Only the prince-elector of Brandenburg voluntarily sided with the Republic.

John De Witt knew that war was coming, and that France was the center of the anti-Dutch combination, but he failed for once to realize the full danger to his beloved Republic. He did not believe in a sudden change of front by Great Britain. Desperately he sought to strengthen the land defenses. Everything he had worked for seemed to crumble before his eyes. The Republic, instead of being respected and at peace with all, was surrounded by enemies. Within the Republic the regime he had helped to build, was disintegrating under the impact of foreign danger. Already young William of Orange, twenty-one years old, had been appointed commander-in-chief for one campaign, a campaign that was to be decisive.

In the spring of 1672, King Louis of France and his generals, the prince of Condé and the viscount of Turenne, took command of an army estimated at one hundred thousand men and marched against the Netherlands. The invasion by the troops of Muenster in 1666 had demonstrated the weakness of the eastern border. So the French commanders planned to march in a semi-circle around the southern Dutch defenses, cross the Rhine and invade Guelderland from the east. The divisions of Muenster would thus naturally form the right wing of the invading force. The Netherlands had little more than 50,000 badly equipped and poorly trained troops with which to oppose the superior forces of the enemy, double their number. In an idle attempt to divert the French attack a strong garrison was placed at Maastricht, whence the enemy lines of communication could be threatened. The French, refusing to become involved in beleaguering operations which might pin down their forces for many weeks, left an observation corps near the town and marched on. They invaded the Brandenburgian territory of Cleve, occupied without much resistance the fortresses held in that district by Netherland troops, crossed the Rhine and then Guelderland's eastern boundary. Twenty miles to the north, the bishop of Muenster marched into Overijssel.

The successive declarations of war by France, England, Muenster, and Cologne-Liége left the Dutch people utterly confounded. The rapid march of the overwhelming French force into Guelderland added to the general panic. The grand pensionary worked feverishly at the construction of new defenses. Prince William, now commanding the army, had disposed his weak forces behind the shallow river of the IJssel; but he knew the position was untenable for he only had 33,000 men to occupy a twenty-mile line. Two possible defense lines further inland were considered. The more eastern, behind the rivulets of the Grebbe and Eem, could be reinforced to some extent by inundations, but these could neither be made complete nor kept at the desired level. For these reasons this line (which was defended in 1940), was abandoned and a second line of inundations on the boundary of the provinces of Holland and Utrecht was prepared. Inundations required time, however, especially in the summer and before the machine age. Would the defenders have time to put the inundations into effect and fortify the passages through the flooded fields? In the first days of June, the French and Allied armies stood poised for the attack on the eastern bank of the IJssel and the Rhine, outnumbering the defenders three to one. If the French army broke through, it would reach the line of the intended inundations within a week. Strategically the war on land was lost for the Netherlands. It was of little avail that De Ruyter in a tremendous battle near Solebay on England's east coast, held the sea against the combined Allied navies.

Strategically, the Netherlands had lost the war, but the French still had to win it tactically. Never in history was a nation saved from utter defeat without the unintentional assistance of its all but victorious foes. At this critical moment, when the prince of Orange, young and without any experience of war, correctly supposed that the IJssel line was untenable, Marshall Turenne, master of strategy, decided to outflank that same position by a difficult manoeuvre instead of attacking in front and breaking through at a score of places. The latter manoeuvre which Condé advised, would have ruined the Republic. Turenne's move was the first step towards saving it. On June 12, a French corps crossed the deep and broad Rhine near Lobith and forced the Dutch troops to withdraw from their half-completed defense works behind the shallow IJssel. The retreat proceeded none too well. With difficulty, Prince William brought part of the army behind the inundations that were in preparation. In those summer days the water rose with desperate slowness; and the peasants of Holland and Utrecht, deprived of a political influence for centuries, resented the saving of a government in which they had no share at the expense of the land on which they lived.

King Louis, advancing triumphantly through Guelderland and Utrecht, all unknowingly continued to preserve his enemy from destruction. While his advance guards occupied the town of Utrecht, the king with his main force moved leisurely westward from the IJssel as if deliberately intending to give his opponents a little more time for preparation. His ally the bishop of Muenster showed more energy, he occupied the whole province of Overijssel and lost no time in forcing the States of that province to recognize him as their future lord. While Louis marched west, he led his troops north against Friesland and Groningen.

Even though Louis's slowness gave the Dutch a few days respite, the situation was desperate. On June 21, when Utrecht capitulated to the French, revolution broke out in Zeeland where the people forced the aristocracy to restore the young prince of Orange to the dignity of his ancestors. On the night of the same day John De Witt was attacked in the streets of the Hague and severely wounded. A week later, his regime collapsed. The urban population of Holland revolted and the ruling caste, unprotected against the fury of the masses, capitulated. William became stadhouder of Holland. In the absence of De Witt, the States of Holland gave way to panic. Leiden took the lead in demanding peace at any price. The majority of the States voted to send a special embassy to King Louis, a decision which was subsequently adopted by the States General although in an irregular way by less than a majority. The embassy left for French headquarters while Amsterdam protested violently, calling for a last ditch defense, and the young stadhouder worked day and night to bring the inundation line into a defensible condition. Louis who advanced towards Utrecht, was probably convinced that the war was over and that the States General would submit to any demands. Consequently he put forward extravagant claims which he failed to support by vigorous military action.

His troops were now in front of the half-completed inundation. The prince of Orange had raised a new army by taking sailors and marines from the navy, by calling out the city guards of adjoining towns, and by arming some of the peasantry. A few thousand Spanish cavalry reinforced his motley troops. Displayed behind the inundations they were quite impressive, and King Louis allowed himself to be bluffed into a belief that the new defenses were very strong. Having scattered half his army in garrisoning useless strongholds, he sat down with the rest of it in front of the inundations. When the negotiations with the French were broken off and unity was restored in the administration of the Republic, the inundations were completed, the soldiers and citizens regained courage, and Louis XIV had allowed his opportunity to pass forever. Bishop Bernhard did his best to do his share of the common task, but the citizens of Groningen returned the fire of his artillery with such vigor that he too desisted. In the second part of the summer the greatest danger had passed. The enemy's progress was halted. The fall rains greatly strengthened the inundation line. King Louis, tired of waiting for surrender, returned to Paris. Brandenburg created a diversion which caused Turenne with part of the French troops, to leave the Netherlands. The time for counterattacks had come.

Not military strength, not even natural defenses like the flooding of the fields, had saved the Republic, but only the grim determination of its leaders—first De Witt, then the prince of Orange—and of the cities of Amsterdam and Groningen and the naval commanders. They impressed the French generals by a power that was only potential, not real. One among them was punished in a most horrible way for his mistakes, which had been far more those of his class than of himself. John De Witt, knowing that his regime had collapsed beyond hope of recovery, asked for his dismissal at the beginning of August. But his opponents were not satisfied. His brother was put on trial and condemned on insufficient grounds. By a plot the former pensionary was lured to the "Gevangenpoort" where his brother was jailed, the city guards of the Hague were mobilized and the cavalry, stationed there to maintain order, called off. A few leaders of the mob then dragged the two brothers out of jail to be murdered in the most beastly way by the city guards. It was the revenge of the middleclass upon the fallen aristocracy. The ousting of De Witt, whose policy had failed, was understandable and justified. His brutal murder remains one of the darkest spots in Netherland history. Once the middleclass had started on the path of revolution, they sought to exploit the opportunity to the full. In some places demands were made that the burgher-aristocracy share the government with representatives of the city guards and guilds, a foreshadowing of things to come. The prince of Orange restored "order," by which he understood the traditional form of government, under his control instead of that of the leading group in Holland.

In 1673 the war shifted to other theaters. The intervention of Brandenburg and Austria further reduced the chances of a French offensive against the now really strong line of inundations. So the best policy for the Allies seemed to be to gain command of the sea to land troops and attack Holland from the west. But here De Ruyter stood guard, forcing the Allies in fierce battles to give up any such design. With the evacuation of the eastern provinces in the fall of 1673, the invasion of the Netherlands came to an end. Next year King Charles II, violently accused of absolutist designs by the British people, made peace. Muenster and Cologne, in a hopeless position between the Netherlands and Brandenburg, did the same. The war with France dragged on until 1678, but it was fought in the southern Netherlands, where Prince William led the armies of a Dutch-Spanish-Austrian coalition against the French forces under Luxembourg. The Republic had found its place in European politics, siding with the weaker powers against Louis XIV, the great aggressor. The series of English wars came to a close. Although the Dutch conception of the freedom of the sea had not triumphed, English claims to sovereignty over the sea had been definitely defeated. Emerging victorious from a struggle in which they had been surrounded by enemies, the Netherlands had reasserted the independence recognized in 1648.

Prince William had another task besides leading the armies. The Republic of the Netherlands had to be reorganized. Holland proposed to reduce the reconquered provinces of Guelderland, Utrecht, and Overijssel to nonvoting members of the Union. That would have transformed the Republic into a Hollandish State. William opposed this, for he did not want to increase the power of the already too influential sea province. The States of Guelderland, dreading the overbearing attitude of the unconquered provinces, offered the ducal crown of their territory to Prince William. Once more a chance to regularize the constitution of the Republic presented itself. William III would have liked to accept the crown, but he wanted the other provinces to follow suit. The States of Zeeland, otherwise so zealous in promoting the interests of Orange, objected. Afraid to oppose the Prince's wishes openly, they appealed to his religious convictions by quoting the Bible:

"Then the men of Israel said unto Gideon: Rule thou over us, both thou and thy sons and son's sons also, for thou hast delivered us from the hand of Midean. And Gideon said unto them: I will not rule over you, neither shall my sons rule over you: the Lord shall rule over you."

William had it in his power to force the consent of the reluctant provinces, both Holland and Zeeland; but he preferred to secure control of public affairs by other means, and contented himself with continuing the quotation of the States of Zeeland:

> "And the children of Israel remembered not the Lord their God who had delivered them out of the hands of all their enemies, on every side: neither shewed they kindness to the House of Jerubbaal, namely Gideon, according to all the goodness which he had shewn unto Israel."

Having dropped the idea of becoming monarch of the Netherlands, Prince William reorganized the constitution of the re-conquered provinces in such a way that his influence in their affairs became paramount, especially in regard to their voting in the States General. With full control over three of the seven votes in that body and with his adherents in power in the other provinces, he became the absolute leader of the Republic's foreign policy and that was all that interested him. The States of Holland, Zeeland, Utrecht, Guelderland, and Overijssel decided to make the office of stadhouder hereditary in the family of William III. His prestige in Europe rose far above that of any of his predecessors and reached its peak in 1688 when he conducted the "Glorious Revolution" and was elected King of Great Britain. The matrimonial alliance between the families of Stuart and Orange, renewed by the marriage of William with Mary, daughter of the duke of York, later James II, did not on this occasion make the House of Orange a tool of the ambitious policy of the Stuarts but brought about a union of English tradition and Netherland freedom in the final triumph of the parliamentary regime in England.

From the time of his ascent to the British throne, William was the recognized leader of the European coalition against the aggressor-king of France. The Netherland Republic took a prominent part in these conflicts. The army, restored to its former efficiency and brought to a fighting force of 50,000 to 70,000 men, had an important share in the battles fought in Brabant and Flanders. The territory of the Republic was safe from attack. The navy took part in the operations against the French in the Channel and in the Mediterranean and against the Swedes in the Baltic. Dutch ships and Dutch sailors had a share in the conquest of Gibraltar by the British in the war of the Spanish Succession in 1704. An attempt to prevent this war, which broke out after his death, was William's last great diplomatic undertaking. He saw the failure of this attempt, but not the ultimate victory of his principles.

William loved the Netherlands, where he stayed whenever he could leave England. But he was not greatly interested in the administration of his own country. His only concern was to have the support, moral and financial, of the burgher-aristocracy for his European policy. He permitted and even encouraged the formation of cliques. Sometimes sorely tempted to resort to strong action against Amsterdam, where the tradition of passive neutrality secured by an alliance with France persisted for a long time, he always came to friendly agreement in the end. William's administration was, in a sense, a reconciliation of the aristocratic class and the Orangist movement. Both prince and aristocrats distrusted popular political influence, and they were united in considering themselves far above the masses. Many adherents of De Witt's policy had been ousted from office in the critical years after 1672, and there remained some resentment against Orange because of this. But William's administration was long—nearly thirty years—and a new generation grew up, accustomed to new conditions. The Netherland history of this period concerns other matters than the reform of government or foreign policy.

CHAPTER X

Ideals of the Eighteenth Century

THE XVIIIth century is usually looked upon as a period of decline in Netherland history. Compared to the glorious age between 1625 and 1675, it seems dull and inert. The contrast is that of a mighty roaring river and a placid inland lake where movement is only on the surface. The atmosphere is dreamy and unreal, not vigorous and refreshing as a hundred years before. This is plain even in a superficial survey of such widely different fields as painting and foreign policy. Painting is the best beloved of Netherland arts and XVIIth century Dutch political influence the pride of the Netherland burgher, so the XVIIIth century stood little chance of winning the favor of posterity. Hence the constant glorification of the XVIIth and deprecation of the XVIIIth century in national history.[43]

There is no doubt that XVIIIth century Dutch history attracts the reader less than that of the age before, so unconsciously the earlier events are placed in the most favorable and later events in the least favorable light. This tendency is historically misleading. We admire Erasmus who, in a turbulent period, described the conversation of friends in a beautiful garden as the height of civilized entertainment; yet we are disgusted with his XVIIIth century followers who put his theory into practice. We are anti-militarist but loathe the least militarist society and government in all Netherland history. There is something purely sentimental and irrational in the attitude of most Netherlanders towards this period.

In what respect did the XVIIIth century represent a decline, compared to the preceding period? If it represented a decline, when did it set in? Is there nothing in which the XVIIIth century was superior to the XVIIth? These questions must be answered before we can judge the relative importance of the two periods. In painting the XVIIIth century has nothing to offer that can possibly compare with the achievements of the preceding decades. To be sure, there were still many good painters. The traditions and models handed down by their predecessors saved the art from complete decay. But beyond question there was a sharp decline which continued beyond the XVIIIth century and reached its lowest level in the early part of the XIXth. Then a new school arose, which has become famous all over the world through the works of Van Gogh and others. No one knows why art flourishes in one period and declines in another. Capricious change of taste, because of which the XVIIIth century had little use even for Rembrandt's masterpieces, may have strangled Netherland productivity. The bold realism of XVIIth century art did not appeal to ensuing genera- tions which, living in an unreal world of comfort and pleasure, preferred miniature decorations and the small finely executed products of craftsman- ship. The change in taste, reflected in artistic production was not abrupt. The last forty years of the XVIIth century, when the power of the Republic reached its peak, saw the slow beginning of a decline in art. Political and artistic decline are by no means related. The revolution of 1572 had seen the dawn of Holland's greatest period; the heroic defense of 1672 scarcely evoked an echo in the world of culture.

Rembrandt's death coincided with a sharp decline in the art of painting, just as Vondel's decease in 1679 did in the history of literature. But here the movement was not so rapid, and if the literary output of the XVIIIth century did not attain the same high level as that of the preceding hundred years, the popularity of the art itself was undiminished. It even suffered from overpopularity, which led to mass production of verse. The unreality of many aspects of this later Dutch civilization makes its literature the more difficult for modern realists to digest. That there was a great deal of interest not only in contemporary writers but also in those of the past is shown by the magnificent editions of the Dutch classics published in the early XVIIIth century. The growing interest in pre-classic literature made possible editions of medieval works which would hardly have commanded attention fifty years before. The last decades of the XVIIth century saw the busy Netherland world of traders and shopkeepers, of artists and crafts- men, transformed into a new one of bankers and merchant princes—gentle- men of leisure interested in letters and in the collection of curios, which might be objects of art or singular items of the most diverse nature. This change fostered scientific progress for, as painting was considered a skilled craft and literary production a pastime, the study of science became the proper occupation for a man of independent means who wanted to be useful to society. Emphasis was placed on mechanics rather than on physics, but the solution of practical problems led naturally to discussions and in- vestigations of fundamental principles.

Ever since the XVIth century mathematics and physics had found ardent students in the Netherlands. Problems of navigation and of military en- gineering had occupied generations of Dutch scientists. John De Witt had devoted his mathematical talent to problems of finance, and shortly before his downfall he wrote his *Evaluation of Life Insurance,* one of the first texts propounding the mathematical theory upon which all insurance depends. For thirty years (1617–1649), Descartes lived in the Netherlands, where he wrote his *Discourse on Reason,* that profoundly influenced Netherland research. After the close of the XVIIth century the work was continued by generations of scientists, who were only occasionally connected with the universities. While professors could study mathematics, they could rarely study physics, for their pitifully meager salaries did not provide the means to carry on experiments. In spite of Leiden's worldwide reputation, university professors were not esteemed socially. The scientist who did not happen to be heir to a considerable estate was faced with the choice between becoming a skilled worker (grinding lenses, for instance, like Baruch De Spinoza); becoming a physician, which might offend his conscience as the prevailing practice of medicine was of dubious value; or living and dying in poverty on bad terms with his more practical relatives and neighbors, like Jan Swammerdam, the brilliant observer of insect life.[44] This conflict of conscience was most serious. Descartes' rationalist methods of scientific research laid bare the quackery of medical remedies, sacred by tradition and so deeply imbedded in popular belief that some of them persist to the present day.

The teaching of Descartes' philosophy had been forbidden at Leiden University in 1656. The wording of the decree was significant, for it was issued only to prevent violent dissent among the members of Leiden's faculty. John De Witt himself studied Descartes' works on geometry with apparent satisfaction. Spinoza's works, permitted to circulate in the time of the grand pensionary, were forbidden in the reaction that followed the crisis of 1672. The wave of rationalism could not be stopped by any such measures and its principles continued to be applied both in the sciences and outside the world of abstract thought. While Swammerdam, a strict rationalist in his methods of insect life, sought to combine the results of his work with deep religious faith, Christian Huyghens, the greatest Dutch physicist of the pre-modern period, unhesitatingly rejected anything that was not based on reason, in all fields of knowledge. At this time the study of mathematics was considered dangerous to the faith of budding theologians. This antithesis was to some extent a direct continuation of that between Erasmianism and dogmatism in the XVIth century.

Christian Huyghens was the typical gentleman-mechanic who made theoretical discoveries while seeking the solution of practical problems. Navigators were struggling with the determination of exact longitude at sea, which required an exact instrument for measuring time. This resulted in the discovery of the pendulum clock and, although for various technical reasons the instrument did not prove satisfactory, its discovery led to many innovations. The polishing of lenses and the theoretical exploration of optics were also combined in Huyghens' work. However, his research work is of less interest in Netherland history than the place Huyghens himself held in the community of his day. The son of Constantijn Huyghens, secretary to three princes of Orange, poet, scholar and diplomat—certainly one of the most remarkable men in XVIIth century Holland—Christian was accustomed to a leisurely and independent life, which he found it difficult to maintain after his father's death. To accept a professorship would have been a social degradation. So he chose the position of head of the Academy of Sciences, created by King Louis XIV of France, and lived for fifteen years in Paris. Thus the brilliant gentleman-mechanic, first physicist of his age, became himself an article in the curio cabinet of a monarch who cared no more for science than a collector cares for an odd piece of furniture his servant has picked up in an antique shop. Huyghens learned that, like other items, a "human curiosity" can be discarded at the owner's whim. Back in Holland, the great man prolonged his gentleman's life with difficulty, until he died, cynical and alone, in 1695.

Scientific research provided a bond between Netherlanders of various classes. Like poetry, mathematics and physics were interests that regardless of rank brought together people who had leisure. The famous microscope builder, Anthony Leeuwenhoek, originally a shopkeeper and later provided because of his scientific distinction with several semi-honorary positions by the government of Delft, had the same access to learned circles as Huyghens the aristocrat. Like Spinoza and Huyghens, Leeuwenhoek devoted much of his time to grinding lenses, an art in which he became a master. His scientific reputation was based on observations made with the microscopes he constructed with his own hands. Among other discoveries, he was the first to describe human blood corpuscles. Here again we find closely related the work of the skilled mechanic and the physicist.

The Netherlands were an ideal place to collect "curiosities." Ships from the East and West Indies brought an immense variety of objects and natural specimens into the country. The directors of the East India Company instructed their government at Batavia to collect rare plants and seeds for the Botanic Garden in Leiden. The Company's factory in Nagasaki, Japan, provided Japanese objects of art. Porcelain was imported in such quantity that a well assorted collection of china became the general fashion. Other collections, even more admired by contemporaries, appear singular to us. In those early days of anatomical research, physician-anatomists opened their "anatomic cabinets" to the public, who came to see dissected human bodies and other anatomic marvels, just as crowds now visit Madame Tussaud's Chamber of Horrors or the neat collections of bones of long-deceased Capucin monks in one of Rome's most frequented churches. This general curiosity about the phenomena of nature had its advantage in spreading interest and encouraging research in medicine and biology, even in archeology and ethnology. The wealthiest of the collectors sent to the far corners of the world for more material and even defrayed the cost of long voyages undertaken for that purpose. In the last quarter of the XVIIth century Amsterdam counted among its burgomasters one mathematician of no small ability, Johan Hudde, and the greatest promoter of scientific geography of the century, Nicholas Witsen.

Nicholas Witsen was the most remarkable of these all-round promoters of learning. Born in 1641, he belonged to an influential Amsterdam family which gave him as a youth opportunities that determined his future career. When he was fifteen, he accompanied his father on a diplomatic mission to England. Cromwell, noticing the boy's interest, showed him *his* curiosities, including such items as the axe with which King Charles I had been beheaded. From objects of this type, Witsen turned quickly to more useful interests. At the Amsterdam Athenaeum he studied astronomy and philosophy, tried his hand at poetry—he wrote a comedy, now long forgotten—and learned engraving. A series of etchings illustrating Ovid's *Metamorphoses* are known to be his work. Skilled craftsmanship had always a place in education in the XVIIth century, and the division of time between study and handiwork, between work and play, was certainly better balanced than in the twentieth century Netherlands. Young Witsen went to Leiden to study law; all Holland's young aristocrats studied law at Leiden. But his interest turned rather to the philosophy of Descartes and Professor Golius' courses on oriental languages. Golius also taught mathematics, a combination that becomes understandable from the fact that the learned professor was the first European to discover the relation between medieval Persian and Chinese chronology. Witsen completed his law studies, but in the meantime had published treatises on economics.

The great opportunity of his youth came in 1664, when he accompanied an embassy to Russia. He was a gentleman in the suite of the ambassadors, with plenty of time to study the land and the people. In Moscow he decided to collect information about the peoples living between Russia and China. In those days the Russians did not give great freedom to foreign diplomats. Witsen was even discouraged from learning Russian. Hearing that a Kalmuck prince from the boundaries of Asia was in Moscow, he found an opportunity to meet him. "His language," Witsen said, "sounded like the cackling of a turkey." He could not gather much information from the prince, for the meeting had to be secret. He was not permitted to see maps of Siberia which he knew to exist in the imperial palace. This was enough to determine him to fill in the blanks in the maps of Asia and to draw a detailed picture of that country. He spent twenty years on this task. His position as a director of the East India Company enabled him to have information collected from Japanese and Chinese geographers. Letters from Jesuit missionaries in China were of invaluable assistance. Most useful of all was his friendship with the new czar of Russia, Peter the Great. From all these sources he compiled his *North and East Tartary* with a large map of Siberia, both works amazingly accurate for that time.

Witsen's work, interesting and characteristic as it is, would not deserve so large a place in this book had it not been for the multiplicity of his activities and their truly astounding consequences. Twice he sent Cornelis De Bruyn, the painter, on far journeys to make drawings of the remains of the ancient world, first to Egypt, Syria and Anatolia; then via Russia to Persia to visit the ruins of Persepolis, and on to Batavia. His botanical experiments mark the starting point of a revolution in the Malay world. By the middle of the XVIIth century Europe was acquainted with coffee. The center of production was southern Arabia and the African area opposite, across the Red Sea. Coffee trees were brought from India both to Batavia and to Amsterdam. Witsen experimented with the coffee plants he received in Amsterdam and succeeded in producing a small quantity of beans, which the burgomasters tasted and declared "rather flat." Apparently Amsterdam's climate was not right! But Witsen's interest encouraged the principal estate owners around Batavia to continue their experiments in Java. At his request, the directors of the Company offered a reward for the successful production of coffee in Java. A few years later the first Java coffee arrived in Amsterdam and the social and agricultural transformation of Java had begun.

This interest in botanical and agricultural experiments was combined with a traditional Netherland interest in gardening. Here the American thinks, of course, of the tulips and bulb fields of Haarlem. The tulips that originated in the Near East are said to have been introduced shortly after 1573 by Charles de l'Ecluse, the famous botanist and first director of Leiden's Botanic Gardens. In the XVIIth century tulip growing became a mania, which in 1636 culminated in the wildest speculation, more than ten thousand guilders being paid for a rare specimen. Around 1700, Haarlem became, as it still is, the center of bulb-growing. From there bulbs were exported to England, Spain, Italy, and many other countries. About the same time, Holland's city aristocracy and wealthy merchant class adorned the most beautiful parts of the countryside—along the Vecht in Utrecht and the fertile dry ground between the dunes and the polders—with their country houses and estates. Literature celebrated pastoral life, painters visualized ideal landscapes and the descendants of Holland's sea captains, now rich and with plenty of leisure, fled from the city into a dream world. Moreover, a desire *to create* seized these men who had amassed fortunes from the outwardly unproductive handling of merchandise and apparently still more sterile banking enterprises. Their eagerness to bend nature to the needs of humanity, by discovering its laws and increasing its beauty and productivity, was expressed in a new utilitarianism, which has left deep traces in Netherland history. It was not agriculture in the broad sense of the word that interested the utilitarian gentlemen. Hardly any technical books on agriculture were published in the Netherlands before 1750, while in neighboring countries, especially Germany, such publications were popular. But treatises on gardening were numerous. The Botanical Gardens of Leiden University and those of Amsterdam were the most famous in Europe. It was horticultural not agricultural production that caught the fancy of Holland's society.

Around 1700, Holland, with its dykes and canals, its thousands of windmills, neat farms, well-kept cattle, numerous quaint towns, comfortable houses and well dressed people, its curiosities gathered from East and West, its flowers and rare plants, looked like a large "curio cabinet" itself. Foreigners came to marvel at the little territory that wielded such wide power across the world. The picture of Holland as tulip land, with oddly dressed people, was formed in the minds of non-Hollanders at that time, and has survived until the present, to hinder the understanding of Netherland problems today. But this was a later development. In the XVIIIth century there was much to learn in Holland. Four hundred foreign students in medicine at Leiden University were not exceptional.

Of the foreigners visiting the Netherlands, the most interesting was Peter the Great of Russia. The czar had learned about the marvels of Holland from Dutch artisans, traders, and physicians in the foreign colony of Moscow. A Hollander built his first boats and taught him how to sail a ship. Dutch workers built wharves at Archangelsk; and Peter who loved to talk with Dutch sea captains there was filled with such admiration for the Netherlanders that he began to imitate the clothing, language, and manners of his sailor friends. These were not those of the best western way of life, and a natural affinity between sailors of the land of Schiedamgin and the emperor of the vodka-producing country resulted in scenes better imagined than described. In 1697 Peter undertook his famous trip through western Europe. Impatient to arrive in Holland, the czar left his numerous suite behind and hurried west. First he visited Zaandam, northwest of Amsterdam, a great whaling and ship building center. In the belief that he could remain incognito, this six-foot-and-a-half-inch giant, who spoke a few words of broken Dutch and was well known to several workers and sailors of the town, pretended to be looking for a job and rented one of the smallest houses of the place. As was to be expected, the Zaandammers took quite an interest in him, and the czar furious at not having his own way and accustomed to direct methods, used his fists liberally on the too-curious spectators. The Dutch workers, unwilling to be thrashed even by an Imperial Majesty, responded in kind. Peter moved to Amsterdam. Here Burgomaster Nicholas Witsen, with whom the czar had corresponded for a long time, was at hand to assist him. As a director of the East India Company, he provided the czar with living quarters on one of the wharves of the Company, where he was well protected from popular curiosity. Here Peter the Great worked for four months. This gave him an opportunity to visit all the curiosities of the city: the anatomical cabinets, which for a time gave him the idea of becoming a physician; collections of art, the workshops of engravers—here too he tried to learn the craft in a few days;—and numerous factories and storehouses. Whatever interested him, he wanted to buy and ship to Russia. Hundreds of artisans were recruited to modernize his empire. So deep an impression did Netherland civilization make on the czar that he decided to make the small country on the North Sea, the model of the modern Russia of his dreams. Dutch was to be *the* foreign language studied in Russia. The Russian navy was reorganized on the pattern of the Dutch. This Netherland influence lasted only as long as Czar Peter reigned. In other parts of the world the effects of Netherland utilitarianism were more lasting.

In the last years of Governor-General Maetsuycker's rule a change came over Batavia and its small Dutch population. For fifty years Dutch and Chinese had been living cooped up within the little town. Outside its walls was the jungle where His Excellency the Governor-General occasionally hunted the tiger or the rhinoceros, and where lawless elements—the district had no settled population—lurked in the hope of capturing a Chinese or killing a Hollander. But towards 1681 the picture changed. Enterprising Chinese had cleared some ground and worked small sugar plantations and mills. A motley crowd of Indonesians, including all tribes and peoples except the Javanese, built their villages under the protection of Batavia's artillery and tilled the soil, growing rice for the townspeople. The Batavian Dutch, too, turned to agriculture and many estates were developed outside the walls. These settlers were no longer the die-hard, narrow-minded traders of Coen's time. Then there was a group of broad-minded men, whose influence became predominant in 1684, when Johannes Camphuijs was appointed governor-general. There was Pieter van Hoorn, who had gone to the imperial court of Peking as an ambassador and had published a didactic poem propounding the teachings of Confucius, a hitherto unheard-of tribute to the wisdom of the "blind and ignorant heathen." Camphuijs himself was an author who wrote on the history of Batavia, composed a description of Japan, and encouraged learning. Johan van Hoorn, Pieter's son, governor-general from 1704-1709, was one of the first officials of the Company who showed real interest in native affairs. Georges Chastellein built three large estates during his life time, one of which he bequeathed to his former slaves, whose descendants to the present day form the Christian community of Depok and hold the estate in common ownership. These were the men with whom Witsen was in contact; Chastellein was the first to produce coffee on his plantations. They all dreamed of changing the Company's system completely, of attracting Netherland colonists and giving greater freedom of commerce to Dutch citizens in the colony. Both in Java and in the Netherlands the monopoly of the Company was sharply criticized, but too many vested interests were involved for any radical change to be made.

The introduction of the coffee tree was the beginning of an economic revolution in Java. The Dutch Company had previously confined itself to acquiring and exporting the natural products of the islands, introducing no innovations. With coffee production the Company started on a new course, exploitation of the *potential* instead of the *existing* resources of the country. Under the new system Java, the only island on which the Company controlled a large area of land, gained prominence over the older centers of production such as Amboina and Ternate in the Moluccas. Around 1677 the Batavian Government had acquired sovereignty over the mountainous districts south of Batavia. The native district chiefs, called "Regents" by the Dutch in imitation of the aristocratic class in Holland, became the Company's vassals. Instead of delivering given quantities of rice and a certain number of laborers to their native overlords, they now delivered a certain amount of produce, which the Company, never forgetting its "exclusively commercial" character, pretended to buy but at fixed prices decidedly advantageous to the buyers. In the first years of coffee production the Batavian government, as yet without experience in this particular matter, fixed the price rather high, with the result that the new crop spread amazingly, and great wealth was amassed in the hands of some of the Javanese "Regents." Faced with a new problem, the directors in Amsterdam, after long deliberation, but little foresight, decided to maintain their traditional policy of keeping the quantity transported low and prices high, instead of giving free scope to production and enlarging the turn-over in Europe by lowering prices. To be sure the choice was not an easy one and there were many problems connected with such a change in commercial policy, but the policy adopted by the directors of limiting coffee production and drastically lower prices was basically wrong, and harmed the interests of the Company as much as it exasperated the native population.

The economic ideas of the liberal group around Camphuijs were definitely rejected by the authorities at home. Their influence in political developments in the East Indies is discernible in the system of administration applied to the newly acquired Preanger districts in West Java. The Statutes of Batavia had granted certain privileges to the Chinese inhabitants of Batavia in matters of private law. Faced with the problem of administering justice to a large indigenous population, Batavia had decreed in 1708 that the native judiciary should be left intact and that cases between Indonesians could be settled before their own courts and according to native law. Since it was of the highest importance that Dutch officials, to whom the supervision of native rulers was entrusted, should know the content of native law, some of them took up its study. This was the beginning of a new field of learning—the study of *adat*-law, the Indonesian customary law—in which progress was made in the XIXth and XXth centuries. Frederik Gobius was the first to penetrate the complexities of this new subject. He was the first to realize that among the Javanese both the ancient customary law and the later Mohammedan law were in force and must be clearly distinguished. Several generations of law students had passed before the full implications of this were understood.

The estates of Witsen's friends in Batavia were the beginning of modern Java, the island of multifarious export crops produced by combined European-Indonesian efforts. In these same years around the turn of the century, Governor Simon Van der Stel wrought a similar change in the economic structure of the still halting colony of the Cape. Van der Stel, born on the island of Mauritius and thus a native *Afrikaander* married into the Amsterdam family of Six, one of whose members was the friend and protector of Rembrandt. Van der Stel promoted colonization vigorously, but he wanted it to be purely Dutch. In the twenty years of his administration he brought the number of settlers at the Cape up to around 800, of whom 150 were French Huguenots driven from their native land by Louis XIV's harsh decrees of persecution. Cattle breeding was their main occupation. The records indicate that these 800 people owned 3,000 head of cattle and 30,000 sheep. Wine growing was also encouraged, but was more successful in quantity than in quality. Even the sailors of the East Indiamen made wry faces at Capetown's beverage. Van der Stel, who really made the tiny African settlement into a colony, lived and worked in the style of his Dutch and Batavian contemporaries. Planting trees and experimenting with new crops were a passion with him. The Company's vegetable garden in Capetown became a beautiful botanic garden of great scientific interest. The Governor's estate impressed Dutch and foreign visitors by the fine architecture of his house, the model of Cape-colonial style.

The conceptions that animated this Netherland civilization at the turn of the century naturally changed the outlook of the people on many problems that had agitated the nation sixty-odd years before. Religious tolerance, rarely accepted in theory, became a general practice. Complaints by the synods of the official church against "Popish impudence" and against Anabaptists or Jews ceased in the time of John De Witt. The Mennonites of Groningen and Friesland had shown such patriotic zeal in the critical months of 1672, that the States of Friesland decided to grant them official freedom of worship. Even the Catholics, mistrusted as potential fifth columnists for France, had proved better patriots in 1672 than might have been expected after the unjust oppression to which they had been subjected. Freedom of worship was not granted them until a century later, but in practice they were able to follow their own rites by paying protection to the police officers. When a schism occurred in connection with the Jansenist movement in France and Belgium, the States of Holland even took official cognizance of the existence of a Roman Catholic Church within the boundaries of the Republic. This action may have been prompted by the hopes of seeing Netherland Catholics form a national Church, which would have removed some obstacles to their being granted greater freedom of worship. It brought to light the existence of excellent personal relations between prominent Catholic priests and members of the burgher-aristocracy. The schism, which failed to gain support among the Catholics, resulted in the renewal—but as a dead letter—of previous decrees against the presence of Jesuits in the Netherlands. Members of the States General, which banished Jesuit missionaries from the country, maintained correspondence with learned followers of St. Ignatius all over the world.

The tolerant attitude of the Netherland city governments, especially that of Amsterdam, provided a haven of refuge for thousands of Jews when the persecution of these people broke out again in eastern Europe. The great Cossack revolution in Poland, a national revolt of Ukranians against Poles and Jews, drove thousands of Israelites to the west. In Amsterdam, where the older Portuguese Jewish settlements flourished, new congregations were established. German-Jewish, Polish-Jewish, and Lithuanian-Jewish groups founded their own synagogues, which later were united. The newcomers were far more numerous, but also much poorer than the earlier Jewish immigrants from the southwest. There was sufficient freedom of worship and trade to make Amsterdam a point of attraction for the persecuted. The new synagogue of the Portuguese congregation begun in 1670, cost 186,000 guilders to build, an enormous sum for the time. The building is so large and conspicuous that its very existence was a monument to freedom of worship in an otherwise still intolerant age. Latir Jews continued to come in during the XVIIIth century and Amsterdam was soon the first big city in western Europe with a sizeable percentage of Jewish population.

The ruling class were determined not to submit to dictation from the official church. The burgomasters of Amsterdam protected Balthazar Bekker, a minister driven from Friesland because of his Cartesian opinions whose book, *The Haunted World,* had stirred up discussion in 1691. In this work he sought to dispel superstitious beliefs in sorcery and witchcraft, giving rational explanations for extraordinary phenomena of nature The States of Friesland protected the small sect of the Labadists, Christian communists, who had selected a country house in that province in which to carry out their social-religious experiment. Later some of the Labadist: moved to America, part of them to Pennsylvania (William Penn had visited their Frisian home on one of his travels on the Continent), and other: to Surinam. In this tropical country the socialist community rapidly disintegrated; and the Labadists, though champions of equality, were ever accused of being the worst of all slave-owners. The relative tolerance practised in the XVIIth century gradually developed into an accepted principle of tolerance. Before the end of the XVIIIth century and the French Revolution, demands for the equality of Catholics and Protestants were formulated.

In regard to religious problems, the XVIIIth century represents a stabilization of XVIIth century trends. The same is true of nearly all phases o Netherland life. The half century between 1650 and 1700 was marked by extensive research in mathematics, physics, botany, and medicine, mostly carried on outside the universities. In the ensuing fifty years the results o this research were recorded, systematized, and spread by the universities The story of William 'sGravesande, professor at Leiden and famous physicist, illustrates the transition from the amateur gentleman-physicist to the professor and research worker. 'sGravesande had studied and practised law but devoted most of his time to mathematics, and in 1717 was asked to take the chair of mathematics at Leiden University. Here he pursued hi researches but, as the university had no money to spend on laboratories, he made his own instruments, and his biographer asserts that these were o such excellent quality that they were still in use in the university laboratory in 1876! He did his share in spreading the knowledge of the preceding generation of physicists by publishing a complete edition of Christian Huyghens' works. Herman Boerhaave, the greatest physician of his time and an eminent teacher of medicine, was the editor of Swammerdam's book on insect life. Thus, the academic world adopted and spread the knowledge of the amateurs who had pioneered a generation before. To collect and publish the knowledge of preceding generations was the typical and productive task of the XVIIIth century. Boerhaave was by no means an innovator in his field. His eminent ability to teach others what older scholars had discovered, and his textbooks, translated into most European languages, established his rank among contemporary professors of medicine.

Not only in the fields of physics and medicine, but also in philology and other sciences, the XVIIIth century edited and published the work of preceding centuries. Balthasar Huydecooper edited the works of Vondel and of medieval authors. Peter Burman published standard editions of the classics with XVIIth century commentaries. In philology, new vistas were opened by Albert Schultens, who continued the Arabic and Hebrew studies that had flourished at Leiden since the beginning of the XVIIth century. Schultens was the first to perceive the interrelation of the Semitic languages and to interpret the Hebrew of the Bible through comparative Semitic philology. Lambert Ten Cate of Utrecht was the first to publish an etymological dictionary of the Dutch language. In this period when the East India Company still flourished, and oriental studies were naturally of great interest, a work in five folio volumes on the Malay archipelago found enough subscribers to make its publication possible. François Valentijn, former minister of the Church of Amboina and Batavia, who produced this compilation, included in it texts by Rumphius and Camphuijs. In the political field, attention turned again to the period of De Witt whose diplomatic correspondence was published.

Within ten years, the historian Johaanes Wagenaar published his enormous twenty-volume history of the Netherlands. Wagenaar determined the tradition of Netherland history for a hundred years to come, and his influence is still noticeable in Dutch textbooks. For him Netherland history was the story of the people of the Seven Provinces. It includes only political events. Neither Rembrandt nor Spinoza is once mentioned in his twenty volumes. And to Wagenaar, the people meant the "decent people"—the ruling caste and occasionally the middleclass. Princes and their deeds had of course to be recorded, but with little interest. The common people were never mentioned, except to refer to their "unruliness." In other words, Wagenaar's book was an historical plea for the rule of the oligarchy, whose authority derived from the consent of the middleclass as well as from their own position. In support of this Tacitus' story of Civilis and his Batavi is quoted at length, but middleclass citizens must not "abuse" their right to remonstrate with the oligarchs. If their remonstrance is rejected, they must admit having been misinformed. In such an interpretation, it was easy to admit popular influence in theory, for it was bound to remain illusory in practice.[45]

So in all its aspects the XVIIIth century was a period of crystallization and certainly not a period of decline as has so often been alleged. It differed from the XVIIth century, but the change had come gradually through a long period of transition beginning shortly after 1650. The main criticism by patriotic historiographers against the XVIIIth century Netherland community, however, is that it lost its hold on international affairs and forfeited the influential position the Republic had maintained throughout the XVIIth century and even up until 1715. The leaders of the Republic neglected the army and navy and refused to share responsibility in settling Europe's problems. When an explanation is offered of this political apathy, it usually is that a rapid decline in trade and industry set in with the turn of the century. To complete our comparison between the two periods under discussion, we must examine the extent to which criticism of later Netherland foreign policy is justified, as well as actual economic developments between 1700 and 1800.

In the light of the historical development, described in the preceding chapter, the foreign policy of the Republic after the death of the Stadhouder-King William (1702) appears perfectly logical. The Republic took an energetic part in the War of the Spanish Succession to keep France out of the southern Low Countries. The Netherlands, having a greater interest than any other country in the fate of the Belgian provinces, were determined to have the deciding voice in any discussions concerning them. Seventy years before, the merchants of Holland had been reluctant to allow their stadhouder to conquer all or part of Belgium. They had secured economic control over the maritime trade of Belgium, but refused to incorporate the country in the Union, either as a free member or a subject territory. In the first decade of the XVIIIth century, they decided to secure economic and military control over the area once for all. When that was accomplished without damage to the alliance with Britain, the object of forty years of war seemed to have been achieved. France was humiliated and a repetition of the catastrophe of 1672 made impossible. In the Baltic, Sweden's power was crumbling before Russia and her allies, and the future safety of the Baltic trade seemed to be guaranteed. Already Netherland ships were finding their way to the new port of St. Petersburg. In the Mediterranean only the Barbary pirates still caused annoyance. The gates to both inland seas were open, and the North Sea and the Channel were protected by the alliance with Britain. In this happy position, the Netherlands seemed to be at liberty to resume their favorite foreign policy of neutrality.

In the War of the Spanish Succession, the duke of Marlborough, commander-in-chief of the allied Dutch and British armies, conquered the Belgian provinces. The States General immediately assumed political control over the conquered area in spite of Austria's protests. If Belgium were to be transferred to another ruler, the States would do it and determine the conditions to which the new ruler must agree. Unfortunately, they let the right moment for making peace go by, and when they finally reached an agreement, they were forced to drop several of their initial demands. Belgium, as part of the Austrian Habsburg monarchy, was to be occupied by a joint Dutch and Austrian force, supported partly from Belgian funds. The economic supremacy of the Netherlands over Belgium was rigorously maintained. The States General had hoped to acquire full possession of the district of Venlo and Roermond along the Meuse, which had once belonged to the duchy of Guelders, but were disappointed. They received only the town of Venlo, all the remainder of the territory being divided between Austria and Prussia.

Notwithstanding this setback, the main objective of the Netherlands seemed to be achieved. The Republic, keeping a watchful eye on the new Austrian regime in Brussels, relapsed into blissful peace, which the leaders hoped would permit them to restore the national finances and give the people an opportunity to devote their energy to industry and commerce. So they shut their eyes as far as possible to the diplomatic problems created by Spain's attempt to rebuild her empire in Italy. However, they grew very energetic the moment the Emperor created a Belgian East India Company to revive that country's foreign trade. With Britain's help this "impudent" competition from a miserably weak neighbor was forcibly suppressed. The Republic sank back into ease, satisfied with having again demonstrated her influence over the Belgian provinces, when war broke out over the Polish succession. It mattered little to the Republic whether King Louis XV's father-in-law or Emperor Charles's friend from Saxonia presided over the unruly Polish Diet. The States General demanded that the war be waged elsewhere than on Belgium's traditional battlefields, and the belligerents were pleased to acquiesce.

The policy of the Netherland Republic in the XVIIIth century has often been described as undignified, but was by no means so. In a sense the very limitation of its aims and directness of its tactics lent it dignity. Yet it was weak because (and here the XVIIIth century leaders are less to blame than their predecessors)—it completely neglected the eastern boundary. The XVIIIth century harvested the evil fruits of XVIIth century negligence. In the war of 1672, Dutch garrisons in Rhineland towns had been driven out by the French, and the sovereign of these towns, the prince-elector of

Brandenburg in his capacity of duke of Cleve, refused to allow them to return. Once the Dutch troops had withdrawn, the age-old rights of the States of Cleve were rapidly and rudely abolished by the Hohenzollerns. The last appeals for help from their towns and nobility went unheeded by the States General. In 1715, the Hohenzollerns, now kings of Prussia, acquired part of Upper Guelders. Towns like Guelders, which for seven centuries had been part of one of the Lowland provinces, were separated forever from the Low Countries. Districts west of the Meuse were also brought under Prussian control, which now spread across both the lower Meuse and the Rhine. The Netherlands were hemmed in on their southeastern border by the rising military power of Germany. In 1744, the same thing happened in the northeast, when East Friesland fell to King Frederick II of Prussia. The Netherland garrisons maintained in Emden and Leeroort on the river Ems were forced to leave. With the advent of Prussian rule, High German became the official language of these districts. The use of Dutch was vigorously opposed, Dutch literary and artistic influence in northern Germany ceased to exist, and with the rapid rise of literary standards in Germany the cultural relations between the two countries were reversed. The States General believed that they had secured the Republic against all possible dangers from the south. They had no inkling of danger from the east.

The political arrangements by which the Republic, theoretically allied with Britain, allowed France to buy Dutch neutrality in her wars with Austria by guaranteeing the integrity of Belgium, admirably suited Netherland wishes. Through connivance with France, the astute merchant-diplomats enjoyed security on land. The combination was too subtle, however, to withstand the shock of a grave crisis. As the success of their diplomacy had strengthened the Dutch aristocracy's false belief in their mastery of foreign policy, the awakening was all the more rude. The year 1740 brought the crisis. France supported the princes-electors of Bavaria, Saxonia, and Brandenburg-Prussia in their claim against Maria Theresa, heiress to the Austrian Empire. King George II of Great Britain, as elector of Hannover, sided with the Habsburgs. The Netherland Republic decided to remain neutral so long as France and Great Britain were not formally involved in the war, a policy made easier by the friendly promise of the French Government not to invade Maria Theresa's Belgian territory. When in 1744 France declared war on both Austria and Britain and actually invaded Belgium, the Republic vainly tried to remain neutral. She was obliged, however, to help Britain resist a Jacobite invasion organized from France, and to pay subsidies to various German princes to align them in the common front against France and Prussia. Thereupon France invaded the Netherlands proper, and notwithstanding a spirited resistance on the frontier, the defense crumbled so rapidly that a repetition of 1672 seemed near. A general desire for peace and the French king's lack of ambition saved the Republic from greater disaster. The peace concluded in 1748 restored the Netherlands in all their possessions but damaged their prestige irretrievably.

The military defeats inflicted by the armies of France in 1745 and 1747 were not nearly so serious as those inflicted in 1666 by the petty Westphalian principality of Muenster. Yet the latter was without consequence, while the former reduced the Republic to the rank of a secondary power. The paradox had many causes, foremost among which was the changed internal political status of the Republic. For a short survey of this internal development, we have to go back to the year 1702, when Stadhouder William III died. In that year the uncontrolled oligarchy of De Witt's day had been restored, not altogether out of principle but more or less accidentally, since the stadhouder left no descendants.[46] He left his personal estate to his cousin John William of Nassau, stadhouder of Friesland, whose inheritance was disputed by other relatives of the House of Orange, including the Hohenzollerns, descendants of Frederick Henry through his daughter. The Frisian branch of the Nassau family had never enjoyed any great prestige outside the northern provinces. In Holland they were looked down upon, as any country squire from the East might be by Amsterdam's burgher-aristocrats. John William, who was rapidly gaining prestige because of his heroic conduct in the War of the Spanish Succession, met his death on a stormy night when the ferry boat on which he was crossing the Moerdijk capsized. His posthumous son inherited his political offices in the northern provinces and, by a settlement with his Prussian relatives, the estates of the House of Orange on Netherland soil. The principality of Orange went to the Hohenzollerns, who ceded it to France; but the title of Prince of Orange was used both by the Netherland Nassaus and the kings of Prussia.

In these circumstances a revival of the "True and Only Freedom" of De Witt's time was natural. Once in control, the city oligarchs quickly recovered their old taste for power and revived the political ideals of De Witt, who thus obtained an honorable place in Netherland forty years after his brutal assassination. As long as the War of the Spanish Succession lasted, the States General proved equal to their task. After the war had been brought to a moderately successful conclusion, the leaders of the Republic devoted their energies to a reduction of armaments and a restoration of the finances of the State. For the first time in many decades the credit of the Netherlands was seriously impaired. For several years the interest on the national debt of Holland could not be paid in full. The only way to restore the public finances acceptable to the oligarchs was by wholesale disarmament and economy. Another method which might have brought considerable relief was a reform of the tax system and a reduction of profiteering by city officials—but the ruling caste stubbornly refused even to consider it. While the States of Holland could not meet their obligation to the Union, burgomasters of Amsterdam sold public offices for scores of thousands of guilders or appropriated them for their own families. The common man was heavily taxed by excise levies on food and other necessities. The wealthier class sometimes paid heavy property taxes and when need was direct, contributed to a forced loan at low interest—which brought sizeable amounts to the treasury.

Administration abuses made any thorough reform of the financial and tax system impossible. The Netherlands in this respect were probably no worse, perhaps even better than France or England, but the Republic had to husband its resources more carefully than these larger and more populous kingdoms. In the Netherlands, the administration became particularly hateful to the people because it served the interests only of a small group of self-appointed dictators of the country. The ruling caste grew smaller and smaller. Dominant cliques within the caste tended to form a superaristocracy and some offices, for instance that of secretary to the States General, virtually became hereditary. In Friesland, where remnants of the ancient democratic system had survived throughout the ages, many of the farm sites with votes were bought or held under mortgages by a few families, who thus controlled the voting in the States Assembly. The irony of history turned this system against its protagonists, who, when they were in financial difficulties, had to approach merchants who in turn took mortgages on their estates and thus secured the final and deciding voice in provincial politics!

The oligarchy, incapable of any sacrifice for the national cause, was obviously not prepared to follow a consistent policy. The army and navy disintegrated, the navy more than the army, for Britain was an ally and France a potential enemy. The provinces no longer contributed to the equipping of new ships, though this was more necessary than ever. The steadily increasing size of warships presented a difficult problem for none of the Dutch ports except Flushing possessed a harbor deep enough to permit large ships of the line to enter. These ships could not reach Amsterdam through the shallow waters of the Zuiderzee and could not enter the Meuse. Important harbor works and the construction of naval bases near Flushing and at Holland's northern point were indicated, but because the projects would hurt vested interests, they were doomed regardless of national interest.

Here we touch upon one of the greatest contrasts between the XVIIth and XVIIIth century Netherlands. In the XVIIth century the leading class knew that it had to fight and work to maintain the Republic's newly acquired political prestige. They competed strenuously and successfully in trade and industry. Money that poured in as the result of hard work was readily spent to protect the sources of wealth. In the XVIIIth century the prestige of the Republic was established, and the ruling class expected to maintain that prestige by diplomatic means. Money was still plentiful, but the sources of wealth were no longer the same. Those who had money wanted to enjoy it, not to win more in a constant bitter struggle against relentless competition. As a French diplomat said, the Republic resembled Tantalus. Standing in wealth up to the lips she was unable to reach it herself, when for others there was plenty.

If the economic position of the Netherlands had dropped so far from the XVIIth-century level as traditional historiography of a few decades ago had it, money would not have been plentiful. As a matter of fact, the deterioration in trade and shipping did not occur until the latter part of the century. Not only did the absolute volume of trade not decline, but until 1700 it even increased to a level never reached before. It was the place held by Netherland trade and shipping in general European commerce that changed. *Proportionally* Netherland activities lagged behind those of other countries, especially Britain. The policy of economic protection inaugurated by most European States in the second half of the XVIIth century now took effect. Next to Britain, France and Germany were the principal competitors of the Netherlands. These nations enjoyed a great advantage over Holland in that they had a more or less independent industrial production, which the Netherlands never could have. Netherland manufacturing had always been a finishing industry for the products of other countries, such as linen and woollen goods from England and later from Silesia. Once the producers of these goods began to expand their own industrial activities, the position of the Netherlands was greatly weakened. The amount of Netherland capital still exceeded that of the country's industrial competitors, but it was of little use in bolstering industry. The relatively "high" wages paid in Leiden and Haarlem precluded effective competition with the exploitation of human misery in the Oder Valley or the growing industrial cities of England. The condition of labor in Leiden and Haarlem was bad enough, but, as a French visitor noted, even the poorest Dutch worker lived far better than the people of the same class in France. And conditions in France were certainly better than in Silesia and probably better than in England. The shifting of textile manufacturing to the rural districts of Brabant and Overijssel gave Dutch industrialists some respite.

Local conditions there permitted ruthless exploitation. How ruthless is revealed in an official document of 1785, which stated:

> "People who know the peasants of Brabant must acknowledge that they are deprived of all the comforts in life that are properly the part of human beings. They drink sour buttermilk or water, they eat potatoes and bread without butter or cheese, they are miserably clothed, they sleep on straw. A prisoner in Holland lives better than a peasant in Brabant."

The industrial decline of Leiden and Haarlem destroyed Holland's economic position in Europe. It deprived the leading provinces of one of the principal elements of well-being. This decline progressed rapidly after 1730. Poor as they were, it reduced the masses of workers in the two towns to still greater poverty, and made them dependent on charity. Many must have left the towns, for contemporary reports tell of houses being torn down and streets and lots being turned into meadows and gardens. We do not know, however, where they went. Not many sailed overseas. Numbers may have gone to the peatmoors of the northeastern provinces, which were just then being rapidly developed and where new villages were formed.

A natural consequence of the industrial development of the larger western European countries was a tendency to establish direct contact with the consumers of their products. So far Netherland merchants had been intermediaries in European trade. Technical difficulties, the small size and slow speed of freighters, imperfect methods of merchandise preservation, lack of capital on the part of the exporters—all these things had made recourse to intermediaries essential. Some of these difficulties were now being overcome. Moreover, Great Britain was even more favorably located than the Netherlands to act as intermediary. Only lack of capital prevented the British from superseding the Netherland trade entirely within a few decades. London easily surpassed Amsterdam as the main shipping center of northern Europe, and even Hamburg fed by a constant stream of merchandise from the interior of Germany rivaled the Dutch commercial capital. The only port in the Netherlands to profit from these new conditions was Rotterdam, favored by its location at the mouth of the Rhine. The production of the Rhineland and Ruhr naturally sought an outlet along the main waterway, and thus Rotterdam was able to gain on Amsterdam.

Amsterdam's economic position would rapidly have become desperate had it not been for the East and West Indian trade which now was of greater *proportional* significance to Netherland economy than it had been, and for Amsterdam's abundant capital supporting its merchants. This same wealth permitted the East and West India Companies to carry on. The latter, reorganized out of the first West India Company that foundered in 1674, was of a strictly limited character. It no longer enjoyed a monopoly of trade on the American Continent, and one of its most important possessions, Surinam, had been transferred to a new enterprise, the shares of which were equally divided between the city of Amsterdam, a prominent oligarch, François van Aerssen van Sommelsdijk, and the Company. Surinam sugar plantations worked with negro slaves brought such huge profits that many XVIIIth century economic experts thought this little district of greater importance to the Netherlands than the whole Dutch Asiatic empire.[47] It is probable that by the middle of the century more than thirty thousand slaves were being used on four hundred plantations, entirely financed by Dutch capital. Between fifty and seventy million guilders were estimated to have been advanced to the planters against mortgages on their estates.

The claim that Surinam was more important to the Netherlands than the Asiatic empire is untenable. It is true that the East India Company was passing through a critical period, that the reserve of more than twenty million guilders built up in Batavia was rapidly dwindling and that the Company had to borrow money from Amsterdam banks to carry on its trade. The exhaustion of the Batavian reserve was due to protracted warfare resulting from the East Indian Government's intervention in the disputes of the princes of Mataram, Java's principal sultanate. By these wars the Company obtained sovereign rights over the northern coastlands of the island, but little economic advantage. Rather indiscreetly the Directors in Amsterdam continued to pay large dividends to avoid a drop of the Company's shares on the Amsterdam Stock Exchange, but it became increasingly difficult to know whether these dividends were paid out of real profits from the East Indies or out of money borrowed in Holland. By 1779 the directors had burdened their enterprise with a debt of eighty-five million guilders nearly all incurred in the XVIIIth century. This debt and the loss of the Batavian reserves exceeded the total sum paid in dividends during the XVIIIth century, and there was some truth in the criticism of contemporary experts who asserted that the prosperity of the Company was merely apparent. Many proposals for reform were made and some even reached the stage of timid initial application. There were experts in the Indies who understood how wrong the whole system was. The officials were underpaid and thus obliged to resort to illicit trading; the limitation of production to keep prices at ever higher levels aroused the hatred of the natives. The organization needed reorganization from the bottom up. But the directors stood by their principles. Vain efforts were made to stop illicit trading, which reached fantastic proportions. Ships are said to have foundered from the enormous weight of "packages and presents" carried surreptitiously for "relatives" at home. The directors resorted to drastic penalties and once, in 1721, to mass execution in Batavia. It was without avail. Their policy only created general unrest in Batavia, which led to the awful massacres of 1740, when Dutch and Indonesians attacked the Chinese inhabitants of the city and murdered thousands of them in an outburst of uncontrolled fury.

Although recognized by all as evil and attacked both in the Netherlands and in Batavia, the system survived because it served the private interests of the ruling clique in Amsterdam. Manipulating the Company's shares on the Stock Exchange and borrowing from the province of Holland, so that the debts of the Company were transferred to the taxpayers, provided wonderful profits which the directors and their caste were loathe to forego. The East India trade might have flourished, but it was deliberately kept at the prescribed level.

While industry declined, while trade and shipping remained stationary, Holland became increasingly important as the money market of Europe. The bankers of Amsterdam played a primordial role in the maintenance of Netherland commerce; their financial resources and wide connections were indispensable to foreign merchants shipping goods abroad, who could rely on having their drafts paid promptly in Amsterdam. Until 1763, all settlements between London and Russia were made in Amsterdam. For decades Amsterdam was the clearing house of all Europe. This gradually reduced the Amsterdam merchants to the position of commission agents, but it took half a century and more for the change to be completed. Amsterdam was also an excellent source of funds for governments and in the long run foreign loans proved attractive and profitable. British bonds were preferred. Britain's expenditures for her armies on the Continent during the Seven Years' War were largely met by loans from Amsterdam bankers. A recent study estimates that the Dutch held a large share of the British public debt around 1760. At that time the debt was nearly 150,000,000 pounds, and the Dutch share so large that British experts feared a catastrophe if their foreign support failed. We may assume that perhaps a billion guilders were invested by Dutch capitalists in British funds alone. To these investments must be added loans floated by France, Austria, Prussia, and Russia in the Amsterdam market.

Thus the significance of the Amsterdam market in international politics becomes clear. Changed economic conditions undoubtedly influenced Netherland foreign policy. XVIIth century shipping and colonization could be protected by ships and soldiers, but XVIIIth century investments could not. Neutrality was the international policy most favorable to Amsterdam's bankers. "Standing quietly in the midst of turbulent waters" gave these gentlemen excellent opportunities. The problems of war and peace, however, were not going to be settled in accordance with the wishes of financial circles; worse, they were not going to be settled in accordance with the needs of national safety and independence.

In the XVIIth century internal political conflicts centered around strong personalities, Oldenbarnevelt and Prince Maurice, John De Witt and William III. Hence the strong personal note in these conflicts and the tragic ends of the defeated. Constitutional problems underlay those conflicts, but personalities overshadowed political issues. In one century the Republic changed twice from oligarchic to semi-monarchical rule, without altering the constitution. However keen the rivalry between the leaders, however great the differences of opinion, the interest of the state predominated. Oldenbarnevelt, supported by France in his conflict with Maurice, never thought of checking his adversary by subordinating national policy to that of France. John De Witt acquiesced in an agreement with Cromwell that aimed at eliminating the prince of Orange from public influence, but he did not seek peace with Cromwell to strengthen his own political position but only because peace was so badly needed by the nation. He never dreamed of subordinating his foreign policy to the requirements of party politics in 1672, and his opponent, Prince William, who was offered monarchical authority over the Netherlands by the enemies of the nation, spurned this offer to continue De Witt's policy of last ditch defense.

All this was changed in the XVIIIth century. The economic interest of the nation demanded neutrality. The political commitments of the state and its interest in the fate of Belgium demanded at least some participation in international affairs. This necessarily meant defending the Dutch military positions in Belgium and siding with Britain against France. It also meant reinforcing the army and navy and placing them under unified command. But this was directly opposed to the private interests of the leading oligarchs, for it would have forced them to share their power with the prince of Orange. It was also opposed to their sentiments and intellectual leanings, which were definitely for France rather than England. Foreign policy was subordinated to party interest, a very dangerous attitude in a small country surrounded by great powers. Nothing contributed more to the rapid decline of the Netherland Republic in the second half of the XVIIIth century than this complete predominance of party over national interests. While "neutralists" and "Orangists" bitterly contested the issues of foreign policy, while French troops overran the Belgian provinces and invaded Dutch Brabant, the middleclass people of the Netherlands, determined to get at the root of the evil, made their first assault on the prerogatives of the oligarchy and on the traditional form of government.

In 1747, a revolt caused by the military catastrophe at the hands of France forced the oligarchs after some resistance to appoint William IV of Nassau-Orange to be stadhouder and commander-in-chief of the army and navy.[48] The Frisian branch of the House of Nassau thus succeeded to the position of the Holland branch. For the first time all the provinces were united under *one* stadhouder, an important progress in the unification of the Republic and also in the growth of monarchical institutions. The office of stadhouder was again proclaimed hereditary, this time in the male or female line. This also applied to the command of the armed forces. A great innovation was the appointment of the new stadhouder as Chief Director of the East and West India Companies. For the first time in history a prince of Orange gained influence in the Dutch overseas territories, and this was considered as only the beginning of a complete reorganization of the administration.

The "burghers," traders, shopkeepers, and artisans of the city, were in feverish agitation. The city guards held political meetings where programs of reform were drafted. The people of Friesland and Groningen, mindful of ancient liberties and democratic forms of government, sought their restoration; and the townspeople of Holland and Utrecht followed with violent demands that the influence of the guilds or city guards in local administration be restored, or at least a council created among the elected officers of the guards to express the wishes of the people and control the "maintenance of the privileges"—that is, check arbitrary and financial exploitation by the oligarchy. These people looked to the prince of Orange to carry out their political wishes more or less according to law. The agitators all belonged to the middleclass and had enough to lose to make them shun violence. The masses of the wage-earners were not asked to share in this bourgeois revolution.

The result was a tragic failure. The prince of Orange, intelligent but weak and strictly traditional in his views, was the worst possible revolutionary leader. After weeks of oratory and vituperation, excited meetings and agitation in the streets, the unrest evaporated after Prince William, offering many embarrassed excuses to the ruling oligarchy, had changed the membership of the City Council of Amsterdam, "I am sorry," he said to one of the burgomasters, "that I must ask you to leave, but I cannot help it." To which the burgomaster replied, "I know it, Your Highness. I myself am convinced that you must discharge me." In this apologetic way "reform" was accomplished and revolution frustrated. The fact that the townspeople permitted this lends a tragic-comic note to the whole episode, which has done more to make Netherlanders ashamed of their

XVIIIth century history than the loss of foreign prestige and of trade.

The saddest aspect of it all was the fact that all parties believed reform necessary—except perhaps the prince of Orange who believed in the magic power of his name—but none wanted reform by any of the others. As early as 1717 the oligarchy had contemplated a modification of the governmental system. Simon van Slingelandt, secretary of the Council of State, put forward a plan for the reorganization of that antiquated body to make it again a central executive authority. The report of the able and learned gentleman was read and filed. That was all. A partial readjustment of customs duties was the only reform achieved before the revolutionary convulsions of 1747. The stadhouder worked feverishly at numerous plans but completed none. His irresolute nature and distrust of stronger characters whose predominance he feared, prevented him from accomplishing any reforms in the few years of his great power. A second plan for the formation of a central executive in the form of "departments" to be organized for the various branches of administration, each under its own director, was rejected.

The stadhouder died in 1751, and his offices, now hereditary, fell to his son under the regency of the princes of Orange. For the first time the functions of stadhouder were exercised by a woman, a British princess of the House of Hannover, daughter of King George II. Against her weak authority the oligarchy rapidly reasserted its influence. In spite of the personal ties between the Court of St. James and that of The Hague, the Netherland Republic remained neutral in the Seven Years' War, when France and Austria fought Britain and Prussia for the mastery of America and India and northern Germany. France and Austria being allies, Belgium for once escaped being the general battlefield. With Belgium secure, the Netherlands looked passively on while the future of Europe, America and India was being determined in seven bloody years of war. This time, the passivity of the Republic was complete. It made no serious attempt to protect its shipping from unprecedented British interference, and did not even dare to refuse passage to French troops.

This attitude had an immediate and serious result in Asia, where the Dutch Company's fleets had ruled the Indian Ocean throughout the XVIIth century. When rumors of Holland's total collapse had spread in 1672 to the ends of the Asiatic world, Batavia had stood like a rock. British squadrons were driven from the Indian seas. If the defense of the homeland failed, it was said, scores of thousands of Hollanders would come to Java and the Moluccas to build a new Netherland. In the Seven Years' War, the Company hardly dared to move while the French and British were fighting for India. Dutch outposts in Bengal were overrun, a relief expedition from Batavia was attacked by British ships and troops on the Ganges and utterly defeated. The Anglo-Dutch alliance in Europe no more prevented the British from overrunning the Dutch sphere of influence than a similar alliance a century and a half before had hindered the Dutch from driving the British from the Malay archipelago.

The Republic had not the strength to resist these foreign incursions, and the States General could not agree to reinforce either the army or the navy. Rather than give preference to the army or the navy, opposing factions in the States General allowed both branches of the service to deteriorate. Rather than strengthen the national treasury, the bankers and merchants of Amsterdam invested hundreds of millions in British, Prussian, and French bonds. The Hague became the center of intrigue in Europe. The princely court was accused of working for British interests, but the charge was brought by those who themselves neglected national interests in the hope of obtaining commercial privileges from the king of France. In one respect the Amsterdam merchants were right. Passive neutrality brought the Netherlands enormous profits, as Amsterdam became more than ever the clearing house of Europe. The prestige of the oligarchy grew; that of the House of Orange declined after the death of the princess regent. The States took the unusual step of assuming the regency themselves until 1766, when young William, fifteen years old, was supposed to be able to exercise his functions, which were as important as ever. Having tasted power again, it was unthinkable that the oligarchy would submit to the will of a child or his favorite advisors. The result was polite cooperation; each party refrained from pressing issues disagreeable to the other. The defense of the Republic, a sad but dire necessity in the late XVIIIth century, when the whim of an absolute monarch or the fretful vapors of a mistress could cause an international catastrophe, were neglected to obviate irksome dissent.

The crisis came in 1776, when Britain was faced with the American Revolution and saw her old enemies rally to seek revenge for earlier defeats. The Netherland Republic suddenly found herself in a most favorable position. The British, anxious to keep the Netherlands neutral even if they did not obtain their help to which they were entitled by treaty, offered to make great concessions to Dutch trade in the Caribbean, which meant allowing the Dutch West Indies to become the headquarters of the most profitable smuggling that could be imagined. The island of St. Eustachius was the main base for blockade runners carrying arms and ammunition to the American revolutionary armies. A working agreement with Britain was easily reached, but it called for a firm attitude towards France, which also wanted the cooperation of the Netherlands. The French hoped to use the Dutch possessions in India and Ceylon as bases for the reconquest of their power in India. Sad to say, the Americans and their fight for freedom never figured in the political combinations of the Netherland leaders.

Prince William V, closely related to the British Royal family and highly conservative, had no sympathy for the Americans and regarded them as "rebels." The Orangist leaders shared his views completely. The anti-Orangist oligarchs were no better informed on the real significance of what was happening on the other side of the Atlantic. Many of them had read the rationalist philosophers of the late XVIIth and the XVIIIth centuries: Locke, Hume, Montesquieu, Voltaire and Rousseau. Countless editions of these works had been published in the Netherlands to avoid French censorship, but the majority of the ruling class objected to the new ideas and granted a request of the Reformed Church that Rousseau's *Contrat Social* and Voltaire's *Essai sur la Tolérance* be banned by the States Assembly.

The American struggle against British rule that preceded the Declaration of Independence, had entirely escaped the attention of the Dutch public. Of the many political pamphlets then published in Holland, not one dealt with American problems. The Netherlanders of 1770 looked upon the Corsicans and later upon the Poles as epic fighters for freedom. America was just too far away. The suppression of the Order of the Jesuits interested the sons of the *Gueus* more than the coming war of liberation in the West. Indeed, these Netherlanders looked towards the past, without much attention to what the future might bring. After the American war had broken out, British propaganda flooded the Netherlands with anti-American literature. The British Parliamentary opposition also saw to it that their point of view was put before the Dutch. French pamphlets were read more generally, because the leading class were familiar with the language. Some time passed, however, before a single American publication was translated into Dutch.[49]

The principles of the American Revolution were of no interest to the leading classes of the Netherlands. The economic opportunity offered by the breaking of Britain's trade monopoly in the Atlantic colonies was a different matter, worthy of more attention. Amsterdam merchants were most anxious to be the first to reap the fruits of Britain's loss. Moreover, was not this war, in which Britain surrounded on all sides by enemies seemed about to succumb, a miraculous opportunity to restore the balance of power in the North Sea and to regain Holland's ancient supremacy? John Adams, who came to the Netherlands in 1780, rightly saw that anti-British sentiment was at the bottom of the pro-American attitude of the Dutch. He found little real interest in his country. It was the large and enormously profitable business done at St. Eustachius that caused the commander of that Dutch port to fire a salute to the American flag on November 16, 1776, the first foreign authority to do so. There were a few exceptions to the attitude of the ruling class. Out of sympathy for the ideals of the Revolution, Johan Van der Capellen sought contact with Benjamin Franklin, and propagated American views among his countrymen. With the progress of time and of political unrest in the Netherlands, with the growing success of the Revolution, more fervent admirers of the new freedom rose to preach American doctrine to the people of the Republic. Peter van der Kemp, a former Mennonite minister, was one of them. But France, Britain and the American Revolution were all less important to the narrow minds of nearly all Dutch politicians than their own petty party quarrels.

The Republic faced a grave crisis. The States General had to decide whether to follow a passive policy towards Britain's efforts to supervise all neutral trade and search all neutral ships. If not, they must prepare for naval war, seriously and immediately. If they chose to recognize the right of search, they must reinforce the army to prevent a possible French attack. On the one hand they would lose the enormous profits from their smuggling trade in the Caribbean. On the other they would hardly be able to supply the Americans with arms and gun powder to be used against their British ally. It was an awkward choice. A gentlemen's agreement with Britain might offer a way out, but in that case what chance would Amsterdam have for American business after Britain's expected defeat? However these considerations weighed less than the fear that alliance with Britain and reinforcement of the army might increase the stadhouder's prestige, or that opposition to Britain would be an unkind act towards the stadhouder's relatives. Neither John De Witt nor William III had ever known such scruples.

The stadhouder was willing to compromise so as to safeguard Netherland commercial interests without involving the nation in a war with Britain. He might have saved the situation if his political opponents had been willing to be saved by him, but that was the last thing they wanted. Not content with sacrificing some of the commercial advantages of neutrality to secure others, they wanted everything; above all they wanted others to fight their war, if war should come. To be sure, preparations were made to reinforce the navy, plans were agreed to for the construction of new ships. But every member of the government knew or should have known, that those ships could not be ready in a few months; that the wharves and ports were inadequate to accommodate large ships; that the new vessels would be too small to engage the British; that against one hundred twenty-two British ships of the line the whole existing Dutch navy numbered no more than eleven, most of which were not in a condition to put to sea. The greed and resentment of the anti-Orangists prepared the ground for French intrigues, which were masterfully conducted by King Louis's diplomats. A promise that the inhabitants of towns supporting an anti-British policy would be favored by French custom-officers created a pro-French landslide in the States of Holland. By accepting this bribe, Holland's towns virtually destroyed the political individuality of their province, not to speak of violating the spirit and letter of the Union of Utrecht which demanded a common front towards the outside world. The Republic did not go to war against Britain; she stumbled into a war the significance of which her leaders failed to see.[50]

The anti-Orangist oligarchy that dragged the nation into war, caused the ruin of the once flourishing Netherland Republic. Dutch shipping, already lagging far behind its British competitors, received a death blow. Only once did a Dutch squadron put to sea to escort merchantmen, but before the convoy had gone far it was forced back after a violent engagement, in which the Dutch men-of-war acquitted themselves honorably. But the losses in ships, merchandise and money were not the worst. Even the plundering and total destruction of St. Eustachius, the smuggling center in the Caribbean, by Admiral George B. Rodney was only a minor accident in the general disaster. To this day the ruins on the small West Indian island testify to the savagery with which the famous British commander wreaked his vengeance; indeed, the Opposition in the House of Commons took Rodney severely to task for his wanton devastation.

Far worse was the fact that the Republic at home and abroad fell into a state of complete vassalage to France. Only the timely arrival of a French fleet saved the Dutch colony at the Cape from being conquered by the British. The same fleet also saved most of Ceylon. Another French fleet reconquered the Dutch settlements in the West Indies already occupied by British troops. From the Gulf of Mexico to Ceylon, French garrisons guarded Dutch possessions, as so many pledges that the ruined Republic would not desert the French cause. In Europe the southern frontier of the Netherland state was deprived of the traditional protection it had enjoyed by the occupation of Belgian fortresses and a general supervision of Belgian affairs. Joseph II of Austria undertook to free his Belgian territory from all outside interference. He brutally ordered the Dutch troops to withdraw and no opposition was possible to his demands. France was unwilling to risk war in Europe for the sake of her newest dependent and offered no assistance. The prince of Orange, who had married Wilhelmina of Prussia, a Hohenzollern princess, in 1767 vainly appealed to his uncle, King Frederick II, as if that shrewd cynical old politician would ever have modified his foreign policy for the sake of a niece's husband. Fearing a renewal of the Seven Years' War and that Prussia might once more be attacked by a ring of enemies, he wanted the king of France as his friend, and advised his nephew to shape his foreign policy to that of France.

Each month that the war lasted, the situation of the Netherlands grew worse. The directors of the East India Company who for a century had deliberately maintained an antiquated system of trade because of its advantage to themselves, saw the collapse of the financial house of cards that had given their enterprise a false appearance of prosperity. Without a cent in their treasury and without a pound of coffee or spice in their warehouses, they were unable to meet their payments. While the Company in the Netherlands had to ask for a moratorium, the storehouses of Batavia were packed with many million guilders worth of coffee. Even then the directors refused to allow Batavia to sell direct to neutral traders.

At this propitious moment the oligarchic clique attacked the prince of Orange, blaming all this misery on his neglect of national interests. The prince had it in his power to save the Republic, if the ruling clique had been willing to cooperate with him. Britain, by no means bent on fighting the war to a finish, had offered complete restoration of Netherland rights and territories. But the oligarchs, allied with France for better or for worse, convinced that a separate peace with Britain would cause an Orangist landslide, preferred to let the nation suffer rather than lose the opportunity to accuse the prince of every political crime short of high treason. The only meritorious act in this mistaken policy—the recognition of the United States as a sovereign state in April, 1782, the second European recognition of American independence—was spoiled by the reluctance of Amsterdam bankers to provide the new state with substantial loans. The outcome was that the Republic let pass the opportune moment for making peace and then, abandoned by all its allies, had to cede Negapatnam, its most important fortress on the coast of India, and throw the Molucca seas open to British shipping. A first breach had been made in the East India's Company's monopoly in southeastern Asia. Soon after a British settlement was founded at Penang on the coast of Malaya, an event which marked the beginning of British occupation of that area.

After the war, trade and shipping partially revived. The East India Company did not. In the fifteen years between 1780 and 1795 its debts rose to 127,000,000 guilders, fifty percent more than all the debts incurred in the one hundred and sixty years preceding the catastrophe of 1780. The West India Company had been moribund for decades and could not possibly recover. By the irony of history, in this last hour of the Republic's existence as a result of measures taken during the war, the Dutch navy regained some efficiency, and at the moment of national collapse this branch of the armed services was in better shape than it had been for three-quarters of a century. The Republic's political prestige was lost forever. What remained of it after the war was destroyed by squabbling political factions in the next three years.

Three men now dominated the old oligarchy—the pensionaries of Haarlem, Amsterdam, and Dordrecht. This triumvirate subordinated all its political actions to the elimination of the stadhouder's influence. They knew that France would never trust Prince William because of his English family ties, so the foreign policy of the Republic was to be strongly pro-French, because French influence would back the oligarchy against the Orangists. No price was too high to pay. France herself in utmost distress and within only a few years of the revolution, still dreamed of further crippling Britain's sea power. Having lost her colonies, France hoped the Dutch possessions would provide substitute bases for the next war. French officers would be sent out to reorganize the Dutch East Indian army in Java; plans drafted for a joint attack on the British positions in India, and so forth. That such plans could but endanger the Netherland colonies and make the Republic a shield for France—a shield on which all British blows would fall—did not bother the triumvirate. The scheme which involved the reorganization of the Dutch army by French officers, was obnoxious to the prince of Orange; that was enough to recommend it.

Poor William V was more hated, more bitterly denounced as "tyrant" and "oppressor" than any Netherland leader since the days of Alva. Not overintelligent, physically sluggish, suspicious and stubborn, with a love of minute detail, irresolute of character, he was the least tyrannical of tyrants. Convinced of the importance of his family in Netherland history, he found no better retort to the insults of the triumvirate than a threat to leave the Republic and withdraw to his possessions in Nassau on the middle-Rhine, as if this were the greatest punishment he could inflict on his opponents. By her energy and persuasion, Princess Wilhelmina prevented this, but he did leave the province of Holland, where he was exposed to the daily pin pricks of the three pensionaries and their clique. Unlike his predecessors, the prince of Orange could not count on popular support in his conflict with the oligarchy. The middleclass still resented the desertion of William's father in 1747, when the first revolutionary attack was made on the power of the oligarchy. After 1747, under the influence of French and British political philosophers, a timid trend towards democracy had developed among the burghers. It grew after the Anglo-Dutch war and under the influence of American independence. A flood of political pamphlets, newspapers, and books spread the new ideas among the middle classes. The principle of popular sovereignty was understood by the Netherlanders, who had advocated it in slightly different form in their struggle against the king of Spain.

The triumvirate gladly took advantage of popular enthusiasm against the "tyrant." But the masses were not satisfied with attacks on the stadhouder; they found the oligarchy equally obnoxious. The "usurpation" of civic liberties by the oligarchs was violently denounced and the restoration of freedom demanded. The guilds and the city-guards were to regain the political influence they were supposed to have exercised in medieval times. The democrats founded clubs, societies and free corps which boisterously took to military training. For a time it seemed that thousands of volunteers all over the country might rise in armed revolt to expel their political opponents from the country. The free corps and clubs formed national unions and held national congresses. Such things were unheard of in the traditional provincialism of the Republic. Be that as it may, the movement lacked leadership and conviction. It was not a movement of the masses but of the middleclass. The have-nots were carefully excluded from the "democratic" organizations. All the members of the clubs and free corps were willing to do was join in armed demonstrations and overthrow a local government. Violence was discussed, but hardly ever resorted to. However well it sounded to proclaim one's willingness to die for the ideal of popular government, it was an entirely different matter to do so, leaving wife, children, and business behind on this earth. The Dutch middleclass was definitely dissatisfied and wanted a change. It was neither desperate nor destitute, a fact which prevented the patriot free corps from becoming the predecessors of the French Jacobins.

Both the oligarchs and the democrats called themselves "Patriots." An Orangist party did not exist, but it could be created. The material was at hand in the masses left out of political consideration by the "Patriots"; in those members of the oligarchy connected with the Orangist movement by tradition or who recognized that a thorough reform could only be achieved by the evolution of the Republic into a constitutional monarchy; in officers and men of the army and navy, who always favored the prince as their commander-in-chief. The Orangist party was organized by the British ambassador at The Hague. Here too, foreign intervention was decisive; the new movement was set up to counteract French political influence in the Netherlands. If the Orangists gained the upper hand, the Republic would switch its allegiance from France to Britain.

The stadhouder obtained additional support from the oligarchs of certain provinces who dreaded the effects of the democratic movement. The States of Guelderland instructed him to suppress revolutionary agitation in their province and, whenever William was ordered to act, he acted promptly. His troops occupied Guelderland and part of Utrecht. Thereupon the States of Holland recalled the troops paid by them from the army of the Union and deployed those troops with armed volunteers along the eastern boundary of the province. Civil war seemed near but did not occur. The States of Holland did not want to attack and the stadhouder did not move unless asked to do so. Thus, the Netherlands lost their last chance to settle their political differences among themselves. The fate of the "Patriots" was sealed. In France the political convulsions preceding the revolution had begun. In Prussia, the old king Frederick II had died and was succeeded by the brother of the princess of Orange, Frederick William II. Britain's prestige was growing, and the Orangist masses in Holland grew more clamorous every week. The opportunity to accomplish a democratic reform of the Netherlands from within had passed. The forces of reaction were too strong. Not they however, but a Prussian military expedition restored the authority of the House of Orange.

An insignificant incident, the refusal of the States to permit Princess Wilhelmina to enter Holland, resulted in a Prussian demand for reparation of the "insult" to His Majesty the King of Prussia—because an armed "Patriot," sword in hand, had guarded His Majesty's sister before she recrossed the boundary of the province. Reparation was refused, of course, for the princess had not been insulted and the matter was purely an internal one. But King Frederick William was not to be denied and assured of British approval and French impotence, he ordered his troops to invade the Republic. The Netherland army under the prince of Orange cooperated with the invaders; the Patriot defenses crumbled without a blow. Amsterdam alone was too proud to surrender without resistance, and some fighting took place on the approaches to the inundation by which the city protected itself. Threatened by an Orangist revolt, the defenders capitulated.

The prince of Orange was restored to all his functions. The Prussians left, but not until they had presented a bill for their expenditures, which at the energetic and indignant protest of Princess Wilhelmina, was reduced to the singular amount of 402,018 guilders and 10 pennies. The States of Holland added a tip of twenty percent, and made it half a million. A storm of Orangist enthusiasm swept over the country, but now reduced to complete vassalage. It could not avoid concluding a strict alliance with both Prussia and Britain. Thousands of Patriots went into exile in France. There, in poverty and amid the turmoil of revolution, they shook off the inhibitions that had made their democratic movement of the eighties a farce. The change came too late. The revolution in the Netherlands was to be made, not by reformed "Patriots" but by the armies of the French republic.

CHAPTER XI

The Second Netherland State

THE thirty years following the revolution of 1789 are in many respects the darkest in Netherland history. In those three decades the old republican state, the pride of Oldenbarnevelt and John De Witt, was torn down. Meanwhile, as a small group of former "Patriots" experimented with new political institutions, the Netherlands lost more of their freedom and independence year by year, until the country as a political entity was utterly destroyed. From the depths of that humiliation the nation rose again to build a second Netherland state. The vicissitudes of Netherland political life in the years of "Restoration" (1787–1795), of destruction and experimentation (1795–1800), are of very little interest. Action always lagged far behind the roar of oratorical protest. The absurd contrast between the energy spent in words and that spent in deeds was so great that often, as in 1747 and 1787, the effect is tragi-comical.

In 1787, the stadhouder, William V, was restored to the full exercise of his functions. A few half-hearted attempts at reform in Europe and the Asiatic empire remained without effect. The historical studies of Adriaan Kluit, a professor of Leiden University, were the most remarkable product of this counter-revolutionary trend. For more than one hundred and fifty years official historians had presented the oligarchic point of view and defended the sovereignty of the States Assemblies with arguments from Tacitus, which were supposed to show that sovereignty in the Low Countries had always belonged to the leading classes. The democratic patriots advocated the theory that sovereignty rested originally with the people and had been usurped by the oligarchy. Against both opinions Kluit formulated his theory of monarchy as the source of all authority. To prove his point, he made a thorough study of medieval Dutch history, the first historian in the Netherlands to do so. His well documented works remained the basis of all later research on the early periods of Holland's history. His theory on sovereignty was taken up and put to political use in the XIXth century.

Two years after the restoration of the stadhouder, revolution broke out in France. In 1793, Britain became involved in the Franco-Austrian war and the Dutch Republic obediently followed her powerful ally. French revolutionary armies conquered Belgium. With them was a "Batave legion" of Dutch "Patriot" exiles organized for the liberation of their native land. The French, under Dumouriez, penetrated into North Brabant but then withdrew to be defeated by the Austrians and driven from Belgian soil. Again the danger had passed. The ruling Orangist party was given a few years respite, but it had become evident that the Republic could not defend herself effectively. The motley German mercenary regiments hired after the catastrophe of 1787 from the princes of Ansbach and similar purveyors of "war equipment" were not dependable. The "Patriots," who for six years had lived in prudent political retirement, regained courage and under the cover of literary clubs reorganized their party. The swift advance of General Jourdan's army in 1794 brought French troops back into Brabant and, in the first days of 1795, a division under General Pichegru crossed the frozen rivers and invaded the heart of Holland. The poorly disciplined Dutch army disintegrated. Herman Daendels, once a lawyer and a bellicose Patriot leader in the tiny town of Hattem in Guelderland, who, in exile, had become a high ranking officer in the French army, rode on ahead of the invading troops to arrange a "revolution" and a voluntary reversal in Dutch politics before the French could occupy the Netherlands and proclaim it conquered land.

The revolution that followed was a "velvet" revolution, as some fanatics returned from exile complained. It developed without any untoward incidents. In Amsterdam a "Revolutionary Committee" under Rutger Jan Schimmelpenninck, a lawyer, went to Town Hall and politely replaced the oligarchic city government, calling itself the "Provisional Representatives of the People." Its example was followed all over the Netherlands. The prince of Orange, discouraged and powerless, decided to leave for England with his family. In Zeeland, where French troops could not so easily penetrate, the ruling class proved most accommodating. They resigned in a body and then resumed their seats, no longer as the States of Zeeland ruling by sacred traditions, but as the "Provisional Representatives of the People of Zeeland." The revolution was an accomplished fact.

There is an outward similarity between these events and those of 1940. In reality there is a basic difference. In 1940, the government itself left the national territory in Europe to continue the struggle against the invaders. In the occupied Netherlands no government remained; only an administration. In 1795, whatever the extent of his power, the prince of Orange, as stadhouder, was *not* the head of the government, let alone the sovereign of the state. He took refuge abroad where he sought to organize an Orangist-Netherland movement. The *Sovereigns,* the States of the provinces, submitted to foreign occupation, but the ruling oligarchy consented almost without protest to make place for new persons who reorganized the state. There was no doubt about the legality of the new government. Whatever may have been the sentiments of the masses who remained largely apathetic, the majority of the intellectuals backed the revolution. It was also supported by most dissenters, especially by the Catholics, who expected now to obtain equality of civic and religious rights.

In England, the stadhouder organized an anti-revolutionary movement and, as Chief Director of the East and West India Companies, sent a circular letter to all Dutch commanders overseas, ordering them to admit British troops to the territories and positions under their control. These British troops were to occupy the Dutch colonies for the duration of the war under an agreement between the British and Netherland states—the latter represented by the prince—guaranteeing restitution after the war. Under this agreement a number of Dutch ports in the West Indies were surrendered to the British. In the East Indies only the fortresses on the southern coast of India, on Sumatra, and in Malaya obeyed the stadhouder's orders. All other colonial administrations, including the government of Batavia, decided to recognize the government in The Hague, despite the fact that their sympathies were not with the revolution.

The British brought legal uncertainty to an end by formally declaring war on the new Dutch Republic (September 15, 1795). A declaration of war necessarily implies recognition of the enemy as a sovereign state. Prussia, in concluding a peace treaty with France at Basle on March 5, 1795, had already deserted her Orangist ally. These facts again throw into strong relief the difference between 1795 and 1940. The Netherland government of 1795 could not face the crisis of foreign invasion with the same determination as that of 1940. Patriotism had suffered from decades of internal confusion in which the aid of foreign powers had been shamelessly accepted for particular political aims.

The "Patriots" of 1787 again ruled the Netherlands. Their ideals of eight years before (such as restoring the guilds and city guards to political influence), now seemed to them memories of a distant past, no more related to their present condition than beliefs of the stone age. They ridiculed the ancient federal republic with its multifarious institutions, its complicated machinery, its cherished charter freedoms. As the source of freedom, the parchment and ink of royal decrees were replaced by theories taken from Rousseau and the orators of the French revolution. The French Republic "One and Indivisible" was the model upon which the institutions of the Seven Provinces were to be formed. To tear down the old structure was easy. The Union of Utrecht was buried in the archives. The nobility were refused access to the States Assemblies; the office of stadhouder and grand pensionary were abolished as were the privileges of the former oligarchy; the East and West India Companies were liquidated and their possessions and debts transferred to the state; a war of extermination was waged against all heraldic emblems, liveries, titles, and whatever else was reminiscent of former class distinctions. More constructive was the admittance of the provinces of Drente and the oppressed people of Brabant to the States General for the first time.

The work of destruction cleared the way for radical reforms. The autonomy of towns and rural districts was erased by a stroke of the pen. The provinces were no longer sovereign; in future the minority in the States General was to submit to the majority. Reconstruction was easy so long as it meant only the pasting of new labels on old forms. The Rights of Man and of the Citizen were solemnly proclaimed; towns and rural districts were re-named; the slogan "Liberty, Equality, Fraternity" was printed and painted on all posters; finally the name of the state was changed to the "Batave Republic." Civilis and his warriors, so long the patron saints of the oligarchy, were appropriated by the new democracy. Few people suffered personally from the revolution. Some were arrested or exiled, among the latter William Bilderdijk, the only outstanding personality of the time in Dutch literature.

These innovations were dearly bought. France had helped the Patriots to victory but not out of pure brotherly love. She sought payment in money, territory and political privileges. Maastricht and Zeeland-Flanders were lost, French garrisons placed in the principal Netherland fortresses, and a huge war contribution was levied on the liberated Dutch sister republic. This did more than anything else to revive anti-French sentiment.

A National Convention elected by the people, Jews and Orangists excepted, toiled for years to frame a constitution. The discussions grew interminable, the stream of oratory flowed unchecked, and with factions evenly balanced, the Convention might have sat until Doomsday, writing a Constitution in many volumes—indeed their final draft was known as the "big book"—if French bayonets had not abruptly put an end to it. The leaders of the Federalist opposition were arrested, the French Constitution of 1795 was translated into Dutch and promulgated in a locally adapted version, and the Batave Republic was blessed with a new political organization. A second display of French military prowess enforced its adoption; a third, three years later (1801) abolished it in favor of an organization more congenial to the new French ruler, Napoleon Bonaparte. The dictator was dissatisfied, however, with the accomplishments of his new regime and by his orders, Rutger Jan Schimmelpenninck, former lawyer and revolutionary leader, found himself invested with full power, the title of grand pensionary, a military escort, and a suite of liveried footmen.[51]

His task was not to rule the Netherlands in their own interest as he had hoped to do, but to pave the way for a "king of Holland" in the person of Napoleon's brother, Louis Bonaparte. "The Netherlands" was now "Holland," a development that could have been foreseen for two centuries; but the House of Orange was replaced by a vainglorious if good-natured Corsican. The climate of the Netherlands did not suit him, and his rheumatism drove him from one residence to another in a futile attempt to escape the country's humidity and chilliness. The new monarch appointed numerous marshals and high ranking officials, adorned the breasts of his favorite officers with magnificent decorations, and created a new Dutch nobility from the descendants of the pre-republican aristocracy and the ranks of the former city oligarchy. Former "Patriots," who had once foamed against "tyranny and aristocracy," had no objection to being incorporated into this new nobility, created for the glory of a Corsican intruder. Even Bilderdijk, the defiant exile of 1795, returned to teach King Louis Dutch and become his court poet. Louis, intelligent but powerless against his brother the emperor, succeeded in gaining some popularity among his subjects by a display of sympathy with the needs of the Netherlanders and by an idle pretense of political independence. Netherlanders must not forget, however, that all the difficulties this king-by-the-grace-of-his-brother encountered in the four years of his reign sprang from his sincere desire to be more Dutch than French. For this reason the emperor dismissed him from his royal office as unceremoniously as he would have thrown out a valet, and incorporated the luckless Netherlands into the French state. The work of destruction begun by the revolutionists of 1795 had reached unexpected completion.

The political evolution was too rapid for people to adapt themselves to the successive changes. General political apathy overcame the masses. Resistance was limited to putting off as long as possible all changes or reforms, good or bad, demanded by the French dictator. Napoleon raged that "a people who refused to create an army had no right to independence," but he forgot that the Netherlands' will to independence would not have found adequate expression in the creation of an auxiliary corps for the emperor's bloody campaigns. He scolded Holland, calling her "an English province" because she refused to commit economic suicide by sacrificing all her foreign trade for the benefit of France. The Dutch had sold their colonies to Britain, he said, but what difference was there whether the Dutch flag was replaced by the tricolor or the Union Jack?

For generations every child in every Dutch school learned of the "French period" as one of degradation and inactivity, marking the lowest political ebb in Netherland national history. The unfortunate coincidence that with very few exceptions Netherland poets of the time produced merely bombastic rhetoric while claiming to excel Hooft and Vondel, has irritated posterity even more. Schimmelpenninck, whose rapid evolution from patriot-revolutionary to "Count of the Empire" rightly shocked the solid Dutch shopkeepers, and Herman Willem Daendels, who rose from small-town lawyer to "Marshal of the Empire" and reformer of the East Indian administration, caught the fancy of the next generation far less than the dramatic figure of the Corsican conqueror. Yet, the "French period" was something more in Netherland history than the lowest point of national life. In the fifteen years between 1795 and 1810 a new Netherland state was created and the foundations laid for some national institutions of which Dutch people are proud today.

The revolution destroyed provincialism and broke down the barriers that held the people of the small Netherland country apart in nine different local groups, each with its own local chauvinism that obscured broader national views. For centuries the people of Guelderland, of Zeeland, of Holland had clung stubbornly to provincial independence. In 1797, after three years' discussion in which the "Federalists," who presumably represented the majority of the Netherland people, put up a strong though losing fight, provincial autonomy had disappeared. For a while the provinces ceased even to exist, being replaced by arbitrarily delimited "departments," after the French model. This was too great a change and three years later the historic territorial divisions were restored, but provincialism had died. Hollanders, Zeelanders, Groningers were all Netherlanders now, or "Bataves" if revolutionists, or "Hollanders" if they bowed to foreign usage. Only in Friesland, where since the earliest Middle Ages provincial nationalism has been stronger than anywhere else, has it survived to some extent until the present, fostered by the persistence of the Frisian language in the rural districts. The lack of opposition to the political unification of the Netherlands once it was begun, is noteworthy. The reforms filled a need long felt but that tradition was reluctant to accept.

Political unification required a complete reform of local provincial administration. This was carried out in the tenth year of the revolution, but the new system was constantly changed until 1813, the year of liberation. In one respect, the Napoleonic system survives to this day: the enormous reduction of provincial influence in the administration. The excessive provincialism of the republican period had produced a reaction. Subsequent legislators have always hesitated to give power to provincial authorities.

Centralization also required a complete reform of finance and taxation.

The debts of all the provinces were amalgamated, and the millions owed by the former East India Company added to the total. This made a nice lump sum of about 600,000,000 guilders, increased by ten years of war to 1,100,000,000 guilders. The annual interest on this debt alone amounted to more than 30,000,000 guilders, which left not a cent of the state's income for the cost of administration or for further war expenditures. The "Patriots" found a financial expert, Isaac Gogel, who devised for the Netherlands the first modern system of taxation, which equitably distributed the incidence of taxation and doubled the income of the state.

Centralization of the government made possible a reorganization of the navy which as regards ships and equipment was better in this period of greatest humiliation than at any time during the XVIIIth century. The rank and file of the sailors, however, refused to risk their lives for a pro-French and anti-Orangist state. For the first time the army became a truly national institution, composed of Netherlanders and commanded by Netherlanders. It received its training under the Corsican on the battlefields of Europe. Centralization also entailed a total reorganization of the judiciary and the creation of a supreme court for the whole nation (1801), the introduction of a new criminal code, (mainly based on Roman-Dutch law), and of a civil code (based on the French Code Napoleon).

The first Constitution of the Batave Republic instituted a Department of Education (1798), a great novelty in XVIIIth century Europe. Educational reform, widely discussed in the Netherlands before the revolution under the influence of Rousseau, and of the reforms accomplished in Westphalia and Prussia by North German educators, could now break through the resistance of traditional institutions. Laws organizing education for the Netherland masses were promulgated in 1801 and 1803, and in 1806 they were put into effect. Qualification tests for teachers were introduced, new text books written, pedagogic methods studied and propagated. The general aim of Netherland education was "to form the mental abilities of the children and to develop in them civic and Christian virtues." Far-reaching educational reforms helped to maintain the high rank of the Netherlands among civilized nations. Many of these reforms were introduced rather dictatorially, but their effects were nonetheless beneficial. The second Netherland state could not have been built after the liberation without this preparatory work.

Besides these reforms, the revolution brought democracy in its modern sense to the Netherlands. The old democratic institutions of the Middle Ages had gradually disappeared, and the XVIIIth century had disposed of their last remnants in Friesland. Only in Drente had a semblance of democratic rural administration survived. The local autonomy that had persisted in the *Waterschappen*—drainage districts—had largely lost its democratic character. Here the revolution first democratized and then sought to suppress the institution, but practical difficulties happily prevented this and the *Waterschappen* remained an effective part of Netherland administration. In local and national government the French theories of 1797 prevailed, and the franchise was given to every Netherland male over twenty. Many historians contend that this enfranchisement was too rapid to be effective, that the people were not ripe for it. This seems hardly correct. In 1797 the draft of a constitution was submitted to a general plebiscite. Of 400,000 potential voters 137,000 went to the polls—one out of three—which, for a people without political experience and with a large percentage of illiterates was by no means bad. Moreover, Jews representing at least 20,000 voters were excluded, as were Orangists. A second plebiscite brought the number of voters up to 165,000. Even modern democracies at times find it difficult to get more than forty or fifty percent of their electorate to the polls. Then the number of voters dropped rapidly. In 1801 only 67,000 appeared at the polls, and in 1809 no more than 14,000—this time out of a restricted electorate of 350,000. This is easily explained by the conviction of the franchise holders that however they voted, the decrees submitted for their approval would be put into effect by virtue of Napoleon's military power behind them. One of the democratic rights given to the people was that of petition and the Dutch people knew how to use it; more than 200,000 names appeared on a petition for the maintenance of the ministers of the Reformed Church on the payroll of the state.

The National Convention of 1796 granted equality of rights to dissenters and Catholics and, after some hesitation, to Jews. Its attempts at a complete separation of Church and State failed. A privileged but no longer a dominating position was reserved for the Dutch Reformed Church. King Louis Bonaparte, officially a member of the Roman Catholic Church, promoted the interests of his co-religionists wherever he could without offending his Reformed subjects. In view of former conditions, it is not surprising that Catholics generally were among the most revolutionary and most democratic elements of the citizenry. Jews, who numbered about 80,000, mostly in Amsterdam, also viewed the revolutionary movement with favor, although their status had been more satisfactory than that of Catholics. Even among Baptists and other Protestant dissenters, a reaction against the former predominance of the Reformed Church lent support to the liberal groups. This growing party formation was rudely opposed by the French dictatorial regime, but it was not without future consequences.

The French period was by no means a social revolution, for the structure of Netherland society was hardly touched. There was no large-scale shifting of property rights, or complete overthrow of the leading classes as in France. The actual administration was taken out of the hands of the oligarchs to be entrusted to middleclass intellectuals but, as early as 1801 by order of Napoleon Bonaparte the revolutionary government began to encourage the return of patriot oligarchs to public office. Many Orangist oligarchs also joined the new regime after the peace treaty of 1806, when even the prince of Orange seemed satisfied to give up all claims to his Netherland offices and possessions. The elevation of Louis Bonaparte to the throne and the creation of a new nobility by this improvised monarch brought a rush of former oligarchs to the feet of His Corsican Majesty in the hope of being admitted and having their former rank restored. They showed striking lack of human dignity, but they retained their social privileges.

The French period was one of internal growth restricted by foreign domination. Not for a moment were the Netherlands permitted to follow their own course in national or international politics. Several times the Batave Republic sought to escape from strangling French control and return to a policy of neutrality between France and Britain, but Napoleon was far too alert for that. In exchange for their "cooperation," the Bataves gained a few minor advantages, such as the incorporation in the territory of the Republic of all former Prussian enclaves, a leftover of the faint-hearted Netherland policy in the Cleve-Juliers problem of 1609. Out of the Prussian debacle of 1806 King Louis even annexed East Friesland. The latter acquisition was valueless. Netherland influence had become extinct in the small country, and King Louis's officials met with distrust and opposition. The mistakes of the XVIIth century could not be rectified by the weak Netherland state of 1806.

The peace treaty of 1802 between France and Britain restored to the Netherlands all their lost colonies except Ceylon, and desperate attempts were made to save them from again falling into British hands. The leaders of the Batave Republic vainly sought to remain neutral when Franco-British hostilities were renewed in 1803, but Napoleon would permit no such combinations. The result was that by 1812 the Netherland flag was hauled down all over the world except, by the irony of history, in the island of Deshima near Nagasaki in Japan. The conservative Japanese authorities were obdurate in their determination to deal with Holland and Holland alone, whether a Netherland state existed or not. Under their protection, Commander Hendrick Doeff kept the Dutch flag flying over Deshima's trading post. The renewal of the war prevented the full development of the revolution in Java, where sudden and complete administrative and economic reform had finally come in 1808.

Java, the only important colony left to the Netherlands in 1805, three years after the renewal of conflict, was for sixteen years virtually isolated from the home country. The East India Company had been dissolved in 1796, and its territories had become part of the Netherland state. There was little change in Batavia during the first ten years of the new regime. A local demonstration of "revolutionists" was rapidly suppressed and its originators punished. The principles of "Liberty, Equality, and Fraternity" were never put into practice in the tropical Netherlands. The economic position of Batavia improved rapidly after the monopoly system had been modified by the necessities of war. Cut off from the Netherlands, the Batavian government was obliged to sell Java's products to neutrals. For a decade American trade with Batavia flourished, giving "Java coffee" the reputation that still makes its name valuable for advertising purposes in the United States. There was no lack of money in Batavia while this trade prospered and the friendship of the principal native rulers guaranteed internal security. Leading a semi-autonomous existence, the Batavian Government could take some liberties in international affairs, and it denied its resources to French military "advisors" sent from Europe to convert the island into an operational base against Britain.

Meanwhile, the republican government at home was discussing theories of colonial administration. Should Java be thrown open to free enterprise or not? Should the ancient forms of communal land-ownership be preserved, or should individual property rights be introduced in the hope of stimulating competition in accordance with economic theories then prevailing in Europe? On the whole, conservatism predominated in the council halls of The Hague. The East Indies were to be administered for "the greatest possible welfare of the inhabitants, the greatest possible advantage of Dutch commerce, and the greatest possible profit of the finances of the Netherland state,"—three aims difficult to reconcile. The principle that "colonies are maintained for the benefit of the mother country" easily prevailed. Batavia could ignore these theoretical discussions, and Bonaparte considered Java important only as a base for attack on British India.

For this purpose, Herman Willem Daendels, the ex-lawyer, ex-general, was sent to the Far East although he had not the slightest knowledge of Javanese affairs. There he thoroughly shook up the lazy, conservative and far from honest Dutch officials left over from the days of the Company. In a few years, he raised an army, built roads and defense works, organized a political administration instead of the former Company system based on commercial traditions, reorganized the judiciary, extended the compulsory production of coffee, and threw a large part of Java open to private enterprise. Government land was sold along with the natives in their villages and the governor general, faithful to the economic if not to the political principles of Liberalism, proclaimed "all protection of the native peasants to be merely an encouragement to laziness." He contended that free labor contracts between the planter-capitalists and the native workers would produce the greatest possible productivity. The former patriot, who had thundered against the "tyranny" of poor good-natured Prince William V became the worst of dictators. In 1811 his regime came to an end and a few weeks later Java was conquered by a strong force under Lord Minto, governor-general of British India. Whatever the merits and mistakes of Daendels, he had opened a new period in East Indian history.

For fifteen years the pro-French party in the Netherlands had carried on under the greatest difficulties. Their hands were never free, beset as they were with insoluble problems. Rich as the Netherlands were, no government could survive indefinitely when forced by foreign pressure to spend twice the amount of its revenues. Trade and industry came to a standstill. In the few months of 1802 and 1803 when peace prevailed, no less than four thousand Dutch merchantmen took to sea, many of them only to fall into British hands before they could return. Bonds issued by foreign government through Amsterdam banks before the war amounted to more than 650,000,000 guilders. The forty million guilders interest due on these bonds every year was never paid. Some bankers had exported part of their capital to the United States. The new American Republic, in dire need of capital, found a plentiful source in the money market of Amsterdam after the stabilization of her credit by Alexander Hamilton's financial reorganization. Dutch capital financed public works such as bridges and canals, and was invested in Hamilton's Society for the Establishment of Useful Manufactures. The largest of these Dutch capitalist concerns was the Holland Land Company, through which three Amsterdam bankers invested one and a half million guilders in land in upper New York State. About three million acres, still recognizable on the map by Dutch place-names—Amsterdam, Rotterdam, Batavia—became the property of this Company. Their investments brought only small returns. Besides American investments, large sums were safely deposited in London, and all through the French period Amsterdam bankers were able to continue transactions which preserved at least a part of Holland's economic power for the future. Agriculture and inland trade with Westphalia, the Rhineland, and Belgium alone flourished.

Misery and unemployment caused dissatisfaction; and the thoughts of the people turned to the past, when the House of Orange had been the traditional palladium of liberty and prosperity. But the prince—the son of William V—was powerless, and had sought refuge with his Hohenzollern relatives. On his estates in Silesia he waited for better times. The incorporation of the Netherlands in the French empire brought no financial relief. The most important innovations of Napoleon were a State Police, a necessary attribute of dictatorship; compulsory military service, which sent about twenty-eight thousand Netherlanders to bleed on a hundred battlefields from Lisbon to Moscow; the French Code Napoleon, which replaced the newly introduced Dutch Code; and the introduction of French as the official language, to be used in preference to or along with Dutch. Anti-French feeling among the people rose high. Some political leaders silently prepared for the restoration of independence. Only a few fanatic militarists, blind devotees of war, were really loyal to the Emperor. In general, apathy weighed heavily upon the nation. A visit by Napoleon brought the people cheering into the streets—not without some official encouragement—but the regular visits of French recruiting sergeants brought the peasants out with scythes and pitchforks, in futile efforts to save their children from Armageddon. A restoration of independence was impossible until Napoleon's power was broken by his enemies. His defeat in Russia caused some unrest; his defeat at Leipzig, a revolt.

The leader of the national movement was Gijsbrecht Karel van Hogendorp, a member of the former Orangist faction in the oligarchy. Hogendorp received enthusiastic support from some other members of the aristocracy, some officers of the army, navy, and merchant marine, part of the burgher class at The Hague, and the common people in Amsterdam; but in general the well-to-do classes were hesitant, and the former oligarchy fearful. The latter refused to take courageous action, and so forfeited all right to a leading role in the new Netherland state. An Orangist independence movement spread over the western part of the country, while in the eastern provinces the people warmly welcomed the advance units of a liberating allied army, bands of Cossacks and Prussian infantry. The prince of Orange entered The Hague on November 30, 1813. In two weeks' time the Netherlands were free. Popular uprisings and the allied invaders had driven out the enemy, whose troops, mostly of poor quality, had run away for fear of being cut off from the main body of the French army. Dutch volunteers engaged in a few skirmishes and contented themselves with surrounding and blockading the fortresses still under French control. But everywhere and unequivocally, even in the former "lands of the Generality" in Brabant, where people had little reason to cherish memories of the pre-French period, the masses expressed their determination to rebuild a free Netherland state.

This was undertaken by Prince William VI, son of Stadhouder William V, who had left in 1795 and died in exile. With the assistance of Hogendorp and others he hastily reorganized an administration, retaining the whole structure built up in the French period; began to build up an army and navy to give the Netherlands their rightful place among the allied nations and reasonable freedom of action in international affairs. In four months, 12,000 men were armed, equipped and trained—not a bad achievement if we consider that their armament had to be collected piecemeal or borrowed from Britain. Meanwhile an internal issue of the utmost importance had been settled. After some hesitation, the prince of Orange dropped all idea of restoring the ancient institutions and he accepted the sovereignty of the Netherlands, with the title of Sovereign Prince. But, as he expressed it himself in his first proclamation, "only under the guarantee of a wise constitution that will safeguard your freedom against eventual abuses." Thus, the long internal constitutional conflict, as old as the Republic of the Netherlands, came to an end with a reconciliation of monarchical and constitutional principles.

It remained to be determined what and whose this "freedom" was. Hogendorp seriously considered a partition of political influence between the new sovereign and the former oligarchy. In his proclamation to the people calling them to arms against the oppressor, he inserted the significant lines: "All leading people will have a part in the new government; the common people will have a holiday with entertainment at public expense." A "holiday" was a nice reward to offer for the fighting and work to be done. The "leading men" of the Batave tribe who had haunted the historians of the Republic since Grotius' time, were not yet laid in their long-forgotten graves, despite the efforts of Professor Kluit. Yet the "leading men" showed little interest in taking a share in political affairs. Several members of the committee appointed to draft a constitution under Hogendorp, preferred to let the ghosts of the past rest in peace and, in the mocking words of Talleyrand, "to lay the new sovereign in Napoleon's bed."

The few years of French domination had already created a bureaucracy whose ideal of service was to dictate laws from behind an office desk. In a way a belated revenge for Philip of Spain! This was much to the liking of the new sovereign, an ambitious, self-opinionated man whose temperament precluded a free exchange of ideas with others and whose enormous capacity for work predisposed him in favor of a bureaucratic administration. So in the new constitution the rights of the people were overshadowed by the power of the executive. His ministers were merely his servants. The Assembly of the States General was revived and its members elected by the provinces. They were no longer to represent these provinces but were

to act as an independent body, deciding by a majority. The influence of
the new States General was limited, however, for they exercised only a
limited control over public finances and their authority was not to be compared to that of the king. In case they were restored by Britain, the colonies
were to be administered at the pleasure of the sovereign. The States of the
various provinces, representing only a very small part of the people, were
purely formal institutions unable to withstand the powerful provincial
governors appointed by the sovereign.[52]

The new monarch found it easy to seize the reins of his administration
and surround himself with congenial advisors. Hogendorp did not long
enjoy his confidence. Cornelis van Maanen, a narrow-minded official—a
revolutionary who had become a servile official of the pro-French government and had held aloof from the national movement until he was sure
that going over would not hurt his interests—became the prince's principal
advisor. The choice indicated the predilection of the new ruler, and it
explains much of what was to come.

Foreign and not home affairs were the prince's first concern. His state
was established but what were its boundaries? Again the all-important
question of the eastern and southern frontier of the Netherlands had to be
faced. The ancient coastland tradition that "Holland lived by the sea and
should not be bothered with continental affairs" still survived. It was the
Amsterdam point of view, which persisted in considering Netherland territory as a mere glacis protecting the great port. In the XVIIth century
this conception had prevented territorial expansion to the south and east.
The princes of Orange had always been interested in the Netherlands as
a whole and given due consideration to frontier problems. An opportunity
to settle the problem seemed now to offer itself. The French Revolution had
incorporated both the Austro-Belgian provinces and the old bishopric of
Liége in the French Republic. Napoleon had erased all political entities that
existed before 1795 on the left bank of the Rhine and in Westphalia. These
territories had become "free," the restoration of their former rulers not
being contemplated by the great powers. Austria was no longer interested
in her former Belgian territory and the political extermination of the petty
German princes was convenient both to their peoples and to the great
powers. What was to be the fate of those territories?

Nobody thought it necessary to consult the inhabitants. In Great Britain
the opposition had criticized the recognition of the prince of Orange before
the Dutch people had expressed their preference for a monarchy or a
republic, but that had been a mere political gesture. No one even *thought*
of consulting the wishes of the liberated peoples. For many years, against
the wishes of his father, the old stadhouder, Prince William had planned

to restore Lowland unity as it existed in 1576. Such a reunion admirably suited British interests in 1798 and later years, when Britain was so dominated by fear of French expansionism that she wanted to create a strong bulwark on the French northern frontier. Every time post-victory settlements were discussed among the Allies of 1803, 1805, and 1809, Britain showed her desire for a union of the northern and southern Low Countries or for a division of the southern provinces between the Netherlands and one of the stronger German states, either Austria or Prussia. For a few years the British Government—a startling fact today!—worked to establish the Prussians in Brussels, Namur, and Ostende. The Netherlands were to receive Antwerp, Malines, and all land north of a line connecting these two cities with Maastricht.[53] Russia suggested the incorporation of both the Netherlands and Belgium into Prussia—which would have saved them from Hitler's invasion the worst possible way—but later Czar Alexander, under Polish influence, objected to the aggrandizement of Prussia. Neither Austria nor Prussia were particularly interested in acquiring territory west of the Meuse and neither objected in principle to the unification of the Low Countries.

Prince William, aware of this favorable disposition of the great powers, boldly advanced his own demands. They were amazingly large. Besides the unification of the Low Countries, he asked for all the territory between the north bank of the Moselle and the left bank of the Rhine. This would have made Coblenz the southeastern frontier-fortress of his kingdom. The prince even hoped to acquire a bridgehead on the right bank of the Rhine by the restoration and enlargement of his patrimonial domain of Nassau. He contended that only by such a wide extension of Dutch territory could the new Netherland kingdom be made secure. There was little likelihood that the ambitions of the first Dutch sovereign would be gratified. But his demands influenced British opinion. Lord Castlereagh first projected a southern boundary for the Netherlands including Antwerp, Malines, Maastricht, Juliers, and either Cologne or Duesseldorf, the remaining part of the southern Low Countries being reserved for Austria or Prussia.[54] After the refusal of both powers to commit themselves to the defense of the Low Countries by the acquisition of territory there, the British statesman projected a new line following the present northern boundary of France to the Sambre, then the course of that river to Charleroi, from where it was to follow the Meuse roughly with Dutch bridgeheads for the fortresses of Namur, Liége and Maastricht. Near Maastricht it was to run due east towards the Rhine, including Aachen, Juliers, and Cologne, into the Netherlands. The districts south of this line between the Meuse and the Rhine (including Luxemburg) he wanted to become Prussian, in order to interest both the Netherlands and Prussia in keeping France within the boundaries assigned to her.

The trouble with these plans, which did not go far enough to suit the wishes of Prince William, was that neither Prussia nor Austria was willing to accept them. Austria would gladly have left a considerable part of the land between the Meuse and the Rhine in the hands of France, simply to preserve France as a counterweight against Prussia. The Berlin government preferred expansion to the east (in Saxony and Poland) rather than to the west. As these wishes suited neither Austria nor Russia, Prussia sought compensation in a westward expansion, and this was fatal to Prince William's grandiose expectations. Prussia claimed that an aggrandizement increasing her population by four million souls had been promised to her, and four million souls she was going to have—souls being as easily shifted, apparently, as cattle. The powerful and victorious czar of Russia was willing to consent to any settlement of western European affairs on the sole condition that Great Britain and the Netherlands take over his debt to the Amsterdam banking house of Hope and Company, amounting to eighty million guilders. After some bargaining, the two western states bought the Imperial consent for fifty millions. The solution finally adopted was the union of Belgium and the Netherlands in the "Kingdom of the United Low Countries." The eastern boundary from the North Sea to the Meuse was to be largely identical with the pre-revolutionary demarcation. South of Nijmegen the boundary would follow the Meuse at "a gun-shot's distance" as far as the old principality of Valkenburg and from here it would coincide roughly with the eastern limits of the old duchy of Limburg. William, now King William I of the Low Countries, ceded his rights to his hereditary lands of Nassau in exchange for the duchy of Luxemburg, but the Netherlands and Luxemburg were only united by a personal union. The principality, then including both the present grand-duchy and the Belgian province of Luxemburg, was to be a member of the newly formed German confederation and its capitol was to be garrisoned by Prussian troops as a Federal German fortress.

The arrangement of 1815 deprived the Netherlands of their last chance for expansion over the duchy of Cleve and minor principalities in the Westphalian border area, such as Bentheim which then had close cultural ties with its western neighbor. To exchange these possibilities for a personal union with Luxemburg was a bad bargain indeed. Luxemburg, although united with the Low Countries since the first Duke Philip of Burgundy, had never taken part in Lowland affairs. It did not send its representatives to the States General in the Burgundian period; it was never counted among the "seventeen provinces"; it did not take part in the national revolt of 1576; it is geographically separated from the Low Countries by the difficult mountainous area of the Ardennes forest; it had no linguistic or cultural ties with the Lowlands. The acquisition by the House of Orange of the grand-duchy of Luxemburg with a Prussian garrison in its capital, an open boundary towards France, and its membership in the German confederation, could be only a burden to the Netherlands. However, King William sought to assimilate Luxemburg into his kingdom, practically as another province. The king's territorial ambitions had succeeded in extending his lands as far as the Moselle, but this merely weakened the new state. Yet it would be wrong to blame King William alone for the outcome of these negotiations. Prussia had excellent bargaining claims to territory on both banks of the Rhine, once part of Cleve, and to territory west of the Meuse and around Venlo, granted to her through the weakness of Holland's oligarchy in the War of the Spanish Succession. For this weakness the new Netherland kingdom had to suffer.

By separate agreement Great Britain consented to restore to the Netherlands most of their former overseas possessions. The western section of Guyana, Cape Colony, and Ceylon were to remain British. The Amsterdam merchants deplored the loss of Guyana where they had considerable investments, but the nation lost most in South Africa. The Cape was the only national overseas settlement where large numbers of Netherlanders could make a new home. Great Britain was under no moral or legal obligation to restore the colonies. The promise, made to the late Stadhouder William V in 1795, was annulled by the Treaty of Amiens, which was accepted by all parties concerned, even by Prince William, the stadhouder's son, then in exile in Germany. In restoring the colonies, Britain was prompted by the desire to strengthen the new Lowland state for it was to serve as "Britain's sentry on the continent" against France. Important in the return of the colonies was the disappointing financial result of British administration in Java and the Moluccas. Thomas Stamford Raffles, governor of Java during the British interregnum, vehemently protested against the cession of his beloved island and pointed out its future economic possibilities. This mattered little to the British statesmen whose attention was wholly concentrated on Europe. They knew little and cared less about Java.

The great powers agreed upon the reunion of the Low Countries. In the Netherlands apathy was stronger than antipathy to the proposal, but few were in favor of it. In Belgium the Catholic clergy and higher aristocracy—descendants of the aristocrats who had once been the colleagues of Prince William I of Orange—were definitely opposed to the plan. Their interests and their convictions alike called for a restoration of Austrian-Habsburg sovereignty, with privileges for the Catholic Church and diplomatic and military careers for the aristocrats. The liberal bourgeoisie, upper middleclass and intellectuals, regretted the secession from France. Thoroughly Frenchified during the revolutionary and Napoleonic eras, they had nothing in common with the Protestant, Dutch-speaking Netherlands and their burghers. The lower middleclass and the masses were more in favor of reunion, but who considered their opinion?

The Netherland constitution of 1814 was modified to suit the wishes of the Belgian leaders, for instance by the institution of an Upper Chamber, a sort of House of Lords, where the Merodes, the Aerschots, the Lignes could sit in state to discuss problems of high policy. Even so, the majority of the "notable people" of Belgium, convened by the king, rejected the constitution. King William ignored this vote of nonconfidence—he could hardly have done otherwise—but having forced acceptance of the constitution, he failed to heed the warning expressed in this vote and to make concessions to the large majority of the southern middleclass that had opposed his government. In fifteen years the union was broken, in spite of the great advantages Belgium gained from William's rule.

During the fifteen years that elapsed between the Congress of Vienna and the secession of Belgium, art, culture and politics were at a low ebb in the northern Low Countries. The southern provinces profited from the great romantic movement in France. In the north both French and German influence infiltrated, but only weakly. The citizens entrusted public affairs with confidence to "Father William," who indeed had their interest at heart but disliked to entrust power to others. The Netherlands which thirty years before had been a republic teeming with internal strife when adjacent monarchies were blessed with "enlightened despots," found themselves under an enlightened paternalism which vainly sought to rouse them from their economic lethargy. King William worked day and night; he invested millions of his own money in economic enterprises, loaned other millions to the state for public works. Canals were dug connecting the ports of Amsterdam and Rotterdam with the sea and providing shorter inland waterways intersecting the rivers; roads were built (which popular tradition in the Netherlands still ascribes to Napoleon!); manufactures were started, shipbuilding revived and the East Indian trade partly resuscitated through the establishment of the *Nederlandsche Handelmaatschappij* (the Netherland Society of Commerce).

But the Netherlanders remained lethargic. King William urged them forward but all attempts at restoring the ancient staple trades and shipping failed. The people had hoped that shipping would revive of its own accord as soon as the sea was free. For generations the Dutch had held a prominent place in all overseas trade; surely the world could not get along without the old-fashioned Dutch tramps on all the seven seas. But the world did get along without them and quite well at that. Even the East Indies seemed to get along without Dutch trade. The Netherland Society of Commerce was established on purpose to regain economic influence in territory which politically had been returned by Britain, but which economically was still wholly within her sphere of influence. It was doubtful how long the political authority of the Netherlands could be maintained under such circumstances. The Asiatic empire began to crumble from the moment of its re-establishment. Not that there was any difficulty in restoring Dutch authority over Java, for this was done without any disturbance or resistance. Some opposition manifested itself in the Moluccas when the natives of these islands became fearful of a restoration of the old monopoly system.

It was not the natives, but certain Britishers who proved dangerous to the re-established Batavian government. Thomas Stamford Raffles, back in the Indies as governor of British Sumatra, a small strip of territory on the southwestern coast of the island, harassed the Dutch whenever he could and persisted in setting up new British outposts in territory that was clearly Dutch under the treaty of 1814. After numerous raids and equally numerous rebukes from his own superiors, he finally founded Singapore on the southern point of Dutch Malaya. It was a master stroke. Long and tedious negotiations ended with an exchange of territory in 1824. Malaya became British and British Sumatra became Dutch. The British promised to refrain from further incursions into the East Indian islands. The Batavian Government was then faced with a revolt of part of Java under a prince of Djokjakarta and bothered little about Malaya or Sumatra, so good relations were re-established. However, the urge to restore the Netherlands as the center of the spice and coffee trade was naturally strengthened by these events.

Commerce had changed since the middle of the XVIIIth century, and the full results of that transformation now became apparent. Producers of export goods sought direct contact with their consumers, and business men from Russia or Germany ordered their merchandise direct from the producing areas without resorting to intermediate markets like the Netherlands. Traditional methods of handling merchandise in Dutch ports further prevented a recovery of Holland's former commercial position. The XIXth century brought an enormous increase in the volume of merchandise transported, and the out-of-date regulations prevailing in Amsterdam and Rotterdam were a hindrance to mass exchange. Finally the increase in the tonnage of merchant ships made entrance to Dutch harbors impossible. Dutch trade and shipping continued to decline until the second half of the XIXth century.

Poverty was general. Of two million inhabitants, seven hundred thousand were dependent upon charity, if contemporary reports are reliable. Societies were founded to take the destitute of the cities back to the countryside. Colonies were started in the peat districts of Friesland and Groningen. These methods proved only palliatives for the needs of the masses. For the first time there was mass emigration from the Netherlands to America, under the combined effect of poverty and religious persecution. That too occurred in the XIXth century in the Netherlands, albeit in a comparatively mild form. Proportionally the number of emigrants remained far below that of many other European countries at the same time, and Dutch immigrants arriving in the United States were never so completely destitute as many of the Irish and Germans. Yet the departure of more than thirty thousand people in forty years for unknown lands where foreign tongues were spoken presents a striking contrast to the XVIIth century when it was difficult to find a few thousand settlers for New Netherland.

Religious persecution has been mentioned as one of the causes of this emigration. King William, becoming more autocratic with the passing of time, had incorporated all Dutch Reformed churches into one National Church, over which the State exercised a certain supervision. The new national Church was dominated by a rationalist interpretation of dogma. The Synod of Dordrecht, the foundation of the Church in Republican times, was abhorred as a monument of intolerance and narrow-mindedness. Official Calvinism became formal, traditional and lifeless, without strength of faith. Willem Bilderdijk, the poet-historian, was one of the first to raise his voice against this trend. After the restoration he devoted his time to lectures on Netherland history at the university of Leiden. Holding no official position, he gathered small classes of voluntary students around him and for their benefit expounded his views in the form of a running and violently critical commentary on Wagenaar's history. Wagenaar had presented the oligarchic-republican view of the past. Bilderdijk, taking as a basis the work of Kluit but exaggerating wildly, denounced all oligarchic leaders as criminals, fools or worse, and lauded without measure the House of Orange and Unionist factions in the Republic. He scoffed at Grotius and his theory of the *Antiquity of the Batave Republic*. Civilis, so long the idol of republicanism, was put in his proper place as a mere rebel against mighty emperors. The long buried sovereignty of the provincial States Assemblies was covered with invective. Despite his strong bias, the force of his personality and his burning conviction aroused in his youthful listeners sentiments and ideas that contributed greatly to the shaping of future Netherland social institutions.

Bilderdijk became one of the originators of a religious revival among the intellectual classes. Another movement among the rural population of the northern and eastern provinces called for a return to the principles of Dordrecht, a dogmatic and strict ecclesiastical discipline. To its adherents state interference in religious affairs was as abhorrent as it had been to the first Calvinists. State interference, they contended, undermined dogma and fostered laxity of discipline. In separation from the official Reformed Church they saw the only possibility of reform. King William opposed this on legal grounds. Gradually a conflict developed which led to the persecution of the separatists and their emigration to the United States, where in Michigan and Iowa their descendants continue to follow the religious traditions of their ancestors. It is safe to say however, that without stringent poverty among the rural classes, emigration would never have drawn so many overseas.

This religious conflict came to a head after 1830. In nearly all fields of spiritual activity, the first twenty years of William's reign were lifeless. An Amsterdam Chief of Police—both man and office left over from Napoleonic days—objected to performances of Shakespeare and Schiller. "Something in between the Greek and the French drama" seemed to him suitable for the Amsterdam public. So he sought to combine his function of chief of police with that of playwright, but with poor artistic results. Even so, for the public his art was not too low, but rather too high. The quiet, pious Amsterdam burghers preferred shows with a great display of costumes and ballets. Some promise was shown in literature and painting, but it was not until the middle thirties that anything original was done in the world of letters, and painting had to wait another decade or so. Music was "no longer an art but merely a pastime" according to a contemporary critic, and it was not until 1840 that Beethoven's Ninth Symphony was performed in the Netherlands. Foreigners said that the only music Dutchmen enjoyed was the tinkling of coins and of church bells, but there was an orchestra in Amsterdam's aristocratic club *Blaas en Strijklust,* freely translated: "The Friends of Blowing and Bowing." These enthusiasts did not achieve much and German musicians—it was the time of Schubert, Mendelssohn and Schumann—came to the rescue of Dutch music-lovers. A German Opera Company brought Mozart and Weber to Amsterdam. Around 1830 new blood began to circulate in the lifeless body of Dutch art, but it was not thoroughly animated for a long time.

Music had greater appeal in Brussels than in Amsterdam. Brussels has probably the unique distinction of having begun a successful revolution in an opera house. The performance of Auber's *La Muette de Portici* in August 1830 was the beginning of the anti-Netherland revolt that ended with the disruption of the recently united Low Countries. From the stage sounded the inflammatory, though somewhat bombastic lines:

"For a slave what peril counts,
Better death than live in chains.
Off the yoke that stifles us!
Perish aliens at our hands,
Holy lore of native land
Give me courage, give me pride!
To my country, life I owe,
And she owes me liberty!"

Wild applause, general commotion among the audience, which was taken up by crowds of young people in the street, and the revolution was started.

In 1830 the Belgians were not, of course, the "slaves of foreigners," nor were they living miserably. They had benefited perhaps more than the Netherlanders from King William's reign, for his economic policy of tariff barriers served the industrial interests of Belgium better than the commercial interest of Holland. The port of Antwerp, in chains for two centuries, was free for the first time since 1585. It became so much more prosperous than Amsterdam and Rotterdam, that it provoked the jealousy of its northern competitors. Religious worship was free in Belgium, although King William made a great mistake in tampering with the Catholic Church, its relations with Rome and its seminaries. Belgium was far more populous than the Netherlands—three and a half million inhabitants against two millions. In spite of centuries of economic restriction, its prosperity if not its wealth was considered greater than that of the Netherlands. King William had caused dissatisfaction among the higher classes by forcibly promoting the use of the Dutch language in the Flemish speaking provinces. Such grievances added to political objections to the absolute character of the monarchy outweighed what economic advantages the Belgian middle class and industrial interests derived from the union. A lack of mutual understanding had been fostered by the economic and political events of the two preceding centuries, and King William was not the right man to deal with such a delicate situation. Add to it the religious antithesis and the old self-centered attitude of the province of Holland, whose interests had been impaired rather than fostered by the union. Of all these factors a group of pro-French Belgians decided to take advantage.

The "uprising" following the performance of *La Muette de Portici* was organized, but the movement immediately got out of hand and assumed the aspect of a proletarian revolution in which the poorest elements of the cities vented their anger against the wealthier classes. France had known similar proletarian uprisings and even in Britain the masses were in ebullition. Factories and machines were destroyed. The government hesitated and failed to subdue the opposition either by blandishment or by force. They allowed the middleclasses in Brussels to take the restoration of order into their own hands; subsequently they attacked Brussels only to withdraw their troops; finally they succeeded in antagonizing their own partisans. This development was not unpleasing to strong groups in the North. It found natural support in France and unexpected sympathy in Britain, where the trend of foreign policy had changed and France was no longer considered a danger. The forcible protection of Dutch shipping by King William threatened to revive the Netherlands as a possible rival for control of the North Sea. Without Britain's support the union of North and South could never have been accomplished; and against her will it could hardly survive the slightest strain.

The events of 1830 rent asunder the entire political structure of the Low Countries. The issue was settled in a few weeks. The Netherlands and Belgium were again to be separated. Only the terms of separation remained to be determined. Nine years elapsed before both parties finally consented to an agreement which had been drafted in 1831 after the intervention of France and Britain. The conditions of the agreement may be considered favorable to the northern state, for some districts where the revolution had gained the upper hand, the towns of Venlo and Roermond on the Meuse for instance, were restored to its sovereignty. This was due to a short campaign in which Netherland troops defeated the newly formed Belgian army. Although the large majority of Northerners was quite satisfied to be separated from Belgium, King William persisted in refusing his consent in the vain hope that a change in the international situation might provide an opportunity to obtain better terms. This policy merely burdened the Netherland state with unnecessary military expenditures. As the unsettled dispute dragged on, he gradually lost the popular affection he had won by fifteen years of constant labor for the economic welfare of the country. The final arrangement of 1839 left the Netherlands all the territory they possessed before 1795 and in addition a strip of land connecting Maastricht and the old county of Valkenburg with Venlo and Brabant. The duchy of Luxemburg was divided, half of its territory going to Belgium.

The arrangement of 1839 left the Netherlands with a very weak southeastern boundary. At one place the strip of Dutch soil between the Belgian and German frontiers was only three miles wide. To make matters worse, the province of Limburg, although remaining an integral part of the Netherlands, became a member of the German confederation. This confusing relationship lasted until 1868. The treaty of 1839 declared Belgium a neutral state, with its integrity guaranteed by Britain, France, and Prussia. This guarantee was not extended to the Netherlands, nor did they join in guaranteeing Belgian neutrality, but the natural effect of the new situation was that they too fell back into complete and passive neutrality. Great Britain had been King William's strongest supporter in the unification of the Low Countries, and Great Britain was also one of the principal agents of its dissolution. The close political connection that had existed between the Netherlands and Britain for fifteen years between unification and dissolution ceased to exist. Netherland neutrality, albeit a long standing political tradition, was now the result of resentment and weakness. It took decades for the nation to overcome the blows of 1830 and 1839 which reacted severely upon its political self-esteem. In some respects the events of 1839 and later years were a success for the cautious, Hollandish, burgherclass conception of the Netherland state over the more national and more daring aspirations represented in former days by the princes of Orange and their adherents. These events placed the land provinces completely under the influence of Holland. They also invited stronger German cultural and economic ties which had previously been much less close than those with France and Britain.

The experiment of 1815 had been most unfortunate. Whatever the desirability or possibility of a reunion between north and south, the way in which the problem was handled in 1815 was definitely wrong. It would have been difficult to choose a less opportune moment for reunion, than immediately after the Napoleonic period, when the peoples of north and south had drifted farther apart than ever before. In theory the union of the Low Countries in 1815 was an integral fusion of two existing units, but even King William realized that this did not correspond to reality, and that his was a dual monarchy. The ingenious constitutional prescription that The Hague and Brussels should serve alternately as residences of the king and the States General made this clear. Moreover, the new kingdom contained elements such as the city of Liége which had never before been incorporated into either of the Low Countries. This purely French center might eventually find its place in a Belgian state, but would never fit into a predominantly Dutch speaking entity. The bond of language made the South share in all French Catholic and French Liberal movements, in which the North took little or no interest. If the reunion was to be undertaken, it should have been in the form of a federation, not of a complete fusion. But fusion held greater attraction for the Northerners. Their national debt had risen to 1,726,000,000 guilders or nearly 850 guilders per inhabitant. As the payment of interest on this huge sum was utterly beyond the capacity of the nation, the government extended a decree of Napoleon, under which two-thirds of the debt was "postponed" without interest. The southern provinces had a debt of 26,000,000 guilders, less than seven and a half guilders per inhabitant. That was why the Northerners favored total fusion. The financial advantages derived from fusion proved to be only temporary.

The separation left the Netherlands in a most difficult position. The public debt had again risen. In addition to the "postponed debt," the state owed 1,324,000,000 guilders. The public income was barely sufficient to meet the regular expense of the administration. King William, who had kept all financial matters in his own hands, who had stretched the terms of the Constitution to exclude public control of the budget, had to leave the solution of this problem to his successor. For years he had hoped that sooner or later the "fabulous wealth" of the Indies would come pouring in again, as it was supposed to have done in the good old days, and that Javanese labor and tropic fertility would restore the finances of his state. To this end he introduced a new system of exploitation in Java, the so-called "Culture System", no great returns from which resulted until after the old king had ceded his crown to his son. King William knew how dissatisfied his subjects were with the outcome of his administration. It embittered him, for he felt that his subjects had left all public cares to him, taking no perceptible interest, only to blame him for having ruled alone when his work proved a failure. He abdicated in 1840 and withdrew to Berlin, where he died three years later. His son William II succeeded him.[55]

When King William I retired, the paternal system of government disappeared. William II disliked to surrender authority even to the States General, but being more versatile than his father he could more easily adapt himself to circumstances. A restoration of public finances was the only real reform he attempted until the year of revolution (1848) convinced him that the time for constitutional reform had come. Of his own volition and out of a high sense of public duty, he ordered a study made of essential changes in the country's political institutions. The work of the committee appointed for this purpose received force of law with the revision of the Constitution agreed to on November 3, 1848. The second Netherland state had become a parliamentary monarchy.

CHAPTER XII

The Democratic Kingdom

THE crisis of 1830 was a severe blow to the kingdom of the Netherlands and affected its power and international prestige. The constitutional reform of 1848 marked the beginning of a revival which slowly restored the nation's position in world affairs. To understand the Netherland nation of today, its national consciousness and pride, one must know the Netherlands of 1840 and appraise the progress made in the past one hundred years. Not the glorious memory of XVIIth century power, but the joy and pride of having transformed the dull narrow-minded community of 1840 into the enlightened and progressive democracy of 1940 is the living source of Netherland patriotism. While the "burgher" of the middle 1800's dreamt of Michiel de Ruyter and John De Witt and basked in the glory of the past, the modern Netherlanders are proud of the great achievements and high culture of their *own* generation.

The kingdom inherited by King William II in 1840 was composed of the same three territorial units that today form the Netherland State—the Netherlands in Europe, the Netherlands West Indies (now officially designated as "Surinam and Curaçao"), and the Netherlands East Indies. Besides these, the Netherlands still possessed a small colony on the African Gold Coast. No attempt was made to develop it after the abolition of the slave trade, and in 1873 it was ceded to Britain in exchange for certain rights in Sumatra. The territory of the European Netherlands is so small— 13,000 square miles—compared to the West Indian area of more than 55,000 square miles and the East Indian island world covering no less than 735,000 square miles, that its economic dependence on the East and West Indies seemed a foregone conclusion, especially in the XIXth century, when the home country had lost so much of its commercial and political importance. To form a reasoned judgment on the European Netherlands, a prior investigation into the interrelations of the overseas territories and their value to the homeland is necessary.

In 1840 as in 1940, the three units comprising the Netherland State formed a single political entity. But, contrary to what now obtains, none of the overseas territories in 1840 enjoyed autonomy. With the sole exception of the East Indian judiciary they were entirely subject to the home country and were administered from Europe. The government of Batavia never enjoyed any autonomy except that which slow and difficult communications confer on a distant executive, however subordinate to higher authority at home. The history of the West Indies was different. For more than a hundred years Surinam, once a British settlement, had possessed some degree of self-government, and the colonists elected a representative council. After the restoration of 1816, this elective body was transformed into a cooptating council, modeled on Dutch oligarchic lines. In 1828, even this remnant of popular influence was destroyed and Surinam was placed under the absolute rule of a governor appointed by the king. Curaçao and the other Dutch West Indian islands were subordinate to the same executive until 1845. The restoration of the former council in 1832 brought no change, as only plantation owners or their representatives were eligible. As nearly all plantations were owned by bankers and capitalists in Amsterdam, the council actually represented only absentee-owners and not the inhabitants of the colony.

The Constitution of 1815 gave the king absolute and exclusive control over the colonies, the word "exclusive" having been inserted into the paragraph against the wishes of Van Hogendorp who drafted the constitution. The king was even relieved of rendering any account to the States General of eventual revenues from the colonies or of how these revenues were spent. Between 1815 and 1848, the colonies were no concern of the Netherland nation, but only of the king. The constitution of 1848 reversed the situation, giving full control over colonial affairs to the States General. It did not provide for or even contemplate colonial autonomy. It did, however, establish distinct colonial administration which made it possible to introduce autonomy.

Any grant of autonomy raises the question whether the colonies are "ripe" for it. What were conditions in the Netherland overseas territories in the middle of the XIXth century? The West Indian possessions were virtually bankrupt. The slave trade, once the chief source of Curaçao's prosperity, had come to an end at the beginning of the century. The British abolished slavery in 1834. Fourteen years later the French followed suit. The Dutch lagged behind. The conservatives retarded emancipation until 1862, when a law to that effect was finally passed by the States General. By that time Curaçao was economically dead. For more than sixty years after 1850, the population remained stationary and did not exceed 32,000. Prosperity burst upon the island after the last war, when international oil companies built refineries there for Venezuelan oil. As late as 1880, out of a total Curaçao budget of half a million guilders, the Netherland Government had to contribute 150,000. The plight of Curaçao's island dependencies—

Aruba, Bonaire, San Saba, St. Eustachius and St. Martin—was even worse.

In the XVIIIth century the last three islands had been centers of sugar production and, during the American war of Independence, had profited enormously from smuggling ammunition to the revolutionists. In the XIXth century these sources of income had dried up, and the population of the islands dwindled. St. Eustachius' 10,000 inhabitants fell to only 1,400 in 1914, and since then their number has further declined. St. Martin lost half its inhabitants. Bonaire and Aruba suffered less. During the XIXth century their populations increased slowly, making a precarious living from agriculture and cattle raising. On these two islands the inhabitants are nearly all of mixed Negro and Indian blood, while the three Dutch Windward Islands are partly inhabited by whites. Around 1860 both groups were equally destitute. Only the Jewish community of Curaçao maintained some degree of prosperity; but many of its members, seeing their economic opportunities diminish, left for more promising areas.

Economically these islands could not support themselves. The discovery of phosphate deposits on Curaçao in 1875 gave some financial relief, but by the end of the century the colony was again in dire need of assistance. "Paternal" administration under the exclusive control by the Crown had left unpleasant memories. It had been, as a member of the Dutch parliament said "a period of continuous neglect, compulsion, and arbitrary rule"; but it is doubtful whether the islands could have flourished under *any* system. The causes of decay were beyond government control.

In Surinam, conditions were no better. Before emancipation there were about 50,000 inhabitants, of whom 36,000 were slaves. The plantations were all near the coast. The interior was thinly settled by bush negroes, descendants of run-away slaves, and a few thousand aboriginal Indians. Sugar had been the main source of agricultural wealth. It was ruined by the rise of European beet production. After emancipation the surviving plantations suffered from lack of labor. The condition of the plantations became hopeless, and the question was again raised whether Surinam could not provide a home for Netherlanders, who at this time were going by the thousand to the United States. An experiment was tried with a group of some four hundred Dutch peasants. Half of them died in the first few months. Neglect on the part of the administration was one of the causes of the catastrophe. The remainder wandered through the more accessible parts of the colony and finally settled in three places where five hundred of their descendants still live. In the opinion of Dutch colonial authorities, this showed that white colonization was impracticable although, compared to the experiences of the first British settlers in Virginia or of American pioneers in the Far West, the result was not discouraging. One thing appeared certain:

if Europeans were to make Surinam a land of white settlers, they could not suffer the competition of colored immigrants whose lower standard of life would make lucrative farming impossible for them. However, the colonial administration indulged in a series of experiments in colonization, which soon deprived white people of any chance. The first Dutch peasants came in 1845. A few years later some 500 settlers from the Island of Madeira were brought in, followed by 2,500 Chinese. The Chinese deserted the farms and plantations to devote their energies to more congenial tasks like shopkeeping. Then in 1873 the Government sought to meet the labor shortage by importing more than 30,000 British Indians. Shortly afterwards the influx of Javanese began. These successive waves of immigration made Surinam an ethnological and linguistic curiosity but added little to its productivity. As before, the colony remained dependent upon subsidies from home, which between 1870 and 1910 varied from 16,000 to 720,000 guilders annually.

From the above it will be clear that neither Surinam nor the island group was really "ripe" for autonomy. The Administration Act of 1865 however, introduced partial self-government by granting both territories colonial "States Assemblies," elected by a small number of franchise holders. The franchise, dependent on the payment of income tax, was exercised in Curaçao by about five percent of the population and in Surinam by one percent. Prior to the last war, this arrangement seemed satisfactory. With unexpected prosperity the post-war period was to bring new problems to some of the territories.

The Netherland State certainly derived neither luster nor power from its West Indian possessions in the XIXth century. The East Indies presented a totally different picture. King William I had begun by a fairly liberal administration of the East Indies. Many of the East India Company's institutions had disappeared during the French period and the ensuing British occupation. Daendels had reorganized the administration; and Raffles the system of taxation. The latter reform had completely transformed the character of European rule. The Company had levied taxation in the form of "forced deliveries," the compulsory production and delivery to Batavia's storehouses of products of commercial value. These taxes had been levied through native rulers and district chiefs, who retained their share and employed what methods they pleased to collect the produce. Raffles imposed taxation directly on the producer and although levying it in the form of agricultural produce, he was satisfied with such products as the native peasants grew for their own needs. Raffles's system was adapted from the tax methods used by the British in Bengal, and its introduction in Java was prompted by a sincere desire to improve the fate of the poor Javanese peasants, who had been terribly exploited by their local chiefs for the benefit both of the Dutch overlords and of the chiefs themselves. The main defect of Raffles's system was that it did not bring in sufficient income to maintain the administration. So in the mountainous districts south of Batavia, administratively set apart from the rest of Java for this purpose, compulsory coffee production was maintained under the old system.

King William I had to solve the problem of providing the East Indian administration with sufficient income without draining the Netherlands, as the East India Company had done in the last decades of its existence. The Company had found some returns, however inadequate, from Asiatic products. King William could expect even less returns. Java produced quantities of coffee, but after the Napoleonic wars the bottom had fallen out of the market. The spices of the Moluccas no longer brought the former high prices now that the monopoly of the islands had been broken by India. The British had surrendered political control over the Malay archipelago but still held first place in that area as importers and traders. To exclude the British from the Dutch Indies by barriers of any kind was explicitly forbidden by the treaty of London under which the colonies had been restored to the Netherlands. To all these problems were added Javanese unrest in Djocjakarta and intrigues by Mr. Raffles. Around 1826 the situation was so hopeless that withdrawal from the East seemed the most sensible policy for the Netherlands to follow.

In these circumstances the "Culture System" was introduced on the advice of Johannes van den Bosch, governor general of the Indies from 1830 until 1833. This system combined the tax methods of the Company and of Raffles, requiring each producer to devote a certain amount of land and labor to the production of commercially valuable crops. Fortunately for the Netherlands, prices again rose in Europe after the post-Napoleonic depression, and soon enormous quantities of sugar and coffee began to fill the warehouses of Amsterdam, which regained its position as a world market for colonial products. Chronologically, the culture system belongs to the reign of King William I; but it did not produce its effect until the reign of William II. The remittances from Batavia to the Netherland treasury during the first fifteen years of the new system were, in principle, applied to the settlement of East Indian debts to the home country, amounting to more than 168,000,000 guilders. This figure included the 134,000,000 taken over in 1796 from the East India Company by the State. During the reign of King William II, returns from the East Indies averaged 14,000,000 guilders a year, rising in the next decade to an average of 28,000,000. The Culture System gave the East Indies new significance for the Netherlands. For the first time a clear and sizeable profit was being derived, that did not disappear into the pockets of a few people but alleviated the financial burden of the whole population.

The new system of exploitation focused Dutch interest on the island of Java, where alone it was fully applied. The Moluccas were of less interest than Java, and the other Dutch outposts in the archipelago had more political than economic significance. So long as Java remained a gold mine for Dutch finances, the government hesitated to expand its rule over less developed regions. This permitted further encroachments upon Netherland rights in the archipelago. In 1846 a British adventurer settled on Borneo's north coast, where he acquired the island of Labuan for his government and the succession to the throne of the native sultanate of Sarawak for himself. Protests by Netherland authorities were ignored. Great Britain, after 1830, had little interest in fostering good relations with the Netherlands.

In the Dutch Asiatic empire, exploited solely for the benefit of the Netherlands, there could be no question of autonomous institutions. Batavia still maintained its old principle of dual administration by which native rulers and political administration continued under Dutch supervision. This system implied respect of native laws and customs, and the administrative segregation of Netherlanders, Chinese and Indonesians. The Administration Act of 1854 sanctioned all these institutions, despite protests by a small group of progressives under the leadership of Walter van Hoevell, a former minister of the Reformed Church in the Indies. They denounced the Culture System as pernicious, but failed to obtain the support of the Liberals as a group. Van Hoevell was the first to state the principles that "the welfare of the colonists should be above all, and before all." The Administration Act of 1854 went no further than to guarantee the traditional rights of the natives to elect their headmen, to enjoy village autonomy and to maintain their own customary laws. As for the Netherlanders, the Act stipulated that they should be subject to laws as closely resembling those of the Netherlands as circumstances permitted.

The Culture System was utterly incompatible with the principles of liberalism. "Prosperity through compulsion"—the fundamental idea of Governor General Van den Bosch—did not and could not go hand in hand with "prosperity through individual liberty." Opposition from progressive groups pointed to the hardships wrought by the System; to famines in several districts; to arbitrary acts by officials; to oppression by native district chiefs, who forced the villagers to work far beyond the legally required limit so as to increase their bonus from additional production, and similar abuses. On the other hand, real prosperity did result from the compulsory system, and numerous new crops (tea and chincona for instance) were introduced into the Indies. The area under production increased; the population more than doubled between 1815 and 1858, growing from 5,000,000 to 11,700,000! These results would hardly have been possible if the System had caused general and constant misery. But however bright the financial picture, there was another and darker side. Apart from the exploitation of the Indonesians, the ambition of Batavian officials under pressure from the home government to increase the yearly returns was reflected in the extreme penuriousness of the East Indian administration. Education, public works, even the protection of Netherland rights outside Java, were all neglected for the benefit of the Dutch treasury.[56]

The financial returns the Netherlands in Europe drew from the Indies made even Liberals reluctant to change so profitable a system. Around 1850 conditions in the Netherlands were such that the eventual loss of twenty million guilders of public income would have been disastrous. In 1849 the kingdom in Europe had 3,000,000 inhabitants as against 2,800,000 in 1840 and 2,000,000 in 1815. Until 1870 the increase of population was slow, only 27,000, or less than one percent a year. From that year to 1890 the increase was 70,000 or about one and a half percent annually, reaching a total of 5,000,000 in 1899. The growth was not equal in all parts of the kingdom. The "big cities"—Amsterdam in 1849 had only 224,000 inhabitants—grew faster than the countryside; and the density of population increased far more in Holland, now divided into the two provinces of North and South Holland, than in the eastern and southern provinces. In the cities the population doubled in the second half of the century. Rotterdam grew from 90,000 inhabitants to 286,000. The three southern provinces lagged far behind, with an increase of only 32 to 36 percent in fifty years. Immigration played a very small part in the increase in population, the total number of foreigners in the Netherlands never exceeded 50,000 in the second half of the XIXth century. Of these 30,000 were Germans and 13,000 or 14,000 were Belgians. The number of foreign immigrants about balanced that of Dutch emigrants, an average of 4,000 annually.

This steadily increasing population had to find employment within the narrow boundaries of the Netherlands. Of the arable soil 33 percent was pasture land, 23 percent cultivated and, in 1833, 27 percent fallow. After fifty years that last percentage was reduced to 21, much of the land remaining uncultivated being barren. In 1849, the Netherlands with its 230 inhabitants to the square mile, was already one of the most densely populated areas in Europe. Before the end of the century this figure rose to 380. Commerce, shipping, and industry had to be increased to provide employment. In the middle of the century nearly one-third of the population lived by agriculture and cattle-raising. This proportion could not be maintained with the steadily rising birth rate. New drainage works could give little and only temporary relief. Between 1815 and 1840, 68,000 acres of land were won by dyking-in and drainage. In the next twenty-five years the total rose to more than 150,000 acres, including the land reclaimed in 1852 by drainage of the Haarlemmermeer, the 79,000-acre inland sea south of Haarlem.

The 1840's saw a deep depression in Netherland agriculture. After 1850 a steady rise of prices brought relief to the peasantry; but the absence of any surplus arable soil obliged shipping and industry to absorb the excess of available labor. But shipping and industry were so backward that competition with foreign countries seemed impossible. In Britain and other countries, sailing vessels were being rapidly replaced by steamships, but in the Netherlands only one ship out of a hundred was a steamer. Industry was wholly dependent upon the outside world for raw materials. The cotton manufacturers of Overijssel could not compete with British producers. During the period of the Culture System the import of Netherland cotton goods into the Indies declined, while that of British goods increased. Even the fisheries, the original source of Netherland prosperity, were affected by the general depression. Many cumbersome regulations dating from the Middle Ages prevented this branch of industry from regaining its former prosperity. Even when ships entered Dutch ports (not without difficulty because of their condition) transportation inland was lacking because railroads had not been developed. The *trekschuit,* the river-steamer, the mail coach seemed good enough in a country where distances were so short.

Under these circumstances the mass of the people had little to expect. Wages of one guilder a day were normal, as was the exploitation of child labor. The hardships of the laboring class were simply ignored by the self-satisfied bourgeoisie. There was still plenty of capital in the Netherlands, but little spirit of enterprise among the middleclass. Inertia and tradition militated against economic progress. In the years around 1850 the Netherland State was unable to make ends meet without revenues from Java. In 1849 the Netherland budget in Europe was a little more than 70,000,000 guilders. Netherland taxpayers provided 50,000,000, the Indies 20,000,000. As a contemporary said, the Indies were "the cork that kept the Netherlands afloat." Taxation amounted to 17 guilders per head of the population and its incidence was such that it was almost equally divided among all citizens, poor or rich. Twenty-eight millions obtained through indirect taxes and excise placed a burden of forty or fifty guilders annually on a working class family. Such conditions obliged poor parents to send their children to work, regardless of other considerations. Of the 70,000,000 guilders collected from all sources, fifty percent was spent on the interest and sinking fund of the national debt. Another 18,000,000 were spent for defense, one-third on the navy and two-thirds on the army. The Department of the Interior, including Education, had to be satisfied with a meager four millions. The average income of teachers, as late as 1850, was 200 guilders a year, with free housing and profits from the sale of books and writing material to the pupils.

The Netherland intellectuals of 1850 looked to the past. They were satisfied to belong to the nation of Vondel, of Cats, of Rembrandt, of Michiel de Ruyter, of John De Witt. Painters studied their XVIIth century models with care, and too often merely imitated them. Writers composed historical novels about the Golden Age and the heroic fight against Spain. Everard Potgieter, by far the most talented writer of the period, vainly sought to re-awaken the Netherland intellectual world by contrasting the self-satisfied mediocrity of his time to the greatness of the Golden Age. He withdrew from literary activity for many years in disappointment. Other men of outstanding talent and originality, Conrad Busken Huet and Edward Douwes Dekker, could find no place in Netherland society. A number of medieval monuments were destroyed to make way for structures with no character of their own. And everywhere ancient city walls were torn down to be replaced by neat little parks and boulevards where the burgher paraded his smugness on Sunday afternoons. No real change occurred until 1870.

Intellectual life was as dull as economic conditions were difficult in the years between 1848 and 1870. Yet, at that very time the foundations of the political organization of the Netherland nation were being laid. The constitutional revision of 1848 shifted the center of political gravity from the Crown to the States General. It also revived the democratic trend of 1795 by transferring the election of members of the Second Chamber from the Provincial States to the people. The First Chamber, formerly appointed by the king, was now elected by the Provincial States from the wealthiest citizens. This form of election to the First Chamber was the only concession made to provincial traditions; in all other matters the autonomy of the provinces was restricted. The new constitution made ministers responsible to Parliament, but nowhere provided that to appear and speak there ministers should be members. This was an important difference from the British system. It permitted the appointment to the Cabinet of eminent specialists, who had never taken part in political life. It also permitted the formation of extra-parliamentary cabinets, which did not start with majority support, but through their administration hoped to secure a majority for each individual measure on its merits. These extra-parliamentary cabinets became quite a feature of Netherland political life. King William III had recourse to this means to preserve direct influence over the administration of the country. Later, in the XXth century, when the splitting-up of political parties rendered the formation of a majority block impossible, extra-parliamentary cabinets were the only possible solution.

The Liberals, who before 1849 only formed a small group in the Netherlands, had seen their political aspirations materialize under the influence of events abroad—the revolutions in France and in Germany. Once they had achieved their aims, they found wide support among the franchiseholders. Again it must be emphasized that the franchise was restricted to a small fraction of the population; even after the passing of the electoral law, which granted votes to taxpayers assessed for a certain amount, the electorate was only three and a half percent of the population, or about 100,000 voters. However, thanks to the Liberal reform, a new class of society gained control of public affairs. Once more in Netherland history, the middleclass supplanted the aristocracy. In 1572, middleclass men, Calvinists for the most part, had thrown the Burgundian-Habsburg oligarchy out of office, only to become oligarchs themselves. They were attacked by the middleclass in 1747 and in 1784, and thrown out in 1795. Hogendorp had contemplated restoring the former oligarchy in 1814; and although he did not succeed, it regained at least part of its power by entering the service of King William I. In 1848 the burgher class again attacked the existing aristocracy, entrenched behind the monarchy, and succeeded in gaining control. Fifty years later, the lower middleclass was to begin its attack on the democrats of 1848, and the struggle between these two groups formed the background of internal political developments until 1940. The upper classes first resisted the Liberal middleclass, to join it later when the pressure from below increased by the labor element drove the middleclass to the conservative side in politics.

The political struggle of the XVIIth and XVIIIth centuries was continued into the XIXth. The connection is clearly visible and can be traced even in the political conflicts of the last few decades. Dutch Liberals of the 1850's and '60's were not an organized political party in our sense of the word. They were merely a group of individuals having certain opinions in common, who fought their electoral campaigns individually and presented a common front in parliament on questions of principle. There was no regular party leadership, at most only an understanding among prominent Liberals. But the Liberals were infinitely better organized than their opponents, who were merely individuals with conservative views, most of them without well-defined political programs of their own. This reflects a very similar political division in the time of the Republic. If the opponents of Oldenbarnevelt and John De Witt had not found a rallying point in the House of Orange, they would never have had a chance against the oligarchy. Much the same thing occurred in the middle of the XIXth century. Against the Liberals were the Conservatives who simply abhorred the idea of giving political influence to "the mob." Against them, were a number of Calvinists who, as in 1618, though on less dogmatic grounds, opposed complete religious equality. The reorganization of the Catholic Church in the Netherlands and the re-establishment of episcopal sees, vacant since 1572 or 1579, aroused a storm which forced the Liberals out of the administration. The Liberals were also opposed, if not by the Crown, at least by the personal sentiment of King William III. Without his help, the motley conservative group would not have stood a chance.

There is no better proof of this than the experience of Groen van Prinsterer, the only man who had the intelligence, the knowledge, and the conviction to create a Conservative party with a program based on well-considered principles. For many years Director of the Archives of the Royal Family, he started the publication of a long series of volumes, the "Archives or unpublished correspondence of the House of Orange-Nassau," which proved an invaluable source for Netherland historians. Groen applied the principles of Bilderdijk, though with far greater objectivity. To him as to Bilderdijk, the theory of the "sovereignty of the people" was abhorrent because revolutionary and conducive to mob rule. In his interpretation of Netherland history he saw the House of Orange, defenders of Calvinist freedom and rights of established social groups, as predestined to monarchy, finally attained in the person of William I. He saw the Netherlands as a Calvinist State, the religious character of which should be maintained as a source of national existence. From a dogmatic point of view he rejected sovereignty of the people as being based on the anti-religious, rationalist philosophy of the XVIIIth century. God, not the people, was sovereign. The law of God revealed in Christian doctrine assigned to each individual his rights and his duties. Only a political order based upon divine law can endure. Sovereignty of the people means the tyranny of the majority, a "totalitarian" regime that ignores the fundamental rights and duties of man. Groen's political program was no platform, it was a creed. Principles rather than aims were expressed in the name of his party: the Anti-Revolutionary Party, anti-revolutionary standing for anti-Rousseau, anti-rationalist.

Groen found but few adherents. His abstract theological-political ideals did not appeal to the burgher class. He could not rally the Conservatives around him, for the upper classes generally did not share his convictions, and the masses who had participated in the anti-Catholic movement of 1853, were more against what was unusual than in favor of any definite theological or political principle. Yet Groen inaugurated a new chapter in Netherland politics. His method of approach to political problems was adopted by the majority of party leaders in the later part of the century, and his basing of political opinion on more fundamental considerations of creed and philosophy was followed so rigorously that by the second decade of the XXth century political and religious divisions in the Netherlands ran largely parallel.

In one point of his historical interpretation of national policy, Groen was definitely mistaken. This was his view of the origin of the Netherland nation. Not only did he ignore all national development before the Great Revolt but he made this Revolt and with it the nation, dependent on the Calvinist struggle. That is why he saw its Calvinism as its basic trait. The declaration of freedom of 1581 however assigned political and not religious reasons for the revolt, and the Haec Libertatis Ergo of the beleaguered town of Leiden professed the same motives. Not Groen van Prinsterer but the Liberals represented the tradition of 1572.

The political leader of the Liberals was John Rudolf Thorbecke, a true representative of the burgher class that now came to power. He was the son of a tobacconist of Zwolle in Overijssel, and by energy and intelligence he succeeded in completing his studies at Leiden University. They were followed by a trip through Germany, where he visited numerous universities. About the middle of the XIXth century Dutch learned circles were impressed by the scientific innovations made in German universities and the methodical results obtained there. Philology, theology, philosophy and history borrowed heavily from German sources. Thorbecke fell under this influence which helped him to give to Netherland constitutional practices, adapted from English and French models, a character of their own. His biographers have noted strong romantic traits in his apparently cool and calculating character. Von Savigny's historical political philosophy, of which he learned through Eichhorn, made a deep impression on him. In the first years after his return to the Netherlands his scientific interest shifted from philosophy to history, then to the science of government, and finally to politics. He was the first to give clear expression to Liberal wishes in regard to constitutional reforms, and to him King William II entrusted the chairmanship of the Committee appointed to revise the Constitution. His prestige among the Liberals made his leadership inevitable, whatever the personal feelings of the monarch.

Leadership in a Netherland cabinet could rest only on personal qualities. The Constitution did not provide for a Premiership like later the constitution of France and like political tradition in Britain. The "Council of Ministers" decided matters of general policy, and the presidency of the Council changed periodically. Such "government by council" was well suited to Netherland tradition, but made strong administration more difficult. The constitutional practice inaugurated by Thorbecke, permits the statesman who forms the Cabinet to retain a position slightly superior to his colleagues, but all attempts to make this tacitly acknowledged leadership official have so far been defeated in parliament. Thorbecke formed three Liberal Cabinets. The last time he took office he was a dying man. But in the two preceding administrations and by his leadership of the Liberal Party, he created the Netherland parliamentary system of government. The laws implementing certain provisions of the constitution were promulgated under his administration. He created the provincial and communal governments. He showed how the franchise was to be extended, by including all who could possibly be given the right to vote; that representation should be as democratic as circumstances permitted. He created new economic opportunities by making new entrances to the ports of Amsterdam and Rotterdam from the sea. He made the Netherlands a free-trade area. He put an end to long discussions of the problem of slavery by forcing Parliament to accept abolition. For the burgher class he created advanced schools, similar to American high schools, where middleclass children could receive the education they would need in industry and trades. Nearly all of his creations survive with only a few essential modifications. In opposition, he succeeded in putting an end to royal interference in elections and in conflicts between ministers and parliament, by insisting on the observance of constitutional methods. No wonder his opponents, especially the rank and file of old-fashioned traditionalists, held the fate of Oldenbarnevelt and John De Witt up to him as a warning! Finally, by his example, he educated his followers to independent political thinking, which inevitably led the younger generation away from him towards more progressive ideals.

This split in the Liberal ranks first became apparent when the East Indian administration was up for discussion. Thorbecke, who put practical solutions before his own predilection, did not believe the time "ripe" for a sweeping reform of the system of government controlled agriculture in Java. He needed the revenue from Batavia for public works in Europe, especially the construction of railroads. But reform could not long be postponed. Van Hoevell kept hammering at the evils of the Culture System and the corruption it produced. Public opinion was aroused by Edward Douwes Dekker, a former official of the East Indian government who in 1859 under the pseudonym of Multatuli ("I suffered much") published his *Max Havelaar,* a fiery accusation of the East Indian regime. This book was the first really vibrant literary production to appear in the Netherlands after a century of dullness. It was widely read, but not believed. After others had convinced the thinking public of the errors of the East Indian administration and had secured its reform, *Max Havelaar* was given credit for the reform. Douwes Dekker left the Netherlands and wandered through Europe, publishing violent attacks on conservatism, on established institutions and on the creed of the masses. His work remained fragmentary. He wanted to picture "the struggle between low and high, between nobleness of soul and scoundrelism." "Away with coziness, with simplicity and sweetness of mind," was his battle-cry. By a fatal overestimation of his own work and personality, Douwes Dekker could "sound the trumpet" for the attack but could never lead it. Nevertheless he foreshadowed things to come. Isaac Fransen van der Putte, one of the younger generation of Liberals held the office of Minister of Colonies in Thorbecke's second administration. He advocated a complete reversal of East Indian policy, which led to such dissension among the Liberal majority that Thorbecke was forced to resign. Van der Putte embarked on his reforms, but the power of the Liberal Party had been temporarily broken. The cleavage in the Liberal Party offered the king a last opportunity to attempt monarchical rule. After it was defeated the problem of the Indies was revived again.

Within twenty years Netherland public opinion had changed greatly. Around 1850, Van Hoevell could hardly mention odd sounding Javanese names without provoking laughter among the less intelligent of the dignified members of Parliament. In 1869 and 1870 the discussion of agrarian reform in Java revealed a thorough study of the subject, and many members of Parliament proved to be well acquainted with the facts. The result was a highly interesting debate that ended in a compromise which proved to be one of the wisest of Dutch parliamentary decisions. All compulsory production was abolished, and the Indies were thrown open to private enterprise. To prevent the poor Javanese peasantry from being reduced to pauperism by western greed, the ownership of the soil was to be determined according to native customary law, which did not permit nonmembers of Indonesian village communities to acquire title to cultivated land or to wild land in the vicinity of the villages. Jungle lands in uninhabited territory, mostly outside of Java, were declared government property to be leased under long term contracts. The agrarian law of 1870 has been most beneficial to the people of the Indies by protecting the property rights of the small peasants, who make up 90 percent of the population. East Indian problems proved more susceptible to happy compromise than the political issues of the home country. Around 1870 a new political division occurred which for the time being weakened the existing parties, without offering any new possibility of majority rule. The Conservative Party, reduced to a handful of members, was resigned to constitutional monarchy, but feared that "progress might be too fast." It could not possibly influence affairs. The party had indeed no reason for existence after it ceased to express any political conviction. Some of the Liberals satisfied with the existing system of government and afraid of "mob rule" if the franchise were extended further, voted with the Conservatives in Parliament and helped to defeat a number of bills. But beyond voting down government measures they were unable to accomplish anything. The defection of this unprogressive group was not the worst blow the Liberal movement suffered in these years. The fate of the Liberal movement was decided by the defection of its Catholic supporters.

The Roman Catholics had strongly supported the Patriot movement in 1780 and 1795. Thanks to the reforms of the French period, they had become full citizens of the Netherland state. Obviously, their interest demanded that they support the Liberals despite the deep gulf between the Catholic creed and the religious neutrality of Thorbecke and his adherents. There were times when the great Liberal leader could obtain a seat in Parliament only by running in a predominantly Catholic constituency. Liberals and Catholics had jointly opposed the policies of Groen van Prinsterer. Neither group would recognize Groen's claim that the Netherlands were a Calvinist state, born of a Calvinist movement, with its freedom anchored in Calvinist doctrine. But their negative cooperation was obviously bound to collapse whenever a positive policy was opposed to Groen's ideas.

The break occurred over the question of education. Groen had demanded that the state, being Calvinist, provide public education on a Reformed basis. In his view the existing regulations under which only public schools were supported by the state, and Calvinist teaching of religion and history was forbidden, "paved the way for Roman Catholic penetration." A return to the educational monopoly of the Dutch Reformed Church was impossible, nor did Groen desire such reversion to the past. He did not expect a religious revival from outward institutions, but only from the spirit. The fact that forty percent of the Netherland people did not belong to the Reformed Church or to any Calvinist organization, had obviously to be taken into account. Groen's ideal was that the state should maintain separate schools for Catholics and Israelites wherever required, and that education in all other public schools should be either based explicitly on the Reformed dogma or strongly imbued with Calvinist historical tradition. This system was acceptable neither to the Liberals nor to the Catholics. But here agreement ceased between these two sections of the Liberal party.

In principle, the Catholics were as much opposed to the existing school system as Groen van Prinsterer, but they wanted freedom to establish their own denominational schools and have them subsidized from the public funds. Their main argument seemed irrefutable: education being the exclusive concern of the state and paid for by the taxpayer's money, ought to be organized according to the taxpayer's wishes. Groen and the Catholic leaders claimed that more than sixty percent of the people disliked the existing system, but could not express their wishes because they did not have the franchise. The *voting* population, the Liberal-minded bourgeoisie, was quite satisfied with the existing education and refused to consider the opinions of the religious groups. A peculiar situation had now developed. Groen, who demanded a denominational school system on the basis of the nation's historical tradition and religious convictions, could not appeal to the nation as a whole. That would have required the extension of the franchise to artisans, shopkeepers, and peasants, and the leader of the anti-revolutionary party opposed democracy on principle. His Liberal opponents who favored democracy on principle, refused to heed to the will of the people on education. They were so fully convinced that they were right in this regard that they planned to use the existing school system to educate the people towards their views. A contradiction such as existed in both political groups between means and aims could only spell catastrophe.

The first to profit from this confusion were the Catholics. This group of Netherlanders had so long lived on sufferance, in political and cultural obscurity, that the majority of the people was firmly convinced that no further contribution to intellectual life could spring from Catholic sources. A certain type of popular literature and history fostered this belief. This general prejudice materially hampered cultural activity among the Dutch Catholics. When William Nuyens, the son of a physician in West Friesland, desired to study history, he was first obliged to become a physician to provide himself with independent means, and then while carrying on his practice, to take up historical research which made him one of the leaders of the Catholic revival. So Catholics in the XIXth century Netherlands continued to work under conditions that had been almost universal two hundred years before. They wrote, studied history and art, edited newspapers and other publications, while earning their living as booksellers, physicians, or in some other profession. Nuyens was a physician and an historian; the bookseller A. J. Alberdingk Thijm became an outstanding art critic and revived the glory of Vondel, himself a poet and shopkeeper.

France strongly influenced Catholic cultural life. Many Catholics read and admired the works of Montalembert who sought a reconciliation between Catholicism and Liberal principles of government; but Louis Veuillot, the leader of the Ultramontane Catholic faction, wielded far wider and

more lasting influence. Under his influence a change, in many respects re-
grettable, took place. Dutch Catholics turned from more liberal to strictly
ultramontane views. Deprived of their civic rights for centuries and regarded with some suspicion by the authorities in the first half of the XIXth
century, Dutch Catholics considered themselves bound to display excessive
zeal in defense of the rights of the Church, whether essential or not, as for
instance the temporal power of the Pope. At times the spirit of the Crusades seemed revived. In proportion to its population, the Netherlands
provided more volunteers for the Papal army in 1864, than any other nation. More than five thousand young men left for Italy, where many participated in the battle of Mentana. Not unnaturally, this Ultramontane enthusiasm was intolerant of Catholics who did not fully share all the political views of the leaders.

Between this Catholic reaction and the Liberals, all cooperation was impossible, and events in Italy between 1864 and 1870 caused a definite break
between the former allies in Dutch politics. Pope Pius IX condemned Liberalism in 1864 in his encyclical *Qanta Cura* and the *Syllabus* that accompanied it. The Dutch Liberals rejoiced over the destruction of the Papal
state. Imprudently and gratuitously the Liberal majority in Parliament decided to express its satisfaction with this event by abolishing Dutch
diplomatic representation at the Vatican. The Catholics resisted the motion
furiously but vainly. From that time on the Dutch Legation at the Vatican
became an internal political issue of curious significance, quite out of
proportion to its diplomatic importance.

The Ultramontane trend among Dutch Catholics, expressed in the
panegyric literature of Herman Schaepman, priest and professor of Church
history in the archdiocese of Utrecht, did not neutralize another and
stronger Catholic aspiration, that of becoming full members of the greater
Netherland community. Whatever the intention of the author, Groen's
interpretation of Dutch history placed them beyond the pale. The interpretation of Robert Fruin, leading Liberal historian, left them in the position of converts who had sinned both against the nation and the most
sacred principles of freedom and tolerance. Against these writers, William
Nuyens defended a new Catholic interpretation of the Great Revolt in
which he claimed for his co-religionists of the XVIth century, a place
among the defenders of freedom equal to that of the Calvinists and Eras-
mians. The literary controversy around the history of the Great Revolt
grew into a political struggle, when the tricentenary of the capture of Brill
by the Sea Beggars was celebrated in 1872.

These conflicts of historical opinion may seem irrelevant to the development of the Netherland nation. Yet they do help to explain the political

confusion of the period from 1870 to 1890, when a clear majority could rarely be found in parliament to support any administration. Extra-parliamentary cabinets or opportunist combinations had to be resorted to, and the development of parliamentary life on the British model was prevented. Moreover, these conflicting trends gain deeper significance when we compare them with certain statistics of Church membership. At the middle of the century the Reformed Church claimed more than 54% of the Dutch people as members. By 1899 its membership had dropped to 48.5% of the population. By 1920 it was reduced to 41.6% and by 1930 its position as the most numerous religious denomination in the Netherlands had been lost to the Roman Catholic Church. The latter claimed 36% of the population in 1930. Half of them were in the provinces of Brabant and Limburg, which were 95% and 98% Catholic. The change in religious trend is made even more clear by the following figures: from 1869 to 1930 the total population of the Netherlands increased 121.7% and the total membership of the Dutch Reformed Church, only 39.6%. This discrepancy was only partly offset by the growth of the minor Calvinist denominations, for even including them, the increase of the combined Calvinist Churches amounted only to 75%, lagging far behind the population growth. The Roman Catholics with an increase of 120% in total membership in the same sixty years suffered only a slight loss. The proportional strength of the other Protestant denominations, Lutherans and Baptists, also showed a decline of about 50%, but the number of their adherents was extremely small to begin with. The most important factor in this development was the natural increase in the proportion of the population belonging to no Church or religious organization, from virtually zero in 1869 to 2.3% in 1899 and to 13% in 1930.

If we bear in mind that membership in an established Church is often a matter of social tradition, it is evident that Groen's ideal of the Netherlands as a Calvinist state did not respond to reality, and that the popular trend was in the opposite direction. It is also evident that confidence must have grown among the Catholics with their increasing proportional strength. New leaders, unwilling to follow in the wake of Liberal policy, were certain to find a response among the masses of Catholics. Calvinist leaders bent on reviving the reformed religion had no choice but to break away from the traditionalism of the Dutch Reformed Church and appeal to the masses of peasants and small burghers who were still actively attached to the creed of their ancestors. Leaders on both sides had to liberalize their movements, a decision which shocked their old followers perhaps more than their opponents. In both Calvinist and Catholic camps leaders recognized the danger of the incipient irreligious trend. Anxious to preserve the religious character of the nation, they had to go to the people before the masses were captured by other and perhaps anti-religious movements.

The Calvinists were more easily democratized than the Catholics. The latter had few capable leaders. The clergy were excluded by the traditional conservatism of the Catholic Church, and among the laity an intellectual class hardly existed. The Catholic gentry of the provinces of Brabant and Limburg and the industrialists of Tilburg in Brabant or Maastricht in Limburg leaned strongly towards Liberalism. In 1880, the Catholics found their first political leader in Herman Schaepman from Overijssel. But for many years Schaepman stood virtually alone among Catholics as a defender of democracy. His co-religionists supported him in asserting the right to denominational schools and on other general issues; they deserted him time and again when he spoke for democracy. His leadership was recognized and his ideals accepted only after his death.

Among the Calvinists the role of democratic leader fell to Abraham Kuyper, a minister of the Church who had turned from modernist views to orthodoxy. Kuyper could work on a far broader basis than Schaepman, for he included as the objects of democratization both the Church and the political party. He led orthodox Calvinists in an attack on the established Reformed Church and founded the Christian Reformed Churches, in which the individual congregations were to have complete autonomy. Half a million members of the Reformed Church went over to the new congregations. Kuyper appealed to the "small people" not to tolerate the "ecclesiastical and political tyranny of a privileged oligarchy," by which he meant the prosperous, Liberal burgher class. Through masterful leadership he worked up an enthusiasm which in a few years made him the most prominent political figure of the country. He completely transformed the small intellectual group organized by Groen into a mass movement with slogans, popular campaigns, and party publications. His ideal was a total rebirth. Not only the political predominance of the Liberals, but also their intellectual monopoly was to be broken. Kuyper demonstrated the power of democracy when, with donations from the poor, he founded a university to give his co-religionists intellectual and spiritual leaders. The money was collected in scores of thousands of small gifts, a few guilders, a few dimes, sometimes a few cents. Many universities have been endowed by millionaires who have hardly missed the millions they bestowed on their foundations. Very few owe their existence, as did Kuyper's foundation, to the masses.

A new era had dawned in the history of the second Netherland state. The thoughts of Netherlanders no longer turned to the past, but to the future. In literature, in art, in science, the nation regained some of its past glory, not by imitation but by initiative. The revival of letters, of which Douwes Dekker and Busken Huet had been the heralds, began around 1880. First English romanticism, then French naturalism inspired this new literature. French influences also strongly influenced the revival of painting. But as in politics, both these arts soon manifested tendencies towards democracy and new social conceptions. The individualists who dominated literature around 1880 soon made way for the preachers of new social gospels. And in the world of painting, Vincent Van Gogh pictured the people as he saw them, without romanticism or sentimentality but with shocking directness that cried aloud for change.

Some reformers believed that the creation of a better world demanded a total break with tradition. A "Society for the Propagation of Atheism," founded in Amsterdam (*De Dageraad*), caused a stir in the conventional Dutch world. Its effect was not very great, but it was connected with the first Marxist movement in the Netherlands. A Dutch section of the first International was founded in 1869, but gained only a handful of adherents from the laboring class. Revolutionary trends were still abhorrent to the working class, and the first Trade Unions, organized in 1866 and backed by younger members of the Liberal Party, were moderate in their aims and methods. The backwardness of Dutch industry did not provide great chances for the new General Workingmen's Federation formed by the Unions.

But after 1860 industry began to expand rapidly. Eastern Overijssel developed its cotton manufactures, which found a ready market in the Indies after the abolition of the Culture System. Tilburg in Brabant, which had inherited the wool industry of Leiden, became another important center, and Maastricht in Limburg further developed its ceramic industry. In all these industrial centers workers lived under pitiful conditions, which prompted some of the younger Liberals to broaden their political and social activities to include the cause of the common man. One of these younger Liberals, Samuel van Houten, was the first to present a bill to restrict child labor. It was adopted in 1874, the first Dutch social legislation.

Thus around 1880 the three major political groups in the Netherlands were feeling their way towards democracy. In each of these three groups a conservative section resented the democratic tendencies of the new leaders. Two of the three, the Anti-Revolutionaries and the Liberals were political parties, while the third group, the Catholics, had only formed a defensive front against the educational policy of the Liberals. Catholic leaders were still debating the advisability of a Catholic Party. Theoretically cooperation among the progressive elements of the three groups was possible. Had it been realized, a two-party system might have resulted. Practically, cooperation was impossible because of the overshadowing educational question. The denominational groups closed ranks as soon as the problem of equality for denominational schools arose. This is not so strange; but it is remarkable that the Liberals, for whom the maintenance of the public schools in a privileged position could hardly have been a matter of principle, stubbornly refused to reconsider their attitude, and also drew up in battle formation whenever this palladium of Liberal tradition was threatened. The idea that by compromising on this point they might attract the social-minded and democratic elements of the Catholic group and perhaps prevent the splitting up of the Dutch nation into political parties corresponding to religious tenets, seems never to have occurred to the younger Liberals. The expansion of such denominational parties is naturally limited, but they have a firm hold on their followers and can only with difficulty be supplanted.

Discussions of the school system in 1879 broadened the gap between the denominational and the Liberal groups. The result was the "monstrous alliance" of Catholics and Calvinists against their common opponent. Within thirty years of the popular unrest of an Anti-Popery campaign caused by Catholic bishops taking up residence in the Netherlands, this seemed hardly credible. For a while the new allies showed distrust of each other, but with the passage of time their bonds became stronger. This alliance was beneficial in that it bridged an old antagonism that had been strong enough to split up the Burgundian Lowland state three hundred years before. The wars of religion were buried. But it doomed the political basis of the Constitution of 1848.

Parliament, instead of being composed of two political parties with alternative majorities, became to some extent representative of religious communities. The educational problem not only diverted political development from its natural course, but also split the new labor movement. The General Workmen's Association, created with the assistance of Liberal leaders, advocated Liberal ideas on education. The immediate effect was the resignation of many members who in politics belonged to the Anti-Revolutionary Party. The Catholics lagged behind in labor unionism. A few leaders, among whom Alphonse Ariens, a priest in the textile district of Overijssel, was the most outstanding character, sought to create a Christian workingmen's movement; but the rank and file of the *voting* Catholics were far too conservative to approve, and the clergy, if not opposed to the new idea, were generally hesitant. They followed the lead of the Protestants in forming their own Unions on a denominational basis when Marxism returned to the field and the first Socialist leaders began a feverish agitation to organize the working class as a combat force against capitalism.[57]

A leading position among the Marxists was held by Ferdinand Domela Nieuwenhuis, a former Lutheran minister, who had left the Church and turned to radicalism. His ardent wish to work for the poor and his individualism, which resented all political or ecclesiastical ties, drove him from the pulpit to the dwellings of the poor, where he preached Socialism, as he conceived Christ to have preached the Gospel of brotherly love. He believed in revolution and despised politics. His Socialism was a creed, the only possible reasonable creed, and he broke with fellow Socialists rather than sacrifice the slightest of his beliefs. Preaching a new creed, he clashed with the defenders of other creeds, but most of all with tradition. His Social Democratic Society separated from the General Workingmen's Association and formed the first Marxist party in the Netherlands. In the years around 1880 a severe crisis ruined Dutch agriculture. The countryside of Friesland and the peat districts of Groningen and Drente were especially hard hit. The farmers of Friesland and the peat diggers of Groningen enthusiastically welcomed Nieuwenhuis, as a prophet of paradise. Against his attacks on accepted religion and established order, Protestant and Catholic workers rallied around their own leaders. By 1890 the working class, like the political world, was divided into numerous groups, some denominational, some a-religious, some anti-religious. This lasted until 1940 and, as far as we can judge, may revive again after the liberation of the Netherlands.

Many Netherlanders have deplored this division of the nation along religious lines, and superficial observers have blamed the ecclesiastical diehards for making all other issues subservient to that of education. But there was no reason why, while the Liberals persisted in their educational views, their opponents should abandon theirs. For a nation to believe that the education is of paramount public interest is not a sign of political incapacity —it marks progress beyond the political squabbles of the XVIIIth century and does not compare unfavorably with the politics of any of the adjacent great powers. Their thoroughness and insistence in discussing the fundamental principles rather than the superficial aspects of a problem were characteristic of the strong religious convictions of the Dutch people. This tendency was not always congenial to parliamentary methods of administration, but as it required each member of the community to account to himself for his political actions it was essentially democratic. In fact, it has proved the main bulwark of the Netherland nation against Nazi indoctrination.

The worst effect of this political system was that groups having common principles divided on secondary issues, while a general re-grouping on new lines remained as impossible as ever. This was the case in the middle nineties, when the proposed extension of the franchise tore both the Liberal and the Anti-Revolutionary parties apart. The more conservative Anti-Revolutionaries formed the Christian Historical Party; the more progressive Liberals formed the Free-Democratic Group. There was no possibility of re-grouping the more Conservative Liberals and more liberal Anti-Revolutionaries in a new conservative front. The Social Democratic group also fell apart over a similar issue. Nieuwenhuis was adamant in the ideal of revolution; in 1894 the majority of the Socialists led by Pieter Jelles Troelstra, formed the Social Democratic Labor Party and plunged into parliamentary activity and the struggle for universal suffrage. Even the Catholic Party might have been divided as only its leader Schaepman defended democracy; but behind him was the authority of Rome. In 1891 Pope Leo XIII had pronounced the condition of the working man to be of great concern to all followers of the Church, thus breaking with the conservatism of the older generation of the clergy.

Pressure by all democratic elements in the various parties brought about a gradual extension of the franchise. In 1870 there were only 100,000 voters in a population of 3,500,000. Tax qualifications restricted the number of franchise holders to about 12% of the male population above the age of twenty-five. A constitutional revision in 1887 broadened the franchise by granting the right to vote to men with certain educational qualifications, at the same time lowering the tax qualification. A law of 1896 redrafted these qualifications and the number of voters in 1900 amounted to 570,000 out of a population of 5,200,000, or about 49% of the male population above the age limit. Prosperity and intellectual progress in the next ten years increased this to 63%, but also intensified the demand for universal suffrage. Only general trends in modern Dutch economic life can be indicated here; other books, recently published in the United States have devoted long chapters to the revival of Dutch prosperity after 1870 and especially after 1900.[58] Trade with Germany assumed a new aspect after the establishment of the German empire in 1870. The huge industrial development of the Ruhr basin revived the transit trade along the Rhine. Rotterdam became the principal port of the Netherlands. The merchant fleet of Amsterdam remained not far below that of its southern competitor, but the tonnage handled in Rotterdam far surpassed that of the northern port. Amsterdam retained a large share in the East Indian trade. The former residences of its merchant kings, the stately houses along its canals, became the home offices of numerous East Indian enterprises. After the abolition of the Culture System, an ever-growing influx of Dutch capital into the Indies gave the overseas territories an entirely new significance for the

Netherlands. The sugar production of Java, which rose from 150,000 to 380,000 tons within fifteen years, and to 1,400,000 tons, forty-four years after the abolition of the Culture System, was financed wholly by Dutch capital. The same was true of the tea and quinine plantations. The British had only a minor share in tobacco production. Rubber was not produced in quantity until after the First World War. The only branch of East Indian production financed from the first by international capital were the oil fields of Sumatra and Borneo, opened in 1889.

Though Netherland investments in the Indies were considerable, those in the United States were not much less important. Dutch capital had large interests in American railroads, especially west of the Mississippi and in Illinois and Wisconsin. It is impossible even to guess the amount invested in this way after 1860. Another favorite investment was in mortgage banks that provided capital to farmers both in Canada and in the western United States. Later, large numbers of shares in American oil companies, in steel works, and in automobile factories were bought by holding companies in Amsterdam. Dealings in American shares were a most important feature on the Amsterdam Stock Exchange. In 1939, Dutch investments in the United States were estimated at $600,000,000.[59] This would indicate that Netherland investments in the United States were slightly larger than those in industrial and agricultural enterprises in the Indies. A few figures illustrating the increase of deposits in savings banks may also be given, as they indicate the prosperity of the masses. In 1860, there were 136 savings banks in the Netherlands, with total deposits amounting to 5,500,000 guilders. In 1900, there were 252 privately owned savings banks besides the Government Postal Savings Banks, and deposits had risen to 164,500,000 guilders. Ten years later the total sum was 275,000,000 guilders. After the First World War it was nearly half a billion, and in 1937, nearly a billion guilders.

This increase in prosperity was matched by a new eclosion of cultural life, that has been described in recent publications in the United States.[60] Five Netherland physicists, among them the great Hendrik Anton Lorentz, were awarded the Nobel Prize. Johan Huizinga, the greatest of contemporary Dutch historians, gained wide renown. Johan Hendrik Kern became world famous for his knowledge of Sanskrit, Indonesian languages and Buddhism and restored the university of Leiden to its rank as a great center of oriental studies. Christian Snouck Hurgronje, who had attracted wide attention of students of Islam by his visit to Mecca in 1884—at a time when the intrusion of "Infidels" was likely to be punished by death—became a leading figure in Islamitic studies and Indonesian ethnology. Cornelis van Vollenhoven, the interpreter of Indonesian *adat*-law, revived the tradition of Grotius and won recognition as an outstanding authority in the field of international law. N. J. Krom brought the ancient and medieval history of the Indies to light from fragments of chronicles and from inscriptions. J. C. Kapteyn and W. De Sitter made Leiden a center of astronomical research, from which their students spread all over the world. There are few important observatories in the United States today where one of them is not to be found.

The Netherlands have not produced another painter of Van Gogh's stature but painting is studied widely and evokes more general interest than any other cultural activity. Another art which flourished was music. Progress since the early XIXth century was so great that in the first forty years of the XXth century Amsterdam became an "unique center of the musical world." After the last war architecture took a new turn with large rehousing projects in many cities, that gave the Netherlands a "garden city" aspect. Social reform had started late, but this was compensated by rapid improvement after the adoption of social laws promoted first by the younger Liberals and then under denominational auspices. By 1901, control over public affairs was definitely lost by the Liberals. The "Coalition" of Anti-Revolutionaries, Catholics, and the Christian-Historical Party, came to power after the first election of the XXth century, and Abraham Kuyper, anti-revolutionary leader, became "prime minister." [61] For once the use of this term is accurate. Kuyper sought to create a premiership which, until then was unknown to Dutch constitutional tradition. The new prime minister had already rendered immeasurable service to his followers and to the nation in general. He had brought the strictly orthodox Calvinist peasants and fishermen out of the cultural isolation into which they had withdrawn as a mistaken defense against modern trends of thought. He had brought the people of the remotest sections to participation in national political and cultural life. He had helped democracy to victory and he had helped to do away with one of the most disastrous divisions in the Netherlands, the antagonism of Calvinists and Catholics based on events that happened three hundred years before.

But as a national leader Kuyper was not a success. In politics he remedied only minor defects. Moreover, he had the bad luck of having to deal with the only extensive railroad strike that ever occurred in the Netherlands; and the way he handled it made his name hateful to the majority of workers. There had been no violence or excess of any sort, yet Kuyper had a law passed prohibiting future railroad strikes without providing the wages and working conditions asked by the leaders of the working class.

A new departure inspired by Kuyper's administration and proclaimed by the queen must be recorded. In her speech from the throne in September 1901, Queen Wilhelmina said in regard to the overseas territories, "The Netherlands have a moral duty to fulfill towards the people of the Indies." This declaration did not produce any immediate change in the Far East, but it was a principle that once established profoundly modified the relations between the component parts of the kingdom of the Netherlands. Liberal reform had abolished the Culture System, but hope had not been abandoned that the Indies would become sufficiently prosperous to permit excess public income to be transferred to the Netherlands without injury to the colonies. That hope had rapidly faded. The last revenue had been received in 1877. A war broke out in the Indies which taxed its resources to the utmost.

Under the treaty of 1824 with Britain the government of Batavia was obliged to suppress piracy in Sumatran waters, and decided to stop the constant raids of Achinese pirates by occupying Achin. It was believed that the sultan, one of the most powerful Indonesian princes, would acknowledge Dutch supremacy and assist in putting down piracy. The grave decision to attack Achin was prompted by fear that foreign powers might otherwise occupy the northern point of Sumatra and endanger the Dutch position in the Archipelago. War broke out in 1873. It was soon apparent that Achin could not easily be conquered, and that the eventual submission of its sultan would not end the conflict with other partisan leaders. Twenty years later during the administration of Kuyper fighting still continued. Hendrik Colijn, later minister and national leader, played an important part in the campaigns by which General Van Heutsz forced the last partisans to capitulate.

After this onerous war, no likelihood remained of renewed revenue from Batavia. Moreover, ideas on the subject had changed radically. Conrad Th. van Deventer, a former East Indian lawyer and financier, demanded the restitution of monies taken from the Indies under the Culture System and outlined the new policy expressed in the declaration of 1901. If revenue could no longer be expected from Batavia, grants from Amsterdam to Batavia were now within the range of possibility. A first grant of forty million guilders—for the improvement of economic conditions in Java—was made in 1905, and in 1912 the complete financial separation of the East Indian and the European administrations was effected by law.

The new East Indian policy included the extension of Dutch administration to all areas within the boundaries of the empire as determined in the treaties with Great Britain of 1829 and 1871 and with Portugal—concerning Timor—of 1860. This strengthening of Dutch control was accompanied by a first attempt to organize a popular educational system. Public health measures were another aspect of the new political trend, which in Dutch colonial history is known as the "ethical policy." It was a policy in which most Netherlanders concurred, irrespective of party. The Socialists, under the leadership of their colonial expert Henri van Kol, advocated even more radical reforms and immediate plans for self-government in the Indies.

The first half of the XXth century will be known in Dutch history as the age of Queen Wilhelmina. In 1890, after reigning forty-two years, King William III had died. Until her majority in 1898 his daughter reigned under the regency of her mother, Queen Emma. The outstanding political feature of the first decade of that period was the rapid rise of the Social Democratic movement in the form of a political party which consistently expressed revolutionary aims while showing a marked preference for gradual evolution. The German Socialist Party under the leadership of August Bebel was then the model for similar parties in all the states adjacent to Germany. Troelstra, the most prominent Dutch leader, was deeply impressed by the success of Socialist mass organization in Germany and by Eduard Berstein's conceptions of revisionist Marxist Socialism. In his idealism he imagined that the fraternization of the working classes of Europe was near. Signs of internal dissension in his own party ought to have warned him, but he continued what seemed a triumphant progress until the war of 1914 completely disillusioned him and broke him physically.

In 1897 the Socialist Party had only two representatives in the Second Chamber. In 1901 there were four, and 39,000 voters supported this ticket. In 1905 the Socialist representatives had increased to seven, backed by 65,000 voters out of a total of 625,000. Ten percent of the franchise holders were already won over. The number of representatives remained stationary in the next election but popular support grew and, as a consequence, the election of 1913 brought the Socialists eighteen seats and made them one of the strongest groups in Parliament. In 1909 a rift in the Socialist ranks between the advocates of revolution and those of evolution led to the secession of a small group of radicals. This was the origin of the later Communist Party in the Netherlands. The new group included some of the best intellects of the party but very few of the rank and file.

Liberal and conservative cabinets alternated until 1917.[62] As long as the Liberal Party was represented in strength the orthodox parliamentary system worked fairly well. But with the last war came a wide change in political conceptions expressed in 1917, by a revision of the Constitution. Democracy triumphed. The last war brought more than an inner political reorientation; it brought the Netherlands back into world politics, from which for over eighty years they had tried to escape.

The history of Netherland foreign policy during the second half of the

XIXth century is easily written. Of this period an American historian said, "the Dutch developed the small power policy to a point little short of perfection. The determination of the Dutch to play a passive role in world politics was so strong as to amount almost to an obsession." [63] Historians obliged to describe Dutch foreign policy between 1840 and 1914, find difficulty in holding the attention of their readers so numerous are the "treaties of conciliation and arbitration." The ease with which these treaties were concluded, when war as an instrument of policy lay under no moral ban, shows that no important issue divided the Netherlands from any other State. There was still some resentment in Belgium over the Scheldt clauses of the treaty of 1839, but it never became dangerous. There was some anxiety in the Netherlands over irresponsible utterances by German historians who were inflated by Prussia's power and Bismarck's political successes. Heinrich von Treitschke, a prophet of Prussianism, devoted a number of his university lectures in 1869 to the history of the Netherlands and although he grudgingly admitted the existence of a historically determined Dutch nation, separated from Germany by natural causes, he made spiteful remarks on the arrogance of Grotius and the shopkeeper mentality of the Dutch, adding a few rhetorical threats to any who might dare to hamper the development of the new German State.[64]

The year in which these words were spoken gave them particular significance. In 1867 and 1868 King William III, as grand duke of Luxemburg, had become involved in a most unpleasant conflict between France and the new North German Confederation. The Netherlands themselves were not concerned. The problem was whether King William could sell to France his sovereignty over the grand duchy, which belonged to him *personally*. Such a sale, transferring a people without their consent to the allegiance of an alien power, is a dubious transaction in itself, but in 1867 nobody questioned King William's right to sell if he wished. The issue was that earlier agreements involved other powers, chiefly Prussia which still maintained a garrison in Luxemburg under the treaties of 1815. The negotiations between William, grand duke of Luxemburg and Napoleon III led to an international dispute which was settled by the mediation of Great Britain at a conference in London. King William withdrew his consent to the transfer of Luxemburg as soon as it became clear that such an action might lead to war.

Naturally, King William availed himself of the Netherland diplomatic service in the negotiations leading to the settlement of London; naturally, the Netherland Parliament was opposed to having the Netherlands involved in a dispute over Luxemburg. The opposition might have dropped the matter had not a constitutional conflict already been in progress. The imprudence of the Minister of Foreign Affairs provided the opposition with an effective weapon against the cabinet and the foreign issue was made the occasion of an internal conflict.

This foreign incident marked a new high in the policy of passive neutrality. The policy of abstention practiced in preceding centuries by Amsterdam's merchants now became a sacred dogma. The arguments supporting it were new. XVIIth century neutrality had been defended on the ground that only when the vital interests of the Dutch nation (usually the commercial interests of the merchant class) were involved, was active participation in European politics justified. The XIXth century doctrine was based chiefly on the claim, "We are powerless anyway." The cult of passive neutrality reconciled the Dutch to political impotence. "Nations too weak to harm the interests of their neighbors are always prompted by noble motives." This became the gist of Dutch foreign policy in the XIXth century. There may be some doubt whether lack of military power is really synonymous with lofty ideals, but there can be no doubt about the peculiarly difficult position of the Netherlands. In the long run, it was this position that imposed modesty of aim and method, that fostered a deeper understanding of the problems of war and peace, of disarmament and international arbitration, than existed in many powerful states, where war was not without attractions until it became reality. Dutch studies of international relations were a natural continuation of the tradition handed down by Erasmus, Grotius and other Netherlanders. Because of them, The Hague was made the seat of two world conferences on disarmament, of the International Court of Arbitration, and later of the Permanent Court of International Justice.

The Dutch people became accustomed to being spectators of world politics and they had a ringside seat in the European arena. Sometimes the action became so violent as to make this close vicinity rather uncomfortable, and the spectators restrained themselves with difficulty from rushing on the stage. This was the case in 1899, during the Boer War. The descendants of the Dutch colonists on the Cape had never valued their racial and linguistic ties with the Netherlands very highly. Reminiscences of the old days of the East India Company were not pleasant. The Boers had become complete "isolationists," culturally as well as politically. Relations between the orthodox Boers and the liberal Dutch Reformed Church had been infrequent and were intensified only after Kuyper's ecclesiastical reforms. But by 1885, when the Transvaal Republic, restored to independence by Gladstone, again felt the pressure of British imperialism and when attempts to organize the republic into a well-administered state failed for lack of trained personnel and of capital, the Boers turned to the Netherlands for resources to offset British penetration.

When war broke out in 1899, the sympathy of all Netherlanders without exception was with the Boers. With some this sympathy remained platonic, with others it flared into enthusiasm and a demand for intervention. The dividing line between these two groups coincides remarkably with that which two centuries previously had separated Oligarchs and Orangists. The Liberals, who were in power in 1899, strongly opposed anything beyond peaceful demonstrations of sympathy. They saw no Netherland interest at stake in the South African conflict, and only grave risks to be incurred by antagonizing Great Britain, the one naval power able to injure Dutch interests in the Far East. Economic considerations outweighed sentimental affections. The opposition, the small burgher class who were largely enlisted in Kuyper's party, demanded action—not war, but emphatic intervention. This group expected the queen, animated by the traditions of the House of Orange, to take the lead. They hardly realized the risks involved in such a policy, but concentrated their resentment, religious, partisan, and national, against the more coolly calculating upper class.

The charge that the Liberals had deliberately left their South African brethren to their fate was a natural weapon in the election campaign of 1901.[65] But once the Liberals had been defeated and the leadership of the state had fallen to Kuyper, the interventionists quickly realized their impotence. Intervention was possible only in the form of a joint protest by many states as in 1863 against Russia in favor of the Polish insurgents. In 1900, no state wanted to be the first to protest. None of the great powers would take the lead, as each hoped to see his neighbor involved in a quarrel with Britain. If the Netherlands took the lead, they would not only risk the loss of the Indies, but would become subservient to some other great power, probably Germany. To try to save the Boers at the certain cost of Netherland independence did not make sense.

The Netherland government under Kuyper weakly attempted to render such service to the Boers as they could. This modest display of activity had far-reaching consequences in foreign politics. The attitude both of the Government and the people created an impression of strong anti-British feeling among the Netherlanders. Other powers sought to profit from the situation. In a letter to Queen Wilhelmina on March 27, 1900, the German emperor, William II, spoke of the "necessity of having a strong fleet sailing the seas." "As soon as this is realized," he added, "the flags of the House of Orange and of the House of Brandenburg will fly side by side on the

Oceans as in the days of old!" Imperial fantasy played havoc with history, for there never were such "days of old," but the meaning was clear. Antagonism between Britain and Germany was growing, and to oppose the one was to invite unwelcome attentions from the other. At that time Great Britain was no more able to protect the Netherlands against the German army, than Germany was to protect the Indies against the British navy. That settled the issue in favor of neutrality.

But the ball had been started rolling. Every incident in Netherland politics was interpreted by diplomatic gossip as an attempt at penetration by one of the great powers. If there were no attempts at penetration, there was at least pressure. Documents already published from the archives of London, Paris, and Berlin, as well as the memoirs of many diplomats show how close was the attention given to the Netherlands and the Indies. An impudent word or gesture by a high Dutch official, and London and Paris imagined the Netherlands a member of the Triple Alliance of Berlin, Rome, and Vienna. Any ripple in British-German relations, and the advisability of occupying the North Sea coast was discussed by Prussian generals, who apparently had their own version of the flags of Orange and Brandenburg flying side by side. Kuyper's pro-Boer agitation and some of his actions had, rightly or wrongly, created the impression that he sympathized with Germany. From this rather scanty evidence, generals and diplomats in both camps drew the unwarranted conclusion that the Netherlands would not oppose the passage of German troops and this set tongues wagging and brains working in all the capitals of Europe. The Netherland government reacted in the only possible way by reinforcing the army and permanent defenses. In 1876 a system of defense against a possible overland invasion had been created. It hinged on a line of inundations running through the province of Utrecht. Advanced posts were built to hold up the invading forces while the inundations were effected. This system was to be completed by modern coastal defenses.

A storm of protests broke over the construction of the latter. They were said to be undertaken at the express demand of the German General Staff to provide Germany with greater security against British landings, and there is little doubt that German complaints had been made about the state of these coastal defenses. The whole affair was slightly absurd, for in case of an Anglo-German conflict, the British army would certainly prefer the well-equipped ports of its French ally to the treacherous sandy coasts of Holland and Zeeland. While a violent discussion raged in numerous European newspapers, the editors of which, we are told, received some compensation from the secret funds of various governments, the agents of the great munition makers of Europe intrigued in the Netherlands for orders.

Thanks to Hendrick Colijn in these trying circumstances, a reorganization of the Dutch army was carried through.

These diplomatic sensations had another more important result. For more than sixty years, since 1890, the Netherland people had lived in a defeatist frame of mind. Was there really any purpose in a spirited defense, if the country were invaded? The doubts of foreign diplomats as to any Dutch reaction to invasion, were certainly based on the fact that the nation had shown so little interest in its own defenses. Shortly before 1914 a more determined attitude prevailed. The worst phase of the policy of passive neutrality had passed.[66]

In 1914, Belgium was invaded and for four years was a theater of war. The Netherlands escaped Belgium's fate by a narrow margin. The German armies moved round the southern point of Limburg instead of passing through as provided in an alternative plan. In the British Cabinet it was proposed to rush aid to Belgium via the Scheldt that is through Netherland territory, but this was rejected. Again and again the nation was on the verge of being drawn into the conflict. Fortunately, none of the belligerents was seriously interested in a change in the status of the Netherlands. In fact, the existence of this bit of neutral territory between the belligerents was in many respects convenient to both parties.

The Dutch army was mobilized at the first signs of approaching war. This mobilization, ordered on July 31, 1914, preceded by a few hours those of France, Russia and Germany. The military force assembled was impressive, but as was revealed long afterwards its equipment was in pitiful condition. There was a lack of ammunition and no provision had been made for its manufacture; the guns were of most diverse models, requiring different types of shells; and the permanent fortifications were hopelessly out of date. "The traditional bravery of the Dutch soldier will make up for their deficient equipment," was the sole consolation offered to young officers who complained about the armament of their troops. To be sure, the government started feverishly to improve defenses, but the absence of war industries and indeed of all heavy industry, made the nation dependent for its military supplies on the belligerents.[67] Communications with the United States soon became insecure, and the Dutch buying in small quantities could not compete with the British and French in the American munitions market. Gradually the material condition of the army improved but the progress of time and the long suspense made it increasingly difficult to keep up the spirit of the troops, which at first had been excellent.

Four years of mobilization had placed a heavy financial burden on the people, but this was offset by a sudden increase in prosperity. Before the war, in 1913, the total revenue of the Dutch state in Europe had amounted to 227,423,000 guilders. Expenditures had exceeded that amount by 11,-300,000 guilders. In 1916, after two years of war in Europe, the government's revenue had risen to 310,000,000, an increase of 40%, and its expenditures to 532,531,000, an increase of more than 100%. In 1918, the situation was still worse. A revenue of 561,000,000 amounted to little more than half of the expenditures which were 1,051,000,000 guilders. After the war public finances were stabilized at a level of about 700,000,000 guilders annual revenue. Taxation had increased enormously during the war, but the nation carried the heavier burden of the 1920's more easily perhaps than it had the far lighter one of 1913. The rise in revenue and expenditure was due in part to widespread currency devaluation, in part to increased prosperity.

For about two years internal politics came to a standstill. All efforts were concentrated on defense. Then as the war continued and people became accustomed to periodical crises caused by repeated attempts of the belligerents to wrest concessions from neutrals, normal political life resumed its course. In a short time it became evident that democratic tendencies had been greatly strengthened by events abroad. A revision of the constitution, planned before the war, was carried into effect in 1917. This revision introduced universal suffrage and provided for woman suffrage to be enacted by Parliament, as was done in 1919. It reorganized the First Chamber by making the qualifications of candidates the same for both houses. Finally, it reorganized the electoral system by proportional representation. Another section granted complete equality to public and private schools. All schools meeting the legal requirements would be subsidized equally from the public funds. Twenty years after this revision which satisfied prolonged popular demand, the majority of elementary schools were denominational.[68]

The introduction of universal suffrage was one of the chief demands of the Socialist Party. It did not however bring them the gains they expected. The party which derived the greatest benefit was the Roman Catholic. It soon formed the strongest party in Parliament, with 30 out of 100 seats. The Socialists who had 18 seats, won 22, becoming the second largest party. The older political groups seemed to be on the decline. The year 1917 brought a socialist revolution in Russia; the next year another in Germany. Under their influence the revolutionary ideal revived in the hearts of some members of the Social Democratic Party, who for more than twenty years had suppressed it as impractical.

Hunger, especially among the poorer sections of the population in the large cities, caused revolutionary outbreaks in the early months of 1918. Troops intervened and people were shot. A few units of the army, bored by standing at arms for years, were on the verge of mutiny. The possibility of a successful revolution seemed great, and Pieter J. Troelstra called upon his followers to force the government to give way to a Socialist administration. He stood alone among the leaders of Socialism, and counter-demonstrations had restored political stability in a few days. The small Communist group staged a demonstration in Amsterdam, where shots were fired and one man killed. That was all. But the attempted revolution did great harm in internal politics. It created deep distrust between the democratic, denominational parties and the Social Democrats, making cooperation infinitely more difficult than it had been.

This most unfortunate incident strengthened the hands of conservative elements in the Netherlands. In 1918, the Liberals seemed crushed beyond all hope of recovery. Their three factions together had only fifteen seats out of a hundred in the Chamber. Apparently the Liberal era had come to an end. This was only partly true. The indirect influence of the Liberal groups remained strong, for most leaders of finance and of commerce and the majority of higher officials, especially in the judiciary and in the foreign service were their adherents. They no longer formed a popular party, but a burgher aristocracy, and although the political power of this aristocracy was small, its social and economic strength was enormous. One must realize this to understand the internal developments in the Netherlands after 1920. The leaders of the denominational parties usually controlled political power, but they could exercise it only through high administrative officials and with the help of economic leaders who belonged to the Liberal minority.[69]

The new political leaders were naturally influenced by their surroundings, and at times it seemed that the change of leadership had been a triumph for Liberal economic conceptions. Many members of the denominational parties, although unable to give precise reasons for their discontent, grew restless and balked at their own leadership. The old antithesis between the burgher aristocracy and the burgher democracy seemed to be revived. The Liberals, who in their early years had represented the anti-oligarchic tradition of 1572, 1747 and 1795, were now firmly established in the higher positions of the country and tended to close and narrow their ranks just as the revolutionaries of 1572 had done when they had gained power. The expectation that Liberal control would be broken by the new regime was sadly disappointed. The twenty years between the two world wars constituted a period of uninterrupted "Rightist" rule. From what has been said before it is evident that the terms "Rightist" and "Leftist" in Dutch political history do not mean "conservative" and "progressive-democratic," but indicate a basic difference in the conception of state and society. The Rightist groups adhere to the religious point of view that both state and society are subject to divine laws; the Leftists ignore religious conceptions as fundamentals of government and statesmanship. The elections of 1918 did not give the Rightist groups an absolute majority. Their predominance in the following four-year period was dependent upon the opposition between the two Leftist groups, the Liberals and the Socialists. From 1922 until the outbreak of the war in 1940 the Rightists *did* have a clear majority, but dissension among the three parties composing that majority prevented the regular working of the parliamentary system. The consequence was that a few men dominated internal Dutch politics. Although a premier is unknown to the constitution, the founder of the Cabinet holds a pre-eminent position in the Council of Ministers. Parliamentary cabinets being the exception, he must have extraordinary personal influence, which further strengthens his position.

The Rightists started on their twenty-year period of administration with a cabinet under Ruys de Beerenbrouck. Ruys, a nobleman of Guelderland, was the first Catholic to hold this prominent position in Netherland politics since the founding of the kingdom. There had been Catholic ministers, but never Catholic leadership. After the elections of 1922 the Cabinet continued with certain changes as the second Ruys Government. In this Cabinet the Ministry of Finance fell to Dirk J. De Geer, a descendant of the great promoter of Swedish industry in the XVIIth century. A proposal to strengthen the navy led to his resignation, and he was replaced by Hendrik Colijn. Again the Cabinet was reconstructed as the third Ruys Ministry. It made way for the first Colijn administration after the elections of 1925. After three and a half months this Cabinet fell in a sudden outburst of long buried antagonism between Calvinists and Catholics. It was succeeded by the first De Geer Cabinet. The elections of 1929 resulted in the formation of the fourth Ruys Cabinet with De Geer again in the post of Minister of Finance. This Cabinet faced the storm of the economic depression, which caused the formation of a new administration on a broader basis, the second Colijn Cabinet. This Cabinet was succeeded after the elections of 1937 by the third Colijn Cabinet. The year 1939 brought a "national government," in which Socialists participated for the first time. It was formed by former minister De Geer and was thus the second De Geer Cabinet.

In this whole period only three men succeeded in forming administrations. Others were asked, but failed. This might have been natural under a two-party system, but not in a country where in 1929 thirty-seven political groups presented candidates at the polls, and representatives of nine parties were elected. This was the result of proportional representation. By 1933, *thirteen* parties were represented in a parliament numbering only one hundred members. This enormously increased the difficulty of forming a cabinet. The modest salaries paid to members of the government did not attract people who could earn many times more in less disagreeable offices. Strong personalities who might have been attracted by the power connected with office, did not welcome a task where freedom of action was hindered by the absence of a regular parliamentary majority.

Only a total revision of the existing party system could bring relief. As it was, the dissatisfaction of party members was rarely expressed by shifting their allegiance to other parties. They formed new parties! For religious reasons the ultra-democratic group among the Catholics would not join the Socialists. They formed a Catholic Democratic Party which was occasionally represented in parliament. The "anti-popery" Calvinists never dreamed of abandoning the maxims of Groen and Kuyper, but formed three or four new parties, each of which in its own way stood for a purified political Calvinism. It was a representative of one of these groups who brought down the first Colijn Cabinet by forcing his co-religionists in parliament to vote "for or against Rome." The Communists barked at the heels of the Socialists, to be attacked themselves by ultra-radical anarchist groups. The Liberals alone succeeded in reforming their badly broken line, and this saved them from what might have been complete elimination by 1922. In between larger groups and their rebellious satellites were ranged "independents," the "Farmers Party," the "National Revival Group,"—forerunners of Fascism in something more than name—and so many others.

In spite of the rank growth of the prevailing system, a general reorganization of political alliances was out of the question. The educational issue had been decided in favor of the denominational groups, and many of the Leftists were glad to be rid of the problem. All political parties, except the Liberals, had anchored their programs so firmly in theology or philosophy that only by breaking this relation could conditions be changed. Few problems involving fundamental principles arose after 1920. The Catholics dropped their demand for the suppression of the last traces of religious inequality so as not to irritate their Protestant allies; and the latter took care not to overemphasize the official Calvinist character of the nation. Tradition and fear of the unknown kept the masses of the people in the political allegiances of their fathers. It was as much a sin for a Socialist to vote the Catholic ticket, as for a Catholic to vote for a Socialist.

Proportional representation made party ties more binding as elections were no longer contests between candidates but between programs. The power of party leaders increased. Compulsory voting—introduced by the constitutional revision of 1917—further strengthened their hands by sending thousands to the polls who had little personal interest in the elections. Small groups of electors whose task it was in the primaries to bring new candidates to the front or to eliminate representatives who were no longer wanted, could get no further by the greatest exertion than adding a new name at the tail end of the party list. Candidates favored by the party leaders were given well protected places at the top of the list. Proportional representation had its merits, but with the progress of time it became clear that an intermediary system combining the advantage of proportional representation with direct contact between the individual candidate and the people of his district must be devised.

The twenty years between the two wars can be divided into three periods. The first was that of transition from the pre-war to the post-war system. It ended with the second constitutional revision in 1922. The second ran from 1922 to the depression, which occurred in the Netherlands in 1931. The third continued until the invasion of 1940.

The first period, when Ruys de Beerenbrouck was leader of the administration with Mgr. Nolens, the leader of the Catholic faction in parliament as his "eminence grise," was one of optimism, of work for a better future, and of generous spending. At the very outset the administration was confronted with a most delicate problem. Belgium, no longer neutral after the German invasion of 1914, complained to the Paris Peace Conference that her defense was seriously impaired by the line of the Belgian-Dutch boundary drawn under the agreement of 1839. She asked that the Dutch province of Limburg and the districts of Zeeland-Flanders situated south of the Scheldt, be turned over to her in exchange for German territory to be annexed by the Netherlands. The Hague immediately retorted that the Netherlands, at peace with Germany, could not annex the territory of their neighbor; quite apart from this consideration they were unwilling to cede one square inch of territory. After a few anxious months, the Netherland government saw its steadfastness rewarded by a decision of the Conference against territorial changes in the Low Countries.

This first post-war period brought rapid advances in social legislation, and finally another revision of the Constitution. Only five years had elapsed since the revision of 1917, but in these five years much had happened. All the German ruling houses had been dethroned. Among these princes were the next heirs to the throne of the Netherlands after Queen Wilhelmina's only daughter, Princess Juliana. In those same years, a stream of publications from the archives of Petrograd and Berlin revealed the dangers of leaving questions of war and peace to the arbitrary decisions of monarchs. No one, to be sure, could accuse Queen Wilhelmina of having interfered with foreign policy, let alone having abused her constitutional right to declare war, but the times demanded that this right be transferred to the representatives of the people. Finally, a new conception of colonial administration had developed which required readjustment of the relation between the Netherlands and the East Indies. These were the points covered by the revision of 1922.

With the exclusion of all of Queen Wilhelmina's distant relatives from the succession, a new problem arose; what course should be followed if the only remaining heir to the throne died? After prolonged discussion a motion to decide the eventual question of monarchy or republic by a plebiscite was defeated, and a paragraph was inserted in the Constitution giving the States General the power to elect a new king. The conclusion of treaties with foreign powers and the power to declare war, were made subject to the approval of the States General. More important was a slight change in the first article of the Constitution. This article had formerly read: "The Kingdom of the Netherlands consists of the Kingdom in Europe and its possessions overseas." This was changed to: "The Kingdom of the Netherlands consists of the Kingdom in Europe, the Netherlands Indies, Surinam, and Curaçao." This opened the way for complete equality between the Netherlands and the Netherlands colonies.

The first steps in this direction had been taken in 1916, when the Netherland government proposed and parliament passed a bill for limited self-government in the Indies. A "People's Chamber" was instituted which had little legislative power and did not represent the masses of Indonesia's inhabitants, but obliged the East Indian administration to give an account of its actions to the public. The scope of the reform was widened a few years later, and a larger representation was granted to Indonesians elected by local representative councils. Thus the reform of the central East Indian administration was closely connected with the decentralization of government authority and the introduction of local self-government. The constitutional revision of 1922 paved the way for further reforms and necessitated a revision of the Administrative Act of 1854, which was replaced in 1925 by the East Indian Constitution.

This new Act limited the participation of European authorities in East Indian affairs to a few well defined cases. The Dutch Parliament at home retained the power to veto the East Indian budget as a whole, but the details could be discussed only by the People's Council, which received quasi-parliamentary rights and in practice widened its influence still further. The assurance that their opposition to unpopular executive decisions would probably be backed by the parliamentary opposition at home, gave critics of the East Indian administration in Batavia a moral support that the governor-general could not ignore. The share of Indonesians in the government was increased in 1927, when a majority of seats in the People's Council was reserved for Indonesians, and five seats more, out of a total of sixty, set aside for representatives of non-Indonesians, such as Chinese and Arabs.

Besides this officially fostered autonomy, nationalism was growing in the Indies, and had done so in Java since 1912. It sprang from two different sources: Javanese pride in their cultural traditions, and Mohammedanism. The former was important to the higher class Javanese; the latter was associated by the masses with an agitation against Chinese predominance in retail trade. Originally neither movement was revolutionary, but the second fell under the influence of the extreme radicalism that spread over the world after the last war. Its chances were spoiled, however, by a premature revolt which was easily suppressed in 1926.[70]

Never had the importance of the East Indies to the Netherlands in Europe been so great as in the years following the last war. Previously only a trickle of emigrants had gone to the East. Most of them returned after twenty years or so in the tropics, some having acquired wealth. When the Indies were opened to free enterprise the picture changed. The number of Europeans living in the East Indies doubled within thirty years after 1870. Around 1930 there were probably 50,000 Netherlanders born in Europe living in the East. In the years of prosperity between 1920 and 1930 most of them stayed only a short time, so that there was a constant flow back and forth between Europe and Asia. Today there is hardly anyone among the city population of the Netherlands without friends or relations who are or have been in the Indies. Contact between the two parts of the kingdom became intimate. The boom period also caused an increased influx of Dutch capital—much of which was lost in the depression—and by 1930 the East Indian Government had floated many loans in Amsterdam to a total of about one billion guilders.

Far greater were the returns from East Indian enterprises. In 1926 agricultural enterprises alone, largely in the hands of Netherlanders, paid dividends of 187,000,000 guilders. To this sum must be added 132,000,000 guilders from other enterprises and 40,000,000 guilders for payments to directors and senior staff in Europe. Free enterprise, without resorting to the crude methods of the XIXth century, had earned 359,000,000 guilders in one year. In the same year, the East Indian Government paid 93,000,000 guilders in pensions and furlough allowances. Most of this money also went to the Netherlands. It is evident that most of this income represented only the normal interest on the billions of guilders invested in the Indies, the rest being the ordinary reward of labor. Even so, investments in the Indies were highly profitable—but only for so long as the boom lasted.

In view of the financial importance of the East Indies, the government considered a strengthening of Dutch naval forces in the archipelago of primary importance. A storm of protest rose. The administration—the second

Ruys Cabinet—was violently attacked for proposing new armaments only a few months after the Netherlands' entry into the League of Nations, which had evoked dreams of general disarmament. Moreover, the first post-war boom was already on the decline. The second Ruys Cabinet stuck to their guns. To strengthen the government, Hendrik Colijn was made minister of Finance, but the anti-militarist agitation increased in violence. Colijn, formerly a high executive of the *Bataafsche,* a subsidiary of the Shell group, was not exactly the person to placate the Socialist and Liberal Democratic opposition. "International Trusts," "colonial imperialism," militarism," and other terms adorned with choice epithets were used by the opposition. With an economic crisis threatening the Netherlands, it was indeed not easy to explain why hundreds of millions should be spent on battleships and cruisers, which it would cost hundreds of millions more to maintain. Yet, there were urgent reasons for the government's decision. The independence of the country was at stake. During the first decade of the XXth century the Netherlands had been unable to move without endangering the independence of the home country or risking the overseas territories. The Indies needed a naval force of their own capable of protecting the island world whatever happened in Europe. The events of 1940 have demonstrated this clearly. Astute Dutch politicians reasoned that the Netherlands in Europe, a point of vital strategic interest, would be protected by the mutual distrust of its neighbors for each other. This comfortable if not convincing thought did not apply to the kingdom in Asia. But the people did not see matters in this light and, under popular pressure, ten members of the Catholic Party joined the opposition. The Navy Bill was defeated.

Unfortunately, this led to another period of political unrest. In 1925, an Anti-Popery outburst broke the coalition of the Catholic and Christian Historical Parties, and with it all hope for a strong administration. For four years, reduction of expenditure was the first concern of the government. It was a time of prosperity, but the leaders of the state proceeded cautiously. They could not have maintained their positions without the tacit support of the Anti-Revolutionary and Catholic Parties, among which caution and a desire to consolidate achievements had replaced earlier democratic endeavors. The third period, which started with the depression of 1931, brought this clearly to light. The economic crisis came later to the Netherlands than to most countries. The national economic structure was basically sound, but in the midst of the general catastrophe, escape was impossible. There was a huge loss on American investments and a goodly portion of the billions of guilders laid out there vanished forever. The East Indies, deprived of markets for their raw material, were severely hit. In 1932 the dividends sent to Europe from the East fell to 31,000,000 guilders and then to 26,000,000, or less than ten percent of what they had been. Losses affected production and trade in the home country. The most serious aspect of the crisis for the Netherlands was the total collapse of the German economy, for trade relations between the Netherlands and Germany had been close. In 1928 Germany provided 27% of all Netherland imports and took 23% of the total exports. More than two billion guilders, invested by Netherlanders in German loans, enterprises and institutions were blocked and virtually lost. The crisis of 1931 and the subsequent German restrictions on the transfer of money to foreign countries broke the backbone of Netherland economic life, after the catastrophe in the United States and in the Indies had destroyed its outer structure. Unemployment rose to fantastic proportions. Out of a total population of eight millions 500,000 people were without work.

Even so, the Netherlands was spared the worst. No major banking concern or industrial enterprise collapsed. No one was in danger of starvation. Help was provided by government agencies, and additional relief by private charity. In these circumstances the leadership of the Ruys Cabinet proved too weak. In 1933 the reins of government fell again to Hendrik Colijn, who remained in office until 1939. Colijn, the successor of Abraham Kuyper, the hero of the "small people," as leader of the anti-revolutionary party, set to work to rebuild Netherland economic life. He succeeded by strict adherence to conservative economic doctrine. Even after Great Britain had set the example, he postponed devaluation as long as he could and carried through a policy of "adaptation," or reduction of the standard of living which among certain classes made him the best hated man in the country. Yet he scored remarkable electoral successes. In 1927, the Anti-Revolutionary group in the Second Chamber had only 13 members. In 1933 it had 14 and 17 in 1937. The thousands of electors who transferred their votes to the Calvinist-democratic group were certainly not all converts to the theological and social views of its founders. Most of them came from the decaying Liberal groups. They did not vote the Anti-Revolutionary ticket, they voted for Colijn. By his economic policy, Colijn made the Anti-Revolutionary group the standard-bearers of conservatism. Revolt among his own followers threatened and the gains of the small "Anti-Popery" faction was a sign of trouble.

Colijn's policy may have been initially sound. It is a matter of opinion whether it should have been maintained as long as it was. It had some very unpleasant and undemocratic aspects that should have been avoided, or remedied by Parliament. But Colijn carried on. At times, the days of the old oligarchy seemed to have returned. In the words of Wagenaar already quoted, "the wisdom of those who knew and could judge alone decided what was the true interest of the masses." This attitude was given exaggerated expression in Colijn's broadcast after the Munich crisis of 1938, when he comforted his listeners with the assurance that the immediate danger of war had passed and concluded, like a father speaking to little children, "and now go to bed without fear, and sleep well."

The opposition to Colijn failed to crystallize. There was unrest in the Catholic Party; dissatisfaction among Anti-Revolutionaries; and the Socialists, left without influence on public affairs, vainly sought to arouse the masses with plans to provide work for all, and with attacks on the "ultra-capitalist" system of Colijn. The growing tension of foreign relations, the influx of political refugees from Germany, and the constant agitation of Nazis and anti-Nazis created additional discontent. Then it was that imitators of Hitler and Mussolini thought the moment ripe to swing the Dutch people into line with the totalitarian front.

The Nazi and Fascist organizers made a fundamental mistake. They imported from abroad a dictatorial form of leadership totally alien to the Dutch mentality. They might have seen that the country was already restive under the strong personal leadership of Mr. Colijn. They might have studied history and found on every page that Netherlanders were strong individualists and would never bow to a makeshift dictator. Anton Mussert, leader of the National Socialist Movement, was the only one of a number of would-be dictators who gained any considerable following.

This he achieved by the vagueness of his principles, by shifting from one point of view to another, so that all the discontented elements who thought "what this country needs is a Hitler," could join without sacrificing their personal opinions. Mussert's elusive attitude is nowhere clearer than in his approach to the Jewish issue, where he shifted from neutrality to anti-semitism according to his momentary relations with his German prototypes. Mussert's party reached its peak in the 1935 election when it obtained 8% of the votes cast. Then Hitler's brutality in dealing with political opponents—Socialists and Catholics—and his persecution of the Jews caused a vehement reaction. Two years after its initial success the party was reduced to 4.2%, and two years later it had fallen to 3.7%. This caused Mussert to turn to violent revolution with foreign support for the achievement of his aims. The financing of his political campaigns and of his newspapers became increasingly difficult. At this time he probably accepted money from Berlin to continue and it is noteworthy that he became violently anti-semitic.

Viewed from the political angle, the picture of the contemporary Netherlands is not impressive, but the antithesis between cultural and political development is remarkable. While the latter was rigid, slow and traditional, the former was vivid, restless, always innovating. Literature attracted more attention in those twenty years than perhaps ever before. Dutch publishers showed amazing industry and enterprise, and succeeded in finding a buying public for many serious works, even at high prices. In painting there were no really great artists, but here also interest was general. Even from a social point of view the outlook in the Netherlands was bright, in spite of the misery caused by the depression. Infant mortality was 3.9% lower than in any other country. The death rate placed the Netherlands in the front rank with Canada and New Zealand, and there was a remarkable contrast between the birth rate in the Netherlands and that of neighboring countries. The latter was at least 25% and sometimes 50% higher in the Netherlands and stood at 20 per 1,000 inhabitants. Indeed, the problem of over-population became more and more threatening. Under the German occupation the population has passed the nine million mark and the density of population, about 640 per square mile, exceeds that of any of the United States, except Rhode Island.

This population trend was foreseen, and the Netherland people undertook the gigantic task of extending the inhabitable area of the country by draining the Zuiderzee. The labor, the cost and the technical difficulties involved in this fantastic project have often been recorded. When the work is completed—two of the four *polders* are ready now—900 square miles will have been added to the territory of the kingdom. Begun in 1918 the work progressed rapidly up to the invasion, and even war has not prevented its continuance. When the Zuiderzee has been finally drained, the Dutch people will have recovered from the sea an area larger than that lost in the course of the last five thousand years. The total losses since earliest times are estimated at 2,243 square miles. The square miles recovered before 1917 numbered 1,305. The draining of the Zuiderzee will leave a net gain of about thirty-eight square miles.

Epilogue on the War

IN 1940 war came to the Netherlands for the first time in more than a hundred years. The last campaign fought by Netherland troops in Europe had been the ten days war against Belgium in 1831, in which less than 300 Dutch soldiers were killed. After 1839, the Netherlands had gone back to neutrality. Since the Burgundian period, neutrality had been an axiom of foreign policy for large groups of Netherlanders. On this policy the entire nation was in virtual agreement, opinions varying only as to the degree of passivity towards world events.

From 1890 until 1920 the foreign policy of the Netherlands had been completely passive. In 1920, when the kingdom joined the League of Nations, this passive neutrality was deliberately discarded. The importance of this departure from traditional policy is borne out by the debates preceding it in parliament. Under the Covenant of the League, the Netherland state bound itself to take part in armed conflicts, at least by allowing foreign troops to pass through their territory and by joining in economic sanctions. A strong group of representatives contended that the advantages to be derived from membership in the League did not justify such a reversal of traditional policy. The majority protested that the country of Hugo Grotius could not stand aloof from an organization for the maintenance of peace, when an attempt was made to substitute law for force in the settlement of international disputes. "Idealists," was the retort of their opponents. "Small nations should hesitate to assume far-reaching international commitments, they must leave these matters to the great powers who have the force and therefore the responsibility. Small nations must not attempt to play a role in international politics." Some of these arguments had been raised in the XVIIth and XVIIIth centuries by the merchant princes of Amsterdam, and it is striking to find the historian of Amsterdam, the late Professor Brugmans, strongly supporting these views.[71] The "idealists" were in the majority, but the opposition did not fail to point out vacancies in the new council of world affairs. Were the Netherlands to give up their neutrality, while great powers like the United States did not? The government took this criticism to heart and only took action when it seemed clear that the League was not to be merely an instrument of French hegemony, and that other great powers, especially Great Britain, would cooperate. The same debate recurred when the protocol of Geneva came up for discussion.

The "idealists" were obviously right. When Great Britain and France, the two most powerful neighbors of the Netherlands joined the League and the door was left ajar for Germany to join, the Netherlands could not afford to stand aloof. Although the nation might feel secure with all danger from the east removed and Belgian pretensions successfully resisted, there was no guarantee that conditions would remain so favorable. From the Dutch point of view the general situation had deteriorated in the Southwest Pacific. Japan had gained enormously by the European War. China, in constant turmoil since the revolution of 1911, displayed unusual interest in Chinese citizens abroad, hundreds of thousands of whom lived in the East Indies.

During the third decade of the century Netherland participation in League affairs was cautious. The Dutch representatives at many international conferences contributed to the common task to the best of their ability. Major political conflicts or questions of principle did not arise. During these ten years the Netherlands were chiefly concerned with some of the after effects of the Treaty of Versailles. The Peace Conference had decided to leave unchanged the Dutch-Belgian boundary and had left the settlement of other problems arising from Belgium's new international status to direct negotiations between the two Lowland kingdoms. Other changes resulted from the new control of the Rhine in which France had gained an important part.

Long negotiations with Belgium led to the drafting of a treaty which was accepted by both foreign offices and ratified by the Belgian Parliament. When its provisions became known, a storm of protest rose in the Netherlands. The treaty was said to be unduly favorable to Belgium. The main objection was an undertaking to build at Dutch expense a canal from Antwerp to Moerdijk, south of Dordrecht, to give direct access from the lower Rhine to the Belgian port. It was contended that this canal would ruin Rotterdam, an obvious exaggeration, and that there was no reason why Dutch taxpayers should pay for a canal useful only to Belgium, an equally obvious truth. The Second Chamber of the States General accepted the treaty after prolonged debate. The First Chamber rejected it, the most momentous decision that body had taken in the hundred and thirty years of its existence. The Belgian problem remained unsettled.

Numerous opponents of the treaty were undoubtedly influenced by the very close political and military ties between Belgium and France during those ten years. Belgium was depicted as a French outpost, a pawn of that great power in European politics. Strength was lent to this view by the fact that the Netherlands had to resist claims of the Rhine-Navigation Commission—controlled by a French-Belgian majority—to control Dutch territorial waters under the Treaty of Versailles, to which the Netherlands were not a party. Too cordial cooperation with Belgium might suggest that the Netherlands had also been drawn into the French bloc. This criticism although exaggerated was comprehensible in a country that had sacrificed its neutrality on the altar of a world peace and not for any particular group of nations.

In 1925, the sixth assembly of the League of Nations took up the problem of disarmament. A preparatory committee was appointed. On this committee the Netherland delegate, Mr. John Loudon, was elected chairman. The story of the Disarmament Conference need not be told here. While agreeing on the principle of disarmament the great powers could not agree on its application, and were suspected by the other powers of making the conference a diplomatic battleground to test their strength. At the actual Disarmament Conference in 1932, total rather than partial limitation of war material was supported whole-heartedly only by the Scandinavian States and the Netherlands. The attitude of the great powers continued to arouse the criticism of smaller states. Finally at the suggestion of the Spanish representative, de Madariaga, this resulted in the formation of an eight power group—Spain, Switzerland, Czechoslovakia, Belgium, Sweden, Norway, Denmark and the Netherlands—to oppose the growing tendency of the great powers to settle important questions among themselves, leaving the smaller states no alternative but to accept their decision.

The Disarmament Conference was a last desperate effort to arrive at cooperation between the European powers. The hope that the states of Europe might form an alliance or even a federation had faded a few years previously. In 1930 M. Briand had again suggested that the powers of Europe consider the establishment of such a federal bond without, as he said, "affecting the sovereignty of any of the nations belonging to the organization." In view of recent events, the reply of the Netherlands has great significance, especially as they were the only state to stress a point now considered of primary importance. Their answer was that the proposed cooperation could succeed only in so far as States were willing to limit the exercise of their sovereign rights. "A conception of sovereignty leaving no room for the voluntary acceptance of certain limitations must be declared incompatible with the very nature of international relations." The modern attitude that sovereignty is not absolute, but relative and naturally limited, is clearly expressed here. The Netherlands, in agreement with a number of other powers, disapproved of Briand's plan in that it seemed to create a European bloc that might lead to inter-continental friction.

Dreams of a more peaceful and prosperous Europe vanished in the depression that shook the whole economic and political structure of Europe to its very foundations. The years from 1930 to 1933 form a real turning point in Dutch history. The Netherlands, relatively secure in Europe, faced a grave crisis in the Far East. Japan started to attack white supremacy in Asia as soon as Europe was shaken by the economic catastrophe. Her attack was both military and economic. The Japanese army invaded Manchuria, and Japan began to undersell European and American producers, conquering new markets and fresh spheres of influence. One of the main objects of Japan's economic attack was the Netherlands Indies, where imports from Japan were only 11% of the total import in 1929, rising in 1934 to 34%. In the same period exports of Dutch cotton goods to the Indies fell from 25 to 7% of the total import. Japan's progress was continuous. It was difficult to object to Japanese imports in an area the Netherlanders themselves had always proudly proclaimed to be open to free competition, even though the Japanese trade was completely one-sided. Japan exported to the Indies, but did not import from them any substantial amount of raw materials. Japanese penetration tended further to upset the already precarious economic position of the islands and seriously impaired the welfare of the population. Moreover, the concomitant military attack on China revealed broader and more sinister aims.

The proposal of the U.S. Secretary of State, Mr. Stimson, that all powers interested in the Far East should consult on ways and means to prevent Japanese aggression from gaining momentum, was all to the advantage of the Netherlands. But as soon as Washington's invitation to take part in such a consultation reached The Hague, the deplorable consequences of the rejection of the Naval Bill in 1925 became evident. The extreme weakness of East Indian defenses, a mere police force, prevented the Netherlands from supporting Mr. Stimson's move. Not even a gesture of sympathy with the American point of view was feasible when it became known that the London Foreign Office did not intend to associate itself with Mr. Stimson's views. The Manchuria affair was a death blow to collective security. That any great power could violate the status quo with impunity, if it did not antagonize enough other great powers, was the lesson of the Far Eastern crisis. In the past the Netherlands had relied largely upon Great Britain to maintain the status quo in the East Indies. The events of 1931 and 1932 indicated a radical change in Far Eastern relations, and the Netherlands were faced with new problems.

A strengthening of the Dutch army and navy in the Far East was urgently needed, but the possibility of large armament credits seemed more remote than ever before. The Netherlands in Europe were confronted with extensive unemployment, and the revenues of the East Indian administration had been cut in half by the economic crisis. The World Economic Conference in London of 1933 failed. Mr. Colijn vainly warned the delegates that ruthless economic warfare threatened. He was able to point out that while others *talked* about trade barriers the Netherlands and Belgium had begun to reduce customs duties by the treaty of Ouchy-Lausanne of 1932. Public opinion in both countries reacted favorably and business circles eagerly discussed a customs union of the Low Countries.

A few months later the kingdom of the Netherlands took another interesting initiative. On September 29, 1933, at the fourteenth assembly of the League of Nations, it called attention to the problem of German refugees, and urged international collaboration for their re-settlement. The results were meager. Then came the fateful year of 1935, which tested the League of Nations sanctions against aggression. The Netherlands among others voted for sanctions and an oil embargo against Italy, while the majority of the great powers held aloof. There was considerable internal opposition to this participation in the Ethiopian conflict. The Netherlands had now departed from the strict neutrality so scrupulously observed until 1920, and various powerful groups in the nation demanded the adoption of a position like that of Switzerland, which enjoyed a privileged neutral status within the League. These groups found adherents not only among the few pro-Fascists, but also among business men who feared the deterioration of foreign trade. But the government, supported by parliament and the majority of the nation, faithfully executed its obligations under the Covenant.

The pitiful result of the sanctions against Italy, played into the hands of the "isolationists." Great Britain and France prepared to acknowledge the new situation in Ethiopia, if not *de jure,* at least *de facto.* The smaller nations felt duped by this arbitrary decision of the great powers. Their disillusion was voiced by the Danish Minister of Foreign Affairs speaking in the name of his own country and of the Netherlands, Norway, Spain, Sweden and Switzerland. In a broadcast he declared that the confidence of the small states in the effectiveness of the League's measures had been greatly shaken, but that they would uphold international law as long as possible. Consequently, when an Ethiopian delegation sought admission to the meeting of the League in the fall of 1936 and when Italian opposition to such admission was apparently supported by France and Great Britain on the ground that the Ethiopian credentials were invalid, several of the smaller states—including the Netherlands and one of the British dominions, backed the attempt of the Soviet Union to have the Ethiopian delegation admitted. The Russian proposal was adopted by an overwhelming majority, but the disillusion of the smaller powers was complete. The system of collective security had collapsed.

Soon afterwards the Netherlands met with further disappointment in their promotion of international cooperation. The "Oslo group" held a trade-barrier conference at The Hague in July 1937 to study the reduction of tariffs and quota in international trade. There was some difficulty in formulating practicable plans for the group as a whole, but the individual member states set an example by reducing tariffs and modifying the quota system not only for other members of the group, but also for the great powers, Britain, France and Germany, and in one instance the United States. The great powers showed a singular lack of appreciation for these gestures of good will. Their negative attitude smothered the movement for the removal of trade barriers before it could develop.

Economic cooperation by the Oslo powers might have led to political cooperation. The declaration made by the Danish Minister of Foreign Affairs after the collapse of the anti-Italian sanctions seemed to anticipate such a possibility. It was further indicated by the change in the character of the League of Nations. From a supposedly world organization, it had become a mere bloc of nations, dominated by France and Great Britain and more or less supported by Russia, but opposed to the ex-members of the League, Japan, Germany and Italy. The great powers did not always place League interests above their own, and the smaller nations who had participated in the sanctions against one of them felt they had been let down by the great powers. A basic change of attitude among them was the result. Their best chance of security now lay in the formation of a bloc of small nations.

This was no easy task as the prospective members of such a bloc were scattered. Czechoslovakia and Poland had alliances with one or more of the great powers and were in a different position to that of Scandinavia and the Low Countries. National traditions hampered effective cooperation among the five States concerned. The government in Berlin, growing bolder with the progress of German rearmament, watched developments on its northern and eastern boundaries sharply. Newspaper reports of political cooperation by the Oslo states caused Goebbels to denounce the scheme as an "encirclement of Germany." In January 1937, Hitler took personal notice of the situation when he offered "to recognize Belgium and the Netherlands as neutral regions for all time" and to guarantee their territorial integrity. The Netherlands rejected this suggestion which, whatever its value, would have modified the international status of the country. The integrity of the Dutch territory was not subject to discussion. It was not dependent on alien guarantees and the acceptance of Hitler's offer would have given Germany the right to supervise the international relations of the Netherlands.

The Oslo states never attempted organized political cooperation although their action was occasionally concerted, as for instance with regard to the recognition of the king of Italy as emperor of Ethiopia. It is sad to record that not even a limited coordination of effort between Belgium and the Netherlands was realized. Both states hurriedly strengthened their defenses, both revised their relationship to the League of Nations in an effort to return to their pre-war neutrality policy. In March 1937, the Foreign Minister of the Netherlands officially declared that the article of the covenant providing for free passage through the territory of member states of troops engaged against a power declared by the League to be an aggressor, was no longer considered binding by the Netherlands. Belgium was released from its obligations under the treaty of Locarno by Britain and France, and returned to neutrality. The Scandinavian states adopted a similar policy.

The League of Nations had failed. The smaller countries are commonly blamed for having returned to neutrality at a time when war was rapidly approaching and the liberty of their peoples was at stake. It is easy to be wise after the event. Should the small nations have gone to war against Germany by themselves? They were obviously not strong enough, and had they been strong enough there would have been no need to resort to war. Should they have allied themselves with the great powers? What had been the attitude of Great Britain in 1931? Of France in 1935? Of the United States and Great Britain on the oil embargo against Italy? By remaining neutral they could at best only delay their destruction. By overt action they would only have hastened it and played into Hitler's hands. He would have had some sort of justification for the attacks he planned. To be effective the military cooperation between the Low Countries and the western powers ought to have been prepared two or three years before the war, yet who can blame them for not siding with Britain and France in 1937 and 1938? What would have been the fate of the Netherlands if they had done so? That of Czechoslovakia?

In the closing days of August 1939 the German government ordered its ambassador at The Hague to deliver a lengthy statement of its willingness to respect the neutrality of the Netherlands. The conditional character of the declaration was overemphasized. The British government submitted an identical statement, in shorter form and clearer terms. It also contained the conditional clause, "so long as Dutch neutrality is respected by the enemy." Such declarations were little more than assurances of momentary peaceful intentions. Neutrality cannot be exactly defined. New prob-

lems are bound to arise from modern warfare to demand constant clarification and the interpretation, adopted by the neutral state, may not be acceptable to all the belligerents. Recognition of the neutrality of a neighboring state would seem to imply, therefore, a willingness to discuss new problems in a friendly spirit, with the avowed intention of arriving at a peaceful settlement.

The Netherlands were beset by many problems during the few months they were allowed to remain neutral. Shipping and imports of essential foodstuffs and raw materials were hampered—unduly so in the opinion of the Netherland Foreign Office—by the allied blockade. Ships were sunk by German torpedoes and German mines, and reparations often refused. The air above the Netherlands was used by the war planes of both sides in violation of international agreements. Apologies were occasionally tended. None of these violations of neutrality was considered sufficient to justify entering the war. The government in The Hague held them to be intentional or unintentional acts of individuals transgressing their orders, or, in the case of the blockade, to be based on a different interpretation of international law, that called for negotiation before action. A *casus belli* would arise only if one of the belligerents invaded the territory of the Netherlands deliberately and in force.

Despite its gravity the notorious incident at Venlo on November 9, 1940, when two British subjects accompanied by an officer of the Dutch army were shot and kidnaped on Dutch soil, was looked upon as an act of the Gestapo without the knowledge of the German government. It took a good deal of imagination to accept this theory. The German Foreign Office may have been unaware of the plot, as Mr. van Kleffens suggests in his book on the Netherlands and the war, but this can hardly be believed of the Nazi leaders.[72] The German authorities never denied the shooting and kidnaping on Dutch soil, and even sought to justify their action by accusing the Netherland Foreign Office of participation in a British plot "to murder Hitler." The British agents captured at Venlo were firmly convinced that they had established contact with anti-Nazi German officers. The conference planned at Venlo was at least the third in a series of unofficial negotiations between the British and the "anti-Nazis." There is little doubt that the latter were in reality agents of the Gestapo. The British Intelligence Service had fallen into a trap set by the Hitler government to obtain information as to eventual peace conditions. The Netherlands were involved only to the extent that the Intelligence Section of the Dutch General Staff refused to permit such negotiations unless their own representatives were present. In doing this the General Staff went as far as it could to foster peace negotiations, well aware that only a timely peace could save the Low Countries from war. The distribution of German Panzer divisions along the eastern boundary left no doubt as to the direction and aims of the coming attack.

About the time of the Venlo incident, the queen of the Netherlands and the king of Belgium made a joint offer of mediation to the belligerents. This unusual gesture was prompted by reports from Germany that a general attack was planned for early in the morning of Sunday, November 12th. These reports were based on troop movements observed during preceding days. It was difficult to believe that the German General Staff would start operations in the worst season of the year, when the roads of southeastern Belgium are nearly impassable, the soil of the Netherlands is saturated with water, and days are shortening rapidly. The alarm was so serious, however, that all defense lines in the Low Countries were manned, which was exactly what the German General Staff wanted as it gave their agents an excellent opportunity to complete their data. The excellence of the German espionage system was revealed a few months later when a briefcase lost by a German diplomat enroute to Berlin was picked up by a working man and handed over to the Dutch authorities. It contained a lengthy and minute description of Dutch defenses.

Under these circumstances there could be no reasonable objection to an exchange of views between Dutch and Belgian military authorities. Yet the only document available on Dutch-Belgian military cooperation indicates that no staff talks were undertaken. On March 30, 1940, the Dutch commander-in-chief, General Winkelman, forwarded a memorandum to Brussels, to be transmitted to the Belgian government immediately after the beginning of hostilities. This memorandum explained the disposition of the Dutch troops, which had been withdrawn to the western section of the country when it became evident that the Belgians would concentrate their troops along the "K.W. line" between Namur and Antwerp, instead of defending the Meuse line. These dispositions, General Winkelman added, could not be changed at the last minute and the Netherlands and Belgium would be obliged to fight their own battles without concerted action. General Winkelman deplored the fact that the Belgian withdrawal to the "K.W. line" prevented the establishment of an unbroken front from the Zuiderzee to the Ardennes. Events in France showed that this unbroken front strategy suited German tactics admirably. The "hinge" at which the Belgian and Dutch sections of the line joined would have been on the flat, sandy ground south of Weert, exactly the spot best suited for an attack by mechanized forces and easily within the reach of the German Army east of the Meuse. The inevitable breakthrough here would have put an end to organized Lowland resistance on the first or second day.

From this point of view, the absence of coordinated military action may have been beneficial to the Allied cause.

The invasion of Norway in April 1940 might have dissipated the last scruples of the Lowland governments in regard to joint military arrangements. A coordination of defense with France and Britain might then have been considered perfectly justified. Mr. Colijn, no longer in office, urged it upon the Netherland Government. Neutrality had lost its *raison d'être*. The difficulty was to convince the people that participation in the war had become inevitable. This done, what would the Low Countries gain by their drastic change of attitude? The German army stood poised for the attack. It could easily have fought the two campaigns in Norway and in the Netherlands together. What help was to be expected from Britain and France? Active participation would burden the governments in The Hague and Brussels with direct responsibility for the extension of hostilities, and give enemy propaganda a valuable opportunity to influence opinion in the United States. If the governments of the two Lowland countries were ready to abandon neutrality, would it be wise to do so? Could the western powers provide effective aid? The best answer to this is another quotation from Mr. Eelco van Kleffens. "Twice," he writes, "I had a discussion on the subject with the British Prime Minister, Mr. Churchill. He was completely frank and various measures of assistance were at once taken, but they could not be extensive enough to save the situation. . . . These discussions . . . gave me the certainty that even if we could have had any prearranged plans with the Allies for common defense . . . we would have obtained no more help than we obtained now. No more was available." Evidently the most prudent policy was to remain neutral, strengthen the defenses, and wait.

The attack came on May 10, at dawn. The invading army is estimated by a Swiss military authority at more than twenty divisions, forming the XVIIIth army, under General von Kuechler. This estimate seems high. Dutch military intelligence reported nearly forty German divisions between the North Sea and Aachen, but the majority were intended for the invasion of Belgium through the Dutch province of Limburg. This would have left some eighteen divisions for the attack on the Dutch positions. This is only a guess. Our information on events after May 10 is still of the scantiest.

The Dutch army consisted of eleven ordinary divisions, one light mechanized division, regiments of territorial and supply troops, altogether about 300,000 men. Of these one brigade was posted in the extreme northeastern corner, near Delfzijl, to guard the narrow entrance into the Netherlands between the sea and the peatmoors, through which Louis of Nassau had

invaded the northern provinces in 1568. This weak force could only delay
the attack. Four hours' resistance was the most the Dutch High Command
dared to expect. South of the peatmoors of Drente the boundary was virtually undefended. A line of machine gun nests behind the River IJssel
about fifty miles to the west formed the first line of resistance. Near Arnhem, this line ran close to the frontier. It was continued beyond the Rhine
to the Waal and from there behind the Waal-Meuse canal to the Meuse
itself. It followed that river as far as the Belgian frontier. A similar Belgian
line ran behind the Meuse to Maastricht, where it joined the strong fortifications behind the Albert Canal. This was the outer ring of the defense.
Behind it a second line running from the Zuiderzee followed the rivulets
Eem and Grebbe, crossed the Rhine, Waal, and Meuse, being strengthened between the rivers by inundations, and then ran due south through
Brabant towards the Belgian frontier. There it ended, rather abruptly from
a strategic point of view. The plan called for a cordon of troops to be drawn
up east-west along the Belgian frontier, but this can have been no more
than a token force. The memorandum of General Winkelman already
mentioned shows that positions south of the riverbelt were only weakly
held, and most troops had been withdrawn behind the Eem-Grebbe-Waal-
Merwede-Haringvliet line. This front could be shortened by further withdrawing the troops from the Grebbe to behind the inundations running
from Naarden via Utrecht to Gorkum. The First Army Corps, which had
guarded the coast during the months of neutrality, was to form a general
reserve.

The Dutch General Staff clearly saw the necessity of withdrawing its
army behind the inundations where it became apparent that direct coordination of defense with the Belgians was impossible. Under these circumstances it is difficult to understand why the main body of the army was
ordered to make its stand behind the weaker Grebbe line instead of behind
the inundations. The leaders of 1672, faced with a similar problem, rejected
the idea of resistance at the Grebbe for exactly the reasons that caused the
collapse of that line in 1940. In his memorandum General Winkelman had
said that he preferred the Grebbe because it offered better possibilities for
counterattack. These tactics were courageous but unrealistic in view of the
overwhelming superiority of the enemy in numbers and equipment. The
inundation line had been extensively written up in the months preceding
the battle. It was claimed to be impassible, and the sudden defeat of the
Dutch army led to unfounded criticism of this means of defense. Indications are not lacking that the Germans considered the inundations a formidable obstacle. They adopted the same method of defense against the
Anglo-American invasion in 1944. In 1940 the Germans used large scale

parachutist attacks far in advance of their motorized columns to neutralize the Dutch positions from the rear. This was the only case in the summer campaign of 1940 in which paratroop attacks were made on a large scale. In less than twelve hours the Germans dumped at least one and possibly two airborne divisions on the western provinces of the Netherlands. The only other place on the western front at which paratroops were used in any number was west of Maastricht, in the attack on the fortress of Eben-Eymael, and there the attackers came down in companies rather than divisions. The mission of the airborne troops was to surround and conquer The Hague, capture the queen and government, and occupy all bridges and roads connecting The Hague with the mainland of Brabant at Delft, Rotterdam, Dordrecht, and Moerdijk. The way would thus be paved for Panzer troops to take the bridges over the Meuse near Grave by surprise and rush forward through 's Hertogenbosch. The road between that town and Moerdijk is narrow and winding, but as the Netherlanders did not expect any immediate penetration there, it was not obstructed and could be passed in a few hours. The main invading force was to make a simultaneous frontal attack on the Grebbe line and in the north on the new dyke between Friesland and Holland. If all went well for Hitler, the strategic points in the Netherlands would be occupied in twenty-four hours and the Dutch army surrounded. But things did not go according to plan.

The paratroop attack came as a complete surprise. In an hour the three main airfields around The Hague were occupied by the invaders. Farther to the south the airport of Waalhaven was captured and used to bring reinforcements. Fighting broke out at the bridges of Dordrecht. At Moerdijk the attack was successful, supported as it was by troops landing from barges that had moved down the rivers before the real invasion began. All kinds of disguises, even Dutch uniforms were used to camouflage the penetration of these advance units. A ship which had entered Rotterdam a few days before flying the Swedish flag, debarked artillery for the paratroops landed at Rotterdam. Confusion reigned in southern Holland. Colonel Moorman, commandant of The Hague, hastily gathered all available troops to protect the Government and break the ring around the capital. The First Army Corps was ordered to turn inland from the coast, and the British and French were asked for help. But the entrances to the Dutch rivers were blocked by magnetic mines dropped from German planes during the night. Everything depended on a single factor: would the Dutch reserves be able to wipe out the airborne invaders before the main enemy forces joined them along the Moerdijk bridges?

The story of the subsequent fighting has often been told. The Dutch forces fought splendidly and did more than had been expected of them.

A German attempt to rush armored trains over the Meuse bridges to prevent their destruction and disrupt fortified positions in the rear, failed. Only one train got through, rushed on into central Brabant and then, being too far in advance of the infantry, moved back only to be destroyed near the village of Mill. Dutch machine gun nests which prevented the crossing of the Meuse were silenced by artillery fire from inside Germany, and the Nazi infantry got across in rubber boats but not without losses. In the southern part of Limburg the Germans crossed at Roermond and captured the Belgian Meuse bridge at Maeseyck; they crossed also at Maastricht where the bridges had been blown up but little resistance was offered. By the end of the day German troops had engaged the Netherlanders along the Peel line, which was also threatened by a flanking movement from the south. The enemy advance here did not exceed ten to fifteen miles, and the Moerdijk bridges were still far away.

Farther to the north the invaders were held up during the morning by the defenders of the Maas-Waal canal. They crossed in the afternoon. The same thing happened in Guelderland and Overijssel, where rearguard actions slowed down the invasion so that only by the end of the day did the enemy occupy Arnhem. His advance units were feeling their way to the Grebbe line. In the far north, the garrison of Delfzijl blocked the way of the invaders for a number of hours and during the afternoon succeeded in partly disengaging themselves. Speeding back towards the Zuiderzee, they crossed the new dyke during the night.

During this whole day the Germans sought desperately to achieve their objects around The Hague. New waves of paratroops descended. The first drifted down in the early afternoon. Small parties of German soldiers were landed from planes on the beaches north of The Hague, but had the bad luck to arrive just as the Dutch destroyer Van Galen was cruising by, and its guns blew their planes to pieces. One airfield was reconquered, the two others rendered useless. The German general commanding the airborne division, General von Sponeck, was shot down with his plane and killed. The attacks on Delft were beaten off and the paratroops annihilated. In Rotterdam a violent counterattack by Dutch marines threw the invaders back to the airport. The destroyer Van Galen supported the attack with its guns until it fell a victim to dive bomber attacks. For hours the small ship braved the German bombs, going down only after the thirty-second attack. Around Dordrecht, Dutch and German forces were locked in fierce fighting for the bridges. Only at Moerdijk was the enemy in complete control.

However precarious its position, the Dutch high command could feel fairly satisfied at the end of the first day. Its plans had been completely upset by the airborne invasion, but the enemy's attempt to annihilate Dutch resistance on the very first day had been completely frustrated. If the British and French came in time, part of the country might be held. Again that evening and night the Germans launched air attacks on The Hague and Rotterdam. Side by side with German paratroopers, fifth columnists went to work. Dutch Nazis and German residents fought Dutch troops in the streets of both cities during the morning hours of May 11. Allied troops failed to appear as soon as the Dutch had hoped. General Henri Giraud's Seventh Army was hurrying through Flanders to Zeeland and Antwerp. As his columns entered Brabant, they were fiercely attacked by German planes. His advance units easily reached the railroad between 's Hertogenbosch and Eindhoven, but the main body of his motorized forces only got as far as Breda in the morning of May 12. His principal objective was to retake the Moerdijk bridges. This would enable us to cut off and eliminate the Germans clinging to the airport and bridges of Rotterdam.

The fate of the Netherlands depended on the results of the second and third days of fighting. May 11 dawned with fierce German attacks all along the line. In the north the bridgehead covering the entrance to the great dyke was bombed and shelled; the Dutch defenders were driven by dive bombers from behind the inundations protecting it and in the afternoon, an attempt was made to storm the dyke itself, but the Germans were repulsed with bloody losses. Here the Dutch positions seemed safe. In the center contact was made along the Grebbe line in the morning. Its southern end was under heavy artillery fire in the afternoon. Bombardment was followed by infantry attacks on the outer bulwark of Wageningen which was taken. In Brabant, the Dutch had occupied new positions behind the canal from the Meuse to Helmond, the *Zuid Willemsvaart,* where they were shelled and attacked during the afternoon. In the evening they withdrew to avoid an encircling movement from the south. German Panzers entered Tilburg, apparently from the southeast. The French advance units joined in the retreat. The result was catastrophic, for with the occupation of 's Hertogenbosch a direct route to Moerdijk was opened to the German motorized troops.

According to the German communiqué an armored S.S. division was ordered to push along this road, and the selection of such specially trained and toughened fighters indicates the importance attached by the German High Command to this forward thrust. The operation was risky, for Giraud's Seventh Army might attack the Panzers on their flank. The impetuous French commander must have considered such an attack, for on Sunday, May 12, at ten o'clock in the morning he ordered the town of Breda evacuated. He planned to use the old residence of the Nassaus as a bulwark to hold up the advance of the Germans coming from the east, while his left wing struck out to the northeast to engage the paratroops holding the Moerdijk bridge for the Panzers. Forty thousand civilians moved out of the town, on foot, as the use of cars or vehicles was forbidden. Fortunately most of them did not go far, but remained hidden in the woods south and southwest of the town. About ten thousand reached Antwerp, and a few thousand were carried along in the stream of refugees flooding the roads into France and finally reached the shores of the Mediterranean beyond Montpellier. Suddenly, however, Giraud changed his drastic plan. His left wing had attacked the German Moerdijk bridgehead near Zevenbergen, and the Dutch defenders of the Peel, now badly disorganized, were being reformed behind the French army. General Giraud ordered his mechanized units to withdraw to his main army, now in position before Antwerp along the Dutch-Belgian boundary. His position was difficult, his communications with French General Headquarters were of the poorest. At one moment he tried to reach them by telephone via The Hague and the Dutch embassy in Paris! His decision to rejoin the main Anglo-Belgian-French line from Antwerp to the Meuse may have been perfectly justified, but it left Zeeland uncovered. Looking back it may be asked what the Seventh Army achieved? In the actual event, it merely wore out its mechanized equipment and exhausted its men.

The S.S. Panzer division pushing on Moerdijk reached its objective in the course of the third day. The Dutch position was breached immediately. The German strategic plan had succeeded, albeit with two full days' delay. This was the more to be deplored because at other points the Dutch defense had been relatively successful. The central part of Holland was cleared of paratroops. The southern half of Rotterdam was lost, but a front had been established running east and west through the city. The river Meuse, where luxury liners were burning and freighters sinking, formed the battle line. In the north the defenders of the great dyke had scored complete success. The Germans collected barges and small steamers to cross the Zuiderzee and land on the undefended eastern shores of Holland, but the Dutch organized a "Zuiderzee Fleet" consisting of one torpedo boat, three gunboats, two minesweepers, and small craft, supported by British and French torpedo boats. This weak force had great difficulty in resisting the constant attacks of German dive bombers, but it succeeded in preventing all attempts to cross the Zuiderzee.

That same day the principal battle of the campaign was fought on the Grebbe. The Germans attacked the line again at its southern point. Their main objective was the small and beautiful town of Rhenen. This was a full dress onslaught, with dive bombers and fighter planes machine gunning the Dutch positions, followed by tanks and flame throwers preceding the infantry. The Dutch line was broken at one point. A counterattack was partially successful, but the Dutch commander realized that his troops could not possibly hold out. On the morning of May 13 the general situation was so unsatisfactory that, at the urgent request of the commander-in-chief, the queen decided to leave the country to continue the struggle from London and to administer from there the overseas territories. No defense was possible against the German armored troops crossing the Moerdijk bridges in force. During the day the German attack was renewed on all sides. The northeastern front, the dyke and the Zuiderzee were still firmly held by the defenders. In the center the Grebbe line was again broken. The Dutch retreated a few miles, counterattacked unsuccessfully, and then withdrew towards the inundation line. Near Dordrecht the valiant defenders of the bridges were overwhelmed by Panzer troops, who cleared the way to Rotterdam.

The government decided to follow the queen to London. Full powers were given to the commander-in-chief, General Winkelman. He could not long conceal the seriousness of the situation. The weakened defenders of the Grebbe had no time to regroup behind the inundations. The official Dutch report indicates that in the confusion, the Germans succeeded in breaking through this line at one point. By noon on May 14, the fifth day of the campaign, General Winkelman decided to capitulate. After he had sent a flag of truce and negotiations had started, the German air force criminally bombarded the center of Rotterdam "to break a passage for the armored troops," who no longer needed it. This murderous air assault was meant to intimidate the population. The capitulation had already been decided before the bombardment, because the Dutch positions were hopeless. The effect of the bombardment was the reverse of what the Germans intended. Great as was the loss in life and property to the Dutch, it cost the Germans far more. By the wanton destruction of the city they brought the same evil upon themselves.

General Winkelman surrendered with all the troops in the Fortress of Holland. In Zeeland the campaign continued. The remnants of the Dutch Peel army, combined with French units, retarded the occupation of the islands for five days more. Details of the fighting are imperfectly known. The German air force bombed Flushing to prevent the French from withdrawing to Belgium, and Middelburg for no reason whatever. Treasures of art and history were lost in this little town. Culturally its destruction was a far greater loss than that of Rotterdam. On May fourteenth all was over in the European Netherlands.

The war continued from England; the Dutch flag was still flying in the East and West Indies. Two years later Batavia fell to the Japanese, after a bitter struggle in which the renown of the Dutch navy, air force, and army spread through all the United Nations. The Indies were never wholly lost. In southern New Guinea, in the primitive town of Merauke Dutch authority has remained intact to this day, and with the American offensive making rapid progress, it may be assumed that the Dutch red, white, and blue will never be hauled down in this little corner of the world.

To write a "history" of the Netherlands under German occupation is still impossible. We have a great deal of information; some and in many respects the most important parts of it cannot be divulged. We know of the despair of the people in the sad summer months of 1940, of the political and spiritual revival that followed, culminating in the great strike of February 1941. We know that the methods of the invaders under that arch-traitor Seyss-Inquart have changed for the worse since the first few months, when there was a great display of moderation. Cruder methods were employed after the great strike, but only cautiously as Germany's younger soldiers were in Russia, and the occupation forces consisted of older men and half trained S.A. members. With the rebuilding of a western German army repression became harsh. The persecution of the Jews, the destruction of coastal towns and villages for defense purposes, the flooding of large areas for the same reason, the resistance of the underground workers and the activity of the underground press, all this must find its place in a history of the occupied Netherlands; in another volume to be published after the war.

It is evident that none of the great traditions of the Dutch nation described in these pages has been lost. Those traditions are a potent force in the reconstruction of the Netherland state and society. The thoroughness of the Dutch, their prudence in action, their unshakable confidence in their own conception of the good life, their deep religious faith, their Erasmian tradition of tolerance, their yearning for social justice, their abhorrence of vain display, have all been made clear under German occupation. Upon these foundations, the kingdom of the Netherlands will be rebuilt.

Notes

[1] A chronology of the oldest Netherland history is difficult to give. The older dates are necessarily hypothetical but the following estimates do not seem exaggerated:

ab. 30,000 B. C. Last glacial period in the Netherlands (only in the northern part).

ab. 20,000 B. C. Last glacial period in Europe, the Netherlands a tundra-area. Oldest inhabitants of the Netherlands (reindeer-hunters of the Cro-Magnon race).

ab. 15,000–
8,000 B. C. Period of the palaeolithicum (rare traces of habitation).

ab. 8,000–5,000 Warmer climate, western part of the Netherlands submerged by the sea. No habitation (?).

ab. 5,000 Warm period. Sea breaks through the Straits of Dover and forms a wall of dunes along Dutch coast.

ab. 2,500–2,000 Climate is dry. Inhabitants in Drente (Hunebed-people) and in southern Limburg.

ab. 1,500 Wandering tribes spread over central Netherlands.

ab. 1,000 Beginning of the Iron Age. Germanic and Celtic immigrations.

ab. 500 Beginning of the moist, warm period of the Sub-Atlanticum (present climate).

300–500 A. D. Period of highest floods.

[2] The anthropological problems of the Netherlands and the literature pertaining to them are discussed by D. J. H. Nyessen, *The Passing of the Frisians. Anthropogeography of Terpia*, The Hague, 1927. The outstanding experts on Dutch archeology are J. H. Holwerda, *Nederlands vroegste geschiedenis*, Amsterdam, 1918, and *Die Niederlanden in der Vorgeschichte Europas*, Leipzig, 1915; and A. E. van Giffen, *De Hunebedden in Nederland*, 2 vols. Utrecht, 1925–1927 and *Die Bauart der Einzelgräber, ein Beitrag zur Kenntnis der älteren individuellen Grabhügelkulturen in den Niederlanden*, Leipzig, 1930. Holwarda presented his latest views on the subject in volume I of the *Geschiedenis van Nederland* edited by H. Brugmans, Amsterdam, 1935.

[3] On the relations between the Frisians and the Anglo-Saxons P. C. Boeles, *"Friesland tot de elfde eeuw*, The Hague, 1927.

[4] There are various theories on the origin and initial form of the mark, but a discussion of them does not belong to Netherland history proper.

[5] "Frisia" indicates the whole original Frisian area, from Bruges in Flanders to Hamburg and beyond in Schleswig.

[6] For the meaning of the name "Holland," see Robert Fruin, *De etymologie van Holland* (*Verspreide Geschriften*, vol. VIII, p. 139) and the *Middelnederlandsch Woordenboek* ed. by E. Verwijs-S. Verdam, vol. III, The Hague, 1894.

[7] J. van Mierlo in *Geschiedenis der Letterkunde der Nederlanden*, ed. by F. Baur, vol. I, 's Hertogenbosch, 1939, defends the existence that an older Dutch literature than the one that has come down to us, but this remains largely theory.

[8] The definition quoted in the text was formulated by the late professor I. H. Gosses in the *Handboek tot de Staatkundige Geschiedenis van Nederland*, The Hague, 1927 (sec. ed.).

[9] The problem of the "discovery" referred to in the text, has been widely discussed, but the latest research on this point makes the role played by Willem Beukelszoon rather doubtful.

[10] The impact of the Hundred Years' War on the political situation in the Low Countries

has been thoroughly studied by Prof. Henry S. Lucas (University of Washington) in his book, *The Low Countries and the Hundred Years' War,* Ann Arbor, 1929.

This book deals minutely with the first decades of the conflict.

[11] The following families reigned over the countries of Holland and Zeeland: from 922 (traditional date) to 1299 the native descendants of the Gerulfs and Dirks of Kennemerland; from 1299 to 1345, the Avesnes of Hainaut; from 1345 to 1433, the Wittelsbachs of Bavaria; from 1433, the Burgundians of the House of Valois.

[12] Each province had its groups of partisans, all known in Dutch history under traditional, often enigmatic names. In Holland the *Hoekschen* opposed the *Kabeljauwschen,* in Friesland the *Schieringers* opposed the *Vetkoopers.* The partisans in Guelder and Utrecht derived their name from the leading aristocratic families in the former, the *Heeckerens* stood against the *Bronkorsten;* in the latter, the *Lichtenbergs* against the *Lokhorsten.*

[13] Prof. E. Lousse of the university of Louvain delivered a series of lectures on the organization of the medieval state, published in mimeographed copies, *L'Etat corporatif au moyen âge et à l'époque moderne,* 1938. His thesis emphasizes the "corporative" character of the medieval state, but the use of this term explains little and tends to confuse the historical issue. In 1933 he published a program of studies on the origin of the States Assemblies in the Low Countries, in the *Revue de l'histoire ecclésiastique de Louvain.*

[14] The Burgundian dynasty was represented in the Low Countries by Duke Philip I (the Bold), who ruled Burgundy from 1363 and Flanders from 1385 to 1404. His son, John (Jean sans Peur) succeeded him in Burgundy and Flanders, 1404–1419, his second son Anthony in Brabant and Limburg, 1404–1415. His grandson, Philip II (the Good), succeeded his father in Burgundy and Flanders, 1419–1467; his cousins in Brabant and Limburg (1430) and in Holland, Zeeland and Hainaut (1433). All these domains were inherited by Philip's son, Charles the Bold, 1467–1477.

[15] The older Dutch historians never went deeply into the origins of the Dutch nation. A narrative of political development seemed sufficient. H. Pirenne, in his *Histoire de Belgique,* 7 vols., Bruxelles, 1902–'37, sought to prove that from the earliest days the southern part of the Low Countries had formed an economic bloc, more or less distinct from the adjacent territories. P. Geyl, in his *Geschiedenis van den Nederlandschen Stam,* vol. I–III, Amsterdam, 1930–1937, deliberately based his narrative on the assumption that from early days the modern Dutch-Flemish linguistic unit had formed a national unit. J. Huizinga, in his articles on Burgundy and the origin of the Netherland nation, attaches great importance to incidental political factors (J. Huizinga, *Uit de voorgeschiedenis van ons nationaal besef* in De Gids, 1912, vol. I, p. 432, id. *Burgund, eine Krise des romanisch-germanischen Verhältnisses,* in *Historische Zeitschrift,* vol. 148, 1933, p. 1, and id. *L'État Bourguignon, ses rapports avec la France, et les origines d'une nationalité néerlandaise* in *Moyen Age,* vol. 40, 1930.

[16] Georges Chastellain wrote a chronicle of the dukes of Burgundy for the period of 1419–1470 (*Oeuvres,* publiés par Kervijn de Lettenhove, Brussels, 1863–1866 in 8 vols.).

[17] An American historian, A. Hyma, wrote an excellent book on the development of this religious movement: *The Christian Renaissance,* Grand Rapids, 1924.

[18] Maximilian of Habsburg married Mary of Burgundy in 1477. After her death in 1482 he ruled the Low Countries as regent until 1494, when his son Philip III (the Handsome) succeeded him.

[19] Charles succeeded his father Philip in 1506, and ruled until 1555, for the first nine years under the regency of his grandfather Maximilian who entrusted the Governership of the Low Countries to his daughter Margaret of Austria. In 1515 Charles took Lowland affairs into his own hands, to entrust direct control again to Margaret until her death in 1530. From 1530–1555 Charles's sister Mary of Hungary was Governess.

[20] The identity of the "seventeen provinces" has been discussed by generations of historians. No contemporary sources enumerate them. One of the latest interpretations of this enigmatic number is that "seventeen" should be taken to mean "many" or "all," in the same way as we speak of the "seven seas" (Huizinga in his article in *Moyen Age,* quoted above).

[21] For the position of the nobility of Holland, see the important article by H. Enno van

Gelder, *De Hollandsche adel in den tijd van den opstand* in *Tijdschrift voor Geschiedenis*, vol. 45, 1930, p. 114.

[22] On these economic and social matters much light has been spread by the research of W. van Ravesteyn, *Onderzoekingen over de economische en sociale ontwikkeling van Amsterdam*, Amsterdam, 1916. For exact data on the herring fisheries see, H. Enno van Gelder, *Gegevens betreffende de haringvisscherij op het eind van de zestiende eeuw* in *Bijdragen van het Historisch Genootschap*, vol. 32, 1918, p. 134.

[23] The text of Erasmus letter, quoted above, is copied from H. M. Allen's edition of Erasmus letters (*Opus Epistolarum Desiderii Erasmi Roterodami*, letter of Aug. 31, 1523, vol. V, Oxford, 1924). P. Frédéricq in his *Corpus documentorum inquisitionis haereticae pravitatis Neerlandicae*, Ghent—The Hague 1879–1906, vol. IV, p. 225 quotes the same letter after an edition of Zwingli's letters. The words following "steadfastness" until "I know it is glorious" are *omitted* in this early edition which entirely changes the meaning of the text. Netherland and Belgian historians quote the letter after Frédéricq.

[24] The literature on William of Orange is abundant. The best general biography is that of P. J. Blok, *Willem I*, 2 vols. Amsterdam, 1909. W. Rachfahl described the early years of William's career up to 1572 in minute detail: *Wilhelm von Oranien*, Halle—The Hague, 1906–1924, 4 vols. An interesting sketch of William's personality, his attitude towards the problems of his time, is given by A. van Schelven, *Willem van Oranje*, Amsterdam, 1933. The Trecentenary of William's birth in 1933 brought a mass of new literature reviewed by Miss M. W. Jurriaanse in *Nijhoffs Bijdragen*, Series VII, vol. 4, 1934. It also led to a discussion between H. E. van Gelder and J. Gorris on the attitude of William towards religion (Gorris in *Historisch Tijdschrift*, 1933 and Van Gelder in *Tijdschrift voor Geschiedenis*, 1933).

[25] The latest and most acceptable explanation of the term *Gueus* and its use in the war of independence is given by J. D. M. Cornelissen, *Waarom zij Geuzen genoemd werden* (*Historische Studiën* published by the *Historisch Tijdschrift*, Tilburg, 1938).

[26] Prince Maurice was appointed to the Stadhouderate in 1585 and died in 1625.

[27] A review of successive historical interpretations of the Great Revolt is given by J. Romein in *De Tachtigjarige Oorlog*, Amsterdam, 1941. Among modern Dutch historians H. Enno van Gelder, an outstanding expert on this period of Dutch history, sees the revolt as a revolutionary movement by part of the people, and the "fight for freedom" as a civil war. P. Geyl (*The Revolt of the Netherlands, 1555–1609*, London, 1932, and *The Netherlands Divided, 1609–1648*, London, 1938) looks upon the revolt as a national movement, headed by William of Orange. J. C. De Pater, in his article *De Religie als factor bij de vorming van den Nederlandschen Staat* in *Nijhoffs Bijdragen*, VII, 8, 1937, and in his greater work on the war, (vol. III and vol. IV of the *Geschiedenis van Nederland*, edited by H. Brugmans, Amsterdam, 1935–1938), thinks religious motives were the most important. J. Romein and others pay special attention to economic causes and the social tensions created by economic changes. In this book an attempt is made to reconcile some of these opinions.

[28] The reasons for the war as propounded by Netherlanders themselves in the XVIth century, have been studied by A. C. J. De Vrankrijker in his interesting book, *De Motiveering van den Opstand*, Nijmegen, 1933.

[29] All possessions of William of Orange in the Low Countries were confiscated by the king of Spain in 1567. Some the prince regained through the liberation of his territory from the Spaniards. His lands outside the Low Countries were heavily mortgaged after his expeditions of 1568 and 1572. Part of the debts incurred by the Nassau family for the liberation of the Netherlands, were refunded by the States General in 1598. The family estates on Spanish territory were restored to William's oldest son, Philip William, who remained a Catholic and loyal to Spain. After the death of that prince, these estates fell to prince Maurice and full possession thereof was guaranteed to the House of Orange by the treaties between the Republic and Spain. The income derived by the princes of Orange from services rendered to the Republic further increased their wealth. However, Stadhouder William II was so generous in his support of his brother-in-law, Charles II, that at his death the family was in difficult circumstances.

[30] Not without reason had the spiritual directors of Calvinism, Theodore de Bèze and Calvin

himself, complained of the religious indifference of the States of the Netherland provinces who refused to use their political power to serve the "true Christian creed." More than once had the Protestant clergy led the assault against the Erasmianism of the ruling class; but the latter under the indomitable Oldenbarnevelt in private life a firm believer, had weathered every storm.

[31] E. Baasch, in his *Holländische Wirtschaftsgeschichte*, Jena, 1927, surveys social conditions in Dutch industry in the XVIIth and XVIIIth centuries, from Dutch sources. Here an extensive bibliography will be found.

[32] This dark picture of Dutch social conditions may surprise readers who are accustomed to see the XVIIth century as the "Golden Age" of Netherland civilization. It must be said, however, that social conditions in the Netherlands, bad as they were, were better than in most of the adjacent countries.

[33] For an exposé of Dutch XVIIth century "imperialism," see J. E. Elias, *Het Voorspel van den eersten Engelschen Oorlog*, 2 vols. The Hague, 1920.

[34] A survey of the development of the Jewish Dutch communities and their economic activities had been published by H. J. Bloom, *The economic activities of the Jews in Amsterdam in the XVIIth and XVIIIth centuries*, Williamsport, Pa., 1937.

[35] Werner Sombart makes this ridiculous assertion in *Die Juden und das Wirtschaftsleben*, 2nd ed. Leipzig, 1918, p. 30 (also in English translation).

[36] This was pointed out by J. Huizinga in his booklet, *Die höllandische Kultur des siebzehnten Jahrhunderts, ihre sozialen Grundlagen und nationale Eigenart*, Jena, 1933.

[37] Frederick Henry succeeded his brother Maurice in 1625 and died in 1647.

[38] William was *stadhouder* from 1647 until 1650.

[39] See P. De La Court, *Interest of Holland*, first published at Amsterdam, 1662. A French translation with the misleading title, *Mémoires de Jean De Witt* was printed at The Hague in 1709.

[40] The first Anglo-Dutch War was fought from 1652 to 1654, the second from 1665 to 1667, and the third from 1672 to 1674.

[41] This subject of Dutch German relations has been little studied. A preliminary study has been made by R. E. von Gronow, *Die öffentliche Meinung in Deutschland gegenüber Holland nach 1648*, Marburg, 1914.

[42] The organization of the Dutch navy in the XVIIth century has been thoroughly studied by J. E. Elias, *Schetsen uit de geschiedenis van ons Zeewezen*, 6 vols., The Hague, 1916–1930 (first published in *Nijhoffs Bijdragen*).

[43] The last decades of the XVIIth century form a period of transition. The "Golden Age" really came to an end after the war of 1672–1676. So, many personalities who chronologically belong to the XVIIth century, are mentioned in this chapter entitled "Ideals of the Eighteenth century."

[44] Interesting biographical sketches of some of the scientists, mentioned here, can be found in J. Romein, *Erflaters onzer Beschaving*, 4 vols., Amsterdam, 1938–1940.

[45] J. Wagenaar's *Geschiedenis des Vaderlands* was first published in 21 vols., Amsterdam, 1749–1760.

[46] William III died in 1702, but Holland, Zeeland and the majority of the provinces did not appoint a new *stadhouder* until 1747. John William Friso, of the Frisian branch of the Nassaus, was appointed *stadhouder* in Friesland, Groningen, and Drente.

[47] The importance of the West Indian colonies is pointed out by the prominent XVIIIth century writer on economic conditions in the Netherlands, E. Luzac, *Holland's Rijkdom*, 4 vols., Leiden, 1780–1783.

[48] William IV, succeeded his father John William Friso in Friesland in 1711. In 1718, he became *stadhouder* of Groningen and in 1722 of Drente and Guelderland.

[49] H. Colenbrander in his three volumes on the Patriot movement (*De Patriotten tijd*, 3 vols., The Hague, 1897–'99) and F. van Wijk in his book, *De Republiek en Amerika*, Leiden, 1921 have thoroughly analyzed the attitude of the Netherland government and people towards the American War of Independence.

[50] The fourth Anglo-Dutch War was fought from 1780 to 1784.

[51] In the French period constitutional changes in the Netherlands were rapid. In 1795 the "Batave Republic" was proclaimed. In 1798 the first Constitution was approved. In 1801, the Constitution was changed to strengthen the executive. In 1804 an authoritarian regime was introduced under Schimmelpenninck as "grand pensionary." This was replaced in 1806 by a monarchy with Louis Bonaparte as "king of Holland." In 1810 the Netherlands were incorporated into the French empire. In 1813 they were liberated.

[52] King William I entered the Netherlands in November 1813, and was proclaimed "Sovereign of the State" on December 5, 1813. The new Constitution was approved in 1814. In 1815, after the union of the Netherlands and Belgium, William took the title of king. The same year a new constitution was adopted. The year 1939 brought the definite separation of Belgium from the Netherlands. King William abdicated in 1840.

[53] For these diplomatic developments, see G. J. Renier, *Great Britain and the establishment of the kingdom of the Netherlands, 1813–1815*, London, 1930, pp. 15–16, 21, 30, 33–37, 217, 221.

[54] Renier, o.c.p. 212 sq.

[55] King William succeeded his father in 1840. He died in 1849.

[56] The Culture System was adopted in 1830 and abolished by the agrarian laws of 1869 and 1870.

[57] The term "socialism" in Dutch politics refers always to Marxist socialism, the term "communism" to Marxism as formulated by the Third International.

[58] B. Landheer, *The Netherlands*, University of California Press, Berkeley, 1943, and Hendrik Riemens, *The Netherlands, the story of a Free People*, New York, 1943.

[59] The United States Federal Reserve Bank, in a report on foreign holdings in this country, gave a figure of 1,780,000,000 dollars as the amount of Dutch investments in the United States. Of this amount, only 600,000,000 were investments in the true sense of the word.

[60] See A. J. Barnouw and B. Landheer, *Contribution of Holland to the Sciences*, New York, Querido, 1943.

[61] The third Thorbecke Cabinet resigned in 1872, shortly before the death of the great Liberal Statesmen. It was succeeded by the Liberal De Vries-Cabinet (1872–'74), then by a Conservative Cabinet (Heemskerk, 1874–'77), again by a Liberal administration (Kappeyne, 1877–'79). The divided Liberals permitted successive Conservative administrations: Van Lijnden van Sandenburg, 1879–'83, and Heemskerk, 1883–'87. After the revision of the Constitution in 1887 and the extension of the franchise, the "Rightists," the combined Anti-revolutionary and Catholic groups, formed their first administration (Mackay, 1888–'91). The Liberals remained in office for ten years after a victory at the polls in 1891: Cabinets Tienhoven, 1891–'94, Roëll, 1894–'97, and Pierson, 1897–1901.

[62] The Rightist administration of Abraham Kuyper (1901–'05) was followed by a Liberal Cabinet (De Meester, 1905–'08), which in turn was succeeded by the Rightist administration of Heemskerk Jr. 1908–'13. In 1913 the Rightists were defeated in the general elections but the Leftists, now a heterogeneous combination of Liberals and Socialists, could not unite on a common program of action, the Socialists being unwilling to take part in the administration. An extra-parliamentary Cabinet, headed by Cort van der Linden, took charge of the administration until the constitutional revision of 1917 was approved and new elections were held.

[63] A. Vandenbosch, in B. Landheer, *The Netherlands*, p. 135.

[64] H. von Treitschke, *Die Republik der Vereinigten Niederlande* in vol. III of his *Historische und Politische Aufsätze*.

[65] The Netherland government (Liberal administration-Pierson) sent the cruiser "Gelderland" to Lourenço Marques to bring President Kruger of the South African Republic safely to Europe. The British government made no attempt to prevent this display of sympathy with the cause of the Boers.

[66] The question is often asked why the two Lowland kingdoms did not concert their action for joint defense against eventual aggression. Such a move was impossible before 1914, because of the international status of Belgium whose neutrality was guaranteed by the adjacent

great powers. Belgium was *obliged* to remain neutral, the Netherlands of their own volition accepted neutrality as their foreign policy.

[67] The best source for the study of the Netherland difficulties during the last war, are the memoirs of N. Bosboom, minister of defense, 1913–1916: *In moeilijke omstandigheden,* Amsterdam, 1933.

[68] The Dutch system of education has been explained by the author of this book in an article on *Education in the Netherlands,* in the *Encyclopedia of Modern Education,* New York, Philosophic books Inc. 1943.

[69] A history of the Netherlands in the twenty years that preceded the present war, is still to be written. The above opinions naturally represent the authors personal view on the political development in that period.

[70] A survey of the development of the nationalist movement in the East Indies was given by this author in his book *Nusantara, a history of the East Indian archipelago,* Cambridge, Harvard University Press, 1943.

[71] H. Brugmans, *Geschiedenis van Nederland onder Koningin Wilhemina,* Amsterdam, 1938.

[72] Eelco van Kleffens, *Juggernaut over Holland,* New York, Columbia University Press, 1941.

Bibliography

Abbreviation: BVG = Bijdragen von Vaderlandsche Geschiedenis en oud-heidkunde, formerly known as Nijhoff's Bijdragen.

H. Pirenne, *Bibliographie de l'histoire de Belgique,* Brussels, 1932 (third edition), gives a complete survey of all the important books and articles on both Dutch and Belgian history during the medieval and sixteenth century. The *Handboek tot de Staatkundige Geschiedenis van Nederland,* by I. Gosses and N. Japikse (second edition, The Hague, 1927) gives detailed bibliographies after each chapter. The *Repertorium van tijdschriftartikelen en verhandelingen betreffende de vaderlandsche geschiedenis en oudheidkunde,* of L. D. Petit continued by H. Ruys, enumerates all articles published before 1930 (4 vols. Leiden, 1900–1939). The *Revue d'histoire ecclésiastique de Louvain,* listed all important books and articles on the same subject currently. In this bibliography only more important, recent publications will be enumerated. The *Rijks-geschiedkundige Publicatiën* published by order of the government of the Netherlands, are devoted to the publication of historical source-material. The same is done by the "Historisch Genootschap" of Utrecht in its *Werken* and its *Bijdragen en Mededeelingen.*

GENERAL HISTORY:

P. J. Blok, *History of the People of the Netherlands,* 5 vols. New York, 1898–1912, provides a great deal of useful information. The latest general history of the Netherlands is: H. Brugmans (editor), *Geschiedenis van Nederland,* 8 vols. Amsterdam, 1935–'38. An excellent short survey: H. Enno van Gelder, *Histoire des Pays Bas* (begins with XVIth century), Paris, 1930. Special points of view: P. Geyl, *Geschiedenis van den Nederlandschen Stam,* 3 vols. (incomplete), Amsterdam, 1930–'37, and J. Romein, *De Lage Landen bij de Zee,* Utrecht, 1934. By far the best book on political history is the *Handboek* of Gosses and Japikse, mentioned above. A modern survey in English: George Edmundson, *History of the Netherlands,* Cambridge, 1922. Indispensable is H. Pirenne's *Histoire de Belgique,* 7 vols. Brussels, 1902–'37. A synopsis of cultural development in the form of biographical sketches: J. and A. Romein, *De Erflaters onzer Beschaving,* Amsterdam, 1935–'40. The recent publications of H. Riemens, *The Netherlands, Story of a Free People,* New York, 1943, and B. Landheer (editor), *The Netherlands,* Berkeley, Calif., 1943, contain historical sections. Naval history: J. C. Mollema, *Geschiedenis van Nederland ter Zee,* Amsterdam, 1939. On the general history of the Netherlands in Asia: F. W. Stapel, *Geschie-*

denis van Nederlandsch Indië, Amsterdam 1930; F. W. Stapel (editor), *Geschiedenis van Nederlandsch Indië,* 4 vols. (incomplete), Amsterdam, 1937 sq.; E. S. De Klerck, *History of the Netherlands Indies,* 2 vols. Rotterdam, 1938; B. H. M. Vlekke, *Nusantara, a history of the East Indian archipelago,* Cambridge, Mass., 1943.

A general history of the Netherlanders in the Western Hemisphere does not exist.

Economic history: H. Differee, *Geschiedenis van den Nederlandschen handel,* Amsterdam, 1905–'08; Ernst Baasch, *Holländische Wirtschaftsgeschichte,* Jena, 1927 (begins with XVIth century, extensive bibliography).

History of learning: A. Barnouw and B. Landheer (editors), *The Contribution of Holland to the Sciences,* New York, 1943. On the House of Orange: N. Japikse, *Geschiedenis van het Huis van Oranje Nassau,* 2 vols. The Hague, 1937–'38 (also in German translation).

On Netherland historiography: S. De Wind, *Bibliotheek van Nederlandsche Geschiedschrijvers,* Middelburg, 1817; J. Romein, *Noordnederlandsche Geschiedschrijving in de Middeleeuwen,* Haarlem, 1932; H. Kampinga, *De opvattingen over onze oudere vaderlandsche geschiedenis by Hollandsche historici der XVIe en XVIIe eeuw,* The Hague, 1917; J. C. Breen, *P. C. Hooft als Geschiedschrijver der Nederlandsche historiën,* J. D. M. Cornelissen, *Hooft en Tacitus,* Nijmegen, 1938, R. Castendijk, *Johan Wagenaar en zijn Vaderlandsche historie,* Schiedam, 1927; K. H. De Jong, *Bilderdijk's Geschiedenis des Vaderlands,* Leiden, 1932; G. W. Kernkamp, *Van Menschen en tijden,* Haarlem, 1931.

PRE-MEDIEVAL HISTORY:

J. P. De Vries (editor), *Volk van Nederland,* sec. ed. Amsterdam, 1938; J. H. Holwerda, *Nederlands Vroegste Geschiedenis,* Amsterdam, 1918; and the same, *"Die Niederlande in der Vorgeschichte Europas,* Leipzig, 1915; A. E. van Giffen, *De Hunebedden in Nederland,* 2 vols. Utrecht, 1925–'27; A. W. Bijvanck, *De Oorsprong van het Nederlansche Volk en de Archeologie van Nederland,* in: *Jaarboek van de Nederlandsche Maatschappy van Letterkunde,* 1935–'36; D. J. H. Nyessen, *The Passing of the Frisians,* The Hague, 1927; P. C. Boeles, *Friesland tot de Elfde Eeuw,* The Hague, 1927.

MIDDLE AGES:

The *Instituut voor Middeleeuwsche Geschiedenis aan de Rijks-Universiteit Utrecht,* published a series of works on Dutch medieval history under the leadership of Prof. O. Oppermann. We mention here: R. R. Post, *Geschiedenis der Utrechtsche bischopsverkiezingen tot 1353,* Utrecht, 1933, and W. Kienast, *Die deutschen Fürsten im Dienste der Westmächte,* 2 vols. Utrecht, 1924.

On the origin of the provinces, besides the literature indicated by Gosses and Japikse in the *Handboek,* P. C. Boeren, *Iets naders over de oudste graven van Wassenberg-Gelre,* in BVG. 7th series, vol. 6 (1935) and J. Formsma, *De Wording van Stad en Lande tot 1536,* Assen, 1930. On relations with France and England, H. S. Lucas, *The Low Countries and the Hundred Years' War,* Ann

Arbor, 1929. On trade relations with the Hansa: Fr. Vollbehr, *Die Holländer und die deutsche Hanse*, in: *Pfingstblätter des hansischen Geschichtsvereins*, vol. XXI, 1930, and Z. W. Sneller, *Deventer, die Stadt der Jahrmärkte*, in the same series, vol. XXV, 1932. On Geert Groote and the "Devotio Moderna": W. Mulder, *Gerardi Magni Epistolae*, Antwerpen, 1933 and A. Hyma, *The Christian Renaissance*, Grand Rapids, 1924. On the origin of the States Assemblies: E. Lousse, *Het Ontstaan der middeleeuwsche standencolleges*, in: *Historisch Tijdschrift*, 1935.

ON THE ORIGIN OF THE NETHERLAND NATION AND THE BURGUNDIAN MONARCHY:

J. Huizinga, *Uit de Voorgeschiedenis van ons Nationaal Besef*, in: *De Gids*, 1912, vol. I; the same, *Burgund, eine Krise des romanisch-germanischen Verhältnisses*, in: *Historische Zeitschrift*, vol. 148, 1933; the same, *L'Etat bourguingon, ses rapports avec la France et les orgines d'une nationalité néerlandaise*, in: *Moyen Age*, vol. XL, 1930; the same *Erasmus*, (English version), New York, 1924; O. Noordenbos, *Erasmus en de Nederlanden*, in: BVG. 7th series, vol. 7, p. 193. The Netherlands under Charles V: J. S. Theissen, *De Noordelijke Nederlanden onder Karel V*, Amsterdam, 1912; W. van Ravesteyn, *Onderzoekingen over de economische en sociale ontwikkeling van Amsterdam in de XVIe en het eerste kwart der XVIIe eeuw*, Amsterdam, 1916. See also the article of H. Enno van Gelder in *Tijdschrift voor Geschiedenis*, 1928 and following years.

THE EIGHTY YEARS' WAR:

The enormous volume of literature on this subject is classified in Pirenne's *Bibliographie*. Only a few of the latest books and articles will be enumerated here.

J. Romein, in cooperation with others, published a magnificent volume on the eighty years' war in occupied Holland: *De Tachtigjarige Oorlog*, Amsterdam, 1941. The trecentenary of William's birth brought a new biography: A. A. van Schelven, *Willem van Oranje*, Amsterdam, 1933, and a great number of articles on the founder of the dynasty of Orange. P. Geyl's description of the war, was published in an English version: P. Geyl, *The Revolt of the Netherlands, 1555–1609*, London, 1932, and *The Netherlands Divided*, London, 1938. A. A. van Schelven studied the problem of religious toleration in the Netherlands in his article: *De ontwikkeling der politieke tolerantie in de Nederlanden*, in: *Tijdschrift voor Geschiedenis*, 1931. Political theory of the revolution was studied by J. van der Grinten, *Het Plakkaat van Verlatinghe*, in: BVG. 7th series, vol. 2, p. 161 and by A. J. C. De Vrankrijker, *De Motiveering van den Opstand*, Nijmegen, 1933. Some recent opinions on the basic causes of the Great Revolt and the separation of North and South: J. C. H. De Pater, *De Religie als factor bij de vorming van den Nederlandschen Staat*, in: BVG. 7th series, vol. VIII, 1937, with reply by P. Geyl in the next issue of the same periodical; H. Enno van Gelder, *De oorzaken van de scheiding van de noordelijke en zuidelijke Nederlanden in de 16e eeuw*, in: BVG. 7th series, vol. X, 1938; L. van der Essen, *De historische gebondenheid der Nederlanden,* in: *Nederlandsche Historiebladen,* vol. I, 1938. On military matters: L. van der Essen, *Alexandre Farnèse, prince de Parme,* 4 vols. Brussels, 1933–'37; J. Wijn, *Over het krijgswezen in den tijd van Prins Maurits,* Utrecht, 1934. On the relations of Philip of Spain, his policy in the Lowlands, and the Papacy: B. De Meester, *Le Saint Siège et les Troubles des Pays Bas, 1566–1597,* Louvain, 1934. Dutch-Spanish trade during the war: J. Kernkamp, *De handel met den vijand,* 2 vols. Utrecht, 1931–'34.

THE SEVENTEENTH CENTURY:

Gosses and Japikse lists all important works, published before 1927. A few recent publications: T. P. van der Kooy, *Hollands Stapelmarkt en haar verval,* Amsterdam, 1931; F. Breetvelt-van Veen, *Louis De Geer, 1587–1652,* Amsterdam, 1935; J. E. Elias, *Schetsen uit de geschiedenis van ons zeewezen,* 6 vols. The Hague 1916–1930, the same, *Het voorspel van den eersten Engelschen zeeoorlog,* 2 vols. The Hague, 1920; H. J. Bloom, *The economic activities of the Jews in Amsterdam in the XVIIth and XVIIIth centuries,* Williamsport, Pa., 1937; J. Huizinga, *Die holländische Kultur des siebzehnten Jahrhunderts, ihre socialen Grundlagen und nationale Eigenart,* Jena, 1933; A. Barnouw, *Vondel,* New York, 1927; C. R. Boxer, *Jan Compagnie in Japan,* 1600–1818, The Hague, 1936; A. Hyma, *The Dutch in the Far East,* Ann Harbor, 1942; J. S. Furnivall, *Netherlands India, a study in Plural Economy,* Cambridge, 1939; S. P. l'Honoré Naber, *De West Indische Compagnie in Brazilië en Guinea* (The Hague), 1930; Gustave Cohen, *Ecrivains français en Hollande dans la première moitié du XVIIe siècle,* Paris, 1920; C. Serrurier, *Descartes, Leer en Leven,* The Hague, 1930; W. M. C. Juynboll, *Zeventiende-eeuwsche beoefenaars van het Arabisch in Nederland,* Utrecht, 1932; D. J. Ter Horst, *Daniel Heinsius,* Utrecht, 1934. On John De Witt: N. Japikse, *Jan de Witt,* sec. ed. Amsterdam, 1938; on the crisis of 1672: Mary C. Trevelyan, *William III and the Defence of Holland, 1672–'74,* London, 1930; on the formation of the Dutch boundaries: W. A. Bannier, *De landgrenzen van Nederland,* vol. I (no other published), Leiden, 1900; H. Emmer, *De grenzen van Nederland van de Wielingen tot aan den Rijn,* Haarlem, 1937.

THE EIGHTEENTH CENTURY:

There is little to add to the books, listed by Gosses and Japikse. Besides studies on special subjects of colonial history, there is: R. Geikei and I. Montgomery, *The Dutch Barrier,* Cambridge, 1930; and on the conflict of oligarchy and democracy: C. J. Guibla, *Democratie en Oligarchie in Friesland tijdens de Republiek,* Assen, 1934; Colenbranders books (*De Patriotten tijd, De Bataafsche Republiek* etc.) remain authoritative on the period of the Patriot revolution and the French domination. For relations with the United States: F. van Wijk, *De Republiek en Amerika,* Leiden, 1922; P. J. Van Winter, *Het Aandeel van Amsterdams handel aan den opbouw van het Amerikaansche Gemeenebest,* Amsterdam, 1927. Preparation of national revival: L. G. J. Verberne, *Gijsbert Karel's Leerjaren*, Amsterdam, 1931.

THE NINETEENTH CENTURY:

H. Colenbrander, *Koning Willem I*, Amsterdam, 1937; G. J. Renier, *Great Britain and the Netherlands, 1813–1815, a study in British foreign policy*, London, 1930; R. Steinmetz, *Englands Anteil and der Trennung der Niederlande*, The Hague, 1930.

C. Wilson, *Anglo-Dutch Commerce and Finance in the Eighteenth Century*, Cambridge, 1941. Religious developments: M. E. Kluit, *Het Réveil in Nederland*, Amsterdam, 1936; G. Brom, *Het Wederopleven van de beoefening der Wetenschappen onder de Katholieken in Nederland*.

Financial policy of King William I: H. Riemens, *Het Amortisatie Syndicaat, een Studie over de Staatsfinanciën onder Koning Willem I*, Amsterdam, 1935; W. F. M. Mansvelt, *A Brief History of the Netherland Trading Society, 1824–1924*, The Hague, 1924. On the growth of Liberalism: K. E. van der Mandele, *Het Liberalisme in Nederland*, Arnhem, 1933; I. Brugmans, *Thorbecke*, Haarlem, 1932; J. B. Manger, *Thorbecke en de Historie*, Amsterdam, 1938. Growth of the Anti-Revolutionary Movement: Hendrik Colijn, *Saevis Tranquillus in Undis*, Amsterdam, 1934; *Gedenkboek bij het Vijftigjarig Bestaan der Antirevolutionnaire Partij*, sec. ed. Kampen, 1929. Socialism: P. J. Troelstra, *Gedenkschriften*, 4 vols. Amsterdam, 1927–'31. A history of the Catholic Political Party does not exist.

TWENTIETH CENTURY:

A. Barnouw, *Holland under Queen Wilhelmina*, London, 1923, H. Brugmans, *Geschiedenis van Nederland onder Koningin Wilhelmina*, Amsterdam, 1938. For more literature on the Netherlands in our day, see: B. Landheer, *The Netherlands*, bibliography, p. 440 sq.

THE WAR:

E. Van Kleffens, *Juggernaut over Holland*, New York, 1941.

Index

The names Britain, England, France, Germany, Holland, Low Countries, Netherlands, that occur frequently throughout the text, have been omitted to save space.

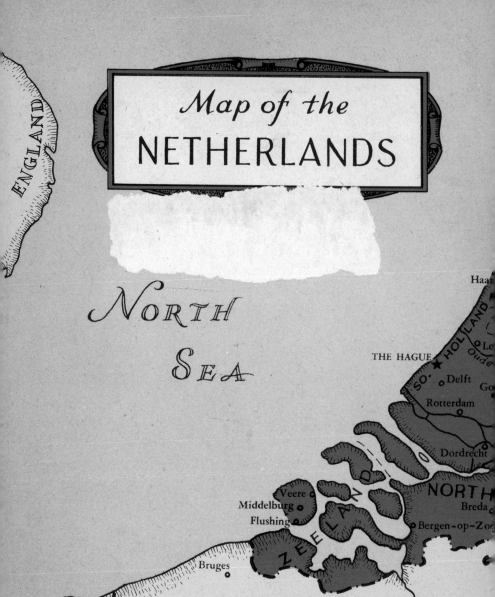

Map of the
NETHERLANDS

ENGLAND

NORTH

SEA

Haar

THE HAGUE ★

SO. HOLLAND

Le

Oude

Delft

Go

Rotterdam

Dordrecht

O

NORTH

Veere

Middelburg

Breda

Flushing

ZEELA

Bergen-op-Zo

Bruges

Antwerp

Schelde

Gand

Lys

Malines

FRANCE

BRUSSELS ★

Louvain

BELG